Praise for *Why the West Rules—for Now*

"Morris is a lucid thinker and a fine writer. . . . [He is] possessed of a welcome sense of humor that helps him guide us through this grand game of history as if he were an erudite sportscaster."

— *New York Times Book Review*

"A formidable, richly engrossing effort to determine why Western institutions dominate the world. . . . Readers will enjoy [Morris's] lively prose and impressive combination of scholarship . . . with economics and science. A superior contribution to the grand-theory-of-human-history genre."

— *Kirkus Reviews* (starred review)

"This is an important book—one that challenges, stimulates and entertains. Anyone who does not believe there are lessons to be learned from history should start here."

— *The Economist*

"[A] stunningly informative, imaginative and engaging account, spanning 50,000 years of the social development of the West and East."

— *Pittsburgh Post-Gazette*

"Accessible and solid . . . It should be in every library." — *Library Journal*

"[Morris] has written the first history of the world that really makes use of what modern technology can offer to the interpretation of the historical process. The result is a path-breaking work that lays out what modern history should look like."

— *Financial Times*

"Here you have three books wrapped into one: an exciting novel that happens to be true; an entertaining but thorough historical account of everything important that happened to any important people in the last ten millennia; and an educated guess about what will happen in the future. Read, learn, and enjoy!"

— Jared Diamond, Professor of Geography at UCLA, and Pulitzer Prize–winning author of *Guns, Germs, and Steel* and *Collapse*

"At last—a brilliant historian with a light touch. We should all rejoice."
– John Julius Norwich, author of *A Short History of Byzantium*

"This is an astonishing work by Ian Morris: hundreds of pages of the latest information dealing with every aspect of change. Then, the questions of the future: What will a new distribution bring about? Will Europe undergo a major change? Will the millions of immigrants impose a new set of rules on the rest? There was a time when Europe could absorb any and all newcomers. Now the newcomers may dictate the terms. The West may continue to rule, but the rule may be very different."
– David S. Landes, author of *The Wealth and Poverty of Nations*

"Deeply thought-provoking and engagingly lively, broad in sweep and precise in detail." – Jonathan Fenby, author of *Modern China: The Fall and Rise of a Great Power, 1850 to the Present*

"The nearest thing to a unified field theory of history we are ever likely to get. With wit and wisdom, Ian Morris deploys the techniques and insights of the new ancient history to address the biggest of all historical questions: Why on earth did the West beat the Rest? I loved it."
– Niall Ferguson, author of *The Ascent of Money*

WHY THE WEST RULES—FOR NOW

WHY THE WEST

RULES—FOR NOW

THE PATTERNS OF HISTORY,

AND WHAT

THEY REVEAL ABOUT

THE FUTURE

IAN MORRIS

EMBLEM

McClelland & Stewart

Cloth edition published 2010
Emblem edition published 2011

Emblem is an imprint of McClelland & Stewart Ltd.
Emblem and colophon are registered trademarks of McClelland & Stewart Ltd.

Published simultaneously in the United States of America by Farrar, Straus and Giroux.

Grateful acknowledgment is made for permission to reprint excerpts from the following previously
published works:

Excerpt from Mark Edward Lewis's partial translation of a poem by Cao Cao reprinted by
permission of the publisher from *The Early Chinese Empires: Qin and Han* by Mark Edward Lewis;
Timothy Brook, General Editor (Cambridge, Mass.: The Belknap Press of Harvard University Press),
copyright © 2007 by the President and Fellows of Harvard College.

To Cambridge University Press for permission to reprint an excerpt from *The Family Instructions
of the Grandfather* from *The Cambridge Illustrated History of China* by Patricia Ebrey (New York:
Cambridge University Press, 1996).

Translation of Daoqian's (Tao Ch'ien's) poem "On the Way to Guizong Monastery" reprinted with
permission from *Commerce and Society in Sung China* by Shiba Yoshinobu (Ann Arbor: Center for
Chinese Studies, University of Michigan, 1970).

To Donald B. Wagner for permission to reprint his translation of excerpts from "Stone Coal" by Su
Shi from his article entitled "Blast Furnaces in Song-Yuan China" in *East Asian Science, Technology,
and Medicine*, no. 18 (2001), pp. 41–74.

Richard Strassberg's translation of Kong Shangren's poem "Trying on Glasses," from *Macao:
Mysterious Decay and Romance* by Ronald Pittis and Susan Henders (eds.), reprinted by permission of
Oxford University Press (China) Ltd.

Excerpt "Here" from *Collected Poems* by Philip Larkin, copyright © 1988, 2003 by the Estate of
Philip Larkin, reprinted by permission of Farrar, Straus and Giroux, LLC, and Faber and Faber Ltd.

Library and Archives Canada Cataloguing in Publication

Morris, Ian, 1960-
Why the West rules – for now : the patterns of history, and what they reveal about the future /
Ian Morris.

Includes bibliographical references and index.
ISBN 978-0-7710-6456-2

1. World history. 2. Civilization – History. 3. Civilization, Western.
4. Civilization, Modern. 5. Comparative civilization. 6. East and West. I. Title.

CB251.M68 2011   909.09821   C2011-901823-3

We acknowledge the financial support of the Government of Canada through the Book Publishing
Industry Development Program and that of the Government of Ontario through the Ontario Media
Development Corporation's Ontario Book Initiative. We further acknowledge the support of the
Canada Council for the Arts and the Ontario Arts Council for our publishing program.

Designed by Abby Kagan

Printed and bound in the United States of America

McClelland & Stewart Ltd.
75 Sherbourne Street
Toronto, Ontario
M5A 2P9
www.mcclelland.com

1 2 3 4 5   15 14 13 12 11

Contents

Illustrations

WHY THE WEST RULES—FOR NOW

INTRODUCTION

ALBERT IN BEIJING

London, April 3, 1848. Queen Victoria's head hurt. She had been kneeling with her face pressed to the wooden pier for twenty minutes. She was angry, frightened, and tired from fighting back tears; and now it had started raining. The drizzle was soaking her dress, and she only hoped that no one would mistake her shivers for fear.

Her husband was right next to her. If she just stretched out her arm, she could rest a hand on his shoulder, or smooth his wet hair—anything to give him strength for what was coming. If only time would stand still—or speed up. If only she and Prince Albert were anywhere but here.

And so they waited—Victoria, Albert, the Duke of Wellington, and half the court—on their knees in the rain. Clearly there was a problem on the river. The Chinese armada's flagship was too big to put in at the East India Docks, so Governor Qiying was making his grand entry to London from a smaller armored steamer named after himself, but even the *Qiying* was uncomfortably large for the docks at Blackwall. Half a dozen tugs were towing her in, with great confusion all around. Qiying was not amused.

Out of the corner of her eye Victoria could see the little Chinese band on the pier. Their silk robes and funny hats had looked splendid an hour ago, but were now thoroughly bedraggled in the English rain. Four times the band had struck up some Oriental cacophony, thinking that Qiying's litter was about to be carried ashore, and four times had given up. The fifth time, though, they stuck to it. Victoria's stomach lurched. Qiying must be ashore at last. It was really happening.

And then Qiying's envoy was right in front of them, so close that Victoria could see the stitching on his slippers. There were little dragons, puffing smoke and flames. It was much finer work than her own ladies-in-waiting seemed able to do.

The envoy droned on, reading the official proclamation from Beijing. Victoria had been told what it said: that the Grand Exemplar the Cultured Emperor Daoguang recognized the British queen's desire to pay her respects to the imperial suzerainty; that Victoria had begged for the opportunity to offer tribute and taxes, paying the utmost obeisance and asking for commands; and that the emperor agreed to treat her realm as one of his inferior domains, and to allow the British to follow the Chinese way.

But everyone in Britain knew what had really happened. At first the Chinese had been welcome. They had helped fund the war against Napoleon, who had closed the continent's ports to them. But since 1815 they had been selling their goods at lower and lower prices in Britain's ports, until they put Lancashire's cotton mills out of business. When the British protested and raised tariffs, the Chinese burned the proud Royal Navy, killed Admiral Nelson, and sacked every town along the south coast. For almost eight centuries England had defied all conquerors, but now Victoria's name would go down forever in the annals of shame. Her reign had been an orgy of murder, rapine, and kidnapping; defeat, dishonor, and death. And here was Qiying himself, the evil architect of Emperor Daoguang's will, come to ooze more cant and hypocrisy.

At the appropriate moment Victoria's translator, kneeling just behind her, gave a perfect courtier's cough that only the queen could hear. This was the signal: Qiying's minion had reached the part about investing her as a subject ruler. Victoria raised her forehead from the dock and sat up to receive the barbaric cap and robe that signified her nation's dishonor. She got her first good look at Qiying. She did not expect to see such an intelligent- and vigorous-looking middle-aged fellow. Could he really be the monster she had dreaded? And Qiying got his first look at Victoria. He had seen a portrait of her at her coronation, but she was even stouter and plainer than he had expected. And young—very, very young. She was soaked and appeared to have little splinters and bits of mud from the dock all over her face. She did not even know how to kowtow properly. What graceless people!

And now came the moment of blackest horror, the unthinkable. With deep bows, two mandarins stepped from behind Qiying and helped Albert to his feet. Victoria knew she should make no sound or gesture—and in very truth, she was frozen to the spot, and could not have protested had she tried.

They led Albert away. He moved slowly, with great dignity, then stopped and looked back at Victoria. The world was in that glance.

Victoria swooned. A Chinese attendant caught her before she fell to the dock; it would not do to have a queen, even a foreign devil queen, hurt herself at such a moment. Sleepwalking now, his expression frozen and his breath coming in gasps, Albert left his adopted country. Up the gangplank, into the luxurious locked cabin, and on to China, there to be invested as a vassal in the Forbidden City by the emperor himself.

By the time Victoria recovered, Albert was gone. Now, finally, great sobs racked her body. It could take Albert half a year to get to Beijing, and the same to get back; and he might wait further months or years among those barbarians until the emperor granted him an audience. What would she do? How could she protect her people, alone? How could she face this wicked Qiying, after what he had done to them?

Albert never came back. He reached Beijing, where he astonished the court with his fluent Chinese and his knowledge of the Confucian classics. But on his heels came news that landless farm workers had risen up and were smashing threshing machines all over southern England; and then that bloody street battles were raging in half the capitals of Europe. A few days later the emperor received a letter from Qiying suggesting that it might be best to keep a talented prince like Albert safely out of the country. All this violence was as much about the painful transition to modernity as about the Chinese Empire, but there was no point taking chances with such turbulent people.

So Albert stayed in the Forbidden City. He threw away his English suits and grew a Manchu pigtail, and with each passing year his knowledge of the Chinese classics deepened. He grew old, alone among the pagodas, and after thirteen years in the gilded cage, he finally just gave up living.

On the other side of the world Victoria shut herself away in underheated private rooms at Buckingham Palace and ignored her colonial masters. Qiying simply ran Britain without her. Plenty of the so-called politicians would crawl on their bellies to do business with him. There was no state funeral when Victoria died in 1901; just shrugs and wry smiles at the passing of the last relic of the age before the Chinese Empire.

LOOTY IN BALMORAL

In reality, of course, things didn't happen this way. Or at least, only some of them did. There really was a Chinese ship called the *Qiying*, and it really did sail into London's East India Docks in April 1848 (Figure I.1). But it was not an ironclad gunboat carrying a Chinese governor to London: the real *Qiying* was just a gaily painted wooden junk. British businessmen in the Crown Colony of Hong Kong had bought the little boat a couple of years before and decided that it would be a jolly jape to send it back to the old country.

Queen Victoria, Prince Albert, and the Duke of Wellington really did come down to the river, but not to kowtow before their new master. Rather, they came as tourists to gawk at the first Chinese ship ever seen in Britain.

The ship really was named after the governor of Guangzhou. But Qiying had not accepted British submission in 1842 after destroying the Royal Navy. In reality, he negotiated China's surrender that same year, after a small British squadron sank every war junk it could find, silenced the coastal batteries, and closed the Grand Canal linking Beijing to the rice-rich Yangzi Valley, threatening the capital with starvation.

And Emperor Daoguang really did rule China in 1848. But Daoguang did not tear Victoria and Albert apart: in fact the royal couple lived on in bliss, punctuated by Victoria's moods, until Albert died in 1861. The reality was that Victoria and Albert tore Daoguang apart.

Figure I.1. The real *Qiying*: boatloads of Londoners row out to see the ship in 1848, as recorded by an artist from the *Illustrated London News*.

History is often stranger than fiction. Victoria's countrymen broke Daoguang and shattered his empire for that most British of vices— a cup of tea (or, to be precise, several billion cups of tea). In the 1790s the British East India Company, which ran much of South Asia as a private fiefdom, was shipping 23 million pounds of Chinese tea leaves to London every year. The profits were enormous, but there was one problem: the Chinese government was not interested in importing British manufactured goods in return. All it wanted was silver, and the company was having trouble raising enough to keep the trade going. So there was much joy when the traders realized that whatever the Chinese government might want, the Chinese people wanted something else: opium. And the best opium grew in India, which the company controlled. At Guangzhou—the one Chinese port where foreigners could trade—merchants sold opium for silver, used the silver to buy tea, then sold the tea for even greater profits back in London.

As so often in business, though, solving one problem just created another. Indians ate opium and Britons dissolved it and drank it, consuming ten to twenty tons every year (some of it going to calm babies). Both techniques produced mildly narcotic effects, enough to inspire the odd poet and stimulate a few earls and dukes to new debaucheries, but nothing to worry about. The Chinese, on the other hand, smoked it. The difference was not unlike that between chewing coca leaves and lighting up a crack pipe. British drug dealers contrived to overlook this difference but Daoguang did not, and in 1839 declared war on drugs.

It was an odd war, which quickly degenerated into a personal face-off between Daoguang's drug czar, Commissioner Lin Zexu, and the British superintendent of trade at Guangzhou, Captain Charles Elliot. When Elliot realized he was losing, he persuaded the traders to surrender a staggering seventeen hundred tons of opium to Lin; and he got the traders to agree to this by guaranteeing that the British government would reimburse them for their losses. The merchants did not know if Elliot actually had the authority to promise this, but they grabbed the offer all the same. Lin got his opium; Elliot saved face and kept the tea trade moving; and the merchants got top price (plus interest and shipping) for their drugs. Everyone won.

Everyone, that is, except Lord Melbourne, Britain's prime minister. Melbourne, who was expected to find £2 million to compensate the drug dealers, did *not* win. It should have been madness for a mere naval captain to put a prime minister on the spot like this, but Elliot knew he could rely on the business community to lobby Parliament to recover the money. And so it was that personal, political, and financial interests thickened around Melbourne until he had no choice but to pay up and then send an expedition to make the Chinese government reimburse Britain for the confiscated opium (Figure I.2).

This was not the British Empire's finest hour. Contemporary analogies are never precise, but it was rather as if in response to the U.S. Drug Enforcement Agency making a major bust, the Tijuana cartel prevailed on the Mexican government to shoot its way into San Diego, demanding that the White House reimburse the drug lords for the street value of the confiscated cocaine (plus interest and carriage charges) as well as paying the costs of the military expedition. Imagine, too, that while it was in the neighborhood, a Mexican fleet seized Catalina Island as a base for future operations and threatened to blockade Washington until Congress gave the Tijuana drug lords monopoly rights in Los Angeles, Chicago, and New York.

The difference, of course, is that Mexico is in no position to bombard San Diego, while in 1839 Britain could do whatever it wanted.

Figure I.2. Not their finest hour: British ships blowing Chinese war junks out of the Yangzi River in 1842. At the far right the *Nemesis*, the world's first all-iron warship, is living up to its name.

British ships brushed aside China's defenses and Qiying signed a humiliating treaty, opening China to trade and missionaries. Daoguang's wives were not carried off to London, the way Albert went to Beijing in the scene I imagined at the beginning of this introduction, but the "Opium War" broke Daoguang all the same. He had let down 300 million subjects and betrayed two thousand years of tradition. He was right to feel like a failure. China was coming apart. Addiction soared, the state lost control, and custom crumbled.

Into this uncertain world came a failed civil service candidate named Hong Xiuquan, who had grown up just outside Guangzhou. Four times Hong had trekked to the city to take the arduous civil service entrance exams; four times he had flunked. Finally, in 1843, he collapsed and had to be carried back to his village. In his fevered dreams, angels took him up to heaven. There he met a man who, he was told, was his elder brother, and standing shoulder-to-shoulder the two of them battled demons under their bearded father's gaze.

No one in the village could make sense of this dream, and Hong seemed to forget about it for several years, until one day he opened a little book he had been given in Guangzhou on one of his trips to the examination hall. It summarized the Christians' sacred texts—and, Hong realized, held the key to his dream. The brother in his dream was obviously Jesus, which made Hong God's Chinese son. He and Jesus had chased the demons out of heaven, but the dream seemed to mean that God wanted Hong to expel them from earth, too. Patching together a mix of evangelical Christianity and Confucianism, Hong proclaimed a Heavenly Kingdom of Great Peace. Angry peasants and bandits flocked to his banner. By 1850 his motley crew was defeating the disorganized imperial armies sent against him, and he followed God's will by introducing radical social reforms. He redistributed land, legislated equal rights for women, and even banned footbinding.

In the early 1860s, while Americans slaughtered each other with artillery and repeating rifles in the world's first modern war, the Chinese were doing the same with cutlasses and pikes in the world's last traditional war. For sheer horror, the traditional version far outdid the modern one. Twenty million died, mostly through starvation and disease, and Western diplomats and generals exploited the chaos to push farther into East Asia. In 1854, looking for coaling stations between California and China, the American Commodore Perry forced Japan's ports open. In 1858 Britain, France, and the United States won new concessions from China. Emperor Xianfeng, who understandably hated the foreign devils who had destroyed his father, Daoguang, and were now exploiting his war against Hong, tried to wriggle out of the new treaty, but when Xianfeng got difficult, the British and French governments made him an offer he couldn't refuse. They marched on Beijing and Xianfeng beat an undignified retreat to a nearby vacation spot. The Europeans then burned his beautiful Summer Palace, letting him know they could do the same to the Forbidden City if they felt like it, and Xianfeng caved in. Shattered even more badly than his father had been, he refused to leave his hiding place or meet with officials ever again, and retreated into drugs and sex. He died a year later.

Prince Albert expired just a few months after Xianfeng. Despite spending years campaigning to persuade the British government that poor drains spread disease, Albert probably died from typhoid carried through Windsor Castle's wretched sewers. Sadder still, Victoria—as deeply enamored of modern plumbing as Albert—was in the bathroom when he passed away.

Robbed of the love of her life, Victoria sank deeper into moods and melancholy. But she was not completely alone. British officers presented her with one of the finest curiosities they had looted from the Summer Palace at Beijing: a Pekinese dog. She named him Looty.

LOCKING IN

Why did history follow the path that took Looty to Balmoral Castle, there to grow old with Victoria, rather than the one that took Albert to study Confucius in Beijing? Why did British boats shoot their way up the Yangzi in 1842, rather than Chinese ones up the Thames? To put it bluntly: Why does the West rule?

To say the West "rules" might sound a little strong; after all, however we define "the West" (a question I will return to in a few pages), Westerners have not exactly been running a world government since the 1840s, and regularly fail to get their own way. Many of us are old enough to remember America's ignominious scramble out of Saigon (now Ho Chi Minh City) in 1975 and the way Japanese factories drove Western rivals out of business in the 1980s. Even more of us now have the sense that everything we buy is made in China. Yet it is also obvious that in the last hundred years or so Westerners have shipped armies to Asia, not the other way around. East Asian governments have struggled with Western capitalist and Communist theories, but no Western governments have tried to rule on Confucian or Daoist lines. Easterners often communicate across linguistic barriers in English; Europeans rarely do so in Mandarin or Japanese. As a Malaysian lawyer bluntly told the British journalist Martin Jacques, "I am wearing your clothes, I speak your language, I watch your films, and today is whatever date it is because you say so."

The list could go on. Since Victoria's men carried off Looty the West has maintained a global dominance without parallel in history.

My goal is to explain this.

At first glance, it might not look like I have set myself a very difficult task. Nearly everyone agrees that the West rules because the industrial revolution happened there, not in the East. In the eighteenth century British entrepreneurs unleashed the energies of steam and coal.

Factories, railroads, and gunboats gave nineteenth-century Europeans and Americans the ability to project power globally; airplanes, computers, and nuclear weapons allowed their twentieth-century successors to cement this dominance.

This did not mean that everything had to turn out exactly as it did, of course. If Captain Elliot had not forced Lord Melbourne's hand in 1839, the British might not have attacked China that year; if Commissioner Lin had paid more attention to coastal defenses, the British might not have succeeded so easily. But it does mean that irrespective of when matters came to a head and of who sat on the thrones, won the elections, or led the armies, the West was always going to win in the nineteenth century. The British poet and politician Hilaire Belloc summed it up nicely in 1898:

> *Whatever happens we have got*
> *The Maxim Gun, and they have not.*

End of story.

Except, of course, this is not the end of the story. It just prompts a new question: *Why* had the West got the Maxim gun when the rest had not? This is the first question I address, because the answer tells us why the West rules today; and, armed with the answer, we can pose a second question. One of the reasons people care about why the West rules is that they want to know whether, how long, and in what ways this will continue—that is, what will happen next.

This question grew increasingly pressing as the twentieth century wore on and Japan emerged as a major power; and in the early twenty-first it has become unavoidable. China's economy doubles in size every half-dozen years and will probably be the world's largest before 2030. As I write, in early 2010, most economists are looking to China, not the United States or Europe, to restart the world's economic engine. China hosted spectacular Olympic Games in 2008 and two Chinese "taikonauts" have taken spacewalks. China and North Korea both have nuclear weapons, and Western strategists worry about how the United States will accommodate itself to China's rising power. How long the West will stay on top is a burning question.

Professional historians are famously bad prophets, to the point that most refuse to talk about the future at all. The more I have thought about why the West rules, though, the more I have realized that the part-time historian Winston Churchill understood things better than most professionals. "The farther backward you can look," Churchill insisted, "the farther forward you are likely to see." Following in this spirit (even if Churchill might not have liked my answers), I will suggest that knowing why the West rules gives us a pretty good sense of how things will turn out in the twenty-first century.

I am not, of course, the first person to speculate on why the West rules. The question is a good 250 years old. Before the eighteenth century the question rarely came up, because it frankly did not then make much sense. When European intellectuals first started thinking seriously about China, in the seventeenth century, most felt humbled by the East's antiquity and sophistication; and rightly so, said the few Easterners who paid the West any heed. Some Chinese officials admired Westerners' ingenious clocks, devilish cannons, and accurate calendars, but they saw little worth emulating in these otherwise unimpressive foreigners. If China's eighteenth-century emperors· had known that French philosophers such as Voltaire were writing poems praising them, they would probably have thought that that was exactly what French philosophers ought to be doing.

Yet from almost the first moment factories filled England's skies with smoke, European intellectuals realized that they had a problem. As problems went, it was not a bad one: they appeared to be taking over the world, but did not know why.

Europe's revolutionaries, reactionaries, romantics, and realists went into a frenzy of speculation on why the West was taking over, producing a bewildering mass of hunches and theories. The best way to begin asking why the West rules may be by separating these into two broad schools of thought, which I will call the "long-term lock-in" and "short-term accident" theories. Needless to say, not every idea fits neatly into one camp or the other, but this division is still a useful way to focus things.

The unifying idea behind long-term lock-in theories is that from time immemorial some critical factor made East and West massively and unalterably different, and determined that the industrial revolution would happen in the West. Long-termers disagree—fiercely—on what that factor was and when it began to operate. Some emphasize material forces, such as climate, topography, or natural resources; others point to less tangible matters, such as culture, politics, or religion. Those who favor material forces tend to see "the long term" as being very long indeed. Some look back fifteen thousand years to the end of the Ice Age; a few go back even further. Those who emphasize culture usually see the long term as being a bit shorter, stretching back just one thousand years to the Middle Ages or two and a half thousand to the age of the Greek thinker Socrates and China's great sage Confucius. But the one thing long-termers can agree on is that the Britons who shot their way into Shanghai in the 1840s and the Americans who forced Japan's harbors open a decade later were merely the unconscious agents of a chain of events that had been set in motion millennia earlier. A long-termer would say that by beginning this book with a contrast between Albert-in-Beijing and Looty-in-Balmoral scenarios, I was just being silly. Queen Victoria was always going to win: the result was inevitable. It had been locked in for generations beyond count.

Between roughly 1750 and 1950 nearly all explanations for why the West ruled were variations on the long-term lock-in theme. The most popular version was that Europeans were simply culturally superior to everyone else. Since the dying days of the Roman Empire most Europeans had identified themselves first and foremost as Christians, tracing their roots back to the New Testament, but in trying to explain why the West was now coming to rule, some eighteenth-century intellectuals imagined an alternative line of descent for themselves. Two and a half thousand years ago, they argued, the ancient Greeks created a unique culture of reason, inventiveness, and freedom. This set Europe on a different (better) trajectory than the rest of the world. The East had its learning too, they conceded, but its traditions were too muddled, too conservative, and too hierarchical to compete with Western thought. Many Europeans concluded that they were conquering everyone else because culture made them do it.

By 1900 Eastern intellectuals, struggling to come to terms with the West's economic and military superiority, often bought into this theory, though with a twist. Within twenty years of Commodore Perry's arrival in Tokyo Bay a "Civilization and Enlightenment" movement was translating the classics of the French Enlightenment and British liberalism into Japanese and advocating catching up with the West through democracy, industrialism, and the emancipation of women. Some even wanted to make English be the national language. The problem, intellectuals such as Fukuzawa Yukichi insisted in the 1870s, was long-term: China had been the source of much of Japan's culture, and China had gone terribly wrong in the distant past. As a result, Japan was only "semicivilized." But while the problem was long-term, Fukuzawa argued, it was not locked in. By rejecting China, Japan could become fully civilized.

Chinese intellectuals, by contrast, had no one to reject but themselves. In the 1860s a "Self-Strengthening" movement argued that Chinese traditions remained fundamentally sound; China just needed to build a few steamships and buy some foreign guns. This, it turned out, was mistaken. In 1895 a modernized Japanese army surprised a Chinese fortress with a daring march, seized its foreign-made guns, and turned them on China's steamships. The problem clearly went deeper than having the right weapons. By 1900 Chinese intellectuals were following the Japanese lead, translating Western books on evolution and economics. Like Fukuzawa, they concluded that Western rule was long-term but not locked in; by rejecting its own past China could catch up too.

But some Western long-termers thought there was simply nothing the East could do. Culture made the West best, they claimed, but was not the ultimate explanation for Western rule, because culture itself had material causes. Some believed that the East was too hot or too diseased for people to develop a culture as innovative as the West's; or perhaps there were just too many bodies in the East—consuming all the surplus, keeping living standards low, and preventing anything like the liberal, forward-looking Western society from emerging.

Long-term lock-in theories come in every political coloring, but Karl Marx's version has been the most important and influential. In the very days that British troops were liberating Looty, Marx—then writing a China column for the *New York Daily Tribune*—suggested that politics was the real factor that had locked in Western rule. For thousands of years, he claimed, Oriental states had been so centralized and so powerful that they had basically stopped the flow of history. Europe progressed from antiquity through feudalism to capitalism, and proletarian revolutions were about to usher in communism, but the East was sealed in the amber of despotism and could not share in the progressive Western trajectory. When history did not turn out exactly as Marx had predicted, later Communists (especially Lenin and his followers) improved on his theories by claiming that a revolutionary vanguard might shock the East out of its ancient slumber. But that would only happen, Leninists insisted, if they could shatter the old, fossilized society—at whatever cost. This long-term lock-in theory is not the only reason why Mao Zedong, Pol Pot, and the Kims of North Korea unleashed such horrors on their people, but it bears a heavy burden of responsibility.

Right through the twentieth century a complicated dance went on in the West as historians uncovered facts that did not seem to fit the long-term lock-in stories, and long-termers adjusted their theories to accommodate them. For instance, no one now disputes that when Europe's great age of maritime discovery was just beginning, Chinese navigation was far more advanced and Chinese sailors already knew the coasts of India, Arabia, East Africa, and perhaps Australia.* When the eunuch admiral Zheng He sailed from Nanjing for Sri Lanka in 1405 he led nearly three hundred vessels. There were tankers carrying drinking water and huge "Treasure Ships" with advanced rudders, watertight compartments, and elaborate signaling devices. Among his 27,000 sailors were 180 doctors and pharmacists. By contrast, when Christopher Columbus sailed from Cadiz in 1492, he led just ninety men in three ships. His biggest hull displaced barely one-thirtieth as much water as Zheng's; at eighty-five feet long it was shorter than Zheng's mainmast, and barely twice as long as his rudder. Columbus had no freshwater tankers and no real doctors. Zheng had magnetic compasses and knew enough about the Indian Ocean to fill a twenty-one-foot-long sea chart; Columbus rarely knew where he was, let alone where he was going.

*Some people think Chinese sailors even reached the Americas in the fifteenth century, but, as I will try to show in Chapter 8, these claims are probably fanciful. The closest thing to evidence for these imaginary voyages is a map of the world exhibited in Beijing and London in 2006, purporting to be a 1763 copy of a Chinese original drawn in 1418. The map is not only wildly different from all genuine fifteenth-century Chinese maps but is also strikingly like eighteenth-century French world maps, down to details like showing California as an island. Most likely an eighteenth-century Chinese cartographer combined fifteenth-century maps with newly available French maps. The mapmaker probably had no intention of deceiving anyone, but twenty-first-century collectors, eager for sensational discoveries, have happily deceived themselves.

This might give pause to anyone assuming that Western dominance was locked in in the distant past, but several important books have argued that Zheng He does, after all, fit into long-term lock-in theories: we just need more sophisticated versions. For example, in his magnificent book *The Wealth and Poverty of Nations*, the economist David Landes renews the idea that disease and demography always gave Europe a decisive edge over China, but adds a new twist by suggesting that dense population favored centralized government in China and reduced rulers' incentives to exploit Zheng's voyages. Because they had no rivals, most Chinese emperors worried more about how trade might enrich undesirable groups like merchants than they did about getting more riches for themselves; and because the state was so powerful, they could stamp out this alarming practice. In the 1430s they banned oceanic voyages, and in the 1470s perhaps destroyed Zheng's records, ending the great age of Chinese exploration.

The biologist and geographer Jared Diamond makes a similar case in his classic *Guns, Germs, and Steel*. His main goal is to explain why it was societies within the band of latitude that runs from China to the Mediterranean Sea that developed the first civilizations, but he also suggests that Europe rather than China came to dominate the modern world because Europe's peninsulas made it easy for small kingdoms to hold out against would-be conquerors, favoring political fragmentation, while China's rounder coastline favored centralized rulers over petty princes. The resulting political unity allowed fifteenth-century Chinese emperors to ban voyages like Zheng's.

In fragmented Europe, by contrast, monarch after monarch could reject Columbus's crazy proposal, but he could always find someone else to ask. We might speculate that if Zheng had had as many options as Columbus, Hernán Cortés might have met a Chinese governor in Mexico in 1519, not the doomed Montezuma. But according to long-term lock-in theories, vast impersonal forces such as disease, demography, and geography ruled that possibility out.

Lately, though, Zheng's voyages and plenty of other facts have started striking some people as just too awkward to fit into long-term models at all. Already in 1905 Japan showed that Eastern nations could give Europeans a run for their money on the battlefield, defeating the Russian Empire. In 1942 Japan almost swept the Western powers out of the Pacific altogether, then, bouncing back from a shattering defeat in 1945, changed direction to become an economic giant. Since 1978 China, as we all know, has moved along a similar path. In 2006 China beat out the United States as the world's biggest carbon emitter, and even in the darkest days of the 2008–2009 financial crisis, China's economy kept growing at rates that Western governments would envy in the best of years. Maybe we need to throw out the old question and ask a new one: not *why* the West rules, but *whether* the West rules. If the answer is no, then long-term lock-in theories that seek ancient explanations for a Western rule that does not actually exist seem rather pointless.

One result of these uncertainties has been that some Western historians have developed a whole new theory explaining why the West used to rule but is now ceasing to do so. I call this the short-term accident model. Short-term arguments tend to be more complicated than long-term ones, and there are fierce disagreements within this camp. But there is one thing short-termers do all agree on: pretty much everything long-termers say is wrong. The West has not been locked into global dominance since the distant past; only after 1800 CE, on the eve of the Opium War, did the West pull temporarily ahead of the East, and even that was largely accidental. The Albert-in-Beijing scenario is anything but silly. It could easily have happened.

LUCKING OUT

Orange County in California is better known for conservative politics, manicured palm trees, and long-time resident John Wayne (the local airport is named after him, despite his dislike of planes flying over the golf course) than for radical scholarship, but in the 1990s it became the epicenter of short-term accident theories of global history. Two historians (Bin Wong and Kenneth Pomeranz) and a sociologist (Wang Feng) at the University of California's Irvine campus* wrote landmark books arguing that whatever we look at—ecology or family structures, technology and industry or finance and institutions, standards of living

---

*Wong left Irvine in 2005, but moved only forty miles, to the University of California's Los Angeles campus; and Wang had a co-author, James Lee, but he, too, teaches just forty miles from Irvine, at the California Institute of Technology in Pasadena.

or consumer tastes—the similarities between East and West vastly outweighed the differences as late as the nineteenth century.

If they are right, it suddenly becomes much harder to explain why
Looty came to London rather than Albert heading east. Some short-
termers, like the maverick economist Andre Gunder Frank (who wrote
more than thirty books on everything from prehistory to Latin American finance), argue that the East was actually better placed to have an
industrial revolution than the West until accidents intervened. Europe,
Frank concluded, was simply "a distant marginal peninsula" in a "Sinocentric world order." Desperate to get access to the markets of Asia, where
the real wealth was, Europeans a thousand years ago tried to batter their
way through the Middle East in the Crusades. When this did not work
some, like Columbus, tried sailing west to reach Cathay.

That failed too, because America was in the way, but in Frank's
opinion Columbus's blunder marked the beginning of the change in
Europe's place in the world system. In the sixteenth century China's
economy was booming but faced constant silver shortages. America
was full of silver; so Europeans responded to China's needs by getting
Native Americans to claw a good 150,000 tons of precious metal out of
the mountains of Peru and Mexico. A third of it ended up in China.
Silver, savagery, and slavery bought the West "a third-class seat on the
Asian economic train," as Frank put it, but still more needed to happen
before the West could "displace Asians from the locomotive."

Frank thought that the rise of the West ultimately owed less to
European initiative than to a "decline of the East" after 1750. This
began, he believed, when the silver supply started shrinking. This set
off political crises in Asia but provided a bracing stimulus in Europe,
where, as they ran out of silver to export, Europeans mechanized their
industries to make goods other than silver competitive in Asian markets. Population growth after 1750 also had different results at each end
of Eurasia, Frank argued, polarizing wealth, feeding political crises,
and discouraging innovation in China but providing cheaper labor for
new factories in Britain. As the East fell apart the West had the industrial revolution that should, by rights, have happened in China; but
because it happened in Britain, the West inherited the world.

Other short-termers, though, disagree. The sociologist Jack Goldstone (who taught for some years at the University of California's
Davis campus and coined the term "California School" to describe the

short-term theorists) has argued that East and West were roughly equally well (or poorly) placed until 1600, each ruled by great agrarian empires with sophisticated priesthoods guarding ancient traditions. Everywhere from England to China, plagues, wars, and the overthrow of dynasties brought these societies to the brink of collapse in the seventeenth century, but whereas most of the empires recovered and reimposed strictly orthodox thought, northwest Europe's Protestants rejected Catholic traditions.

It was that act of defiance, Goldstone suggests, that sent the West down the path toward an industrial revolution. Freed from the fetters of archaic ideologies, European scientists laid bare the workings of nature so effectively that British entrepreneurs, sharing in this pragmatic can-do culture, learned to put coal and steam to work. By 1800 the West had pulled decisively ahead of the rest.

None of this was locked in, Goldstone argues, and in fact a few accidents could have changed the world completely. For instance, at the battle of the Boyne in 1690 a Catholic musket ball ripped through the shoulder of the coat worn by William of Orange, the Protestant pretender to England's throne. "It's well it came no nearer," William is supposed to have said; well indeed, says Goldstone, speculating that if the shot had hit a few inches lower England would have remained Catholic, France would have dominated Europe, and the industrial revolution might not have happened.

Kenneth Pomeranz at Irvine goes further still. As he sees it, the fact that there was an industrial revolution at all was a gigantic fluke. Around 1750, he argues, East and West were both heading for ecological catastrophe. Population had grown faster than technology and people had already done nearly everything possible in the way of extending and intensifying agriculture, moving goods around, and reorganizing themselves. They were about to hit the limits of what was possible with their technology, and there was every reason to expect global recession and declining population in the nineteenth and twentieth centuries.

Yet the last two hundred years have seen more economic growth than all earlier history put together. The reason, Pomeranz explains in his important book *The Great Divergence*, is that western Europe, and above all Britain, just got lucky. Like Frank, Pomeranz sees the West's luck beginning with the accidental discovery of the Americas, creating a trading system that provided incentives to industrialize production;

but unlike Frank, he suggests that as late as 1800 Europe's luck could still have failed. It would have taken a lot of space, Pomeranz points out, to grow enough trees to feed Britain's crude early steam engines with wood—more space, in fact, than crowded western Europe had. But a second stroke of luck intervened: Britain, alone in all the world, had conveniently located coalfields as well as rapidly mechanizing industries. By 1840 Britons were applying coal-powered machines to every walk of life, including iron warships that could shoot their way up the Yangzi River. Britain would have needed to burn another 15 million acres of woodland each year—acres that did not exist—to match the energy now coming from coal. The fossil-fuel revolution had begun, ecological catastrophe had been averted (or at least postponed into the twenty-first century), and the West suddenly, against all odds, ruled the globe. There had been no long-term lock in. It was all just a recent, freakish accident.

The variety of short-term explanations of the Western industrial revolution, stretching from Pomeranz's fluke that averted global disaster to Frank's temporary shift within an expanding world economy, is every bit as wide as the gulf between, say, Jared Diamond and Karl Marx on the long-term side. Yet for all the controversy within both schools, it is the battle lines *between* them that produce the most starkly opposed theories of how the world works. Some long-termers claim that the revisionists are merely peddling shoddy, politically correct pseudo-scholarship; some short-termers respond that long-termers are pro-Western apologists or even racists.

The fact that so many experts can reach such wildly different conclusions suggests that something is wrong in the way we have approached the problem. In this book I will argue that long-termers and short-termers alike have misunderstood the shape of history and have therefore reached only partial and contradictory results. What we need, I believe, is a different perspective.

THE SHAPE OF HISTORY

What I mean by this is that both long-termers and short-termers agree that the West has dominated the globe for the last two hundred years, but disagree over what the world was like before this. Everything revolves around their differing assessments of premodern history. The only way we can resolve the dispute is by looking at these earlier periods to establish the overall "shape" of history. Only then, with the baseline established, can we argue productively about why things turned out as they did.

Yet this is the one thing that almost no one seems to want to do. Most experts who write on why the West rules have backgrounds in economics, sociology, politics, or modern history; basically, they are specialists in current or recent events. They tend to focus on the last few generations, looking back at most five hundred years and treating earlier history briefly, if at all—even though the main issue at dispute is whether the factors that gave the West dominance were already present in earlier times or appeared abruptly in the modern age.

A handful of thinkers approach the question very differently, focusing on distant prehistory then skipping ahead to the modern age, saying little about the thousands of years in between. The geographer and historian Alfred Crosby makes explicit what many of these scholars take for granted—that the prehistoric invention of agriculture was critically important, but "between that era and [the] time of development of the societies that sent Columbus and other voyagers across the oceans, roughly 4,000 years passed, during which little of importance happened, *relative to what had gone before*."

This, I think, is mistaken. We will not find answers if we restrict our search to prehistory or modern times (nor, I hasten to add, would we find them if we limited ourselves to just the four or five millennia in between). The question requires us to look at the whole sweep of human history as a single story, establishing its overall shape, before discussing why it has that shape. This is what I try to do in this book, bringing a rather different set of skills to bear.

I was educated as an archaeologist and ancient historian, specializing in the classical Mediterranean of the first millennium BCE. When I started college at Birmingham University in England in 1978, most classical scholars I met seemed perfectly comfortable with the old long-term theory that the culture of the ancient Greeks, created two and a half thousand years ago, forged a distinctive Western way of life. Some of them (mostly older ones) would even say outright that this Greek tradition made the West better than the rest.

So far as I remember, none of this struck me as being a problem until I started graduate research at Cambridge University in the early 1980s, working on the origins of Greek city-states. This took me among anthropological archaeologists working on similar processes in other parts of the world. They openly laughed at the quaint notion that Greek culture was unique and had started a distinctive democratic and rational Western tradition. As people often do, for several years I managed to carry two contradictory notions in my head: on the one hand, Greek society evolved along the same lines as other ancient societies; on the other, it initiated a distinctive Western trajectory.

The balancing act got more difficult when I took my first faculty position, at the University of Chicago, in 1987. There I taught in Chicago's renowned History of Western Civilization program, ranging from ancient Athens to (eventually) the fall of communism. To stay even one day ahead of my students I had to read medieval and modern European history much more seriously than before, and I could not help noticing that for long stretches of time the freedom, reason, and inventiveness that Greece supposedly bequeathed to the West were more honored in the breach than the observance. Trying to make sense of this, I found myself looking at broader and broader slices of the human past. I was surprised how strong the parallels were between the supposedly unique Western experience and the history of other parts of the world, above all the great civilizations of China, India, and Iran.

Professors enjoy nothing more than complaining about their administrative burdens, but when I moved to Stanford University in 1995 I quickly learned that serving on committees could be an excellent way to find out what was going on outside my own little field. Since then I have directed the university's Social Science History Institute and Archaeology Center, served as chair of the Classics department and senior associate dean of the School of Humanities and Sciences, and run a large archaeological excavation—which all meant plenty of paperwork and headaches, but which also let me meet specialists in every field, from genetics to literary criticism, that might be relevant to working out why the West rules.

I learned one big thing: to answer this question we need a broad approach, combining the historian's focus on context, the archaeologist's awareness of the deep past, and the social scientist's comparative methods. We could get this combination by assembling a multidisciplinary team of specialists, pooling deep expertise across a range of fields, and that is in fact just what I did when I started directing an archaeological excavation on Sicily. I knew nowhere near enough about botany to analyze the carbonized seeds we found, about zoology to identify the animal bones, about chemistry to make sense of the residues in storage vessels, about geology to reconstruct the landscape's formation processes, or about a host of other indispensable specialties, so I found specialists who did. An excavation director is a kind of academic impresario, bringing together talented artists who put on the show.

That is a good way to produce an excavation report, where the goal is to pile up data for others to use, but books-by-committee tend to be less good at developing unified answers to big questions. As a result, in the book you are reading now I take an *inter-* rather than *multi*disciplinary approach. Instead of riding shotgun over a herd of specialists, I strike off on my own to draw together and interpret the findings of experts in numerous fields.

This courts all kinds of dangers (superficiality, disciplinary bias, and just general error). I will never have the same subtle grasp of Chinese culture as someone who has spent a lifetime reading medieval manuscripts, or be as up-to-date on human evolution as a geneticist (I am told that the journal *Science* updates its website on average every thirteen seconds; while typing this sentence I have probably fallen behind again). But on the other hand, those who stay within the boundaries of their own disciplines will never see the big picture. The interdisciplinary, single-author model probably is the worst way to write a book like this—except for all the other ways. To me it certainly seems the least bad way to proceed, but you will have to judge from the results whether I am right.

So what are the results? I argue in this book that asking why the West rules is really a question about what I will call social development. By this I basically mean societies' abilities to get things done—to shape their physical, economic, social, and intellectual environments to their own ends. Back in the nineteenth century and well into the twentieth, Western observers mostly took it for granted that social development was an unquestioned good. Development is progress (or evolution, or History), they implicitly and often explicitly said, and progress—whether toward God, affluence, or a people's paradise—is the point of life. These days that seems less obvious. Many people feel that the environmental degradation, wars, inequality, and disillusionment that social development brings in its train far outweigh any benefits it generates.

Yet whatever moral charge we put on social development, its reality is undeniable. Almost all societies today are more developed (in the sense I defined that word in the previous paragraph) than they were a hundred years ago, and some societies today are more developed than others. In 1842 the hard truth was that Britain was more developed than China—so developed, in fact, that its reach had become global. There had been empires aplenty in the past, but their reach had always been regional. By 1842, however, British manufacturers could flood China with their products, British industrialists could build iron ships that outgunned any in the world, and British politicians could send an expedition halfway around the globe.

Asking why the West rules really means asking two questions. We need to know both why the West is more developed—that is, more able to get things done—than any other region of the world, and why Western development rose so high in the last two hundred years that for the first time in history a few countries could dominate the entire planet.

The only way to answer these questions, I believe, is by measuring social development to produce a graph that—literally—shows the shape of history. Once we do that, we will see that neither long-term lock-in nor short-term accident theories explain the shape of history very well at all. The answer to the first question—why Western social development is higher than that of any other part of the world—does not lie in any recent accident: the West has been the most developed region of the world for fourteen of the last fifteen millennia. But on the other hand, neither was the West's lead locked in in the distant past. For more than a thousand years, from about 550 through 1775 CE, Eastern regions scored higher. Western rule was neither predetermined thousands of years ago nor a result of recent accidents.

Nor can either long-term or short-term theories by themselves answer the second question, of why Western social development has risen so high compared to all earlier societies. As we will see, it was only around 1800 CE that Western scores began surging upward at astonishing rates; but this upturn was itself only the latest example of a very long-term pattern of steadily accelerating social development. The long term and the short term work together.

This is why we cannot explain Western rule just by looking at pre-history or just by looking at the last few hundred years. To answer the question we have to make sense of the whole sweep of the past. Yet while charting the rise and fall of social development reveals the shape of history and shows us what needs to be explained, it doesn't actually *do* the explaining. For that we need to burrow into the details.

SLOTH, FEAR, AND GREED

"HISTORY, *n*. An account, mostly false, of events, mostly unimportant, which are brought about by rulers, mostly knaves, and soldiers, mostly fools." It is sometimes hard to disagree with Ambrose Bierce's comic definition: history can seem to be just one damned thing after an-other, a chaotic jumble of geniuses and dolts, tyrants and romantics, poets and thieves, accomplishing the extraordinary or scraping the barrel of depravity.

Such people stud the pages that follow, which is as it should be. After all, it is flesh-and-blood individuals, not vast impersonal forces, who do all the living, dying, creating, and fighting in this world. Yet behind all the sound and fury, I will argue, the past nevertheless has strong patterns, and with the right tools historians can see what they are and even explain them.

I will use three of these tools.

The first is biology,* which tells us what humans truly are: clever chimps. We are part of the animal kingdom, which is itself part of the larger empire of life, stretching from the great apes all the way down to amoebas. This very obvious truth has three important consequences.

First, like all life-forms, we survive because we extract energy from our environment and turn that energy into more of ourselves.

Second, like all the more intelligent animals, we are curious crea-tures. We are constantly tinkering, wondering whether things are ed-ible, whether we can have fun with them, whether we can improve

---

*Academic biology is a vast field; I draw on its ecological/evolutionary end rather than its molecular/cellular end.

them. We are just much better at tinkering than other animals, because we have big, fast brains with lots of folds to think things through, endlessly supple vocal cords to talk things through, and opposable thumbs to work things through.

That said, humans—like other animals—are obviously not all the same. Some extract more energy from the environment than others; some reproduce more than others; some are more curious, creative, clever, or practical than others. But the third consequence of our animalness is that large groups of humans, as opposed to individual humans, *are* all much the same. If you pluck two random people from a crowd, they may be as different as can be imagined, but if you round up two complete crowds they will tend to mirror each other rather closely. And if you compare groups millions strong, as I do in this book, they are likely to have very similar proportions of energetic, fertile, curious, creative, clever, talkative, and practical people.

These three rather commonsensical observations explain much of the course of history. For millennia social development has generally been increasing, thanks to our tinkering, and has generally done so at an accelerating rate. Good ideas beget more good ideas, and having once had good ideas we tend not to forget them. But as we will see, biology does not explain the whole history of social development. Sometimes social development has stagnated for long periods without rising at all; sometimes it has even gone into reverse. Just knowing that we are clever chimps is not enough.

This is where the second tool, sociology, comes in.* Sociology tells us simultaneously what causes social change and what social change causes. It is one thing for clever chimps to sit around tinkering, but it is another altogether for their ideas to catch on and change society. That, it seems, requires some sort of catalyst. The great science-fiction writer Robert Heinlein once suggested that "Progress is made by lazy men looking for easier ways to do things." We will see later in this book that this Heinlein Theorem is only partly true, because lazy

---

*I use "sociology" as a shorthand term for the social sciences more generally, and draw primarily on those branches that generalize about how all societies work rather than those that focus on differences. This definition cuts across traditional academic distinctions among sociology, anthropology, economics, and political science, and puts great emphasis on areas where biology and the social sciences meet, especially demography and psychology.

women are just as important as lazy men, sloth is not the *only* mother of invention, and "progress" is often a rather upbeat word for what happens. But if we flesh it out a little, I think Heinlein's insight becomes about as good a one-sentence summary of the causes of social change as we are likely to find. In fact, as the book goes on I will start passing off a less pithy version of it as my own Morris Theorem: "Change is caused by lazy, greedy, frightened people looking for easier, more profitable, and safer ways to do things. And they rarely know what they're doing." History teaches us that when the pressure is on, change takes off.

Greedy, lazy, frightened people seek their own preferred balance among being comfortable, working as little as possible, and being safe. But that is not the end of the story, because people's success in reproducing themselves and capturing energy inevitably puts pressure on the resources (intellectual and social as well as material) available to them. Rising social development generates the very forces that undermine further social development. I call this the paradox of development. Success creates new problems; solving them creates still newer problems. Life, as they say, is a vale of tears.

The paradox of development is constantly at work, confronting people with hard choices. Often people fail to rise to its challenges, and social development stagnates or even declines. At other times, though, sloth, fear, and greed combine to push some people to take risks, innovating to change the rules of the game. If at least a few of them succeed and if most people then adopt the successful innovations, a society might push through the resource bottleneck and social development will keep rising.

People confront, and solve, such problems every day, which is why social development has generally kept moving upward since the end of the last ice age. But as we will see, at certain points the paradox of development creates tough ceilings that will yield only to truly transformative changes. Social development sticks at these ceilings, setting off a desperate race. In case after case we will see that when societies fail to solve the problems that confront them, a terrible package of ills—famine, epidemic, uncontrolled migration, and state failure—begins to afflict them, turning stagnation into decline; and when famine, epidemic, migration, and state failure are joined by further forces of disruption, like climatic change (collectively, I call these the five horsemen of the apocalypse), decline can turn into disastrous, centuries-long collapses and dark ages.

Between them, biology and sociology explain most of the shape of history—why social development has generally risen, why it rises faster at some times and slower at others, and why it sometimes falls. But these biological and sociological laws are constants, applying every-where, in all times and all places. They by definition tell us about hu-manity as a whole, not about why people in one place have fared so differently from those in another. To explain that, I will argue through-out this book, we need a third tool: geography.*

LOCATION, LOCATION, LOCATION

"The Art of Biography is different from Geography," the humorist Edmund Bentley observed in 1905; "Biography is about chaps, but Geography is about maps." For many years, chaps—in the British sense of upper-class men—dominated the stories historians told, to the point that history was barely distinguishable from biography. That changed in the twentieth century as historians made women, lower-class men, and children into honorary chaps too, adding their voices to the mix, but in this book I want to go further. Once we recognize that chaps (in large groups and in the newer, broader sense of the word) are all much the same, I will argue, all that is left is maps.

Many historians react to this claim like a bull to a red rag. It is one thing, several have said to me, to reject the old idea that a few great men determined that history would unfold differently in East and West; it is another altogether to say that culture, values, and beliefs were unimportant and to seek the reason why the West rules entirely in brute material forces. Yet that is more or less what I propose to do.

I will try to show that East and West have gone through the same stages of social development in the last fifteen thousand years, in the same order, because they have been peopled by the same kinds of

---

*Geography, like biology and sociology, is a huge and loosely defined field (so loosely defined, in fact, that since the 1940s many universities have decided that it is not an academic discipline at all and have closed their geography departments). I draw more on human/economic geography than on physical geography.

human beings, who generate the same kinds of history. But I will also try to show that they have not done so at the same times or at the same speed. I will conclude that biology and sociology explain the global similarities while geography explains the regional differences. And in that sense, it is geography that explains why the West rules.

Put so bluntly, this probably sounds like as hard-line a long-term lock-in theory as could be imagined, and there have certainly been historians who have seen geography that way. The idea goes back at least as far as Herodotus, the fifth-century-BCE Greek often credited with being the father of history. "Soft countries breed soft men," he insisted; and, like a string of determinists since him, he concluded that geography had destined his own homeland for greatness. Perhaps the most remarkable example is Ellsworth Huntington, a Yale University geographer who marshaled rafts of statistics in the 1910s to demonstrate that his hometown of New Haven, Connecticut, had an almost-ideal climate for stimulating people to greatness. (Only England was better.) By contrast, he concluded, the "too uniformly stimulating" climate of California—where I live—merely produced elevated rates of insanity. "The people of California," Huntington assured readers, "may perhaps be likened to horses which are urged to the limit so that some of them become unduly tired and break down."

It is easy to mock this kind of thing, but when I say that geography explains why the West rules I have something rather different in mind. Geographical differences do have long-term effects, but these are never locked in, and what counts as a geographical advantage at one stage of social development may be irrelevant or a positive disadvantage at another. We might say that while geography drives social development, social development determines what geography means. It is a two-way street.

To explain this a bit better—and to give a quick road map for the rest of the book—I would like to look back twenty thousand years, to the coldest point in the last ice age. Geography then mattered very much: mile-thick glaciers covered much of the northern hemisphere, dry and barely habitable tundras fringed them, and only closer to the equator could small bands of humans make a living by gathering and hunting. Distinctions between the south (where people could live) and the north (where they could not) were extreme, but within the southern zone distinctions between East and West were relatively minor.

The end of the Ice Age changed the meaning of geography. The poles remained cold and the equator remained hot, of course, but in half a dozen places between these extremes—what, in Chapter 2, I will call the original cores—warmer weather combined with local geography to favor the evolution of plants and/or animals that humans could domesticate (that is, genetically modify to make them more useful, eventually reaching the point that the genetically modified organisms could survive only in symbiosis with humans). Domesticated plants and animals meant more food, which meant more people, which meant more innovation; but domestication also meant more pressure on the very resources that drove the process. The paradox of development went straight to work.

These core regions had all been fairly typical of the relatively warm, habitable regions during the Ice Age, but they now grew increasingly distinct, both from the rest of the world and from one another. Geography had favored them all, but had favored some more than others. One core, the so-called Hilly Flanks in western Eurasia, had uniquely dense concentrations of domesticable plants and animals; and since groups of people are all much the same, it was here, where resources were richest and the process easiest, that moves toward domestication began. That was around 9500 BCE.

Following what I hope is common sense, throughout this book I use the expression "the West" to describe all the societies that have descended from this westernmost (and earliest) of the Eurasian cores. The West long ago expanded from the original core in southwest Asia* to encompass the Mediterranean Basin and Europe, and in the last few centuries the Americas and Australasia too. As I hope will become clear, defining "the West" like this (rather than picking on some supposedly uniquely "Western" values such as freedom, rationality, or tolerance, and then arguing about where these values came from and which parts of the world have them) has major consequences for understanding the world we live in. My goal is to explain why a particular set of societies that descend from the original Western core—above all, those of North America—now dominate the globe, rather than societies in another

---

*What, since the nineteenth century, people have rather confusingly called the "Middle East."

part of the West, societies descended from one of the other cores, or, for that matter, no societies at all.

Following the same logic, I use "the East" to refer to all those societies that descend from the easternmost (and second-oldest) of the Eurasian cores. The East also long ago expanded from its original core between China's Yellow and Yangzi rivers, where the domestication of plants began around 7500 BCE, and today stretches from Japan in the north into the countries of Indochina in the south.

The societies that descend from the other cores—a southeastern core in what is now New Guinea, a South Asian one in modern Pakistan and northern India, an African one in the eastern Sahara Desert, and two New World cores in Mexico and Peru—all have their own fascinating histories. I touch on these repeatedly in what follows, but I focus as relentlessly as I can on East-West comparisons. My reasoning is that since the end of the Ice Age, the world's most developed societies have almost always been ones that descended from either the original Western or the original Eastern core. While Albert in Beijing is a plausible alternative to Looty in Balmoral, Albert in Cuzco, Delhi, or New Guinea is not. The most efficient way to explain why the West rules is therefore to zero in on East-West comparisons, and that is what I have done.

Writing the book this way has its costs. A more properly global account, looking at every region of the world, would be richer and more nuanced, and would give the cultures of South Asia, the Americas, and other regions full credit for all the contributions they have made to civilization. But such a global version would also have drawbacks, particularly in loss of focus, and it would need even more pages than the book I did write. Samuel Johnson, eighteenth-century England's sharpest wit, once observed that while everyone admired *Paradise Lost*, "None ever wished it longer than it is." What applies to Milton, I suspect, applies even more to anything I might come up with.

If geography really did provide a Herodotus-style long-term lock-in explanation of history, I could wrap this book up rather quickly after pointing out that domestication began in the Western core around 9500 BCE and in the Eastern core around 7500. Western social development would simply have stayed two thousand years ahead of Eastern and the West would have gone through an industrial revolution while the East was still figuring out writing. But that, obviously, did not happen. As we will see in the chapters that follow, geography did not lock in history, because geographical advantages are always ultimately self-defeating. They drive up social development, but in the process social development changes what geography means.

As social development rises, cores expand, sometimes through migration and sometimes through copying or independent innovation by neighbors. Techniques that worked well in an older core—whether those techniques were agriculture and village life, cities and states, great empires, or heavy industry—spread into new societies and new environments. Sometimes these techniques flourished in the new setting; sometimes they just muddled along; and sometimes they needed huge modifications to work at all.

Odd as it may seem, the biggest advances in social development often come in places where methods imported or copied from a more developed core do not work very well. Sometimes this is because the struggle to adapt old methods to new environments forces people to make breakthroughs; sometimes it is because geographical factors that do not matter much at one stage of social development matter much more at another.

Five thousand years ago, for instance, the fact that Portugal, Spain, France, and Britain stuck out from Europe into the Atlantic was a huge geographical disadvantage, meaning that these regions were a very long way from the real action in Mesopotamia* and Egypt. By five hundred years ago, however, social development had risen so much that geography changed its meanings. There were new kinds of ships that could cross what had always been impassable oceans, which abruptly made sticking out into the Atlantic a huge plus. It was Portuguese, Spanish, French, and English ships, rather than Egyptian or Iraqi ones, that started sailing to the Americas, China, and Japan. It was western Europeans who began tying the world together with maritime trade, and western European social development soared upward, overtaking the older core in the eastern Mediterranean.

---

*Mesopotamia is the ancient Greek name (literally meaning "between the rivers") for Iraq. By convention, historians and archaeologists use Mesopotamia for the period before the Arab invasion of 637 CE and Iraq after that date.

I call this pattern the "advantages of backwardness,"* and it is as old as social development itself. When agricultural villages began turning into cities (soon after 4000 BCE in the West and 2000 BCE in the East), for instance, access to the particular soils and climates that had favored the initial emergence of agriculture began to matter less than access to great rivers that could be tapped to irrigate fields or used as trade routes. And as states kept expanding, access to great rivers started mattering less than access to metals, or to longer trade routes, or to sources of manpower. As social development changes, the resources it demands change too, and regions that once counted for little may discover advantages in their backwardness.

It is always hard to say in advance how the advantages of backwardness will play out: not all backwardness is equal. Four hundred years ago, for instance, it seemed to many Europeans that the booming plantations of the Caribbean had a brighter future than North America's farms. With hindsight we can see why Haiti turned into the poorest place in the western hemisphere and the United States into the richest, but predicting such outcomes is much harder.

One very clear consequence of the advantages of backwardness, though, was that the most developed region within each core moved around over time. In the West it shifted from the Hilly Flanks (in the age of early farmers) southward to the river valleys of Mesopotamia and Egypt as states emerged and then westward into the Mediterranean Basin as trade and empires became more important. In the East it migrated northward from the area between the Yellow and Yangzi rivers to the Yellow River basin itself, then westward to the Wei River and the region of Qin.

A second consequence was that the West's lead in social development fluctuated, partly because these vital resources—wild plants and animals, rivers, trade routes, manpower—were distributed in different ways across each core and partly because in both cores the processes of expansion and incorporation of new resources were violent and unstable, pushing the paradox of development into overdrive. The growth of Western states in the second millennium BCE, for example, made the Mediterranean Sea not only a highway for commerce but

---

*I borrow this term from the economist Alexander Gerschrenkon (although he used it slightly differently).

also a highway for forces of disruption. Around 1200 BCE Western states lost control, and migrations, state failures, famines, and epidemics set off a core-wide collapse. The East, which had no such inland sea, went through no comparable collapse, and by 1000 BCE the West's lead in social development had narrowed sharply.

Over the three thousand years that followed, the same pattern has played out again and again with constantly changing consequences. Geography determined where in the world social development would rise fastest, but rising social development changed what geography meant. At different points the great steppes linking eastern and western Eurasia, the rich rice lands of southern China, the Indian Ocean, and the Atlantic Ocean were all crucially important; and when the Atlantic rose to prominence in the seventeenth century CE, those people best placed to exploit it—at first chiefly the British, then their former colonists in America—created new kinds of empires and economies and unlocked the energy trapped in fossil fuels. And that, I will argue, is why the West rules.

THE PLAN

I have divided the chapters that follow into three sections. Part I (Chapters 1–3) confronts the most basic issues: What is the West? Where do we start our story? What do we mean by "rule"? How can we tell who is leading or ruling? In Chapter 1, I set out the biological basis of the story in the evolution and dispersal of modern humans over the planet; in Chapter 2, I trace the formation and growth of the original Eastern and Western cores after the Ice Age; and in Chapter 3, I break the narrative to define social development and explain how I will use it to measure differences between East and West.*

In Part II (Chapters 4–10), I trace the stories of East and West in detail, asking constantly what explains their similarities and differences. In Chapter 4, I look at the rise of the first states and the great disruptions that wracked the Western core in the centuries down to 1200 BCE. In Chapter 5, I consider the first great Eastern and Western empires and how their social development rose toward the limits of

---

*I present more technical accounts in the appendix to this book and on my website, www.ianmorris.org.

what was possible in agricultural economies; then in Chapter 6, I discuss the great collapse that swept Eurasia after about 150 CE. In Chapter 7, we reach a turning point, with the Eastern core opening a new frontier and taking the lead in social development. By about 1100 CE the East was again pressing against the limits of what was possible in an agricultural world, but in Chapter 8 we will see how this set off a second great collapse. In Chapter 9, I describe the new frontiers that Eastern and Western empires created on the steppes and across the oceans as they recovered, and examine how the West closed the development gap on the East. Finally, in Chapter 10, we will see how the industrial revolution converted the West's lead into rule and the enormous consequences this had.

In Part III (Chapters 11 and 12) I turn to the most important question for any historian: So what? First, in Chapter 11, I pull together my argument that behind all the details of what has happened in the last fifteen thousand years, two sets of laws—those of biology and sociology—determined the shape of history on a global scale, while a third set—those of geography—determined the differences between Eastern and Western development. It was the ongoing interplay between these laws, not long-term lock-ins or short-term accidents, that sent Looty to Balmoral rather than Albert to Beijing.

This is not how historians normally talk about the past. Most scholars seek explanations in culture, beliefs, values, institutions, or blind accident rather than the hard surfaces of material reality, and few would be caught dead speaking of laws. But after considering (and rejecting) some of these alternatives, I want to go one step further, suggesting in Chapter 12 that the laws of history in fact give us a pretty good sense of what is likely to happen next. History has not come to an end with Western rule. The paradox of development and the advantages of backwardness are still operating; the race between the innovations that drive social development upward and the disruptions that drag it down is still on. In fact, I will suggest, the race is hotter than ever. New kinds of development and disruption promise—or threaten—to transform not just geography but biology and sociology too. The great question for our times is not whether the West will continue to rule. It is whether humanity as a whole will break through to an entirely new kind of existence before disaster strikes us down—permanently.

PART I

1

⊚ ⊚ ⊚

BEFORE EAST AND WEST

WHAT IS THE WEST?

"When a man is tired of London," said Samuel Johnson, "he is tired of life; for there is in London all that life can afford." It was 1777, and every current of thought, every bright new invention, was energizing Dr. Johnson's hometown. London had cathedrals and palaces, parks and rivers, mansions and slums. Above all, it had things to buy—things beyond the wildest imaginings of previous generations. Fine ladies and gentlemen could alight from carriages outside the new arcades of Oxford Street, there to seek out novelties like the umbrella, an invention of the 1760s that the British soon judged indispensable; or the handbag, or toothpaste, both of them products of the same decade. And it was not just the rich who indulged in this new culture of consumption. To the horror of conservatives, tradesmen were spending hours in coffee shops, the poor were calling tea a "necessary," and farmers' wives were buying pianos.

The British were beginning to feel they were not like other people. In 1776 the Scottish sage Adam Smith had called them "a nation of shopkeepers" in his *Inquiry into the Nature and Causes of the Wealth of Nations*, but he had meant it as a compliment; Britons' regard for their own well-being, Smith insisted, was making everyone richer. Just think, he said, of the contrast between Britain and China. China had been "long one of the richest, that is, one of the most fertile, best cultivated, most industrious, and most populous, countries of the world," but had already "acquired that full complement of riches which the measure of its laws and institutions permits it to acquire." The Chinese, in short, were stuck. "The competition of the labourers and the interest of the masters," Smith predicted, "would soon reduce them to the lowest rate which is consistent with common humanity," with the consequence that "the poverty of the lower ranks of people in China far surpasses that of the most beggarly nations in Europe . . . Any carrion, the carcase of a dead dog or cat, for example, though half putrid and stinking, is as welcome to them as the most wholesome food to the people of other countries."

Johnson and Smith had a point. Although the industrial revolution had barely begun in the 1770s, average incomes were already higher and more evenly distributed in England than in China. Long-term lock-in theories of Western rule often start from this fact: the West's lead, they argue, was a cause rather than a consequence of the industrial revolution, and we need to look back further in time—perhaps much further—to explain it.

Or do we? The historian Kenneth Pomeranz, whose book *The Great Divergence* I mentioned in the introduction, insists that Adam Smith and all the cheerleaders for the West who followed him were actually comparing the wrong things. China is as big and as varied, Pomeranz points out, as the whole continent of Europe. We should not be too surprised, then, that if we single out England, which was Europe's most developed region in Smith's day, and compare it with the average level of development in the whole of China, England scores higher. By the same token, if we turned things around and compared the Yangzi Delta (the most developed part of China in the 1770s) with the average level of development across the whole of Europe, the Yangzi Delta would score higher. Pomeranz argues that eighteenth-century England and the Yangzi Delta had more in common with each other (incipient industrialism, booming markets, complex divisions of labor) than England did with underdeveloped parts of Europe or the Yangzi Delta did with underdeveloped parts of China—all of which leads him to conclude that long-term theorists get things back-to-front because their thinking has been sloppy. If England and the Yangzi

Delta were so similar in the eighteenth century, Pomeranz observes, the explanation for Western rule must lie *after* this date, not before it.

One implication is clear: if we want to know why the West rules, we first need to know what "the West" is. As soon as we ask that question, though, things get messy. Most of us have a gut feeling about what constitutes "the West." Some people equate it with democracy and freedom; others with Christianity; others still with secular rationalism. In fact, the historian Norman Davies has found no fewer than twelve ways that academics define the West, united only by what he calls their "elastic geography." Each definition gives the West a different shape, creating exactly the kind of confusion that Pomeranz complains about. The West, says Davies, "can be defined by its advocates in almost any way that they think fit," meaning that when we get right down to it, "Western civilization is essentially an amalgam of intellectual constructs which were designed to further the interests of their authors."

If Davies is right, asking why the West rules means nothing more than arbitrarily picking some value to define the West, claiming that a particular set of countries exemplifies this value, then comparing that set with an equally arbitrary set of "non-Western" countries to reach whatever self-serving conclusions we like. Anyone who disagrees with our conclusions can simply choose a different value to exemplify Westernness, a different set of countries exemplifying it, and a different comparison set, coming—naturally—to a different but equally self-serving conclusion.

This would be pointless, so I want to take a different approach. Instead of starting at the end of the process, making assumptions about what count as Western values and then looking back through time to find their roots, I will start at the beginning. I will move forward through time from the beginning until we reach a point at which we can see distinctive ways of life emerging in different parts of the world. I will then call the westernmost of these distinctive regions "the West" and the easternmost "the East," treating West and East for what they are—geographical labels, not value judgments.

Saying we must start at the beginning is one thing; finding it is another altogether. As we will see, there are several points in the distant past at which scholars have been tempted to define East and West in terms of biology, rejecting the argument I made in the introduction that folks (in large groups) are all much the same and instead seeing the people in one part of the world as genetically superior to everyone else. There are also points when it would be all too easy to conclude that one region has, since time immemorial, been culturally superior to all others. We must look into these ideas carefully, because if we make a misstep here at the start we will also get everything about the shape of the past, and therefore about the shape of the future, too, wrong.

IN THE BEGINNING

Every culture has had its own story about how things started, but in the last few years astrophysicists have given us some new, scientific versions. Most experts now think time and space began over 13 billion years ago, although they do not agree on just how that happened. The dominant "inflationary" theory holds that the universe initially expanded faster than the speed of light from an infinitely dense and infinitely small point, while a rival "cyclical" theory argues that it blew up when a previous universe collapsed. Both schools agree that our universe is still expanding, but while inflationists say it will continue to grow, the stars will go out, and eventually infinite darkness and coldness will descend, cyclists claim it will shrink back on itself, explode again, and start another new universe.

It is hard to make much sense of these theories unless you have had years of advanced mathematical training, but fortunately our question does not require us to begin quite so early. There could be neither East nor West when there were no directions at all and when the laws of nature did not exist. Nor could East and West be useful concepts before our sun and planet took shape 4.5 billion years ago. Perhaps we can speak of East and West once the earth's crust formed, or at least once the continents reached something like their current positions, by which point we are already into the last few million years. Really, though, all these discussions are beside the point: East and West cannot mean anything for the question in this book until we add another ingredient to the mix—humans.

Paleoanthropologists, who study early humans, like controversy even more than historians do. Their field is young and fast moving, and new discoveries constantly turn established truths on their heads. If you get two paleoanthropologists into a room they are likely to come out with three theories of human evolution, and by the time the door shuts behind them, all will be out of date.

The boundary between humans and prehumans is necessarily fuzzy. Some paleoanthropologists think that as soon as we see apes that could walk upright we should start speaking of humans. Judging from the fossilized remains of hip and toe bones, some East African apes began doing this 6 or 7 million years ago. Most experts, though, think this sets the bar too low, and standard biological classifications in fact define the genus *Homo* ("mankind" in Latin) by bundling together an increase in brain size from 400–500 cubic centimeters to roughly 630 (our own brains are typically about twice as big) with the first evidence for upright apes smashing stones together to create crude tools. Both processes began among bipedal East African apes around 2.5 million years ago. Louis and Mary Leakey, the famous excavators of Olduvai Gorge in Tanzania (Figure 1.1), named these relatively big-brained, tool-using creatures *Homo habilis*, Latin for "Handy Man." (Until recently, paleoanthropologists, like most people, thought nothing of applying the word "man" to individuals of both sexes; that has changed, but by convention scientists still use single-sex names like Handy Man.)

East and West meant little when *Homo habilis* walked the earth—first, because these creatures lived entirely within the forests of East Africa, and no regional variations had yet developed, and second, because the expression "walked the earth" is actually overly generous. Handy Men had toes and ankles like ours, and certainly did walk, but their long arms suggest that they also spent a lot of time in trees. These were fancy apes, but not much more. The marks their stone tools left on animal bones show that *Homo habilis* ate meat as well as plants, but it looks like they were still quite low on the food chain. Some paleoanthropologists defend a man-the-hunter theory, seeing *Homo habilis* as smart and brave enough to kill game armed with nothing more than sticks and broken stones, but others (rather more convincingly) see in *Homo habilis* man-the-scavenger, following the real killers (like lions) around, eating the bits they didn't want. Microscopic studies show that marks from Handy Man's tools did at least get onto animal bones before those from hyenas' teeth.

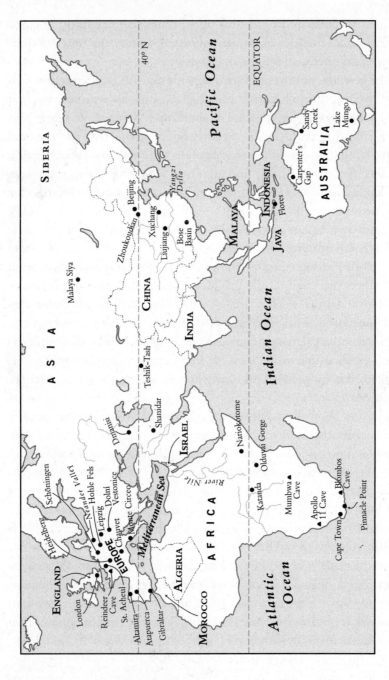

Figure 1.1. Before "East" and "West" meant much: locations in the Old World mentioned in this chapter

For 25,000 generations Handy Men scampered and swung through the trees in this little corner of the world, chipping stone tools, grooming each other, and mating. Then, somewhere around 1.8 million years ago, they disappeared. So far as we can tell this happened rather suddenly, although one of the problems in studying human evolution is the difficulty of dating finds precisely. Much of the time we depend on the fact that the layers of rock containing the fossil bones or tools may also contain unstable radioactive isotopes whose rate of decay is known, so that measuring the ratios between the isotopes gives dates for the finds. These dates, however, can have margins of error tens of thousands of years wide, so when we say the world of *Homo habilis* ended suddenly, "suddenly" may mean a few lifetimes or a few thousand lifetimes.

When Charles Darwin was thinking about natural selection in the 1840s and 1850s he assumed that it worked through the slow accretion of tiny changes, but in the 1970s the biologist Stephen Jay Gould suggested instead that for long periods nothing much happens, then some event triggers a cascade of changes. Evolutionists nowadays divide over whether gradual change (evolution by creeps, as its critics call it) or Gould's "punctuated equilibrium" (evolution by jerks) is better as a general model, but the latter certainly seems to make most sense of *Homo habilis*'s disappearance. About 1.8 million years ago East Africa's climate was getting drier and open savannas were replacing the forests where *Homo habilis* lived; and at just that point, new kinds of ape-men* took Handy Man's place.

I want to hold off putting a name on these new ape-men, and for now will just point out that they had bigger brains than *Homo habilis*, typically about 800 cc. They lacked the long, chimplike arms of *Homo habilis*, probably meaning that they spent nearly all their time on the ground. They were also taller. A million-and-a-half-year-old skeleton from Nariokotome in Kenya, known as the Turkana Boy, belongs to a five-foot-tall child who would have reached six feet had he survived to adulthood. As well as being longer, his bones were less robust than

---

*The word "ape-man," with its Tarzan-and-Jane connotations, was much favored in schoolbooks when I was young. Nowadays paleoanthropologists tend to think it condescending, but it seems to me to capture nicely the ambiguities of these prehuman hominins, and is certainly less of a mouthful.

those of *Homo habilis*, suggesting that he and his contemporaries relied more on their wits and tools than on brute strength.

Most of us think that being smart is self-evidently good. Why, then, if *Homo habilis* had the potential to mutate in this direction, did they putter along for half a million years before "suddenly" morphing into taller, bigger-brained creatures? The most likely explanation lies in the fact that there is no such thing as a free lunch. A big brain is expensive to run. Our own brains typically make up 2 percent of our body weight but use up 20 percent of the energy we consume. Big brains create other problems too: it takes a big skull to hold a big brain—so big, in fact, that modern women have trouble pushing babies with such big heads down their birth canals. Women deal with this by in effect giving birth prematurely. If our babies stayed in the womb until they were almost self-sufficient (like other mammals), their heads would be too big for them to get out.

Yet risky childbirth, years of nurturing, and huge brains that burn up one fifth of our food intake are all fine with us—finer, anyway, than using the same amounts of energy to grow claws, more muscles, or big teeth. Intelligence is much more of a plus than any of these alternatives. It is less obvious, though, why a genetic mutation producing bigger brains gave ape-men enough advantages to make the extra energy costs worthwhile a couple of million years ago. If being smarter had not been beneficial enough to pay the costs of supporting these gray cells, brainy apes would have been less successful than their dumber relatives, and their smart genes would have quickly disappeared from the population.

Perhaps we should blame it on the weather. When the rains failed and the trees the ape-men lived in started dying, brainier and perhaps more sociable mutants might well have gained an edge over their more apelike relatives. Instead of retreating ahead of the grasslands, the clever apes found ways to survive on them, and in the twinkling of an eye (on the timescale of evolution) a handful of mutants spread their genes through the whole pool and completely replaced the slower-witted, undersized, forest-loving *Homo habilis*.

THE BEGINNINGS OF EAST AND WEST?

Whether because their home ranges got crowded, because bands squabbled, or just because they were curious, the new ape-men were the first such creatures to leave East Africa. Their bones have been found everywhere from the southern tip of the continent to the Pacific shores of Asia. We should not imagine great waves of migrants like something out of a cowboy movie, though; the ape-men were surely barely conscious of what they were doing, and crossing these vast distances required even vaster stretches of time. From Olduvai Gorge to Cape Town in South Africa is a long way—two thousand miles—but to cover this ground in a hundred thousand years (the length of time it apparently took) ape-men only needed, on average, to expand their foraging range by 35 yards each year. Drifting northward at the same rate would take them to the threshold of Asia, and in 2002 excavators at Dmanisi in the Republic of Georgia found a 1.7-million-year-old skull that combines features of *Homo habilis* and the newer ape-men. Stone tools from China and fossil bones from Java (then still joined to the Asian mainland) may be almost as old, implying that after leaving Africa the ape-men picked up speed, averaging a cracking pace of 140 yards per year.*

We can only realistically expect to distinguish Eastern and Western ways of life after ape-men left East Africa, spreading through the warm, subtropical latitudes as far as China; and an East-West distinction may be just what we do find. By 1.6 million years ago, there are obvious Eastern and Western patterns in the archaeological record. The question, though, is whether these contrasts are important enough that we should imagine distinct ways of life lying behind them.

Archaeologists have known about these East-West differences since the 1940s, when the Harvard archaeologist Hallam Movius noticed that the bones of the new, brainy ape-men were often found in association with new kinds of flaked stone tools. Archaeologists called the most distinctive of these tools "Acheulean hand axes" ("ax" because they look like axheads, even though they were clearly used for cutting, poking, and pounding as well as chopping; "hand" because they were handheld, rather than being attached to sticks; and Acheulean after the small French town of St. Acheul, where they were first found in large numbers). Calling these tools works of art might be excessive, but their simple symmetry is often much more beautiful than Handy Men's

*In practice they probably jumped a few miles at a time to find good new foraging spots, then stayed put for several years.

cruder flakes and chopping tools. Movius noticed that while Acheulean hand axes were common in Africa, Europe, and southwest Asia, none had been found in East or Southeast Asia. Instead, Eastern sites produced rougher tools much like the pre-Acheulean finds associated with *Homo habilis* in Africa.

If the so-called Movius Line (Figure 1.2) really does mark the beginning of separate Eastern and Western ways of life, it could also provide an astonishingly long-term lock-in theory—one holding that almost as soon as ape-men moved out of Africa, they divided between Western/technologically advanced/Acheulean hand ax cultures in Africa and southwest Asia and Eastern/technologically less advanced/flake-and-chopper cultures in East Asia. No wonder the West rules today, we might conclude: it has led the world technologically for a million and a half years.

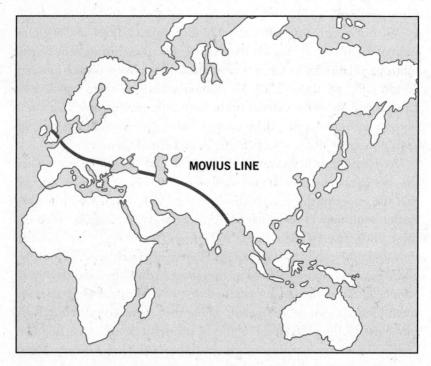

Figure 1.2. The beginnings of East and West? This map shows the Movius Line, which for about a million years separated Western hand-ax-using cultures from Eastern flake-and-chopper-using cultures.

Identifying the Movius Line, though, is easier than explaining it. The earliest Acheulean hand axes, found in Africa, are about 1.6 million years old, but there were already ape-men at Dmanisi in Georgia a hundred thousand years before that. The first ape-men clearly left Africa before the Acheulean hand ax became a normal part of their toolkit, carrying pre-Acheulean technologies across Asia while the Western/African region went on to develop Acheulean tools.

A quick glance at Figure 1.2, though, shows that the Movius Line does not divide Africa from Asia; it actually runs through northern India. This is an important detail. The first migrants left Africa *before* Acheulean hand axes were invented, so there must have been subsequent waves of migration out of Africa, bringing hand axes to southwest Asia and India. So we need to ask a new question: Why did these later waves of ape-men not take Acheulean technology even farther east?

The most likely answer is that rather than marking the boundary between a technologically advanced West and a less-advanced East, the Movius Line merely separates Western regions where access to the sort of stones needed for hand axes is easy from Eastern areas where such stones are rare and where good alternatives—such as bamboo, which is tough but does not survive for us to excavate—are easily available. According to this interpretation, as hand-ax users drifted across the Movius Line they gradually gave Acheulean tools up because they could not replace broken ones. They carried on producing choppers and flakes, for which any old pebble would do, but perhaps started using bamboo for tasks previously done with stone hand axes.

Some archaeologists think finds from the Bose Basin in south China support this thinking. About 800,000 years ago a huge meteor crashed here. It was a disaster on an epic scale, and intense fires burned millions of acres of forest. Before the impact, ape-men in the Bose Basin had used choppers, flakes, and (presumably) bamboo, like other East Asians; but when they returned after the fires they started making hand axes rather like the Acheulean ones—perhaps, the theory runs, because the fires had burned off all the bamboo, in the process exposing usable cobbles. After a few centuries, as the vegetation grew back, the locals gave up hand axes and went back to bamboo.

If this speculation is right, East Asian ape-men were perfectly capable of making hand axes when conditions favored these tools, but normally did not bother because alternatives were more easily available. Stone hand axes and bamboo tools were just two different tools for doing the same jobs, and ape-men all lived in much the same ways, whether they found themselves in Morocco or Malaya.

That makes reasonable sense, but, this being prehistoric archaeology, there are other ways of looking at the Movius Line too. So far I have avoided giving a name to the ape-men who used Acheulean hand axes, but at this point the name we give them starts to matter.

Since the 1960s most paleoanthropologists have called the new species that evolved in Africa about 1.8 million years ago *Homo erectus* ("Upright Man") and have assumed that these creatures wandered through the subtropical latitudes to the shores of the Pacific Ocean. In the 1980s, however, some experts began focusing on subtle differences between *Homo erectus* skulls found in Africa and those found in East Asia. They suspected that they were in fact looking at two different species of ape-men. They coined a new name, *Homo ergaster* ("Working Man"), for those who evolved in Africa 1.8 million years ago and then spread all the way to China. Only when *Homo ergaster* reached East Asia, they suggested, did *Homo erectus* evolve from them. *Homo erectus* was therefore a purely East Asian species, distinct from the *Homo ergaster* who filled Africa, southwest Asia, and India.

If this theory is correct, the Movius Line was not just a trivial difference in tool types: it was a genetic watershed that split early ape-men in two. In fact, it raises the possibility of what we might call the mother of all long-term lock-in theories: that East and West are different because Easterners and Westerners are—and have been for more than a million years—different kinds of human beings.

THE FIRST EASTERNERS: PEKING MAN

This technical debate over classifying prehistoric skeletons has potentially alarming implications. Racists are often eager to pounce on such details to justify prejudice, violence, and even genocide. You might feel that taking the time to talk about a theory of this kind merely dignifies bigotry; perhaps we should just ignore it. But that, I think, would be a mistake. Pronouncing racist theories contemptible is not enough. If we really want to reject them, and to conclude that people (in large groups) really are all much the same, it must be because racist theories are wrong, not just because most of us today do not like them.

Basically, we do not know whether there was just one kind of ape-man on earth around 1.5 million years ago—meaning that ape-men (in large groups) were all much the same from Africa to Indonesia—or whether there was one distinct species of *Homo ergaster* west of the Movius Line and another of *Homo erectus* east of it. Only further research will clear that question up. But we do know, without a shadow of doubt, that within the last million years distinct species of ape-men *did* evolve in East and West.

Geography probably had a lot to do with this. The ape-men that drifted out of Africa around 1.7 million years ago were well adapted to subtropical climes, but as they wandered northward, deeper into Europe and Asia, they had to face longer and harsher winters. Living in the open air, like their African ancestors, became increasingly impractical as they advanced toward a line roughly 40 degrees north of the equator (running from the top of Portugal to Beijing; see Figure 1.1). So far as we can tell, building huts and making clothes were beyond their mental capacities, but they could figure out one response: take shelter in caves. Thus were born the cavemen we all heard about as children.

Cave-dwelling was a mixed blessing for the ape-men, who regularly had to share space with bears and lion-sized hyenas whose teeth could crunch up bones. It was a godsend for archaeologists, though, because caves preserve prehistoric deposits well, allowing us to trace how the evolution of ape-men began diverging in the Eastern and Western parts of the Old World as different adaptations to the colder climates took hold.

For understanding Eastern ape-men, the most important site is Zhoukoudian near Beijing, right on the 40-degree line, occupied on-and-off from about 670,000 through 410,000 years ago. The story of its excavation is an epic in its own right, and forms the backdrop to part of Amy Tan's excellent novel *The Bonesetter's Daughter*. While European, American, and Chinese archaeologists were digging here between 1921 and 1937, the hills around the site became the front line in a brutal civil war among Nationalists, Communists, and assorted home-grown warlords. The excavators often worked to the sound of gunfire and had to dodge bandits and checkpoints to take their finds back to

Beijing. The project finally collapsed when Japan invaded China, Zhoukoudian became a Communist base, and Japanese troops tortured and murdered three members of the team.

Matters then went from bad to worse. In November 1941, when war between Japan and the United States looked certain, a decision was taken to ship the finds to New York for safekeeping. Technicians packed them into two large crates to await collection in a car from the American embassy in Beijing. No one knows for sure if the car ever came, or where, if it did come, it took the crates. One story has it that Japanese soldiers intercepted the U.S. Marines escorting the finds at the very moment bombs started falling on Pearl Harbor, arrested them, and abandoned the priceless finds. Life was cheap in those dark days, and no one paid much attention to a few boxes of rocks and bones.

But all was not lost. The Zhoukoudian team had published their finds meticulously and had sent plaster casts of the bones to New York—an early example of the importance of backing up data. These show that by 600,000 years ago Peking Man* (as the excavators dubbed the Zhoukoudian ape-men) had diverged from tall, lanky Africans like the Turkana Boy toward a stockier form, better suited to cold. Peking Men were typically around five feet three inches tall and less hairy than modern apes, though if you ran into one on Main Street it would certainly be disconcerting. They had short, wide faces, with low, flat foreheads, a heavy single eyebrow, and a big jaw with almost no chin.

Conversation with Peking Man would be a challenge. So far as we can tell, the basal ganglia (the parts of the brain that allow modern humans to combine a small number of mouth movements into an infinite number of utterances) of *Homo erectus* were poorly developed. The well-preserved skeleton of the Turkana Boy also has a neural canal (holding the spinal cord) only three quarters as wide as a modern human's, suggesting that he could not control his breathing precisely enough to talk anything like we do.

That said, other finds suggest—indirectly—that ape-men in the Eastern Old World could communicate, after a fashion. In 1994 archaeologists on the little island of Flores near Java excavated what appeared to be 800,000-year-old stone tools. Eight hundred thousand

---

*Although we now normally transliterate the name of the Chinese capital as Beijing, by convention paleoanthropologists still speak of Peking Man.

years ago Flores was definitely an island, separated from the mainland by twelve miles of ocean; all of which seemed to mean that *Homo erectus* must have been able to communicate well enough to make boats, sail over the horizon, and colonize Flores. Other archaeologists, however, dismayed at the idea of boat-building *Homo erectus*, countered that perhaps these "tools" were not tools at all; maybe they were simply rocks bashed into misleading shapes by natural processes.

The argument could easily have deadlocked, as archaeological debates so often do, but in 2003 Flores yielded up even more astonishing discoveries. A deep sounding exposed eight skeletons, all dating around 16,000 BCE, all belonging to adults, and all under four feet tall. The first of Peter Jackson's films of *The Lord of the Rings* had just come out, and journalists immediately labeled these prehistoric little people "hobbits," after J.R.R. Tolkien's furry halflings. When animal populations are isolated on islands where there are no predators they quite often evolve into dwarf forms, and this is presumably how the "hobbits" came to be so small. To have shrunk to hobbit size by 16,000 BCE, though, ape-men must have colonized Flores many thousands of generations earlier—perhaps even as long as 800,000 years ago, as the stone tools found in 1994 suggest. The implication, once again, is that *Homo erectus* could communicate well enough to cross the sea.

The ape-men at Zhoukoudian, then, could probably make themselves understood much better than chimpanzees or gorillas, and the deposits from the cave suggest that they could also make fire at will. On at least one occasion Peking Men roasted a wild horse's head. Cuts on the skull show they were after its tongue and brain, both rich in fats. They may have been fond of one another's brains too: in the 1930s the excavators inferred cannibalism and even headhunting from bone-breakage patterns. A 1980s study of the plaster casts showed that most of the marks on the skulls were actually caused by the teeth of prehistoric giant hyenas rather than other Peking Men, but one skull—an additional fragment of which was excavated in 1966—definitely shows stone tool marks.

If instead of bumping into a Peking Man on a modern Main Street you could take a time machine back to Zhoukoudian half a million years ago, you would have a disorienting and alarming experience. You would see the cavemen communicating, perhaps with grunts and gestures, but you would not be able to talk to them. Nor could you get through to them by drawing pictures; there is no good evidence that art made any more sense to *Homo erectus* than it does to chimpanzees. The Peking Men that evolved in the Eastern Old World were very different from us.

THE FIRST WESTERNERS: NEANDERTHALS

But were Peking Men also different from the ape-men that were evolving in the Western Old World? The oldest finds from Europe, made in 1994 in a chain of caves at Atapuerca in Spain, date back about 800,000 years (roughly to the time that *Homo erectus* may have taken to boats and colonized Flores). In some ways, the Atapuerca finds were rather like those from Zhoukoudian: many of the bones were crisscrossed with cut marks from stone tools exactly like those that butchery would produce.

The hints of cannibalism grabbed headlines, but paleoanthropologists were even more excited by the ways in which Atapuerca differed from Zhoukoudian. The Atapuerca skulls had bigger brain cavities than those of *Homo erectus* and rather modern-looking noses and cheekbones. The paleoanthropologists concluded that a new species was emerging, which they called *Homo antecessor* ("Ancestral Man").

Homo antecessor helped make sense of a string of finds going back to 1907, when workmen had turned up a strange jawbone in a sandpit in Germany. This species, named Heidelberg Man after a nearby university town, looked much like *Homo erectus* but had heads more like ours, with high, rounded skulls and brains of about 1,000 cc—much bigger than the 800 cc average for *Homo erectus*. It looks as if the pace of evolutionary change accelerated all across the Old World after 800,000 years ago as ape-men entering the cold north encountered wildly different climates where random genetic mutations could flourish.*

Here at last we have some incontrovertible facts. By 600,000 years ago, when Heidelberg Man came onto the scene and Peking Man ruled

---

*That said, Heidelberg Man did live in Africa as well as Europe. Some paleoanthropologists envisage a European origin followed by a spread back into Africa, but others assume that Heidelberg Man, like *Homo habilis* and *Homo ergaster*, evolved in Africa in response to local climate changes, then spread north. Bones rather like Heidelberg Man's have also been found in China, but that evidence is more disputed.

the roost at Zhoukoudian, there were definitely different species of *Homo* in the Eastern and Western parts of the Old World: in the East the small-brained *Homo erectus* and in the West the larger-brained *Homo antecessor* and Heidelberg Man.*

When it comes to brains, size is not everything. Anatole France won the Nobel Prize for literature in 1921 with a brain no bigger than Heidelberg Man's. Yet Heidelberg Man does seem to have been a lot smarter than earlier ape-men or contemporary Peking Man. Before Heidelberg Man showed up, stone tools had barely changed for a million years, but by 500,000 BCE Heidelberg Man was making thinner and therefore lighter versions, striking more delicate flakes using soft (probably wood) hammers as well as just banging rocks together. This suggests better hand-eye coordination. Heidelberg Men and Women also made more specialized tools and began preparing specially shaped stone cores from which they could strike further tools at will, which must mean that they were just a lot better than *Homo erectus* at thinking about what they wanted from the world and how to get it. The very fact that Heidelberg Man could survive at Heidelberg, well north of the 40-degree line, is itself evidence of a smarter ape-man.

Zhoukoudian's occupants changed little between 670,000 and 410,000 years ago, but Western ape-men continued evolving across this period. If you crawl several hundred yards into the dank Spanish caves at Atapuerca, mostly on your belly and sometimes using ropes, you come to a forty-foot drop into the aptly named Pit of Bones—the densest concentration of ape-man remains ever found. More than four thousand fragments have been recovered here since the 1990s, dated between 564,000 and 600,000 years ago. Most belong to teenagers or young adults. What they were doing so far beneath the earth remains a mystery, but like the older Atapuerca deposit, the Pit of Bones has remarkably diverse human remains. The Spanish excavators classify most of them as Heidelberg Man, but many foreign scholars think they look more like yet another species—the Neanderthals.

These most famous of cavemen were first recognized in 1856, when quarry workers in the Neander Valley (Tal or Thal in German) showed

---

*And, of course, an unknown number of hominin species like the Flores hobbits that died out without leaving modern descendants. Another new species was identified in the mountains of central Asia in 2010, and was predictably labeled "the yeti."

a local schoolteacher a skullcap and fifteen bones they had found (excavations in the 1990s recovered a further sixty-two fragments from the workers' waste dump). The teacher showed them to an anatomist, who, with impressive understatement, pronounced them "pre-Germanic."

The Atapuerca finds suggest that Neanderthals emerged gradually across a quarter of a million years. Rather than climate change or expansion into new areas providing conditions for a few mutants to outbreed and replace Heidelberg Man, this may have been a case of genetic drift, with many different kinds of ape-men developing alongside one another. "Classic" Neanderthals appeared by 200,000 years ago and within another hundred thousand years spread over much of Europe and east into Siberia, though so far as we know they did not reach China or Indonesia.

Just how much did Neanderthals differ from Peking Men? They were typically about the same height as Eastern ape-men and were even more primitive-looking, with sloping foreheads and weak chins. They had big front teeth, often worn down from use as tools, set in forward-thrust faces with large noses, the latter perhaps an adaptation to the cold air of Ice Age Europe. Neanderthals were more heavily built than Peking Men, with broader hips and shoulders. They were as strong as wrestlers, had the endurance of marathon runners, and seem to have been ferocious fighters.

Despite having much heavier bones than most ape-men, Neanderthals got injured a lot; the closest modern parallel to their bone-breakage patterns, in fact, comes from professional rodeo riders. Since there were no bucking broncos to fall off a hundred thousand years ago (modern horses would not evolve until 4000 BCE), paleoanthropologists are confident that Neanderthals got hurt fighting—with one another and with wild animals. They were dedicated hunters; analysis of nitrogen isotopes from their bones shows that they were massively carnivorous, getting an amazing proportion of their protein from meat. Archaeologists had long suspected that Neanderthals got some of their meat by eating one another, just like Peking Man, and in the 1990s finds in France proved this beyond a doubt. The bones of half a dozen Neanderthals were found mixed with those of five red deer. The ape-men and deer had been treated exactly the same way: first they were cut into pieces with stone tools, then the flesh was sliced off their bones, and finally their skulls and long bones were smashed to get at their brains and marrow.

The details I have emphasized so far make Neanderthals sound not so different from Peking Men, but there is more to the story than this. For one thing, Neanderthals had big brains—even bigger brains than ours, in fact, averaging around 1,520 cc to our 1,350 cc. They also had wider neural canals than the Turkana Boy, and these thick spinal cords gave them more manual dexterity. Their stone tools were better made and more varied than Peking Men's, with specialized scrapers, blades, and points. Traces of tar on a stone point found embedded in a wild ass's neck in Syria suggest that it had been a spearhead attached to a stick. Wear patterns on tools suggest that Neanderthals used them mostly for cutting wood, which rarely survives, but at the waterlogged German site of Schöningen four beautifully carved seven-foot-long spears turned up near heaps of wild horse bones. The spears were weighted for thrusting, not throwing; for all their smartness, Neanderthals may not have been coordinated enough to use missile weapons.

The need to get up close to scary animals may account for Neanderthals' rodeo-rider injuries, but some finds, especially from Shanidar Cave in Iraq, hint at entirely different qualities. One skeleton showed that a man had survived with a withered arm and deformed legs for years, despite losing his right forearm and left eye (in her bestselling novel *The Clan of the Cave Bear*, Jean Auel based her character Creb—the disabled spiritual leader of a Neanderthal band living in Crimea—on this skeleton). Another man at Shanidar had crippling arthritis in his right ankle, but also managed to get by, at least until a stab wound killed him. Having bigger brains doubtless helped the weak and injured to help themselves; Neanderthals could definitely make fire at will and could probably turn animal skins into clothes. All the same, it is hard to see how the Shanidar men could have coped without help from able-bodied friends or family. Even the most austere scientists agree that Neanderthals—by contrast with all earlier kinds of *Homo* and their contemporaries at Zhoukoudian—showed something we can only call "humanity."

Some paleoanthropologists even think that Neanderthals' big brains and wide neural canals allowed them to talk more or less like us. Like modern humans they had hyoid bones, which anchor the tongue and let the larynx make the complex movements needed for speech. Other scholars disagree, though, noting that Neanderthal brains, while big, were longer and flatter than ours, and that the speech areas were probably less developed. They also point out that although the relevant areas survive on the bases of only three skulls, it looks as if Neanderthals' larynxes were very high in their necks, meaning that despite their hyoid bones they could vocalize only a narrow range of sounds. Maybe they could just grunt single syllables (what we might call the "me Tarzan, you Jane" model), or maybe they could express important concepts—"come here," "let's go hunting," "let's make stone tools/dinner/love"—by combining gestures and sounds (the *Clan of the Cave Bear* model, where Neanderthals have an elaborate sign language).

In 2001 it began to look like genetics might settle things. Scientists found that one British family that for three generations had shared a speech disorder called verbal dyspraxia also shared a mutation on a gene called FOXP2. This gene, it turned out, codes for a protein influencing how the brain processes speech and language. This does not mean that FOXP2 is "the language gene": speech is a bewilderingly complex process involving countless genes working together in ways we cannot yet fathom. FOXP2 came to geneticists' attention because sometimes it just needs one thing to go wrong for a whole system to crash. A mouse chews through a two-cent wire and my twenty-thousand-dollar car won't start; FOXP2 malfunctions and the brain's elaborate speech networks seize up. All the same, some archaeologists suggested, maybe random mutations producing FOXP2 and related genes gave modern humans linguistic skills that earlier species, including Neanderthals, lacked.

But then the plot thickened. As everyone now knows, deoxyribonucleic acid—DNA—is the basic building block of life, and in 2000 geneticists sequenced the modern human genome. What is less well known is that back in 1997, in a scene reminiscent of *Jurassic Park*, scientists in Leipzig, Germany, extracted ancient DNA from the arm of the original Neanderthal skeleton found in the Neander Valley in 1856. This was an extraordinary feat, since DNA begins breaking down immediately upon death, and only tiny fragments survive in such ancient material. The Leipzig team is not about to clone cavemen and open a Neanderthal Park, so far as I know,* but in 2007 the process of

---

*One Harvard anthropologist greeted the publication of the Neanderthal genome by suggesting that a mere $32 million investment would allow us to genetically modify modern human DNA and insert it into a chimpanzee cell to yield a genuine

sequencing a draft of the Neanderthal genome (which was completed in 2009) produced a remarkable discovery—that Neanderthals also had the FOXP2 gene.

Maybe this means that Neanderthals were as chatty as us; or maybe that FOXP2 was not the key to speech. One day we will surely know, but for now all we can do is observe the consequences of Neanderthals' interactions. They lived in bigger groups than earlier types of ape-men, hunted more effectively, occupied territories for longer periods, and cared about one another in ways earlier ape-men could not.

They also deliberately buried some of their dead, and perhaps even performed rituals over them—the earliest signs of that most human quality of all, a spiritual life, *if* we are interpreting the evidence correctly. At Shanidar, for instance, several bodies had definitely been buried, and the soil in one grave contained high concentrations of pollen, which might mean that some Neanderthals laid a loved one's body on a bed of spring flowers. (Rather less romantically, some archaeologists point out that the grave was honeycombed with rat burrows, and that rats often carry flowers into their lairs.)

In a second case, at Monte Circeo near Rome, construction workers in 1939 exposed a cave that had been sealed by a rockfall fifty thousand years ago. They told archaeologists that a Neanderthal skull sat on the floor in the middle of a circle of rocks, but because the workers moved the skull before experts saw it, many archaeologists harbor doubts.

Finally, there is Teshik-Tash in Uzbekistan. Here Hallam Movius (he of Movius Line fame) found the skeleton of a boy encircled, he said, by five or six pairs of wild goat horns. However, the deposits at Teshik-Tash are full of goat horns, and Movius never published plans or photographs of the finds to convince skeptics that these particular ones were in a meaningful pattern.

We need clearer evidence to lay this question to rest. Personally, I suspect that there is no smoke without fire, and that Neanderthals did have some kind of spiritual life. Perhaps they even had medicine women and shamans like Iza and Creb in *The Clan of the Cave Bear*. Whether

---

Neanderthal baby. The necessary technology is not—yet—available, but even when it is, we might hesitate to apply it; as my Stanford colleague Richard Klein, one of the world's leading paleoanthropologists, asked a journalist: "Are you going to put [the Neanderthals] in Harvard or in a zoo?"

that is right or not, though, if the time machine I invoked earlier could transport you to Shanidar as well as to Zhoukoudian, you would see real behavioral differences between Eastern Peking Man and Western Neanderthals. You would also be hard-pressed to avoid concluding that the West was more developed than the East. This may already have been true 1.6 million years ago, when the Movius Line took shape, but it was definitely true a hundred thousand years ago. Again the specter of a racist long-term lock-in theory rears its head: Does the West rule today because modern Europeans are the heirs of genetically superior Neanderthal stock, while Asians descend from the more primitive *Homo erectus*?

BABY STEPS

No.

Historians like giving long, complicated answers to simple questions, but this time things really do seem to be straightforward. Europeans do not descend from superior Neanderthals, and Asians do not descend from inferior *Homo erectus*. Starting around seventy thousand years ago, a new species of *Homo*—us—drifted out of Africa and completely replaced all other forms.* Our kind, *Homo sapiens* ("Wise Man"), did interbreed with Neanderthals in the process. Modern Eurasians share 1 to 4 percent of their genes with the Neanderthals, but everywhere from France to China it is the same 1 to 4 percent.† The spread of modern humans wiped the slate clean. Evolution of course continues, and local variations in skin color, face shape, height, lactose tolerance, and countless other things have appeared in the two thousand generations

---

*Some isolated groups, like the Flores "hobbits," possibly survived until recently. When Portuguese sailors reached Flores in the sixteenth century they claimed to have seen tiny, hairy cave dwellers who could barely talk. More than a hundred years have now passed since a sighting has been claimed, but it is said that similar little people still exist on Java. One of their hairs was recently produced, but on testing, its DNA turned out to be fully human. Some anthropologists believe that we will eventually encounter these last relics of premodern humanity in the shrinking Javanese forests. I have to admit I am skeptical.

†*Homo sapiens* who stayed in Africa, however, did not interbreed with Neanderthals, and modern Africans have no Neanderthal DNA. The implications of this have yet to be explored.

since we began spreading across the globe. But when we get right down to it, these are trivial. Wherever you go, whatever you do, people (in large groups) are all much the same.

The evolution of our species and its conquest of the planet established the biological unity of mankind and thereby the baseline for any explanation of why the West rules. Humanity's biological unity rules out race-based theories. Yet despite the overwhelming importance of these processes, much about the origins of modern humans remains obscure. By the 1980s archaeologists knew that skeletons more or less like ours first appeared around 150,000 years ago on sites in eastern and southern Africa. The new species had flatter faces, more retracted under their foreheads, than earlier ape-men. They used their teeth less as tools, had longer and less muscular limbs, and had wider neural canals and larynxes positioned better for speaking. Their brain cavities were a little smaller than Neanderthals' but their skullcaps were higher and more domed, leaving room for bigger speech and language centers and stacked layers of neurons that could perform massive numbers of calculations in parallel.

The skeletons suggested that the earliest *Homo sapiens* could walk the walk just like us, but—oddly—the archaeology suggested that for a hundred thousand years they stubbornly refused to talk the talk. *Homo sapiens* tools and behavior looked much like those of earlier ape-men, and—again like other ape-men, but utterly unlike us—early *Homo sapiens* seemed to have had just one way of doing things. Regardless of where archaeologists dug in Africa, they kept coming up with the same, not particularly exciting, kinds of finds. Unless, that is, they excavated *Homo sapiens* sites less than fifty thousand years old. On these younger sites *Homo sapiens* started doing all kinds of interesting things, and doing them in lots of different ways. For instance, archaeologists identify no fewer than six distinct styles of stone tools in use in Egypt's Nile Valley between 50,000 and 25,000 BCE, whereas before then a single fashion prevailed from South Africa to the shores of the Mediterranean.

Humans had invented style. Chipping stone tools this way, rather than that way, now marked a group off as different from their neighbors; chipping them a third way marked a new generation as different from their elders. Change remained glacial by the standards we are used to, when pulling out a four-year-old cell phone that can't make movies, locate me on a map, or check e-mail makes me look like a fossil, but it was meteoric compared to all that had gone before.

As any teenager coming home with hair dyed green or a new piercing will tell you, the best way to express yourself is to decorate yourself, but until fifty thousand years ago, it seemed that almost no one had felt this way. Then, apparently, almost everyone did. At site after site across Africa after 50,000 BCE archaeologists find ornaments of bone, animal tooth, and ivory; and these are just the activities that leave remains for us to excavate. Most likely all those other forms of personal adornment we know so well—hairstyles, makeup, tattoos, clothes—appeared around the same time. A rather unpleasant genetic study has suggested that human body lice, which drink our blood and live in our clothes, evolved around fifty thousand years ago as a little bonus for the first fashionistas.

"What a piece of work is a man!" gasps Hamlet when his friends Rosencrantz and Guildenstern come to spy on him. "How noble in reason! how infinite in faculty! in form and moving how express and admirable! in action how like an angel! in apprehension how like a god!" And in all these ways, how unlike an ape-man. By 50,000 BCE modern humans were thinking and acting on a whole different plane from their ancestors. Something extraordinary seemed to have happened—something so profound, so magical, that in the 1990s it moved normally sober scientists to flights of rhetoric. Some spoke of a Great Leap Forward;* others of the Dawn of Human Culture or even the Big Bang of Human Consciousness.

But for all their drama, these Great Leap Forward theories were always a little unsatisfactory. They required us to imagine not one but two transformations, the first (around 150,000 years ago) producing modern human bodies but not modern human behavior, and the second (around 50,000 years ago) producing modern human behavior but leaving our bodies unchanged. The most popular explanation was that the second transformation—the Great Leap—began with purely neurological changes that rewired the brain to make modern kinds of speech possible, which in turn drove a revolution in behavior; but just what this rewiring consisted of (and why there were no related changes to skulls) remained a mystery.

*Mao Zedong coined this phrase in 1957 to describe his radical experiment in industrialization and collectivization in China. It was one of the worst disasters in world history, and by the time Mao called it off in 1962 maybe 30 million people had starved (I return to it in Chapter 10). This makes "Great Leap Forward" rather an odd term to describe the emergence of fully modern humans, but it has caught on.

If there is anywhere that evolutionary science has left room for supernatural intervention, some superior power breathing a spark of divinity into the dull clay of ape-men, surely it is here. When I was (a lot) younger I particularly liked the story that opens Arthur C. Clarke's science-fiction novel *2001: A Space Odyssey* (and Stanley Kubrick's memorable, if hard to follow, movie version). Mysterious crystal monoliths drop from outer space to Earth, come to upgrade our planet's ape-men before they starve into extinction. Night after night Moon-Watcher, the alpha ape-man in one band of earthlings, feels what Clarke calls "inquisitive tendrils creeping down the unused byways of his brain" as a monolith sends him visions and teaches him to throw rocks. "The very atoms of his simple brain were being twisted into new patterns," says Clarke. And then the monolith's mission is done: Moon-Watcher picks up a discarded bone and brains a piglet with it. Depressingly, Clarke's vision of the Big Bang of Human Consciousness consists entirely of killing things, culminating in Moon-Watcher murdering One-Ear, the top ape-man in a rival band. Next thing the reader knows, we are in the space age.

Clarke set his *2001* moment 3 million years ago, presumably to account for the invention of tools by *Homo habilis*, but I always felt that the place where a good monolith would really do some work was when fully modern humans appeared. By the time I started studying archaeology in college I had learned not to say things like that, but I couldn't shake the feeling that the professionals' explanations were less compelling than Clarke's.

The big problem archaeologists had in those far-off days when I was an undergraduate was that they simply had not excavated very many sites dating between 200,000 and 50,000 years ago. As new finds accumulated across the 1990s, though, it began to become clear that we did not need monoliths after all; in fact, the Great Leap Forward itself began to dissolve into a series of Baby Steps Forward, spread across tens of thousands of years.

We now know of several pre-50,000-BCE sites with signs of surprisingly modern-looking behavior. Take, for instance, Pinnacle Point, a cave excavated in 2007 on the South African coast. *Homo sapiens* moved in here about 160,000 years ago. This is interesting in itself: earlier ape-men generally ignored coastal sites, probably because they could not work out how to find much food there. Yet *Homo sapiens* not only headed for the beach—distinctly modern behavior—but when they got there they were smart enough to gather, open, and cook shellfish. They also chipped stones into the small, light points that archaeologists call bladelets, perfect as tips for javelins or arrows—something that neither Peking Man nor Europe's Neanderthals ever did.

On a handful of other African sites people engaged in different but equally modern-looking activity. About a hundred thousand years ago at Mumbwa Cave in Zambia people lined a group of hearths with stone slabs to make a cozy nook where it is easy to imagine them sitting around telling stories, and at dozens of sites around Africa's coasts, from its southern tip to Morocco and Algeria in the north (and even just outside Africa, in Israel), people were sitting down and patiently cutting and grinding ostrich eggshells into beads, some of them just a quarter of an inch across. By ninety thousand years ago people at Katanda in the Congo had turned into proper fishermen, carving harpoons out of bone. The most interesting site of all, though, is Blombos Cave on Africa's southern coast, where in addition to shell beads, excavators found a 77,000-year-old stick of ocher (a type of iron ore). Ocher can be used for sticking things together, waterproofing sails, and all kinds of other tasks; but in recent times it has been particularly popular for drawing, producing satisfyingly bold red lines on tree bark, cave walls, and people's bodies. Fifty-seven pieces turned up at Pinnacle Point, and by 100,000 BCE it shows up on most African sites, which probably means that early humans liked drawing. The truly remarkable thing about the Blombos ocher stick, though, is that someone had scratched a geometric pattern on it, making it the world's oldest indisputable work of art—and one made for producing more works of art.

At each of these sites we find traces of one or two kinds of modern behavior, but never of the whole suite of activities that becomes familiar after 50,000 BCE. Nor is there much sign yet that the modern-looking activities were cumulative, building up gradually until they took over. But archaeologists are already beginning to feel their way toward an explanation for the apparent baby steps toward fully modern humanity, driven largely by climate change.

Geologists realized back in the 1830s that the miles-long, curving lines of rubble found in parts of Europe and North America must have been created by ice sheets pushing debris before them (not, as had previously been thought, by the biblical flood). The concept of an "ice age" was born, although another fifty years passed before scientists understood exactly why ice ages happen.

Earth's orbit around the sun is not perfectly round, because the gravity of other planets also pulls on us. Over the course of a hundred thousand years our orbit goes from being almost circular (as it is now) to being much more elliptical, then back again. Earth's tilt on its axis also shifts, on a 22,000-year rhythm, as does the way the planet wobbles around this axis, this time on a 41,000-year scale. Scientists call these Milankovich cycles, after a Serbian mathematician who worked them out, longhand, while interned during World War I (this was a very gentlemanly internment, leaving Milankovich free to spend all day in the library of the Hungarian Academy of Sciences). The patterns combine and recombine in bewilderingly complex ways, but on a roughly hundred-thousand-year schedule they take us from receiving slightly more solar radiation than the average, distributed slightly unevenly across the year, to receiving slightly less sunlight, distributed slightly more evenly.

None of this would matter much except for the way Milankovich cycles interact with two geological trends. First, over the last 50 million years continental drift has pushed most land north of the equator, and having one hemisphere mostly land and the other mostly water amplifies the effects of seasonal variations in solar radiation. Second, volcanic activity has declined across the same period. There is (for the time being) less carbon dioxide in our atmosphere than there was in the age of the dinosaurs, and because of this the planet has—over the very long run and until very recently—steadily cooled.

Through most of Earth's history the winters were cold enough that it snowed at the poles and this snow froze, but normally the sun melted this ice every summer. By 14 million years ago, however, declining volcanic activity had cooled Earth so much that at the South Pole, where there is a large landmass, the summer sun no longer melted the ice. At the North Pole, where there is no landmass, ice melts more easily, but by 2.75 million years ago temperatures had dropped enough for ice to survive year-round there, too. This had huge consequences, because now whenever Milankovich cycles gave Earth less solar radiation, distributed more evenly across the year, the North Pole ice cap would expand onto northern Europe, Asia, and America, locking up more water, making the earth drier and the sea level lower, reflecting back more solar radiation, and reducing temperatures further still. Earth then spiraled down into an ice age—until the planet wobbled, tilted, and rotated its way back to a warmer place, and the ice retreated.

Depending on how you count, there have been between forty and fifty ice ages, and the two that spanned the period from 190,000 through 90,000 BCE—crucial millennia in human evolution—were particularly harsh. Lake Malawi, for instance, contained just one-twentieth as much water in 135,000 BCE as it does today. The tougher environment must have changed the rules for staying alive, which may explain why mutations favoring braininess began flourishing. It may also explain why we have found so few sites from this period; most protohumans probably died out. Some archaeologists and geneticists in fact estimate that around 100,000 BCE there were barely twenty thousand *Homo sapiens* left alive.

If this new theory is correct, the population crisis would have done several things at once. On the one hand, by shrinking the gene pool it would have made it easier for mutations to flourish; but on the other, if *Homo sapiens* bands became smaller they would die out more easily, taking any advantageous mutations with them. If (as seems likely from the tiny number of sites known from this period) there were also fewer bands, groups would meet less often and have less chance to pool their genes and knowledge. We should probably imagine that for a hundred thousand years tiny bands of protohumans eked out livings in Africa in unfriendly and unpredictable environments. They did not meet, interbreed, or exchange goods and information very often. Genetic mutations flourished in these isolated pockets of people, some producing humans very like us, some not. Some groups figured out harpoons, many made beads, but most did neither, and the specter of extinction haunted them all.

These were dark days for *Homo sapiens*, but around seventy thousand years ago their luck changed. Eastern and southern Africa became warmer and wetter, which made hunting and gathering easier, and humans reproduced as rapidly as their food sources. Modern *Homo sapiens* had been evolving for a good hundred thousand years, with a lot of trial, error, and extinctions, but when the climate improved, those populations with the most advantageous mutations took off, outbreeding less brainy humans. There were no monoliths; no Great Leap Forward; just a lot of sex and babies.

Within a few thousand years early humans reached a tipping point that was as much demographic as biological. Instead of dying out so often, bands of modern humans grew big enough and numerous enough to stay in regular contact, pooling their genes and know-how. Change became cumulative and the behavior of *Homo sapiens* diverged rapidly from that of other ape-men. And once that happened, the days of biological distinctions between East and West were numbered.

OUT OF AFRICA—AGAIN

Climate change is rarely simple, and while *Homo sapiens'* homelands in eastern and southern Africa were getting wetter seventy thousand years ago, North Africa was drying out. Our ancestors, multiplying rapidly in their home ranges, chose not to spread in that direction; instead, little bands wandered from what is now Somalia across a land bridge to southern Arabia, and then to Iran (Figure 1.3). At least, this is what we think they must have done. There has been relatively little archaeological exploration in South Asia, but we have to assume bands of modern humans moved this way, because by 60,000 BCE they had reached Indonesia, taken to boats, crossed fifty miles of open water, and wandered as far as Lake Mungo in southern Australia. The colonists

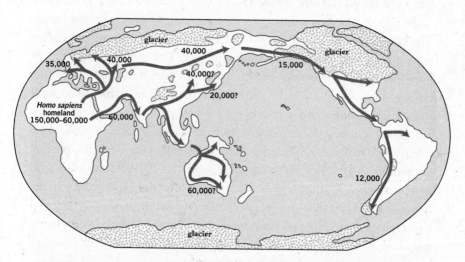

Figure 1.3. The unity of mankind restored: the spread of fully modern humans out of Africa between roughly 60,000 and 12,000 years ago. The numbers show how many years ago humans arrived in each part of the world and the coastlines represent those of the late Ice Age, around 20,000 years ago.

moved fifty times faster than *Homo erectus/ergaster* had done when they left Africa, averaging more than a mile a year compared to the earlier ape-men's thirty-five yards.

Between fifty thousand and forty thousand years ago a second wave of migrants probably moved through Egypt into southwest and central Asia, spreading from there into Europe. Clever enough to make themselves delicate blades and bone needles, these modern humans cut and sewed fitted clothing and built houses out of mammoth tusks and skins, turning even the frigid wastes of Siberia into a home. Around 15,000 BCE humans crossed the land bridge linking Siberia and Alaska and/or sailed in short hops along its edge. By 12,000 BCE they had left coprolites (scientist-speak for dung) in caves in Oregon and seaweed in the mountains of Chile. (Some archaeologists think humans also crossed the Atlantic along the edge of ice sheets then linking Europe and America, though as yet this remains speculative.)

The situation in East Asia is less clear. A fully modern human skull from Liujiang in China may be 68,000 years old, but there are some technical problems with this date, and the oldest uncontroversial remains date back only to around 40,000 BCE. More digging will settle whether modern humans reached China relatively early or relatively late,* but they certainly reached Japan by twenty thousand years ago.

Wherever the new humans went, they seem to have wrought havoc. The continents where earlier ape-men had never set foot were teeming with giant game when *Homo sapiens* arrived. The first humans to enter New Guinea and Australia encountered four-hundred-pound flightless birds and one-ton lizards; by 35,000 BCE these were extinct. The finds from Lake Mungo and a few other sites suggest that humans arrived around 60,000 BCE, meaning that humans and megafauna coexisted for twenty-five millennia, but some archaeologists dispute the dates, putting humanity's arrival just forty thousand years ago. If they are right, the great beasts disappeared suspiciously quickly after humans arrived. In the Americas, the first human colonists fifteen thousand years ago met camels, elephants, and huge ground sloths; within four thousand years these, too, were all extinct. The coincidence between the coming of *Homo sapiens* and the going of the giant animals is, to say the least, striking.

---

*Some Chinese archaeologists think modern humans evolved independently in China. I discuss this idea below.

There is no direct evidence that humans hunted these animals to extinction or drove them off their ranges, and alternative explanations for the extinctions (like climate change or comet explosions) abound. But there is less debate over the fact that when modern humans entered environments already occupied by ape-men, the ape-men became extinct. Modern humans had entered Europe by 35,000 BCE, and within ten thousand years Neanderthals had vanished everywhere except the continent's mountainous fringes. The latest Neanderthal deposits known to us, from Gibraltar in southern Spain, date to around 25,000 BCE. After dominating Europe for 150,000 years, the Neanderthals simply disappeared.

The details of how modern humans replaced ape-men, though, are crucial for deciding whether racial explanations for Western rule make sense. We do not know, yet, whether our ancestors actively killed less intellectually gifted species or just outcompeted them for food. At most sites, modern human deposits simply replace those associated with Neanderthals, suggesting that the change was sudden. The main exception is Reindeer Cave in France, where phases of Neanderthal and modern human occupation apparently alternated between 33,000 and 35,000 years ago, and the Neanderthal layers contain stone foundations for huts, bone tools, and necklaces of animal teeth. The excavators suggested that Neanderthals learned from modern humans and were moving toward a Dawn of Neanderthal Consciousness. Several finds of ocher on Neanderthal sites in France (twenty pounds of it in one cave) may point the same way.

It is easy to imagine heavily muscled, low-browed Neanderthals watching the quicker, talkative newcomers painting their bodies and building huts, then struggling to repeat these actions with their clumsy fingers, or perhaps trading freshly killed meat for jewelry. In *The Clan of the Cave Bear*, Jean Auel imagined modern humans contemptuously chasing off Neanderthal "Flatheads," while Neanderthals just tried to stay out of the way of "the Others"—except, that is, for Ayla, an orphaned five-year-old human girl whom the Neanderthal Cave Bear clan adopt, with transformative results. It is all fantasy, of course, but it is as plausible as anyone else's guess (unless we follow those unromantic archaeologists who point out that sloppy excavation is the most economical explanation for the interleaved Neanderthal and human deposits at Reindeer Cave, meaning that there is no direct evidence for Flatheads learning from Others).

The bottom line is sex. If modern humans replaced Neanderthals in the Western Old World and *Homo erectus* in the Eastern regions without interbreeding, racist theories tracing contemporary Western rule back to prehistoric biological differences must be wrong. But was that what happened?

In the heyday of so-called scientific racism in the 1930s, some physical anthropologists insisted that modern Chinese people were more primitive than Europeans because their skulls had similarities (small ridges on top, relatively flat upper faces, nonprotruding jaws, shovel-shaped incisors) to those of Peking Man. So, too, these anthropologists pointed out, the skulls of Australia's indigenous peoples had similarities— ridges around the back for attaching neck muscles, shelflike brows, receding foreheads, large teeth—with those of Indonesian *Homo erectus* a million years ago. Modern Easterners, these (Western) scholars concluded, must have descended from these more primitive ape-men, while Westerners descended from the more advanced Neanderthals; and that might well explain why the West rules.

No one puts things so crudely today, but if we are serious about asking why the West rules we have to confront the possibility that *Homo sapiens* interbred with premodern peoples, and that Eastern populations remain biologically less advanced than Western. We will never be able to excavate copulating cavemen to see whether *Homo sapiens* merged their genes with Neanderthals in the West and with Peking Man in the East, but fortunately we do not need to, because we can observe the consequences of their trysts in our own bodies.

Each of us has inherited our DNA from all the ancestors we ever had, which means that in theory geneticists could compare the DNA of everyone alive and draw a family tree going back to humanity's most recent shared ancestor. In practice, though, the fact that half the DNA in your body comes from your mother's line and half from your father's makes disentangling the information as difficult as unscrambling an egg.

Geneticists found a clever way around this problem by focusing on mitochondrial DNA. Rather than being reproduced sexually, like most DNA, mitochondrial DNA is transmitted solely by women (men inherit mitochondrial DNA from their mothers but do not pass it on). Once upon a time we all had the same mitochondrial DNA, so any difference between the mitochondrial DNA in my body and that in yours must be the result of random mutations, not sexual mixing.

In 1987 a team led by the geneticist Rebecca Cann published a study of mitochondrial DNA in living people from all over the world. They distinguished about 150 types within their data and realized that no matter how they shuffled the statistics, they kept getting three key results: first, that there is more genetic diversity in Africa than anywhere else; second, that the diversity in the rest of the world is just a subset of the diversity within Africa; and third, that the deepest—and therefore oldest—mitochondrial DNA lineages all come from Africa. The conclusion was unavoidable: the last female ancestor shared by everyone in the world must have lived in Africa—African Eve, as she was immediately dubbed. As Cann and her colleagues observed, she was "one lucky mother." Using standard estimates of mutation rates in mitochondrial DNA, they concluded that Eve lived 200,000 years ago.

Throughout the 1990s paleoanthropologists argued over the Cann team's conclusions. Some questioned their methods (there are thousands of ways to arrange the scores, in theory all equally valid) and others their evidence (most of the "Africans" in the original study were actually African-Americans), but no matter who redid the samples or the numbers, the results came out much the same. The only real change was to push Eve's lifetime closer to 150,000 years ago. To clinch matters, African Eve got company at the end of the 1990s when technical advances allowed geneticists to examine nuclear DNA on the Y chromosome. Like mitochondrial DNA, this is reproduced asexually, but is transmitted only through the male line. The studies found that Y-chromosome DNA also has the greatest variety and deepest lineages in Africa, pointing to an African Adam living between sixty thousand and ninety thousand years ago, and an origin for non-African variants around fifty thousand years ago.* In 2010, geneticists added one more detail: immediately after they left Africa, *Homo sapiens* copulated enough

---

*If it sounds odd that African Adam lived a hundred thousand years after African Eve, that is because the names do not mean anything. These were not the first *Homo sapiens* man and woman; they are just the most recent ancestors to whom everyone alive today can trace genes. On average, men have just as many offspring as women (obviously, since we all have one father and one mother), but the number of children per man varies more around that average than does the number of children per woman, since some men father dozens of babies. The relatively large pool of men with no children means that men's genetic lines die out more easily than women's, and the surviving male lines therefore converge on a more recent ancestor than the female ones.

with Neanderthals to pick up a trace of their DNA, and they then spread this mix across the rest of the planet.

But some paleoanthropologists remain unconvinced, insisting that genetics counts for less than the skeletal similarities they see between Western *Homo sapiens* and Neanderthals and between Eastern *Homo sapiens* and *Homo erectus*. In place of the out-of-Africa model they propose a "multiregional" model. Maybe, they concede, the initial Baby Steps Forward did happen in Africa, but population movements between Africa, Europe, and Asia then promoted such rapid gene flows that beneficial mutations in one place spread everywhere within a few thousand years. As a result, slightly different kinds of modern humans evolved in parallel in several parts of the world. That would explain both the skeletal and the genetic evidence, and would also mean that Easterners and Westerners really are biologically different.

Like so many theories, multiregionalism can cut two ways, and some Chinese scientists have insisted that China is exceptional beause—as the *China Daily* newspaper puts it—"modern Chinese man originated in what is present-day Chinese territory rather than Africa." Since the late 1990s, though, the evidence has tipped steadily against this idea. There has been relatively little analysis of ancient DNA in East Asia, and still less that offers cheer to the multiregionalists. The authors of one Y-chromosome study even conclude that "the data do not support even a minimal *in situ* hominid contribution to the origin of anatomically modern humans in East Asia." In Europe, initial studies of Neanderthal mitochondrial DNA found zero overlap with human mitochondrial DNA (whether found in 24,000-year-old skeletons or in living, breathing Europeans), suggesting that Neanderthals and *Homo sapiens* did not—perhaps could not—interbreed at all. The unraveling of the full Neanderthal genome has now shown that this went too far, and that Neanderthals did once inspire enough passion among *Homo sapiens* to make a small mark on our DNA; but it also showed that that mark is exactly the same all the way from France to China. Everywhere in Eurasia, people (in large groups) are all much the same.

The debate over multiregional origins drags on, and as recently as 2007 new finds from Zhoukoudian and from Xuchang were being trumpeted as showing that modern humans must have evolved from *Homo erectus* in China. Even as the publication announcing these finds was being printed, however, other scholars drove what looks to be the final nail into the multiregionalist coffin. Their sophisticated multiple-regression analysis of measurements from more than six thousand skulls showed that when we control for climate, the variations in skull types around the world are in fact consistent with the DNA evidence. Our dispersals out of Africa in the last sixty thousand years wiped the slate clean of all the genetic differences that had emerged over the previous half million years.

Racist theories grounding Western rule in biology have no basis in fact. People, in large groups, are much the same wherever we find them, and we have all inherited the same restless, inventive minds from our African ancestors. Biology by itself cannot explain why the West rules.

PREHISTORIC PICASSOS

So if the racial theories are wrong, where *did* East and West begin? The answer has seemed obvious to many Europeans for more than a hundred years: even if biology does not enter into it, they have confidently asserted, Europeans have just been culturally superior to Easterners ever since there were such things as modern humans. The evidence that convinced them began to appear in 1879. Charles Darwin's *On the Origin of Species*, published two decades earlier, had made fossil-hunting a respectable hobby for gentlemen, and like so many of his class, Don Marcelino Sanz de Sautuola took to looking for cavemen on his estates in northern Spain. One day, with his daughter in tow, he visited the cave of Altamira. Archaeology is not much fun for eight-year-olds, so while Sautuola fixed his eyes on the ground, little Maria ran around playing games. "Suddenly," she told an interviewer many years later, "I made out forms and figures on the roof." She gasped: "Look, Papa, bulls!"

All archaeologists dream of an "Oh my God" moment—the instant of absolute disbelief, when time stands still and everything falls away in the face of the unbelievable, awe-inspiring discovery. Not many archaeologists actually have one, and maybe no archaeologist ever had one quite like this. Sautuola saw bison, deer, layer upon layer of multicolored animals covering twenty feet of the cave's ceiling, some curled up, some cavorting, some leaping gaily (Figure 1.4). Each was

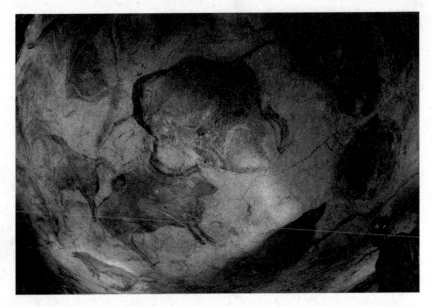

Figure 1.4. "After Altamira, all is decadence . . ." Just part of the stunning Ceiling of Bulls discovered by eight-year-old Maria Sanz de Sautuola in 1879, which ruined her father's life and took Picasso's breath away.

beautifully, movingly rendered. When Picasso visited the site years later, he was stunned. "None of us could paint like that," he said. "After Altamira, all is decadence."

Sautuola's first reaction was to laugh, but quickly he became "so enthusiastic," Maria recalled, "that he could hardly speak." He gradually convinced himself that the paintings really were ancient (the latest studies suggest some are more than 25,000 years old). Back in 1879, though, no one knew this. In fact, when Sautuola presented the site at the International Congress of Anthropology and Prehistoric Archaeology in Lisbon in 1880, the professionals laughed him off the stage. Everyone knew that cavemen could not produce such art; Sautuola, they agreed, was either a liar or a sucker. Sautuola took this—rightly— as an attack on his honor. He died a broken man eight years later. His "Oh my God" moment ruined his life.

Not until 1902 did Sautuola's main critic actually visit Altamira and publicly recant, and since then several hundred prehistoric painted caves have been found. Chauvet Cave in France, one of the most spectacular of all, was discovered as recently as 1994, so well preserved that it looked like the artists had just stepped out for a quick bite of reindeer and would be back at any moment. One of the paintings at Chauvet is thirty thousand years old, making it one of the earliest traces of modern humans in western Europe.

Nothing quite like these cave paintings has been found anywhere else in the world. The modern human migration out of Africa had swept away all distinctions created by the Movius Line and all biological divergences between earlier species of ape-men; but should we locate the true beginning of a special (and superior) Western tradition thirty thousand years ago in a uniquely creative culture that filled northern Spain and southern France with prehistoric Picassos?

The answer, perhaps surprisingly, lies in the frozen wastes of Antarctica. Every year snow falls there, burying previous snows, and compressing them into thin layers of ice. These layers are like a chronicle of ancient weather. By separating them, climatologists can measure their thickness, telling us how much snow fell; establish the balance between isotopes of oxygen, revealing temperatures; and compare the amounts of carbon dioxide and methane, illuminating greenhouse effects. But drilling cores through the ice sheets is one of the toughest assignments in science. In 2004 a European team finished extracting an Antarctic core almost two miles deep, going back an astonishing 740,000 years, to the days when Neanderthals were still a twinkle in some ape-man's eye. The scientists did this despite temperatures that plunged to $-58°F$ in winter and never got above $-13°$, being forced to start over when the drill jammed in 1999, and having to use a plastic bag filled with ethanol as a makeshift drill bit for the final hundred yards.

The results these supermen and -women of science extracted from the ice make one thing very clear: the world the Altamira artists lived in was cold. Temperatures had started tumbling again after modern humans left Africa, and around twenty thousand years ago—when more artists were daubing ocher and charcoal on cave walls than ever before or since—the last ice age reached its chilling climax. Average temperatures stood $14°F$ below those of recent times. That made a staggering difference. Mile-thick glaciers covered northern Asia, Europe, and America, locking up so much water that the sea level was more than three hundred feet lower than today. You could have walked from Africa to England, Australia, or America without ever laying eyes on the sea. Not that you would have wanted to visit many of these places;

at the edges of the glaciers winds howled and dust storms raged across vast arid steppes, frigid in winter and barren in summer. Even in the least forbidding regions, within 40 degrees of the equator, short summers, meager rainfall, and reduced levels of carbon dioxide in the air limited plant growth and kept animal (including human) populations low. Things were as bad as in the worst days before modern humans left Africa.

Life was easier in what are now the tropics than it was in Siberia, but wherever archaeologists look, they find that people adapted to the Ice Age in rather similar ways. They lived in tiny bands. In colder environments, a dozen people was a big group; in the milder regions, twice that many might stick together. They learned when different plants ripened and where to find them; when animals migrated ahead of the seasons and where they could intercept them; and they followed both around the landscape. Those who did not learn these things starved.

Such tiny bands would have struggled to reproduce themselves. Like modern hunter-gatherers in marginal environments, they must have come together from time to time to exchange marriage partners, trade goods, tell stories, and perhaps speak to their gods, spirits, and ancestors. These gatherings would have been the most exciting social events on the calendar. We are guessing, of course, but many archaeologists think these festival days lie behind western Europe's spectacular cave paintings: everyone put on their best skins and beads, painted their faces, and did what they could to decorate their holy meeting places, making them truly special.

The obvious question, though, is why—if these hard facts of life applied all across Africa, Asia, and Europe—we find such spectacular cave paintings only in western Europe. The traditional answer, that Europeans were more culturally creative than anyone else, seems to make a lot of sense, but we might do better to turn the question around. The history of European art is not a continuous catalogue of masterpieces running from Chauvet to Chagall; the cave paintings died out after 11,500 BCE and many millennia passed before we know of anything to equal them.

Looking for the roots of Western rule in a thirty-thousand-year tradition of European creativity is obviously mistaken if this tradition in fact dried up for thousands of years. Perhaps we should ask instead why the cave paintings ended, because once we do so it starts to look like the astonishing finds from prehistoric Europe have as much to do with geography and climate as with any special Western culture.

Through most of the Ice Age, northern Spain and southern France were excellent hunting grounds, where herds of reindeer migrated from summer to winter pastures and back again. But when temperatures started rising about fifteen thousand years ago (more on this in Chapter 2) the reindeer stopped migrating this far south in winter, and the hunters followed them northward.

It cannot be a coincidence that western European cave painting declined at just the same time. Fewer and fewer artists crawled under the ground with their animal-fat lamps and sticks of ocher. Sometime around 13,500 years ago the very last artist walked away. He or she probably did not realize it, but on that day the ancient tradition died. Darkness fell in the caves, and for millennia only bats and dripping water disturbed their tomblike silence.

Why did beautiful cave paintings not move steadily northward across Europe after 11,500 BCE as hunters followed the retreating reindeer? Probably for the very good reason that northern European hunters did not have such convenient caves to paint. Northern Spain and southern France have a tremendous number of deep limestone caves; northern Europe has far fewer. The efforts prehistoric peoples made to decorate their meeting places rarely survived for us to find unless hunting grounds coincided with deep caves. Whenever this happy coincidence failed to arise, people must have gathered nearer to or even above the surface. Exposed to wind, sun, and rain for twenty thousand years, few traces of their artwork survive.

"Few traces" is not the same as "no traces," though, and sometimes we get lucky. At the wonderfully named Apollo 11 Cave in Namibia, slabs of stone with drawings of rhinos and zebras peeled off the wall, fell to the floor, and were preserved under deposits that formed between 19,000 and 26,000 years ago, and some Australian examples are even older. At Sandy Creek, mineral deposits that built up over part of a carving on a cave wall can be dated to about 25,000 years ago and fragments of pigment are 26,000 to 32,000 years old, while at Carpenter's Gap part of a painted cave wall fell into 40,000-year-old occupation debris, making it even earlier than Chauvet.

None of the African or Australian examples compares aesthetically with the best French and Spanish work, and there are quite a few deep

caves outside western Europe that do not have paintings (like Zhoukoudian, reoccupied twenty thousand years ago). It would be silly to
claim that all humans put equal effort into cave. art, let alone that all
artistic traditions are equally successful. But given the preservation issues and the fact that archaeologists have been looking longer and
harder in Europe than anywhere else, the survival of anything at all on
other continents suggests that all modern humans, everywhere, shared
the urge to create art. Where the conditions for cave painting were not
so good as in western Europe, people may have put their energy into
other media.

Figure 1.5 shows nicely that while cave art clusters in western
Europe, stone, clay, and bone models of humans and animals are more
common farther east. If the economics of publishing allowed it, I could
show pictures of dozens of quite extraordinary figurines, found everywhere from Germany to Siberia. Since it does not, I will limit myself

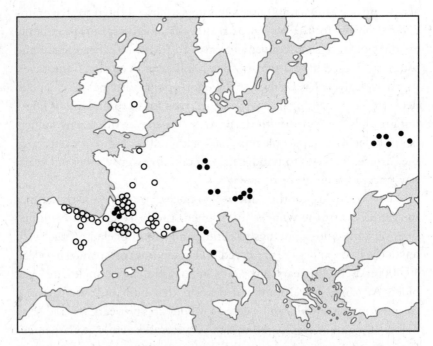

Figure 1.5. The beginnings of Western culture? The open circles show
cave paintings 12,000 or more years old, and the solid circles
show finds of portable art of the same age.

to the most recent discovery, found in 2008 at Hohle Fels in Germany (Figure 1.6)—a two-inch-tall statuette of a woman with no head but with gigantic breasts, carved 35,000 years ago from mammoth ivory. Around the same date hunters at Malaya Síya near Lake Baikal in Siberia—surely one of the most inhospitable spots on earth—took time to engrave pictures of animals on bones; and by 25,000 BCE groups up to 120 strong were gathering in huts of mammoth bone and skin at Dolní Vestonice in the Czech Republic, where they made thousands of clay figurines of animals and, again, large-breasted women. In East Asia the artistic record remains thin, but the earliest find—a tiny model bird carved perhaps fifteen thousand years ago from a deer antler, discovered at Xuchang in 2009—seems so sophisticated that we can be confident that future excavations will reveal a flourishing Ice Age artistic tradition in China, too.

Ice Age humans outside western Europe, lacking the conditions that made Chauvet and Altamira what they were, apparently found

Figure 1.6. The urge to create: a two-inch-tall, 35,000-year-old headless statuette of a huge-breasted "Venus," carved from mammoth ivory, found in 2008 at Hohle Fels in Germany

other outlets for their creativity. There is precious little evidence that earlier ape-men felt any creative urges at all, but imagination seems to be hardwired into *Homo sapiens*. By fifty thousand years ago humans had the mental faculties to seek meaning in the world and the skills to represent these meanings in art and (probably, though we cannot observe it) poetry, music, and dance. Once again, people (in large groups) all seem to be much the same, wherever we find them. For all its splendor, Altamira did not make the West different from the rest.

Technological, intellectual, and biological differences accumulated for more than a million and a half years after the first ape-men left Africa, dividing the Old World into a Neanderthal/*Homo sapiens* West and a *Homo erectus* East. Around a hundred thousand years ago the West was characterized by relatively advanced technology and even hints of humanity, while the East looked increasingly backward; but when fully modern humans moved out of Africa sixty thousand years ago they swept all this away. By the time the last ice age reached its climax twenty thousand years ago, "east" and "west" were just directions in which the sun rose and set. Far more united the little bands of humans scattered from Britain to Siberia—and (relatively) soon to cross over into America—than divided them. Each band foraged and hunted, roaming over huge areas as plants ripened and animals came and went. Each must have known its territory intimately and have told stories about every rock and tree; each had its own art and traditions, tools and weapons, spirits and demons. And each surely knew that their gods loved them, because they were, in spite of everything, still alive.

Humans had come as far as they were likely to in such a cold, dry world; and there, we must suspect, things would have stayed, had the earth not wobbled under their feet.

2

⊙ ⊙ ⊙

THE WEST TAKES THE LEAD

GLOBAL WARMING

Though the cavemen shivering around their campfires twenty thousand years ago could not know it, their world had begun moving back toward warmth. Over the next ten thousand years the combination of climate change and their own superfast brains would transform geography, generating distinct regional ways of life that have continued to this very day. East and West began to mean something.

The consequences of global warming were mind-boggling. In two or three centuries around 17,000 BCE the sea level rose forty feet as the glaciers that had blanketed northern America, Europe, and Asia melted. The area between Turkey and Crimea, where the waves of the Black Sea now roll (Figure 2.1), had been a low-lying basin during the Ice Age, but glacial runoff now turned it into the world's biggest freshwater lake. It was a flood worthy of Noah's ark,* with the waters rising

*In their 1999 book *Noah's Flood*, the geologists William Ryan and Walter Pitman suggested that the Black Sea flood did inspire the Bible story. They dated the flood around 5600 BCE, but more recent studies have shown that the basin was probably flooded by freshwater between 16,000 and 14,000 BCE and then turned salty after the Mediterranean broke through, somewhere around 7400 BCE. It is unlikely that such an early catastrophe inspired the Noah story, and the submergence of what is now the Persian Gulf may be a more plausible source for the flood narratives in ancient literature.

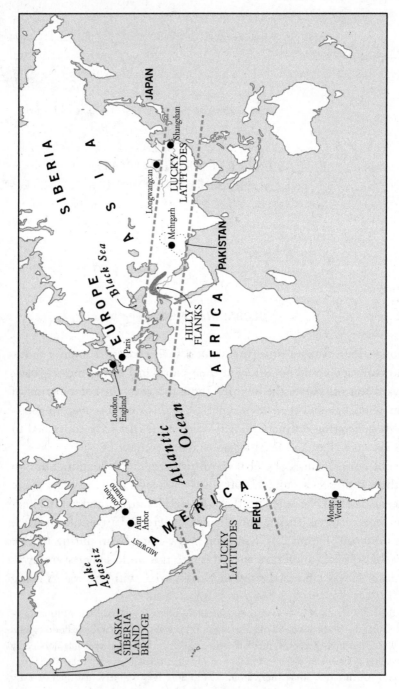

Figure 2.1. The big picture: this chapter's story seen at the global scale

six inches per day at some stages. Every time the sun came up, the lakeshore had advanced another mile. Nothing in modern times begins to compare.

Earth's changing orbit set off a wild seesaw of warming and cooling, feast and famine. Figure 2.2 shows how the ratios between two isotopes of oxygen in the Antarctic ice cores mentioned in Chapter 1 zigzagged back and forth as the climate changed. Only after about 14,000 BCE, when melting glaciers stopped dumping icy water into the oceans, did the world clearly start taking two steps toward warmth for every one back toward freezing. Around 12,700 BCE these steps turned into a gallop, and within a single lifespan the globe warmed by about 5°F, bringing it within a degree or two of what we have known in recent times.

Medieval Christians liked to think of the universe as a Great Chain of Being, from God down to the humblest earthworm. The rich man in his castle, the poor man at his gate—all had their allotted places in a timeless order. We might do better, though, to imagine an anything-but-timeless Great Chain of Energy. Gravitational energy structures the universe. It turned the primeval cosmic soup into hydrogen and helium and then turned these simple elements into stars. Our sun works as a great nuclear reactor converting gravitational into electromagnetic

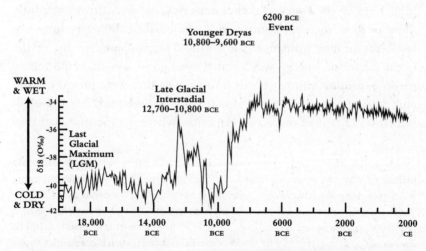

Figure 2.2. A story written in ice: the ratio between oxygen isotopes in air bubbles trapped in the Antarctic ice pack, revealing the swings between warm/wet and cold/dry weather across the last twenty thousand years

energy, and plants on Earth photosynthesize a tiny portion of this into chemical energy. Animals then consume plants, metabolizing chemical energy into kinetic energy. The interplay between solar and other planets' gravities shapes the earth's orbit, determining how much electromagnetic energy we get, how much chemical energy plants create, and how much kinetic energy animals make from it; and that determines everything else.

Around 12,700 BCE, Earth leaped up the Great Chain of Energy. More sunlight meant more plants, more animals, and more choices for humans, about how much to eat, how much to work, and how much to reproduce. Every individual and every little band probably combined the options in their own ways, but overall, humans reacted to moving up the Great Chain of Energy in much the same ways as the plants and animals they preyed upon: they reproduced. For every human alive around 18,000 BCE (maybe half a million) there were a dozen people in 10,000 BCE.

Just how people experienced global warming depended on where they lived. In the southern hemisphere the great oceans moderated the impact of climate change, but the north saw dramatic contrasts. For foragers in the pre–Black Sea Basin, warming was a disaster, and things were little better for people living on coastal plains. They had enjoyed some of the Ice Age world's richest pickings, but a warmer world meant higher sea levels. Every year they retreated as waves drowned a little more of their ancestral hunting grounds, until finally everything was lost.* Yet for most humans in the northern hemisphere, moving up the Great Chain of Energy was an unalloyed good. People could follow plants and other animals north into regions that were previously too cold to support them, and by 13,000 BCE (the exact date is disputed) humans had fanned out across America, where no ape-man had trod

---

*Some people believe that wondrous civilizations, richer than Atlantis, flourished on the coastal plains of the Ice Age but were forgotten after 12,700 BCE when the rising sea engulfed them. Archaeologists generally ignore this idea, not because they are trying to hide the truth, but because it is just not plausible. Apart from anything else, it requires us to believe that no one from the interior highlands (that is, areas that still lie above the water) ever traded with the lost cities or imitated their achievements. Despite more than a hundred years of excavations, no wonderful works from lost civilizations have turned up. Trawlers regularly dredge up Ice Age stone tools and mammoth bones from the seabed but advanced artifacts stubbornly refuse to come to light.

before. By 11,500 BCE people reached the continent's southern tip, scaled its mountains, and pushed into its rain forests. Mankind had inherited the earth.

THE GARDEN OF EDEN

The biggest beneficiaries of global warming lived in a band of "Lucky Latitudes" roughly 20–35 degrees north in the Old World and 15 degrees south to 20 degrees north in the New (see Figure 2.1). Plants and animals that had clustered in this temperate zone during the Ice Age multiplied wildly after 12,700 BCE, particularly, it seems, at each end of Asia, where wild cereals—forerunners of barley, wheat, and rye in southwest Asia and of rice and millet in East Asia—evolved big seeds that foragers could boil into mush or grind up and bake into bread. All they needed to do was wait until the plants ripened, shake them, and collect the seeds. Experiments with modern southwest Asian wild grains suggest that a ton of edible seeds could have been extracted from just two and a half acres of plants; each calorie of energy spent on harvesting earned fifty calories of food. It was the golden age of foraging.

In the Ice Age, hunter-gatherers had roamed the land in tiny bands because food was scarce, but their descendants now began changing their ways. Like the largest-brained species of several kinds of animals (whether we are talking about bees, dolphins, parrots, or our closest relatives, apes), humans seem to clump together instinctively. We are sociable.

Maybe big-brained animals got this way because they were smart enough to see that groups have more eyes and ears than individuals and do better at spotting enemies. Or maybe, some evolutionists suggest, living in groups came before big brains, starting what the brain scientist Steven Pinker calls a "cognitive arms race" in which those animals that figured out what other animals were thinking—keeping track of friends and enemies, of who shared and who didn't—outbred those whose brains were not up to the task.

Either way, we have evolved to like one another, and our ancestors chose to exploit Earth's movement up the Great Chain of Energy by forming bigger permanent groups. By 12,500 BCE it was no longer unusual to find forty or fifty people living together within the Lucky Latitudes, and some groups passed the hundred mark.

In the Ice Age, people had tended to set up camp, eat what plants and kill what animals they could find, then move on to another location, then another, and another. We still sing about being a wandering man, rambling on, free as a bird, and so on, but when the Great Chain of Energy made settling down a serious possibility, hearth and home clearly spoke to us more strongly. People in China began making pottery (a bad idea if you plan to move base every few weeks) as early as 16,000 BCE, and in highland Peru hunter-gatherers were building walls and keeping them clean around 11,000 BCE—pointless behavior for highly mobile people, but perfectly sensible for anyone living in one place for months at a stretch.

The clearest evidence for clumping and settling comes from what archaeologists call the Hilly Flanks, an arc of rolling country curving around the Tigris, Euphrates, and Jordan valleys in southwest Asia. I will spend most of this chapter talking about this region, which saw humanity's first major movement away from hunter-gatherer lifestyles—and with it, the birth of the West.

The site of 'Ain Mallaha in modern Israel (Figure 2.3; also known as Eynan) provides the best example of what happened. Around 12,500 BCE, now-nameless people built semisubterranean round houses here, sometimes thirty feet across, using stones for the walls and trimming tree trunks into posts to support roofs. Burned food scraps show that they gathered an astonishing variety of nuts and plants that ripened at different times of year, stored them in plaster-lined waterproof pits, and ground them up on stone mortars. They left the bones of deer, foxes, birds, and (above all) gazelle scattered around the village. Archaeologists love gazelles' teeth, which have the wonderful property of producing different-colored enamel in summer and winter, making it easy to tell what time of year an animal died. 'Ain Mallaha has teeth of both colors, which probably means that people lived there year-round. We know of no contemporary sites like this anywhere in the world outside the Hilly Flanks.

Settling down in bigger groups must have changed how people related to one another and the world around them. In the past humans had had to follow the food, moving constantly. They doubtless told stories about each place they stopped: this is the cave where my father died, that is where our son burned down the hut, there is the spring where the spirits speak, and so on. But 'Ain Mallaha was not just one

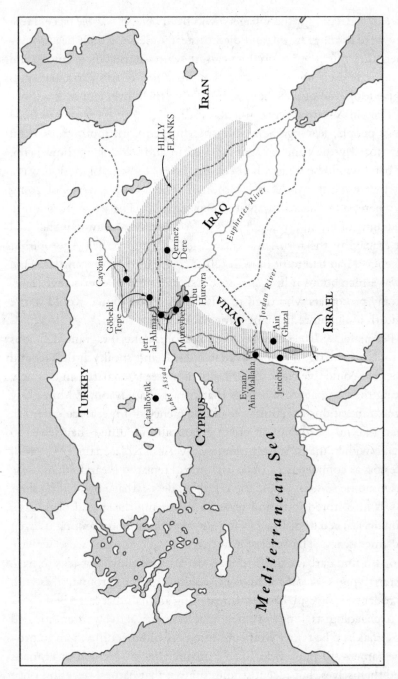

Figure 2.3. The beginning of the West: sites in and around the Hilly Flanks discussed in this chapter

place in a circuit; for the villagers who lived here, it was *the* place. Here they were born, grew up, and died. Instead of leaving their dead somewhere they might not revisit for years, they now buried them among and even inside their houses, rooting their ancestors in this particular spot. People took care of their houses, rebuilding them over and over again.

They also started worrying about dirt. Ice Age foragers had been messy people, leaving their campsites littered with food scraps. And why not? By the time maggots moved in and scavengers showed up, the band would be long gone, seeking the next source of food. It was a different story at 'Ain Mallaha, though. These people were not going anywhere, and had to live with their garbage. The excavators found thousands of rat and mouse bones at 'Ain Mallaha—animals that had not existed in the forms we know them during the Ice Age. Earlier scavengers had had to fit human refuse into a broader feeding strategy. It was a nice bonus if humans left bones and nuts all over a cave floor, but any proto-rats who tried to rely on this food source would starve to death long before humans came back to replenish it.

Permanent villages changed the rules for rodents. Fragrant, delicious mounds of garbage became available 24/7, and sneaky little rats and mice that could live right under humans' noses fared better in this new setting than big, aggressive ones that attracted attention. Within a few dozen generations (a century would be plenty of time; mice, after all, breed like mice) rodents in effect genetically modified themselves to cohabit with humans. Sneaky (domestic) vermin replaced their big (wild) ancestors as completely as *Homo sapiens* had replaced Neanderthals.

Domestic rodents repaid the gift of endless garbage by voiding their bowels into stored food and water, accelerating the spread of disease. Humans learned to dislike rats for just this reason; some among us even find mice scary. The scariest scavengers of all, though, were wolves, who also find garbage irresistible. Most humans see drawbacks to having terrifying, *Call of the Wild*–type monsters hanging around, so as with the rodents, it was smaller, less threatening animals that fared best.

Archaeologists long assumed that humans actively domesticated dogs, making the tamer wolf cubs into pets and breeding them to produce tamer-still pups who liked humans almost as much as humans liked themselves, but recent studies suggest that natural selection once again worked without our conscious input. Either way, though, the interaction of wolves, garbage, and humans created the animals we call dogs, which could kill the disease-bearing rodents that competed with them for scraps and even fight with true wolves, earning their place as man's best friend. Woman's, too: around 11,000 BCE an elderly woman was buried at 'Ain Mallaha with one hand resting on a puppy, both of them curled up as if asleep.*

DAILY BREAD

In the introduction to this book I spun out the science-fiction writer Robert Heinlein's one-liner that "progress is made by lazy men looking for easier ways to do things" into a general sociological theory that history is made by lazy, greedy, frightened people (who rarely know what they're doing) looking for easier, more profitable, and safer ways to do things. This principle kicked in with a vengeance in the Hilly Flanks at the end of the Ice Age, creating a distinctive Western way of living, with higher social development than in any other part of the world.

We can probably praise (or blame) women for this. In modern hunter-gatherer societies women do most of the plant gathering while men do more hunting. Judging from the tendency for men's graves to contain more spear- and arrowheads while women's have more grinding tools, things were similar in prehistory, too, which suggests that the answer to the question that has dominated this book so far—when and where we should start speaking of a Western way of life distinct from other ways—grew out of the ingenuity of women living in the Hilly Flanks nearly fifteen thousand years ago.

Wild cereals are annual plants. That is, they grow, produce seeds, and die in one season, then their seeds grow into new plants the next year. When a plant ripens, the rachis (little stalks attaching individual seeds to the plant) weaken and one by one the seeds fall to the ground, where their protective husks shatter and they germinate. For foragers fifteen thousand years ago the simplest way to harvest such seeds was to take a basket and shake the plants so the almost-ripe seeds fell into

---

*A touching scene, so long as we do not ask how the puppy came to be available for burial at just the same time as its mistress.

it. The only problem was that every seed on every wild plant in every stand ripened at different times. If gatherers got to a stand late in the season, most of the seeds would already have fallen and germinated or been eaten by birds. If they came too early the rachis would still be strong and most seeds would be too firmly attached to shake loose. Either way, they lost most of the crop. They could, of course, visit the stand repeatedly, but then they would have less time to visit other stands.

We don't know whether sloth (not wanting to walk from stand to stand), greed (just wanting more food), or fear (of hunger or of someone else getting to the plant first) was the inspiration, but someone, very likely a woman, had a bright idea: Why not take some of the best seeds and replant them in a particularly fertile spot? Then, she presumably thought, if we look after them—turning the soil, pulling up weeds, maybe even watering the plants—we can rely on them to be there every year, and even to give us better yields. Life is good.

Once again, the earliest direct evidence comes from the Hilly Flanks, and indirectly we can thank the Ba'ath Party for it. The Ba'athists are best known as Saddam Hussein's murderous political movement in Iraq, but they first seized power next door in Syria in 1963. After purging their rivals they set about modernizing Syria. Damming the Euphrates to create the fifty-mile-long Lake Assad that now generates most of Syria's electricity was a big part of this. Foreseeing that the dam would flood the heart of the Hilly Flanks, the Syrian Directorate General of Antiquities launched an international campaign to study the sites that would be destroyed. In 1971 a British team explored the mound of Abu Hureyra. Finds on the surface suggested there had been a village here around 7000 BCE, and the archaeologists documented this in rich detail; but one trench revealed that this village had been built on the ruins of an older settlement, dating back to 12,700 BCE.

This was a huge bonus. The excavators raced against time, as the floodwaters rose, and against war, as the Syrian army drafted their workers to fight Israel in the 1973 Yom Kippur/Ramadan conflict. By the time the site was drowned, the team had excavated a little over five hundred square feet of the earliest village: a tiny area, but one of the most important in archaeology. They found semisubterranean circular huts, grinding stones, hearths, and thousands of carbonized seeds. Most came from wild grasses, but a handful of plump, heavy rye seeds stood out.

These seeds suggest that people at Abu Hureyra were using hoes to till fields. They were planting seeds beneath the surface rather than just dropping them on it, and this favored larger seedlings, which find it easier to push their way up to the air, over smaller ones, which find this difficult. If the prehistoric cultivators simply ate everything they grew this would not have mattered, but if they saved some of the seeds to plant again next year, big seeds would be slightly overrepresented. At first the difference would not be enough to notice, but if cultivators repeated this often enough, they would gradually change the meaning of "normal" as the average size of seeds slowly increased. Archaeo-botanists (people who study ancient plant remains) call these bigger seeds "cultivated," to distinguish them from wild grains and from the fully domesticated grains we eat today.

By the time the 'Ain Mallahans buried the old woman and her little dog around 11,000 BCE, Abu Hureyrans had replanted rye so often that it gave them bigger seeds. This must have seemed a small thing at the time, but it proved (to use one of archaeology's worst puns) the seed from which the West would grow.

PARADISE LOST

Half a planet away, icily indifferent to puppies and rye, the glaciers kept melting. A hundred thousand years earlier their advance had scoured North America, creating the vast flatness of the Midwest; their retreat now turned these increasingly forested plains into a boggy, mosquito-infested mess. Drunken woodland is what ecologists call it—the ground gets so wet that trees cannot stand up straight. Ridges of boulders and ice that had not melted yet trapped the runoff from glaciers in vast lakes. Geologists have named the biggest of these Lake Agassiz (Figure 2.1) after the Swiss scientist who, back in the 1830s, first realized that there must have been global ice ages. By 10,800 BCE Lake Agassiz covered almost a quarter-million square miles of the western plains, four times the area of modern Lake Superior. Then the inevitable happened: rising temperatures and rising waters undermined the icy spur holding the lake back.

Its collapse was a drawn-out cataclysm, in striking contrast to many modern disaster stories. In the impressively implausible movie *The Day*

After Tomorrow, for instance, Dennis Quaid plays Jack Hall, a scientist (apparently the only one) who has noticed that global warming is going to cause the ice caps to collapse the next day. Summoned to the White House, he tells the president that a superstorm is about to create temperatures of −150°F, switching off the Gulf Stream that bathes northern Europe's coasts with tropical water and keeps London, England, from having winters like London, Ontario. The superstorm will trigger a new ice age, Hall insists, making most of North America uninhabitable. Not surprisingly, the president is skeptical. Nothing gets done. A few hours later the storm erupts, trapping Hall's son in New York. Heroics ensue.

I won't spoil the plot by telling you how the movie turns out, except to say that when Lake Agassiz really turned off the Gulf Stream around 10,800 BCE, things unfolded rather differently. There was no superstorm, but for twelve hundred years, while the lake drained into the Atlantic, the world slid back into ice age conditions. (Geologists call the period 10,800–9600 BCE the Younger Dryas after the waterlogged petals of a little flower called the Arctic Dryas that is common in peat bogs of this date.) The wild cereals that had fed permanent villages in the Hilly Flanks, made garbage heaps possible, and given us mice and dogs now grew less thickly and yielded fewer, smaller seeds.*

Mankind was expelled from the Garden of Eden. Abandoning year-round villages, most people divided into smaller groups and went back to roaming the hillsides in search of their next meal, much like their ancestors at the coldest point of the Ice Age. Animal bones from the Hilly Flanks show that gazelles were getting smaller by 10,500 BCE as people overhunted them, and the enamel on human teeth regularly has telltale ridges indicating chronic childhood malnutrition.

There has never been another catastrophe on quite this scale. To find a parallel, in fact, we have to turn to science fiction. In 1941 Isaac Asimov, then just starting his career, published a story called "Nightfall"

---

*Some archaeologists tell a different story. Tiny beads of glass, carbon, and iridium found on several North Americans sites dating to around 11,000 BCE could only, they suggest, have been produced by intense heat—the kind of heat we would get if debris in a comet's tail hit the earth. These archaeologists picture not gradual melting of glaciers but a sudden blast at the North Pole turning the Gulf Stream off. Not even that, though, would have produced *The Day After Tomorrow*'s superstorm.

in the magazine *Astounding Science Fiction*. He set it on Lagash, a planet with six suns. Wherever Lagashians go, at least one sun is shining and it is always day—except for once every 2,049 years, when the suns line up just right for a passing moon to create an eclipse. The sky darkens and the stars come out. The terrified populace goes mad. By the time the eclipse ends the Lagashians have destroyed their civilization and plunged themselves into savagery. Over the next 2,049 years they slowly rebuild their culture, only for night to fall again and start the whole process over.

The Younger Dryas sounds like "Nightfall" revisited: the earth's orbit generates wild swings between freezing and thawing, which every few thousand years produce disasters like the draining of Lake Agassiz, wiping the slate of history clean. Yet while "Nightfall" is a great story (the Science Fiction Writers of America voted it the best science-fiction story of all time, and for what it is worth it has my vote too) it is not such a good model for historical thinking. In the real world not even the Younger Dryas could wipe the slate clean like "Nightfall." We might do better, in fact, to follow the ancient Greek thinker Heraclitus, who— 2,500 years before Asimov sat down to write—observed, "You can't step into the same river twice." It is a famous paradox: the second time you put your foot into a stream the waters you originally disturbed have flowed on to the sea and the river is not the same river anymore.

In just the same way, you cannot have the same ice age twice. The societies in the Hilly Flanks when Lake Agassiz collapsed around 10,800 BCE were no longer the same as those that had been there during the previous ice age. Unlike Asimov's Lagashians, earthlings did not go mad when nature turned their world upside down. Instead they applied a particularly human skill, ingenuity, and built on what they had already done. The Younger Dryas did not turn the clock back. Nothing ever does that.

Some archaeologists suggest that far from being a Nightfall moment, the Younger Dryas actually speeded innovation up. Like all scientific techniques, those used to date the earliest cultivated rye seeds from Abu Hureyra have built-in margins of error. The site's excavators point out that while the midpoints of the date ranges for the large rye seeds mentioned earlier fall around 11,000 BCE, before the Younger Dryas, they could perfectly well have been harvested five hundred years later, *after* the Younger Dryas began. Perhaps it was not laziness or greed that prompted the women of Abu Hureyra to tend rye; maybe it was fear. As temperatures fell and wild foods declined, Abu Hureyrans may have experimented, discovering that careful tending produced more and bigger seeds. On the one hand, cold, dry weather made it harder to cultivate cereals; on the other, the harsher weather increased incentives to do so. Some archaeologists imagine Younger Dryas foragers carrying bags of seeds around, scattering them in promising-looking spots as insurance against nature letting them down.

Further digging will show whether this is right, but we already know that not everyone in the Hilly Flanks responded to climatic disaster by returning to moving around in search of food. At Mureybet, just upstream from Abu Hureyra, French excavators found a new village established around 10,000 BCE. They exposed only twenty-five square feet of the earliest levels before Lake Assad swallowed this site too, but it was enough to show that the villagers scraped together sufficient wild plants and gazelles to hang on year-round. And in a house dated 10,000–9500 BCE the archaeologists made an unexpected discovery: embedded in a clay bench were the horns of a wild aurochs, the fierce six-foot-tall predecessor of the modern ox, plus the shoulder blades of two more.

No pre–Younger Dryas site has yielded anything quite this odd, but after 10,000 BCE villages filled up with all kinds of surprising things. Take, for example, Qermez Dere in northern Iraq, exposed by bulldozing in 1986. Only two small trenches could be excavated, one of which hit an area for preparing wild foods, much like those known from 'Ain Mallaha or Abu Hureyra. The other trench, though, produced no evidence of domestic activities. Instead it contained a sequence of three roundish chambers, each twelve to fifteen feet across and dug five feet beneath the ancient ground level. The first chamber was plastered and a row of four pillars had been set in the floor, so close together that it was hard to move around the room. One of the pillars was found intact: molded in clay and plaster over a stone core, it tapered and had odd bulges near the top, making it look like a stylized human torso with shoulders. The room had been filled (apparently deliberately) with several tons of earth, containing several groups of big animal bones and unusual objects like stone beads. A new room was then dug, just like the first one, on almost exactly the same spot; it, too, was plastered then filled in with tons of earth. Then a third room was dug in the same place, plastered, and filled in. After dumping a few baskets of soil into this final chamber, people placed six human skulls, minus their jawbones, just above the floor. The skulls were in bad shape, suggesting that they had been in circulation for a long time before being buried here.

What on earth were these people doing? It is a standing joke among archaeologists that whenever we cannot figure out what we have dug up, we say it is religious (having just finished excavating a site on Sicily that I think is religious, I should confess to not finding the joke very funny anymore). The problem, of course, is that we cannot dig up past beliefs; yet that does not mean archaeologists are just making things up when they talk about prehistoric religion.

If we take a fairly commonsense definition of religion as belief in powerful, supernatural, normally unseen beings who care about humans and expect humans to care about them (which seems to apply to so many societies that some evolutionary psychologists think religion is hardwired into the human brain), we should be able to recognize, if not necessarily understand, remains of rituals through which people communicated with a divine world.

Rituals are notoriously culture-specific. Depending on when and where you find yourself, it may be that the mighty ones will listen only if you pour the blood of a live white goat on the right side of this particular rock; or only if you take off your shoes, kneel down, and pray facing in that direction; or if you tell your misdeeds to a man in black who doesn't have sex; and so on. The list is endless. Yet despite their wondrous variety, rituals do have certain things in common. Many require special places (mountaintops, caves, unusual buildings), objects (images, statues, valuable or foreign goods), movements (processions, pilgrimages), and clothes (highly formal, totally disheveled), all heightening the sense of stepping outside the everyday. Feasting, often involving unusual foods, is popular; so too is fasting, which induces altered states of mind. Sleep deprivation, pain, repetitive chanting and dancing, or (the favorite) drugs all do the same job, and may tip truly holy people into trances, fits, and visions.

These sites have it all: strange underground rooms, humanoid pillars, jawless skulls—and while everything in the archaeology of religion is speculative, I find it hard not to see them as religious responses to the Younger Dryas. The world was freezing, plants were dying, and the gazelles were going away; what could be more natural than asking gods, spirits, and ancestors for aid? What could make more sense than identifying special people and creating special places to facilitate communication? The shrine at Qermez Dere looks like an amplifier, turning up the volume on requests for help.

So when the world warmed up at the end of the Younger Dryas, around 9600 BCE, the Hilly Flanks were not the same place they had been when the world had warmed up at the end of the main ice age, three thousand years earlier. Global warming did not step into the same society twice. Sites from the earlier period of warming, such as 'Ain Mallaha, give the impression that people just happily took advantage of nature's bounty, but in the villages that popped up around the Hilly Flanks after 9600 BCE people sank serious resources into religion. Many post-9600 sites have evidence for elaborate treatment of human and aurochs skulls and several have big, underground chambers that look like communal shrines. At Jerf al-Ahmar in Syria, now slumbering alongside so many other sites beneath the waters of Lake Assad, French archaeologists found ten multiroomed houses around a large underground chamber. A human skull was sitting on a bench and in the middle of the room was a headless skeleton. It looks disturbingly like a human sacrifice.

Most spectacular of all is Göbekli Tepe, perched on a hilltop with commanding views across southeast Turkey. Since 1995 its German and Turkish excavators have exposed four sunken chambers, up to ten feet deep and thirty feet across, dating to 9000 BCE or even earlier. Like the smaller, earlier chambers at Qermez Dere, each had been deliberately filled in. Each contained T-shaped stone columns, some seven feet tall, decorated with carved animals. Geomagnetic surveys suggest that fifteen more chambers remain unexcavated; in all there may be two hundred stone pillars at the site, many weighing over eight tons. A twenty-foot-long pillar found unfinished in a quarry weighed fifty tons.

People did all this with nothing more sophisticated than flint tools. While we will never know why this particular hilltop was so sacred, it certainly looks like a regional sanctuary, perhaps a place for festivals where hundreds of people congregated for weeks at a time, carving pillars, dragging them to the chambers, and setting them upright. One thing seems certain, though: never before in history had such large groups worked together.

Humans were not passive victims of climate change. They applied ingenuity, working to get the gods and ancestors on board in the struggle against adversity. And while most of us doubt that these gods and ancestors actually existed, the rituals may well have done some good anyway as a kind of social glue. People who sincerely believed that big rituals in lavish shrines would win the gods' aid were surely more likely to tough it out and stick together no matter how hard times got.

By 10,000 BCE, the Hilly Flanks stood out from the rest of the world. Most people in most places still drifted between caves and campsites, like the one excavated since 2004 at Longwangcan in China, where the only traces of their activity that survive are small circles of baked earth from campfires. A battered piece of shale from this site might be a simple stone spade, perhaps implying that cultivation of crops had begun, but there is nothing like the fat rye seeds of Abu Hureyra, let alone the monuments of Mureybet or Qermez Dere. The most substantial building known from the Americas is a small hut of bent saplings covered with hides, detected by meticulous excavators at Monte Verde in Chile; while in the whole of India archaeologists have not been able to find even that much, and scatters of stone tools are the only traces of human activity.

A distinctive Western world was taking shape.

PARADISE TRANSFORMED

By 9600 BCE Earth was warming up again, and this time around, Hilly Flankers already knew how to get the most from grasses. They quickly (by the standards of earlier times, anyway) resumed cultivation. By 9300 BCE wheat and barley seeds from sites in the Jordan Valley were noticeably bigger than wild versions and people were modifying fig trees to improve their yields. The world's oldest known granaries, clay storage chambers ten feet wide and ten feet tall, come from the Jordan Valley around 9000 BCE. By then cultivation was under way in at least seven pockets in the Hilly Flanks, from modern Israel to southeast Turkey, and by 8500 BCE big-seeded cereals were normal all across the region.

Changes were very slow indeed by modern standards, but over the next thousand years they made the Hilly Flanks increasingly different from any other part of the world. The people of this area were, unknowingly, genetically modifying plants to create fully domesticated crops that could not reproduce themselves without human aid. Like dogs, these plants needed us as much as we needed them.

Plants, like animals, evolve because random mutations occur when DNA is copied from one generation to the next. Once in a while, a mutation increases a plant's chance of reproducing. This is particularly common if the environment is changing too, as happened when permanent villages created niches in which small, tame wolves had advantages over big, fierce ones, or when cultivation gave big seedlings advantages over small ones. I already mentioned that wild cereals reproduce by having each seed ripen and fall to the ground at a different time from the others, whereupon the husk shatters, leaving the seed free to grow. But a few plants—just one per one or two million normal plants—have a random mutation on a single gene that strengthens the rachis connecting the seed to the plant and also the husk protecting the seed. When these seeds ripen they do not fall to the ground and the husks cannot shatter. The seeds literally wait for a harvester to come along and get them. Before there were any harvesters the mutant plants died out each year because their seeds could not get into the soil, making this a most disadvantageous mutation. The same thing happened if humans shook the plants and caught the grains that fell; the mutant seeds would not fall, and once again died out.

Archaeobotanists argue passionately over just what happened to change this situation, but most likely good old-fashioned greed got involved. After investing their energy in hoeing, weeding, and watering the best stands of grasses, women (assuming, again, that it was women) may have wanted to squeeze every last bit of food from their plants. That would have meant visiting each stand to shake the bushes several times, and they would surely have noticed that no matter how hard they shook, some stubborn seeds—the mutants with the tough rachis—just would not drop. What could be more natural than to rip the offending stalk out of the ground and take the whole plant home? Wheat and barley stalks do not weigh much, after all, and I'm fairly sure that's how I would react if confronted by a cereal that would not surrender.

If women then replanted a random selection of their seeds, they would have taken mutant seeds along with normal ones; in fact, the mutants would be slightly *overrepresented*, because at least some normal seeds would already have fallen and been lost. Each year that they replanted they would slightly increase the proportion of mutants in their cultivated stands. This was clearly an agonizingly slow process, quite invisible to the people involved, but it set off an evolutionary spiral just as dramatic as what happened to mice in garbage dumps. Within a couple of thousand years, instead of one plant that waited for the harvester per field of one or two million, they had *only* genetically modified domesticated plants. The excavated finds suggest that even around 8500 BCE fully domesticated wheat and barley were still almost unheard of. By 8000, though, about half the seeds we find in the Hilly Flanks have the tough rachis that would wait for the harvester; by 7500, virtually all do.

Laziness, greed, and fear constantly added improvements. People discovered that planting cereals in a garden one year then protein-rich beans the next replenished the soil as well as varying their diet; in the process, they domesticated lentils and chickpeas. Crushing wheat and barley on coarse grindstones filled bread with grit, which wore people's teeth down to stumps; so they sieved out the impurities. They found new ways to prepare grains, baking clay into waterproof pots for cooking. If we are right to draw analogies with modern agriculturalists, women would have been responsible for most or all of these innovations, as well as for learning to weave linen into clothes. Skins and furs were out.

While women tamed plants, men (probably) took on animals. By 8000 BCE herders in what is now western Iran were managing goats so effectively that bigger, calmer strains evolved. Before 7000 BCE herders turned the wild aurochs into something like the placid cows we know today and tamed wild boars into pigs. Across the next few thousand years they learned not to kill all animals for meat while they were still young but to keep some around for wool and milk, and then—most useful of all—to harness them to wheeled carts.* Previously, moving anything meant picking it up and carrying it, but an ox in harness could deliver three times the draft power of a man. By 4000 BCE the

---

*This sounds like an obvious thing to do, but yoking animals so they can pull carts without strangling themselves while also remaining under a driver's control is a lot harder than it looks.

domestication of plants and animals converged in the ox-drawn plow. People carried on tinkering, but nearly six thousand years would pass before humans added significant new energy sources to this package by harnessing the power of coal and steam in the industrial revolution.

The early farmers of the Hilly Flanks transformed the way people lived. Those of us who quake at the prospect of sitting next to a screaming baby on a long plane ride should spare a thought for female foragers, who regularly carry their infants with them as they walk thousands of miles every year gathering plants. Not surprisingly, they do not want too many children; consciously or not, they space their pregnancies by extending breastfeeding into the child's third or fourth year (producing breast milk prevents ovulation). Ice Age foragers probably followed similar strategies, but the more they settled down, the less they needed to do this. Having more babies in fact became a boon, providing extra labor, and recent skeletal studies suggest that the average woman in an early farming village, staying in one place with stores of food, gave birth to seven or eight babies (of whom maybe four would survive to their first birthday and perhaps three to reproductive age) as compared to the mere five or six live births of her roving ancestresses. The more food people grew, the more babies they could feed; although, of course, the more babies they fed, the more food they had to grow.

Population soared. By 8000 BCE some villages probably had five hundred residents, ten times the size of pre–Younger Dryas hamlets such as 'Ain Mallaha. By 6500 Çatalhöyük in modern Turkey had perhaps three thousand. These were villages on steroids, and they had all the problems that implies. Microscopic analysis of sediments from Çatalhöyük shows that people simply dumped garbage and night soil in stinking heaps between houses, to be trodden into the dust and mud. The filth would have appalled hunter-gatherers but surely delighted rats, flies, and fleas. We can see from tiny pieces of excrement trodden into the dirt floors that villagers also stabled domestic animals in their homes, and human skeletons from the site of 'Ain Ghazal in Jordan show that by 7000 BCE tuberculosis had jumped from cattle to people. Settling down and raising more food increased fertility, but also meant more mouths to feed and more germs to share, both of which increased mortality. Each new farming village probably grew rapidly for a few generations until fertility and mortality balanced each other out.

Yet for all the squalor, this was clearly what people wanted. Little hunter-gatherer bands had had broad geographical horizons but narrow social ones: the landscape changed but the faces did not. The early farmer's world was just the opposite. You might pass your whole life within a day's walk of the village where you were born, but what a place it was—full of shrines where the gods revealed themselves, festivals and feasts to delight the senses, and gossipy, nosy neighbors in solid houses with plastered floors and waterproof roofs. These buildings would strike most people today as cramped, smoky, smelly hovels, but they were a big step up from sharing damp caves with bears or huddling out of the rain under skins stretched over branches.

Early farmers tamed the landscape, breaking it into concentric circles—at the center was home; then came the neighbors; then the cultivated fields; then the pastures, where shepherds and flocks trekked between summer and winter grazing; and beyond them the wild, an unregulated world of scary animals, savages who hunted, and who knew what monsters. A few excavations have found stone slabs incised with lines that, at least to the eye of the believer, look a bit like maps of fields divided by tiny paths; and around 9000 BCE villagers in Jerf al-Ahmar and some of the neighboring sites now under Lake Assad seem to have been experimenting with a kind of protowriting, scratching images of snakes, birds, farm animals, and abstract signs on little stone tokens.

By imposing such mental structures on their world, Hilly Flankers were, we might say, domesticating themselves. They even remade what love meant. The love between husband and wife or parent and child is natural, bred into us over millions of years, but farming injected new forces into these relationships. Foragers had always shared their knowledge with their young, teaching them to find ripe plants, wild game, and safe caves, but farmers had something more concrete to pass down. To do well, people now needed property—a house, fields, and flocks, not to mention investments like wells, walls, and tools. The first farmers were apparently quite communal, sharing food and perhaps cooking collectively, but by 8000 BCE they were building bigger, more complicated houses, each with its own storerooms and kitchens, and perhaps dividing the land into privately owned fields. Life increasingly focused on small family groups, probably the basic unit for transmitting property between generations. Children needed this material inheritance, because the alternative was poverty. Transmitting property became a matter of life and death.

There are signs of what can only be called an obsession with ancestors. We perhaps see it as early as 10,000 BCE, with the jawless skulls of Qermez Dere, but as farming developed, it escalated. Burying multiple generations of the dead under house floors became common, mingling bodies in ways that seem to express very physically the link between property and descent. Some people went further, disinterring bodies after the flesh decayed, removing the skulls, and reburying the headless corpses. Using plaster, they modeled faces on the skulls, sticking shells in the eye sockets and painting in details like hair.

Dame Kathleen Kenyon, a formidable woman in the man's world of 1950s archaeology, was the first to document this horror-movie custom in her excavations at the famous site of Jericho on the West Bank, but plastered skulls have now been found in dozens of settlements. What people did with the skulls is less clear, since we only find ones that have been reburied. Most were placed in pits, though at Çatalhöyük one young woman was buried around 7000 BCE hugging to her breast a skull that had been replastered and painted red no fewer than three times.

Such intimacy with corpses makes most of us squeamish but clearly mattered a lot to early farmers in the Hilly Flanks. Most archaeologists think it shows that ancestors were the most important supernatural beings. The ancestors had passed on property, without which the living would starve; in return the living honored them. Possibly ancestral rituals clothed the transmission of property in a holy aura, justifying why some people owned more than others. People may also have used skulls for necromancy, summoning ancestors to ask when to plant, where to hunt, and whether to raid neighbors.

Ancestor cults flourished all over the Hilly Flanks. At Çatalhöyük almost every house had bodies under the floor and ancestral skulls plastered into the surfaces and walls. At 'Ain Ghazal two pits were found containing life-size statues and busts made from bundles of reeds coated with plaster. Some had twin heads; most were painted with giant, staring eyes. Most striking of all, around 8000 BCE people at Çayönü in southeast Turkey built what its excavators labeled a "House of the Dead," with sixty-six skulls and more than four hundred skeletons stashed behind an altar. Chemists identified deposits on the altar as hemoglobin crystals from human and animal blood. More human blood was caked on clay bowls, and two other buildings also had bloodstained altars, one with the image of a human head carved on it. The mind fairly boggles. It sounds like a slasher movie—struggling victims tied to altars, priests tearing their jugulars open with razor-sharp flint blades and sawing off their heads for storage, worshippers drinking their blood . . .

Or maybe not. Nothing archaeologists dig up can prove or disprove such flights of fancy. Still, the statues and the House of the Dead seem to imply the emergence of religious specialists who somehow persuaded everyone that they had privileged access to the supernatural. Perhaps they could fall into trances or fits; perhaps they could just describe their visions better. Whatever the reason, priests may have been the first people to enjoy institutionalized authority. Here, perhaps, we see the beginnings of entrenched hierarchy.

Whether that is true or not, hierarchy developed fastest *within* households. I have already observed that men and women had had different roles in foraging societies, the former more active in hunting and the latter in gathering, but studies of contemporary groups suggest that domestication sharpens the sexual division of labor, tying women to the home. The high mortality/high fertility regime required most women to spend most of their lives pregnant and/or minding small children, and changes in agriculture—changes that women themselves probably pioneered—reinforced this. Domesticated cereals need more processing than most wild foods, and since threshing, grinding, and baking can be done in the home while supervising infants, these logically became women's work.

When land is abundant but labor is scarce (as in the earliest days of cultivation), people normally cultivate large areas lightly, with men and women hoeing and weeding together. If population increases but the supply of farmland does not, as happened in the Hilly Flanks after 8000 BCE, it makes sense to work the land more intensively, squeezing more from each acre by manuring, plowing, and even irrigating. All these tasks require upper-body strength. Plenty of women are as strong as men, but men do increasingly dominate outdoor work and women indoor work as agriculture intensifies. Grown men work the fields; boys tend the flocks; and women and girls manage the ever more sharply defined domestic sphere. A study of 162 skeletons dating around

7000 BCE from Abu Hureyra revealed striking gender distinctions. Both men and women had enlarged vertebrae in their upper backs, probably from carrying heavy loads on their heads, but only women had a distinctive arthritic toe condition caused by spending long periods kneeling, using their toes as a base to apply force while grinding grain.

Weeding, clearing stones, manuring, watering, and plowing all increased yields, and inheriting a well-tended field, rather than just any bit of land, made all the difference to a household's fortunes. The way religion developed after 9600 BCE suggests that people worried about ancestors and inheritance, and we should probably assume that it was at this point that they began reinforcing their rituals with other institutions. With so much at stake, men in modern peasant cultures want to be sure they really are the fathers of the children who will inherit their property. Foragers' rather casual attitudes about sex yield to obsessive concern with daughters' premarital virginity and wives' extramarital activities. Men in traditional agricultural societies typically marry around the age of thirty, after they have come into their inheritance, while women generally marry around fifteen, before they have had much time to stray. While we cannot be sure that these patterns originated at the dawn of farming, it does seem rather likely. By, say, 7500 BCE a girl would typically grow up under the authority of her father, then, as a teenager, exchange it for the authority of a husband old enough to be her father. Marriage would become a source of wealth as those who already had good lands and flocks would marry others in the same happy situation, consolidating holdings. The rich got richer.

Having things worth inheriting meant having things worth stealing, and it is surely no coincidence that evidence for fortifications and organized warfare mushrooms in the Hilly Flanks after 9600 BCE. Modern hunter-gatherer life is famously violent; with no real hierarchy to keep their passions in check, young hunters often treat homicide as a reasonable way to settle disagreements. In many bands, it is the leading cause of death. But to live together in villages, people had to learn to manage interpersonal violence. Those that did so would have flourished—and have been able to harness violence to take things from other communities.

The most remarkable evidence comes from Jericho, famous for the biblical story of the walls that tumbled down when Joshua blew his trumpet. When Kathleen Kenyon dug there fifty years ago, she did find walls—but not Joshua's. Joshua lived around 1200 BCE, but Kenyon uncovered what looked like fortifications eight thousand years older. She interpreted these as a defensive bastion, twelve feet high and five feet thick, dating to around 9300 BCE. New studies in the 1980s showed that she was probably mistaken, and that her "fortification" actually consisted of several small walls built at different times, perhaps to hold back a stream; but her second great find, a stone tower twenty-five feet tall, probably really was defensive. In a world where the most advanced weapon was a stick with a pointed stone tied to the end, this was a mighty bulwark indeed.

Nowhere outside the Hilly Flanks did people have so much to defend. Even in 7000 BCE, almost everyone outside this region was a forager, shifting seasonally, and even where they had begun to settle down in villages, such as Mehrgarh in modern Pakistan or Shangshan in the Yangzi Delta, these were simple places by the standards of Jericho. If hunter-gatherers from any other place on earth had been airlifted to Çayönü or Çatalhöyük they would not, I suspect, have known what hit them. Gone would be their caves or little clusters of huts, replaced by bustling towns with sturdy houses, great stores of food, powerful art, and religious monuments. They would find themselves working hard, dying young, and hosting an unpleasant array of microbes. They would rub shoulders with rich and poor, and chafe under or rejoice in men's authority over women and parents' over children. They might even discover that some people had the right to murder them in rituals. And they might well wonder why people had inflicted all this on themselves.

GOING FORTH AND MULTIPLYING

Fast-forward ten thousand years from the origins of hierarchy and drudgery in the prehistoric Hilly Flanks to Paris in 1967.

To the middle-aged men who administered the University of Paris campus in the dreary suburb of Nanterre—the heirs of traditions of patriarchy stretching back to Çatalhöyük—it seemed obvious that the young ladies in their charge should not be allowed to entertain young gentlemen in their dorm rooms (or vice versa). Such rules have probably never seemed obvious to the young, but for three hundred generations teenagers had had to live with them. But not anymore. As winter closed in, students challenged their elders' right to dictate their love lives. In January 1968 Daniel Cohn-Bendit, nowadays a respected Green Party member of the European Parliament but then a student activist known as "Danny the Red," compared the minister for youth's attitudes to the Hitler Youth's. In May students took on armed police in running street-fights, paralyzing downtown Paris with barricades and burning cars. President De Gaulle met secretly with his generals to find out whether— if it came to a new Bastille Day—the army would stand by him.

Enter Marshall Sahlins, a youngish anthropology professor from the University of Michigan. Sahlins had made his name with a series of brilliant essays on social evolution and by criticizing the Vietnam War; now he forsook Ann Arbor ("a small university city made up exclusively of side streets," he unkindly but not unfairly called it) to spend two years at the Collège de France, the Mecca of both anthropological theory and student radicalism. As the crisis deepened, Sahlins sent a manuscript to the journal *Les temps modernes*, required reading for everyone who was anyone on the French intellectual scene. It was to become one of the most influential anthropological essays ever written.

"Open the gates of nurseries, universities, and other prisons," student radicals had scrawled on a wall at Nanterre. "Thanks to teachers and exams competitiveness starts at six." Sahlins's manuscript offered something to the students: not an answer, which the anarchists probably did not want ("Be a realist, demand the impossible" went one of their slogans), but at least some encouragement. The central issue, Sahlins argued, was that bourgeois society had "erected a shrine to the Unattainable: *Infinite Needs*." We submit to capitalist discipline and compete to earn money so we can chase Infinite Needs by buying things we don't really want. We could learn something, Sahlins suggested, from hunter-gatherers. "The world's most primitive people," he explained, "have few possessions *but they are not poor*." This only sounded like a paradox: Sahlins argued that foragers typically worked just twenty-one to thirty-five hours per week—less than Paris's industrial laborers or even, I suspect, its students. Hunter-gatherers did not have cars or TVs, but they did not know they were supposed to want them. Their means were few but their needs were fewer, making them, Sahlins concluded, "the original affluent society."

Sahlins had a point: Why, he asked, did farming ever replace foraging if the rewards were work, inequality, and war? Yet replace foraging
it clearly did. By 7000 BCE farming completely dominated the Hilly
Flanks. Already by 8500 BCE cultivated cereals had spread to Cyprus
and by 8000 had reached central Turkey. By 7000 fully domesticated
plants had reached all these areas and spread eastward to (or, perhaps,
developed independently in) Pakistan. They had reached Greece, southern Iraq, and central Asia by 6000, Egypt and central Europe by 5000,
and the shores of the Atlantic by 4000 (Figure 2.4).

Archaeologists have argued for decades over why this happened,
without much agreement. At the end of a magisterial recent review, for
instance, the strongest generalization that Graeme Barker of Cambridge University felt he could make was that farmers replaced foragers
"in different ways and at different rates and for different reasons, but in
comparable circumstances of challenges to the world they knew."

Yet although the process was messy—going on across millennia
at the scale of entire continents, how could it not be?—we can make

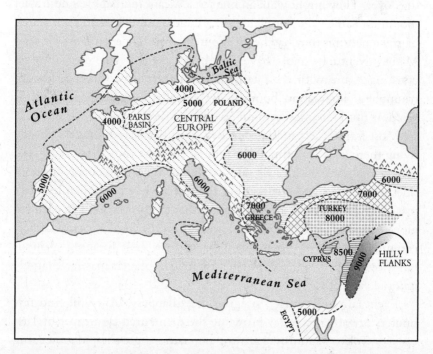

Figure 2.4. Going forth and multiplying, version one: the westward spread of
domesticated plants from the Hilly Flanks to the Atlantic, 9000–4000 BCE

quite a lot of sense of it if we remember that it was, at the end of the day, all about Earth's movement up the Great Chain of Energy. Orbital change meant that Earth captured more of the sun's electromagnetic energy; photosynthesis converted some of that larger share into chemical energy (that is, more plants); metabolism converted some of that larger stock of chemical energy into kinetic energy (that is, more animals); and farming allowed humans to extract vastly more energy from plants and other animals for their own use. Pests, predators, and parasites in turn sucked as much of this newfound energy out of farmers as they could, but there was still plenty left over.

Humans, like plants and other animals, found a major outlet for their extra energy in sexual reproduction. High birthrates meant that new villages could grow rapidly until every square inch of available land was being farmed, whereupon hunger and sickness rose until they canceled out fertility. Energy capture and energy consumption then reached a rough balance. Some villages stabilized like this, always hovering on the edge of misery; in others a few daring souls decided to start over. They might walk an hour to a vacant (perhaps less desirable) spot in the same valley or plain—or trudge hundreds of miles in search of green pastures they had heard about. They might even cross the seas. Many adventurers must have failed, the ragged, starving survivors crawling home with their tails between their legs. Others, though, triumphed. Population boomed until deaths caught up with births again or until colonies spun off colonies of their own.

Most farmers expanding into new territory found foragers already living there. It is tempting to imagine scenes like something out of old Western movies, with cattle raids, scalping, and shoot-outs (with both sides using bows and arrows), but the reality may have been less dramatic. Archaeological surveys suggest that the first farmers in each region tended to settle in different areas from the local foragers, almost certainly because the best farmland and the best foraging grounds rarely overlapped. At least at first, farmers and foragers may have largely ignored each other.

Eventually, of course, foraging did disappear. You will find few hunters or gatherers today prowling the manicured landscapes of Tuscany or Tokyo's suburbs. Farming populations grew rapidly, needing only a few centuries to fill up the best land, until they had no option but to push into the (in their eyes) marginal territories of the foragers.

There are two main theories about what happened next. The first suggests that farmers basically destroyed the original affluent society. Disease might have played a part; rats, flocks, and permanent villages certainly made farmers less healthy than hunter-gatherers. We should not, though, imagine epidemics like those that carried off Native Americans in their millions after 1492. The farmers' and foragers' disease pools had been separated by just a few miles of forest, not uncrossable oceans, so they had not diverged very far.

Yet even without mass kill-offs, weight of numbers was decisive. If foragers decided to fight, as happened on so many colonial frontiers in modern times, they might destroy the odd farming village, but more colonists would just keep coming, swamping resistance. Alternatively, foragers might choose flight, but no matter how far they fell back, new farmers would eventually arrive, chopping down still more trees and breathing germs everywhere, until foragers ended up in the places farmers simply could not use, such as Siberia or the Sahara.

The second theory says none of these things happened, because the first farmers across most of the regions shown in Figure 2.4 were not descendants of immigrants from the Hilly Flanks at all. They were local hunter-gatherers who settled down and became farmers themselves. Sahlins made farming sound deeply unattractive compared to the original affluent society, but in all likelihood foragers rarely faced a simple choice between two lifestyles. A farmer who left his plow and started walking would not cross a sharp line into foragers' territory. Rather, he would come to villages where people farmed a little less intensively than he did (maybe hoeing their fields instead of plowing and manuring), then people who farmed less intensively still (maybe burning patches of forest, cultivating them until the weeds grew back, then moving on), and eventually people who relied entirely on hunting and gathering. Ideas, people, and microbes drifted back and forth across this broad contact zone.

When people realized that neighbors with more intensive practices were killing the wild plants and chasing off the animals that their own foraging lifestyles depended on, rather than attacking these vandals or running away they also had the option of joining the crowd and intensifying their own cultivation. Instead of picking farming over foraging, people probably only decided to spend a little less time gathering and a little more time gardening. Later they might have to decide whether to start weeding, then plowing, then manuring, but this was—to repeat an image from the previous chapter—a series of baby steps rather than a once-and-for-all great leap from the original affluent society to backbreaking toil and chronic illness. On the whole, across hundreds of years and thousands of miles, those who intensified also multiplied; those who clung to their old ways dwindled. In the process, the agricultural "frontier" crept forward. No one chose hierarchy and working longer hours; women did not embrace arthritic toes; these things crept up on them.

No matter how many stone tools, burned seeds, or house foundations archaeologists dig up, they will never be able to prove either theory, but once again genetics has come (partly) to the rescue. In the 1970s Luca Cavalli-Sforza of Stanford University began a massive survey of European blood groups and nuclear DNA. His team found a consistent gradient of gene frequencies from southeast to northwest (Figure 2.5), which, they pointed out, mapped quite well onto the archaeological evidence for the spread of farming shown in Figure 2.4. Their conclusion: after migrants from western Asia brought farming to Europe, their descendants largely replaced the aboriginal foragers, pushing their remnants into the far north and west.

The archaeologist Colin Renfrew argued that linguistics also supported Cavalli-Sforza's scenario: the first farmers, he suspected, not only replaced European genes with southwest Asian ones but also replaced Europe's native languages with Indo-European ones from the Hilly Flanks, leaving just isolated pockets of older tongues such as Basque. The drama of dispossession that ended the original affluent society is inscribed in modern Europeans' bodies and reenacted every time they open their mouths.

At first the new evidence only increased the scholarly arguments. Linguists immediately challenged Renfrew, arguing that modern European languages would differ much more from one another if they had really begun diverging from an ancestral tongue six or seven millennia ago, and in 1996 an Oxford team led by Bryan Sykes challenged Cavalli-Sforza on the genetics. Sykes looked at mitochondrial DNA rather than the nuclear DNA Cavalli-Sforza had studied, and instead of a southeast–northwest progression, like Figure 2.5, identified a pattern too messy to be represented easily on a map, finding six groups of ge-

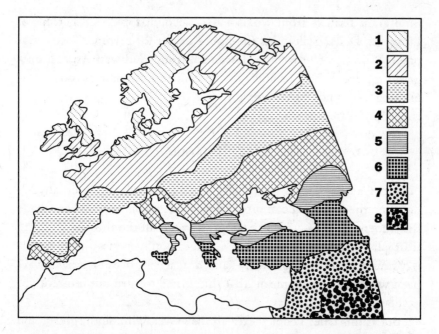

Figure 2.5. A story written in blood: Luca Cavalli-Sforza's interpretation of
Europe's genetic makeup, based on a massive sample of nuclear DNA.
He concluded that this map, showing degrees of genetic similarity of
modern populations to the hypothesized colonists from the Hilly Flanks,
with 8 representing complete similarity and 1 the lowest level of
correspondence (measuring the first principal component in his statistical
manipulation of the results, accounting for 95 percent of the variation in
the sample), showed that colonists descended from the Hilly Flanks
spread agriculture across Europe. But many archaeologists and some
geneticists disagree.

netic lineages, only one of which could plausibly be linked to agricultural migrants from western Asia. Sykes suggested that the other five
groups are much older, going back mostly to the original out-of-Africa
peopling of Europe 25,000 to 50,000 years ago; all of which, he concluded, indicates that Europe's first farmers were mainly aboriginal
foragers who decided to settle down, rather than the descendants of
immigrants from the Hilly Flanks.

The Cavalli-Sforza and Sykes teams squared off fiercely in the pages
of the *American Journal of Human Genetics* in 1997, but since then their
positions have steadily converged. Cavalli-Sforza now calculates that

immigrant farmers from western Asia account for 26–28 percent of European DNA; Sykes puts the figure nearer 20 percent. To say that one of Europe's first farmers descended from southwest Asian immigrants for every three or four who descended from natives is oversimplifying, but is not far wrong.

PREDESTINATION

Neither Cavalli-Sforza's and Renfrew's claims nor Sykes's alternative—nor even the emerging compromise between them—would have made the students at Nanterre very happy, because all the theories treat the triumph of farming as inevitable. Competition, genetics and archaeology imply, has little to do with exams or teachers, because it has always been with us. Its logic means that things had to turn out more or less as they did.

But is this true? People, after all, have free will. Sloth, greed, and fear may be the motors of history, but each of us gets to choose among them. If three-quarters or more of Europe's first farmers descended from aboriginal foragers, surely prehistoric Europeans could have stopped farming in its tracks if enough of them had decided against intensifying cultivation. So why did that not happen?

Sometimes it did. After sweeping from what is now Poland to the Paris Basin in a couple of hundred years before 5200 BCE, the wave of agricultural advance ground to a halt (Figure 2.4). For a thousand years hardly any farmers invaded the last fifty or sixty miles separating them from the Baltic Sea and few Baltic foragers took up more intensive cultivation. Here foragers fought for their way of life. Along the farming/foraging fault line we find remarkable numbers of fortified settlements and skeletons of young men killed by blunt-instrument traumas on the front and left sides of their skulls—just what we would expect if they died fighting face-to-face with right-handed opponents using stone axes. Several mass graves may even be grisly relics of massacres.

We will never know what acts of heroism and savagery went on along the edge of the North European Plain seven thousand years ago, but geography and economics probably did as much as culture and violence to fix the farming/foraging frontier. Baltic foragers lived in a chilly Garden of Eden, where rich marine resources supported dense populations in year-round villages. Archaeologists have unearthed great mounds of seashells, leftovers from feasts, which piled up around the hamlets. Nature's bounty apparently allowed the foragers to have their cake (or shellfish) and eat it: there were enough foragers to stand up to farmers but not so many that they had to shift toward farming to feed themselves. At the same time, farmers found that the plants and animals that had originally been domesticated in the Hilly Flanks fared less well this far north.

We frankly do not know why farming did finally move north after 4200 BCE. Some archaeologists emphasize push factors, proposing that farmers multiplied to the point that they steamrollered all opposition; others stress pull factors, proposing that a crisis within forager society opened the north to invasion. But however it ended, the Baltic exception seems to prove the rule that once farming appeared in the Hilly Flanks the original affluent society could not survive.

In saying this I am not denying the reality of free will. That would be foolish, although plenty of people have succumbed to the temptation. The great Leo Tolstoy, for instance, closed his novel *War and Peace* with an odd excursus denying free will in history—odd, because the book is studded with agonized decisions (and indecisions), abrupt changes of mind, and not a few foolish blunders, often with momentous consequences. All the same, said Tolstoy, "Free will is for history only an expression connoting what we do not know about the laws of human history." He continued:

> The recognition of man's free will as something capable of influencing historical events . . . is the same for history as the recognition of a free force moving the heavenly bodies would be for astronomy . . . If there is even a single body moving freely, then the laws of Kepler and Newton are negated and no conception of the movement of the heavenly bodies any longer exists. If any single action is due to free will, then not a single historical law can exist, nor any conception of historical events.

This is nonsense. High-level nonsense, to be sure, but nonsense all the same. On any given day any prehistoric forager could have decided not to intensify, and any farmer could have walked away from his fields or her grindstone to gather nuts or hunt deer. Some surely did, with immense consequences for their own lives. But in the long run it did not matter, because the competition for resources meant that people who kept farming, or farmed even harder, captured more energy than those who did not. Farmers kept feeding more children and livestock, clearing more fields, and stacking the odds still further against foragers. In the right circumstances, like those prevailing around the Baltic Sea in 5200 BCE, farming's expansion slowed to a crawl. But such circumstances could not last forever.

Farming certainly suffered local setbacks (overgrazing, for instance, seems to have turned the Jordan Valley into a desert between 6500 and 6000 BCE), but barring a climatic disaster like a new Younger Dryas, all the free will in the world could not stop agricultural lifestyles from expanding to fill all suitable niches. The combination of brainy *Homo sapiens* with warm, moist, and stable weather plus plants and animals that could evolve into domesticated forms made this as inevitable as anything can be in this world.

By 7000 BCE the dynamic, expansive agricultural societies at the western end of Eurasia were unlike anything else on earth, and by this point it makes sense to distinguish "the West" from the rest. Yet while the West was different from the rest, the differences were not permanent, and across the next few thousand years people began independently inventing agriculture in perhaps half a dozen places across the Lucky Latitudes (Figure 2.6).

The earliest and clearest case outside the Hilly Flanks is China. Cultivation of rice began in the Yangzi Valley between 8000 and 7500 BCE and of millet in north China by 6500. Millet was fully domesticated around 5500 and rice by 4500, and pigs were domesticated between 6000 and 5500. Recent finds suggest that cultivation began almost as early in the New World too. Cultivated squash was evolving toward domesticated forms by 8200 BCE in northern Peru's Nanchoc Valley and in Mexico's Oaxaca Valley by 7500–6000 BCE. Peanuts appear in Nanchoc by 6500, and while archaeological evidence that wild teosinte was evolving into domesticated corn in Oaxaca goes back only to 5300 BCE, geneticists suspect that the process actually began as early as 7000.

The Chinese and New World domestications were definitely independent of events in the Hilly Flanks, but things are less clear in Pakistan's Indus Valley. Domesticated barley, wheat, sheep, and goats all appear

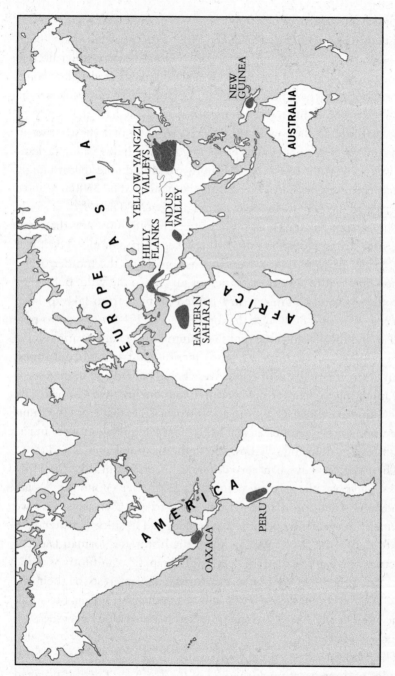

Figure 2.6. Promised lands: seven regions around the world where domestication of plants or animals may have begun independently between 11,000 and 5000 BCE

abruptly at Mehrgarh around 7000 BCE—so abruptly that many archaeologists think that migrants from the Hilly Flanks carried them there. The presence of wheat seems particularly telling, because so far no one has identified local wild wheats from which domesticated wheat could have evolved anywhere near Mehrgarh. Botanists have not explored the region very thoroughly (not even the Pakistani army has much stomach for poking around these wild tribal lands), so there may be surprises in store. And while present evidence does suggest that Indus Valley agriculture was an offshoot of the Hilly Flanks, we should note that it rapidly went its own way, with local zebu cattle domesticated by 5500 BCE and a sophisticated, literate urban society emerging by 2500 BCE.

The eastern Sahara Desert was wetter around 7000 BCE than it is now, with strong monsoon rains filling lakes every summer, but it was still a brutal place to live. Adversity was apparently the mother of invention here: cattle and sheep could not survive in the wild, but foragers could eke out a living if they herded animals from lake to lake. Between 7000 and 5000 BCE the foragers turned themselves into pastoralists and their wild cattle and sheep into larger, tamer animals.

By 5000 BCE agriculture was also emerging in two highland zones, one in Peru, where llama or alpaca were being herded and quinoa seeds were mutating to wait for the harvester, and one in New Guinea. The New Guinean evidence has been as controversial as that from the Indus Valley, but it now seems clear that by 5000 BCE highlanders were burning off forests, draining swamps, and domesticating bananas and taro.

These regions have had very different histories, but, like the Hilly Flanks, each was the starting point for a distinctive economic, social, and cultural tradition that has lasted down to our own day. Here we can finally answer the question that has dogged us since Chapter 1, of how to define the West. We saw there the historian Norman Davies's criticisms of what he called the "elastic geography" of definitions of the West, "designed," as he put it, "to further the interests of their authors." Davies threw the baby out with the bathwater, refusing to speak of the West at all. Thanks to the time depth archaeology provides, we can now do better.

The modern world's great civilizations all go back to these original episodes of domestication at the end of the Ice Age. There is no need to let the intellectual squabbles Davies describes rob us of "the West" as an analytical category: it is simply a geographical term, referring to those societies that descended from the westernmost Eurasian core of domestication, in the Hilly Flanks. It makes no sense to talk about "the West" as a distinctive region before about 11,000 BCE, when cultivation began making the Hilly Flanks unusual; and the concept starts to become an important analytical tool only after 8000 BCE, when other agricultural cores also started appearing. By 4500 BCE the West had expanded to include most of Europe, and in the last five hundred years colonists have taken it to the Americas, the Antipodes, and Siberia. "The East," naturally enough, simply means those societies that descended from the easternmost core of domestication that began developing in China by 7500 BCE. We can also speak of comparable New World, South Asian, New Guinean, and African traditions. Asking why the West rules really means asking why societies descended from the agricultural core in the Hilly Flanks, rather than those descended from the cores in China, Mexico, the Indus Valley, the eastern Sahara, Peru, or New Guinea, came to dominate the planet.

One long-term lock-in explanation springs to mind immediately: that people in the Hilly Flanks—the first Westerners—developed agriculture thousands of years before anyone else in the world because they were smarter. They passed their smartness on with their genes and languages when they spread across Europe; Europeans took it along when they colonized other parts of the globe after 1500 CE; and that is why the West rules.

Like the racist theories discussed in Chapter 1, this is almost certainly wrong, for reasons the evolutionist and geographer Jared Diamond laid out forcefully in his classic book *Guns, Germs, and Steel*. Nature, Diamond observed, is just not fair. Agriculture appeared in the Hilly Flanks thousands of years earlier than anywhere else not because the people living here were uniquely smart, but because geography gave them a head start.

There are 200,000 species of plants in the world today, Diamond observed, but only a couple of thousand are edible, and only a couple of hundred have much potential for domestication. In fact, more than half the calories consumed today come from cereals, and above all wheat, corn, rice, barley, and sorghum. The wild grasses these cereals evolved from are not spread evenly over the globe. Of the fifty-six grasses with the biggest, most nutritious seeds, thirty-two grow wild in southwest Asia and the Mediterranean Basin. East Asia has just six wild species; Central America, five; Africa south of the Sahara, four; North America, also four; Australia and South America, two each; and western Europe, one. If people (in large groups) were all much the same and foragers all over the world were roughly equally lazy, greedy, and scared, it was overwhelmingly likely that people in the Hilly Flanks would domesticate plants and animals before anyone else because they had more promising raw materials to work with.

The Hilly Flanks had other advantages too. It took just one genetic mutation to domesticate wild barley and wheat, but turning teosinte into something recognizable as corn called for dozens. The people who entered North America around 14,000 BCE were no lazier or stupider than anyone else, nor did they make a mistake by trying to domesticate teosinte rather than wheat. There was no wild wheat in the New World. Nor could immigrants bring domesticated crops with them from the Old World, because they could enter the Americas only while there was a land bridge from Asia. When they crossed, before the rising oceans drowned the land bridge around 12,000 BCE, there were no domesticated food crops to bring; by the time there were domesticated food crops,* the land bridge was submerged.

Turning from crops to animals, the odds favored the Hilly Flanks almost as strongly. There are 148 species of large (over a hundred pounds) mammals in the world. By 1900 CE just 14 of them had been domesticated. Seven of the 14 were native to southwest Asia; and of the world's 5 most important domesticates (sheep, goat, cow, pig, and horse), all but the horse had wild ancestors in the Hilly Flanks. East Asia had 5 of the 14 potentially domesticable species and South America just 1. North America, Australia, and Africa south of the Sahara had none at all. Africa, of course, teems with big animals, but there are obvious challenges in domesticating species such as lions, who will eat you, or giraffes, who can outrun even lions.

We should not, then, assume that people in the Hilly Flanks invented agriculture because they were racially or culturally superior. Because they lived among more (and more easily) domesticable plants and animals than anyone else, they mastered them first. Concentra-

---

*As opposed to nonfood crops—a 2005 DNA study suggests that the first colonists of the Americas brought with them from Asia cultivated bottle gourds, which they used as containers.

tions of wild plants and animals in China were less favorable, but still good; domestication came perhaps two millennia later there. Herders in the Sahara, who had just sheep and cattle to work with, needed another five hundred years, and since the desert could not support crops, they never became farmers. New Guinean highlanders had the opposite problem, with just a narrow range of plants and no domesticable large animals. They needed a further two thousand years and never became herders. The agricultural cores in the Sahara and New Guinea, unlike the Hilly Flanks, China, the Indus Valley, Oaxaca, and Peru, did not develop their own cities and literate civilizations—not because they were inferior, but because they lacked the natural resources.

Native Americans had more to work with than Africans and New Guineans but less than Hilly Flankers and people in China. Oaxacans and Andeans moved quickly, cultivating plants (but not animals) within twenty-five centuries of the end of the Younger Dryas. Turkeys and llamas, their only domesticable animals other than dogs, took centuries more.

Australians had the most limited resources of all. Recent excavations show that they experimented with eel farming, and given another few thousand years may well have created domesticated lifestyles. Instead, European colonists overwhelmed them in the eighteenth century CE, importing wheat and sheep, descendants of the original agricultural revolution in the Hilly Flanks.

So far as we can tell, people were indeed much the same everywhere. Global warming gave everyone new choices, among working less, working the same amount and eating more, or having more babies, even if that meant working harder. The new climate regime also gave them the option of living in larger groups and moving around less. Everywhere in the world, people who chose to stay put, breed more, and work harder squeezed out those who made different choices. Nature just made the whole process start earlier in the West.

EAST OF EDEN

Maybe so, the advocate of long-term lock-in theories might agree; maybe people really are much the same everywhere, and maybe geography did make Westerners' jobs easier. Yet there is more to history than weather and the size of seeds. Surely the details of the particular choices people made among working less, eating more, and raising bigger families matter too. The end of a story is often written in its beginning, and perhaps the West rules today because the culture created in the Hilly Flanks more than ten thousand years ago, the parent from which all subsequent Western societies descend, just had more potential than the cultures created in other core regions around the world.

Let us take a look, then, at the best-documented, oldest, and (in our own times) most powerful civilization outside the West, that which began in China. We need to find out how much its earliest farming cultures differed from those in the West and whether these differences set East and West off along different trajectories, explaining why Western societies came to dominate the globe.

Until recently archaeologists knew very little about early agriculture in China. Many scholars even thought that rice, that icon of Chinese cuisine in our own day, began its history in Thailand, not China. The discovery of wild rice growing in the Yangzi Valley in 1984 showed that rice could have been domesticated here after all, but direct archaeological confirmation remained elusive. The problem was that while bakers inevitably burn some of their bread, preserving charred wheat or barley seeds for archaeologists to find, boiling, the sensible way to cook rice, rarely has this result. Consequently it is much harder for archaeologists to recover ancient rice.

A little ingenuity, however, soon got archaeologists around this roadblock. In 1988 excavators at Pengtoushan in the Yangzi Valley (Figure 2.7) noticed that around 7000 BCE potters began mixing rice husks and stalks into their clay to prevent pots cracking in the kiln, and close study revealed surefire signs that these plants were being cultivated.

The real breakthroughs, though, began in 1995, when Yan Wenming of Peking University* teamed up with the American archaeologist Richard MacNeish, as hardcore a fieldworker as any in the world. (MacNeish, who began digging in Mexico in the 1940s, logged an awe-inspiring 5,683 days in the trenches—nearly ten times what I have

---

*Like Peking Man, discussed in Chapter 1, Peking University has kept the older form of its name. In this case, administrators made a conscious decision in the 1980s to keep translating "Beijing Daxue" into Western languages as "Peking University."

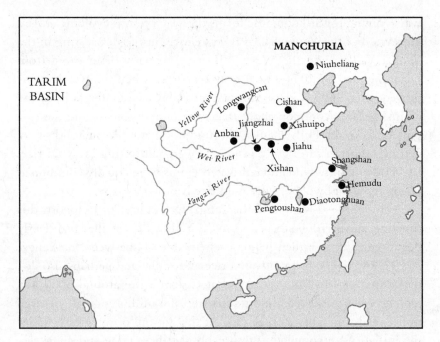

Figure 2.7. The beginning of the East: sites in what is now
China discussed in this chapter

managed to do; and when he died in 2001, aged eighty-two, it was
with his boots on, in an accident while doing fieldwork in Belize. He
reportedly talked archaeology with the ambulance driver all the way to
the hospital.) MacNeish brought to China not only decades of expertise studying early agriculture but also the archaeobotanist Deborah
Pearsall, who in turn brought a new scientific technique. Even though
rice rarely survives in archaeological deposits, all plants absorb tiny
amounts of silica from groundwater. The silica fills some of the plant's
cells, and when the plant decays it leaves microscopic cell-shaped
stones, called phytoliths, in the soil. Careful study of phytoliths can
reveal not just whether rice was being eaten but also whether it was
domesticated.

Yan and MacNeish dug a sixteen-foot-deep trench in Diaotonghuan Cave near the Yangzi Valley, and Pearsall was able to show from
phytoliths that by 12,000 BCE people were uprooting wild rice and
bringing it back to the cave. Rather like the Hilly Flanks, where wild
wheat, barley, and rye flourished as the world warmed up, this was a
hunter-gatherer golden age. There is no sign in the phytoliths that rice

was evolving toward domestic forms the way rye was evolving at Abu Hureyra, but the Younger Dryas was clearly just as devastating in the Yangzi Valley as in the West. Wild rice virtually disappeared from Diaotonghuan by 10,500 BCE, only to return when the weather improved after 9600. Coarse pottery, probably vessels for boiling the grains, became common about that time (2,500 years before the first pottery from the Hilly Flanks). Around 8000 BCE the phytoliths start getting bigger, a sure sign that people were cultivating the wild rice. By 7500 BCE fully wild and cultivated grains were equally common at Diaotonghuan; by 6500, fully wild rice had disappeared.

A cluster of excavations in the Yangzi Delta since 2001 supports this timeline, and by 7000 BCE people in the Yellow River valley had clearly begun cultivating millet. Jiahu, a remarkable site between the Yangzi and Yellow rivers, had cultivated rice and millet and perhaps also domesticated pigs by 7000 BCE, and at Cishan a fire around 6000 BCE scorched and preserved almost a quarter of a million pounds of large millet seeds in eighty storage pits. At the bottom of some pits, under the millet, were complete (presumably sacrificed) dog and pig skeletons, some of the earliest Chinese evidence for domesticated animals.

As in the West, domestication involved countless small changes across many centuries in a range of crops, animals, and techniques. The high water table at Hemudu in the Yangzi Delta has given archaeologists a bonanza, preserving huge amounts of waterlogged rice as well as wood and bamboo tools, all dating from 5000 BCE onward. By 4000, rice was fully domesticated, as dependent on human harvesters as were wheat and barley in the West. Hemudans also had access to domesticated water buffalo and were using buffalo shoulder blades as spades. In northern China's Wei Valley archaeologists have documented a steady shift from hunting toward full-blown agriculture after 5000 BCE. This was clearest in the tools being used: stone spades and hoes replaced axes as people moved from simply clearing patches in the forest to cultivating permanent fields, and spades got bigger as farmers turned the soil more deeply. In the Yangzi Valley recognizable rice paddies, with raised banks for flooding, may go back as far as 5700 BCE.

Early Chinese villages, like Jiahu around 7000 BCE, looked quite like the first villages in the Hilly Flanks, with small, roughly round semisubterranean huts, grindstones, and burials between the houses.

Between fifty and a hundred people lived at Jiahu. One hut was slightly larger than the others but the very consistent distribution of finds suggests that wealth and gender distinctions were still weak and cooking and storage were communal. This was changing by 5000 BCE, when some villages had 150 residents and were protected by ditches. At Jiangzhai, the best-documented site of this date, huts faced an open area containing two large piles of ash, which may be remains of communal rituals.

The Jiangzhai sacrifices—if such they are—look pretty tame compared to the shrines Westerners had already been building for several thousand years, but two remarkable sets of finds in graves at Jiahu suggest that religion and ancestors were every bit as important as in the Hilly Flanks. The first consists of thirty-plus flutes carved from the wing bones of red-crowned cranes, all found in richer-than-average male burials. Five of the flutes can still be played. The oldest, from around 7000 BCE, had five or six holes, and while they were not very subtle instruments, modern Chinese folk songs can be played on them. By 6500 BCE seven holes were normal and the flutemakers had standardized pitch, which probably means that groups of flautists were performing together. One grave of around 6000 BCE held an eight-hole flute, capable of playing any modern melody.

All very interesting; but the flutes' full significance becomes clear only in the light of twenty-four rich male graves containing turtle shells, fourteen of which had simple signs scratched on them. In one grave, dating around 6250 BCE, the deceased's head had been removed (shades of Çatalhöyük!) and replaced with sixteen turtle shells, two of them inscribed. Some of these signs—in the eyes of some scholars, at least—look strikingly like pictograms in China's earliest full-blown writing system, used by the kings of the Shang dynasty five thousand years later.

I will come back to the Shang inscriptions in Chapter 4, but here I just want to observe that while the gap between the Jiahu signs (around 6250 BCE) and China's first proper writing system (around 1250 BCE) is almost as long as that between the strange symbols from Jerf al-Ahmar in Syria (around 9000 BCE) and the first proper writing in Mesopotamia (around 3300 BCE), China has more evidence for continuity. Dozens of sites have yielded the odd pot with an incised sign, particularly after 5000 BCE. All the same, specialists disagree fiercely over whether the crude Jiahu scratchings are direct ancestors of the five-thousand-plus symbols of the Shang writing system.

Not the least of the arguments in favor of links is the fact that so many Shang texts were also scratched on turtle shells. Shang kings used these shells in rituals to predict the future, and traces of this practice definitely go back to 3500 BCE; could it be, the excavators of Jiahu now ask, that the association of turtle shells, writing, ancestors, divination, and social power began before 6000 BCE? As anyone who has read Confucius knows, music and rites went together in first-millennium-BCE China; could the flutes, turtle shells, and writing in the Jiahu graves be evidence that ritual specialists able to talk to the ancestors emerged more than five thousand years earlier?

That would be a remarkable continuity, but there are parallels. Earlier in the chapter I mentioned the peculiar twin-headed statues with giant staring eyes, dating around 6600 BCE, found at 'Ain Ghazal in Jordan; Denise Schmandt-Besserat, an art historian, has pointed out that descriptions of the gods written down in Mesopotamia around 2000 BCE are strikingly like these statues. In East and West alike, some elements of the first farmers' religions may have been extremely long-lived.

Even before the discoveries at Jiahu, Kwang-chih Chang of Harvard University—the godfather of Chinese archaeology in America from the 1960s until his death in 2001—had suggested that the first really powerful people in China had been shamans who persuaded others that they could talk to animals and ancestors, fly between worlds, and monopolize communication with the heavens. When Chang presented this theory, in the 1980s, the evidence available only allowed him to trace such specialists back to 4000 BCE, a time when Chinese societies were changing rapidly and some villages were turning into towns. By 3500 BCE some communities had two or three thousand residents, as many as Çatalhöyük or 'Ain Ghazal had had three thousand years earlier, and a handful of communities could mobilize thousands of laborers to build fortifications from layer upon layer of pounded earth (good building stone is rare in China). The most impressive wall, at Xishan, was ten to fifteen feet thick and ran for more than a mile. Even today it still stands eight feet high in places. Parts of children's skeletons in clay jars under the foundations may have been sacrifices, and numerous pits full of ash within the settlement contained adults in poses suggesting struggle, sometimes mixed with animal bones. These may have been ritual murders like those from Çayönü in Turkey, and there is some evidence that such grisly rites go back to 5000 BCE in China.

If Chang was right that shamans were taking on leadership roles by 3500 BCE, they may have lived in the large houses, covering up to four thousand square feet, that now appeared in some towns (archaeologists often call these "palaces," though that is a bit grandiose). These had plastered floors, big central hearths, and ash pits holding animal bones (from sacrifices?). One contained a white marble object that looks like a scepter. The most interesting "palace," at Anban, stood on high ground in the middle of the town. It had stone pillar bases and was surrounded by pits full of ash, some holding pigs' jaws that had been painted red, others pigs' skulls wrapped in cloth, and others still little clay figurines with big noses, beards, and odd pointed hats (much like Halloween witches).

Two things about these statuettes get archaeologists excited. First, the tradition of making them lasted for thousands of years, and a very similar model found in a palace dating around 1000 BCE had the Chinese character *wu* painted on its hat. *Wu* meant "religious mediator," and some archaeologists conclude that all these figurines, including the ones from Anban, must represent shamans. Second, many of the figurines look distinctly Caucasian, not Chinese. Similar models have been found all the way from Anban to Turkmenistan in central Asia along the path that later became the Silk Road, linking China to Rome. Shamanism remains strong in Siberia even today; for a price, ecstatic visionaries will still summon up spirits and predict the future for adventurous tourists. The Anban figurines might indicate that shamans from the wilds of central Asia were incorporated into Chinese traditions of religious authority around 4000 BCE; they might, some archaeologists think, even mean that the shamans of the Hilly Flanks, going back to 10,000 BCE, had some very distant influence on the East.

Other fragments of evidence suggest this is perfectly possible. The most extraordinary is a set of mummies from the Tarim Basin, almost totally unknown to Westerners until the magazines *Discover, National Geographic, Archaeology,* and *Scientific American* gave them a publicity blitz in the mid-1990s. The mummies' Caucasoid features seem to prove beyond doubt that people did move from central and even western Asia into China's northwest fringes by 2000 BCE. In a coincidence that seems almost too good to be true, not only did the people buried in the Tarim Basin have beards and big noses like the Anban figurines; they were also partial to pointed hats (one grave contained ten woolen caps).

It is easy to get overexcited about a few unusual finds, but even setting aside the wilder theories, it looks like religious authority was as important in early China as in the early Hilly Flanks. And if any doubts remain, two striking discoveries from the 1980s should dispel them. Archaeologists excavating at Xishuipo were astonished to find a grave of around 3600 BCE containing an adult man flanked by images of a dragon and a tiger laid out in clamshells. More clamshell designs surrounded the grave. One showed a dragon-headed tiger with a deer on its back and a spider on its head; another, a man riding a dragon. Chang suggested that the dead man was a shaman and that the inlays showed animal spirits that helped him to move between heaven and earth.

A discovery in Manchuria, far to the northeast, surprised archaeologists even more. Between 3500 and 3000 BCE a cluster of religious sites covering two square miles developed at Niuheliang. At its heart was what the excavators called the "Goddess Temple," an odd, sixty-foot-long semisubterranean corridor with chambers containing clay statues of humans, pig-dragon hybrids, and other animals. At least six statues represented naked women, life size or larger, sitting cross-legged; the best preserved had red painted lips and pale blue eyes inset in jade, a rare, hard-to-carve stone that was becoming the luxury good of choice all over China. Blue eyes being unusual in China, it is tempting to link these statues to the Caucasian-looking figurines from Anban and the Tarim Basin mummies.

Despite Niuheliang's isolation, half a dozen clusters of graves are scattered through the hills around the temple. Mounds a hundred feet across mark some of the tombs, and the grave goods include jade ornaments, one of them carved into another pig-dragon. Archaeologists have argued, with all the ingenuity that lack of evidence brings out in us, over whether the men and women buried here were priests or chiefs. Quite possibly they were both at once. Whoever they were, though, the idea of burying a minority of the dead—usually men—with jade offerings caught on all over China, and by 4000 BCE actual worship of the dead was beginning at some cemeteries. It looks as if people in the

Eastern core were just as concerned about ancestors as those in the Hilly Flanks, but expressed their concern in different ways—by removing skulls from the dead and keeping them among the living in the West, and by honoring the dead at cemeteries in the East. But at both ends of Eurasia the greatest investments of energy were in ceremonies related to gods and ancestors, and the first really powerful individuals seem to have been those who communicated with invisible worlds of ancestors and spirits.

By 3500 BCE agricultural lifestyles rather like those created in the West several millennia earlier—involving hard work, food storage, fortifications, ancestral rites, and the subordination of women and the young to men and the old—seem to have been firmly established in the Eastern core and were expanding from there. The Eastern agricultural dispersal also seems to have worked rather like that in the West; or, at least, the arguments among the experts take similar forms in both parts of the world. Some archaeologists think people from the core area between the Yellow and Yangzi rivers migrated across East Asia, carrying agriculture with them; others, that local foraging groups settled down, domesticated plants and animals, traded with one another, and developed increasingly similar cultures over large areas. The linguistic evidence is just as controversial as in Europe, and as yet there are not enough genetic data to settle anything. All we can say with confidence is that Manchurian foragers were living in large villages and growing millet by at least 5000 BCE. Rice was being cultivated far up the Yangzi Valley by 4000, on Taiwan and around Hong Kong by 3000, and in Thailand and Vietnam by 2000. By then it was also spreading down the Malay Peninsula and across the South China Sea to the Philippines and Borneo (Figure 2.8).

Just like the Western agricultural expansion, the Eastern version also hit some bumps. Phytoliths show that rice was known in Korea by 4400 BCE and millet by 3600, the latter reaching Japan by 2600, but prehistoric Koreans and Japanese largely ignored these novelties for the next two thousand years. Like northern Europe, coastal Korea and Japan had rich marine resources that supported large, permanent villages ringed by huge mounds of discarded seashells. These affluent foragers developed sophisticated cultures and apparently felt no urge to take up farming. Again like Baltic hunter-gatherers in the thousand years between

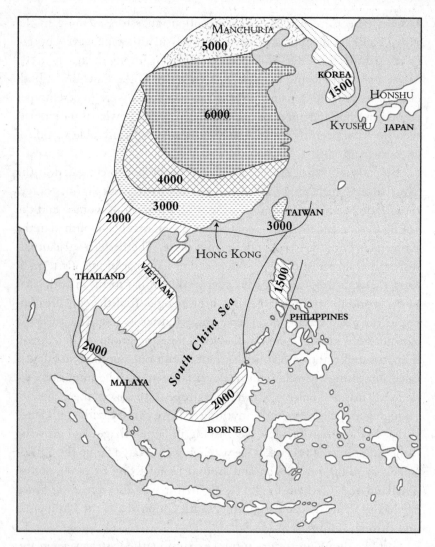

Figure 2.8. Going forth and multiplying, version two: the expansion
of agriculture from the Yellow-Yangzi valleys, 6000–1500 BCE

5200 and 4200 BCE, they were numerous (and determined) enough to
see off colonists who tried to take their land but not so numerous that
hunger forced them to take up farming to feed themselves.

In both Korea and Japan the switch to agriculture is associated with
the appearance of metal weapons—bronze in Korea around 1500 BCE

and iron in Japan around 600 BCE. Like European archaeologists who argue over whether push or pull factors ended the affluent Baltic foraging societies, some Asianists think the weapons belonged to invaders who brought agriculture in their train while others suggest that internal changes so transformed foraging societies that farming and metal weapons suddenly became attractive.

By 500 BCE rice paddies were common on Kyushu, Japan's southern island, but the expansion of farming hit another bump on the main island of Honshu. It took a further twelve hundred years to get a foothold on Hokkaido in the north, where food-gathering opportunities were particularly rich. But in the end, agriculture displaced foraging as completely in the East as in the West.

BOILING AND BAKING, SKULLS AND GRAVES

How are we to make sense of all this? Certainly East and West were different, from the food people ate to the gods they worshipped. No one would mistake Jiahu for Jericho. But were the cultural contrasts so strong that they explain why the West rules? Or were these cultural traditions just different ways of doing the same things?

Table 2.1 summarizes the evidence. Three points, I think, jump out. First, if the culture created in the Hilly Flanks ten thousand years ago and from which subsequent Western societies descend really did have greater potential for social development than the culture created in the East, we might expect to see some strong differences between the two sides of Table 2.1. But we do not. In fact, roughly the same things happened in both East and West. Both regions saw the domestication of dogs, the cultivation of plants, and domestication of large (by which I mean weighing over a hundred pounds) animals. Both saw the gradual development of "full" farming (by which I mean high-yield, labor-intensive systems with fully domesticated plants and wealth and gender hierarchy), the rise of big villages (by which I mean more than a hundred people), and, after another two to three thousand years, towns (by which I mean more than a thousand people). In both regions people constructed elaborate buildings and fortifications, experimented with protowriting, painted beautiful designs on pots, used lavish tombs, were

DATE BCE	WEST	EAST
14,000		Simple pottery
13,000		**END OF ICE AGE**
12,000		
11,000	Dogs ?Cultivated plants	
		YOUNGER DRYAS BEGINS
10,000	Big shrines	
	Cultivated plants	**YOUNGER DRYAS ENDS**
	?Fortification	
9000	Protowriting	
	Big villages	
	Expansion begins (Cyprus)	Dogs
8000	Domesticated animals	
	?Human sacrifice	Cultivated plants
	Full farming	?Fortification
	Towns, big buildings	Protowriting
7000	Simple pottery	
		Big villages
		Domesticated animals
6000	Expansion accelerates	
	Elaborate ceramics	Expansion begins (Manchuria)
		Full farming
		?Human sacrifice
5000		
		Rich grave goods
		Towns, big buildings
4000		Elaborate ceramics
		Big shrines
	Rich grave goods	Expansion accelerates
3000		

Table 2.1. The beginnings of East and West compared

fascinated with ancestors, sacrificed humans, and gradually expanded agricultural lifestyles (slowly at first, accelerating after about two thousand years, and eventually swamping even the most affluent foragers).

Second, not only did similar things happen in both East and West, but they also happened in more or less the same order. I have illustrated this in Table 2.1 with lines linking the parallel developments in each region. Most of the lines have roughly the same slope, with developments coming first in the West, followed about two thousand years later by the East.* This strongly suggests that developments in the East and West shared a cultural logic; the same causes had the same consequences at both ends of Eurasia. The only real difference is that the process started two thousand years earlier in the West.

Third, though, neither of my first two points is *completely* true. There are exceptions to the rules. Crude pottery appeared in the East at least seven thousand years earlier than in the West, and lavish tombs one thousand years earlier. Going the other way, Westerners built monumental shrines more than six thousand years before Easterners. Anyone who believes that these differences set East and West off along distinct cultural trajectories that explain why the West rules needs to show why pottery, tombs, and shrines matter so much, while anyone (me, for instance) who believes they did not really matter needs to explain why they diverge from the general pattern.

Archaeologists mostly agree why pottery appeared so early in the East: because the foods available there made boiling so important. Easterners needed containers they could put on a fire and consequently mastered pottery very early. If this is right, rather than focusing on the pottery itself, we should perhaps be asking whether differences in food preparation locked East and West into different trajectories of development. Maybe, for instance, Western cooking provided more nutrients, making for stronger people. That, though, is not very convincing. Skeletal studies give a rather depressing picture of life in both the Eastern and Western agricultural cores: it was, as the seventeenth-century English philosopher Thomas Hobbes more or less put it, poor, nasty, and short (though not necessarily brutish). In East and West alike early farmers were malnourished and stunted, carried heavy parasite loads, had bad teeth, and died young; in both regions, improvements

*The mean difference was just under 1,700 years; the median, 2,250 years.

in agriculture gradually improved diet; and in both regions, fancier elite cuisines eventually emerged. The Eastern reliance on boiling was one among many differences in cooking, but overall, the similarities between Eastern and Western nutrition vastly outweigh the differences.

Or maybe different ways of preparing food led to different patterns of eating and different family structures, with long-term consequences. Again, though, it is far from obvious that this actually happened. In both East and West the earliest farmers seem to have stored, prepared, and perhaps eaten food communally, only to shift across the next few millennia toward doing these things at the family level. Once more, East-West similarities outweigh differences. The early Eastern invention of pottery is certainly an interesting difference, but it does not seem very relevant to explaining why the West rules.

What of the early prominence of elaborate tombs in the East and the even earlier prominence of elaborate shrines in the West? These developments, I suspect, were actually mirror images of each other. Both, as we have seen, were intimately linked to an emerging obsession with ancestors at a time when agriculture was making inheritance from the dead the most important fact of economic life. For reasons we will probably never understand, Westerners and Easterners came up with different ways to give thanks to and get in contact with the ancestors. Some Westerners apparently thought that passing their relatives' skulls around, filling buildings with bulls' heads and pillars, and sacrificing people in them would do the trick; Easterners generally felt better about burying carved jade animals with their relatives, worshipping their tombs, and eventually beheading other people and throwing them in the grave too. Different strokes for different folks; but similar results.

I think we can draw two conclusions from Table 2.1. First, early developments in the Western and Eastern cores were mostly rather similar. I do not want to gloss over the very real differences in everything from styles of stone tools to the plants and animals people ate, but none of these differences lends much support to the long-term lock-in theory we have been discussing, that something about the way Western culture developed after the Ice Age gave it greater potential than Eastern culture and explains why the West rules. That seems to be untrue.

If any long-term lock-in theory can survive confronting the evidence in Table 2.1, it is the simplest one of all, that thanks to geography the West got a two-thousand-year head start in development, retained that lead long enough to arrive first at industrialization, and therefore dominates the world. To test this theory we need to extend our East-West comparison into more recent periods to see if that is what really happened.

That sounds simple enough, but the second lesson of Table 2.1 is that cross-cultural comparison is tricky. Just listing important developments in two columns was only a start, because making sense of the anomalies in Table 2.1 required us to put boiling and baking, skulls and graves into context, to find out what they meant within prehistoric societies. And that plunges us into one of the central problems of anthropology, the comparative study of societies.

When nineteenth-century European missionaries and administrators started collecting information about the peoples in their colonial empires, their reports of outlandish customs amazed scholars. Anthropologists catalogued these activities, speculating about their diffusion around the globe and what they might tell us about the evolution of more civilized (by which they meant more European-like) behavior. They sent eager graduate students to exotic climes to collect more examples. One of these bright young men was Bronislaw Malinowski, a Pole studying in London who found himself in the Trobriand Islands in 1914 when World War I broke out. Unable to get a boat home, Malinowski did the only reasonable thing; after sulking briefly in his tent, he got himself a girlfriend. Consequently, by 1918 he understood Trobriand culture from the inside out. He grasped what his professors in their book-lined studies had missed: that anthropology was really about explaining how customs fit together. Comparisons must be between complete functioning cultures, not individual practices torn out of context, because the same behavior may have different meanings in different contexts. Tattooing your face, for instance, may make you a rebel in Kansas, but it marks you as a conformist in New Guinea. Equally, the same idea may take different forms in different cultures, like the circulating skulls and buried jades in the prehistoric West and East, both expressing reverence toward ancestors.

Malinowski would have hated Table 2.1. We cannot, he would have insisted, make a grab bag of customs from two functioning cultures and pass judgment on which was doing better. And we certainly cannot write books with chapter titles like "The West Takes the Lead."

What, he would have asked, do we mean by "lead"? How on earth do we justify disentangling specific practices from the seamless web of life and measuring them against each other? And even if we could disentangle reality, how would we know which bits to measure?

All good questions, and we need to answer them if we are to explain why the West rules—even though the search for answers has torn anthropology apart over the last fifty years. With some trepidation, I will now plunge into these troubled waters.

3

⊚ ⊚ ⊚

TAKING THE MEASURE OF THE PAST

ARCHAEOLOGY EVOLVING

Social evolution was still rather a new idea when cultural anthropologists launched the rebellion against it described at the end of Chapter 2. The word's modern sense goes back only to 1857, when Herbert Spencer, a homeschooled English polymath, published an essay called "Progress: Its Law and Cause." Spencer was an odd character, who had already tried his hand at being a railway engineer, a copy editor at the then brand-new magazine *The Economist*, and a romantic partner of the lady novelist George Eliot (none of which suited him; he never held a steady job or married). This essay, though, was an overnight sensation. In it Spencer explained, "From the remotest past which Science can fathom, up to the novelties of yesterday, that in which progress essentially consists, is the transformation of the homogeneous into the heterogeneous." Evolution, Spencer insisted, is the process by which things begin simply and get more complex, and it explains everything about everything:

> The advance from the simple to the complex, through a process of successive differentiations, is seen alike in the earliest changes of the Universe to which we can reason our way back, and in the earliest

changes which we can inductively establish; it is seen in the geologic
and climatic evolution of the Earth; it is seen in the unfolding of every
single organism on its surface, and in the multiplication of kinds of
organisms; it is seen in the evolution of Humanity, whether contem-
plated in the civilized individual, or in the aggregate of races; it is seen
in the evolution of Society in respect alike of its political, its religious,
and its economical organization; and it is seen in the evolution of all
those endless concrete and abstract products of human activity which
constitute the environment of our daily life.

Spencer spent the next forty years bundling geology, biology, psychology, sociology, politics, and ethics into a single evolutionary theory. He succeeded so well that by 1870 he was probably the most
influential philosopher writing in English, and when Japanese and
Chinese intellectuals decided they needed to understand the West's
achievements, he was the first author they translated. The great minds
of the age bowed to his ideas. The first edition of Charles Darwin's *On
the Origin of Species*, published in 1859, did not contain the word "evolution"; nor did the second or third, nor even the fourth or fifth. But in
the sixth imprint, in 1872, Darwin felt compelled to borrow the term
that Spencer had by now popularized.*

Spencer believed that societies had evolved through four levels of
differentiation, from the simple (wandering bands without leaders)
through the compound (stable villages with political leaders) and doubly compound (groups with churches, states, complex divisions of labor, and scholarship) to the trebly compound (great civilizations like
Rome and Victorian Britain). The scheme caught on, though no two
theorists quite agreed on how to label the stages. Some spoke of evolution from savagery through barbarism to civilization; others preferred
evolution from magic through religion to science. By 1906 the forest
of terminologies was so annoying that Max Weber, the founding father

---

*That said, Darwin's vision of evolution was rather different from Spencer's. Spencer
believed that evolution applied to everything, was progressive, and would perfect the
universe; Darwin restricted evolution to biology and defined it as "descent with
modification," the modifications supplied by random genetic mutations and therefore
directionless, sometimes producing complexity out of simplicity and sometimes not.

of sociology, complained about "the vanity of contemporary authors who conduct themselves in the face of a terminology used by someone else as if it were his toothbrush."

Whatever the labels evolutionists used, though, they all faced the same problem. They had a gut feeling that they must be right, but little hard evidence to prove it. The newly forming discipline of anthropology therefore set out to supply data. Some societies, the thinking went, are less evolved than others: the colonized peoples of Africa or the Trobriand Islands, with their stone tools and colorful customs, are like living ancestors, reflecting what civilized people in trebly compound societies must have been like in prehistory. All that the anthropologist had to do (apart from putting up with malaria, internal parasites, and ungrateful natives) was take good notes, and he (not too often she in those days) could come home and fill in the gaps in the evolutionary story.

It was this intellectual program that Malinowski rejected. In a way, though, it is odd that the issue came up at all. If evolutionists wanted to document progress, why not do so directly, using archaeological data, the physical remains left behind by actual prehistoric societies, rather than indirectly, using anthropological observations of contemporary groups and speculating that they were survivals? The answer: archaeologists a century ago just did not know very much. Serious excavation had barely begun, so evolutionists had to combine the skimpy information in archaeological reports with incidental details from ancient literature and random ethnographic accounts—which made it all too easy for Malinowksi and like-minded anthropologists to expose evolutionists' reconstructions as speculative just-so stories.

Archaeology is a young science. As little as three centuries ago, our most ancient evidence about history—China's Five Classics, the Indian Vedas, the Hebrew Bible, and the Greek poet Homer—barely reached back to 1000 BCE. Before these masterpieces, all was darkness. The simple act of digging things up changed everything, but it took a while. When Napoleon invaded Egypt in 1799 he brought with him a legion of scholars, who copied down or carried off dozens of ancient inscriptions. In the 1820s French linguists unlocked the secrets of these hieroglyphic texts, abruptly adding two thousand years to documented history. Not to be outdone, in the 1840s British explorers tunneled into ruined cities in the lands that are now Iraq or, hanging from ropes, transcribed royal inscriptions in the mountains of Iran; before the decade was over, scholars could read Old Persian, Assyrian, and the wisdom of Babylon.

When Spencer started writing about progress in the 1850s, archaeology was still more adventure than science, bursting with real-life Indiana Joneses. It was only in the 1870s that archaeologists began applying the geological principle of stratigraphy (the commonsense insight that since the uppermost layers of earth on a site must have got there after the lower layers, we can use the sequence of deposits to reconstruct the order of events) to their digs, and stratigraphic analysis became mainstream only in the 1920s. Archaeologists still depended on linking their sites with events mentioned in ancient literature to date what they excavated, and so until the 1940s finds in most parts of the world floated in a haze of conjecture and guesswork. That ended when nuclear physicists discovered radiocarbon dating, using the decay of unstable carbon isotopes in bone, charcoal, and other organic finds to tell how old objects were. Archaeologists began imposing order on prehistory, and by the 1970s a global framework was taking shape.

When I was a graduate student in the 1980s one or two senior professors still claimed that when they had been students their teachers had advised them that the only essential tools for fieldwork were a tuxedo and a small revolver. I am still not sure whether I should have believed them, but whatever the truth of the matter, the James Bond era was certainly dying by the 1950s. The real breakthroughs increasingly came from the daily grind of an army of professionals, grubbing facts, pushing further into prehistory, and fanning out across the globe.

Museum storerooms were overflowing with artifacts and library shelves groaning under the weight of technical monographs, but some archaeologists worried that the fundamental question—*what does it all mean?*—was going unanswered. The situation in the 1950s was the mirror image of the 1850s: where once grand theory sought data, now data cried out for theory. Armed with their hard-won results, mid-twentieth-century social scientists, particularly in the United States, felt ready for another crack at theorizing.

Calling themselves neo-evolutionists to show that they were more advanced than fuddy-duddy "classical" evolutionists like Spencer, some social scientists began suggesting that while it was wonderful to have so many facts to work with, the mass of evidence had itself become part of the problem. The important information was buried in messy narrative accounts by anthropologists and archaeologists or in historical documents: in short, it was not scientific enough. To get beyond the forest of nineteenth-century typologies and create a unifying theory of society, the neo-evolutionists felt, they needed to convert these stories into numbers. By measuring differentiation and assigning scores they could rank societies and then search for correlations between the scores and possible explanations. Finally, they could turn to questions that might make all the time and money spent on archaeology worthwhile— whether there is just one way for societies to evolve, or multiple ways; whether societies cluster in discrete evolutionary stages (and if so, how they move from one stage to another); or whether a single trait, such as population or technology (or, for that matter, geography), explains everything.

In 1955 Raoul Naroll, an anthropologist working on a vast multi-university data-gathering project called the Human Relations Area Files, took the first serious stab at what he described as an index of social development. Randomly choosing thirty preindustrial societies from around the world (some contemporary, others historical), he trawled the files to find out how differentiated they were, which, he thought, would be reflected in how big their largest settlements were, how specialized their craftworkers were, and how many subgroups they had. Converting the results to a standard format, Naroll handed out scores. At the bottom were the Yahgan people of Tierra del Fuego, who had impressed Darwin in 1832 as "exist[ing] in a lower state of improvement than [those] in any other part of the world." They scored just twelve out of a possible sixty-three points. At the top were the pre-Spanish-conquest Aztecs, with fifty-eight points.

Over the next twenty years other anthropologists tried their hands at the game. Despite the fact that each used different categories, data sets, mathematical models, and scoring techniques, they agreed on the results between 87 and 94 percent of the time, which is pretty good for social science. Fifty years after Spencer's death, a hundred after his essay on progress, neo-evolutionists looked poised to prove the laws of social evolution.

ANTHROPOLOGY DEVOLVING

So what happened? If neo-evolutionists had delivered the goods and explained everything about social evolution, we would all have heard about it. And more to the point right now, they would already have answered the why-the-West-rules question. That question is, after all, about the relative levels of development of Eastern and Western societies: whether, as long-term lock-in theorists claim, the West pulled ahead long ago, or, as short-term accident theorists would have it, the West's lead is very recent. If neo-evolutionists could measure social development we would not have to mess around with complicated diagrams like Table 2.1. It would just be a matter of calculating Eastern and Western scores at various points since the end of the Ice Age, comparing them, and seeing which theory corresponds better with reality. So why has no one done this?

Largely, I suspect, because neo-evolutionism imploded. Even before Naroll took up his slide rule in the 1950s, the desire to measure societies struck many anthropologists as naïve. The "law-and-order crowd" (as critics called Naroll and his ilk), with their punch cards of coded data, arcane debates about statistics, and warehouse-size computers, seemed strangely divorced from the reality of archaeologists digging trenches or anthropologists interviewing hunter-gatherers; and as the times started a-changing in the 1960s, neo-evolutionism began to look not so much ridiculous as downright sinister. The anthropologist Marshall Sahlins, for example, whose "Original Affluent Society" essay I mentioned in Chapter 2, had begun his career in the 1950s as an evolutionist, but in the 1960s decided that "sympathy and even admiration for the Vietnamese struggle, coupled to moral and political disaffection with the American war, might undermine an anthropology of economic determinism and evolutionary development."

By 1967, when Sahlins was in Paris arguing that hunter-gatherers were not really poor, a new generation of anthropologists—who had cut their teeth on America's civil rights, antiwar, and women's movements, and were often steeped in the counterculture—was staking out much tougher positions. The only thing evolutionists were really doing, they suggested, was ranking non-Western societies by how much they resembled the Westerners doing the measuring, who—amazingly—always gave themselves the highest scores.

"Evolutionary theories," the archaeologists Michael Shanks and Christopher Tilley wrote in the 1980s, "easily slip into ideologies of self-justification or assert the priorities of the West in relation to other cultures whose primary importance is to act as offsets for our contemporary 'civilization.'" Nor, many critics felt, was this confidence in numbers merely a harmless game Westerners played to make themselves feel good; it was part and parcel of the hubris that had given us carpet-bombing, the Vietnam War, and the military-industrial complex. Hey hey, ho ho, LBJ had got to go; and so, too, the professors of ethnocentrism with their arrogance and their mathematics.

The sit-ins and name-calling turned an academic debate into a Manichean showdown. To some evolutionists, their critics were morally bankrupt relativists; to some critics, evolutionists were stooges of American imperialism. Through the 1980s and '90s anthropologists fought it out in hiring, tenure, and graduate admissions committees, ruining careers and polarizing scholarship. Anthropology departments on America's most famous campuses degenerated into something resembling bad marriages, until, broken down by years of mutual recriminations, the couples started leading separate lives. "We no longer [even] call each other names," one prominent anthropologist lamented in 1984. In the extreme case—at Stanford, my own university—the anthropologists divorced in 1998, formally splitting into the Department of Anthropological Sciences, which liked evolution, and the Department of Cultural and Social Anthropology, which did not. Each did its own hiring and firing and admitted and trained its own students; members of one group had no need to acknowledge members of the other. They even gave rise to a new verb, to "stanfordize" a department.

The woes—or joys, depending on who was talking—of stanfordization kept anthropologists entertained in bars at professional conferences for several years, but stanfordizing is not much of a solution to one of the biggest intellectual problems in the social sciences.* If we are going to explain why the West rules we need to confront the arguments on both sides of this issue.

---

*Stanford recognized this in 2007 and staged a shotgun second wedding, putting the two anthropologies back together.

Social evolution's critics were surely right that the law-and-order crowd was guilty of hubris. Like Herbert Spencer himself, in trying to explain everything about everything they perhaps ended up explaining rather little about anything. There was a lot of confusion over what neo-evolutionists were actually measuring, and even when they agreed on just what was supposed to be evolving within societies (which mostly happened when they stuck to Spencer's favorite idea of differentiation) it was not always obvious what ranking the world's societies in a league table would actually accomplish.

Score sheets, the critics insisted, obscure more than they reveal, masking the peculiarities of individual cultures. I certainly found that to be true when I was studying the origins of democracy in the 1990s. The ancient Greek cities that invented this form of government were really peculiar; many of their residents honestly believed that instead of asking priests what the gods thought, the best way to find the truth was to get all the men together on the side of a hill, argue, and take a vote. Giving ancient Greece a score for differentiation does not explain where democracy came from, and burying the Greeks' peculiarity somewhere in an index of social development can actually make the task harder by diverting attention from their unique achievements.

Yet that does not mean that an index of social development is a waste of time; just that it was the wrong tool for that specific question. Asking why the West rules is a different *kind* of question, a grand comparative one that requires us to range across thousands of years of history, look at millions of square miles of territory, and bring together billions of people. For this task an index of social development is exactly the tool we need. The disagreement between long-term lock-in and short-term accident theories is, after all, about the overall shape of social development in East and West across the ten or so millennia that "East" and "West" have been meaningful concepts. Instead of concentrating on this and directly confronting each other's arguments, long-termers and short-termers tend to look at different parts of the story, use different bodies of evidence, and define their terms in different ways. Following the law-and-order crowd's lead and reducing the ocean of facts to simple numerical scores has drawbacks but it also has the one great merit of forcing everyone to confront the same evidence—with surprising results.

WHAT TO MEASURE?

The first step is to figure out exactly what we need to measure. We could do worse than listen to Lord Robert Jocelyn, who fought in the Opium War that made Western rule clear to all. On a sweltering Sunday afternoon in July 1840 he watched as British ships approached Tinghai, where a fort blocked their approach to the Yangzi River mouth. "The ships opened their broadsides upon the town," Jocelyn wrote, "and the crashing of timber, falling houses, and groans of men resounded from the shore. The firing lasted from our side for nine minutes . . . We landed on a deserted beach, a few dead bodies, bows and arrows, broken spears and guns remaining the sole occupants of the field."

The immediate cause of Western rule is right here: by 1840 European ships and guns could brush aside anything an Eastern power could field. But there was, of course, more to the rise of Western rule than military power alone. Armine Mountain, another officer with the British fleet in 1840, likened the Chinese force at Tinghai to something out of the pages of medieval chronicles: it looked "as if the subjects of [those] old prints had assumed life and substance and colour," he mused, "and were moving and acting before me unconscious of the march of the world through centuries, and of all modern usage, invention, or improvement."

Mountain grasped that blowing up ships and forts was merely the proximate cause of Western dominance, the last link in a long chain of advantages. A deeper cause was that British factories could turn out explosive shells, well-bored cannon, and oceangoing warships, and British governments could raise, fund, and direct expeditions operating halfway round the world; and the ultimate reason that the British swept into Tinghai that afternoon was their success at extracting energy from the natural environment and using it to achieve their goals. It all came down to the fact that Westerners had not only scrambled further up the Great Chain of Energy than anyone else but also scrambled so high that—unlike any earlier societies in history—they could project their power across the entire world.

This process of scrambling up the Great Chain of Energy is the foundation of what, following the tradition of evolutionary anthropologists since Naroll in the 1950s, I will call social development—basically, a group's ability to master its physical and intellectual environment to get things done.* Putting it more formally, social development is the bundle of technological, subsistence, organizational, and cultural accomplishments through which people feed, clothe, house, and reproduce themselves, explain the world around them, resolve disputes within their communities, extend their power at the expense of other communities, and defend themselves against others' attempts to extend power. Social development, we might say, measures a community's ability to get things done, which, in principle, can be compared across time and space.

Before we go any further with this line of argument, there is one point I need to make in the strongest possible terms: measuring and comparing social development is not a method for passing moral judgment on different communities. For example, twenty-first-century Japan is a land of air-conditioning, computerized factories, and bustling cities. It has cars and planes, libraries and museums, high-tech healthcare and a literate population. The contemporary Japanese have mastered their physical and intellectual environment far more thoroughly than their ancestors a thousand years ago, who had none of these things. It therefore makes sense to say that modern Japan is more developed than medieval Japan. Yet this implies nothing about whether the people of modern Japan are smarter, worthier, or luckier (let alone happier) than the Japanese of the Middle Ages. Nor does it imply anything about the moral, environmental, or other costs of social development. Social development is a neutral analytical category. Measuring it is one thing; praising or blaming it is another altogether.

I will argue later in this chapter that measuring social development shows us what we need to explain if we are to answer the why-the-West-rules question; in fact, I will propose that unless we come up with a way to measure social development we will never be able to answer this question. First, though, we need establish some principles to guide our index-making.

I can think of nowhere better to start than with Albert Einstein, the most respected scientist of modern times. Einstein is supposed to have

---

*Psychologists use the term "social development" very differently, to refer to children learning the norms of the societies they grow up in.

said that "in science, things should be made as simple as possible, but no simpler": that is, scientists should boil their ideas down to the core point that can be checked against reality, figure out the simplest possible way to perform the check, then do just that—nothing more, but nothing less either.

Einstein's own theory of relativity provides a famous example. Relativity implies that gravity bends light, meaning—if the theory is right—that every time the sun passes between Earth and another star, the sun's gravity will bend the light coming from that star, making the star appear to shift position slightly. That provides an easy test of the theory—except for the fact that the sun is so bright that we cannot see stars near it. But in 1919 the British astronomer Arthur Eddington came up with a clever solution, very much in the spirit of Einstein's aphorism: by looking at the stars near the sun during a solar eclipse, Eddington realized, he could measure whether they had shifted by the amount Einstein predicted.

Eddington set off to the South Pacific, made his observations, and pronounced Einstein correct. Acrimonious arguments ensued, because the difference between results that supported Einstein and results that disproved him was tiny, and Eddington was pushing the instruments available in 1919 to their very limits; yet despite the theory of relativity's complexity,* astronomers could agree on what they needed to measure and how to measure it. It was then just a matter of whether Eddington had got the measurements right. Coming down from the sublime movement of the stars to the brutal bombardment of Tinghai, though, we immediately see that things are much messier when we are dealing with human societies. Just what should we be measuring to assign scores to social development?

If Einstein provides our theoretical lead, we might take a practical lead from the United Nations Human Development Index, not least because it has a lot in common with the kind of index that will help answer our question. The UN Development Programme devised the index to measure how well each nation is doing at giving its citizens

---

*When a member of the Royal Astronomical Society in London tried to compliment Eddington by calling him one of only three people in the world who really understood Einstein's theory, Eddington fell silent; "I'm just wondering," he finally said, "who the third might be."

opportunities to realize their innate potential. The Programme's econ-omists started by asking themselves what human development really means, and boiled it down to three core traits: average life expectancy, average education (expressed by literacy levels and enrollments in school), and average income. They then devised a complicated weight-ing system to combine the traits to give each country a score between zero, meaning no human development at all (in which case everyone would be dead) and one—perfection, given the possibilities of the real world in the year the survey was done. (In case you're wondering, in the most recent index available as I write, that for 2009, Norway came first, scoring .971, and Sierra Leone last, with .340.)

The index satisfies Einstein's rule, since three traits is probably as simple as the UN can make things while still capturing what human development means. Economists still find a lot not to like about it, though. Most obviously, life expectancy, education, and income are not the only things we could measure. They have the advantage of be-ing relatively easy to define and document (some potential traits, like happiness, would be much harder), but there are certainly other things we could look at (say employment rates, nutrition, or housing) that might generate different scores. Even economists who agree that the UN's traits are the best ones sometimes balk at conflating them into a single human development score; they are like apples and oranges, these economists say, and bundling them together is ridiculous. Other economists are comfortable both with the variables chosen and with conflating them, but do not like the way the UN statisticians weight each trait. The scores may look objective, these economists point out, but in reality they are highly subjective. Still other critics reject the very idea of scoring human development. It creates the impression, they say, that Norwegians are 97.1 percent of the way toward ultimate bliss, and 2.9 times as blissful as people in Sierra Leone—both of which seem, well, unlikely.

But despite all the criticisms, the human development index has proved enormously useful. It has helped relief agencies target their funds on the countries where they can do most good, and even the critics tend to agree that the simple fact of having an index moves the debates forward by making everything more explicit. An index of so-cial development across the last fifteen-thousand-plus years faces all the same problems as the UN's index (and then some), but it also, I think, offers some similar advantages.

Like the UN economists, we should aim to follow Einstein's rule. The index must measure as few dimensions of society as possible (keep it simple) while still capturing the main features of social development as defined above (don't make it *too* simple). Each dimension of society that we measure should satisfy six rather obvious criteria. First, it must be relevant: that is, it must tell us something about social development. Second, it must be culture-independent: we might, for example, think that the quality of literature and art are useful measures of social development, but judgments in these matters are notoriously culture-bound. Third, traits must be independent of one another—if, for instance, we use the number of people in a state and the amount of wealth in that state as traits, we should not use per capita wealth as a third trait, because it is just a product of the first two traits. Fourth, traits must be adequately documented. This is a real problem when we look back thousands of years, because the available evidence varies so much. Especially in the distant past, we simply do not know much about some potentially useful traits. Fifth, traits must be reliable, meaning that experts more or less agree on what the evidence says. Sixth, traits must be convenient. This may be the least important criterion, but the harder it is to get evidence for something or the longer it takes to calculate results, the less useful that trait is.

There is no such thing as a perfect trait. Each trait we might choose inevitably performs better on some of these criteria than on others. But after spending many months now looking into the options, I have settled on four traits that I think do quite well on all six criteria. They do not add up to a comprehensive picture of Eastern and Western society, any more than the UN's traits of life expectancy, education, and income tell us everything there is to know about Norway or Sierra Leone. But they do give us a pretty good snapshot of social development, showing us the long-term patterns that need to be explained if we are to know why the West rules.

My first trait is energy capture. Without being able to extract energy from plants and animals to feed soldiers and sailors who did little farming themselves, from wind and coal to carry ships to China, and from explosives to hurl shells at the Chinese garrison, the British would never have reached Tinghai in 1840 and blown it to pieces. Energy capture is fundamental to social development—so much so that back in the 1940s the celebrated anthropologist Leslie White proposed reducing all human history to a single equation: $E \times T \rightarrow C$, he pronounced, where E stands for energy, T for technology, and C for culture.

This is not quite as philistine as it sounds. White was not really suggesting that multiplying energy by technology tells us all we might want to know about Confucius and Plato or artists like the Dutch Old Master Rembrandt and the Chinese landscape painter Fan Kuan. When White spoke of "culture" he in fact meant something rather like what I am calling social development. But even so, his formulation is too simple for our purposes. To explain Tinghai we need to know more.

All the energy capture in the world would not have taken a British squadron to Tinghai if they had not been able to organize it. Queen Victoria's minions had to be able to raise troops, pay and supply them, get them to follow leaders, and carry out a host of other tricky jobs. We need to measure this organizational capacity. Up to a point organizational capacity overlaps with Spencer's old idea of differentiation, but neo-evolutionists learned in the 1960s that it is almost impossible to measure differentiation directly, or even to define it in a way that will satisfy critics. We need a proxy, something closely related to organizational capacity but easier to measure.

The one I have chosen is urbanism. Perhaps that will seem odd; after all, the fact that London was a big place does not directly reflect Lord Melbourne's revenue flows or the Royal Navy's command structure. On further reflection, though, I hope the choice will seem less odd. It took astonishing organization to support a city of 3 million people. Someone had to get food and water in and waste products out, provide work, maintain law and order, put out fires, and perform all the other tasks that go on, day in, day out, in every great city.

It is certainly true that some of the world's biggest cities today are dysfunctional nightmares, riddled with crime, squalor, and disease. But that, of course, has been true of most big cities throughout history. Rome had a million residents in the first century BCE; it also had street gangs that sometimes brought government to a halt and death rates so high that more than a thousand country folk had to migrate into Rome every month just to make up the numbers. Yet for all Rome's foulness (brilliantly evoked in the 2006 HBO television series *Rome*), the organization needed to keep the city going was vastly beyond anything any earlier society could have managed—just as running Lagos (population 11 million) or Mumbai (population 19 million), let alone Tokyo (population 35 million), would have been far beyond the Roman Empire's capabilities.

This is why social scientists regularly use urbanism as a rough guide to organizational capacity. It is not a perfect measure, but it is certainly a useful rough guide. In our case, the size of a society's largest cities has the extra advantage that we can trace it not only in the official statistics produced in the last few hundred years but also in the archaeological record, allowing us to get an approximate sense of levels of organization all the way back to the Ice Age.

As well as generating physical energy and organizing it, the British of course also had to process and communicate prodigious amounts of information. Scientists and industrialists had to transfer knowledge precisely; gunmakers, shipbuilders, soldiers, and sailors increasingly needed to read written instructions, plans, and maps; letters had to move between Asia and Europe. Nineteenth-century British information technology was crude compared to what we now take for granted (private letters needed three months to get from Guangzhou to London; government dispatches, for some reason, needed four), but it had already advanced far beyond eighteenth-century levels, which, in turn, were well head of the seventeenth century. Information processing is critical to social development, and I use it as my third trait.

Last but sadly not least is the capacity to make war. However well the British extracted energy, organized it, and communicated, it was their ability to turn these three traits toward destruction that settled matters in 1840. I grumbled in Chapter 1 about Arthur C. Clarke equating evolution with skill at killing in his science-fiction classic *2001: A Space Odyssey*, but an index of social development that did not include military power would be no use at all. As Chairman Mao famously put it, "Every Communist must grasp this truth: 'Political power grows out of the barrel of a gun.'" Before the 1840s, no society could project military power across the whole planet, and to ask who "ruled" was nonsense. After the 1840s, though, this became perhaps the most important question in the world.

Just as with the UN's human development index, there is no umpire to say that these traits, rather than some other set, are the ultimate way to measure social development, and again like the UN index, any change to the traits will change the scores. The good news, though, is that none of the alternative traits I have looked at over the last few years changed the scores much, and none changed the overall pattern at all.*

If Eddington had been an artist he might have been an Old Master, representing the world at a level of detail painful to behold. But making an index of social development is more like chainsaw art, carving grizzly bears out of tree trunks. This level of roughness and readiness would doubtless have turned Einstein's hair even whiter, but different problems call for different margins of error. For the chainsaw artist, the only important question is whether the tree trunk looks like a bear; for the comparative historian, it is whether the index shows the overall shape of the history of social development. That, of course, is something historians will have to judge for themselves, comparing the pattern the index reveals with the details of the historical record.

Provoking historians to do this may in fact be the greatest service an index can perform. There is plenty of scope for debate: different traits and different ways of assigning scores might well work better. But putting numbers on the table forces us to focus on where errors might have crept in and how they can be corrected. It may not be astrophysics, but it is a start.

HOW TO MEASURE?

Now it is time to come up with some numbers. It is easy enough to find figures for the state of the world in 2000 CE (since it is such a nice round number, I use this date as the end point for the index). The United Nations' various programs publish annual statistical digests that tell us, for instance, that the average American consumes 83.2 million kilocalories of energy per year, compared to 38 million for the average person in Japan; that 79.1 percent of Americans live in cities, as against

---

*I also collected data on the size of population within the largest political unit, standards of living (using adult stature as a proxy), speed of transportation, and scale of largest buildings. Each of these had problems (overlap with other traits, gaps in the data) that made them seem less useful than the four traits I ended up with; but each of them also followed much the same pattern as the four traits I selected.

66 percent of Japanese; that there are 375 Internet hosts per thousand Americans but only 73 per thousand Japanese; and so on. The International Institute for Strategic Studies's annual *Military Balance* tells us, so far as it can be known, how many troops and weapons each country has, what their capabilities are, and how much they cost. We are drowning in numbers. They do not add up to an index, though, until we decide how to organize them.

Sticking to the simple-as-possible program, I set 1,000 points as the maximum social development score attainable in the year 2000 and divide these points equally between my four traits. When Raoul Naroll published the first modern index of social development in 1956 he also gave equal points to his three traits, if only, as he put it, "because no obvious reason appeared for giving one any more weight than another." That sounds like a counsel of despair, but there is actually a good reason for weighting the traits equally: even if I thought up reasons to weight one trait more heavily than another in calculating social development, there would be no grounds to assume that the same weightings have held good across the fifteen-thousand-plus years under review or have applied equally to East and West.

Having set the maximum possible score for each trait in the year 2000 at 250 points, we come to the trickiest part, deciding how to award points to East and West at each stage of their history. I will not go step-by-step through every calculation involved (I summarize the data and some of the main complexities in the appendix at the end of this book, and I have posted a fuller account online),* but it might be useful to take a quick look inside the kitchen, as it were, and explain the procedure a bit more fully. (If you don't think so, you can of course skip to the next section.)

Urbanism is probably the most straightforward trait, although it certainly has its challenges. The first is definitional: Just what do we mean by urbanism? Some social scientists define urbanism as the proportion of the population living in settlements above a certain size (say, ten thousand people); others, as the distribution of people across several ranks of settlements, from cities down to hamlets; others still, as the average size of community within a country. These are all useful approaches, but are difficult for us to apply across the whole period we are

*www.ianmorris.org.

looking at here because the nature of the evidence keeps changing. I decided to go with a simpler measure: the size of the largest known settlement in East and West at each moment in time.

Focusing on largest city size does not do away with definitional problems, since we still have to decide how to define the boundaries of cities and how to combine different categories of evidence for numbers within them. It does, though, reduce the uncertainties to a minimum. When I played around with the numbers I found that combining largest city size with other criteria, such as the best guesses at the distribution of people between cities and villages or the average size of cities, hugely increased the difficulties of the task but hardly changed the overall scores at all; so, since the more complicated ways of measuring produced roughly the same results but with a whole lot more guesswork, I decided to stick to simple city sizes.

In 2000 CE, most geographers classified Tokyo as the world's biggest city, with about 26.7 million residents.* Tokyo, then, scores the full 250 points allotted to organization/urbanism, meaning that for all other calculations it will take 106,800 people (that is, 26.7 million divided by 250) to score 1 point. The biggest Western city in 2000 CE was New York, with 16.7 million people, scoring 156.37 points. The data from a hundred years ago are not as good, but all historians agree that cities were much smaller. In the West, London had about 6.6 million residents (scoring 61.80 points) in 1900 CE, while in the East Tokyo was still the greatest city, but with just 1.75 million people, earning 16.39 points. By the time we get back to 1800 CE, historians have to combine several different kinds of evidence, including records of food supply and tax payments, the physical area covered by cities, the density of housing within them, and anecdotal accounts, but most conclude that Beijing was the world's biggest city, with perhaps 1.1 million souls (10.30 points). The biggest Western city was again London, with about 861,000 people (8.06 points).

The further we push back in time, the broader the margins of error, but for the thousand years leading up to 1700 the biggest cities were

*The figure of 35 million I gave for Tokyo on p. 149 was for the year 2009—and means that between 2000 and 2009 the East's score for organization/urbanism soared from 250 to 327.72 points. I will come back to the acceleration of social development in the twenty-first century, taking Eastern and Western scores well beyond 1,000 points, at the end of this chapter and in Chapter 12.

clearly Chinese (with Japanese ones often close behind). First Chang'an, then Kaifeng, and later Hangzhou came close to or passed a million residents (around 9 points) between 800 and 1200 CE. Western cities, by contrast, were never more than half that size. A few centuries earlier the situation was reversed: in the first century BCE Rome's million residents undoubtedly made it the world's metropolis, while Chang'an in China had probably 500,000 citizens.

As we move back into prehistory the evidence of course becomes fuzzier and the numbers become smaller, but the combination of systematic archaeological surveys and detailed excavation of smaller areas still gives us a reasonable sense of city sizes. As I mentioned earlier, this is very much chainsaw art. The most commonly accepted estimates might be as much as 10 percent off but are unlikely to be much wider of the mark than that; and since we are applying the same methods of estimation to Eastern and Western sites, the broad trends should be fairly reliable. To score 1 point on this system requires 106,800 people, so slightly more than one thousand people will score 0.01 points, the smallest number I felt was worth entering on the index. As we saw in Chapter 2, the biggest Western villages reached this level around 7500 BCE and the biggest Eastern ones around 3500 BCE. Before these dates, West and East alike score zero (you can see tables of the scores in the appendix).

It might be worth taking a moment here to talk about energy capture as well, since it poses very different problems. The simplest way to think about energy capture is in terms of consumption per person, measured in kilocalories per day. Following the same procedure as for urbanism, I start in the year 2000 CE, when the average American burned through some 228,000 kilocalories per day. That figure, certainly the highest in history, gets the West the full compliment of 250 points (as I said earlier in the chapter, I am not interested in passing judgment on our capacities to capture energy, build cities, communicate information, and wage war; only in measuring them). The highest Eastern consumption per person in 2000 CE was Japan's 104,000 kilocalories per day, earning 113.89 points.

Official statistics on energy go back only to about 1900 CE in the East and 1800 in the West, but fortunately there are ways to work around that. The human body has some basic physiological needs. It will not work properly unless it gets about 2,000 kilocalories of food per day (rather more if you are tall and/or physically active, rather less if you are not; the current American average of 3,460 kilocalories of food per day is, as supersized waistbands cruelly reveal, well in excess of what we need). If you take in much less than 2,000 kilocalories per day your body will gradually shut down functions—strength, vision, hearing, and so on—until you die. Average food consumption can never have been much below 2,000 kilocalories per person per day for extended periods, making the lowest possible score about 2 points.

In reality, though, the lowest scores have always been above 2 points, because most of the energy humans consume is in nonfood forms. We saw in Chapter 1 that *Homo erectus* was probably already burning wood for cooking at Zhoukoudian half a million years ago, and Neanderthals were certainly doing so 100,000 years ago, as well as wearing animal skins. Since we know so little about Neanderthal lifestyles our guesses cannot be very precise, but by tapping into nonfood energy sources Neanderthals definitely captured on average another thousand-plus kilocalories per day on top of their food, earning them about 3.25 points altogether. Fully modern humans cooked more than Neanderthals, wore more clothes, and also built houses from wood, leaves, mammoth bones, and skins—all of which, again, were parasitic on the chemical energy that plants had created out of the sun's electromagnetic energy. Even the technologically simplest twentieth-century-CE hunter-gatherer societies captured at least 3,500 calories per day in food and nonfood sources combined. Given the colder weather, their distant forebears at the end of the Ice Age must have averaged closer to 4,000 kilocalories per day, or at least 4.25 points.

I doubt that any archaeologist would quibble much over these estimates, but there is a huge gap between Ice Age hunters' 4.25 points and the contemporary gasoline- and electricity-guzzling West's 250. What happened in between? By pooling their knowledge, archaeologists, historians, anthropologists, and ecologists can give us a pretty good idea.

Back in 1971, the editors of the magazine *Scientific American* invited the geoscientist Earl Cook to contribute an essay that he called "The Flow of Energy in an Industrial Society." He included in it a diagram, much reprinted since then, showing best guesses at per-person energy consumption among hunter-gatherers, early agriculturalists (by which he meant the farmers of southwest Asia around 5000 BCE whom we met in Chapter 2), advanced agriculturalists (those of northwest Europe around 1400 CE), industrial folk (western Europeans around 1860), and late-twentieth-century "technological" societies. He divided the scores into four categories of food (including the feed that goes into animals whose meat is eaten), home and commerce, industry and agriculture, and transport (Figure 3.1).

Cook's guesstimates have stood up remarkably well to nearly forty years of comparison with the results gathered by historians, anthropologists, archaeologists, and economists.* They only provide a starting point, of course, but we can use the detailed evidence surviving from each period of Eastern and Western history to tell us how far the actual societies departed from these parameters. Sometimes we can draw on textual evidence, but in most periods up to the last few hundred years archaeological finds—human and animal bones; houses; agricultural tools; traces of terracing and irrigation; the remains of craftsmen's workshops and traded goods, and the carts, ships, and roads that bore them—are even more important.

Sometimes help comes from surprising directions. The ice cores that featured so prominently in Chapters 1 and 2 also show that airborne pollution increased sevenfold in the last few centuries BCE, mostly because of Roman mining in Spain, and in the last ten years, studies of sediments from peat bogs and lakes have confirmed this picture. Europeans apparently produced nine or ten times as much copper and silver in the first century CE as in the thirteenth century CE, with all the energy demands that implies—people to dig the mines, and animals to cart away the slag; more of both to build roads and ports, to load and unload ships, and carry metals to cities; watermills to crush the ores; and above all wood, as timber to shore up mineshafts and fuel to feed forges. This independent source of evidence also lets us compare levels of industrial activity in different periods. Not until the eleventh century CE—when Chinese documents say that the relentless demands of ironworkers stripped the mountains around Kaifeng so bare of trees that coal, for the first time in history, became an important power source— did pollution in the ice return to Roman-era levels, and only with the

---

*I have made only one substantial modification to Cook's numbers; I think he overestimated the rate of increase in energy capture in southwest Asia after the beginnings of plant domestication, and that his "early agricultural" figure of 12,000 kilocalories per person per day fits better around 3000 BCE than around 5000 BCE, where he placed it.

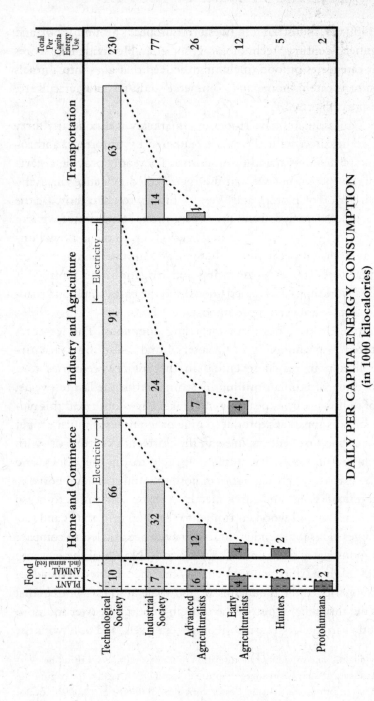

DAILY PER CAPITA ENERGY CONSUMPTION
(in 1000 kilocalories)

Figure 3.1. The Great Chain of Energy in numbers: the geoscientist Earl Cook's estimates of energy capture per person per day, from the time of *Homo habilis* to 1970s America

belching smokestacks of nineteenth-century Britain did pollution push seriously beyond Roman-era levels.

Once again, I want to emphasize that we are doing chainsaw art. For instance, I estimate per-person energy capture at the height of the Roman Empire, in the first century CE, around 31,000 kilocalories per day. That is well above Cook's estimate of 26,000 calories for advanced agricultural societies, but archaeology makes it very clear that Romans ate more meat, built more cities, used more and bigger trading ships (and so on, and so on) than Europeans would do again until the eighteenth century. That said, Roman energy capture could certainly have been 5 percent higher or lower than my estimate. For reasons I address in the appendix, though, it was probably not more than 10 percent higher or lower, and definitely not 20 percent. Cook's framework and the detailed evidence constrain guesstimates pretty tightly, and as with the urbanism scores, the fact that the same person is doing the guessing in all cases, applying the same principles, should mean that the errors are at least consistent.

Information technology and war-making raise their own difficulties, discussed briefly in the appendix and more fully on my website, but the same principles apply as with urbanism and energy capture, and probably the same margins of error too. For reasons I discuss in the appendix, the scores will need to be systematically wrong by 15 or even 20 percent to make a real difference to the fundamental pattern of social development, but such big margins of error seem incompatible with the historical evidence. In the end, though, the only way to know for sure is for other historians, perhaps preferring other traits and assigning scores in other ways, to propose their own numbers.

Fifty years ago the philosopher Karl Popper argued that progress in science is a matter of "conjectures and refutations," following a zigzag course as one researcher throws out an idea and others scramble to disprove it, in the process coming up with better ideas. The same, I think, applies to history. I am confident that any index that stays close to the evidence will produce more or less the same pattern as mine, but if I am wrong, and if others find this scheme wanting, hopefully my failure will encourage them to uncover better answers. To quote Einstein one more time, "There could be no fairer destiny for any theory . . . than that it should point the way to a more comprehensive theory in which it lives on."

WHEN AND WHERE TO MEASURE?

Two final technical issues. First, how often should we calculate the scores? If we wanted to, we could trace changes in social development from year to year or even month to month since the 1950s. I doubt that there would be much point, though. After all, we want to see the over-all shape of history across very long periods, and for that—as I hope to show in what follows—taking the pulse of social development once every century seems to provide enough detail.

As we move back toward the end of the Ice Age, though, checking social development on a century-by-century basis is neither possible nor particularly desirable. We just can't tell much difference between what was going on in 14,000 and the situation in 13,900 BCE (or 13,800 for that matter), partly because we don't have enough good evidence and partly because change just happened very slowly. I therefore use a sliding scale. From 14,000 through 4000 BCE, I measure social development every thousand years. From 4000 through 2500 BCE the quality of evidence improves and change accelerates, so I measure every five hundred years. I reduce this to every 250 years between 2500 BCE and 1500 BCE, and finally measure every century from 1400 BCE through 2000 CE.

This has its risks, most obviously that the further back in time we go, the smoother and more gradual change will look. By calculating scores only every thousand or five hundred years we may well miss something interesting. The hard truth, though, is that only occasion-ally can we date our information much more precisely than the ranges I suggest. I do not want to dismiss this problem out of hand, and will try in the narrative in Chapters 4 through 10 to fill in as many of the gaps as possible, but the framework I use here does seem to me to offer the best balance between practicality and precision.

The other issue is *where* to measure. You may have been struck while reading the last section by my coyness about just what part of the world I was talking about when I generated numbers for "West" and "East." I spoke at some points about the United States and at others about Britain; sometimes of China, sometimes of Japan. Back in Chap-ter 1 I described the historian Kenneth Pomeranz's complaints about how comparative historians often skew analysis of why the West rules

by sloppily comparing tiny England with enormous China and concluding that the West already led the East by 1750 CE. We must, he
insisted, compare like-sized units. I spent Chapters 1 and 2 responding
to this by defining West and East explicitly as the societies that have
descended from the original Western and Eastern agricultural revolutions in the Hilly Flanks and the Yellow and Yangzi river valleys; now
it is time to admit that that resolved only part of Pomeranz's problem.
In Chapter 2, I described the spectacular expansion of the Western and
Eastern zones in the five thousand or so years after cultivation began
and the differences in social development that often existed between
core areas such as the Hilly Flanks or Yangzi Valley and peripheries
such as northern Europe or Korea; so which parts of the East and West
should we focus on when working out scores for the index of social
development?

We could try looking at the whole of the Eastern and Western
zones, although that would mean that the score for, say, 1900 CE would
bundle together the smoking factories and rattling machine guns of
industrialized Britain with Russia's serfs, Mexico's peons, Australia's
ranchers, and every other group in every corner of the vast Western
zone. We would then have to concoct some sort of average development score for the whole Western region, then do it again for the East,
and repeat the process for every earlier point in history. This would get
so complicated as to become impractical, and I suspect it would be
rather pointless anyway. When it comes to explaining why the West
rules, the most important information normally comes from comparing the most highly developed parts of each region, the cores that were
tied together by the densest political, economic, social, and cultural
interactions. The index of social development needs to measure and
compare changes within these cores.

As we will see in Chapters 4–10, though, the core areas have themselves shifted and changed across time. The Western core was geographically actually very stable from 11,000 BCE until about 1400 CE,
remaining firmly at the eastern end of the Mediterranean Sea except
for the five hundred years between about 250 BCE and 250 CE, when
the Roman Empire drew it westward to include Italy. Otherwise, it
always lay within a triangle formed by what are now Iraq, Egypt, and
Greece. Since 1400 CE it has moved relentlessly north and west, first to
northern Italy, then to Spain and France, then broadening to include

Britain, Belgium, Holland, and Germany. By 1900 it straddled the Atlantic and by 2000 was firmly planted in North America. In the East the core remained in the original Yellow-Yangzi zone right up until 1800 CE, although its center of gravity shifted northward toward the Yellow River's central plain after about 4000 BCE, back south to the Yangzi Valley after 500 CE, and gradually north again after 1400. It expanded to include Japan by 1900 and southeast China by 2000 (Figure 3.2). For now I just want to note that all the social development scores reflect the societies in these core areas; why the cores shifted will be one of our major concerns in Chapters 4 through 10.

THE PATTERN OF THE PAST

So much for the rules of the game; now for some results. Figure 3.3 shows the scores across the last sixteen thousand years, since things began warming up at the end of the Ice Age.

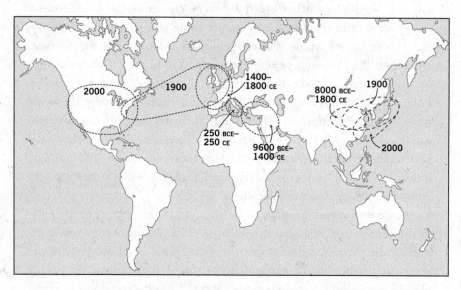

Figure 3.2. Shifting centers of power: the sometimes slow, sometimes rapid relocation of the most highly developed core within the Western and Eastern traditions since the end of the Ice Age

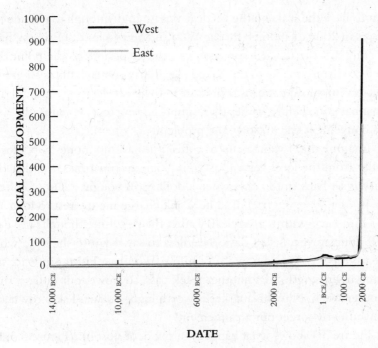

Figure 3.3. Keeping score: Eastern and Western social
development since 14,000 BCE

After all this buildup, what do we see? Frankly, not much, unless your eyesight is a lot better than mine. The Eastern and Western lines run so close together that it is hard even to distinguish them, and they barely budge off the bottom of the graph until 3000 BCE. Even then, not much seems to happen until just a few centuries ago, when both lines abruptly take an almost ninety-degree turn and shoot straight up.

But this rather disappointing-looking graph in fact tells us two very important things. First, Eastern and Western social development have not differed very much; at the scale we are looking at, it is hard to tell them apart through most of history. Second, something profound happened in the last few centuries, by far the fastest and greatest transformation in history.

To get more information, we need to look at the scores in a different way. The trouble with Figure 3.3 is that the upward swing of the Eastern and Western lines in the twentieth century was so dramatic that to have the scale on the vertical axis go high enough to include the scores in 2000 CE (906.38 for the West and 565.44 for the East) we have to compress the much lower scores in earlier periods to the point that they are barely visible to the naked eye. This problem afflicts all graphs that try to show patterns where growth is accelerating, multiplying what has gone before, rather than simply adding to it. Fortunately there is a convenient way to solve the problem.

Imagine that I want a cup of coffee but have no money. I borrow a dollar from the local version of Tony Soprano (imagine, too, that this story is set back in the days when a dollar still bought a cup of coffee). He is, of course, my friend, so he won't charge me interest so long as I pay him back within a week. If I miss the deadline, though, my debt will double every seven days. Needless to say, I fail to show up when the payment is due, so now I owe him two dollars. Fiscal prudence not being my strength, I let another week pass, so I owe four dollars; then another week. Now his marker is worth eight dollars. I skip town and conveniently forget our arrangement.

Figure 3.4 shows what happens to my debt. Just like Figure 3.3, for a long time there is nothing much to see. The line charting the interest becomes visible only around week 14—by which time I owe a breathtaking $8,192. On week 16, when my debt has spiraled to $32,768, the line finally pulls free from the bottom of the graph. By week 24, when the mobsters track me down, I owe $8,260,608. That was one expensive cup of coffee.

By this standard, of course, the growth of my debt in the first few weeks—from one, to two, to four, to eight dollars—was indeed trivial. But imagine that I had bumped into one of the loan shark's foot soldiers a month or so after my fateful coffee, when my debt stood at sixteen dollars. Let us also say that I didn't have sixteen dollars, but did give him a five. Concerned for my health, I make four more weekly payments of five dollars each, but then drop off the map again and stop paying. The black line in Figure 3.5 shows what happened when I paid nothing, while the gray one shows how my debt grows after those five five-dollar payments. My coffee still ends up costing more than $3 million, but that is less than half what I owed without the payments. They were crucially important—yet they are invisible in the graph. There is no way to tell from Figure 3.5 why the gray line ends up so much lower than the black.

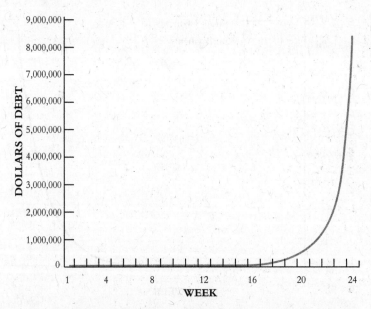

Figure 3.4. The $8 million cup of coffee: compound interest plotted on a conventional graph. Even though the cost of a cup of coffee spirals from $1 to $8,192 across fourteen weeks, the race to financial disaster remains invisible on the graph until week 17.

Figure 3.6 tells the story of my ruin in a different way. Statisticians call Figures 3.4 and 3.5 linear-linear graphs, because the scales on each axis grow by linear increments; that is, each week that passes occupies the same amount of space along the horizontal axis, each dollar of debt the same space on the vertical axis. Figure 3.6, by contrast, is what statisticians call log-linear. Time is still parceled out along the horizontal scale in linear units, but the vertical scale records my debt logarithmically, meaning that the space between the bottom axis of the graph and the first point on the vertical axis covers my debt's tenfold growth from one to ten dollars; in the space between the first and second points it again expands tenfold, from ten to a hundred dollars; then tenfold more, from a hundred to a thousand; and so on to ten million at the top.

Politicians and advertisers have turned misleading us with statistics into a fine art. Already a century and a half ago the British prime minister Benjamin Disraeli felt moved to remark, "There are three kinds of lies: lies, damned lies, and statistics," and Figure 3.6 may strike you

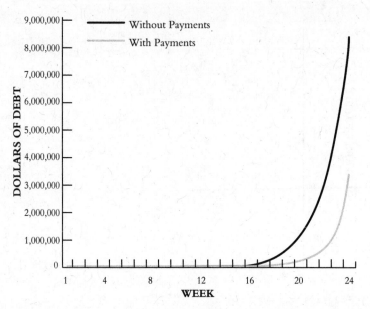

Figure 3.5. A poor way to represent poor planning: the black line shows the same spiral of debt as Figure 3.4, while the gray line shows what happens after small payments against the debt in weeks 5 through 9. On this conventional (linear-linear) graph, these crucial payments are invisible.

as proving his point. But all it really does is highlight a different aspect of my debt than Figures 3.4 and 3.5. A linear-linear scale does a good job of showing just how bad my debt is; a log-linear scale does a good job of showing how things got to be so bad. In Figure 3.6 the black line runs smooth and straight, showing that without any payments the size of my debt accelerates steadily, doubling every week. The gray line shows how after four weeks of doubling, my series of five-dollar payments slow down, but do not cancel out, my debt's rate of growth. When I stop paying, the gray line once again rises parallel to the black one, since my debt is once again doubling every week, but does not end up at quite such a dizzying height.

Neither politicians nor statistics *always* lie; it is just that there is no such thing as a completely neutral way to present either policies or numbers. Every press statement and every graph emphasizes some aspects of reality and downplays others. Thus Figure 3.7, showing social

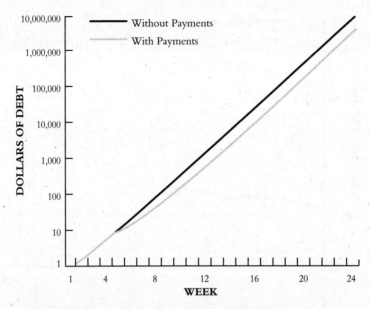

Figure 3.6. Straight roads to ruin: the spiral of debt on a log-linear
scale. The black line shows the steady doubling of the debt if no
payments are made, while the gray shows the impact of the small
payments in weeks 5 through 9 before it goes back to doubling
when the payments stop.

development scores from 14,000 BCE through 2000 CE on a log-linear
scale, produces a wildly different impression than the linear-linear version of the same scores in Figure 3.3. There is much more going on
here than met the eye in Figure 3.3. The leap in social development in
recent centuries is very real and remains clear; no amount of fancy
statistical footwork will ever make it go away. But Figure 3.7 shows
that it did not drop out of a clear blue sky, the way it seemed to do in
Figure 3.3. By the time the lines start shooting upward (around 1700
CE in the West and 1800 in the East) the scores in both regions were
already about ten times higher than they were at the left-hand side of
the graph—a difference that was barely visible in Figure 3.3.

Figure 3.7 shows that explaining why the West rules will mean answering several questions at once. We will need to know why social development leaped so suddenly after 1800 CE to reach a level (somewhere
close to 100 points) where states could project their power globally.

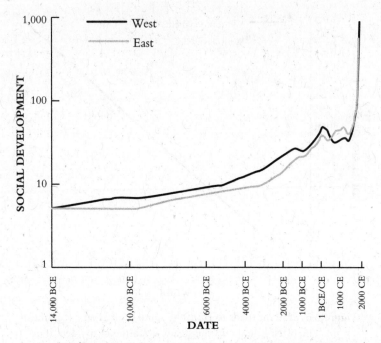

Figure 3.7. The growth of social development, 14,000 BCE–2000 CE, plotted on a log-linear scale. This may be the most useful way to present the scores, highlighting the relative rates of growth in East and West and the importance of the thousands of years of changes before 1800 CE.

Before development reached such heights, even the strongest societies on earth could dominate only their own region, but the new technologies and institutions of the nineteenth century allowed them to turn local domination into worldwide rule. We will also, of course, need to figure out why the West was the first part of the world to reach this threshold. But to answer either of these questions we will also have to understand why development had already increased so much over the previous fourteen thousand years.

Nor is that the end of what Figure 3.7 reveals. It also shows that the Eastern and Western scores were not in fact indistinguishable until just a few hundred years ago: Western scores have been higher than Eastern scores for more than 90 percent of the time since 14,000 BCE. This seems to be a real problem for short-term accident theories. The West's lead since 1800 CE is a reversion to the long-term norm, not some weird anomaly.

Figure 3.7 does not necessarily disprove short-term accident theories, but it does mean that a successful short-term theory will need to be more sophisticated, explaining the long-term pattern going back to the end of the Ice Age as well as events since 1700 CE. But the patterns also show that long-term lock-in theorists should not rejoice too soon. Figure 3.7 reveals clearly that Western social development scores have not *always* been higher than Eastern. After converging through much of the first millennium BCE, the lines cross in 541 CE and the East then remains ahead until 1773. (These implausibly precise dates of course depend on the unlikely assumption that the social development scores I have calculated are absolutely accurate; the most sensible way to put things may be to say that the Eastern score rose above the Western in the mid sixth century CE and the West regained the lead in the late eighteenth.) The facts that Eastern and Western scores converged in ancient times and that the East then led the world in social development for twelve hundred years do not disprove long-term lock-in theories, any more than the fact that the West has led for nearly the whole time since the end of the Ice Age disproves short-term accident theories; but again, they mean that a successful theory will need to be rather more sophisticated and to take account of a wider range of evidence than those offered so far.

Before leaving the graphs, there are a couple more patterns worth pointing out. They are visible in Figure 3.7, but Figure 3.8 makes them clearer. This is a conventional linear–linear graph but covers just the three and a half millennia from 1600 BCE through 1900 CE. Cutting off the enormous scores for 2000 CE lets us stretch the vertical axis enough that we can actually see the scores from earlier periods, while shortening the time span lets us stretch the horizontal axis so the changes through time are clearer too.

Two things particularly strike me about this graph. The first is the peak in Western scores in the first century CE, around forty-three points, followed by a slow decline after 100 CE. If we look a little farther to the right, we see an Eastern peak just over forty-two points in 1100 CE, at the height of the Song dynasty's power in China, then a similar decline. A little farther still to the right, around 1700 CE, Eastern and Western scores both return to the low forties but this time instead of stalling they accelerate; a hundred years later the Western line goes through the roof as the industrial revolution begins.

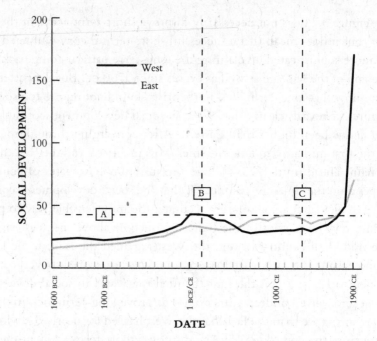

Figure 3.8. Lines through time and space: social development across
the three and a half millennia between 1600 BCE and 1900 CE,
represented on a linear-linear plot. Line A shows a possible threshold
around 43 points, which may have blocked the continuing
development of the West's Roman Empire in the first centuries CE
and China's Song dynasty around 1100 CE, before East and West
alike broke through it around 1700 CE. Line B shows a possible
connection between declining scores in both East and West in the
first centuries CE, and line C shows another possible East-West
connection starting around 1300 CE.

Was there some kind of "low-forties threshold" that defeated Rome
and Song China? I mentioned in the introduction that, in his book *The
Great Divergence*, Kenneth Pomeranz argued that East and West alike ran
into an ecological bottleneck in the eighteenth century that should, by
rights, have caused their social development to stagnate and decline. Yet
they did not, the reason being, Pomeranz suggested, that the British—
more through luck than judgment—combined the fruits of plundering
the New World with the energy of fossil fuels, blowing away traditional
ecological constraints. Could it be that the Romans and Song ran into
similar bottlenecks when social development reached the low forties but

failed to open them? If so, maybe the dominant pattern in the last two thousand years of history has been one of long-term waves, with great empires clawing their way up toward the low-forties ceiling then falling back, until something special happened in the eighteenth century.

The second thing that strikes me about Figure 3.8 is that we can draw vertical lines on it as well as horizontal ones. The obvious place to put a vertical line is in the first century CE, when Western and Eastern scores both peaked, even though the Eastern score was well below the Western (34.13 versus 43.22 points). Rather than (or as well as) focusing on the West hitting a low-forties ceiling, perhaps we should be looking for some set of events affecting both ends of the Old World, driving down Roman and Han Chinese social development scores regardless of the levels they had reached.

We could put another vertical line around 1300 CE, when Eastern and Western scores again followed similar patterns, although this time it was the Western score that was much lower (30.73 as against 42.66 points). The Eastern score had already been sliding for a hundred years, but the Western score now joined it, only for both lines to pick up after 1400 and accelerate even more sharply around 1700. Again, instead of focusing on the scores hitting a low-forties ceiling in the early eighteenth century, perhaps we should look for some global events that started pushing Eastern and Western development along a shared path in the fourteenth century. Perhaps the industrial revolution came first to the West not because of some extraordinary fluke, as Pomeranz concluded, but because East and West were both on track for such a revolution; and then something about the way the West reacted to the events of the fourteenth century gave it a slight but decisive lead in reaching the takeoff point in the eighteenth.

It seems to me that Figures 3.3, 3.7, and 3.8 illuminate a real weakness in both long-term lock-in and short-term accident theories. A few of the theorists focus on the story's beginning in the agricultural revolution, while the great majority look only at its very end, in the last five hundred years. Because they largely ignore the thousands of years in between, they rarely even try to account for all the spurts of growth, slowdowns, collapses, convergences, changes in leadership, or horizontal ceilings and vertical links that jump out at us when we can see the whole shape of history. That, putting it bluntly, means that neither approach can tell us why the West rules; and that being the case, neither can hope to answer the question lurking beyond that—what will happen next.

SCROOGE'S QUESTION

At the climax of Charles Dickens's *A Christmas Carol*, the Ghost of Christmas Yet to Come brings Ebenezer Scrooge to a weed-choked churchyard. Silently, the Ghost points out an untended tombstone. Scrooge knows his name will be on it; he knows that here, alone, unvisited, he will lie forever. "Are these the shadows of the things that Will be, or are they shadows of the things that May be, only?" he cries out.

We might well ask the same question about Figure 3.9, which takes the rates of increase in Eastern and Western social development in the twentieth century and projects them forward.* The Eastern line crosses the Western in 2103. By 2150 the West's rule is finished, its pomp at one with Nineveh and Tyre.

The West's epitaph looks as clear as Scrooge's:

WESTERN RULE
1773–2103
R.I.P.

Yet are these really the shadows of the things that Will be?

Confronted with his own epitaph, Scrooge fell to his knees. "Good Spirit," he begged, grabbing the specter's hand, "assure me that I yet may change these shadows you have shown me, by an altered life!" Christmas Yet to Come said nothing, but Scrooge worked out the answer for himself. He had been forced to spend an uncomfortable evening with the Ghosts of Christmas Past and Christmas Present because he needed to learn from both of them. "I will not shut out the lessons that they teach," Scrooge promised. "Oh, tell me I may sponge away the writing on this stone!"

---

*The 1,000-point maximum score I set for the year 2000 CE does not, of course, mean that that is the highest development will ever rise. By my calculations, between 2000 and 2010, the year in which I am writing, Western development climbed from about 906 to about 1,060 points, and Eastern from about 565 to about 680 points.

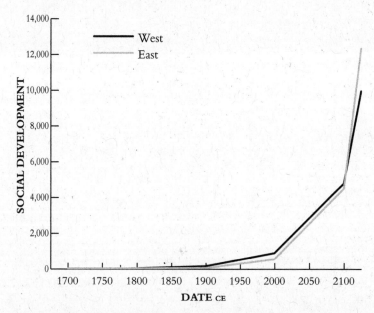

Figure 3.9. The shape of things to come? If we project the rates at which Eastern and Western social development grew in the twentieth century forward into the twenty-second, we see the East regain the lead in 2103. (On a log-linear graph, the Eastern and Western lines would both be straight from 1900 onward, reflecting unchanging rates of growth; because this is a linear-linear plot, both curve sharply upward.)

I commented in the introduction that I'm in a minority among those who write on why the West rules, and particularly on what will happen next, in not being an economist, modern historian, or political pundit of some sort. At the risk of overdoing the Scrooge analogy, I would say that the absence of premodern historians from the discussion has led us into the mistake of talking exclusively to the Ghost of Christmas Present. We need to bring the Ghost of Christmas Past back in.

To do this I will spend Part II of this book (Chapters 4–10) being a historian, telling the stories of East and West across the last few thousand years, trying to explain why social development changed as it did, and in Part III (Chapters 11 and 12) I will pull these stories together. This, I believe, will tell us not only why the West rules but also what will happen next.

PART II

◎ ◎ ◎

PART II

4

◎ ◎ ◎

THE EAST CATCHES UP

THE ELEPHANT IN THE ROOM

There is an old South Asian story about six blind men who meet an elephant. One grabs its trunk, and says it is a snake; another feels its tail, and thinks it is a rope; a third leans against a leg, and concludes it is a tree; and so on. It is hard to avoid thinking of this fable when reading long-term lock-in or short-term accident theories of Western rule: like the blind men, long-termers and short-termers alike tend to seize one part of the beast and mistake it for the whole. An index of social development, by contrast, makes the scales fall from our eyes. There can be no more nonsense about snakes, ropes, and trees. Everyone has to recognize that he or she is hanging on to just one piece of a tusker.

Figure 4.1 sums up what we saw impressionistically in Chapter 2. At the end of the last ice age, climate and ecology conspired to set social development rising earlier in the West than in the East, and despite the climatic catastrophe of the Younger Dryas, the West maintained a clear lead. Admittedly, back in these early times before 10,000 BCE our chainsaw art is very rough-and-ready indeed. In the East it is hard to detect any measurable change in social development for more than four thousand years, and even in the West, where development was clearly higher by 11,000 BCE than it had been in 14,000, the

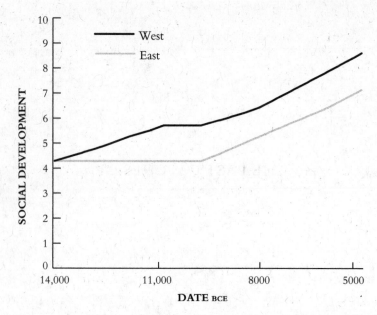

Figure 4.1. The shape of things so far: the West's early lead in social development between 14,000 and 5000 BCE, as described in Chapter 2

subtleties of the changes are lost to us. Yet although the light the index casts is flickering and dim, a little light is better than none, and it reveals a very important fact: just as long-term lock-in theories predict, the West got a head start and held on to it.

But Figure 4.2, continuing the story from 5000 through 1000 BCE, is less straightforward. It differs as much from Figure 4.1 as, say, a rope from a snake. Like ropes and snakes, the two graphs do have similarities: in both graphs the Eastern and Western scores close higher than they started and in both, Western scores are always higher than Eastern. The differences, though, are just as striking. First, the lines rise much faster in Figure 4.2 than in Figure 4.1. In the nine thousand years between 14,000 and 5000 BCE the Western score doubled and the Eastern score increased by two-thirds, but in the next four thousand years—less than half the period covered by Figure 4.1—the Western score tripled and the Eastern increased two-and-a-half times. The second difference is that for the first time in history, we actually see social development falling in the West after 1300 BCE.

In this chapter I try to explain these facts. I suggest that the acceleration and the West's post-1300 BCE decline were in fact two sides of

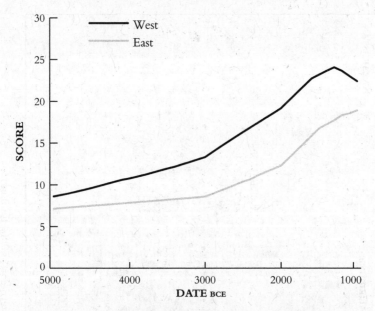

Figure 4.2. Onward, upward, farther apart, and closer together:
the acceleration, divergence, and convergence of Eastern and
Western social development, 5000–1000 BCE

the same process, which I call the paradox of development. In the
chapters that follow we will see that this paradox plays a major part in
explaining why the West rules and in telling us what will happen next.
But before we can get to that we need to look into exactly what happened between 5000 and 1000 BCE.

HOTLINES TO THE GODS

Between 14,000 and 5000 BCE Western social development scores doubled and farming villages spread from their starting point in the Hilly
Flanks deep into central Asia and to the shores of the Atlantic. Yet by
5000 BCE agriculture had hardly touched Mesopotamia, the "land between the rivers" that we now call Iraq, even though it was just a few
days' walk from the Hilly Flanks (Figure 4.3).

In a way, that is not surprising. Since 2003 news flashes have made
the world all too familiar with Iraq's harsh environment. Summer temperatures soar over 120°F, it hardly ever rains, and deserts press in on

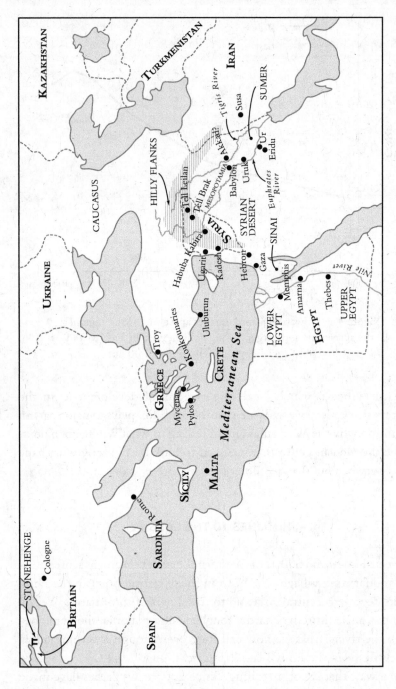

Figure 4.3. The expansion of the Western core, 5000–1000 BCE: sites and regions mentioned in this chapter.

every side. It is difficult to imagine farmers ever choosing to live there, and back around 5000 BCE Mesopotamia was even hotter. It was also wetter, though, and the main problem for farmers was not how to find water but how to manage it. Monsoon winds off the Indian Ocean brought some rain, though barely enough to support agriculture; but if farmers could control the summer floods of the mighty Tigris and Euphrates rivers and bring the waters into their fields at the right time to fertilize their crops, the possibilities were endless.

The people who carried agricultural lifestyles over horizon after horizon across Europe, or who adopted agriculture from farming neighbors, were constantly tinkering with tradition to make farming work in new settings. Making techniques developed for rain-fed agriculture in the Hilly Flanks work for irrigated farming in Mesopotamia took more than tinkering, though. Farmers had to start almost from scratch. For twenty generations they improved their canals, ditches, and storage basins; and gradually they made Mesopotamia's marginal lands not just livable, but actually more productive than the Hilly Flanks had ever been. They were changing the meaning of geography.

Economists sometimes call this process the discovery of advantages of backwardness. When people adapt techniques that worked in an advanced core to operate in a less-developed periphery, the changes they introduce sometimes make those techniques work so well that the periphery becomes a new core in its own right. By 5000 BCE this was happening in southern Mesopotamia, where elaborate canals supported some of the world's biggest towns, with perhaps four thousand souls. Such crowds could build much more elaborate temples, and in one town, Eridu, we can trace superimposed temples on brick platforms from 5000 through 3000 BCE, always using the same basic architectural plan but getting bigger and more ornate through time.

So many advantages accrued to Mesopotamia that people in the old core back in the Hilly Flanks started emulating the dynamic new societies in the floodplains. Around 4000 BCE inhabitants of Susa, in a plain nestling in the Hilly Flanks in southwest Iran, outdid even Eridu by building a brick platform 250 feet long and 30 feet high. It probably supported a grand temple, although its nineteenth-century excavators, a little vague on the finer points of archaeological technique, hacked through the site and destroyed the evidence. But even they could not miss all the signs of increasingly complex organization, including some of the world's earliest copper ornaments as well as stamps and clay impressions that may indicate administrative control of goods, and images that some scholars interpret as "priest-kings." Archaeologists often imagine that a regional chief lived at Susa, which was much bigger than the villages around it. The outlying villagers may have come to Susa to worship the gods, acknowledge their lord, and exchange food for ornaments and weapons.

Or, of course, they may not have—it is hard to tell from such a poorly excavated site. But archaeologists are forced to rely on Susa to understand this period because contemporary Mesopotamian towns are deeply buried under silt from six thousand years of Euphrates and Tigris floods, making them hard to study (plus there has, for obvious reasons, been little new research in Iran since the 1979 Islamic Revolution or in Iraq since Saddam Hussein's 1990 invasion of Kuwait). Comparable changes were probably under way all along the Euphrates and Tigris after 4500 BCE, but only after 3800 do they become clearly visible to archaeologists.

Just why towns got bigger and more complex remains controversial. The sixth millennium BCE, when farmers first moved into Mesopotamia, saw Earth reaching the warmest, wettest point in its endlessly changing orbit round the sun and its wobbly rotation around its own axis, but by 3800 BCE the world was cooling again. Good news for Mesopotamian farmers, you might think; but you would be wrong. Cooler summers meant that the rain-bearing monsoons blowing off the Indian Ocean got weaker. Rain fell less often and less predictably, and Mesopotamia started looking more like the parched place we see on CNN. Problems compounded one another: declining spring rains meant shorter growing seasons, which meant that crops ripened before the Euphrates and Tigris flooded each summer. The systems Mesopotamian farmers had painstakingly built up across two thousand years no longer worked.

Climate change forced tough choices on Mesopotamians. They could bury their heads in the sand as it encroached on their fields and carry on as usual, but the price of doing nothing would be hunger, poverty, and perhaps starvation. Or they could migrate to regions less dependent on the monsoon; but it is no small thing for farmers to abandon their well-tended fields. In any case, the Hilly Flanks—the obvious place to go—was already packed with villages. In 2006 archaeologists at Tell Brak in northeast Syria uncovered two mass graves of young men dating to around 3800 BCE, apparently the victims of massacres. Moving back to the crowded, violent Hilly Flanks might not have been a very attractive option.

If enough Mesopotamians had done nothing or run away, this new core would have collapsed. However, a third possibility presented itself. People could abandon their villages but stay in Mesopotamia, congregating in a few big sites. That seems counterintuitive: if crop yields are falling, cramming more people into smaller spaces should make things worse. But some Mesopotamians seem to have figured out that if more of them worked together they could run larger irrigation systems and store floodwaters until the crops were ready. They could feed more miners to dig copper from the ground; more smiths to make ornaments, weapons, and tools; and more traders to carry these goods around. So successful were they that by 3000 BCE bronze (an alloy of copper and a little tin) had largely replaced stone for weapons and most tools, sharply increasing fighters' and workers' effectiveness.

Getting to that point, though, required organization. Centralized administration was the answer. By 3300 BCE people were scratching onto little clay tablets such sophisticated records of their activities that most archaeologists call the symbols writing (even if as yet only a tiny scribal elite could read them). Little villages that could not support such sophisticated activities went to the wall while one site, Uruk, turned into a true city with maybe twenty thousand residents.

Mesopotamians were inventing management, meetings, and memoranda—the curses of life for so many of us today, and hardly the stuff of soaring narratives of human achievement. Yet as will become clear in the next few chapters, these were often the most important motors of social development. Organization turned villages in the Hilly Flanks and along the banks of the Yellow River into cities, states, and empires; failures of organization caused their fall. Managers are simultaneously the heroes and the villains of our story.

The birth of management as the monsoons dried up must have been traumatic. We should probably picture bedraggled, defeated columns of the hungry slouching toward Uruk under a dusty sky, like Okies but without the jalopies, let alone the New Deal. We should probably also imagine angry villagers refusing to cede power to self-important bureaucrats who tried to requisition their fields or crops. Violence must often have been the outcome. Uruk could easily have broken apart; perhaps plenty of rival towns did.

We will never know the stories of the ancient managers who pulled Uruk through, but archaeologists suspect that they were tied to temples. Many pieces of evidence point this way, propping one another up like the poles in a tepee. For instance, excavations at temples have uncovered stacks of uniform-sized dishes known as "bevel-rimmed bowls," probably for distributing food. The earliest clay tablets scratched with crude symbols come mostly from temples, and the symbol for "rations" on them is a sketch of a bevel-rimmed bowl. And when writing systems developed to the point they could record such information, they tell us that temples controlled broad acres of irrigated land and the labor to work them.

The temples themselves mushroomed into huge monuments, dwarfing the communities that built them. Long flights of stairs led to hundred-foot-high enclosures where specialists took counsel with the gods. If the tenth-millennium shrines that we saw in Chapter 2 were amplifiers for messages to the spirits, the mighty sanctuary of fourth-millennium Uruk was a public address system worthy of Led Zeppelin. The gods would have to be deaf not to hear.

It was these shouts to the gods that originally drew me to archaeology. In 1970 my parents took my sister and me to see a film of Edith Nesbit's Edwardian classic *The Railway Children*. I think I liked it, but the short feature that ran before it blew my mind (as people used to say in those days). Until that evening I had been obsessed with Apollo 11 and wanted to be an astronaut, but the B movie—a documentary (of a sort) based on Erich von Däniken's book *Chariots of the Gods?*—made me realize that archaeology was the way to go.

Like Arthur C. Clarke in *2001* (which, like *Chariots of the Gods?*, was published in 1968), von Däniken claimed that space aliens had visited Earth in ancient times and taught humans great secrets. Von Däniken differed from Clarke, though, in insisting that (a) he was not making this up and (b) the aliens kept coming back. They had inspired Stonehenge and Egypt's pyramids; the Hebrew Bible and Indian epics had described their spacecraft and nuclear weapons. The reason so many early civilizations had kings who claimed to talk to superhuman beings in the sky, von Däniken insisted, was that early kings *did* talk to superhuman beings in the sky.

While the evidence is thin (to put it mildly), the argument is certainly economical. Plenty of people believe it, and von Däniken sold 60 million books. He still has plenty of fans. Just a few years ago, while minding my own business standing over a barbeque, I was accused—in all seriousness—of belonging to a secret cabal of archaeologists that suppresses these facts.

Scientists are often criticized for taking the wonder out of the world, but they generally do so in the hope of putting truth in its place. In this case the truth of the matter is that we do not need spacemen to explain Mesopotamia's godlike kings any more than we need a *2001* moment to explain the evolution of *Homo sapiens*. Religious specialists had been important since agriculture began, and all the signs are that now, when the mighty ones seemed to have forsaken humanity by taking rain away, Mesopotamians instinctively looked to priests claiming special access to the gods to tell them what to do. Organization was the key to survival in those tough times, so the more that people did what the priests said, the better things would go (provided the priests gave reasonably sound advice).

Two processes must have fed back on each other, their logic just as circular as von Däniken's but even more convincing. Ambitious men claiming to have special access to the gods said they needed wonderful temples, elaborate ceremonies, and great wealth to make the gods hear them. Once they got these, they could turn around and point to their wonderful temples, elaborate ceremonies, and great wealth to prove that they were indeed close to the gods—after all, who but someone the gods loved would have such things? By the time scribes were recording such matters, around 2700 BCE, Mesopotamian kings even claimed gods as their ancestors. Sometimes, as (I suspect) at Uruk, entrusting power to men who had hotlines to the gods worked wonders; and when it failed, as it often must have done, it of course left little for archaeologists to dig up.

Uruk became not only a city but also a state, with centralized institutions imposing taxes, making decisions binding the whole community, and backing them up with force. A few men (but apparently no women) occupied the top positions, and a larger group of warriors, landowners, merchants, and literate bureaucrats assisted them. For nearly everyone the rise of the state meant surrendering freedoms, but that was the price of success in hard times. Communities that paid the price could muster more people, wealth, and power than pre-state societies.

Cities and states drove social development upward in Mesopotamia after 3500 BCE and then spread outward, just as farming villages had once done in the Hilly Flanks. Uruk-style material culture (bevel-rimmed bowls, writing tablets, lavish temples) spread into Syria and Iran. The debates over how this happened are much like those over the initial spread of farming. There was probably colonization from the densely populated, highly organized south of Mesopotamia to the lightly settled, less centralized north: Habuba Kabira in central Syria, for instance, looks like someone cloned an Uruk neighborhood and dropped it down a thousand miles away. Tell Brak, by contrast, which was a large town long before bevel-rimmed bowls were dreamed up, looks more like a local community picking and choosing among customs invented at Uruk. Villagers struggling to make ends meet and seeing Mesopotamian cities' success may have allowed local priests to turn themselves into kings; and ambitious priests, seeing Uruk's religious leaders flourishing, perhaps talked, tricked, or bullied fellow villagers into giving them similar powers. Either way, people who preferred village life must have found state formation just as hard to resist as foragers had found farming all those thousands of years before.

THE GODS MADE FLESH

While the first farmers were sweating to make crops grow on Mesopotamia's plains around 5000 BCE, even more intrepid folk were striking out from the Jordan Valley across the Sinai Desert to try their luck along the Nile River. Egypt had few domesticable native plants and had lagged behind the Hilly Flanks in adopting agriculture, but once the right seeds and animals were imported, the new lifestyle flourished. The Nile flooded at just the right time for crops each year, and large, rain-fed oases supported farming far into what is now desert.

These advantages meant, though, that the retreat of the monsoon around 3800 BCE hit Egypt even harder than Mesopotamia. Many Egyptians abandoned their oases and squeezed into the Nile Valley, where water was plentiful but land was scarce, particularly where the valley narrowed in Upper Egypt.* As in Mesopotamia, management was the answer. Excavated tombs suggest that Upper Egyptian village leaders had both military and religious roles. Successful chiefs grew rich as their villages captured more land; unsuccessful chiefs disappeared; and by 3300 BCE three small states had formed. Each had a rich cemetery where its early kings—if that is not too grand a title for them—were laid to rest in tombs that aped Mesopotamian architecture, accompanied by gold, weapons, and Mesopotamian imports.

The kingdoms fought until, by 3100 BCE, only one still stood. At that point, the scale of royal monuments exploded and the distinctive Egyptian hieroglyphic script abruptly appeared. Writing was probably limited to a narrow scribal group, as in Mesopotamia, but right from the beginning Egyptian texts contain narratives as well as bureaucratic accounts. One remarkable carving says that an Upper Egyptian king named Narmer conquered Lower Egypt around 3100 BCE, while another suggests the involvement of someone called the Scorpion King.[†] Later texts also mention a conqueror named Menes (perhaps the same person as Narmer). But although the details are confused, the basic story is clear: around 3100 BCE the Nile Valley was united into the largest kingdom the world had yet seen, with maybe a million subjects.

Upper Egyptian material culture spread rapidly down the Nile Valley after 3100 BCE. As with the expansion of farming thousands of years earlier and the spread of Uruk culture in contemporary Mesopotamia, Lower Egyptians may (voluntarily or out of the need to compete) have emulated Upper Egyptian lifestyles. This time, though, there is also clear evidence that the Upper Egyptian population, organized into a state, had grown faster than the village-based peoples of Lower Egypt and that political unification consisted partly of south-to-north colonization.

Despite having so much in common, the Uruk expansion in Mesopotamia after 3500 BCE and the Upper Egyptian expansion after 3300 had different consequences. First, just as Narmer/Menes/the Scorpion

---

*Confusingly for those of us used to modern maps with north at the top, Egyptians thought in terms of the Nile; the river flowed down from "Upper Egypt" in the south toward "Lower Egypt" in the north.

†The *Scorpion King* movies, sad to say, bear not even a passing resemblance to the little we know of the real Scorpion King.

King was subduing Lower Egypt around 3100 BCE, the Uruk expansion was abruptly ending. Uruk itself burned and most of the new sites with Uruk-style material culture were abandoned. Why is a mystery. When texts start recording more information, around 2700 BCE, the southern Mesopotamians, now calling themselves Sumerians, were divided into thirty-five city-states, each with its own godlike king. Uruk's unraveling left unified Egypt as the major Western core.

Why Egypt and Mesopotamia diverged remains unexplained. Maybe Egypt, with its single river valley and delta, a few oases, and desert all around it was just easier to conquer and hold than Mesopotamia, with its two rivers, multiple tributaries where resistance could fester, and surrounding hills full of viable rivals. Or maybe Narmer et al. just made better decisions than the now-nameless kings of Uruk. Or maybe some entirely different factor was decisive. (I will come back to this question below.)

There is a further big difference between Mesopotamia and Egypt. While Sumerian kings claimed to be *like* gods, Egyptian kings claimed to *be* gods. The movie and TV series *Stargate*, spun off from von Däniken's books, offer a simple explanation: Narmer and company really were spacemen, while Uruk's kings were merely friends of spacemen. But appealingly straightforward as that is, there is just no evidence for it, and quite a lot suggesting that the pharaohs (as Egypt's kings were called) in fact worked very hard to promote the image of their own divinity.

Self-divinization strikes most of us as psychotic, and was no trivial thing five thousand years ago either. So how did it happen? Narmer and his friends left no accounts (gods do not need to explain themselves), and our best clue comes from much later stories about Alexander the Great of Macedon. Alexander conquered Egypt in 332 BCE and had himself proclaimed pharaoh. Caught up in a power struggle with his own generals, he found it useful to spread the rumor that he, like earlier pharaohs, really was a god. Few Macedonians took this very seriously, so Alexander raised the stakes. When his army reached what is now Pakistan, he rounded up ten local sages and ordered them—on pain of death—to answer his deepest questions. When he got to sage number seven, Alexander asked, "How can a man become a god?" The philosopher answered simply: "By doing something a man cannot do." It is easy to imagine Alexander scratching his head and wondering: *Do*

I know anyone who's done something lately that no man could do? The answer, he may have told himself, was obvious: *Yes. Me. I just overthrew the Persian Empire. No mere mortal could do that. I am a god and I should stop feeling bad about killing my friends when they contradict me.*

Alternatively, Alexander or his supporters may have made the whole story up, but in a way its reality matters less than the fact that in the 320s BCE the best way for a king to sell the idea he was divine was through superhuman military prowess. We can only guess whether this was already the best way three thousand years earlier, but in unifying the Nile Valley the Scorpion King, Narmer, and/or Menes had certainly done things no mortal could be expected to do. Perhaps fusing a godlike king with a great conqueror made self-divinization plausible.

Nor was this the only coup the pharaohs pulled off. Upper Egypt's first kings must have developed managerial skills like Uruk's, getting people to give them resources and to accept central management, but the pharaohs now co-opted local elites from the whole Nile Valley to be their managers. The pharaohs built a new capital at Memphis, strategically placed between Upper and Lower Egypt, and had regional grandees come to them. At Memphis the pharaohs dispensed patronage, giving petty aristocrats who bought into the system incentives to keep it going. Local lords extracted revenues from the peasants, trying to take as much as they could without making the peasants' lives impossible, then passed income up the chain, in return for which royal favor came back down it again.

The pharaohs' success depended partly on politicking and back-scratching and partly on pageantry, and for that being gods, rather than just friends of gods, surely made things easier. What local bigwig would not want to work for a god? To be on the safe side, though, the pharaohs also created a powerful symbolic language. Soon after 2700 BCE the artists of King Djoser designed styles for carving hieroglyphs and representing god-kings that survived for five hundred years. Djoser understood the theological delicacy of an immortal being seen to die, and designed the ultimate symbol of Egyptian kingship—the pyramid—to hold the sacred corpse. King Khufu's 450-foot-high Great Pyramid, built around 2550 BCE, remained the world's tallest building until Cologne Cathedral in Germany nudged past it in 1880 CE. It is still the heaviest, weighing something like a million tons.

Thousands of laborers worked on it for decades, quarrying stone, floating it down the Nile, and dragging it into place. The so-called workmen's village at the foot of the pyramids was among the world's biggest cities in its day. Feeding workers and moving them around required a quantum leap in the size and reach of the bureaucracy, and joining the gangs must have been a transformative experience for villagers who had perhaps never left home before. If anyone doubted pharaoh's divinity before the pyramids, they surely did not afterward.

The Sumerian city-states in Mesopotamia moved in similar directions but more slowly and cautiously. Each city, the texts say, was divided into "households" containing many monogamous families. Each household had one family at its head, organizing its land and labor, with the other families ranked, some working in the fields and others in crafts, fulfilling quotas in return for rations. The biggest and richest households were theoretically headed by gods, and might command thousands of acres and hundreds of workers. The men who ran these households for the gods were normally the city's leaders, with the king heading the household of the city's patron god. It was the king's job to promote his patron god's interests. If the king did well, his god must be flourishing too; if he performed poorly, the god's stock fell.

After 2500 BCE this began to be a problem. Improved agriculture allowed people to rear larger families, and population growth drove competition for good land and more effective ways to fight for it. Some cities defeated and took over others. The theological implications were as thorny as the death of Egyptian god-kings: if a king looked after his patron god's interests, what did it mean if another king, acting for a different god, took over? Some priests proposed a "temple-city" theory, making the religious hierarchy and gods' interests independent from kings. Successful kings responded by claiming to be more than merely gods' representatives. Around 2440 BCE one king announced that he was his patron god's son, and poems began circulating about how King Gilgamesh of Uruk had traveled beyond this world in search of immortality. These coalesced into the *Epic of Gilgamesh*, the world's oldest surviving literary masterpiece.

Rulers sought new venues to display their majesty, and the greatest archaeological find ever made in Mesopotamia, the Royal Cemetery of Ur, was probably one of these. Its spectacular gold and silver grave goods, like the pharaohs' pyramids, hint at more-than-mortal stature for the dead; and the seventy-four people poisoned to accompany Queen Puabi to the next world suggest that struggles over rulers' relationships to the gods could be bad news for ordinary Sumerians.

Conflict came to a head around 2350 BCE. There were violent coups, armed conquests, and revolutionary redistributions of property and sacred rights. In 2334 a man called Sargon (which, rather suspiciously, means "legitimate ruler"; he probably took this name after he seized power) founded a new city called Akkad. It may lie under Baghdad, and—no surprise—remains unexcavated, but clay tablets from other sites say that rather than fighting other Sumerian kings Sargon plundered Syria and Lebanon until he could pay for a full-time army of five thousand men. He then turned on the other Sumerians, subduing their cities through diplomacy and violence.

Textbooks often call Sargon the world's first empire-builder, but what he and his Akkadian successors did was really not so different from what Egypt's unifiers had done eight centuries earlier. Sargon himself did not become a god, but after defeating a rebellion around 2240 BCE his grandson Naram-Sin announced that eight of Sumer's gods wanted him to join their ranks. Sumerian artists started representing Naram-Sin as horned and larger than life, traditional attributes of divinity.

By 2230 BCE the twin Western cores in Sumer and Egypt had massively eclipsed the original core in the Hilly Flanks. Responding to ecological problems, people had created cities; responding to competition between cities, they had created million-strong states, ruled by gods or godlike kings and managed by bureaucracies. As struggles in the core drove social development upward, a network of cities spread over the simpler farming villages of Syria and the Levant and through Iran to the borders of modern Turkmenistan. On Crete people would soon start building palaces too; imposing stone temples rose upward on Malta; and fortified towns began dotting the southeastern coast of Spain. Farther north and west farmers had filled every ecologically viable niche, and on the farthest fringe of the Western world, where the Atlantic pounds Britain's cold shores, people invested an estimated 30 million hours of labor in the most enigmatic monument of all, Stonehenge. One of von Däniken's spacemen visiting Earth around 2230 BCE would probably have concluded that there was little further need for alien interventions: these clever chimps were pushing social development steadily upward.

THE WILD WEST

A return trip fifty years later might have shocked the spaceman. From one end of the Western core to the other states were falling apart and people were fighting and leaving their homes. For the next thousand years a series of disruptions (a neutral-sounding word covering a horrible variety of massacres, misery, flight, and want) sent the West on a wild ride. And when we ask who or what disrupted social development, we get a surprising answer: social development was itself to blame.

One of the main ways people try to improve their lot has always been by moving information, goods, and themselves around. What is abundant here may be scarce—and valuable—over there. The result has been increasingly complex webs tying communities together, operating at every level of society. Four thousand years ago temples and palaces owned some of the best land, and instead of dividing it among peasant families, each trying to grow everything they needed, centralized bureaucracies hung on to this land and told people what to grow. A village with good cropland might grow just wheat, while one on a hillside could tend vines, with a third specializing in metalwork; and bureaucrats could redistribute the products, skimming off what they needed, storing some against emergencies and parceling the rest out as rations. This had begun at Uruk by 3500 BCE; a thousand years later it was the norm.

Kings also gave one another self-interested gifts. Egypt's pharaohs, rich in gold and grain, gave these goods to minor rulers of Lebanese cities, who reciprocated with fragrant cedar, since Egypt lacked good wood. Failing to give an appropriate gift was a major faux pas. Gift exchange was rooted as much in psychology and status anxiety as in economics, but it moved goods, people, and ideas around quite effectively. The kings at each end of these chains and plenty of merchants in between got rich.

Nowadays we tend to assume that "command economies" with a king, dictator, or politburo telling everyone what to do must be inefficient, but most early civilizations depended on them. Perhaps in a world lacking the trust and laws that make markets work, they may be the best option available. But they were never the only option, and humbler independent traders always flourished alongside royal and priestly enterprises. Neighbors bartered, swapping cheese for bread or help digging a latrine for babysitting. Town and country folk traded at fairs. Tinkers loaded pots and pans on donkeys and plied their routes. And at a kingdom's edges, where sown fields faded into deserts or mountains, villagers exchanged bread and bronze weapons with shepherds or foragers for milk, cheese, wool, and animals.

The best-known account of this comes from the Hebrew Bible. Jacob was a successful shepherd in the hills near Hebron in what is now the West Bank. He had twelve sons, but played favorites, giving the eleventh—Joseph—a coat of many colors. In a fit of pique, Joseph's ten older brothers sold the gaudily dressed apple of their father's eye to passing slave traders headed for Egypt. Some years later, when food was scarce in Hebron, Jacob sent his ten oldest sons to Egypt to trade for grain. Unknown to them, the governor they confronted there was their brother Joseph, who, although a slave, had risen high in pharaoh's service (admittedly after a spell in jail for attempted rape; he was, of course, framed). In a perfect illustration of the difficulty of knowing when to trust traders, the brothers showed no surprise when the disguised Joseph pretended to think they were spies and threw them in prison. The story ends happily, though, with Jacob, his sons, and all his flocks moving into Egypt. "And they gained possessions in it," says the Good Book, "and were fruitful and multiplied exceedingly."

The Joseph story is probably set in the sixteenth century BCE, by which time people whose names are now lost had been following the same script for two thousand years. Amorites from the fringes of the Syrian Desert and Gutians from the mountains of Iran, coming as traders and laborers, were familiar faces in Mesopotamia's cities; so, too, "Asiatics," to use the Egyptians' contemptuous catch-all term, in the Nile Valley. Rising social development intertwined the cores' economies, societies, and cultures with those of neighboring regions, enlarging the cores, increasing their mastery of their environments, and driving up social development. But the price of growing complexity was growing fragility. This was, and remains, a central piece of the paradox of social development.

Around 2200 BCE, when the god-king Naram-Sin's equally divine son Sharkalisharri ruled much of Mesopotamia from his throne room in Akkad, something started going wrong, and Harvey Weiss, a Yale University archaeologist who excavated the site of Tell Leilan in Syria, thinks he knows what it was. Tell Leilan was a city of twenty thousand people in Sargon's day, around 2300 BCE, but a ghost town a century later. Searching for explanations, the geologists on Weiss's team discovered from microscopic studies of sediments that the amount of dust in the soil at Tell Leilan and neighboring sites increased sharply just before 2200 BCE. Irrigation canals silted up, probably because of declining rainfall, and people drifted away.

A thousand miles away, in the Nile Valley, something was also going wrong. In the story of Joseph the pharaoh relied on dream interpreters to predict agricultural yields, but real pharaohs had a device called the Nilometer, which measured the river's floods and gave advance warning of good and bad harvests. Inscriptions recording some of its readings show that floods fell sharply around 2200 BCE. Egypt, too, was getting drier.

Back around 3800 BCE drier weather had propelled Uruk to greatness and set off wars that unified Egypt, but in the more complicated, interconnected world of the late third millennium BCE, abandoning sites such as Tell Leilan also meant taking away the business that Amorites and Asiatics depended on. It would have been as if Joseph's brothers had come down to Egypt to buy grain but found no one home. They could have gone back to Hebron and told their father he had to starve, or they could have pushed farther into pharaoh's land, trading or working for food when they could, fighting for it or stealing it when they could not.

Under other circumstances the Akkadian and Egyptian militias might have slaughtered such nuisances (economic migrants or criminals, depending on your point of view), but by 2200 BCE these armed forces were themselves unraveling. Some Mesopotamians saw their Akkadian kings as cruel conquerors, and when the supposedly divine Sharkalisharri failed to cope very well with the problems he faced in the 2190s BCE many priestly families stopped cooperating with him. His armies melted away; generals proclaimed themselves kings in their own right; and Amorite gangs took over entire cities. In less than a decade the empire disintegrated. It was every town for itself—

as a Sumerian chronicler put it, "Who then was king? Who was not king?"

In Egypt tensions between court and aristocracy had also been mounting, and King Pepy II, who had sat on the throne for sixty years, proved unequal to the challenges. While his courtiers schemed against him and one another, local elites took matters into their own hands. By the time a coup set up a new dynasty in Lower Egypt around 2160 BCE there were dozens of independent lords and ungovernable Asiatic bands rampaging around the countryside. Worse still, the high priests of the great temple of Amen at Thebes in Upper Egypt took on progressively grander titles, eventually sliding in and out of civil war with the Lower Egyptian pharaoh.

By about 2150 BCE Egypt and Akkad had decomposed into petty statelets, fighting outlaws and each other for shares of the peasants' shrinking output. Some warlords prospered but the general tone of the few surviving texts is desperate. There are also hints that the crisis reverberated beyond the core. It is hard for archaeologists to tell when events in one region are linked to those in another, and we should never underestimate simple coincidence, but it is hard not to detect a broader pattern in the fiery destruction of the biggest buildings in Greece, the end of the Maltese temples, and the abandonment of Spain's coastal fortresses, all between 2200 and 2150 BCE.

The larger, more complex systems of the Western core depended on regular flows of people, goods, and information, and sudden changes—like the drier weather at Tell Leilan or Pepy's senility—disrupted these. Disruptions such as the drought and migrations after 2200 BCE did not *have* to produce chaos, but they effectively rolled the dice of history. In the short term, at least, anything could have happened. If Pepy had had an adviser like Joseph he might have turned hard times to his advantage; if Sharkalisharri had cut better deals with his generals and priests his empire might have endured. Instead, the main result in Mesopotamia was that the city of Ur exploited Akkad's collapse, carving out a new empire, smaller than Akkad's but better known to us because its compulsive bureaucrats produced so many tax receipts. Forty thousand have been published, and thousands more await study.

Shulgi, who took Ur's throne in 2094 BCE, pronounced himself a god and instituted a cult of personality. He even gave Ur a new musical form, the "Shulgi Hymn," praising his skill at everything from singing to prophesy and making him sound unnervingly like North Korea's dictator-cum–movie director Kim Jong Il. Yet despite Shulgi's talents, within a few years of his death in 2047 BCE his empire, too, imploded. In the 2030s raiding became such a problem that Ur built a hundred-mile wall to keep the Amorites out, but in 2028 cities started pulling out of Ur's tax system anyway, and state finances collapsed around 2020. In a rerun of the fall of Akkad, famines raged as some generals tried to requisition grain for Ur and others declared themselves independent. "Hunger filled the city like water," says the Sumerian poem *The Lamentation over Ur*. "Its people are as if surrounded by water, they gasp for breath. Its king breathed heavily in his palace, all alone, its people dropped their weapons . . ." In 2004 BCE raiders sacked Ur and carried its last king into slavery.

While Mesopotamia fell apart, however, Egypt came together again. The Theban high priests of Upper Egypt, now acting as kings in their own right, defeated their main rivals in 2056 BCE and mastered the whole Nile Valley in 2040. By 2000 BCE the Western core looked much like it had done a thousand years earlier, with Egypt unified under a god-king and Mesopotamia split into city-states under kings who were at best merely godlike.

By this point, more than four thousand years ago, the Western core's dizzy, wild ride had already laid bare some of the fundamental forces that drive social development. Social development is not a gift or curse laid on humanity by Clarke's monolith or von Däniken's aliens; it is something we make ourselves, just not in ways of our own choosing. As I suggested in the introduction, the bottom line is that we are lazy, greedy, and fearful, always looking for easier, more profitable, or safer ways to do things. From the rise of Uruk to the Theban reunification of Egypt, sloth, avarice, and/or fright drove every upward nudge of social development. But people cannot nudge things any way they like; each nudge builds on all the earlier nudges. Social development is cumulative, a matter of incremental steps that have to be taken in the right order. The chiefs of Uruk around 3100 BCE could no more have organized the kind of bureaucracy that Ur boasted under Shulgi a millennium later than William the Conqueror could have built computers in medieval England. As the Yankee saying goes, you can't get there from here. This cumulative pattern also explains why increases in social development keep speeding up: each innovation builds on earlier ones and contributes to later ones, meaning that the higher social development rises, the faster it can continue rising.

Yet the course of innovation never did run smooth. Innovation means change, bringing joy and pain in equal measures. Social development creates winners and losers, new classes of rich and poor, new relations between men and women and old and young. It even creates whole new cores when the advantages of backwardness empower those who had previously been marginal. Its growth depends on societies becoming larger, more complicated, and harder to manage; the higher it rises, the more threats to itself it creates. Hence the paradox: social development creates the very forces that undermine it. When these slip out of control—and particularly when a changing environment multiplies uncertainty—chaos, ruin, and collapse may follow, as came to pass around 2200 BCE. And as we will see in the chapters that follow, the paradox of social development largely explains why long-term lock-in theories cannot be correct.

THE BAND OF BROTHERS

Despite the chaos that swept over the Western core after 2200 BCE, this was no Nightfall moment. The collapses after 2200 do not even register on the graph in Figure 4.2.* That may understate the scale of the disruptions, but even so, one thing is very clear: by 2000 BCE Western social development was almost 50 percent higher than it had been in 3000 BCE. Social development kept rising and Western societies got bigger and more sophisticated.

The cores changed in other ways, too. No Mesopotamian ruler ever again claimed to be a god after 2000 BCE, and even in Egypt some of the shine came off the pharaohs. Second-millennium-BCE statues

---

*This is partly because our archaeological data are very coarse-grained and partly for technical reasons. Because the data are so patchy, I have measured social development in the third millennium BCE at quarter-millennium intervals, and the points at 2250 and 2000 BCE happen to miss much of the chaos. Second, the Western region had two separate cores, one in Mesopotamia and one in Egypt, where the collapses followed slightly different rhythms. In 2100 BCE Egyptian social development was lower than it had been in 2200 BCE, but Mesopotamia had recovered from its initial collapse; by 2000 BCE Mesopotamia had collapsed again, but Egypt had recovered.

and poetry portray pharaohs as more warlike, world-weary, and disappointed than those of the third millennium. And in what must be a related process, state power contracted: although palaces and temples remained important, more land and trade were now in private hands.

The most important reason why the disruptions did not set the clock back, though, was that the core kept expanding through the crises, drawing in peripheries that found new advantages in their backwardness and pushed their way into the core. From Iran to Crete people adapted Egyptian- and Mesopotamian-style palaces and redistributive economies to fluid, often-violent frontiers with rain-fed agriculture. On the whole, frontier kings relied more on military power than those in the irrigation-fed cores and made fewer claims to divinity; it was perhaps hard to seem godlike when the rulers of Egypt and Sumer looked so much grander.

Once again, rising social development changed the meanings of geography. Access to a great river basin was crucial for development in the third millennium BCE, but in the second millennium living on the old core's northern edge became an even greater advantage. Herders in what is now Ukraine had domesticated horses around 4000 BCE, and two thousand years later horse tamers on the steppes of modern Kazakhstan started yoking these powerful beasts to light, two-wheeled chariots. A few steppe herders riding around in chariots did not concern the core, but if someone with the resources to pay for thousands of chariots got hold of them it would be a different story. Chariots were not tanks, crashing through enemy lines (the way directors of sword-and-sandals movies like to portray them), but armies with masses of fast-moving chariot-mounted archers could make old-fashioned shoving matches between infantry obsolete.

Chariots' advantages seem obvious, but armies that have done well with one tactical system are often slow to adopt another. Setting up a corps of well-trained charioteers would throw the pecking order of all-infantry armies into chaos, empowering a whole new elite, and though the evidence is patchy, the Egyptians and Mesopotamians, with their entrenched hierarchies, seem to have adopted the new battle systems only sluggishly. New northern states such as the mysterious Hurrians, who apparently migrated into northern Mesopotamia and Syria from the Caucasus after 2200 BCE, were more flexible. The Hurrians' steppe connections gave them easy access to the new weapons, and their looser social structure probably raised fewer barriers to adoption. Neither they nor the Kassites of western Iran, the Hittites of Anatolia,* the Hyksos of modern Israel and Jordan, and the Mycenaeans of Greece were as organized as Egypt or the Mesopotamian city of Babylon, but for a while that did not matter, because chariots gave these formerly peripheral peoples such an edge in war-making that they could plunder or even take over their older, richer neighbors. The Hyksos steadily moved into Egypt, building their own city around 1720 BCE and seizing the throne in 1674. In 1595 Hittites sacked Babylon, and soon Kassites were taking over Mesopotamia's cities. By 1500 BCE the Hurrians had carved out a kingdom called Mittani and Mycenaeans had conquered Crete (Figure 4.4).

These were turbulent times, but in the long run the upheavals served only to enlarge the core, not to drive development down. In Mesopotamia, the main upshot of the enslavements, deportations, massacres, and dispossessions was that northern immigrants replaced local rulers. In Egypt, where Theban-led rebels kicked the Hyksos out in 1552 BCE, not even that much changed. But by 1500 BCE new kingdoms had taken shape around the northern fringe of the old core, their development rising so quickly that they forced their way into an enlarged version of that core. So tightly were the great states now linked that historians call the next three hundred years the International Age.

Trade boomed. Royal texts are full of it, and fourteenth-century letters found at Amarna in Egypt show the kings of Babylon, Egypt, and the newly powerful states of Assyria, Mittani, and the Hittites jockeying for position, asking for gifts, and marrying off princesses. They created a shared diplomatic language and addressed one another as "brother." Second-tier rulers, excluded from the club of great powers, they called "servants," but rank could be renegotiated. Ahhiyawa (probably Greece), for instance, was a borderline great power. There are no Ahhiyawan letters in the Amarna archive, but when a Hittite king listed "the kings who are equal to me in rank" in a thirteenth-century treaty he named "the king of Egypt, the king of Babylonia,

---

*Ancient historians generally call the land that is now Turkey by the Greek name Anatolia (meaning "Land of the East"), since the Turks—who originally came from central Asia—settled Anatolia only in the eleventh century CE.

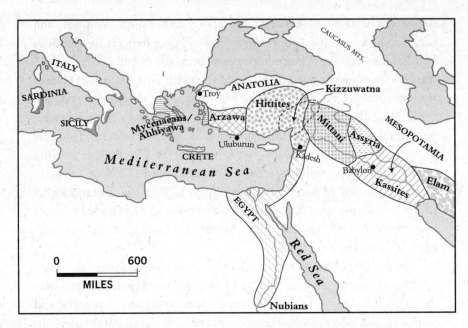

Figure 4.4. The band of brothers: the Western core's International Age
kingdoms as they stood around 1350 BCE, after the Hittites and Mittani
had gobbled up Kizzuwatna but before the Hittites and Assyrians
destroyed Mittani. The gray areas in Sicily, Sardinia, and Italy show
where Mycenaean Greek pottery has been found.

the king of Assyria, and the king of Ahhiyawa"—only to think better
of it and scratch Ahhiyawa off the list.

The more the "brothers" had to do with one another, the tougher
their sibling rivalry got. The Hyksos invasion in the eighteenth century BCE had traumatized the Egyptian elite, shattering their sense that
impassable deserts shielded them from attack; determined to prevent
any repeat, they upgraded their rather ramshackle militias into a permanent army with career officers and a modern chariot corps. By 1500
BCE they had pushed up the Mediterranean coast into Syria, building
forts as they went.

An ancient arms race broke out by 1400 BCE and the devil took the
hindmost. Between 1350 and 1320 BCE the Hittites and Assyrians swallowed up Mittani. Assyria intervened in a Babylonian civil war, and by
1300 the Hittites had destroyed Arzawa, another neighbor. Hittite and
Egyptian kings waged a deadly cold war, full of spies and covert op-

erations, to control Syria's city-states. In 1274 BCE it turned hot, and the biggest armies the world had yet seen—perhaps thirty thousand infantry and five thousand chariots on each side—clashed at Kadesh. Ramses II, the Egyptian pharoah, apparently blundered into a trap. Since he was a god, this naturally presented no problem, and in an account posted in no fewer than seven temples, Ramses tells us that he went on a Rambo-like rampage:

> His Majesty [Ramses] slew the entire force of the Foe of Hatti [another name for the Hittites], together with his great chiefs and all his brothers, as well as all the chiefs of all the countries that had come with him, their infantry and their chariotry falling on their faces one upon the other. His Majesty slaughtered them in their places; they sprawled before his horses; and his majesty was alone, none other with him.

The "vile Chief of Hatti," says Ramses, then begged for peace (as well he might).

Extracting military history from a god-king's bombast is tricky, but all our other evidence suggests that, contrary to his boasts, Ramses barely escaped the Hittite ambush that day. The Hittites kept advancing down the coast until 1258 BCE, stopping only because they had picked new fights, one with Assyria in the mountains of southeast Anatolia and another with Greek adventurers on Anatolia's west coast. Some historians think that Homer's *Iliad*, the Greek epic poem written down five centuries later, dimly reflects a war in the 1220s BCE in which a Greek alliance besieged the Hittite vassal city of Troy; and far to the southeast, an even more terrible siege was under way, ending with Assyria sacking Babylon in 1225 BCE.

These were savage struggles. Defeat could mean annihilation—men slaughtered, women and children carried into slavery, cities reduced to rubble and condemned to oblivion. Everything, therefore, was sacrificed for victory. More militarized elites emerged, far richer than their predecessors, and their internal feuds took on a new edge. Kings fortified their palaces or built themselves whole new cities where the lower orders would not disturb their tranquillity. Taxes and demands for forced labor rose sharply and debt spiraled as aristocrats borrowed to finance lavish lifestyles and peasants mortgaged harvests to stay alive. Kings described themselves as their people's shepherds but spent more time fleecing their flocks than protecting them, fighting to control labor and carrying off whole peoples to work on their building projects. The Hebrews toiling on pharaoh's cities, distant descendants of Jacob's sons who had migrated to Egypt with such high hopes, are merely the best known of these slave populations.

So it was that state power grew after 1500 BCE and the Western core expanded with it. Pottery made in Greece has been found around the shores of Sicily, Sardinia, and northern Italy, suggesting that other, more valuable (but archaeologically less visible) goods were moving long distances too. Archaeologists diving off the Anatolian coast have recovered astonishing snapshots of the mechanics of trade. A ship wrecked at Uluburun around 1316 BCE, for instance, was carrying enough copper and tin to make ten tons of bronze, as well as ebony and ivory from tropical Africa, cedar from Lebanon, glass from Syria, and weapons from Greece and what is now Israel; in short, a little of everything that might fetch a profit, probably gathered, a few objects at a time, in every port along the ship's route by a crew as mixed as its cargo.

The shores of the Mediterranean Sea were being drawn into the core. Rich graves containing bronze weapons suggest that village chiefs were turning into kings in Sardinia and Sicily, and texts reveal that young men left their villages on these islands to seek their fortunes as mercenaries in the core's wars. Sardinians wound up in Babylon and even in what is now Sudan, where Egyptian armies pushed south in search of gold, smashing native states and building temples as they went. Still farther afield, chiefs in Sweden were being buried with chariots, the ultimate status symbols from the core, and were putting other imported military hardware—particularly sharp bronze swords— to deadly use.

As the Mediterranean turned into a new frontier, rising social development once again changed what geography meant. In the fourth millennium BCE the rise of irrigation and cities had made the great river valleys in Egypt and Mesopotamia into more valuable real estate than the old core in the Hilly Flanks, and in the second millennium the explosion of long-distance trade made access to the Mediterranean's broad waterways more valuable still. After 1500 BCE the turbulent Western core entered a whole new age of expansion.

TEN THOUSAND *GUO* UNDER HEAVEN

Archaeologists often suffer from an affliction that I like to call Egypt envy. No matter where we dig or what we dig up, we always suspect we would find better things if we were digging in Egypt. So it is a relief to know that Egypt envy affects people in other walks of life too. In 1995 State Councillor Song Jian, one of China's top scientific administrators, made an official visit to Egypt. He was not happy when archaeologists told him that its antiquities were older than China's, so on returning to Beijing he launched the Three Dynasties Chronology Project to look into the matter. Four years and $2 million later, it announced its findings: Egypt's antiquities really are older than China's. But now at least we know exactly how much older.

As we saw in Chapter 2, agricultural lifestyles began developing in the West around 9500 BCE, a good two thousand years earlier than in China. By 4000 BCE farming had spread into marginal areas such as Egypt and Mesopotamia, and when the monsoons shifted southward after 3800 BCE these new farmers created cities and states out of self-preservation. The East had plenty of dry, marginal zones too, but farming had barely touched them by 3800, so the arrival of cooler, drier weather did not lead to the rise of cities and states. Instead, it probably made life easier for villagers by making the warm, wet Yangzi and Yellow river valleys a little drier and more manageable. Hard as it is to imagine today, the Yellow River valley was mostly subtropical forest around 4000 BCE; elephants trumpeted down what are now the car-choked streets of Beijing.

Instead of a transition to cities and states like Egypt and Mesopotamia, fourth-millennium-BCE China saw steady, unspectacular population growth. Forests were cleared and new villages founded; old villages grew into towns. The better people did at capturing energy, the more they multiplied and the greater pressure they put on themselves; so, like Westerners, they tinkered and experimented, finding new ways to squeeze more from the soil, to organize themselves more effectively, and to grab what they wanted from others. Thick fortifications of pounded earth sprouted around the bigger sites, suggesting conflict, and some settlements were laid out in more organized ways, suggesting community-level planning. Houses got bigger and we find more objects in them, pointing to slowly rising standards of living; but differences between houses also increased, perhaps meaning that richer peasants were distinguishing themselves from their neighbors. Some archaeologists think that the distribution of tools within houses reveals emerging gender distinctions too. In a few places, notably Shandong (Figure 4.5), some people—mostly men—found their last resting place in big graves with more offerings than others, and a few even had elaborate carved jade ornaments.

Beautiful as these jades can be, it must still be hard for archaeologists excavating Chinese sites of around 2500 BCE to avoid the odd pang of Egypt envy. They find no Great Pyramids or royal inscriptions. Their discoveries in fact look more like what archaeologists find on sites in the Western core that date around 4000 BCE, shortly

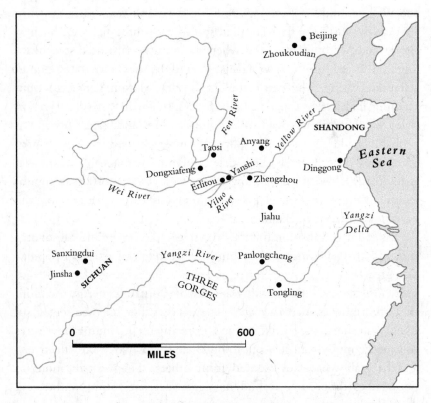

Figure 4.5. The expansion of the Eastern core, 3500–1000 BCE:
sites mentioned in this chapter

before the first cities and states emerged. The East was moving along a path like the West's, but at least fifteen hundred years behind; and, staying on schedule, between 2500 and 2000 BCE the East went through transformations rather like those the West had seen between 4000 and 3500 BCE.

All along the great river valleys the pace of change accelerated, but an interesting pattern emerged. The fastest changes came not on the broadest plains with the richest soils but in cramped spaces, where it was hard for people to run away and find new homes if they lost struggles for resources within villages or wars between them. On one of Shandong's small plains, for instance, archaeologists found a new settlement pattern taking shape between 2500 and 2000 BCE. A single large town grew up, with perhaps five thousand residents, surrounded by smaller satellite towns, which had their own smaller satellite villages. Surveys around Susa in southwest Iran found a similar pattern there some fifteen hundred years earlier; this, perhaps, is the way things always go when one community wins political control.

To judge from the lavish send-offs some men got in their funerals, genuine kings may have been clawing their way up the greasy pole in Shandong after 2500 BCE. A few graves contain truly spectacular jades and one has a turquoise headdress that looks a lot like a crown. The most remarkable find, though, is a humble potsherd from Dinggong. When this apparently unremarkable fragment of gray pottery initially came out of the ground the excavators just tossed it in a bucket with their other finds, but when they cleaned it back at the lab they found eleven symbols, related to yet different from later Chinese scripts, scratched on its surface. Is this, the excavators asked, the tip of an iceberg of widespread writing on perishable materials? Did Shandong's kings have bureaucrats managing their affairs, like the rulers of Uruk in Mesopotamia a thousand years earlier? Maybe; but other archaeologists, pointing to the unusual way the inscription was identified, wonder whether it has been wrongly dated or is even a fake. Only further discoveries will clear this up. Yet writing or no, whoever ran the Shandong communities was certainly powerful. By 2200 BCE human sacrifices were common and some graves received ancestor worship.

Who were these top people? Taosi, a site four hundred miles away in the Fen River valley, may provide some clues. This is the biggest settlement known from these times, with perhaps ten thousand inhabitants. A huge pounded-earth platform may have supported one of China's first palaces, though the only direct evidence is a decorated fragment of a destroyed wall found in a pit. (I will return to this in a moment.)

Thousands of burials have been excavated at Taosi, and these hint at a steep social hierarchy. Nearly nine out of every ten graves were small, with just a few offerings. Roughly one in ten was bigger, but about one in a hundred (always male) was enormous. Some of the giant graves held two hundred offerings, including vases painted with dragons, jade ornaments, and entire pigs, sacrificed but not eaten. In a striking parallel to Jiahu, the prehistoric cemetery discussed in Chapter 2, the very richest graves contained musical instruments: clay or wood drums with crocodile skins, large stone chimes, and an odd-looking copper bell.

When I talked about Jiahu in Chapter 2, I mentioned the archaeologist Kwang-chih Chang's theory that Eastern kings developed from prehistoric shamans who used alcohol, music, and repetitive rituals to convince themselves (and others) that they traveled to spirit worlds and talked to ancestors and gods. Jiahu had not been excavated when Chang developed this idea, and he could trace evidence only back to about 3500 BCE; but pointing to Taosi and similar sites, he suggested that it was between 2500 and 2000 BCE that ancient China's religious and royal symbols crystallized. About two thousand years later the *Rites of Zhou*, a Confucian handbook on ceremonies, would still list all the instrument types found in the Taosi graves as appropriate for elite rituals.

Chang believed that other literature produced around the same time as the *Rites of Zhou* also reveals memories of the period before 2000 BCE. One of the most significant, if also most cryptic, passages may come in the *Springs and Autumns of Mr. Lü,** a survey of useful knowledge compiled in 239 BCE by one Lü Buwei, chief minister of the state of Qin. Lü pronounced, "The Way of Heaven is round; the Way of Earth is square. The sage kings took this as their model." The sage kings were said to be descendants of the high god Di, and the last of these sage kings, Yu, was supposed to have saved mankind by dig-

---

Springs and Autumns was a popular name for Chinese history books, meaning in effect "Years." "Annals" might be a good translation.

ging drainage ditches when the Yellow River flooded. "But for Yu," another text said, "we should have been fishes." The grateful people made Yu their king, the story runs, and he founded China's first fully human dynasty, the Xia.

Lü Buwei believed in his book's accuracy, reportedly suspending a thousand pieces of gold above it outside his city's main market and offering the money to anyone who could show that he needed to add or remove a single word. (Fortunately, publishers no longer require this of authors.) But despite Lü's touching faith, King Yu sounds about as credible as Noah, the West's version of a blameless man who saved humanity from floods. Most historians think the sage kings were entirely fictional. Kwang-chih Chang, though, suggested that Lü's book preserved genuine, albeit distorted, information about the late third millennium BCE, the age when something resembling kingship was taking shape in the East.

Chang saw a link between Lü's story that the sage kings took the roundness of heaven and squareness of earth as their model and the *cong*, a type of jade vessel that appeared in rich graves in the Yangzi Delta region around 2500 BCE then spread to Taosi and other sites. A *cong* is a square block of jade with a cylindrical opening drilled through it, the circle and square expressing the union of heaven and earth. The circle-square remained a potent emblem of royal power until the fall of China's last dynasty in 1912 CE. If you brave the crowds at the Forbidden City in Beijing and peer into the dark interiors of the palaces, you will see the same symbols—square throne base, round ceiling—repeated over and over again.

Perhaps, Chang suggested, memories of ancient priest-kings, men who claimed to move between this and the spirit world and used *cong* to symbolize their power, survived into Lü's day. Chang called the years 2500–2000 BCE "the Age of Jade *Cong*, the period when shamanism and politics joined forces and when an elite class based on its shamanistic monopoly came into being." The most spectacular *cong* were surely royal treasures; the biggest example, engraved with images of spirits and animals, has been dubbed by archaeologists (whose humor is nothing if not predictable) the King *Cong*.

If Chang was right, religious specialists turned themselves into a ruling elite between 2500 and 2000 BCE, much as they had done in Mesopotamia a thousand-plus years earlier, with jade, music, and temples on beaten-earth platforms as amplifiers for their messages to the gods. One site even had a shrine (admittedly small, just twenty feet across, and only on a low platform) shaped like a *cong*.

By 2300 BCE Taosi looked like an Uruk in the making, complete with palaces, platforms, and chiefs on their way to becoming godlike. And then, suddenly, it didn't. The elite compound was destroyed, which is why the only trace of a palace is the fragment of a painted wall found in a garbage pit that I mentioned earlier. Forty skeletons, some dismembered or with weapons stuck in them, were dumped in a ditch where the palace had stood, and some of the biggest graves in the cemetery were looted. Taosi shrank to half its previous size and a big new town grew up just a few miles away.

One of the frustrating things about archaeology is that we often see the results of what people did but not the causes. We can spin yarns (Barbarians burn Taosi! Civil war destroys Taosi! Internal feuds tear Taosi in two! New neighbor sacks Taosi! And so on.) but can rarely tell which is true. In this case, the best we can do is to observe that the fall of Taosi was part of a larger process. By 2000 BCE the biggest sites in Shandong had also been abandoned and population was falling across northern China—at just the same time, of course, that drought, famine, and political collapse were racking Egypt and Mesopotamia. Could climate change have brought on an Old World–wide crisis?

If Taosi had recorded flood levels with a Yellow Riverometer like Egypt's Nilometer, or if Chinese archaeologists had done micromorphological studies like those at Tell Leilan in Syria, we might be able to say, but these kinds of evidence do not exist. We might scour the literary accounts written two thousand years after these events for information, though as with the stories about sage kings, we cannot tell how much their authors really knew about such early times.

"During the reign of Yu," the *Springs and Autumns of Mr. Lü* says, "there were ten thousand *guo* under heaven." Translating *guo* as "chiefdom," a small political unit based on a walled town, many archaeologists think this is quite a good description of the Yellow River valley between 2500 and 2000 BCE. Some scholars go on to argue that there really was a King Yu, who ended the age of ten thousand *guo* and imposed the rule of a Xia dynasty on them. The literary sources even provide a climatic cause, though instead of a Mesopotamian-style dust bowl they speak of torrential rain in nine out of ten years, which was why Yu needed to drain the Yellow River valley. Something like this certainly could have happened; until two decades ago, when the Yellow River started running dry in places, people regularly called it "China's sorrow" because it flooded most years and changed course on average once each century, ruining or killing peasants by the thousands.

Maybe the story of Yu is based on a real catastrophe around 2000 BCE. Or maybe it is just a folktale. We simply don't know. Once again, though, while the causes of change are obscure, its consequences are clear. While the towns of Shandong and the Fen Valley bounced back by 2000 BCE (Taosi even got a monumental platform twenty feet tall and two hundred feet across), the advantages of backwardness—so important in Western history—now kicked in, and even more impressive monuments began filling a former backwater, the Yiluo Valley.

We do not have enough evidence to know why, but the Yiluoans did not simply copy Taosi. Instead they created a whole new architectural style, replacing the big buildings that were easy to see and approach from every angle, which had been customary for a thousand years in northern China, with closed-in palaces, their courtyards surrounded by roofed corridors with only a few points of entry. They then tucked the palaces away behind tall rammed-earth walls. Interpreting architecture is a tricky business, but the Yiluo style may mean that relationships between rulers and ruled mutated in new and perhaps more hierarchical directions as priestly leadership spread to the fluid frontier in the Yiluo Valley.

We might think of this as the East's Uruk moment, when one community left all rivals behind and turned itself into a state with rulers who could use force to impose their decisions on and raise taxes from their subjects. That community was Erlitou, which exploded into a true city with 25,000 residents between 1900 and 1700 BCE. Many Chinese archaeologists believe Erlitou was the capital of the Xia dynasty said to have been established by the sage king Yu. Non-Chinese scholars on the whole disagree, pointing out that the literary references to the Xia only begin a thousand years after Erlitou was abandoned. Perhaps, they suggest, the Xia—along with King Yu—were made up. These critics accuse Chinese scholars of at best being gullible about mythology and at worst of peddling propaganda, bolstering modern China's national identity by pushing its origins as far into antiquity as possible. Not surprisingly, these arguments get nasty.

The debate is mostly beside the point for the questions we are discussing here, but we cannot avoid it completely. For my own part, I tend to suspect that there really was a Xia dynasty, and that Erlitou was its capital, even if the stories about Yu are largely folktales. As we will see in the next section, whenever we can check them, it's clear that later Chinese historians did rather well at transmitting names; I just cannot imagine Yu and the Xia being invented out of whole cloth.

Whatever the truth, though, Yu, the Xia, or whoever ruled Erlitou could command labor on a whole new scale, building a string of palaces and perhaps an ancestral temple on stamped-earth platforms in the new, closed-in style. One platform, supporting Palace I, must have taken something like a hundred thousand workdays to complete. A quarter of a mile from it archaeologists found slag, crucibles, and molds from bronze casting strewn across two acres. Copper had been known since 3000 BCE, but long remained a novelty item, used mostly for trinkets. When Erlitou was established around 1900 BCE, bronze weapons were still rare, and stone, bone, and shell remained normal for agricultural tools well into the first millennium BCE. The Erlitou foundry thus represented a quantum leap over earlier craft activity. It churned out weapons and craftsmen's tools, which must have helped with the city's success, but also produced remarkable ritual objects—bells like the earlier example from Taosi; plaques with inlaid turquoise eyes, animals, and horns; and ritual vessels a foot or more in diameter. The shapes invented at Erlitou (*jia* tripods, *ding* cauldrons, *jue* pouring cups, *he* pitchers for heating wine) became the East's ultimate amplifiers for religious messages, displacing jade *cong* and dominating rituals for the next thousand years.

These great vessels have been found only at Erlitou, and if Chang was right that royal power flowed from the king's claim to stand at the junction of this and supernatural worlds, bronze ritual vessels were probably as important to Erlitou's power as bronze swords. The king of Erlitou had the loudest amplifier; lords of lesser *guo* might have concluded that it made sense to cooperate with the man the spirits could hear best.

For the king, though, bronze vessels must have been a headache as well as a tool. They were hugely expensive, requiring armies of craftsmen and ton upon ton of copper, tin, and fuel—all in short supply in the Yiluo Valley. In addition to carving out a small kingdom (guessing from the pattern of settlements, some archaeologists estimate that it covered about two thousand square miles), Erlitou may have sent out colonists to grab raw materials. Dongxiafeng, for instance, set in copper-rich hills a hundred miles west of Erlitou, has Erlitou-type pottery and great mounds of debris from copper smelting, but no palaces, rich graves, or molds for casting vessels, let alone the vessels themselves. The archaeologists may just have dug in the wrong places, but they have been looking there a long time; most likely copper was mined and refined at Dongxiafeng then sent back to Erlitou—the East's first colonial regime.

ANCESTOR-IN-CHIEF

Backwardness may have advantages, but it has disadvantages too, not least that as soon as a periphery forces its way into an older core it finds itself confronting new peripheries similarly intent on forcing their way in. Erlitou was the most dazzling city in the East by 1650 BCE, its temples gleaming with bronze cauldrons and echoing with chimes and bells, but a mere day's walk beyond the Yellow River would have taken an adventurous urbanite into a violent world of fortresses and feuding chiefs. Two skeletons found in a pit just forty miles from the big city show unmistakable signs of scalping.

Relations between Erlitou and this wild frontier may have been rather like those between Mesopotamia's Akkadian Empire and the Amorites, with trading and raiding profitable to both parties—until something upset the balance. The upset in the East shows up in the form of a fortress called Yanshi, built around 1600 BCE just five miles from Erlitou. Later literary sources say that around this time a new group, the Shang, overthrew the Xia dynasty. The earliest finds from Yanshi combine Erlitou styles of material with traditions from north of the Yellow River, and most Chinese archaeologists (and this time many non-Chinese too) think the Shang crossed the Yellow River around 1600 BCE, defeated Erlitou, and built Yanshi to dominate their humbled but more sophisticated foes. Yanshi bloomed into a great city as Erlitou declined, until around 1500 BCE the Shang kings, perhaps deciding that they did not need to watch their former enemies quite so closely, moved fifty miles east to a new city at Zhengzhou.

Anything Erlitou could do, it seems, Zhengzhou could do better, or at least bigger. Zhengzhou had an inner city about the same size as Erlitou but also an entire square mile of suburbs with their own enormous stamped-earth wall. By one estimate this would have taken ten thousand laborers eight years to build. "They tilted in the earth with a rattling," a later poem says of the construction of such a wall, "They pounded it with a dull thud. / They beat the walls with a loud clang, / they pared and chiseled them with a faint ping-ping." Zhengzhou must have reverberated with rattles, thuds, clangs, and ping-pings. The city also needed not one but several bronze foundries, just one of which left an eight-acre waste dump. Zhengzhou's ritual vessels continued Erlitou traditions but, naturally, were grander. One bronze cauldron buried in a hurry around 1300 BCE (perhaps during an attack) was three feet tall and weighed two hundred pounds.

Zhengzhou also expanded Erlitou's colonialism. Four hundred miles away, beyond the Yangzi River, miners tore up the valleys of Tongling in search of copper, burrowing a hundred plank-lined shafts into the rock, disfiguring the landscape with 300,000 tons of slag. The objects they left behind (so well preserved that archaeologists have even found their wood and bamboo tools and reed sleeping mats) are just like those from the Shang capital. When Uruk-style material culture had expanded through Mesopotamia after 3500 BCE, some sites looked like they were cloned from Uruk itself, right down to their street plans; likewise, Shang colonists built a kind of miniature Zhengzhou, complete with palaces, rich burials, and bronze ritual vessels in fully developed Shang style at Panlongcheng, astride the easiest route from Tongling to the Shang heartland.

Only around 1250 BCE, though, do the Shang really come alive for us. According to legend, in 1899 (CE, that is) a relative of Wang Qirong, director of the Imperial Academy in Beijing, caught malaria and sent a servant to buy decayed turtle shell, a traditional Chinese remedy.* Wang's sick relative was an educated man, and when he saw a row of

---

*I say "according to legend" because the trail leading to Zhoukoudian, the great prehistoric site discussed in Chapter 1, is said to have begun the same year in much the same way, when a German naturalist, trapped in Beijing by civil unrest, recognized a "dragon bone" in a druggist's store as an early human tooth. The coincidence is slightly suspicious.

symbols scratched on the shell his servant brought home he guessed that they were an ancient version of Chinese. He sent the shell to Wang for a second opinion, and Wang guessed that the inscription dated back to the Shang dynasty.

Buying more shells, Wang made rapid progress on decipherment, but not rapid enough. In summer 1900 popular anger against Western-ers erupted in the Boxer Rebellion. The dowager empress backed the rebels and put imperial officials, including Wang, in charge of mili-tia bands. The Boxers besieged the foreign embassy compound, but twenty thousand alien troops—Japanese, Russian, British, American, and French—descended on Beijing. Swept up in the disaster, his life in ruins, Wang, his wife, and his daughter-in-law poisoned themselves and jumped down a well.

Wang's inscribed bones came into the hands of an old friend. Within a decade he, too, was dead, after disgrace and exile to China's desolate west, but in 1903 he managed to publish the inscriptions as a book. It set off bone frenzy. Foreign and indigenous scholars scrambled to buy up turtle shells; one was offering three ounces of silver per inscribed word, at a time when laborers in Beijing were earning just one sixth of an ounce per day. The bad news was that this set off a rash of illicit digging, with armed gangs shooting it out in potato fields over frag-ments of ancient turtle shells. The good news, though, was extraordi-nary. Not only had Wang been right that these burned shells and bones were China's oldest texts; but they also turned out to name kings who matched exactly those listed by the first-century-BCE historian Sima Qian as the last rulers of the Shang dynasty.

Antiquities dealers tried to keep the source of the bones secret, but soon everyone knew they came from the village of Anyang, and in 1928 the Chinese government launched its first official archaeological excavation there. Unfortunately, it immediately ran into the same problems as the Peking Man excavations at Zhoukoudian. Warlords and bandits fought across the neighborhood; tomb robbers with home-made pistols had firefights with police; and the Japanese army closed in. The biggest-ever find of inscriptions, a pit containing seventeen thousand bones, was made just an hour before the 1936 excavation season was due to end. Archaeologists struggled for an additional four days and nights to get the artifacts out of the ground, knowing they might never be able to return. Most of their finds disappeared during the decade of war that followed, but the bronze vessels and inscriptions made it to Taiwan after the 1949 Communist takeover. And it was all worthwhile; the Anyang excavations transformed early Chinese history.

The excavations showed that Anyang was the final Shang capital, established around 1300 BCE. Its walled settlement, located only in 1997, covered nearly three square miles, but like Zhengzhou it was dwarfed by its suburbs. Temples, cemeteries, and bronze foundries sprawled across another dozen square miles, an area one-third the size of Manhattan. One foundry, excavated in 2004, covered ten acres, but at the core of this ritual landscape, dominating what was recorded in the inscriptions, was a different activity: the kings' efforts to cajole their ancestors into helping them.

The excavated inscriptions begin in the long reign of King Wuding (1250–1192 BCE), and from the information they contain we can piece together the rituals that produced them. The king would put questions to his ancestors, summoning their spirits from their great tombs on the other side of the river that ran through Anyang. Pressing a heated stick against a shell or bone, he would interpret the cracks it produced, and specialists would inscribe the results on the "oracle bone."

The rites made Wuding ancestor-in-chief, hosting parties for spirits of recently dead kings and corralling them into hosting their own ancestors, who in turn—for really serious matters—would host all the spirits on up to Di, the high god. The idea that the silent turtle could make the ancestors' voices heard perhaps went back six thousand years to sites like Jiahu, discussed in Chapter 2, but the Shang kings of course made it bigger and better. Archaeologists have found more than 200,000 oracle bones at Anyang, and David Keightley, the leading Western scholar of the inscriptions, calculates some 2 million to 4 million were originally made, consuming a hundred thousand turtles and oxen. The rituals also involved binge drinking, perhaps to put the king and diviners into the right frame of mind for talking to spirits.

Shang kings tried to get on the right side of the spirits with spectacular funerals to mark their predecessors' transition to ancestorhood. Eight royal tombs have been found, one for each king from 1300 through 1076 BCE, with an unfinished ninth for Di Xin, still on the throne when the dynasty fell in 1046. All were looted, but the cemeteries are still overwhelming—not so much for the few thousand tons of earth moved for each tomb, which were paltry by Egyptian standards, but for the real Shang funeral specialty: violence.

Ancient Chinese literature speaks of people "following in death" at elite funerals, but nothing prepared the Anyang excavators for what they found. Tomb 1001, probably Wuding's resting place, contained about two hundred corpses—9 at the bottom of the shaft, each in its own pit with a dead dog and a deliberately broken bronze blade; 11 more on a ledge around the shaft; between 73 and 136 (it's hard to tell from the hacked-up body parts) scattered on ramps into the tomb; and 80 more on the surface next to the grave. About five thousand sacrificial pits have been identified around the tombs, typically holding several murdered humans (mostly men, some with their joints worn down by hard labor) and animals (from birds to elephants). Nor did the doomed go quietly. Some were beheaded; others had limbs chopped off or were severed at the waist; others still were found bound and contorted, surely buried alive.

The numbers are staggering. The oracle bones mention 13,052 ritual killings, and if Keightley is right that we have found only 5–10 percent of the inscriptions, in all a quarter of a million people may have perished. Averaged out, that would be four or five per day, every day, for 150 years. In reality, though, they were bunched around big funerals in great orgies of hacking, screaming, and dying, when the cemeteries literally ran with blood. Nearly three thousand years later, Aztec kings in Mexico waged wars specifically to take prisoners to feed their bloodthirsty god Quetzalcoatl; the Shang may have done the same for their ancestors, particularly against people they called the Qiang, more than seven thousand of whom are listed as victims in the oracle bones.

Wuding and his colleagues, like great kings in the West, talked to spirits in another world while dealing death in this one. It was the combination of worship and war that made them kings, and the funerals that turned kings into ancestors were full of martial symbolism. Even after being plundered, tomb 1004 (perhaps for King Lin Xin, who died around 1160 BCE) still contained 731 spearheads, 69 axes, and 141 helmets; and when Wuding spoke directly to the high god Di, it was usually about fighting. "Crackmaking on day forty-one, Zheng divined," says a typical oracle bone. "If we attack the Mafang, Di will confer assistance on us."

By Western standards Shang armies were small. The largest mentioned in the oracle bones is ten thousand men, just a third the size of Ramses' army at Kadesh. Place-names in the inscriptions also suggest that Wuding directly administered quite a small stretch of the Yellow River, plus a few far-flung colonies such as Panlongcheng. He apparently ran not an integrated, tax-paying, bureaucratically managed state like Egypt, but a looser group of allies who sent tribute to Anyang—cattle, white horses, bones and shells for divining, and even humans for sacrifice.

Sima Qian, the first-century-BCE historian who listed the Shang kings, made early Chinese history sound simple. After the sage kings, culminating in Yu the ditch digger, came the Xia, then the Shang, and then the Zhou (the three dynasties of the Three Dynasties Chronology Project). From them China developed, and nothing else was worth mentioning. But while archaeology has shown that Erlitou and Anyang were indeed peerless in their age, it has also shown that Sima Qian's account oversimplified things. Like the Egyptians and Babylonians, the Xia and Shang had to deal with dozens of neighboring states.

Archaeologists are just beginning to unearth these other states' impressive remains, especially in southern and eastern China. As recently as 1986 we had little idea that a rich kingdom had flourished around 1200 BCE far up the Yangzi River in Sichuan; but then archaeologists found two pits stuffed with treasures at Sanxingdui. There were dozens of bronze bells, a couple of six-foot-high statues of men with crowns and huge, staring eyes, and elaborate bronze "spirit trees" twice that height, their branches full of delicate metal fruit, leaves, and birds. The excavators had stumbled onto a lost kingdom, and in 2001 a major city came to light in nearby Jinsha. By some estimates, half of all the house and highway construction in the world in the 2010s and 2020s will happen in China, and there is no telling what the salvage archaeologists, racing to stay one step ahead of the backhoes, will turn up next.

We find it easy to think of the Hittites, Assyrians, and Egyptians as distinct peoples, because ancient texts preserve their different languages and we are used to the West being divided into multiple national states. In the East, though, Sima Qian's story line that Chineseness began with the Xia and radiated outward makes it all too tempting to imagine these early states, which nowadays lie within a single modern

nation, as "always" being Chinese. In reality, ancient East and West probably had rather similar networks of jostling states, sharing some beliefs, practices, and cultural forms while differing in others. They
traded, fought, competed, and expanded. As our evidence accumu-
lates, the processes through which social development rose in the ancient East and West are coming to look more and more similar. Perhaps
there was once a wooden hall at Anyang holding letters on silk and
bamboo like the inscribed clay tablets at Amarna in Egypt, recording
diplomatic correspondence with foreign rulers who spoke alien tongues.
The king of Jinsha may have called Wuding his "brother" as they
exchanged thoughts on whether to treat the rulers of Shandong as
equals; and maybe Wuding even arranged to send some unsuspecting
Shang princess as a bride to a petty court on the Yangzi, there to
swelter and bear children far from her family and loved ones. We will
never know.

THINGS FALL APART

I would like to bring von Däniken's spacemen back into the story once
more. Even if the collapse of Egypt and Mesopotamia after 2200 BCE
had taken the aliens by surprise, as I suggested earlier, they would have
felt nothing but satisfaction had they brought their flying saucer back
to orbit the world of Wuding and Ramses II around 1250 BCE. This
time their work really did seem to be done. Western social development had reached twenty-four points on the index, nearly three times
where it stood in 5000 BCE.

The average Egyptian or Mesopotamian harnessed probably 20,000
kilocalories per day, as compared to 8,000 around 5000 BCE, and the
biggest cities, such as Thebes in Egypt or Babylon, had maybe eighty
thousand residents. There were thousands of literate scribes and burgeoning libraries. The greatest armies could muster five thousand
chariots, and it would have been a fair guess that one state (maybe
Egypt, or perhaps the Hittites) would soon create a core-wide empire.
New states, with their own palaces, temples, and godlike kings, would
develop in Italy, Spain, and beyond; then the empire in the core would
swallow these, too, until one great realm filled the map in Figure 4.3.
The East would continue tracking Western developments a millennium

or two behind. It would probably go through disruptions like the West's, and the West would probably face more upsets too; but like the earlier episodes, these would barely slow the rising tide of social development. The West would retain its lead, figure out fossil fuels within a couple of thousand years, and go on to global rule.

So when nearly every major city in the Western core, from Greece to what we now call the Gaza Strip, went up in flames around 1200 BCE, the aliens would have assumed it was another disruption like 2200 or 1750 BCE—a big one, to be sure, but nothing to worry about in the long term. Even when disaster engulfed the palaces so suddenly that their scribes barely had time to record it, the aliens would lose no sleep.

An unusual clay tablet from around 1200 BCE found in the ruined palace at Pylos in Greece opens with the ominous line "the watchers are guarding the coasts"; another from the same site, written in evident haste, seems to be describing human sacrifices meant to forestall an emergency, but then trails off, unfinished. At Ugarit, a rich trading city on the Syrian coast, archaeologists found a batch of clay letters lying in a kiln where scribes had intended to dry them before they were filed. Ugarit was sacked before anyone could come back and get the texts. These letters from the city's dying days make grim reading. One is from the Hittite king, begging for food: "it is a matter of life and death!" In another, Ugarit's king writes that while his troops and ships were away supporting the Hittites, "the enemy's ships came here; my cities were burned, and they did evil things in my country."

Darkness fell all around, yet so long as Egypt still stood, hope remained. In a temple he built in his own honor, Pharaoh Ramses III set up an inscription that seems to pick up the story from Ugarit: "The foreign countries had made a conspiracy in their islands," it says. "No land could stand before their arms." These foreigners—the Peoples of the Sea, Ramses calls them—had overwhelmed the Hittites, Cyprus, and Syria. Now, in 1176 BCE, they came against Egypt. But they had not reckoned with the god-king:

> Those who reached my frontier, their seed is not, their heart and their
> soul are finished for ever and ever . . . They were dragged in, enclosed,
> and prostrated on the beach, killed, and made into heaps from tail to

head . . . I have made the lands turn back from [even] mentioning Egypt; for when they pronounce my name in their land, then they are burned up.

Ramses III's Peoples of the Sea were probably also the villains in the Pylos and Ugarit stories. They included, Ramses says, Shrdn, Shkrsh, Dnyn, and Prst. Egyptian hieroglyphics did not record vowels, and identifying who these names refer to is a cottage industry among historians. Most think Shrdn was pronounced "Sherden," an ancient name for Sardinians, and the Shkrsh were Sheklesh, Egyptian for Sikels (Sicilians). Dnyn is less clear, but could mean Danaans, a name Homer would later use for Greeks. With Prst we are on firmer ground: it means Peleset, the Egyptian name for the Philistines of biblical fame.

This is quite a cocktail of Mediterranean peoples, and historians argue endlessly over what brought them to the Nile Delta. The evidence is spotty, but some archaeologists point to signs of higher temperatures and lower rainfall in every part of the Western core after 1300 BCE. Drought, they suggest, reran the 2200 BCE scenario, setting off migrations and state failure. Others think that earthquakes threw the core into turmoil, providing opportunities for plunder and pulling raiders in from the frontier. There were also changes in how people fought; new swords for slashing and deadlier javelins might have given swarms of irregular, lightly armed infantry from the peripheries the weapons they needed to defeat the core's gleaming but inflexible chariot armies. And disease might have played a part too. A terrible plague had spread from Egypt to the Hittites in the 1320s BCE. "The Land of Hatti, all of it, is dying," one prayer said, and although surviving texts do not mention plague again, if it was anything like epidemics in better-documented periods it would have kept returning. By 1200 BCE populations were apparently falling in the core.

The hard truth is that we just don't know the specific causes of the crisis, although the underlying dynamic seems clear enough: a sudden shift in relations between the core and its expanding frontiers. As had been the case so often before, expansion was a two-edged sword. On the one hand, the new frontier in the Mediterranean fueled surging social development, but on the other, it unveiled new advantages of backwardness and set off disruptions—migrations, mercenaries, and unmanageable new tactics—that challenged the established order. And in the thirteenth century BCE, it seems that the great powers in the core began losing control of the frontier they had created.

Whether they were pushed or pulled and whether the motor was climate change, earthquakes, changes on the battlefield, or plagues, people began moving into the core in overwhelming numbers. Already in the 1220s BCE Ramses II had fortified Egypt's borders, settling migrants in closely controlled towns or enlisting them in his army, but it was not enough. In 1209 BCE Pharaoh Merneptah had to fight not only the Sherden and Sheklesh, whom Ramses III would confront again in the 1170s BCE, but also Libyans and people named Akaiwasha—perhaps Ahhiyawans from Greece?—who joined forces to raid Egypt from the west.

The victorious Merneptah joyfully recorded that he cut off 6,239 uncircumcised penises to tally the enemy dead, but even while he was counting them the storm was engulfing the north. Greek, Hittite, and Syrian cities burned. Later legends talk of migrations into Greece around this time, and archaeology hints at out-migration too. Pottery found around Gaza, where the Philistines settled in the twelfth century BCE, is almost identical to vases from Greece, suggesting that the Philistines began as Greek refugees; and more Greeks settled on Cyprus.

Migration may have snowballed as refugees from devastated areas joined it. It looks like it was a shapeless movement, with disconnected plundering and fighting going on everywhere at once. The Syrian collapse apparently pushed people called Arameans into Mesopotamia, and despite Ramses' claims of victory, former Peoples of the Sea settled in Egypt. Like Greece, Egypt experienced out- as well as in-migration. The biblical story of Moses and the Israelites fleeing Egypt and eventually settling in what is now the West Bank probably reflects these chaotic years. It may not be a coincidence that the first nonbiblical reference to Israel is Merneptah's pronouncement in his 1209 BCE inscription that he left that land "wasted, bare of seed."

The sheer scale of the migrations that began in the 1220s BCE dwarfed earlier disruptions, but as late as the 1170s aliens watching from their flying saucers could still plausibly have hoped that this episode might turn out like earlier ones. After all, Egypt had not been pillaged, and in Mesopotamia the Assyrians actually expanded their kingdom as rival states folded. But as the twelfth century wore on and the upheavals continued, it slowly became clear that this disruption was something altogether new.

In Greece the palaces destroyed after 1200 BCE were not reoccupied and the old bureaucracy disappeared. Fairly wealthy aristocrats did preserve something like the old ways, often relocating to easily defended sites on mountains or small islands, but a new wave of destructions hit them around 1125 BCE. When I was a graduate student I had the doubly good fortune (not only was the archaeology fascinating, but I also met my future wife there) to dig on one of these sites, a fortified hilltop at Koukounaries on the island of Paros.* Its chief had enjoyed a fine lifestyle with great views, wonderful beaches, and a throne decorated with ivory inlays, but around 1100 BCE disaster struck him down. His villagers had stockpiled stones to fling at attackers and brought their animals behind the walls (we found donkey skeletons amid the ruins), but fled ahead of the flames when someone—we never learned who—stormed the citadel. Similar scenes played out all over Greece, and in the eleventh century BCE the survivors built only simple mud huts. Population, craftsmanship, and life expectancy all declined; a dark age set in.

Greece was the extreme case, but the Hittite Empire also went under, and Egypt and Babylon struggled to control migrants and raiders. Famines spread as villagers abandoned their fields. Because farmers could not pay taxes, states could not raise troops; and because there were no troops, raids went unchecked and local strongmen carved out little dukedoms. By 1140 BCE Egypt's empire in what is now Israel faded away. Abandoned by their paymasters, garrison troops turned into peasants or bandits. "In those days there was no king in Israel," says the book of Judges, the Israelites' account of their own part in this breakdown; "all the people did what was right in their own eyes."

By 1100 BCE Egypt itself was fragmenting. Thebes broke away; immigrants created principalities in the Nile Delta; and soon Ramses XI, the official god-king, was being told what to do by his own vizier,

---

*I'd like to thank Dr. Demetrius Schilardi of the Archaeological Society of Athens once again for his generosity in inviting us onto his excavation from 1983 through 1989.

who seized the throne in 1069. For several centuries few of Egypt's shadowy pharaohs fielded large armies, put up monuments, or even wrote much down.

Assyria, which early on looked like the big winner, lost control of the countryside as movements of Aramean peoples increased. By 1100 BCE the fields lay fallow, the treasury had run empty, and hunger stalked the land. The situation gets harder to read as the bureaucrats committed less to writing, rather suddenly stopping altogether after 1050. By then Assyria's cities were empty and its empire just a memory.

The Western core had contracted by 1000 BCE. Sardinia, Sicily, and Greece largely lost contact with the wider world, and warrior chiefs carved up the carcasses of the Hittite and Assyrian empires. Cities survived in Syria and Babylonia, but were a sad comedown from second-millennium-BCE metropolitan centers such as Ugarit. A cluster of little states survived in Egypt, but these were weaker and poorer than the glorious empire of Ramses II. And for the first time, social development actually fell. The numbers for every trait slid: by 1000 BCE people captured less energy, lived in smaller cities, fielded weaker armies, and used less writing than their predecessors had done around 1250. Scores fell back to where they had been six hundred years before.

CHARIOTS, NOT OF THE GODS

Around 1200 BCE, while King Wuding still sat on the throne, the Shang elite found something new to destroy in their funerals: chariots. These show up in a couple of dozen twelfth- and eleventh-century tombs at Anyang (complete, needless to say, with slaughtered horses and crews). Shang chariots are so like those that appeared in the Western core five hundred years earlier* that most archaeologists agree that both must have shared an origin in the chariots invented in Kazakhstan around 2000 BCE. Chariots took two or three centuries to reach the Hurrians and to alter the balance of power in the West; they needed eight to cross the greater distance to the Yellow River valley.

---

*The only real difference is that Chinese chariots had more spokes in their wheels than Western ones.

Like the Egyptians and Babylonians, the Shang were slow to adopt the new weapon. They must have learned about chariots from the peoples they called the Gui and Qiang who lived to their north and west, and oracle bones mention these neighbors using chariots in battle. In Wuding's day the Shang themselves used chariots only for hunting, and even then not very well. The fullest account describes Wuding crashing while chasing rhinoceros. He walked away, but a certain Prince Yang was hurt so badly that a whole set of oracle bones records efforts to exorcise the spirits causing his pain. A hundred years later the Shang were using a few chariots in battle, but instead of massing them like the Hittites and Egyptians, they scattered them among the infantry, probably for officers to ride around in.

Shang relations with their northwestern neighbors seem rather like Mesopotamian relations with the Hurrians and Hittites five hundred years earlier. Like the Mesopotamians, the Shang traded and fought with their neighbors, playing them off against one another. One of these groups, the Zhou, is first mentioned in the oracle bones as an enemy around 1200 BCE. They then show up as allies, but by 1150 BCE they were enemies again, now apparently living in the Wei Valley. While they were falling in and out of friendship with the Shang, the Zhou seem also to have been adapting and adopting those elements of Shang culture that suited them. By 1100 BCE they were forming their own state, complete with palaces, bronze vessels, divination, and rich tombs. One Zhou nobleman had a chariot team slaughtered, Shang-style, at his funeral, and Zhou kings even married Shang princesses. But then—again like the Mesopotamians dealing with their chariot-riding Hurrian and Hittite neighbors—the Shang lost control of the situation. The Zhou apparently put together an alliance of northwestern peoples, and by 1050 BCE were threatening the great Shang capital of Anyang itself.

Like the ancient Western states, the Shang state unraveled rather quickly when things went wrong. The oracle bones suggest that the Shang elite's internal dynamics had been in turmoil since about 1150 BCE, leaving the king more powerful but with fewer aristocratic supporters. By 1100 the Shang colonies in the south may have broken away, and many allies closer to home (like the Zhou) had defected.

In 1048 BCE the Shang king Di Xin could still muster eight hundred lords to block a Zhou attack, but two years later it was a different story. The Zhou king Wu massed three hundred chariots and swung around to take Anyang from the rear. A probably contemporary poem makes it sound like these Zhou chariots were decisive:

> *The war chariots gleamed,*
> *The team of white-bellies* was tough . . .*
> *Ah, that King Wu*
> *Swiftly fell upon Great Shang,*
> *Who before daybreak begged for a truce.*

Di Xin committed suicide. Wu won over some Shang leaders, executed others, and left Di Xin's son as a vassal king. Wu's political arrangements soon ran into trouble, as we will see in Chapter 5, but by then the gap in social development between East and West had narrowed sharply. The West had got a two-thousand-year head start over the East in agriculture, villages, cities, and states, but across the third and second millennia BCE the West's lead steadily shrank to just a thousand years.

As long ago as the 1920s most Western archaeologists thought they knew why China had started catching up: it was because the Chinese had copied almost everything—agriculture, pottery, building, metallurgy, chariots—from the West. Sir Grafton Elliot Smith, a British anatomist in Cairo, was so enthusiastic that he even managed to give Egypt envy a bad name. Wherever in the world he looked and whatever he looked at—pyramids, tattooing, stories about dwarfs and giants—Elliot Smith saw the copying of Egyptian archetypes, because, he convinced himself, Egyptian "Children of the Sun" had carried a "heliolithic" ("sun and stone") culture around the world. When we get right down to it, Elliot Smith concluded, we are all Egyptians.

Some of this seemed fairly nutty even at the time, and since the 1950s archaeology has steadily disproved nearly all Elliot Smith's claims. Eastern agriculture arose independently; Easterners used pottery thousands of years before Westerners; the East had its own traditions of monumental building; even human sacrifice was an independent Eastern invention. Yet despite all these findings, some important ideas clearly did move from West to East, above all bronzeworking. That

---

*Horses, that is.

metal, so important at Erlitou, is first seen in China not in the developed Yiluo Valley but in arid, windswept Xinjiang far to the northwest, probably after being brought across the steppes by the Western-looking people whose burials in the Tarim Basin I mentioned earlier. Chariots, as we have seen, probably entered the same way, just five hundred years after they had reached the Western core from the steppes.

But while West-to-East diffusion probably explains some of China's catch-up, the most important factor by far was not Eastern copying but the Western collapse. Eastern social development was still a thousand years behind the West's in 1200 BCE, but the Western core's implosion effectively wiped out six centuries' worth of gains. By 1000 BCE the East's development score was only a few hundred years behind the West's. The great Western collapse of 1200–1000 BCE began the first turning point in our story.

HORSEMEN OF THE APOCALYPSE

Just why the Western core broke down, though, remains one of history's greatest mysteries. If I had a cast-iron answer, I would of course have mentioned it by now, but the sad fact is that unless some stroke of luck provides a whole new kind of evidence, we will probably never know.

All the same, looking systematically at the disruptions of social development described in this chapter is rather illuminating. Table 4.1 summarizes what strike me as their most important features.

We know so little about the disruptions that undid the Uruk expansion in the West around 3100 BCE and Taosi in the East around 2300 that we should probably leave them out of the discussion, but the four cases of upheavals that remain break down into two pairs. The first pair—the Western crisis after 1750 BCE and the Eastern crisis around 1050—was, we might say, man-made. Chariot warfare shifted the balance of power; ambitious newcomers pushed into the cores; violence, migration, and regime change ensued. The main outcome, in both cases, was a shift in power toward formerly peripheral groups, with development continuing to move upward.

The second pair—the Western crises of 2200–2000 and 1200–1000 BCE—was quite different, most obviously because nature magnified

DATE BCE	MIGRATION	STATE FAILURE	FAMINE	DISEASE	CLIMATE CHANGE
West:					
3100		X			
2200	X	X	X		X
1750	X	X			
1200	X	X	X	?X	X
East:					
2300		X			
1050	X	X			

Table 4.1. The horsemen of the apocalypse: the documented dimensions
of disasters, 3100–1050 BCE

human folly. Climate change was largely beyond human control, and
was at least partly responsible for the famines in these periods (though
if the biblical story of Joseph is any guide, poor planning probably
contributed too). This second pair of disruptions was much more severe than the first, and we might draw a tentative conclusion from this:
that when the four horsemen of the apocalypse—climate change, famine, state failure, and migration—ride together, and especially when a
fifth horseman of disease joins them, disruptions can turn into collapses, sometimes even driving social development down.

Yet we cannot conclude that the orbital tilts and wobbles behind
climate change straightforwardly *caused* collapse. The drought that afflicted the Western core around 2200 BCE seems to have been harsher
than that around 1200, yet the core muddled through between 2200
and 2000 while it fell apart between 1200 and 1000 BCE. The drought
starting around 3800 BCE may have been worse than either 2200 or
1200, but it had relatively little impact in the East and actually drove
social development upward in the West.

This suggests a second possibility: that collapse comes out of the
interactions between natural and human forces. I think we can probably be more specific about this: bigger, more complex cores generate
bigger, more threatening upheavals, increasing the risk that disruptive

forces such as climate change and migration will set off thoroughgoing collapses. Around 2200 BCE the Western core was already large, with palaces, godlike kings, and redistributive economies covering the whole area from Egypt to Mesopotamia. When drought and migrations out of the Syrian Desert and Zagros Mountains shook up this region's internal and external relationships, the results were horrific, but because the twin core areas of Egypt and Mesopotamia were not very tightly linked, each stood or fell independently. By 2100 BCE Egypt had partly collapsed, but Mesopotamia revived; and when Mesopotamia partly collapsed around 2000 BCE, Egypt revived.

In 1200 BCE, by contrast, the core had expanded into Anatolia and Greece, reached the oases of central Asia, and even touched Sudan. Migrations apparently began on the unstable new Mediterranean frontier, but in the twelfth century BCE peoples were on the move everywhere from Iran to Italy. The snowball they created was much, much bigger than anything previously seen, and rolled across a more interconnected core that had more to go wrong. Raiders burned the crops at Ugarit because the king had sent his army to help the Hittites; disasters in one place compounded those in another in ways that had not happened a thousand years earlier. When one kingdom fell, it affected others. Chaos extended across the eleventh century BCE and finally dragged everyone down.

The paradox of social development—the tendency for development to generate the very forces that undermine it—means that bigger cores create bigger problems for themselves. It is all too familiar in our own age. The rise of international finance in the nineteenth century (CE) tied together capitalist nations in Europe and America and helped push social development upward faster than ever before, but this also made it possible for an American stock market bubble in 1929 to drag all these countries down; and the staggering increase in financial sophistication that helped push social development up in the last fifty years also made it possible for a new American bubble in 2008 to shake virtually the whole world to its foundations.

This is an alarming conclusion, but we can also derive a third, more optimistic, point from the troubled history of these early states. Bigger, more complex cores generate bigger, more threatening disruptions but also offer more, and more sophisticated, ways to respond to them. The world's financial leaders pounced on the crash of 2008 in ways that had been unimaginable in 1929, and as I write (in early 2010), seem to have averted a meltdown like that of the 1930s.

As social development moves upward it sets off a race between ever more threatening disruptions and ever more sophisticated defenses. Sometimes, as happened in the West around 2200 and 1200 BCE, the challenges overwhelm the responses available. Whether because leaders make mistakes, institutions fail, or the organization and technology are just not there, problems spiral out of control, disruption turns into collapse, and social development goes backward.

Before the collapse of 1200–1000 BCE, Western social development had been running well ahead of Eastern for thirteen thousand years. There was every reason to think the West's lead was permanent. After the collapse, the West's lead was wafer-thin; another such setback could wipe it out altogether. The paradox of social development, played out so brutally and so often between 5000 and 1000 BCE, showed that nothing lasts forever. No simple long-term lock-in theory can tell us why the West rules.

5

◎ ◎ ◎

NECK AND NECK

THE ADVANTAGES OF DULLNESS

Figure 5.1 may be the dullest diagram ever. Unlike Figure 4.2, it has no great divergences, disruptions, or convergences—just two lines drifting along in parallel for nearly a thousand years.

Yet while Figure 5.1 may be plain vanilla, the things that *don't* happen in it are crucial for our story. We saw in Chapter 4 that when the Western core collapsed around 1200 BCE, its lead in social development shrank sharply. It took Western development five centuries to claw its way back up to twenty-four points, where it had stood around 1300 BCE; if it had collapsed again when it hit this level, that would have wiped out the East-West gap altogether. If, on the other hand, Eastern development had collapsed when it reached twenty-four points, that would have restored the West's pre-1200 BCE lead. In reality, as Figure 5.1 shows, neither of these things happened. Eastern and Western social development kept rising in parallel, in a neck-and-neck race. The mid first millennium BCE was one of history's turning points because history failed to turn.

But what *does* happen in Figure 5.1 matters too. Social development almost doubled in both East and West between 1000 and 100 BCE. Western development passed thirty-five points; it was higher when

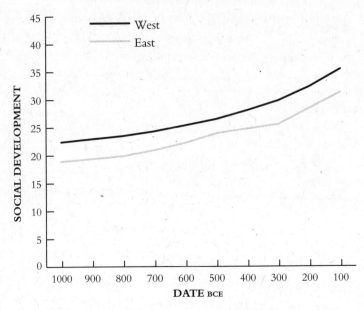

Figure 5.1. The dullest diagram in history? Social development,
1000–100 BCE

Julius Caesar crossed the Rubicon than it would be when Columbus crossed the Atlantic.

Why did the Western core not collapse around 700 BCE, or the Eastern around 500 BCE, when each hit twenty-four points? Why did social development rise so high by 100 BCE? Why were the Eastern and Western cores so alike by this point? These are the questions I try to answer in this chapter, although the obvious follow-up questions—why, if social development was so high in 100 BCE, did ancient Rome or China not colonize the New World? Or have an industrial revolution?—must wait till Chapters 9 and 10, when we can compare what happened after 1500 CE and what didn't happen in antiquity. Right now, though, we need to see what *did* happen.

KINGSHIP ON THE CHEAP

In a nutshell, the Eastern and Western cores avoided collapse in the first millennium BCE by restructuring themselves, inventing new institutions that kept them one step ahead of the disruptions that their continuing expansion itself generated.

There are basically two ways to run a state, what we might call high-end and low-end strategies. The high end, as its name suggests, is expensive. It involves leaders who centralize power, hiring and firing underlings who serve them in return for salaries in a bureaucracy or army. Paying salaries requires a big income, but the bureaucrats' main job is to generate that income through taxes, and the army's job is to enforce its collection. The goal is a balance: a lot of revenue goes out but even more comes in, and the rulers and their employees live off the difference.

The low-end model is cheap. Leaders do not need huge tax revenues because they do not spend much. They get other people to do the work. Instead of paying an army, rulers rely on local elites—who may well be their kinsmen—to raise troops from their own estates. The rulers reward these lords by sharing plunder with them. Rulers who keep winning wars establish a low-end balance: not much revenue comes in but even less goes out, and the leaders and their kin live off the difference.

The biggest event in the first millennium BCE in both East and West was a shift from low-end toward high-end states. States had been drifting that way since the days of Uruk; mid-third-millennium-BCE Egyptian pharaohs already had enough bureaucratic muscle to build pyramids, and a thousand years later their successors organized complex armies of chariots. But the scale and scope of first-millennium-BCE states dwarfed all earlier efforts. The activities of states—management and fighting—therefore dominate this chapter.

Eastern and Western states took different routes toward the high end during the first millennium BCE, but both were bumpy. Eastern states, created so much later than Western ones, were still near the low end of the spectrum around 1000 BCE. The Shang state had been a loose collection of allies who sent turtles and horses to Anyang and sometimes showed up for wars; and when King Wu overthrew the Shang in 1046 BCE his Zhou state was perhaps even looser. Wu did not annex the Shang kingdom, because he had no one to run it. He simply put a puppet king over the Shang and went home to the Wei Valley (Figure 5.2).

This is a cheap way to control former enemies when it works, but in this case sibling rivalry, a perennial problem in low-end organizations,

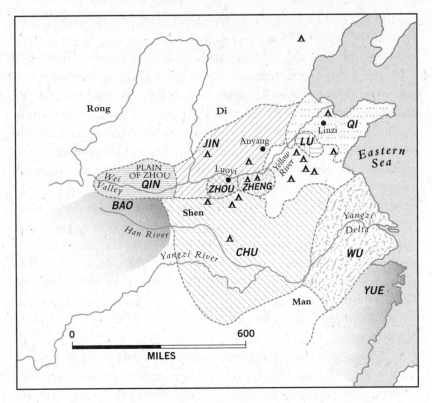

Figure 5.2. Low-end kingship in the East: sites from the first half
of the first millennium BCE mentioned in the text. Triangles
mark major Zhou colonies.

soon undid it. Wu could not rely on his family to do what he wanted.
He died in 1043 BCE, leaving behind three brothers and a son. According to the Zhou dynasty's official version, written of course by the
winners, Wu's son Cheng was too young to rule, so the Duke of Zhou,
Wu's younger brother, loyally agreed to serve as regent (many historians think the duke actually launched a coup). King Wu's two elder
brothers reacted by joining forces with the remnants of the Shang regime to resist the duke.

In 1041 BCE the Duke of Zhou won this civil war and killed his
elder brothers, but he realized he could neither rule the Shang as
cheaply as Wu had hoped nor leave them to plot against him. He came
up with a brilliant low-end solution: he would send members of the
Zhou royal clan to set up virtually independent city-states along the

Yellow River valley (between twenty-six and seventy-three of them, depending on which ancient author we believe). These cities did not pay taxes to him, but he did not have to pay them to be there either.

The Zhou kingdom really was a family business—one that had much in common with that most famous of family businesses, the Mafia. The king, effectively the Zhou family's *capo di tutti capi*, lived off huge estates in the Plain of Zhou, running them with a rudimentary bureaucracy, while his subsidiary rulers—"made men," in the Mob's terms—lived in their own fortified cities. When the king called on them, these lords provided him with muscle, showing up with chariots and troops so the king could shake down his enemies. When the fighting was over the mobsters shared the plunder and went home. Everyone was happy (except the plundered enemies).

Like bosses in *la cosa nostra*, Zhou kings offered emotional as well as material incentives to keep their captains loyal. In fact, they invested heavily in legitimacy, which is often the only thing that separates kings from gangsters. They convinced the subsidiary rulers that the king—as head of the family, master of divination and the ancestor cult, and the contact point between this and the divine world—had a right to call on them.

The more a king could rely on his kinsmen's loyalty, of course, the less he had to rely on sharing plunder. Zhou kings actively promoted a new theory of kingship: that Di, the high god in heaven, chose earthly rulers and had bestowed his mandate on the virtuous Zhou because he was disgusted by the Shang's moral failings. Stories about King Wu's virtue grew so elaborate that by the fourth century BCE the philosopher Mencius was claiming that rather than fighting the Shang, Wu had merely proclaimed, "I come to bring peace, not to wage war on the people." Immediately, "the sound of people knocking their heads on the ground [in submission] was like the toppling of a mountain."

Few—if any—Zhou lords can have believed such silliness, but the mandate-of-heaven theory did encourage them to go along with the kings. It could also be turned on its head, though: if the Zhou ceased to behave virtuously, heaven could withdraw its mandate and bestow it on someone else. And who, if not the lords, was to say whether the kings' behavior met heaven's standard?

Zhou aristocrats liked to inscribe lists of the honors they received on the bronze vessels they used in rituals to honor their ancestors, revealing nicely the combination of material and psychological rewards. One, for instance, describes how King Cheng (reigned 1035–1006 BCE) "made" a follower in an elaborate ceremony, granting him his own lordship and lands. "In the evening," the inscription says, "the lord was awarded many ax-man vassals, two hundred families, and was offered use of the chariot team in which the king rode; bronze harness-trappings, a dustcoat, a robe, cloth, and slippers."

While it worked, the Zhou racket was highly effective. Kings mobilized quite large armies (hundreds of chariots by the ninth century BCE) and won general agreement that the ancestors wanted them to squeeze protection money from "barbarian enemies" who surrounded the Zhou world. Farmers within the Zhou realm, increasingly safe from attack, worked their fields and fed growing cities. Instead of taxing the farmers, the lords extracted labor dues. In theory, fields were laid out in three-by-three grids, like tic-tac-toe boards, with eight families working the outer fields for themselves and taking turns to work the ninth field, in the middle, for their lord. Reality was doubtless messier, but the combination of peasant labor, plunder, and extortion made the elite rich. They buried one another in spectacular tombs, and while they sacrificed fewer people than the Shang aristocrats, they buried far more chariots. They cast and inscribed astounding numbers of bronze vessels (some thirteen thousand examples have been excavated and published), and although writing remained an elite tool, it spread beyond its narrow Shang-era uses.

The system had one weakness, however; it depended on a steady diet of victories. The rulers delivered for nearly a century, but in 957 BCE King Zhao failed. Failure was not something anyone wanted to write down, so all we know about it comes from a throwaway comment in the *Bamboo Annals*, a chronicle buried in a tomb in 296 BCE and rediscovered when the tomb was plundered nearly six centuries later. It says that two great lords followed King Zhao against Chu, a region south of the Zhou realm. "The heavens were dark and tempestuous," says the chronicler. "Pheasants and hares were terrified. The king's six armies perished in the River Han. The king died."

All at once the Zhou lost their army, their king, and the mystique of the mandate of heaven. Maybe, the lords apparently concluded, the Zhou were not so virtuous after all. Their problems compounded: after 950 BCE inscriptions on bronze vessels found at the eastern end of the

Yellow River stop professing loyalty to the Zhou, and as the kings struggled to keep these vassals in line they lost control of "barbarian enemies" in the west, who began threatening the Zhou cities.

With the supply of newly conquered territories running low, elite
conflict over land apparently increased. Faced with a meltdown in his
low-end state, King Mu turned toward higher-cost solutions by building up a bureaucracy after 950 BCE. Some Zhou kings (we aren't sure
which ones) then used their administrators to transfer land between
families, perhaps to reward loyalty and punish betrayal, but the aristocracy pushed back. Piecing together the story from brief accounts on
bronze vessels, it sounds like someone deposed King Yih in 885 BCE,
only for the "many lords" to restore him; and then Yih went to war
with the greatest of these lords, Marquis Ai of Qi, boiling him alive in
a bronze cauldron in 863. In 842 the "many lords" struck back, and
King Li, like some Mob boss going to the mattresses as treacherous
captains try to take him out, fled into exile.

At the other end of Eurasia, Western kings were also building
low-end states in the tenth and ninth centuries BCE. How the Western
core pulled out of its post-1200 BCE slump is almost as unclear as how
the slump began, but the inventiveness born of desperation probably
played a part. The collapse of long-distance trade had forced people to
fall back on local resources, but some vital goods—above all tin, essential for making bronze—were just not available in many places.*
Westerners therefore learned to use iron instead. Smiths on Cyprus,
which had long been home to the world's most advanced metallurgy,
had already figured out before 1200 BCE how to extract a serviceable
metal from the ugly red and black iron ores that crop up all around the
Mediterranean, but so long as bronze was available iron remained
merely a novelty item. The drying up of the tin supply changed all
that, making it iron or nothing, and by 1000 BCE the new, cheap metal
was in use from Greece to what is now Israel (Figure 5.3).

Back in the 1940s Gordon Childe, one of the giants of European
archaeology, suggested, "Cheap iron democratized agriculture and industry and warfare too." Another sixty years of excavations has left us
little clearer about exactly how this worked, but Childe was certainly
right that iron's easy availability made metal weapons and tools more

---

*The Western core's main tin source was in southeastern Anatolia.

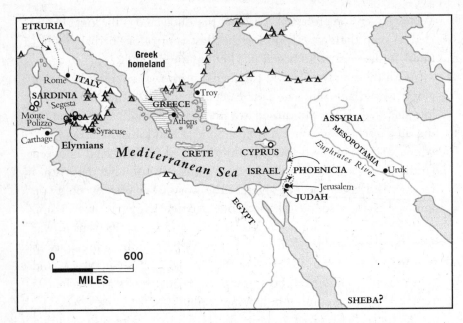

Figure 5.3. Low-end kingship in the West: sites of the first half of the first millennium BCE mentioned in the text. Triangles mark major Greek colonies; open circles, major Phoenician colonies. The Greek homeland is shaded.

common in the first millennium BCE than they had been in the second; and when trade routes revived, no one went back to bronze for weapons or tools.

The first part of the Western core to revive after the dark age may have been Israel, where, the Hebrew Bible says, the tenth-century BCE kings David and Solomon created a "United Monarchy" stretching from the borders of Egypt to the Euphrates. Its capital at Jerusalem boomed, we are told, and Solomon feted the queen of distant Sheba (perhaps in Yemen) and sent trading missions across the Mediterranean. While smaller and weaker than the International Age kingdoms, the United Monarchy sounds more centralized than the contemporary Zhou family business, extracting taxes and drawing in tribute from all around. It may have been the strongest state in the world until its components, the peoples of Israel and Judah, abruptly parted ways on Solomon's death around 931 BCE.

Unless, that is, none of these things actually happened. Many biblical scholars believe there was no United Monarchy. The whole thing was a fantasy, they argue, dreamed up by Israelites centuries later to console themselves about the dire situation in their own day. Archaeologists have certainly had trouble finding the great building projects that the Bible says David and Solomon undertook, and debates have become alarmingly fierce. In the normal run of things, even the most dedicated archaeologists have been known to doze off in seminars about the chronology of ancient storage vessels, but when one archaeologist suggested in the 1990s that pots normally dated to the tenth century BCE were in fact made in the ninth century—which would mean that monumental buildings previously associated with Solomon, in the tenth century, must also date a hundred years later, in turn meaning that Solomon's kingdom was a poor and undistinguished place and the Hebrew Bible has the story wrong—he provoked such rage that he had to hire a bodyguard.

These are troubled waters. Not having a bodyguard, I will get out of them quickly. It seems to me that the biblical account, like the Chinese traditions about the Xia and Shang discussed in Chapter 4, may be exaggerated but is unlikely to be totally fanciful; and evidence from other parts of the Western core also suggests that revival was under way by the late tenth century BCE. In 926 Sheshonq I, a Libyan warlord who had seized the Egyptian throne, led an army through Judah (the southern part of modern Israel and the West Bank) in what looks like an attempt to restore the old Egyptian Empire. He failed, but in the north a still greater power was also stirring. After a hundred-year gap during the dark age, Assyrian royal records restarted in 934 BCE under King Ashur-dan II, giving us a glimpse of a gangster state that made the Zhou look angelic.

Ashur-dan was very conscious that Assyria was recovering from a dark age. "I brought back the exhausted peoples of Assyria who had abandoned their cities and houses in the face of want, hunger, and famine, and had gone up to other lands," he wrote. "I settled them in cities and houses . . . and they dwelt in peace." In some ways Ashur-dan was an old-fashioned king, seeing himself as the earthly representative of Assyria's patron god Ashur, much as Mesopotamian kings had been doing for two thousand years. Ashur, though, had had a makeover during the dark age. He had become an angry god; in fact, a very angry god, because although *he* knew he was top god, most mortals failed to grasp this. Ashur-dan's job was to make them grasp it by turning the world into Ashur's hunting ground. And if hunting for Ashur made Ashur-dan rich, that was fine too.

Within Assyria's heartland the king commanded a small bureaucracy and appointed governors called Sons of Heaven, giving them huge estates and labor forces. These were high-end practices that would have been familiar to any International Age ruler, but the Assyrian king's real power had low-end sources. Rather than taxing Assyria to pay for an army to do Ashur's hunting, the king relied on the Sons of Heaven to provide troops, rewarding them—as Zhou kings did with their lords—with plunder, exotic gifts, and a place in royal rituals. The Sons of Heaven leveraged this position to win thirty-year terms of office, effectively turning their estates into hereditary fiefs and their laborers into serfs.

Just like Zhou rulers, Assyrian kings were hostages to the lords' goodwill, but so long as they won wars that did not matter. The Sons of Heaven provided much bigger armies than Zhou vassal kings (according to royal accounts, fifty thousand infantry in the 870s BCE and more than a hundred thousand in 845, plus thousands of chariots), and the kings' relatively high-end bureaucracy provided the logistical support to feed and move these hosts.

Not surprisingly, the rulers of Assyria's smaller, weaker neighbors generally preferred buying protection to being impaled on pointed sticks while their cities burned. An offer from the Assyrians was normally one they couldn't refuse, particularly since Assyria often left submissive local kings in power rather than using the Zhou strategy of replacing them with colonists. Defeated kings could even end up profiting; if they loaned Assyria troops for its next war, they could get a cut of the plunder.

Client kings might be tempted to back out of their deals, though, so Assyria focused their minds with holy terror. Those who submitted did not have to worship Ashur, but they did have to recognize that Ashur ruled heaven and told their own gods what to do—which made rebellion a religious offense against Ashur as well as a political one, giving the Assyrians no choice but to punish it as savagely as possible. Assyrian kings decorated their palaces with carved scenes of horrific brutality, and their glee in cataloguing massacres rapidly becomes mind-numbing. Take, for instance, Ashurnasirpal II's account of the punishments meted out to rebels around 870 BCE:

I built a tower over against his city gate and I flayed all the chiefs who had revolted, and I covered the tower with their skin. Some I walled up within the tower, some I impaled upon the tower on stakes, and others I bound to stakes around the tower . . .

Many captives from among them I burned with fire, and many I took as living captives. From some I cut off their noses, their ears, and their fingers, of many I put out the eyes. I made one pile of the living and another of heads, and I hung their heads from tree trunks round about the city. Their young men and maidens I burned up in the fire. Twenty men I captured alive and I walled them up in his palace . . . The rest of the warriors I consumed with thirst in the desert.

The political fortunes of the Eastern and Western cores were moving in different directions in the ninth century BCE, with Zhou rule unraveling while Assyria was reviving after the dark age, but both cores experienced constant warfare, growing cities, more trade, and new, low-cost ways to run states. And in the eighth century BCE they found something else in common: both discovered the limits of kingship on the cheap.

THE WINDS OF CHANGE

It's an ill wind, the saying goes, that blows nobody any good. Never was this truer than around 800 BCE, when minor wobbles in Earth's axis generated stronger winter winds all over the northern hemisphere (Figure 5.4). In western Eurasia, where the main winter winds are "westerlies" blowing from the Atlantic, this meant more winter rain. This was good for people in the Mediterranean Basin, where the commonest cause of death had always been intestinal viruses that flourish in hot, dry weather, and the main problem for farmers was that the winter winds might not bring enough rain for good harvests. Cold and rain were better than sickness and hunger.

The new climate regime was bad, though, for people north of the Alps, where the main killers were respiratory diseases that flourished in the cold and damp and the main agricultural problem was a short summer growing season. As the weather changed between 800 and 500 BCE population fell in northern and western Europe but rose around the Mediterranean.

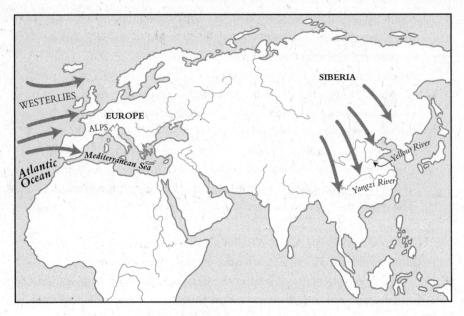

Figure 5.4. The chill winds of winter: climate change in the
early first millennium BCE

In China the winter winds blow mainly from Siberia, so when they grew stronger after 800 BCE they made the weather drier as well as cooler. This probably made agriculture easier around the Yangzi and Yellow rivers by reducing flooding, and population kept growing in both valleys, but it made life harder for people on the increasingly arid plateau north of the Yellow River.

Within these broad patterns there were countless local variations, but the main result was like the episodes of climate change we saw in Chapter 4; the balances within and between regions shifted, forcing people to respond. The author of a standard textbook on paleoclimatology says of these years, "If such a disruption of the climate system were to occur today, the social, economic, and political consequences would be nothing short of catastrophic."

In East and West alike the same amount of land had to feed more mouths as population grew. This generated both conflicts and innovations. Both could potentially be good for rulers; more conflicts meant more chances to help friends and punish enemies, more innovations meant more wealth being generated, and the engine behind both—more people—meant more laborers, more warriors, and more plunder.

All these good things could come to kings who kept control, but the low-end kings of the eighth century BCE found that difficult. The big winners, best placed to exploit new opportunities, were often local bosses—the governors, landlords, and garrison commanders on whom low-end kings relied to get things done. This was bad news for kings.

In the 770s BCE Eastern and Western kings alike lost control of their vassals. The Egyptian state, more or less unified since 945 BCE, split into three principalities in 804 and devolved by 770 into a dozen virtually independent dukedoms. In Assyria, Shamshi-Adad V had to fight to secure his succession to the throne in 823 BCE, then lost control of his client kings and governors. Some Sons of Heaven even waged wars in their own names. Assyriologists call the years 783 through 744 BCE "the interval," a time when kings counted for little, coups were common, and governors did what they liked.

For local aristocrats, minor princes, and little city-states, this was a golden age. The most interesting case is Phoenicia, a string of cities along the modern Lebanese coast, whose inhabitants had been prospering as middlemen since the Western core revived in the tenth century BCE, carrying goods between Egypt and Assyria. Their wealth attracted Assyrian attention, though, and by 850 the Phoenicians were paying protection money. Some historians think this pushed Phoenicians to venture into the Mediterranean in search of profits to buy peace; others suspect that the growing population and pull of new markets in the Mediterranean was more important. Either way, by 800 BCE Phoenicians were voyaging far afield, setting up trade enclaves on Cyprus and even building a little shrine on Crete. By 750 the Greek poet Homer could take it for granted that his audience knew (and mistrusted) "Phoenician men, famous for their ships, gnawers at profit, bringing countless pretty things in each dark hull."

The Greek population grew fastest of all, though, and Phoenician explorers and traders may have pulled hungry Greeks along in their wake. By 800 BCE someone was carrying Greek pottery to southern Italy, and by 750 Greeks as well as Phoenicians were settling permanently in the western Mediterranean (see Figure 5.3). Both groups liked good harbors with access via rivers to markets in the interior, but the Greeks, who came in much greater numbers than the Phoenicians, also settled as farmers and grabbed some of the best coastal land.

Native groups sometimes resisted. Some, such as the tribesmen of Etruria and Sardinia in Italy, already had towns and long-distance trade before the colonists came; now they built cities and monuments, organized low-end states, and intensified agriculture. They created alphabets based on the Greek model (which the Greeks, in turn, had adapted from Phoenicia between 800 and 750 BCE). These alphabets were easier to learn and use than most earlier scripts, which had needed hundreds of signs, each representing a consonant-plus-vowel syllable; and much easier than the Egyptian hieroglyphic or Chinese scripts, which needed thousands of signs, each expressing a separate word. By the best guess, in the fifth century BCE 10 percent of Athenian men could read simple statements or write their own name—far more than anywhere in the East or West at any earlier time.

We know much more about the spread of cities, states, trade, and writing into first-millennium-BCE Europe than about the spread of agriculture four or five thousand years earlier (discussed in Chapter 2), but the arguments over what happened in each case are strangely similar. Some archaeologists claim that colonization from the eastern Mediterranean in the first millennium BCE caused the rise of cities and states farther west; others respond that native peoples transformed their own societies in resistance to colonialism. Members of the latter group, mostly younger scholars, sometimes accuse the former group of projecting onto the ancient world nostalgia for the self-proclaimed civilizing missions of modern colonial regimes; while some of the former group, mostly of an older generation, reply that their critics are more interested in posing as champions of the oppressed than in finding out what really happened.

The name-calling is admittedly tame compared to the rage that the archaeology of Israel generates (so far as I know no one has needed a bodyguard yet), but by the genteel standards of classical scholarship it counts as bitter controversy. It was enough to draw me in, anyway, and in an effort to make sense of the issues I spent my summers between 2000 and 2006 excavating a Sicilian site called Monte

Polizzo.* This was an indigenous town occupied between 650 and 525 BCE by people called Elymians. It was so close to Phoenician and Greek colonies that we could see them from the summit of our hill, making it an ideal place to test competing theories of whether colonization or indigenous development caused the western Mediterranean takeoff. And after seven summers of picking, troweling, sieving, counting, weighing, and eating too much pasta, our conclusion is: it was a bit of both.

This is, of course, pretty much the same conclusion archaeologists have reached about the expansion of agriculture thousands of years earlier. In each case, social development rose in both the core and in the peripheries around it. Traders and colonists left the core, whether pushed out by rivals or pulled by tempting opportunities, and some people in the peripheries actively copied core practices or independently created their own versions. The result was that higher levels of social development spread outward from the core, overlaying earlier systems and being transformed in the process as people in the peripheries added their own twists and discovered the advantages in their backwardness.

At Monte Polizzo local initiatives were clearly important. For one thing, we suspect that our site was destroyed by fellow Elymians from Segesta, who created their own city-state in the sixth century BCE. But the arrival of Greek colonists was also critical, since Segestan state formation was partly a response to Greek competition for land and was massively shaped by Greek culture. Segestan aristocrats struggled to look like serious rivals to the Greeks, borrowing Greek practices to do so. In fact, they built such a perfect example of a Greek-style temple in the 430s BCE that many art historians think they must have hired the architects who designed the Parthenon at Athens. Segestans also inserted themselves into Greek mythology, claiming (as Romans did too) to be descendants of Aeneas, a refugee from the fall of Troy. By

*I'd like to take this opportunity to thank once again for all their support my co-directors Sebastiano Tusa (formerly superintendent of archaeology for Trapani Province), Kristian Kristiansen (University of Gothenburg), Christopher Prescott (University of Oslo), Michael Kolb (Northern Illinois University), and Emma Blake (University of Arizona), superintendents Rossella Giglio and Caterina Greco, the people of Salemi (especially Giovanni Bascone and Nicola Spagnolo), the many donors who made the Stanford project possible, and all the students and staff who took part in the project.

the fifth century BCE colonial cities in the western Mediterranean such as Carthage (a Phoenician settlement) and Syracuse (a Greek one) rivaled any in the old core. Etruscan social development was not far behind, and dozens of groups like the Elymians trailed not far behind them.

A rather similar process of state breakdown in the core combined with expansion on the periphery also unfolded in the East as population grew. Around 810 BCE the Zhou king Xuan lost control of his lords, who saw less and less reason to cooperate with him as they themselves grew richer and stronger. Xuan's capital in the Plain of Zhou slid into factional conflicts and raiders from the northwest plundered deep into his kingdom. When Xuan's son You inherited the throne in 781 BCE he tried to stop the rot, apparently engineering a showdown with his surly vassals and his father's too-powerful ministers, who may have been conspiring with You's firstborn son and the boy's mother.

At this point the story descends into the kind of folktale that fills so many of our ancient sources. Sima Qian, the great historical scholar of the first century BCE, recounts a bizarre tale that an earlier Zhou king had once opened a thousand-year-old box of dragon saliva, from which a black reptile appeared. For reasons that Sima Qian leaves unclear, the king's response was to have several palace women strip naked and yell at the monster. Rather than running away, it impregnated one of them, who gave birth to a reptilian daughter but then abandoned her. Another couple, fleeing the Zhou capital to escape the king's anger over a wholly unrelated matter, carried this snake-child off to Bao, one of the rebellious vassal states in the Zhou kingdom.

The point of this odd story is that in 780 BCE the people of Bao decided to try to broker a deal with King You by sending him the dragon's offspring—now grown into a beautiful young woman named Bao Si—as a concubine. You was very happy about this, and the next year Bao Si bore him a son. This, apparently, was why You decided to get rid of his firstborn son and senior wife.

All went well for You until 777 BCE, when his exiled son fled to another restless Zhou vassal state and You's most senior minister joined the boy there. At this point a group of vassals made an alliance with northwestern people whom the Zhou called the Rong (the name simply means "hostile foreigners").

King You, heedless of all this, had turned his attention to a more immediate problem: how to make Bao Si laugh (not surprisingly, given her background, she was rather humorless). Only one thing seemed to work. You's predecessors had set up watchtowers so that if the Rong attacked, drums and fires could warn the many lords, who would rush to the rescue with their retinues. Sima Qian says,

> King You lit the beacons and beat the great drums. As the beacons were to be lit only when intruders drew near, the many lords all came. Upon their arrival, there were no intruders, thus Lady Bao Si laughed out loud. The king was pleased, so he lit the beacons several times. Afterwards, since this was not reliable, the many lords became more reluctant to come.

King You was the original boy who cried wolf, and when the Rong and rebellious Shen really did attack in 771 BCE, the many lords ignored the beacons. The rebels killed You, burned his capital, and put his estranged son on the throne with the title King Ping.

It is hard to take this story too seriously, but many historians think it does preserve memories of real events. In the 770s BCE, the same decade that Egyptian and Assyrian rulers lost control, it would seem that population growth, resurgent local power, dynastic politics, and external pressures came together in China to produce an even sharper setback for monarchy.

The vassals who left King You to his fate in 771 BCE perhaps wanted only to demonstrate their strength, install Ping as a figurehead, and carry on ignoring the monarchy. Their decision to bury their bronze ritual vessels all around the Wei valley, where archaeologists have recovered them in huge numbers since the 1970s, suggests that they planned to return as soon as the Rong went home laden with plunder from You's palace. But if this was their thinking, they were badly mistaken. The Rong came to stay, and the many lords were forced to install King Ping as head of a government-in-exile at Luoyi in the Yellow River valley.* It soon became clear that the Zhou king, Son of Heaven

*Historians conventionally call the years 1046–771 BCE the Western Zhou period; the period from the royal family's eastward migration in 771 until 481, 453, or 403 BCE (different historians choose different end-points) they speak of as the Eastern

as he might be, was impotent now he had lost his estates in the Wei Valley, and the earls of Zheng, the strongest of the "vassals," started to test their erstwhile kings. In 719 BCE one earl took the heir to the throne hostage; in 707 another earl even shot the king with an arrow.

By 700 BCE the Zhou court was almost irrelevant to the dukes, earls, viscounts, and marquises of the former colonies (one ancient source says there were now 148 of them). The leading "vassals" still claimed to be acting on behalf of the Zhou king, but in reality fought one another for supremacy without consulting their supposed ruler, making and breaking treaties at will. In 667 BCE Marquis Huan of Qi, temporarily dominant, even summoned his rivals to a conference where they acknowledged him as their leader (though they continued to fight him and everyone else). The next year Marquis Huan browbeat the king of Zhou into naming him *ba*, an "overlord" who would (theoretically) represent Zhou's interests.

Marquis Huan earned this standing largely by protecting weaker states from attacks by peoples they considered foreign—in the north, the Rong and Di, and in the south, groups known as Man. Yet the main (and surely unintended) consequence of these wars was rather similar to Phoenician and Greek colonization of the western Mediterranean, drawing the Rong, Di, and Man into the core and hugely expanding it in the process.

In the seventh century BCE states along the northern edge of the core recruited Rong and Di as allies, cementing these ties by intermarriage. Many Rong and Di leaders became versed in Zhou literature and deliberately attached themselves to border states such as Qi, Jin, and Qin, which grew much larger. In the south some Man created their own large state, Chu, as they fought with Jin and Qi in the seventh century. By the 650s BCE Chu was a full member of the interstate community, attending its conferences; and, rather like the Segestans and Romans in the West who claimed to descend from Aeneas, Chu's leaders started saying that they, like the other states in the Eastern core, had begun as a colony of Zhou. A distinct Chu material culture emerged by 600 BCE, combining core and southern elements.

Zhou. To make things more confusing, historians also regularly call 722–481 BCE the Spring and Autumn period after the main chronicle of these years, *The Springs and Autumns of the State of Lu*, and call 480–221 BCE the Warring States period.

Chu became such a power that in 583 BCE the state of Jin decided to make alliances with other Man peoples to build up enemies in Chu's rear. In 506 one of these allies, the state of Wu, was strong enough to smash Chu's army; so strong, in fact, that in 482 the Marquis of Jin yielded his status as *ba* to Viscount Fuchai of Wu—who, like the kings of Chu, now claimed Zhou ancestry. By then yet another southern state, Yue, had also become a major power. Its viscounts tried to trump Wu ideologically by claiming descent from the earliest dynasty of all, the Xia; and in 473 BCE, after Viscount Fuchai of Wu hanged himself while Yue's armies besieged his capital, Yue's viscount took his place as *ba*. Despite its political breakdown, the Eastern core had expanded just as dramatically as the Western.

TOWARD THE HIGH END

The years 750–500 BCE were the turning point when history didn't turn. In 750 BCE Western social development was pushing twenty-four points, just where it had been on the eve of the great collapse in 1200 BCE; by 500 BCE so, too, was the East's. Just as happened around 1200, the climate was changing, peoples were migrating, conflict was escalating, new states were pushing into the cores, and old states were coming apart. New collapses seemed entirely possible, but both cores instead restructured themselves, developing the economic, political, and intellectual resources to manage the challenges that faced them. That is what makes Figure 5.1 so dull—and so interesting.

We see the changes first in Assyria. The upstart who usurped the throne in 744 BCE under the name Tiglath-Pileser III at first looked much like all the other pretenders who had pulled the same stunt since the 780s, yet in less than twenty years he catapulted Assyria from a broken, low-end state to a dynamic, high-end one. Along the way he converted himself, like some mafioso going legitimate, from a gangster boss into a great (but brutal) king.

His secret was cutting the aristocratic Sons of Heaven out of the deal. Tiglath-Pileser did this by creating a standing army, paid by and loyal to him alone, instead of having his lords provide troops. The surviving texts do not say how he did this, but somehow he dragooned prisoners of war into forming a personal army. When it won battles,

Tiglath-Pileser used the loot to pay his own troops directly instead of sharing it with his lords. Supported by the army, he then broke the nobles' power, subdividing top offices and filling many with captured eunuchs. Eunuchs had two advantages—they could not have sons to pass their positions to, and were held in such contempt by the traditional aristocracy that they were unlikely to lead rebellions. Above all, Tiglath-Pileser hugely expanded the bureaucracy to run his state, stepping over the old elite to create administrators loyal entirely to him.

All this was expensive, so Tiglath-Pileser regularized his finances. Instead of shaking down foreigners by showing up periodically and demanding payoffs, he insisted on regular contributions—basically, taxes. If a client king argued, Tiglath-Pileser replaced him with an Assyrian governor. In 735 BCE, for instance, King Pekah of Israel joined Damascus and other Syrian cities in a tax revolt (Figure 5.5). Tiglath-Pileser came down on them like a wolf on the fold. He destroyed Damascus in 732 BCE, installed a governor, and annexed Israel's fertile

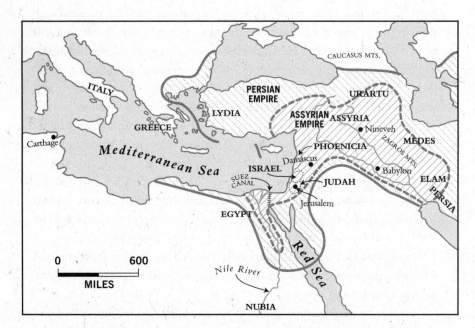

Figure 5.5. The first high-end empires. The broken line marks the maximum extent of the Assyrian Empire, around 660 BCE, and the solid line the maximum extent of the Persian Empire, around 490 BCE.

northern valleys. Pekah's unhappy subjects assassinated him and enthroned the pro-Assyrian King Hoshea instead.

All went well until Tiglath-Pileser died in 727 BCE. Hoshea, assuming that the new Assyrian system would die with him, stopped paying, but Tiglath-Pileser's institutions proved robust enough to survive a change at the top. In 722 Assyria's new king, Shalmaneser, devastated Israel, killed Hoshea, installed a governor, and deported tens of thousands of Israelites. Between 934 and 612 BCE Assyria in fact forcibly moved some 4.5 million people from one place to another. Deportees filled Assyria's armies, built its cities, and worked on projects to raise the empire's productivity—damming rivers, planting trees, tending olives, and digging canals. The labor of the dispossessed fed Nineveh and Babylon, each of which grew to a hundred thousand residents, dwarfing earlier cities and sucking in resources from all around. Social development surged upward; by 700 BCE Assyria was stronger than any previous state in history.

Did Tiglath-Pileser change the course of history by heading off collapse in the eighth century? At one time historians unhesitatingly said yes, but nowadays most shy away from attributing so much to the will of unique great men. In this case, they are probably right. Great Tiglath-Pileser might have been, if that is the label we want to use for ruthlessness, but he was not unique. All over the Western core late-eighth-century-BCE rulers hit on centralization as the solution to their woes. In Egypt, Nubians from what is now Sudan reunited the country even before Tiglath-Pileser seized Assyria's throne, and over the next thirty years instituted reforms he would have recognized. By the 710s BCE even little Judah's King Hezekiah was doing the same.

Rather than a single genius changing history, this looks like desperate men trying out every idea that came along, with the best solutions winning. It was centralize or perish; rulers who failed to get local chiefs under control were crushed by those who succeeded. Hezekiah, worried about Assyria, felt compelled to strengthen Judah; Assyria's new king, Sennacherib, worried about Hezekiah's strength, felt compelled to stop him. In 701 BCE Sennacherib plundered Judah and carried off its people. He spared Jerusalem, whether because (as the Hebrew Bible says) the Angel of the Lord smote the Assyrians or because (as Sennacherib's account says) Hezekiah agreed to pay more tribute.

Either way, Sennacherib's victory brought him face-to-face with a harsh new reality: every war that Assyria won simply generated new enemies. When Tiglath-Pileser annexed northern Syria in the early 730s BCE, Damascus and Israel organized against him; when Shalmaneser conquered Damascus and Israel between 732 and 722 BCE, Judah became the front line; and cowing Judah in 701 BCE merely made Egypt a threat, so in the 670s Assyria overran the Nile Valley. Egypt, though, turned out to be a country too far, and by the time the Assyrians withdrew ten years later, problems were plaguing all their frontiers. Destroying Urartu, their main enemy to the north, had exposed them to devastating raids from the Caucasus; sacking Babylon, their main enemy to the south, only generated wars with Elam, farther southeast; and destroying Elam in the 640s BCE merely freed the Medes of the Zagros Mountains to become a threat and allowed Babylon to regain its strength.

In his influential book *The Rise and Fall of the Great Powers*, the Yale University historian Paul Kennedy argued that in the past five hundred years, the need to fight great wars has consistently forced European states to overreach, undermining their strength so much that they collapsed. Despite leaping to a high-end model with huge revenue flows, a professional army, and a bureaucracy, and despite defeating all rivals, Assyria ended up as a poster child for such imperial overreach. By 630 BCE it was in retreat everywhere, and in 612 BCE a league of Medes and Babylonians sacked Nineveh and divided its empire.

Assyria's abrupt fall repeated a pattern we saw in Chapter 4, in which military upheavals enlarge a core by giving previously peripheral peoples the chance to push their way in. Media adopted many of Assyria's institutions and policies; Babylon once again became a great power; and Egypt tried to re-create its long-lost empire in the Levant. The tussle over Assyria's carcass also kept the expansionary dynamic going. Median centralization turned another peripheral people, the Persians of southwest Iran, into a formidable power. In 550 BCE the Persian warlord Cyrus overthrew the Medes, his path smoothed by Median factional fighting. (The Median king rather foolishly put the army he sent against Cyrus under a general whom he had previously forced to eat the flesh of his own murdered son. The general promptly defected, the army collapsed, and Cyrus took over.)

Like Assyrian kings before them, Persia's rulers believed they were on a mission from God. As they saw it, their family, the Achaemenids, represented the earthly interests of Ahuramazda, the god of light and truth, in his eternal struggle with darkness and evil. Other people's gods, they convinced themselves, saw the justice of their cause, and wanted them to win. Thus, when Cyrus took Babylon in 539 BCE he claimed (apparently sincerely) to have done so to liberate Babylon's gods from corrupt rulers who neglected them. When he followed this up by sending the Jews back to Jerusalem, whence the Babylonians had carried them into captivity in 586 BCE, the authors of the Hebrew Bible even confirmed Cyrus' high opinion of himself. Their own god, they insisted, thought of Cyrus as "my shepherd . . . my anointed . . . whose right hand I have grasped to subdue nations before him and strip kings of their robes."

Cyrus led his armies to the Aegean Sea and the borders of what are now Kazakhstan, Afghanistan, and Pakistan. His son Cambyses conquered and held Egypt, then, in a story quite as bizarre as anything in Sima Qian, his distant relative Darius seized the throne in 521 BCE. According to the Greek historian Herodotus, Cambyses misinterpreted a dream as meaning that his brother Smerdis was plotting against him, and had Smerdis secretly murdered. To Cambyses' horror, though, a priest—who happened to be named Smerdis too, and happened to look exactly like the dead Smerdis—now seized the throne, pretending to be the real Smerdis. Cambyses jumped onto his horse to rush home and reveal the fraud (and the fact that he had murdered his own brother) but accidentally stabbed himself in the thigh and died. Meanwhile, Fake Smerdis was exposed when one of his wives discovered that he had no ears (Fake Smerdis' ears having been cut off as a punishment some time earlier). Seven noblemen then murdered Fake Smerdis and held a contest for the throne: each plotter brought his horse to a chosen place, the plan being that whoever's horse neighed first when the sun rose would become king. Darius won (he cheated).

Remarkably, this turned out to be as good a way to choose a king as any,* and Darius quickly proved himself to be a new Tiglath-Pileser.

---

*If it's true, that is. Most historians suspect that Darius actually murdered the genuine Smerdis and overthrew a priestly clique around him.

So effectively did he maximize revenue from his realm of perhaps 30 million subjects, Herodotus recorded, that "the Persians like to say that Darius was a shopkeeper . . . [who] made a profit on everything."

Darius followed the money, which drew him west, to where rising social development had revived the Mediterranean frontier. By 500 BCE traders acting for themselves rather than working for palaces and temples had created a vibrant economy, driving the costs of seaborne transport down so much that they could make profits by shipping bulk goods such as food as well as luxuries. Around 600 BCE people in Lydia, in western Anatolia, started stamping lumps of metal to guarantee their weight, and by Darius' day this innovation—coinage—was in widespread use, speeding up commerce still further. Living standards rose: by 400 BCE the average Greek consumed perhaps 25–50 percent more than his or her predecessor had done three centuries earlier. Houses were bigger, diets more varied, and people lived longer.

Darius tapped into this Mediterranean economy by hiring Phoenicians to man Persia's first fleet, cutting a Suez canal linking the Mediterranean and Red seas, and grabbing control of Greek cities. According to Herodotus, he sent spies to scope out Italy and even considered attacking Carthage.

By the time Darius died in 486 BCE, Western social development was a good 10 percent higher than the twenty-four points it had reached around 1200 BCE. Irrigation farming in Egypt and Mesopotamia had steadily increased yields; Babylon may have had 150,000 residents (the city was so big, says Herodotus, that when Cyrus captured it, it took days for the news to reach some neighborhoods); Persian armies were so big (again, according to Herodotus) that they drank whole rivers dry; and, as we have already seen, perhaps as many as one Athenian man in ten could write his name.

Eastern scores were also reaching twenty-four points, and processes of state restructuring and centralization much like those the West had known since the eighth century BCE were under way. The breakdown of Zhou authority since 771 BCE had been a mixed blessing for the rulers of the former vassal states. It set them free to fight one another, which they did with a vengeance, but breakdown did not stop at that point. The dukes and viscounts who had formerly been unruly vassals, obligated to the Zhou king but exploiting the fact that he relied on them for troops, now found that their own aristocrats were every bit as unruly as they had been. One solution was to end-run the aristocrats by bringing outsiders into the state, as Tiglath-Pileser had done when he filled his army with prisoners of war. Four big states on the edges of the Zhou world (Jin, Qi, Chu, and Qin; see Figure 5.2) started doing this in the seventh century and grew strong.

As early as 690 BCE Chu, less fettered by Zhou-era aristocratic norms than states in the Yellow River valley, created new administrative districts with governors reporting directly to the palace. Other states copied this. In the 660s BCE Marquis Xian, ruler of Jin, tried a more drastic solution, massacring the heads of his state's leading families and appointing ministers who, he hoped, would be more obedient. Other states copied this too. In 594 Marquis Xuan of Lu found another path around his peers; by remitting the peasants' labor dues to their local lords, he effectively gave them title to the land they worked, in return for military service and taxes paid directly to him. Other states, I hardly need add, rushed to copy this policy as well.

Modernizing rulers created bigger armies, fought harsher wars, and capitalized on economic growth like that in the West. Peasants, more willing to work to improve land when it was their own, pushed up yields by developing better crops and investing in ox-drawn plows. Iron farm tools spread, and fifth-century-BCE blacksmiths learned to use bellows to heat iron ore to 2,800°F, at which point it melted and could be cast.* Craftsmen in Wu even manipulated iron's carbon content to produce true steel.

Cities boomed—Linzi in Lu probably had fifty thousand residents by 500 BCE—and as in the West, their demand encouraged private merchants to bring them food. In 625 BCE a minister in Lu abolished border checkpoints to make trade easier. Waterborne commerce flourished and Jin and the Zhou court at Luoyi introduced bronze coins, independent from their invention in the West. In another parallel with the West, economic growth raised living standards but also increased inequality. Tax rates drifted upward, from 10 percent in the early sixth century to 20 percent a hundred years later. Lords built icehouses in their palaces; peasants slid into debt.

---

*By the first century BCE cast iron was common in China; wrought iron, made by heating ore to 1,650°F and repeatedly hammering the soft "bloom" this produces, was the only technique known in the West until the fourteenth century CE.

When Western economic expansion took off in the sixth century BCE, kings had already reasserted their power, but in the East growth just exacerbated the rulers' problems, since the ministers who replaced their fractious lords normally themselves came from powerful lineages. Ministers were often better placed than their masters to capture the fruits of growth, and regularly developed into rivals. In 562 BCE three ministerial lineages in Lu effectively sidelined the marquis, and in the 480s one took over the state. In Jin ministers waged a fifty-year, three-way civil war, partitioning the state in 453 BCE.

By this time, though, rulers (and those ministers who usurped power from them) had found a solution. If aristocratic ministers were as problematic as the nobles they replaced, why not go outside the state altogether, recruiting administrators from other states? These hired hands, known as *shi*—usually translated "gentlemen"—lacked the political connections to become rivals. Many, in fact, came from quite humble backgrounds, which was why they were looking for employment in the first place. The proliferation of *shi* attests to both the centralization of power and the spread of literacy. In their thousands *shi* shuffled scrolls and counted beans in quiet county offices, drifting from state to state as jobs opened up.

A happy few *shi* caught the attention of earls or marquises and rose to high station. In an interesting contrast with Western bureaucracies it was these men, rather than the rulers who hired them, who became the main characters in the literature of the day, cast as virtuous advisers helping rulers prosper by keeping them on the straight and narrow. The *Zuozhuan*, a commentary on historical documents assembled around 300 BCE, is full of such characters. My favorite is Zhaodun, a high minister to Duke Ling of Jin. "Duke Ling was no true ruler," the *Zuozhuan* says, with some understatement. "From his terrace he shot at people with a crossbow and watched them flee the bolts.* When his

---

*There is a problem here: Zhaodun's story is set around 610 BCE, but crossbows became common only in the mid fifth century. Some historians conclude from such discrepancies that the *Zuozhuan* is really a bundle of folktales, growing by accretions as they were retold over the centuries, expressing generalized ideals but telling us little about real advisers and rulers. This, though, may be too skeptical. While much in the Zhaodun story is clearly fantastic, the compilers of the *Zuozhuan* apparently had access to good sources and seem to give us at least some sense of institutional and intellectual changes.

cook prepared a dish of bears' paws that was not thoroughly done, he killed him, stuffed the body in a casket, and had his women carry it through the audience chamber."

Zhaodun remonstrated so much with Duke Ling that the ruler finally sent an assassin to silence the tiresome adviser. But when the hit man reached Zhaodun's house at dawn, the worthy *shi* was already dressed in his court robes and hard at work. Caught between horror at murdering such a good man and shame at disobeying his ruler, the killer took the only decent way out, committing suicide by smashing his head against a tree.

Further adventures followed. Duke Ling set an ambush, but Zhaodun escaped when his footman killed an attack dog with one punch and it turned out that one of the duke's troops was a man Zhaodun had saved from starvation years before. In the end, as in all *Zuozhuan* stories, Duke Ling gets his comeuppance, although as also often happens in this moralistic text, Zhaodun got blamed for not preventing it.

Other (presumably better-behaved) rulers prospered, though, and new styles of architecture speak of their growing power in the fifth century BCE. Whereas Zhou kings had built palaces on beaten-earth platforms just three or four feet high, the lords now went vertical, moving toward the high end in the most literal sense. One palace in Chu reportedly sat on a platform five hundred feet tall, said (implausibly) to reach the clouds. Another, in northern China, was called "The Platform Reaching Midway to Heaven." Rulers fortified their palaces, apparently fearing their own people as much as enemy states.

By 450 BCE Eastern rulers, like Western ones, were moving toward high-end models, raising taxes and permanent armies and managing these complex transactions with bureaucracies loyal to them alone but also independent enough to survive their deaths. Their economies were booming and social development had passed twenty-four points. In the West the core had expanded and the Persian Empire had united most of it; in the East similar processes were under way. Of the 148 states that emerged from the fall of the Zhou in 771 BCE, only 14 remained standing by 450 BCE, and just 4—Jin, Qi, Chu, and Qin— dominated the scene.

In Chapter 4, I imagined von Däniken's spacemen predicting around 1250 BCE that the cores would keep expanding and that a single empire would emerge in each. If they had come back around 450 BCE they might have felt vindicated; their prediction had not been wrong after all. Just the timing had been off.

THE CLASSICS

The aliens might also have been interested to see that earthlings were losing their taste for pretending to have hotlines to superhumans. For thousands of years godlike kings had anchored the moral order in chains of ritual, linking the humblest villager to rulers who touched heaven by sacrificing on ziggurats or slaughtering captives in cemeteries. But now, as godlike kings reinvented themselves as chief executives, the enchantment was going out of the world. "Would that I had died before or been born later," complained the seventh-century Greek poet Hesiod, "for now is truly an age of iron . . . Righteousness and Indignation, their loveliness wrapped in robes of white, depart the wide-avenued earth. They abandon mankind to join the deathless gods on Olympus; bitter sorrows will be left for mortal men; and there will be no more aid against evil."

But that was only one way of seeing things. From the shores of the Aegean to the Yellow River basin, other thinkers began developing radical new views of how the world worked. They spoke from the margins—socially, because most stood on the lower rungs of the elite; and geographically, because most came from small states on the fringes of power.* Despair not, they said (more or less); we do not need godlike kings to transcend this sullied world. Salvation is within us, not in the hands of corrupt, violent rulers.

Karl Jaspers, a German philosopher struggling at the end of World War II to make sense of the moral crisis of his own day, called the centuries around 500 BCE the "Axial Age," meaning they formed an axis around which history turned. In the Axial Age, Jaspers portentously

---

*Not all, though. The Mahavira (roughly 497–425 BCE), founding father of Jainism, came from Magadha, India's most powerful state. Zoroaster, whom some historians include among the Axial Age masters, was Iranian, although he lived—probably some time between 1400 and 600 BCE—while Persia was still marginal to the Western core. (I do not discuss Zoroaster here because the evidence is so messy.)

declared, "Man, as we know him today, came into being." Axial Age writings—Confucian and Daoist texts in the East, Buddhist and Jain documents in South Asia, and Greek philosophy and the Hebrew Bible (with its descendants the New Testament and the Koran) in the West—became the classics, timeless masterpieces that have defined the meaning of life for countless millions ever since.

This was quite an achievement for men like the Buddha and Socrates who wrote little or nothing down. It was their successors, sometimes distant ones, who recorded, embellished, or just plain made up their words. Often no one really knew what the founders themselves had thought, and their bitterly feuding heirs held councils, issued anathemas, and cast one another into the outer darkness over this question. The greatest triumph of modern philology has been to reveal that in between splitting, fighting, damning, and persecuting one another, the successors found time to write and rewrite their sacred books so many times that sifting the texts for their original meaning can be virtually impossible.

The Axial texts are also very varied. Some are collections of obscure aphorisms; others, witty dialogues; others still, poems, histories, or polemics. Some texts combine all these genres. And as a final challenge, the classics all agree that their ultimate subject, a transcendent realm beyond our own sordid world, is indefinable. Nirvana—literally "blowing out," a state of mind in which the passions of this world are snuffed out like a candle—cannot be described, said the Buddha; even trying is inappropriate. For Confucius, *ren*—often translated "humaneness"—was similarly beyond language. "The more I look up to it, the higher it is; the more I penetrate it, the harder it becomes; I see it ahead of me and suddenly it is behind . . . in speaking about it can one avoid being hesitant?" Likewise, when pressed to define *to kalon*, "the good," Socrates threw up his hands: "it's beyond me, and if I try I'll only make a fool of myself." All he could do was tell parables: the good is like a fire that casts shadows that we mistake for reality. Jesus was equally allusive about the Kingdom of Heaven, and equally fond of parables.

Most indefinable of all was *dao*, the "Way" that Daoists follow:

> *The Way that can be spoken of is not the true Way;*
> *The name that can be named is not the true name . . .*

Both may be called mysterious.
Mysterious and still more mysterious,
The gateway of all subtleties!

The second thing the classics agreed on was how to attain transcendence. There is more to Confucianism, Buddhism, Christianity, and so on than bumper-sticker slogans, but one I saw on a car outside my favorite coffee shop while I was writing this chapter summed things up nicely: "Compassion is revolution." Live ethically, renounce desire, and do unto others as you would have them do unto you, and you will change the world. All the classics urge us to turn the other cheek and offer techniques to train the self in this discipline. The Buddha used meditation; Socrates favored conversation. Jewish rabbis* urged study; Confucius agreed, and added punctilious observation of ritual and music. And within each tradition, some followers leaned toward mysticism while others took a down-to-earth, folksy line.

The process was always one of *self*-fashioning, an internal, personal reorientation toward transcendence that did not depend on godlike kings—or even, for that matter, gods. Supernatural powers, in fact, often seem beside the point in Axial thought. Confucius and the Buddha refused to talk about divinities; Socrates, though professing piety, was condemned partly for failing to believe in Athens's gods; and rabbis warned Jews that God was so ineffable that they should not mention his name or praise him too much.

Kings fared even worse than gods in Axial thought. Daoists and the Buddha were largely indifferent to them, but Confucius, Socrates, and Jesus openly upbraided rulers for ethical shortcomings. Axial critiques troubled the good and the great, and the new questions being raised about birth, wealth, gender, race, and caste could be positively countercultural.

In picking out these similarities between the Eastern, Western, and South Asian classics I am not trying to gloss over their equally real differences. No one would mistake the Tripitaka (the "Three Baskets" of the Buddhist canon) for Plato's *Republic* or Confucius' *Analects*, but neither would anyone mistake Confucius' *Analects* for competing Chi-

---

*The rabbinic schools flourished particularly in the first century BCE and the first few centuries CE.

nese classics such as the Daoist *Zhuangzi* or the "Legalist" *Book of Lord Shang*. The years 500–300 BCE were, in Chinese tradition, "the age when a hundred schools of thought contended," and I want to take a moment to look at the extraordinary range of ideas within this single regional tradition.

Confucius took the eleventh-century-BCE Duke of Zhou as his model of virtue and defined his goal as being to restore the moral excellence of the duke's time by reinstating its system of ritual. "I transmit but do not create," Confucius said. "I am an admirer of antiquity." Archaeology, though, suggests that Confucius actually knew rather little about the duke's distant era. It was not the duke but a broad and much later "ritual revolution" around 850 BCE that had given Zhou society restrained, carefully graded rites, assigning all members of a broad elite to places in a hierarchy. Then, around 600 BCE, rituals had changed again as a few superpowerful men began being buried with huge wealth, setting themselves above the rest of the elite.

Confucius, one of the educated but not particularly rich *shi*, was probably reacting against this second change, idealizing the stable ritual order that flourished between 850 and 600 BCE and projecting it back onto the Duke of Zhou. "To subdue oneself and return to ritual," Confucius insisted, "is to practice humaneness (*ren*)." This meant caring more about the living family than about ancestors; valuing honest reverence over showy sanctimony; esteeming virtue, not descent; performing rituals accurately with simple equipment; and following precedent. Confucius insisted that if he could persuade just one ruler to practice *ren*, everyone would imitate him and the world would find peace.

The fifth-century-BCE thinker Mozi, however, disagreed completely. As he saw it, Confucius had misunderstood *ren*. It meant *doing* good, not *being* good, and was about everyone, not just your family. Mozi rejected rituals, music, and the Duke of Zhou. Even though people are hungry and suffering violence, he said, Confucians "act like beggars, scoff food like hamsters, ogle like he-goats, and waddle about like castrated pigs." Dressing in coarse clothes, sleeping rough, and eating gruel, Mozi went among the poor and preached *jian ai*, a combination of universal sympathy and rigid egalitarianism. "Regard another's state as you regard your own, another's family as you regard your own, and another's person as you regard your own," he said. "The reason why the world's calamities, dispossessions, resentments, and hatreds arise is lack of *jian ai*." Mozi undertook diplomacy to avert wars, walking until his sandals disintegrated. He even sent his cultlike following of 180 young men to fight to the death to defend an unjustly attacked state.

The thinkers who are normally grouped under the heading of Daoists, however, were as unimpressed by Mozi as they were by Confucius. The Way of the Universe is change, they argued: night into day, joy into sorrow, life into death. Nothing is fixed, nothing definable. Humans eat beef, deer eat grass, centipedes eat snakes, owls eat rats; who can say which is the best diet? What Confucians call true, Daoists noted, followers of Mozi call false, but in reality everything is connected to everything else. No one knows where the Way leads. We must become one with the Way, but cannot do so through frantic activity.

Zhuangzi, one of the Daoist masters, told a story about another great Daoist named Liezi. After seeking the Way for years, Liezi realized he was learning nothing, and returned home.

> For three years [says Zhuangzi] he did not go out. He cooked for his wife and tended the pigs as if they were humans. He showed no interest in his studies. He cast aside his desires and sought the truth. In his body he became like the ground itself. In the midst of everything he remained enclosed with the One and that is how he remained until the end.

Zhuangzi thought that Liezi made Confucius' and Mozi's activism look ridiculous—and dangerous. "You can't bear the sufferings of this one generation," Zhuangzi imagined someone saying to Confucius, "therefore you go and cause trouble for ten thousand generations to come. Do you set out to be this miserable, or don't you realize what you are doing? . . . What is wrong cannot but harm and what is active cannot fail to be wrong." Mozi, by contrast, struck Zhuangzi as "one of the good of this world," but someone who took the fun out of life. "Mohists wear skins and coarse cloth, wooden shoes or hemp sandals, never stop night and day, and view such fervent activity as their highest achievement." Yet this only produced "A life that is laborious and a death that is insignificant . . . Even if Mozi himself could stand it," Zhuangzi asked, "how can the rest of the world be expected to live this way?"

Mozi rejected Confucius; Zhuangzi rejected Confucius *and* Mozi; but the so-called Legalist Tradition rejected them all. Legalism was the anti-Axial option, more Machiavellian than Machiavelli. *Ren*, *jian ai*, and *dao*, Legalists felt, all missed the point. Trying to transcend reality was stupid: godlike kings had yielded to managerial, efficiency-seeking ones, and the rest of us should get with the program. For Lord Shang, a fourth-century-BCE chief minister of Qin and Legalism's guiding light, the goal was not humaneness; it was "the enrichment of the state and the strengthening of its military capacity." Do not do unto others as you would have them do unto you, said Lord Shang, because "If in enterprises you undertake what the enemy would be ashamed to do, you have the advantage." Neither be good nor do good, because "A state that uses the wicked to govern the good always enjoys order and becomes strong." And waste no time on rituals, activism, or fatalism. Instead draw up comprehensive law codes with brutal penalties (beheading, burial alive, hard labor) and impose them rigidly on everyone. Like a carpenter's square, Legalists liked to say, laws force messy materials to conform.

Chinese Axial thought ranged from mysticism to authoritarianism, and was constantly evolving. The third-century-BCE scholar Xunzi, for instance, combined Confucianism with Mozi's ideas and Daoism and sought middle ground with Legalism. Plenty of Legalists welcomed Mozi's work ethic and the Daoists' acceptance of things. Over the centuries ideas were combined and recombined in kaleidoscopic complexity.

Much the same was true of Axial thought in South Asia and the West. I will not work through these traditions in detail, but even a quick look at the small land of Greece gives a sense of the bubbling cauldron of ideas. Godlike kingship may have been weaker in Greece before 1200 BCE than in the older states of southwest Asia, and by 700 Greeks had rejected it decisively. That, perhaps, was why they went on to confront even more starkly than others in the Axial Age the question of what a good society should look like in the absence of rulers who tapped into another world.

One Greek response was to seek the good through collective politics. If no one had access to supernatural wisdom, some Greeks asked, why not pool the limited knowledge each man does have to create a (male) democracy? This was a distinctive idea—not even Mozi had thought of it—and long-term lock-in theorists often suggest that the Greek invention of male democracy marks a decisive rupture between the West and the rest.

By this point in the book it will probably be no surprise to hear that I am not convinced. Western social development had been higher than Eastern for fourteen thousand years before Greeks started voting on things, and the West's lead barely changed during the fifth and fourth centuries BCE, the golden age of Greek democracy. Only in the first century BCE, when the Roman Empire had made democracy redundant, did the West's lead over the East rise sharply. An even greater problem with the Greek-rupture theory (as will become clear in Chapters 6 through 9) is that democracy disappeared from the West almost completely in the two thousand years separating classical Greece from the American and French revolutions. Nineteenth-century radicals certainly found ancient Athens a useful foil in their debates over how modern democracies might work, but it takes a heroically selective reading of history to see a continuous spirit of democratic freedom stretching from classical Greece to the Founding Fathers (who, incidentally, tended to use the word "democracy" as a term of abuse, just one step above mob rule).

In any case, Greece's real contribution to Axial thought came not from democrats but from the critics of democracy, led by Socrates. Greece, he argued, did not need democracies, which merely pooled the ignorance of men who judged everything by appearances; what it needed was men like himself, who knew that when it came to the one thing that mattered—the nature of the good—they knew nothing. Only such men could hope to understand the good (if, indeed, anyone could; Socrates was not sure) through reason, honed in philosophical debate.

Plato, one of Socrates' followers, produced two versions of the master's model for the good society: *The Republic*, idealistic enough for any Confucian, and *The Laws*, authoritarian enough to warm Lord Shang's heart. Aristotle (one of Plato's pupils) covered a similar range, from the humane *Ethics* to the coldly analytical *Politics*. Some of the fifth-century-BCE thinkers known as Sophists could match Daoists for relativism, just as the visionaries Parmenides and Empedocles matched them for mysticism; and Protagoras was as much a champion of the common man as Mozi.

In the introduction to this book I talked about another long-term lock-in theory, which holds that the West rules today not because ancient Greeks invented democracy per se but because they created a uniquely rational, dynamic culture while ancient China was obscurantist and conservative.* I think this theory is wrong too. It caricatures Eastern, Western, and South Asian thought and ignores their internal variety. Eastern thought can be just as rational, liberal, realist, and cynical as Western; Western thought can be just as mystical, authoritarian, relativist, and obscure as Eastern. The real unity of Axial thought is unity in diversity. For all the differences among Eastern, Western, and South Asian thought, the *range* of ideas, arguments, and conflicts was remarkably similar in each region. In the Axial Age, thinkers staked out the same terrain for debate regardless of whether they lived in the Yellow River valley, the Ganges plain, or the cities of the eastern Mediterranean.

The real break with the past was the shape of this intellectual terrain *as a whole*, not any single feature (such as Greek philosophy) within it. No one was having Axial arguments in 1300 BCE, when the West's social development score first approached twenty-four points. The closest candidate is Akhenaten, pharaoh of Egypt between 1364 and 1347 BCE, who swept aside traditional gods and installed a trinity of himself, his wife, Nefertiti, and the sun disk, Aten. He built a new city full of temples to Aten, composed haunting hymns, and promoted a deeply strange art style.

For a hundred years Egyptologists have argued over what Akhenaten was doing. Some think he was trying to invent monotheism; no less a luminary than Sigmund Freud argued that Moses stole this concept from Akhenaten while the Hebrews were in Egypt. There are certainly striking parallels between Akhenaten's "Great Hymn to the Aten" and the Hebrew Bible's Psalm 104, the "Hymn to God the Cre-

---

*Some intellectual historians and many New Age devotees turn this on its head, keeping the East-West distinction but arguing that Eastern/South Asian thought liberates the human spirit while Western abstraction puts a straitjacket on it.

ator." Yet Akhenaten's religious revolution was anything but Axial. It had no room for personal transcendence; in fact, Akhenaten banned mere mortals from worshipping Aten at all, making the pharaoh even more of a bridge between this world and the divine than he had been before.

If anything, Atenism illustrates the difficulty of making major intellectual changes in societies where god-kings are firmly ensconced. His new religion won no following, and as soon as he died the old gods were brought back. Akhenaten's temples were smashed and his revolution forgotten until archaeologists dug his city up in 1891.

So is Axial thought the secret ingredient that makes Figure 5.1 so dull? Did Confucius, Socrates, and the Buddha guide societies through some intellectual barrier when social development reached twenty-four points in the mid first millennium BCE, while the absence of such geniuses blocked social development in the second millennium?

Probably not. For one thing, chronology is against it. In the West, Assyria became a high-end state and pushed past twenty-four points in the eighth century BCE, but it is hard to see much that is strikingly Axial in Western thought before Socrates, three hundred years later. It is a closer call in the East; there Qin, Chu, Qi, and Jin reached twenty-four points around 500 BCE, just when Confucius was most active, but the main wave of Eastern Axial thought falls later, in the fourth and third centuries BCE. And if South Asianists are right in redating the Buddha to the late fifth century BCE, high-end state formation seems to precede Axial thought there, too.

Geography is also against it. The most important Axial thinkers came from small, marginal communities such as Greece, Israel, the Buddha's home state of Sakya, or Confucius' of Lu; it is hard to see how transcendent breakthroughs in political backwaters affected social development in the great powers.

Finally, logic is against it. Axial thought was a reaction against the high-end state, at best indifferent to great kings and their bureaucrats and often downright hostile to their power. Axial thought's real contribution to raising social development, I suspect, came later in the first millennium BCE, when all the great states learned to tame it, making it work for them. In the East, the Han dynasty emasculated Confucianism to the point it became an official ideology, guiding a loyal class of bureaucrats. In India, the great king Ashoka, apparently genuinely horrified by his own violent conquests, converted to Buddhism around 257 BCE, yet somehow managed not to renounce war. And in the West the Romans first neutralized Greek philosophy, then turned Christianity into a prop for their empire.

The more rational strands within Axial thought encouraged law, mathematics, science, history, logic, and rhetoric, which all increased people's intellectual mastery of their world, but the real motor behind Figure 5.1 was the same as it had been since the end of the Ice Age. Lazy, greedy, and frightened people found easier, more profitable, and safer ways to do things, in the process building stronger states, trading farther afield, and settling in greater cities. In a pattern we will see repeated many times in the next five chapters, as social development rose the new age got the culture it needed. Axial thought was just one of the things that happened when people created high-end states and disenchanted the world.

EDGE EMPIRES

If further proof is needed that Axial thought was more a consequence than a cause of state restructuring, we need only look at Qin, the ferocious state at the western edge of the Eastern core (Figure 5.6). "Qin has the same customs as the [barbarians] Rong and Di," said the anonymous author of *The Stratagems of the Warring States*, a kind of how-to book on diplomatic chicanery. "It has the heart of a tiger or wolf; greedy, loving profit, and untrustworthy, knowing nothing of ritual, duty, or virtuous conduct." Yet despite being the antithesis of everything Confucian gentlemen held dear, Qin exploded from the edge of the Eastern core to conquer the whole of it in the third century BCE.

Something rather similar also happened at the other end of Eurasia, where the Romans—also regularly likened to wolves—came from the edge of the Western core to overthrow it and enslave the philosophers who called them barbarians. Polybius, a Greek gentleman taken to Rome as a hostage in 167 BCE, wrote a forty-volume *Universal History* to explain all this to his fellow countrymen. "Who," he asked, "can be so narrow-minded or lazy that he does not want to know how . . . in

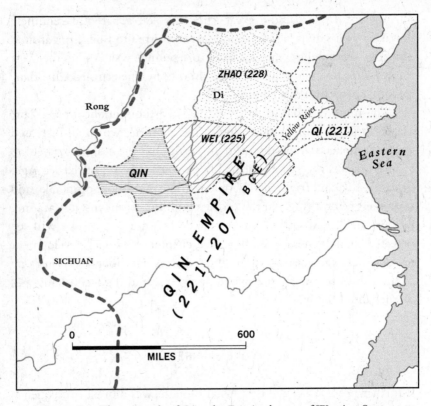

Figure 5.6. The triumph of Qin: the East in the era of Warring States,
300–221 BCE (dates in parentheses show when the main states fell to Qin)

less than fifty-three years [220–167 BCE] the Romans brought under
their rule almost the whole inhabited world,* something without
parallel in history?"

Qin and Rome had a lot in common. Each was a spectacular example of the advantages of backwardness, combining organizational
methods pioneered in an older core with military methods honed on a
violent frontier; each slaughtered, enslaved, and dispossessed millions;
and each drove social development up faster than ever before. Qin and
Rome also exemplify what we might call the paradox of violence:
when the rivers of blood dried, their imperialism left most people, in
both East and West, better off.

*That is, the whole world that Polybius knew about; he had no idea what Qin was
doing.

For both Qin and Rome, the secret of success was simple—numbers. Qin and Rome got there by different paths, but each was just better at raising, arming, feeding, and replacing armies than any rival.

In the East, Qin had for centuries been the weakest of the six great warring states.* It started moving toward high-end organization late, introducing land taxes only in 408 BCE. By then relentless fighting had forced the other states to conscript their subjects, tax them, and use Legalist methods to discipline them. Rulers did everything possible to increase revenues, and the best practices spread quickly, since the alternative to copying was destruction. Around 430 BCE the state of Wei had begun rounding up laborers and digging vast irrigation channels to raise farm output; the other states, including (eventually) Qin, followed suit. Zhao and Wei built walls to protect their valuable irrigated land; so did the others.

In the fourth century BCE Qin caught up. Lord Shang made his name there in the 340s, advising Qin's ruler on how to turn his state into a nightmare of surveillance and discipline:

> [Lord Shang] commanded that the people be divided into tens and fives and that they supervise each other and be mutually liable. Anyone who failed to report criminal activity would be chopped in two at the waist, while those who reported it would receive the same reward as that for obtaining the head of an enemy . . .

This was no mere authoritarian fantasy; records on bamboo strips recovered from the tombs of Qin magistrates show that the laws were enforced in all their savagery.

If it is any consolation, Lord Shang was eventually hoist with his own petard, condemned to be torn apart with his ankles and wrists tied to chariots. By then, though, the high-end Legalist state had triumphed and the Eastern core had become an armed camp. Thirty thousand men had counted as a big army in 500 BCE, but by 250 BCE a hundred thousand was normal. Two hundred thousand was nothing special, and really strong armies were twice that size. Casualties were

---

*The four great powers (Jin, Qi, Chu, and Qin) of the sixth century BCE became six when Jin split into three states (Hann, Wei, and Zhao) after a civil war. Some historians include Yan, around modern Beijing, as a seventh great power.

correspondingly enormous. One text says that a Qin army killed sixty thousand troops from Wei in 364 BCE. The numbers may be exaggerated, but since Qin soldiers were paid by the head (literally; they turned in severed ears to claim bonuses), they cannot be too far from the truth.

So alarming were the forces being unleashed that in 361 BCE the great powers set up regular conferences to negotiate their differences, and diplomats-for-hire, known as "persuaders," appeared in the 350s. A single man might shuttle among several great kingdoms, serving as chief minister for all of them at once, weaving webs of intrigue worthy of Henry Kissinger.

"To jaw-jaw is always better than to war-war," said Winston Churchill, but brute force still beat out bargaining in the fourth century BCE. The problem was Qin. Secure behind mountainous borders that made it hard to attack, and free to use its position at the edge of the core to bolster its manpower by drawing in people from the stateless societies even farther west, its armies constantly pressed into the core. "Qin is the mortal enemy of 'All Under Heaven,'" said *The Stratagems of the Warring States*; it wants "to swallow the whole world."

The other states recognized that they needed to combine against Qin, but four centuries of war had created such mistrust that they could not resist stabbing one another in the back. Between 353 and 322 BCE Wei led a series of coalitions, but as soon as the allies won a few victories they turned on Wei, terrified that it might do better than the rest of them. Wei responded like many a spurned lover or leader, switching its affections to the old enemy, Qin. Between 310 and 284 BCE Qi led a new set of alliances, only to be brought down as Wei had been; then Zhao took the mantle. In 269 BCE Zhao won two great victories over Qin and hope flared in every heart, but it was too little, too late. Qin's King Zheng discovered a terrible new strategy: simply kill so many people that other states could not rebuild their armies. Qin had invented the body count.

Qin generals killed about a million enemy soldiers over the next thirty years. A dismal record of massacres fills the annals, then ends suddenly in 234 BCE, when, we are told, Qin beheaded a hundred thousand men of Zhao. After that no credible enemies remained and the surrender of states replaced slaughters in the annals.

With neither jaw-jaw nor war-war working, Qin's remaining enemies pinned their hopes on murder. In 227 BCE a hit man talked his way past the Qin king Zheng's minders, grabbed Zheng's arm, and lunged at him with a poisoned dagger—only for Zheng's sleeve to tear off in his hand. Zheng ducked behind a pillar, thrashed around to get his ridiculously long ceremonial sword out of its scabbard, then hacked the assassin to bits.

There were no more chances, and Qi, the last independent state, fell in 221 BCE. King Zheng now took the name Shihuangdi, or August First Emperor. "We are the First Emperor," he thundered, "and our successors shall be known as Second Emperor, Third Emperor, and so on, for endless generations." No one argued.

Rome's path to empire was different (Figure 5.7). Persia had already united most of what was then the Western core by the time Darius won the throne in 521 BCE, but his desire to tap the wealth of the Mediterranean frontier set off waves of defensive state formation and created forces that would eventually destroy the Persian Empire.

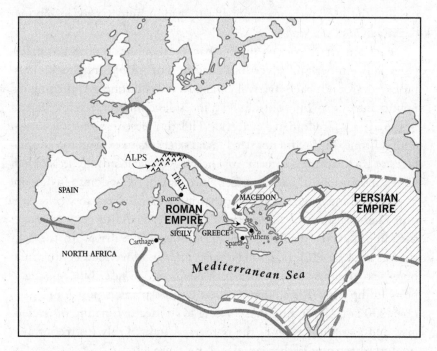

Figure 5.7. Ancient empires in the West: from Persia to Rome, 500–1 BCE. The broken line shows the maximum extent of the western end of the Persian Empire, around 490 BCE, and the solid line shows the extent of the Roman Empire in 1 BCE.

Greek and Italian cities were already very developed, scoring high on energy capture and information technology but less so on organization and military power. So long as Darius tackled them one by one he could bully them into submission, but the bullying itself drove the cities to combine, ratcheting up their organizational and military powers.

Thus, when Darius' son Xerxes led a huge force into Greece in 480 BCE, Athens and Sparta set aside their differences to resist him. The historian Herodotus (and, rather differently, the film *300*) immortalized their extraordinary victory, which left Athens a great power at the head of a league of cities. Rather like what happened when Eastern states tried to ally against Qin, Athenian power scared Sparta even more than the Persians did, and in 431 BCE the terrible Athenian-Spartan conflict known as the Peloponnesian War broke out (immortalized by Thucydides, but so far no movie). By the time the defeated and starving Athenians surrendered their fleet and pulled down their walls in 404 BCE the war had drawn in Sicily and Carthage, and its tentacles had turned parts of the Mediterranean, notably Macedon, into Greek economic dependencies.

Macedon was a sort of ancient banana republic, rich in resources (especially timber and silver) but chaotic. For fifty years Greek cities pushed it around, backing rival claimants to its throne and turning its politics into a soap opera of adultery, incest, and murder, but in 359 BCE Philip II, a Macedonian version of Tiglath-Pileser, seized the kingdom's throne. Philip did not need social scientists to explain the advantages of backwardness to him: instinctively understanding, he adapted Greek institutions to his large, rich, but anarchic kingdom. He dug up silver, hired mercenaries, and got the riotous aristocracy to work with him, then brushed the Greek cities aside. He would surely have done the same to Persia had not a mysterious assassin—driven to the act, rumors said, by Philip's drunken rages and/or a love feud ending in a homosexual gang rape—struck him down in 336 BCE. Not missing a beat, Philip's son Alexander fulfilled Philip's plans in just four years (334–330 BCE), hounding Persia's king to his death, burning his sacred city, and marching as far as the borders of India. Only his troops' refusal to march any farther could stop his conquests.

Alexander was a child of the new, disenchanted world (Aristotle had been one of his tutors) and probably did not realize how difficult it was to fill a godlike king's shoes.* Devout Persians held that their kings were Ahuramazda's earthly representatives in his eternal struggle with darkness; Alexander, therefore, must be an agent of evil. This image problem doubtless lay behind Alexander's tortured efforts (mentioned in Chapter 4) to convince Persians he was godlike. Maybe, given time, he would have succeeded, although the more he tried to impress Persians with his divinity, the more insane he looked to Greeks and Macedonians. And time was short: Alexander dropped dead, perhaps poisoned, in 323 BCE, and his generals fought civil wars, broke up the empire, and gradually became kings (edging toward divinity) in their own right.

Eventually one of their kingdoms might have conquered the others, following Qin's route, but Alexander's successors were as short of time as the great king had been. In the fourth century BCE Macedon had been drawn into Greek conflicts, adapted Greek institutions to its own needs, defeated the Greeks, and then destroyed the great empire of the day; in the second century Rome virtually reran the script.

Rome is a perfect example of how colonization and developments on the periphery combine to expand cores. The city had been heavily influenced by Greece since the eighth century BCE, but grew strong in local struggles with its neighbors and created an odd mix of high- and low-end organization. An aristocratic senate made most big decisions, while assemblies dominated by middling farmers voted on matters of peace and war. Like Qin, Rome was late in moving toward the high end; it began paying its soldiers only in 406 BCE, and probably instituted its first taxes at the same time. For centuries Rome's budget relied mostly on plunder, and instead of taxing defeated enemies it made deals with them, extracting troops to fight more wars.

Romans were as averse to godlike kings as Greeks, but understood all too well the link between conquest and divinity. Really successful generals were awarded triumphs, ticker-tape parades through Rome in chariots pulled by white horses, festooned with images of sanctity, but accompanied by slaves whispering in their ears, "Remember, you are a

---

*Literally: Alexander was a foot shorter than the Persian king, and the first time he jumped on the throne his feet did not reach the ground. They dangled in a most ungodlike way until a courtier rushed up with a footstool.

mortal." The triumph effectively put divine kingship in a box, making the mighty conqueror god for a day—but no more than that.

Old-fashioned as this system looked to Greeks in the third century BCE, its combination of high- and low-end practices generated manpower on a scale to match even Qin. Persia had raised perhaps 200,000 troops to invade Greece in 480 BCE, but after losing them needed decades to refill its treasuries. Rome faced no such constraints. A century of war gave it all the manpower of Italy, and in 264 BCE the senate began a titanic struggle with Carthage to control the western Mediterranean.

The Carthaginians lured Rome's first fleet into a storm, sending it—and a hundred thousand sailors—to the bottom. Rome simply built a bigger fleet. This went down in another storm two years later, so Rome sent out a third armada, only to lose that as well. A fourth fleet finally won the war in 241 BCE because Carthage could not replace its own huge losses. Carthage needed twenty-three years to recuperate, whereupon its general Hannibal marched his elephants over the Alps to attack Italy from the rear. Between 218 and 216 BCE he killed or captured a hundred thousand Romans, but Rome just raised more men and ground him down in a war of attrition. And like Qin, Rome redefined brutality. "The Roman custom," said Polybius, was "to exterminate every form of life they encountered, sparing none . . . so when cities are taken by the Romans you may often see not only the corpses of human beings but also dogs cut in half, and the dismembered limbs of other animals." Carthage finally gave up in 201 BCE.

War-war struck the senate as much better than jaw-jaw. After just one summer's rest, Rome turned on the kingdoms of Alexander's successors in the eastern Mediterranean and by 167 BCE had smashed them. Another generation of grueling wars against guerrillas took its armies deep into Spain, North Africa, and northern Italy. Rome had become the West's sole superpower.

FIRST CONTACT

By 200 BCE the East and West had more in common than at any time since the Ice Age. Each was dominated by a single great empire with tens of millions of subjects. Each had a literate, sophisticated elite

schooled in Axial thought, living in great cities fed by highly productive farmers and supplied by elaborate trade networks. And in each
core social development was 50 percent higher than it had been in
1000 BCE.

This chapter has illustrated nicely the principle that people (in large
groups) are all much the same. Divided by the vast expanses of central
Asia and the Indian Ocean, East and West had followed separate but
similar histories in virtual isolation from each other, differing chiefly
in the fact that the West still narrowly kept the lead in social development
that the geography of domesticable plants and animals had given it at
the end of the Ice Age.

This chapter also illustrates a second major principle, though—that
while geography determines the course of social development, social
development also changes the meanings of geography. The expansion
of the cores was eating away at the distance between them, folding
East and West into a single Eurasian story. This was to have dramatic
consequences.

As late as 326 BCE, when Alexander of Macedon led his troops into
the Punjab (Figure 5.8), even the best-educated Easterners and Westerners knew almost nothing of each other's existence. Alexander assured his
men that they would soon bathe in the waters of Ocean, the great river
that encircled the world (when instead of Ocean the Ganges plain unfolded before them, bristling with fortified cities, they mutinied).

Alexander did a U-turn and headed home, but left various malcon-
tents behind as settlers. In what is now Afghanistan one group set up a
kingdom called Bactria, which by 150 BCE had conquered parts of the
Ganges plain and begun a remarkable fusion of Greek and Indian culture. One Indian text claims to record a Greek-speaking Bactrian
king's conversations with a Buddhist monk, after which the king, along
with plenty of his subjects, converted.

Bactria has a remarkable claim to fame: its disintegration around
130 BCE is the earliest historical event to be mentioned in both Eastern
and Western documents. An ambassador from the Chinese court who
wandered into the kingdom's wreckage just a couple of years later took
wonderful stories back to his emperor, particularly about central Asia's
horses, and in 101 BCE a Chinese expedition battled its way into the
region. Some historians think that the local troops that resisted it may
have included Romans, prisoners of war taken in far-off Mesopotamia

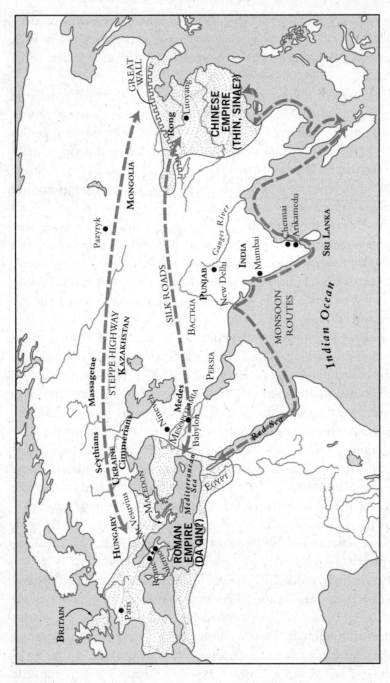

Figure 5.8. Between East and West: the late-first-millennium-BCE tissue of trade linking East and West across the Indian Ocean, Silk Roads, and steppe highway

and traded through countless hands until they found themselves fighting China in the mountains of central Asia.

Less-romantic historians think another two centuries passed before Chinese and Romans actually met. According to an official Chinese history, in 97 CE a Chinese general "dispatched his adjutant Gan Ying all the way to the coast of the Western Sea and back." On this distant shore, wherever exactly it was, Gan visited the kingdom of Da Qin—literally, "Great Qin," so-called because it struck the Chinese as being a grand, distant reflection of their own empire. Whether the Western Sea was the Mediterranean and Da Qin was Rome remain open questions. The least-romantic historians of all think that it was only in 166 CE, when ambassadors from Da Qin's King Andun (surely the Roman emperor Marcus Aurelius Antoninus) reached the Chinese capital at Luoyang, that Chinese and Romans finally stood in the same room.

There may, though, have been more productive meetings, involving kinds of people who struck the educated gentlemen who wrote most of the surviving texts as too despicable to notice—slaves, for instance. In 2010, geneticists announced that mitochondrial DNA from the bones of a man buried at Vagnari in southern Italy in the second century CE suggested that his maternal ancestors had come from East Asia; and archaeologists added that the circumstances of his burial implied that he was an agricultural slave. What miseries carried him or his ancestors so far from home are anyone's guess.

A second such group of despised wanderers consisted of traders—for all we know, the very traders who brought an East Asian slave to Italy. Pliny the Elder, a Roman aristocrat who wrote an immense description of the world and its peculiarities (he was killed in 79 CE, too fascinated by the eruption of Vesuvius to run away from the lava), did bring himself to mention the annual departure of a merchant fleet from Egypt's Red Sea coast for Sri Lanka, and one actual merchant document survives, a roughly contemporary Greek text called *The Voyage on the Red Sea*. This was a kind of traders' handbook, describing the Indian Ocean's ports and winds.

Roman merchants certainly left their mark on India. Almost as soon as British and French colonists settled there in the eighteenth century, in fact, people started bringing them ancient Roman coins, but not until 1943 did the scale of contact become clear. That summer, after decades of neglecting India's cultural heritage—at the height of World

War II and with the end of the Raj in sight—the British Colonial Office decided that it was time to overhaul Indian archaeology. It promptly plucked Brigadier Mortimer Wheeler off the beach at Salerno, where an Anglo-American force had just invaded Italy, and dropped him into New Delhi to administer a million and a half square miles of territory that was almost as archaeologically rich as Egypt.

Wheeler was a larger-than-life character. He fought in both world wars, left a trail of broken hearts across three continents, and revolutionized British archaeology with his meticulous excavations of Roman sites. All the same, eyebrows were raised at this appointment. The British Empire was clearly on its last legs, so why, Indian nationalists asked, inflict on us some pensioned-off Colonel Blimp, more at home on muddy Roman sites in Britain than in the land of the Buddha?

Wheeler had a lot to prove, and as soon as he landed in Mumbai (known to the British as Bombay) he set off on a whirlwind archaeological tour. Arriving at Chennai (colonial Madras) as it sweltered in the heat of the impending monsoon, Wheeler found the government offices closed and decided to kill time at the local museum. "In a workshop cupboard," he wrote in his memoirs,

> my hand closed upon the neck and long handle of a pottery vessel strangely alien to that tropical environment. As I looked upon it I remember recalling that provocative question in the Legislative Assembly at New Delhi: "What has Roman Britain got to do with India?" Here was the complete answer.

Wheeler was holding a fragment of a Roman wine jar dug up at Arikamedu (Pondicherry), eighty miles down the coast. He took the overnight train and after a long, alcoholic breakfast at the town's French legation, went looking for Romans.

> An inner room of the public library contained three or four museum cases. I strode hopefully forward, and, removing the dust with an excessively sweaty arm, peered into them. For the second time within the month, my eyes started in their sockets. Crowded together were fragments of a dozen more Roman amphorae [wine jars], part of a Roman lamp, a Roman intaglio [cameo brooch], a mass of Indian material—potsherds, beads, terracottas—and several fragments of a

red-glazed ware no one trained in the school of classical archaeology could mistake.

As a little bonus, when Wheeler got back to New Delhi with one of the red potsherds in his pocket he ran into two more giants of British archaeology doing war work on aerial photographs. "I casually produced an Arretine sherd," he says, referring to the red-glazed ware from the Arikamedu museum, "and the effect was gratifying—how childishly rewarding is a comprehending audience!"

Excavations soon showed that Mediterranean goods were reaching Arikamedu (and several other ports) by 200 BCE. They increased in quantity for the next three centuries, and recent digs on Egypt's Red Sea coast have also found dried-out coconuts, rice, and black pepper that can only have come from India. By the first century CE goods were also moving between China and India, and from both places to Southeast Asia.

It would be an exaggeration to say that East and West had joined hands across the oceans. This was less a web of connections than a few gossamer-thin threads strung end to end. One trader might ship wine from Italy to Egypt; another might take it overland to the Red Sea; a third might move it on to Arabia; and a fourth might cross the Indian Ocean to Arikamedu. There he might sit down with a local merchant selling silks that had passed through even more hands in their journey from the Yellow River valley.

It was a beginning, though. *The Voyage on the Red Sea* mentions a place called "Thin," probably a corruption of Qin (pronounced Chin), from which the Western name China comes; and a generation later a Greek named Alexander claimed to have visited Sinae, again probably China. By about 100 BCE, thanks partly to China's military advance to Bactria, silks and spices were moving westward and gold and silver eastward along the famous Silk Roads. Only lightweight, expensive goods—such as silk, of course—could remain profitable after being carried for six months across five thousand miles, but within a century or two no self-respecting Roman noblewoman would be caught dead without her silk shawl, and central Asian merchants had set up branch offices in all China's major cities.

There was much for the wealthy aristocrats who ran the Eastern and Western cores to celebrate in these first contacts, but there was much to worry about too, for some of the people on the move struck them as being even nastier than merchants. "They have squat bodies, strong limbs, and thick necks, and are so hideous and deformed that they might be two-legged beasts," the Roman historian Ammianus wrote about these people around 390 CE. He continued:

> Their shape, while horrible, is still human, but their lives are so rough that they do not use fire or cooked food, but live on the wild roots and any kind of half-raw flesh, which they warm slightly by sticking it between their thighs and the backs of their horses.

These people were nomads, utterly alien to landowners such as Ammianus. We have already met their ancestors, the herders of central Asia who domesticated horses around 3500 BCE and hitched them to carts around 2000 BCE, giving birth to the horse-drawn chariots that threw the Western core into chaos after 1750 BCE and reached the East five hundred years later. Climbing onto horses' backs and riding them around sounds easier than attaching them to vehicles, but it was not until about 1000 BCE that the breeding of bigger horses, improvements in horse harnesses, and the invention of small, powerful bows that could be fired from the saddle combined to create a whole new way of life: mounted pastoral nomadism. Taking to horseback transformed geography once again, gradually turning the unbroken band of arid plains stretching from Mongolia to Hungary (both named after nomad peoples) into a "steppe highway" linking East and West.

In some ways these steppe nomads were no different from any other relatively mobile, relatively underdeveloped peoples living along the edges of great empires, going all the way back to Jacob and his sons in the Hebrew Bible. They traded animals and skins for the products of settled society. There could be profits all around: Chinese silks and a Persian carpet adorn the lavish fifth-century-BCE tombs at Pazyryk in Siberia, while in the ninth century BCE the Assyrians imported horses and bows from the steppes and replaced their chariots with cavalry.

But there could also be problems all around. As well as silks and carpets, the Pazyryk tombs contain piles of iron weapons and cups made from the gold-plated skulls of scalped enemies, hinting that the line between trading and fighting was fine. Particularly after 800 BCE, when colder, drier weather reduced pastureland on the steppes, herders who could move their flocks quickly across long distances and fight when they arrived had huge advantages. Entire tribes took to horseback, riding hundreds of miles between winter and summer pastures.

Their migrations created a domino effect. In the eighth century BCE a group called the Massagetae migrated west across what is now Kazakhstan, confronting the Scythian people in their path with the same choice that prehistoric hunter-gatherers had had to make when farmers moved into their foraging lands or Sicilian villagers had had to make when Greek colonists landed on their coasts: they could stand their ground, organizing themselves to fight back and even electing kings, or they could run away. Those who yielded fled across the Volga River, presenting the Cimmerians who already lived there with the same fight-or-flight choice.

In the 710s BCE bands of Cimmerian refugees started moving into the Western core. There were not many of them, but they could do a lot of damage. In agrarian states, many peasants have to toil in the fields to support a few soldiers. At the height of their wars, Rome and Qin had mobilized maybe one man in six, but in peacetime they mustered barely one in twenty. Among nomads, by contrast, every man (and many a woman, too) could be a warrior, born and raised with a horse and bow. This was the original example of asymmetric warfare. The great empires had money, quartermasters, and siege weapons, but the nomads had speed, terror, and the fact that their sedentary victims were often busy fighting one another.

In these years climate change and rising social development once again combined to disrupt the Western core's frontiers, and violence and upheaval were once more the results. The Assyrian Empire, which was still the greatest power in the West around 700 BCE, invited the Cimmerians into the core to help it fight its rivals. At first that worked well, and in 695 BCE King Midas of Phrygia in central Turkey, so rich that Greek legends said he could turn objects to gold just by touching them, committed suicide as the Cimmerians closed in on his capital.

By eliminating buffer states such as Phrygia, though, the Assyrians exposed their heartland to nomad raids, and by 650 BCE Scythians virtually controlled northern Mesopotamia. Their "violence and neglect of law led to total chaos," the Greek historian Herodotus wrote. "They acted like mere robbers, riding up and down the land, stealing everyone's property." The nomads destabilized the Assyrian Empire and helped the Medes and Babylonians sack Nineveh in 612 BCE, then immediately turned on the Medes, too. Not until about 590 BCE did the Medes figure out how to fight such wily, fast-moving foes—according to Herodotus, by getting their leaders drunk at a banquet and murdering them.

The kings of Media, Babylon, and Persia experimented with how to handle nomads. One option was to do nothing, but then nomad raids ruined frontier provinces, cutting the tax take. Buying the nomads off was another possibility, but paying protection could get as pricey as being raided. Preemptive war was a third response, striking into the steppes and occupying the pastures nomads needed to survive, but that was even costlier and riskier. With little to defend, nomads could retreat into the treeless, waterless waste, luring the invaders to destruction when their supplies ran out.

Cyrus, the founder of the Persian Empire, tried preemptive war against the Massagetae in 530 BCE. Like the Medes before him, he fought with the grape: he let the Massagetan vanguard loot his camp, and when they were drunk, slaughtered them and captured their queen's son. "Glutton as you are for blood," Queen Tomyris wrote to Cyrus, "give me back my son and get out of my country with your forces intact . . . If you refuse, I swear by the sun our master to give you more blood than you can drink." True to her word, Tomyris defeated the Persians, cut off Cyrus' head, and stuffed it in a bag of gore.

It was a bad start for preemptive strikes, but in 519 BCE Darius of Persia showed that they could work, defeating a confederation that Persians called the "Pointy-Hatted Scythians" and imposing tribute and a puppet king on them. Five years later he tried it again, crossing the Danube and pursuing other Scythians deep into Ukraine. But like so many asymmetric wars in our own day, it is hard to say who won. Herodotus thought it was a disaster, from which Darius was lucky to escape alive, but the Scythians never again threatened Persia, so clearly something went right.

It took longer for cavalry from the steppes to become a fact of life in the East, just as it had taken chariots longer to reach China than the West, but when the nomadic domino effect did arrive it worked just as viciously. The eastward spread of nomadism had probably been behind the Rong people's attacks on the Zhou in the eighth century BCE, and the northern people absorbed by the states of Qin and Jin in the seventh and sixth centuries BCE must often have been choosing assimilation over fighting incoming nomads. When they did so, the combined pressure of nomad incursions and Chinese states' expansion eliminated buffer societies, just as had happened in the West.

The state of Zhao now became the frontier. Like the Assyrians when they faced the Scythians, Zhao immediately recruited nomadic horsemen to fight its neighbors and trained its own subjects as cavalry. Zhao also developed an antinomad strategy little used in the West, the war of attrition, building walls to keep nomads out (or at least to channel where they traded and raided). This seemed to work less badly than fighting or paying protection, and in the third century BCE walls proliferated. The Qin First Emperor's wall stretched for two thousand miles, costing (according to legend, anyway) one laborer's life for every yard built.*

Being the kind of man he was, the First Emperor lost no sleep over this. In fact, he so appreciated wall-building that he turned this defensive strategy into a weapon, extending his Great Wall to enclose a vast sweep of pasture where nomads had traditionally grazed. Then, in 215 BCE, he followed up with a preemptive war.

The Great Wall sent a clear signal: geography was changing meaning again. The forces that drove the dull upward march of social development in Figure 5.1—rising energy capture, more effective organization, widespread literacy, ever-deadlier armies—were transforming the world. By 200 BCE a single great empire dominated each core, its warriors and traders reaching even into the spaces between the cores. The steppes had gone from being a vast barrier between East and West to a highway linking them, and instead of separate but similar histories, the Eastern and Western cores were beginning to be intertwined. Very few goods, people, or ideas were as yet traveling the whole way from one end of Eurasia to the other, but new geographical realities were taking shape. Over the next few centuries, these would sweep away the great empires that dominated the cores in 200 BCE, throw the upward trends of social development into reverse, and end the West's lead. The paradox of development was entering a whole new phase.

---

*The Qin Great Wall is not the iconic stone barrier you can visit on day trips from Beijing (that one dates mostly to the sixteenth century CE). Nor is it true that the Great Wall can be seen from orbiting spacecraft, let alone from the moon.

6

DECLINE AND FALL

ALL FOR THE BEST

"All is for the best in this best of all possible worlds," says Dr. Pangloss—again, and again, and again—in Voltaire's eighteenth-century comic classic *Candide*. Despite contracting syphilis, losing an eye and an ear, and being enslaved, hanged, and caught in not one but two earthquakes, Pangloss sticks to his story.

Pangloss, of course, was Voltaire's little joke, poking fun at the silliness of contemporary philosophy, but history has thrown up plenty of real-life versions. The great empires that dominated the Eastern and Western cores in the first few centuries CE seem to have been especially rich in them. "When the emperor makes his imperial tour, all is resplendent," one Chinese poet wrote. "Boundless joy reigns for ten thousand years." In the Roman Empire the Greek orator Aristides waxed even more enthusiastic. "For the eternal duration of the empire the whole civilized world prays all together," he declaimed. "Let all the gods grant that this empire and this city flourish forever and never cease until stones float on the sea and trees cease to put forth shoots."

So what would these Panglosses have made of Figure 6.1? After peaking around 1 BCE/CE, social development fell in both East and West. This was collapse on a whole new scale. Not only was it broader

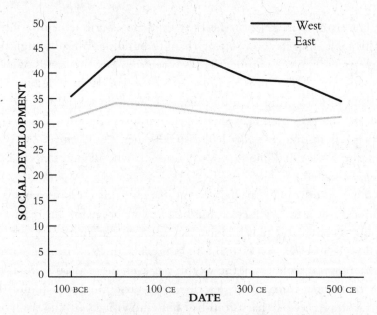

Figure 6.1. An Old World–wide depression: the peak, decline,
and fall of the ancient empires, 100 BCE–500 CE

than ever before, affecting both ends of Eurasia, but it was also longer and deeper. Century after century it dragged on, cutting more than 10 percent off the East's development score by 400 CE and 20 percent off the West's by 500. How this happened, ushering in the end of the West's fourteen-thousand-year-long lead in social development, is this chapter's subject.

THE NEW WORLD ORDER

The ancient empires had not always been full of Panglosses. It took hundreds of years of wars and millions of deaths before the paradox of violence that I mentioned in Chapter 5—the fact that war eventually brought peace and prosperity—made itself clear; and no sooner had the wars of unification ended than the Qin and Roman superstates both turned on themselves in horrific civil wars. Qin got down to this immediately; Rome, more gradually.

Qin's centralized, repressive institutions had been magnificent for conquering but turned out to be less good for ruling. After vanquishing his last enemies in 221 BCE the First Emperor continued conscripting all his male subjects, now setting them to building instead of fighting. Sometimes they were productive, as when they laid thousands of miles of roads and canals; sometimes less so. Sima Qian says that despite convincing himself of his own divinity and spending several fortunes on quacks who promised to make him live forever, the First Emperor—perhaps as insurance—also had 700,000 men spend thirty-six years building his tomb. (The graves of hundreds who died at the site have been excavated.)

The (mostly unexcavated) twenty-square-mile tomb complex is China's answer to Egypt envy. It is best known today for the Terracotta Army, six-thousand-plus life-size clay soldiers that guarded it, discovered by chance by a work team digging wells in 1974. It is one of the archaeological wonders of the world, but even more astonishing is the fact that when Sima Qian described the First Emperor's tomb, this Terracotta Army that has astonished museum visitors around the world did not even get a mention. Sima instead saved his words for the tomb's underground bronze palace, four hundred yards across, surrounded by replicas of the kingdom's rivers in mercury. (Geochemical surveys in 1981 and 2003 confirmed that the soil above the tomb has massively elevated mercury levels.) All those royal concubines who had not given the First Emperor children, Sima Qian says, plus all the artisans who knew the tomb's secrets and possibly the empire's top hundred officials, too, were buried with the emperor in 210 BCE.

The First Emperor's megalomaniacal policies generated resistance at every level. When noblemen complained, he forcibly moved them to his capital; when intellectuals complained, he buried 460 of them alive; and when peasants complained, he cut them in half.*

The reign of terror imploded almost the moment the First Emperor died. One day in 209 BCE, the story runs, heavy rain prevented two lowly officials from delivering conscripts to a garrison on time. The penalty for lateness was, of course, death. "As things stand, we face death whether we stay or run away," Sima Qian reports one of them saying, "while if we were to start a revolt we would likewise face death. Since

---

*This is what Confucian scholars claimed, at least; many modern historians suspect that the gentry embellished the story. The cutting-in-two of peasants, however, seems indisputable.

we must die in any case, would it not be better to die fighting for our country [by rebelling]?"

As they anticipated, both rebels were soon killed, but their insurgency spread. Within months, the warring states had reconstituted themselves. By 206 BCE Qin was finished and the revolt became a terrible civil war. After another four years of slaughter only the peasant-turned-warlord Liu Bang remained standing. He proclaimed the Han dynasty, beheaded eighty thousand prisoners of war, announced universal peace, and eventually took the new name Gaodi ("High Emperor").*

Rome had the opposite problem from Qin. Instead of being too centralized to rule in peace, its institutions were too diffuse. Its senate of rich old men and assemblies of poor citizens had evolved to run a city-state, not an empire, and could not cope with the mountains of plunder, armies of slaves, and gaggle of superrich generals that victory created. In one policy dispute in 133 BCE the august senators smashed up the wooden benches they sat on and used the legs to club one another to death, and by the 80s BCE no one knew for sure who was actually running the empire.

Instead of abruptly collapsing, like Qin, Rome slid in and out of civil war for fifty years. Increasingly armies were loyal to their generals rather than to the state, and the only way the senate could deal with successful generals was by sending them off to attack weaker foreigners (which only made the generals stronger) or by empowering new generals to attack the old ones (which only created new challengers). In 45 BCE Julius Caesar managed to defeat all comers, only to fall to assassins the next year; whereupon the wheel turned again, until in 30 BCE Octavian hunted Antony and Cleopatra down in Egypt, where they committed suicide. Exhausted by constant war, the Roman elite agreed that they would do whatever Octavian (who renamed himself Augustus, "the most august one") said while pretending he was really just a

---

*There are a lot of different ways to refer to Chinese emperors. Each had one or more names of his own (Liu Bang was also known as Liu Ji) and each was also assigned at least one "temple name" (Liu became Gaodi, but was also known as Gaozu, "High Progenitor"). To avoid confusion, I will refer to all emperors by the temple name used in Anne Paludan's useful book *The Chronicle of the Chinese Emperors.* Where there are multiple emperors with the same names, I add the name of their dynasty too (for example, Han Wudi, Liang Wudi, and so on).

private citizen. With everyone's face saved by this odd arrangement, in 27 BCE Augustus declared that the republic had been restored and got down to ruling as an emperor.

By 1 BCE almost the whole of the Eastern and Western cores were under the rule of single empires, but this had not been inevitable. Gaodi, the founder of the Han dynasty, had actually made an agreement to share the Eastern core with his last enemy in 203 BCE, but broke his word, killed his rival, and took everything; and in the 30s BCE it looked as if the Mediterranean would split between a Latin-speaking west, ruled by Octavian from Rome, and a Greek-speaking east, ruled by Antony and Cleopatra from Egypt. Had Gaodi been more honorable, or Antony less addled by liquor and sex, this chapter would have begun differently. In South Asia, things did go differently. Small cities and states developed in the Ganges Valley between 1000 and 600 BCE then shifted toward high-end states like those in the Eastern and Western cores. In the third century BCE these were swallowed into the huge Mauryan Empire, probably the world's biggest state in its day (though Qin would soon surpass it). But instead of going from strength to strength like Rome and China, this empire gradually broke apart over the next hundred years. By Augustus' time South Asia was once again home to a mass of jostling little kingdoms.

"All happy families resemble one another," Tolstoy famously said, "but each unhappy family is unhappy in its own way." So, too, empires. There are countless ways for empires to disintegrate—lost battles, disgruntled governors, uncontrollable grandees, desperate peasants, incompetent bureaucrats—but only one way to stay together: compromise. Han and Roman rulers showed a positive genius for this.

Gaodi won his civil war in 202 BCE only because he cut deals with other warlords, rewarding ten of them by leaving two-thirds of his "empire" as semi-independent kingdoms under their control. To prevent new civil wars, the empire needed to crush these vassal kings, but moving too quickly and scaring them might provoke the very wars the empire needed to prevent—as might moving too slowly and leaving the kings too strong. The Han emperors, however, moved at just the right speed, dismantling the kingdoms by 100 BCE with surprisingly few rebellions.

Han emperors were not as megalomaniacal as the Qin First Emperor, although they had their moments. Jingdi, for instance, was buried in

141 BCE with his own terracotta army (six times as large as the First Emperor's, though only one-third as tall). But with the partial exception of the great conqueror Wudi, Han emperors backed away from claiming immortality and divinity, though they did hang on to the Shang and Zhou kings' role as intermediary between this and the supernatural worlds.

They calibrated this carefully. Getting along with the great families required retreating from royal godliness (although the practical step of tying aristocratic wealth to the court's own success also helped). Placating the gentleman scholars required inserting the throne into an idealized, Confucian model of a hierarchical universe (as well as another pragmatic move, making knowledge of the Confucian classics rather than aristocratic connections the route to administrative office). Maintaining royal authority in the vast countryside required something else again, combining some of the monarchy's pre–Axial Age status as the bridge to the ancestors and gods with more down-to-earth measures such as reducing military service, relaxing the cruelest Qin laws, and making carefully timed tax cuts.

Compromise created peace and unity, which gradually knit the Eastern core into a single entity. Its rulers called it *zhongguo* (the "Middle Kingdom" at the center of the world) or *tianxia* ("All Under Heaven," because nothing beyond its borders mattered), and at this point it really does start making sense to think of the Eastern core as a single entity that modern Westerners, in their own mispronunciation of "Qin," call China. Huge cultural differences remained within All Under Heaven, but the Eastern core had started becoming Chinese.

Rome pursued similar compromises. When the civil wars ended in 30 BCE the victorious Augustus demobilized the conscripts and manned the frontier with career soldiers. Like the Han emperors, he knew that the army could threaten his regime, but whereas China's rulers reacted by staffing their military with convicts and foreigners, in a sense pushing it outside mainstream society, Augustus and his successors decided to keep their enemies even closer than their friends. They made the army a central social institution, but one directly under their own control.

War became the preserve of specialists, and everyone else turned toward the arts of peace. Rome, like China, absorbed its client kings and tied aristocrats' prosperity to the empire's. The emperors walked a tightrope, pretending to be merely first among peers when dealing with the aristocracy, commander-in-chief when dealing with the army, and godlike when dealing with parts of the empire that expected their rulers to be numinous. They substituted a god-when-I'm-dead strategy for the old god-for-a-day compromise: emperors were merely outstanding men until they died, the theory held, whereupon they were clutched to the bosoms of the divinities. Some, like the emperor Vespasian, found it ridiculous; as he collapsed, dying, he joked with his courtiers, "I think I'm becoming a god."

By the first century CE a fusion Greco-Roman culture was developing. Rich men could travel from the Jordan to the Rhine, stopping in similar-looking cities, eating off much the same gold plates, watching familiar Greek tragedies, and making clever allusions to Homer and Virgil, everywhere finding like-minded men who would appreciate their sophistication. The senate admitted more and more provincial worthies, local bigwigs put up inscriptions in Latin and Greek, and even farmers in the fields started thinking of themselves as Romans.

Compromise defused resistance. It would be nice to quote an ancient text on this, but none sums it up quite like the 1979 comedy *Monty Python's Life of Brian*. When Reg (played by John Cleese), chairman of the People's Front of Judea (Official), tries to whip his none-too-zealous followers into an anti-Roman rage, he finds that they prefer talking about the benefits of the empire (especially the wine). Reg throws back at them what has surely become the most famous question ever asked about the Roman Empire: "All right then. Apart from the sanitation, the medicine, education, wine, public order, irrigation, the fresh water system, and public health—what have the Romans ever done for us?" The freedom fighters think for a moment, then one tentatively raises a hand. "Brought peace?" Gasping at this stupidity, Reg answers: "Oh, peace . . . shut up!"

Reg did not get it: peace changed everything, bringing prosperity to both ends of Eurasia. Population soared in both empires and their economies grew even faster. At the most fundamental level, however we count—total product, product per unit of land, or product per unit of labor—agricultural output rose. Han and Roman laws gave greater security in property to landlords and peasants alike. Farmers at all levels took new land under cultivation, extended irrigation and drainage systems, bought slaves or hired laborers, and used more manure and better tools. Egyptian records show that Roman-era farmers could harvest ten pounds of wheat for every pound sown as seed, a spectacular level for premodern agriculture. No statistics survive from China, but archaeological finds and accounts in agricultural handbooks suggest that yields were high here, too, particularly in the Yellow River basin.

Quietly, so quietly in fact that the noblemen who wrote the surviving literature barely remark on it, farmers and artisans pushed energy capture toward a threshold. Virtually all energy previously used in the entire history of humanity had come from muscles or from biomass fuels, but people now tapped into four potentially revolutionary sources—coal, natural gas, water, and wind.

The first two remained very marginal—a few Chinese blacksmiths used coal in iron foundries, and saltmakers in Sichuan piped natural gas through bamboo tubes and burned it to evaporate brine—but not the third and fourth. In the first century BCE Romans and Chinese both came up with waterwheels, using them to power mills to grind grain and bellows to heat up furnaces. The most impressive example known, built at Barbegal in France soon after 100 CE, linked sixteen wheels to generate thirty kilowatts of power, roughly the same as a hundred oxen (or two Model T Fords running at full speed). Most wheels were much smaller, but even an average Roman mill generated as much power as ten strong men turning wheels with their feet.

The most important use of wind- and waterpower came not from the brand-new waterwheels, though, but from improvements to the older technologies of sailing. No one would bother producing thousands of tons of wheat, millions of gallons of wine, and billions of iron nails unless they could move them from farm or foundry to potential buyers. Bigger, better, and cheaper ships (and harbors and canals) mattered as much as plows and waterwheels. Trade and industry grew together.

Figure 6.2 shows this neatly for the West, plotting the rising number of shipwrecks against levels of lead pollution recorded in a 2005 study of lake deposits at Penido Velho in Spain. (I show shipwrecks because no written records survive of ancient shipping, so—unless captains inexplicably got clumsier and steered onto rocks more often as time went on—shipwrecks are the best proxy for the number of voyages; I show lead pollution, a by-product of silver processing, because

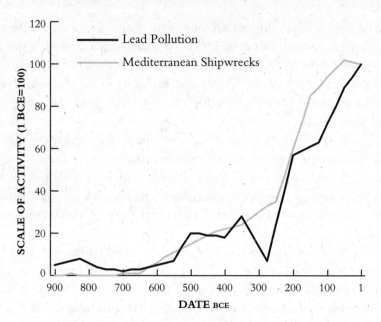

Figure 6.2. Goods and services: the parallel increases in
Mediterranean shipwrecks and in lead pollution in the Spanish lake
of Penido Velho. Numbers of wrecks and amounts of lead have been
normalized so they can be compared on the same vertical scale,
with the amounts of each in 1 BCE being counted as 100.

lead is the easiest isotope for geochemists to study.) The curves rise
together to twin peaks in the first century BCE, showing how strongly
trade and industry were linked (and that ancient Rome was no golden
age for the environment).

We cannot yet compare Figure 6.2 with an equivalent graph for the
East because Chinese archaeologists have not collected much quantifi-
able data. What there is, though, suggests that trade boomed in the
Eastern core after 300 BCE, but not as much as in the Western core.
One recent study, for instance, concludes that the Roman Empire had
roughly twice as much coinage in circulation as the Han and that the
richest Romans were twice as rich as the richest Chinese.

Geography probably had a lot to do with the difference in the
growth of trade. In Rome's empire, 90 percent of the people lived
within ten miles of the Mediterranean Sea. In the second millennium
BCE the Western core's expansion into the Mediterranean Basin had
brought rising development and increasing disruption in equal mea-

sure, but once Rome conquered the entire coastline in the first century BCE it put an end to the disruptions. The sea now allowed cheap water transport to link almost everyone, and development shot up.

In the Han Empire, a much lower proportion of the population lived close to the sea or big rivers, and the rivers were in any case not always navigable. Rome's military expansion secured a new economic frontier where farmers who applied the most advanced techniques to recently conquered lands could sell their crops to feed the cities of Italy and Greece, but in the absence of waterways like those of the Mediterranean, the Qin and Han conquests did this only on a much smaller scale. Some Han emperors worked furiously to improve transport by dredging the Yellow and Wei rivers and bypassing the worst stretches with canals, but centuries would pass before China solved the problem of not having its own Mediterranean Sea.

Two rather similar forces lay behind economic growth in both East and West, one pulling and one pushing the economy upward. The pull factor was the growth of the state. Roman and Han conquerors taxed vast areas, spending most of their income on armies along the frontiers (probably 350,000 troops in Rome and at least 200,000 in China) and gigantic capital cities (probably a million people at Rome and half that number at Chang'an, the Han capital). Both needed to move food, goods, and money from rich, taxpaying provinces to hungry, revenue-consuming concentrations of humanity.

Monte Testaccio ("Mount Potsherd"), a site in the suburbs of Rome, illustrates the scale of this pull factor in the West. This 150-foot-high, weed-covered mound of broken pottery is less dramatic than the Qin First Emperor's tomb, but for hard-core archaeologists it is Italy's answer to Egypt envy. Twenty-five million storage pots, a staggering number, were dumped here across three centuries. Most were used to ship olive oil—200 million gallons of it—from southern Spain to Rome, where urbanites put it on their food, washed with it,* and burned it in their lamps. To stand on Monte Testaccio is to feel awe at

---

*In those days before soap, people who could afford it got clean by oiling up, then scraping themselves down. That may not be to everyone's taste, but compared to using urine as toothpaste (which one Roman poet mentions, albeit in mockery), it was positively hygienic. Genuine soap, and toothpaste, were invented a thousand years later in China.

what hungry humans can do. And this was just one of Rome's artificial hills of garbage.

The second force, which pushed the economy upward, was the familiar one of climate change. Global cooling after 800 BCE had thrown low-end states into chaos and set off centuries of expansion. By 200 BCE continuing orbital changes ushered in what climatologists call the Roman Warm Period. This weakened winter winds—bad news for farmers in the Mediterranean and in China's great river valleys—but the high-end empires that had been created partly in response to the earlier global cooling now gave Eastern and Western societies the resilience not just to survive climate change but also to exploit it. Tougher times increased incentives for diversification and innovation. People tinkered with waterwheels and coal and exploited regional advantages by shipping goods around; high-end states provided roads and harbors to make these profitable and the armies and law codes to make profits secure, on the very sensible assumption that richer subjects will be able to pay more taxes.

High-end empires also pushed beyond the old heartlands into areas where the Warm Period made farming more productive—such as France, Romania, and rainy England in the West, and Manchuria, Korea, and central Asia in the East (Figure 6.3). Without knowing that they were doing it, the empires had effectively hedged their bets, since climate changes that hurt them in the warmer regions helped them in the cooler ones. In Rome, where the Mediterranean made it so easy for traders to move goods between regions, the benefits were surely huge; in China, where the great rivers were less convenient, the benefits must have been smaller, but real all the same.

The payoff from all the wars, enslavements, and massacres of the first millennium BCE was an age of plenty that inspired the Panglossian enthusiasm that opened this chapter. Its fruits were unevenly distributed—there were far more peasants than philosophers or kings—but more people were alive than in any previous age, in bigger cities, and on the whole they lived longer, ate better, and had more things than ever before.

When I began going on archaeological excavations, in 1970s England, I dug on several Roman sites. It could be exhausting work, clearing huge foundations of poured concrete (another Roman invention)

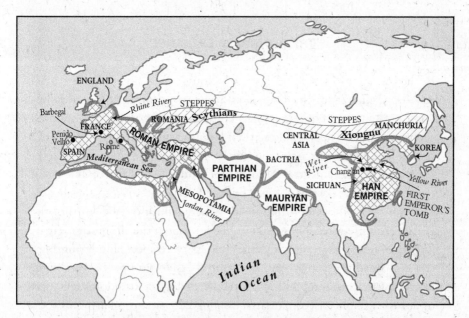

Figure 6.3. Making the most of the weather: the maximum extent of the
Han (c. 100 CE) and Roman (117 CE) empires, incorporating areas that
benefited from global warming

with pickaxes and racing to keep the log books one step ahead of the
flood of finds. But then I started doing a PhD on Greek society around
700 BCE, and in 1983 dug for the first time on a site of that date. It was
a shock. These people just didn't have anything. Finding even a couple
of hunks of rusty iron was a big deal. Compared to earlier populations,
Romans lived in a consumer paradise. Per capita consumption in what
became the western provinces of the Roman Empire rose from a level
near subsistence around 500 BCE to maybe 50 percent above it six or
seven hundred years later.

Similar processes were clearly under way in the East, too, even if, as
I mentioned earlier, they are not yet so well quantified. People in both
cores remained desperately poor by modern standards—half of all babies died before their fifth birthday, few people lived past fifty, and
poor diets typically left adults six inches shorter than us—but compared to all that had gone before, this was a golden age. Small wonder
the ancient empires were crawling with Dr. Panglosses.

THE OLD WORLD EXCHANGE

What the Panglosses could not see, though, was how surging social development within the cores was also transforming the worlds beyond the empires' borders. When empires were strong, they imposed their wills on the peoples along their frontiers, as when Darius of Persia in the sixth century BCE and the Qin First Emperor in the third brought great swaths of the central Asian steppe under their control; but when empires were weak, the nomads pushed back. In the West, the successor states that Alexander the Great's generals built on the ruins of the Persian Empire after 300 BCE could never match the might of their illustrious predecessor, and Scythian raiders were soon plundering Bactria and northern India. Another central Asian group, the Parthians, began infiltrating Iran; and when the Macedonian kingdoms fell apart under the weight of Roman attacks after 200 BCE, the Parthians took full advantage.

The Parthians differed from earlier nomads who had pushed their way into the Western core. Nomads such as the Scythians got rich by robbing or extorting protection money from agrarian empires; they were basically bandits, with no interest in conquering high-end states and managing their bewildering bureaucracies. The Parthian horsemen, by contrast, were only seminomads. They came from the edges of the central Asian steppe rather than its barren heart, and had been living alongside farmers for generations. Their rulers knew how to extract taxes from downtrodden peasants while maintaining the horseback traditions that their military power depended on; and by about 140 BCE they had turned much of the old Persian Empire into a loosely integrated kingdom of their own.

The Parthian monarchs liked to call themselves the heirs of Cyrus and Darius and strenuously assimilated themselves to Western high culture, but in reality theirs was always a low-end state. It could never threaten Rome's existence, although it did administer a short, sharp shock to any Roman who forgot the power of nomadic cavalry. Parthia's horsemen were famous for the "Parthian shot," where a rider pretended to flee, then turned in his saddle to loose arrows at his pursuer. Tactics such as these allowed Parthia to see off the Roman general Crassus, who lost his army and his life in a rash attack in 53 BCE. The

Parthian king, a great admirer of Western culture, was watching a Greek tragedy when Crassus' head was brought to him; his education was good enough that he could get the joke when the lead actor worked the grisly memento into his lines.

Rome's problems with Parthia at the western end of the steppes, however, paled by comparison with China's with the Xiongnu at the eastern end. There the Qin First Emperor's preemptive war in 215 BCE had disastrous results: instead of intimidating the nomads, it set off a political revolution on the steppes, fusing the feuding Xiongnu tribes into the world's first true nomad empire. Rather than taxing peasants to pay for a mounted aristocracy, like the Parthians did, the Xiongnu overlord Maodun funded his ultra-low-end state entirely by plundering China and buying the loyalty of lesser nomad chiefs with captured silk and wine.

Maodun's timing was excellent. He took over the Xiongnu in 209 BCE, right after the First Emperor's death, and for nine years exploited China's civil wars to loot to his heart's content. In 200 BCE the first Han emperor, Gaodi, decided that enough was enough, and led a huge army into the steppe, only to learn that fighting nomads was different from fighting rivals for China's throne. The Xiongnu fell back, letting the Chinese starve in the wilderness, and by the time Maodun turned and sprang an ambush, one-third of Gaodi's men had lost fingers to frostbite. The Chinese emperor barely got out in one piece; and as generally happens in war, most of his men fared worse.

When he realized that attrition, inaction, and preemption were all failing against the Xiongnu, Gaodi came up with a fourth strategy: he would make Maodun family. Tearing his eldest daughter from Chang'an's polished stone chambers and pearl-seeded bedspreads,* Gaodi packed her off to be Maodun's wife, to count out her days in a felt tent on the steppe. A thousand years later Chinese poets still sang of the heartbreak of the Han maiden alone among the fierce horsemen.

This royal marriage initiated what Chinese scholars euphemistically called the harmonious kinship policy, and just in case love was not enough, Gaodi also bought Maodun off with annual "gifts" of

---

*This is how the poet Chuci described the luxuries in an account of Chang'an's palaces in 208 BCE, although these particular delights have not yet turned up in excavations.

gold and silk. Unfortunately the gifts did not really work either. The Xiongnu kept raising the price and then plundering anyway, confident that so long as the costs of the damage were less than the costs of going to war to punish them, Han emperors would do nothing.

Harmonious kinship lasted for sixty increasingly expensive years, until in the 130s BCE the Han court split bitterly over it. Some remembered the disaster of 200 BCE and urged patience; others bayed for blood. In 135 BCE, when his cautious mother died, the young Emperor Wudi joined the sanguinary crowd. Each year from 129 through 119 BCE he sent armies hundreds of thousands strong into the wilderness, and each year barely half their number returned. The cost in lives and treasure was appalling, and Wudi's critics—the educated elite who wrote the history books—concluded that his preemptive war had been a disaster.

But Wudi's campaigns, like those Darius of Persia waged against the Scythians four hundred years earlier (which were also judged a failure by the history writers), transformed the nomad problem. Deprived of gifts and plunder to share with subordinates and with their grazing lands under constant threat, Xiongnu rulers lost control of their allies and started fighting one another. In 51 BCE they acknowledged Han rule, and about a century later broke into two tribes. One retreated northward; the other settled inside the Chinese empire.

By the first century CE the Romans and Han had both gained the initiative against the nomads. The Han started "using barbarians to fight barbarians," as they called it, giving the Southern Xiongnu a place to live (and constant "gifts") in return for military service against other nomads. Rome, protected by the forests, mountains, and farms of eastern Europe from most movements along the steppe highway, only directly faced (semi)nomads in Parthia; and even here, Rome faced them not on the steppe, where nomads had so many advantages, but among the cities and canals of Mesopotamia. Whenever emperors got serious, Rome's legions brushed Parthian resistance aside.

That said, neither Rome's eastern nor China's northern frontier ever entirely settled down. In 114 CE Rome chased the Parthians out of Mesopotamia, getting control of the whole Western core, only to abandon the land between the rivers in 117. Four more times in the second century Rome overran Mesopotamia, and four more times gave it up. Despite its wealth, Mesopotamia was just too far away and too difficult to hold. China, by contrast, found that bringing the Xiongnu inside its territory gradually converted its border from a line on a map into a fluid frontier zone, a Wild North where people came and went as they liked, the government's writ rarely ran, and a good sword mattered more than legal niceties.

The growing entanglements of the nomadic and agrarian empires were altering Eurasia's geography, shrinking the world just a little. The most visible consequence is a huge zone of shared material culture, stretching from Ukraine to Mongolia, through which merchants and warriors passed Eastern and Western ideas, art, and weapons from hand to hand. The most important cargoes moving between East and West, though, were ones that no one could see at all.

In the thousands of years since Old World farmers had started crowding into villages, they had evolved a nasty set of pathogens. Most were highly contagious; many could be fatal. Large populations breathing on one another and sharing body fluids spread diseases rapidly, but sheer numbers also meant that plenty of people happened to have the right antibodies to resist them. Over the millennia these people spread their defenses through the gene pool. Random mutations could still turn dormant diseases back into killers that would burn through the human population like wildfire, but hosts and viruses would then work out a new balance where both could survive.

People exposed for the first time to an unfamiliar package of germs have few defenses against the silent killers. The most famous example is what the geographer and historian Alfred Crosby has called the "Columbian Exchange," the horrific, unintended fallout of Europe's conquest of the New World since 1492 CE. Entirely separate disease pools had evolved in Europe and the Americas. America had unpleasant ailments of its own, such as syphilis, but the small, rather thinly spread American populations could not begin to compete with Europe's rich repertoire of microbes. The colonized peoples were epidemiological virgins. Everything from measles and meningitis to smallpox and typhus—and plenty in between—invaded their bodies when the Europeans arrived, rupturing their cells and killing them in foul ways. No one knows for sure how many died, but the Columbian Exchange probably cut short the lives of at least three out of every four people in the New World. "It appears visibly that God wishes that [the natives] yield their place to new peoples," one sixteenth-century Frenchman concluded.

A similar but more evenly balanced "Old World Exchange" seems to have begun in the second century CE. The Western, South Asian, and Eastern cores had each evolved their own unique combination of deadly diseases in the thousands of years since agriculture had begun, and until 200 BCE these developed almost as if they were on different planets. But as more and more merchants and nomads moved along the chains linking the cores, the disease pools began to merge, setting loose horrors for everyone.

Chinese documents record that mysterious pestilences broke out in an army fighting nomads on the northwest frontier in 161–162 CE, killing a third of the troops. In 165 ancient texts again talk of disease in the army camps; but this time the texts are Roman, describing pestilence in military bases in Syria during a campaign against Parthia, four thousand miles from the Chinese outbreak. Plagues returned to China five more times between 171 and 185 and ravaged the Roman Empire almost as often in those years. In Egypt, where detailed records survive, epidemics apparently killed more than a quarter of the population.

It is hard to figure out just what ancient diseases were, partly because viruses have continued to evolve in the past two thousand years, but mostly because ancient authors described them in such maddeningly vague ways. Just as aspiring writers today can buy books such as *Screenwriting for Dummies* then churn out movies or TV shows to formula, ancient authors knew that any good history needed politics, battles, and plagues. Their readers, like us when we go to movies, had a strong sense of what these plot elements should look like. Plagues needed omens of their approach, gruesome symptoms, and staggering death tolls; rotting corpses, the breakdown of law and order, and heartbroken widows, parents, and/or children.

The easiest way to write a plague scene was to lift it from another historian and just change the names. In the West the archetype was Thucydides' eyewitness account of a plague that hit Athens in 430 BCE. In 2006, a DNA study suggested that this was a form of typhoid fever, though that is not entirely obvious from Thucydides' narrative; and after other historians had recycled his (admittedly gripping) prose for a thousand years, not very much at all is obvious about the epidemics they described.

Despite this fog of uncertainty, Roman and Chinese sources contrast sharply with Indian literature, which mentions no plagues in the second century CE. That may just reflect the educated classes' lack of interest in something as mundane as the deaths of millions of poor people, but more likely the plagues really did bypass India, which suggests that the Old World Exchange spread mostly across the Silk Road and steppes rather than by the Indian Ocean trade routes. That would certainly be consistent with how the epidemics began in China and Rome, in army camps on the frontiers.

Whatever the mechanisms of microbial exchange, terrible epidemics recurred every generation or so from the 180s CE on. In the West the worst years were 251–266, when for a while five thousand people died each day in the city of Rome. In the East the darkest days came between 310 and 322, beginning again in the northwest, where (according to reports) almost everyone died. A doctor who lived through the sickness made it sound like measles or smallpox:

> Recently there have been persons suffering from epidemic sores that attack the head, face, and trunk. In a short time, these sores spread all over the body. They have the appearance of hot boils containing some white matter. While some of these pustules are drying up a fresh crop appears. If not treated early the patients usually die. Those who recover are disfigured by purplish scars.

The Old World Exchange had devastating consequences. Cities shrank, trade declined, tax revenues fell, and fields were abandoned. And as if all this were not enough, every source of evidence—peat bogs, lake sediments, ice cores, tree rings, strontium-to-calcium ratios in coral reefs, even the chemistry of algae—suggests that the weather, too, turned against humanity, ending the Roman Warm Period. Average temperatures fell about 2°F between 200 and 500 CE, and since the cooler summers of what climatologists call the Dark Age Cold Period reduced evaporation from the oceans and weakened the monsoon winds, rainfall declined as well.

Under other circumstances, the flourishing Eastern and Western cores might have responded to climate change just as effectively as they had done when the Roman Warm Period began in the second century BCE. But this time disease and climate change—two of the five horsemen of the apocalypse who featured so prominently in Chapter 4—were riding together. What that would mean, and whether the other three horsemen of famine, migration, and state failure would join them, would depend on how people reacted.

LOSING THE MANDATE OF HEAVEN

Like all organizations, the Han and Roman empires had evolved to solve specific problems. They had learned how to defeat all rivals, govern vast territories and huge populations with simple technologies, and move food and revenue from rich provinces to the armies on their frontiers and the crowds in their great cities. Each, though, did all this in slightly different ways, and the differences determined how they responded to the Old World Exchange.

Most important was how each empire dealt with its army. To confront the Xiongnu from the 120s BCE onward, the Han had developed huge cavalry squadrons, increasingly recruited from the nomads themselves, and as they perfected the "using barbarians to fight barbarians" policy in the first century CE they settled many of these nomads within the empire. This had the double consequence of militarizing the frontier, where Xiongnu fighters lived with little Han supervision, and demilitarizing the interior. Few troops were to be found in the heart of China, except at the capital itself, and fewer still were recruited there. Chinese aristocrats saw little to gain from serving as officers over "barbarians" stationed far from the capital. War became something that distant foreigners did on the emperor's behalf.

The upside for emperors was that they no longer had to worry that powerful noblemen would use the army against them; the downside, that they no longer had much of a stick with which to beat any noblemen who did become troublesome. Consequently, as the state's monopoly on force weakened, aristocrats found it easier to bully local peasants, swallowing their farms into huge estates that the landlords ran as private fiefdoms. There is a limit to how much surplus can be squeezed out of peasants, and when the landlord was so near and the emperor so far away, more surplus was handed over to local masters as rent and less sent to Chang'an as tax.

Emperors pushed back, limiting the size of estates aristocrats could hold and the number of peasants on them, redistributing land to free (and taxable) small farmers, and raising cash from state monopolies on necessities such as iron, salt, and alcohol. But in 9 CE the emperor-landlord tussle turned critical when a high official named Wang Mang seized the throne, nationalized all land, abolished slavery and serfdom, and pronounced that from now on only the state could own gold. His near-Maoist centralization collapsed immediately, but peasant uprisings convulsed the empire, and by the time order returned, in the 30s CE, Han policy had gone through a sea change.

The emperor who replaced Wang Mang, Guangwu (reigned 25–57 CE), came from a propertied family, not one that drew its power from links to the old court. To restore Han authority, Guangwu had to work closely with his fellow magnates, and he threw his lot in with them, initiating a golden age for landowners. Growing as rich as kings and ruling thousands of peasants, these grandees virtually ignored the state and its bothersome taxmen. Formerly Han emperors had moved troublesome landowners to Chang'an so they could keep an eye on them, but Guangwu instead moved the capital to Luoyang (Figure 6.4), where the landowners were strongest and the magnates could monitor the court.*

The elite began rolling back the state and steadily disengaging from its biggest budget item, the army. By the late first century CE, with the Xiongnu no longer a major threat, the great cavalry army that had been built to fight them was being left to fend for itself, which meant plundering the peasants it supposedly protected. By about 150 CE the Southern Xiongnu, theoretically vassals, were more or less independent.

Nor was much effort made to reshape the army to meet new threats being posed by the Qiang, a name the Chinese used loosely for farmers and herders around their western frontier. Thanks perhaps to the clement weather of the Roman Warm Period, Qiang numbers had been growing for generations and small groups had moved into the western provinces, occupying land when they could, fighting and stealing

---

*Historians often call the period 202 BCE–9 CE the Western Han, because the capital was at Chang'an in the west, and the period 25–220 CE the Eastern Han, because the capital was at Luoyang in the east. Others prefer to speak of Former and Later Han.

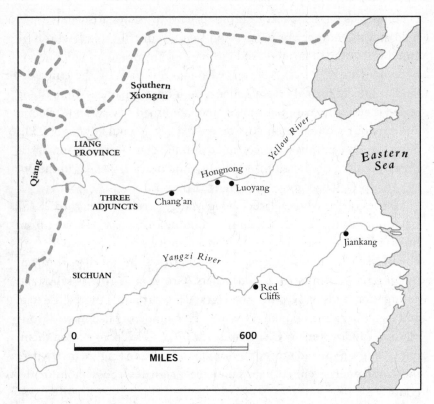

Figure 6.4. The end of the Han dynasty, 25–220 CE: locations
mentioned in the text

when they could not. To keep this under control the frontier needed
garrison troops, not nomadic cavalry, but the landowners of the Luoyang region did not want to pay for them.

Some officials suggested abandoning the western provinces altogether and leaving the Qiang to their own devices, but others feared a
domino effect. "If you lose Liang province," one courtier argued, "then
the Three Adjuncts will be your border. If the people of the Three
Adjuncts move inward, then Hongnong will be the border. If the people of Hongnong move inward, then Luoyang will be the border. If
you carry on like this you will reach the edge of the Eastern Sea, and
that, too, will be your border."

Persuaded, the government stayed the course and spent a fortune,
but infiltration continued. In 94 and again in 108 CE Qiang groups
took over broad swaths of the western provinces. In 110 there was a

general Qiang uprising, and by 150 the Qiang were as much beyond Luoyang's control as were the Xiongnu. On both the western and the northern frontiers local landowners had to organize their own defenses, turning dependent peasants into militias, and the governors, forgotten by the state that had sent them there, also raised their own armies (and plundered their provinces to pay them).

It must have been hard not to conclude that the Han had lost the mandate of heaven, and in 145 CE three separate rebellions demanded a new dynasty. For the great landowning elite, however, the cloud had a thick silver lining. The empire was smaller, tax receipts were dwindling, and the army was, in a sense, being privatized, but their estates were more productive than ever, imperial tax collectors left them alone, and war was but a distant rumor. All was, after all, for the best.

China's Panglosses had a rude awakening when the Old World Exchange burst onto this scene in the 160s. Plagues ravaged the northwest, where the Qiang were moving into the empire, and spread across the land. And rather than responding with strong leadership, the imperial court imploded.

In theory, the hundreds of bureaucrats who filled offices at the palace in Luoyang lived only to put the emperors' wishes into practice, but in practice (like civil servants in many eras) they had their own interests too. Most came from landowning families, and tended to be remarkably good at finding reasons not to do things that landowners found distasteful (like raising money for wars). Any emperor with ideas of his own had to work around them. Some emperors brought in kinsmen, particularly relatives of their multiple wives, to get things done; others turned to eunuchs, whose advantages I mentioned in Chapter 5. Astute emperors used both to great effect, but these agents, too, had their own agendas, and tried to make sure that emperors were not astute. In fact, they so arranged matters that after 88 CE no prince over the age of fourteen ever survived to ascend the throne. Court politics degenerated into backstairs intrigues among senior ministers, eunuchs, and boy emperors' in-laws.

In 168 CE, at the very moment Han China most needed leadership, palace eunuchs staged a coup against the in-laws of the newly installed twelve-year-old emperor, Lingdi. For almost twenty years, while epidemics raged and Xiongnu and Qiang raided, the court launched purge and counterpurge, claiming thousands of lives and paralyzing government. Corruption and incompetence reached new heights. Injustice sparked uprisings, and, unable to muster or command armies, Lingdi's handlers authorized local strongmen to raise troops and do what they thought necessary.

People cried out for explanations of this abrupt descent into chaos, and when neither Confucian rituals nor Daoist mysticism provided them, self-proclaimed visionaries filled the gap. In the Yellow River valley a physician won a great following by teaching that sin caused disease and that confession brought health. In the 170s he went one step further: the dynasty itself, he concluded, was the ultimate source of sin and contagion. It had to go. "When a new cycle of sixty years begins," he pronounced, "great fortune will come to the world."

But great fortune did not come. Instead, when the new calendar cycle began on April 3, 184, things got even worse. Even though pro-Han armies suppressed the rebels (known as Yellow Turbans from their headgear, yellow being the symbol of the new age), imitators popped up all over China. Heaven itself seemed to be showing its displeasure when the Yellow River flooded massively, displacing 365,000 peasants. A "Five Pecks of Grain" movement (promising freedom from sickness to those who confessed their sins and paid five measures of rice) turned Sichuan into an independent Daoist theocracy; the Qiang exploited the chaos and plundered western China again; the special commanders deputized to contain these threats made themselves independent warlords; and when the court did act, it only made things worse.

In 189 Lingdi recalled the mightiest warlord, Dong Zhuo, but Dong wrote back saying, "The Han and barbarian troops under my command all came to me and said . . . 'Our provisions will be cut off, and our wives and children will die of hunger and cold.' Pulling back my carriage, they would not let me go." When Lingdi insisted, Dong called his bluff, returning to Luoyang but bringing his army with him. Lingdi conveniently died as Dong approached, and the courtiers around Lingdi's senior widow (who backed a thirteen-year-old as the new ruler) and the eunuchs (who backed an eight-year-old) set about murdering one another. Dong broke into Luoyang, massacred the eunuchs, murdered the older boy, and set up the younger as Emperor Xiandi. Then he torched Luoyang and wondered what to do next.

The Han were no longer in control, but neither was Dong, because while the emperors' managerial, high-end power had failed, their vaguely divine, low-end power persisted. No one dared proclaim himself emperor while Xiandi lived, but no one dared murder the boy king either. (Warlords, however, were fair game; Dong was assassinated in 192.) As the power brokers squabbled, using Emperor Xiandi as a pawn, the empire broke down into fiefdoms, the Xiongnu and Qiang took over the frontiers, and the high-end institutions that had seemed so solid melted into air.

"My armor has been worn so long that lice breed in it," the warlord and part-time poet Cao Cao wrote sometime after 197.

> Myriad lineages have perished,
> White bones exposed in the fields,
> For a thousand li [roughly three hundred miles] not even a cock
>   is heard.
> Only one out of a hundred survives.
> Thinking of it rends my entrails.

Cao contained his grief long enough, however, to snatch Xiandi and manipulate the boy emperor into making him the main player in northern China.

Cao was a complicated man. He may well have been trying to restore the Han dynasty, casting himself in the time-honored role of wise adviser. Seeing how landlords had undermined the old high-end state, he tried to solve the military problem by settling his soldiers in colonies where some grew food while others trained for war, and the political problem by classifying the gentry into nine ranks, determining their positions in a meritocracy. Like Tiglath-Pileser in Assyria a thousand years earlier, he was cutting the magnates out of the picture, and until 208, when his navy was wiped out at the battle of the Red Cliffs, it looked as if Cao might pull China together again.

Yet despite these efforts, Cao (thanks largely to an enormous fourteenth-century novel called *The Romance of the Three Kingdoms*) has been remembered chiefly as the monster who destroyed the Han. In twentieth-century Peking Opera, actors wearing the Cao mask with its caked white makeup and black-lined eyes were always the villain audiences loved to hate, and in the 1990s Cao went high-tech, jumping to the computer screen as the bad guy in countless video games. He made it to bigger screens as the villain of a TV version of *The Romance* (in eighty-four episodes), and to the biggest screens of all in the costliest Asian-financed film ever made (*The Battle of the Red Cliffs*, costing $80 million; Part One was released to coincide with the 2008 Beijing Olympics).

Cao's bad reputation has more to do with what happened after his death than with his own misdeeds. After the battle of the Red Cliffs a balance developed among three main warlords, and after 220, when Cao's son finally told Emperor Xiandi to abdicate, the country devolved into three kingdoms. The one that Cao founded, though, was always the strongest. It crushed one of its rivals in 264, rebranded itself as the Jin dynasty,* and in 280 raised a huge army and fleet that finished reconquering China.

For the next decade, the post-Han collapse looked like a brief aberration, comparable perhaps to what had happened in the Western core after 2200 or 1750 BCE, when climate change, migrations, and famine caused state collapse but had little impact on social development. But it soon turned out that the fall of the Han was in fact much more like the Western collapse around 1200 BCE, with enormous long-term consequences.

Battlefield victories could reduce the number of surviving warlords to one but could not change China's underlying problems. The aristocracy remained as strong as ever and rapidly undermined Cao's military colonies and meritocracy. Epidemics still raged, and the Dark Age Cold Period was making life harder not only for farmers in the Yellow River valley but also for the Xiongnu and Qiang. Between 265 and 287 a quarter of a million central Asians settled inside the Jin Empire. Sometimes the Jin welcomed the manpower they provided; at other times the authorities simply could not stand up to them.

In this context, little things such as an emperor's love life could assume huge importance. Rather carelessly, the Jin emperor sired twenty-seven sons, and when he died in 289 some of them hired the

---

*Jin had been the name of one of the great warring states of the eighth through fifth centuries BCE. Most of the new states created in the period of disunion in 220–589 CE reused older names to make their rule seem legitimate, apparently unconcerned by the confusion this would cause for students today.

wildest nomads they could find to fight one another. The nomads, no fools, quickly realized that they did not have to settle for the wages they were paid: they could demand any price they liked. When a Xiongnu chief did not get his price in 304, he turned up the heat by announcing that he was founding a new kingdom. The Jin still did not give him everything he wanted, so his son burned Luoyang in 311, desecrated the Jin dynasty's family tombs, and took its emperor prisoner, setting him to serve wine at feasts. Still not getting the loot they thought they deserved, in 316 the Xiongnu destroyed Chang'an, too, and captured the new Jin emperor, putting this prisoner in charge of washing cups as well as serving wine. Tiring of the game after a few months, the Xiongnu killed him and his relatives.

The Jin state collapsed. Bands of Xiongnu and Qiang plundered at will across north China, and the Jin court, with a million followers in its train, fled to Jiankang (modern Nanjing) on the Yangzi River. The northern lands they gave up were home to some of the world's most advanced agriculture, but under the combined impact of high death rates (as epidemics hit home) and high emigration, much now reverted to the wild. That suited the nomads who moved in from the steppes just fine, but for remaining farming communities it meant that famine also reared its head. In happier days, local gentry or the state might have stepped in with aid, but now there was no one to help. To make the misery complete, plagues of locusts devoured what surpluses the villagers still produced. New epidemics, perhaps carried by migrants from the steppes, brought yet more woes to the weakened population. Smallpox probably made its first appearance in China in 317, the year after Chang'an burned.

The wars that Xiongnu and Qiang chiefs waged across this barren landscape were more like giant slave raids than clashes between high-end states. Rulers rounded up peasants, tens of thousands at a time, and herded them into territories around new capital cities, where the bondsmen tilled fields to feed armies of full-time cavalrymen. The horsemen, meanwhile, imported new weapons from the steppes—proper saddles, stirrups, and bigger horses that could charge while wearing armor and carrying armored knights—that made infantry virtually obsolete. Those Chinese aristocrats who did not flee south took to the hills, their dependent peasants crowding into huge stockades that offered the only refuge from marauding horsemen.

The new states forming in north China ("The Sixteen Kingdoms of the Five Barbarians," as Chinese historians contemptuously called them) were highly unstable. In 350, for instance, one state imploded in an orgy of ethnic cleansing, with native Chinese slaughtering Inner Asians. "The dead numbered more than two hundred thousand," the official dynastic history says. "Corpses were piled outside the city walls, where they were all eaten by jackals, wolves, and wild dogs." Other chiefs swarmed into the power vacuum this left. By 383 one lord briefly looked like he might unite all China; but as he closed in on Jiankang, an apparently minor defeat mutated into a panic-stricken rout, and by 385 his entire state had ceased to exist.

Refugees fleeing south from the destruction of Chang'an founded an "Eastern Jin"* state at Jiankang in 317. Unlike the bandit kingdoms in northern China, this boasted a luxurious, sophisticated court and kept up the appearances of how Chinese royalty should live. It sent ambassadors to Japan and Indochina, produced magnificent literature and art, and, most remarkable of all, survived for a century.

But behind the surface glitter, the Eastern Jin kingdom was as bitterly divided as any northern state. The former northern grandees who fled south had little interest in obeying the emperor's commands. Some refugee noblemen clustered in Jiankang, becoming parasitic timeservers and feeding off the royal court; others colonized the Yangzi Basin and carved out estates in this hot, wet new homeland. They drove off indigenous peoples, felled forests, drained swamps, and settled refugee peasants as serfs.

Conflict was endemic at every level. The new noblemen who had fled from the north feuded with older southern families; aristocrats of all stripes struggled against middling magnates; the rich and the middling elites both squeezed the peasantry; Chinese of all classes pushed natives back into the mountains and forests; and everyone resisted the embattled court at Jiankang. Despite all their heartbroken poetry about the lost lands of the north, the landlords of southern China were in no hurry to pay the taxes or surrender the powers that might have allowed a reconquest. The mandate of heaven had been lost.

---

*So called to distinguish it from the "Western Jin" who had ruled all China from Chang'an between 280 and 316 CE.

THE AWFUL REVOLUTION

Unlike the crisis of the twelfth century BCE, the crisis triggered by the Old World Exchange was Eurasia-wide, and its Western component inspired what was arguably the first masterpiece of modern historical writing, Edward Gibbon's *History of the Decline and Fall of the Roman Empire*. His subject, Gibbon declared, was an "awful revolution," one "which will ever be remembered, and is still [in the 1770s] felt by the nations of the earth." He was right: only during his lifetime had Western social development regained the dizzy heights it had reached under the Roman Empire.

The early Roman and Han emperors had faced similar problems but had tried different solutions. Terrified of civil war, Chinese rulers neutralized the army, but then had few weapons against powerful landlords; Roman rulers instead took over the army, putting relatives in command and filling its ranks with citizens. This made it harder for civilians to defy emperors, but easier for soldiers to do so.

It took skill to manage this system, and since plenty of Rome's rulers were unhinged, periodic crashes were unavoidable. Caligula's orgies and decision to make his horse a consul were bad enough, but Nero's fondness for forcing senators to sing in public and murdering anyone who annoyed him was too much. In 68 CE three different factions in the army proclaimed their own generals as emperor and it took a brutal civil war to sort matters out. "Now was revealed," the historian Tacitus noted, "the secret of empire—that emperors could be made outside Rome." Wherever there were soldiers, there could be a new emperor.

The Roman solution did, however, preserve the frontiers (Figure 6.5). The Germans beyond the Rhine and Danube, like the Qiang along China's western border, experienced population growth in the first centuries CE. They responded by fighting one another, trading with Roman towns, and slipping across the rivers into the empire. For all these activities, organizing into larger groups with stronger kings made sense. Like the Han, Rome responded to increasingly porous borders by building walls (most famously Hadrian's across Britain), monitoring trade, and fighting back.

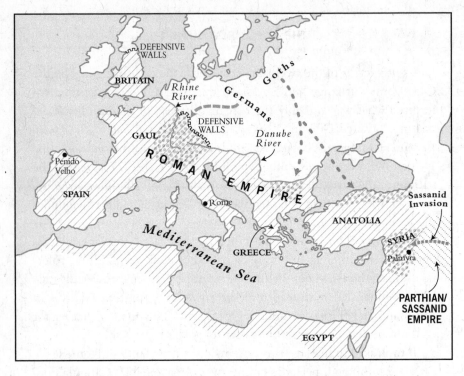

Figure 6.5. Rome's third-century crisis. The dotted areas show where Germanic, Gothic, and Persian raids were common.

In 161 CE, when Marcus Aurelius Antoninus became emperor, Rome still seemed to be in sturdy health, and Marcus looked forward to following his passion—philosophy. Instead, he had to confront the Old World Exchange. The first serious epidemic broke out in army camps on China's northwest frontier the year he ascended the throne, and the very same year a Parthian invasion of Syria forced Marcus to concentrate troops there. Their crowded camps provided the ideal host for disease to spread, and in 165 a pestilence (smallpox? measles? the literary accounts are, as ever, vague) devastated them. It reached Rome in 167, just as population movements far to the north and east were pushing new, powerful Germanic federations across the Danube. Marcus spent the rest of his life—thirteen years—fighting them.*

*He did, though, take the evenings off to write *The Meditations*, one of the classics of Stoic philosophy.

Unlike China, Rome won its second-century frontier wars. Had it not, Rome—like the Han—might have lurched into crisis in the 180s. As it was, though, Marcus' victories affected only the pace of change, not its results, which suggests that armies alone could not halt the collapse. The epidemics' massive death toll had thrown the economy into chaos. Food prices and agricultural wages soared, which made the plagues a boon for the farmers who survived, who could abandon less-productive fields and concentrate on the best land; but as farming contracted and taxes and rents fell, the larger economy went into free fall. The number of shipwrecks in the Mediterranean declines sharply after 200, and pollution in ice cores, lake sediments, and bogs follows after 250 (Figure 6.6). By then everyone was feeling the pinch. Bones from cattle, pigs, and sheep become smaller and scarcer in settlements after 200, suggesting declining standards of living, and by the 220s

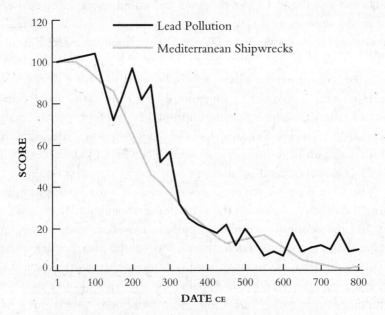

Figure 6.6. Declining and falling: numbers of Mediterranean shipwrecks and levels of lead pollution in the lake bed at Penido Velho, Spain, across the first millennium CE. The downward slopes mirror the upward slopes in the first millennium BCE shown in Figure 6.2. As in Figure 6.2, numbers of wrecks and amounts of lead have been normalized so they can be compared on the same vertical scale, with the amounts of each in 1 CE being counted as 100.

wealthy city dwellers were putting up fewer grand buildings and inscriptions.

Fifty years after Marcus' victories, Rome lost control of its frontiers anyway. Just as victories over the Xiongnu in the first century BCE had paradoxically made it harder for the Han to control their borders, a string of Roman successes undermined Parthia so badly that the regime collapsed before a Persian uprising in the 220s CE. The new Sassanid dynasty that emerged forged a much stronger army and in 244 defeated a Roman force and killed the emperor who led it.

Rushing troops and money to prop up the collapsing eastern front left Rome unable to defend its Danube and Rhine frontiers properly. Instead of sneaking across in little gangs to steal cattle, war bands hundreds or thousands strong now pushed through the denuded lines, burning, looting, and carrying off slaves. The Goths, who had only recently migrated to the Balkans from the shores of the Baltic, raided as far as Greece and in 251 defeated and killed another Roman emperor. By then more epidemics had broken out, perhaps carried by these population movements. When Rome finally mustered another army against Persia, in 259, it hit a new low: the emperor Valerian was captured and thrown in a cage, where he remained for a year, dressed in slave's rags and suffering ingeniously horrible torments. Romans insisted that Valerian's fortitude impressed his captors, but the reality seems to be that the Persians, like the Xiongnu when they captured Chinese emperors, eventually got bored. They flayed Valerian and hung his skin on their capital's walls.

The Old World Exchange and the rise of Sassanid Persia transformed Rome's position. At the very moment that population was falling and the economy stumbling, emperors needed more money and troops than ever before. Their first (not-so-bright) idea, paying for new armies with debased currency, simply made money worthless and accelerated economic collapse. Appalled by the failures of central government, armies took matters into their own hands, proclaiming new emperors with bewildering speed. In contrast to earlier emperors, these men had no whiff of divinity about them at all. Most were tough soldiers, and some were illiterate privates. Few lasted longer than two years, and all died by the sword.

With army factions spending more time fighting one another than defending the provinces, local grandees followed the same path as their

Chinese counterparts, turning the peasants into dependents and organizing them into militias. The Syrian trading city of Palmyra managed
to throw the Persians back, theoretically on Rome's behalf, but its
warrior queen Zenobia (who led her troops in person and regularly
attended city assemblies dressed in armor) then turned on Rome too,
overrunning Egypt and Anatolia. At the other end of the empire a
governor on the Rhine declared an independent "Kingdom of the
Gauls," taking Gaul (modern France), Britain, and Spain with him.

By 270 Rome looked rather like China had done in 220, divided
into three kingdoms. But despite all the turmoil, Rome's situation was
actually less dire. By taking on Persia and the Germans in the 260s,
Palmyra and Gaul bought the empire a breathing space, and the cities
around the Mediterranean—the empire's fiscal backbone—remained
largely secure. So long as goods kept moving by sea, money kept coming into the imperial coffers, and the new, hardheaded military men
who sat on the throne could recover and rebuild. Trading the philosophers' beards and flowing locks of earlier emperors for shaved chins and
crew cuts, they hiked taxes in the regions they still controlled, built a
strike force around armored cavalry, then turned on their enemies.
They smashed Palmyra in 272, Gaul in 274, and most of the Germanic
war bands by 282. In 297 Rome even got some revenge for Valerian by
capturing the Persian royal harem.

The emperor Diocletian (reigned 284–305) exploited this turn-
around with administrative, fiscal, and defensive reforms that adapted
the empire to deal with the new world. The army more or less doubled
in size. The frontiers never entirely settled down, but Rome was now
winning more battles than it lost, blunting Germanic raids with defense in depth and wearing the Persians down in sieges. To handle all
this activity Diocletian split his job into four parts, with one ruler and
a deputy handling the western provinces and another ruler and deputy
the eastern. Predictably, the empire's multiple rulers fought two-, three-,
or four-way civil wars as often as they fought external enemies, but
compared to the twenty-seven-way civil war in China's Jin Empire in
the 290s, this was stability indeed.

A new empire was taking shape. Rome itself ceased to be a capital
city, as decision-making shifted in the western provinces to forward
bases near the frontiers and in the eastern to a grand new city at Constantinople. But in the end, no amount of reorganization could solve

the empire's underlying problems. The economic integration built up over so many centuries had been shaken. The eastern provinces revived in the fourth century, with trade in grain, wine, and olive oil again spreading wealth far down the hierarchy, but the western provinces steadily drifted out of this circuit. Great landlords in western Europe held on to much of the power they had gained during the third century, tying "their" peasants to the land and shielding them from state taxation. As estates grew more self-sufficient, the cities around them dwindled and trade and industry declined further still; and the toughest problems were simply beyond any emperor's ken. Temperatures and rainfall kept declining, whatever rulers said or did; epidemics kept killing; and peoples on the steppe kept moving.

Sometime around 350, a group called the Huns moved west across Kazakhstan, sending dominos tumbling in every direction (Figure 6.7). Just why they inspired such fear is debated. Ancient writers blamed their sheer horribleness; modern scholars more often point to the powerful bows they used. Once again, we can only observe the consequences. Nomads fleeing the Huns broke into India and Iran or retreated west into modern Hungary. That made life difficult for the Goths, who had settled as farmers in what we now call Romania after their third-century raids on the empire. After heated internal debates, the Goths asked Rome for sanctuary inside the empire.

There was nothing new in this. Rome had developed a policy rather like the Han "using barbarians to fight barbarians," routinely admitting immigrants, dividing them into small groups, then enrolling them in the army, settling them on farms, or selling them as slaves. This simultaneously relieved pressure on the frontiers, raised troop numbers, and increased the taxable population. The immigrants, naturally, often had different ideas, preferring to settle as a group inside the empire and continue living as they had before. To prevent this, Rome needed always to have enough troops on hand to overawe the immigrants.

The Goths' arrival at the Danube in summer 376 was a tough call for Emperor Valens, who ruled the eastern provinces from Constantinople. On the one hand, there were too many Goths for comfort. On the other, the potential gains from accepting so many immigrants were enormous, and it might in any case be difficult to keep them out, especially since Valens' best troops were away fighting Persia. He decided to admit the Goths, but almost as soon as they crossed the river his

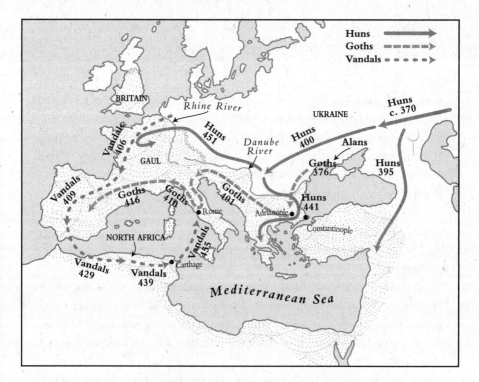

Figure 6.7. Scourges of God: the coming of the Huns and the collapse of the western Roman Empire, 376–476 CE. The map shows three major groups of invaders (Huns, solid lines; Goths, broken lines; Vandals, dotted lines) with the dates of their main movements. There were countless smaller migrations too.

commanders on the ground, more interested in profiteering than in dispersing the immigrants, lost control. Half-starved Goths broke out, looting what is now Bulgaria and demanding a homeland within the empire. Playing hardball, Valens refused to negotiate. He disentangled his army from the Persian front and rushed back to the Balkans—only to make another bad decision, giving battle rather than waiting for his western co-emperor to bring more help.

About fifteen thousand Romans (many of them Germanic immigrants) fought maybe twenty thousand Goths at Adrianople in August 378. Two-thirds of the Romans, including Valens, died in the rout that followed. Back in Augustus' day, losing ten thousand troops would barely have registered; Rome would have called up more legions and taken terrible revenge. By 378, though, the empire was stretched so thin that these men could not be replaced. The Goths were inside the empire and out of control.

A peculiar standoff developed. The Goths were not nomads like the Xiongnu, stealing things and then riding off to the steppes, nor were they imperialists like the Persians, come to annex provinces. They wanted to carve out their own enclave in the empire. But with no siege engines to storm cities and no administration to run them, they needed Roman cooperation; and when that was not forthcoming they rattled around the Balkans, trying to blackmail Constantinople into granting them their own kingdom. Lacking legions to expel them, the eastern emperor pleaded poverty, bribed the Goths, and skirmished with them, until, in 401, he persuaded them that they would get a better deal by migrating westward, whereupon they became his co-emperor's problem.

But all this clever diplomacy ceased to matter in 405 when the Huns resumed their western progress. More dominos fell and more Germanic tribes pressed against Rome's frontiers. The legions, now chiefly made up of Germanic immigrants and led by a half-German general, wore them down in bloody campaigns, and diplomats wove yet more webs, but on New Year's Eve, 406, Rome finally lost control when thousands of Germans poured across the frozen Rhine. There were no more armies to stop them. The immigrants fanned out, taking everything. The poet Sidonius, among the richest of the rich, described the indignities he had to endure when a band moved onto his estate in Gaul. "Why ask for a song to Venus," he wrote to a correspondent living back in Rome, "when I'm stuck in the middle of a long-haired rabble, forced to listen to Germanic speech, keeping a straight face while I praise songs from a swinish Burgundian who spreads rancid butter in his hair? . . . You don't have the stink of garlic and onions from ten breakfasts belched on you early every morning." Plenty would have envied Sidonius, though. Another eyewitness put things more bluntly: "All Gaul is filled with the smoke of a single funeral pyre."

The army in Britain rebelled, taking charge of its own defense, and in 407 what remained of the Rhine armies joined it. By then everything was falling apart. Struggling to get the western Roman emperor's attention amid so many disasters, the Goths invaded Italy in 408 and in 410 sacked Rome itself. They finally got their deal in 416, with the emperor agreeing that if the Goths helped him drive the Germans and assorted usurpers out of Gaul and Spain, they could keep part of the territory.

Rome's frontiers, like China's, had become places where barbarians (as each empire called outsiders) settled and then took imperial pay to defend the empire against more barbarians trying to push their way in. It was a lose-lose situation for the emperors. When the Germanic Goths (now fighting on Rome's side) defeated the Germanic Vandals (fighting against Rome) in Spain in 429, the Vandals crossed to North Africa. It may seem hard to believe, but what is today the Tunisian Sahara Desert was then Rome's breadbasket, ten thousand square miles of irrigated fields, exporting half a million tons of grain to Italy each year. Without this food, the city of Rome would starve; without the taxes on it, Rome could not pay its own Germans to fight enemy Germans.

For another ten years brilliant Roman generals and diplomats (themselves often of German stock) managed to keep the Vandals in check and parts of Gaul and Spain loyal, but in 439 it all came crashing down. The Vandals overran Carthage's agricultural hinterland and Rome's worst-case scenario abruptly materialized.

Rulers in Constantinople were often quite happy to see their potential rivals in Rome struggling, but the prospect of the western parts of the empire actually breaking up alarmed the eastern emperor Theodosius II enough that he mustered a large force to help liberate what is now Tunisia. But as his troops gathered in 441, yet another blow fell. A new king of the Huns, Attila—the "Scourge of God," as Roman authors called him—erupted into the Balkans, leading not just ferocious cavalry but also a modern siege train. (Refugees from Constantinople may have brought him this technology; an ambassador from Theodosius described meeting such an exile at Attila's court in 449.)

As his cities crumbled under the Huns' battering rams, Theodosius canceled the attack on the Vandals. He saved Constantinople—just— but these were dark days for Rome. The city still had perhaps 800,000 residents around 400 CE; by 450 three-quarters had left. Tax revenues dried up and the army evaporated, and the worse things got, the more usurpers tried to seize the throne. Attila chose this moment to decide he had squeezed the Balkans dry, and turned west. The half-Gothic commander of Rome's western armies managed to convince the Goths that Attila was their enemy too, and, leading an almost entirely Germanic force, he dealt Attila the only defeat of his career. Attila died before he could get revenge. Bursting a blood vessel during a drinking bout to celebrate his umpteenth wedding, the Scourge of God went to meet his maker.

Without Attila the loose Hun Empire disintegrated, leaving the emperors in Constantinople free to try to put the western empire back together again, but not until 467 did all the requirements—money, ships, and a Roman strongman worth backing—fall into place. Emptying his treasury, the eastern emperor sent his admiral Basiliskos with a thousand ships to recapture North Africa and heal the western provinces' fiscal backbone.

In the end, the fate of the empire came down to the wind. In summer 468, as Basiliskos closed on Carthage, the breezes should have been blowing westward along North Africa's shore, pushing Basiliskos' ships along. But at the last moment the wind shifted and trapped them against the coast. The Vandals sent burning hulks into the packed Roman vessels, just the tactics that the English would use against the Spanish Armada in 1588. Ancient ships, with their tinder-dry ropes, wooden decks, and cloth sails, could turn into infernos in seconds. Piled on top of one another, panicking to push the fireships away with poles, and with no room to escape, the Romans lost all order. The Vandals came in for the kill, and it was all over.

In Chapter 5 I talked about the great-man theory of history, which holds that it is unique geniuses, such as Tiglath-Pileser of Assyria, not grand impersonal forces, such as the Old World Exchange, that shape events. The other side of the great-man coin is the bungling-idiot theory of history: What, we have to ask, would have happened had Basiliskos had the wits not to get trapped against the coast?* He probably would have retaken Carthage, but would that have restored the Italy–North Africa fiscal axis? Maybe; the Vandals had been in Africa for less than forty years, and the Roman Empire might have been able to rebuild economic structures quickly. Or then again, maybe not. Odoacer, king of the Goths, the strongest strongman in western Europe, already had his eye on Italy. In 476 he wrote to Zeno, the emperor in Constantinople, observing that the world no longer needed two

---

*This assumes, of course, that Basiliskos actually was a bungling idiot. The Romans preferred conspiracy theories, accusing Basiliskos of taking bribes and almost lynching him.

emperors. Zeno's glory was sufficient for everyone, Odoacer said, and he made a proposal: he would run Italy—loyally, of course—on Zeno's behalf. Zeno understood full well that Odoacer was really announcing his takeover of Italy, but also knew it was no longer worth arguing about.

And so the end of Rome came, not with a bang but a whimper. Would Zeno have been any better placed to defend Italy if Basiliskos had recovered Carthage than he actually was in 476? I doubt it. By this point preserving a Mediterranean-wide empire was beyond anyone's power, and the fifth century's frenzied maneuvering, politicking, and killing could do little to change the realities of economic decline, political breakdown, and migrations. The classical world was finished.

SMALLER WORLDS

The Eastern and Western cores had each split in two. In China, the Eastern Jin dynasty ruled the southern part of the old empire, but saw themselves as rightful heirs to the whole realm. Similarly, in the West a Byzantine Empire (so called because its capital, Constantinople, stood on the site of the earlier Greek city Byzantium) ruled the eastern part of the old Roman Empire but claimed its entirety (Figure 6.8).

The Eastern Jin and Byzantine Empires remained high-end states, with bureaucrats, taxes, and salaried armies. Each boasted great cities and learned scholars, and the farms of the Nile and Yangzi valleys were richer than ever. But neither compared with the Roman and Han empires in their heydays. Their worlds were shrinking as northern China and western Europe slid out of the cores.

Disease, migration, and war had dissolved the networks of managers, merchants, and money that had bound each of the earlier empires into a coherent whole. The new kings of fourth-century northern China and fifth-century western Europe were determinedly low-end, feasting with their long-haired warrior lords in the grand halls they had captured. These kings were happy to take taxes from conquered peasants, but without salaried armies to pay, they did not absolutely need this revenue. They were already rich; they were certainly strong; and trying to manage bureaucracies and extract regular taxes from their unruly followers often seemed more trouble than it was worth.

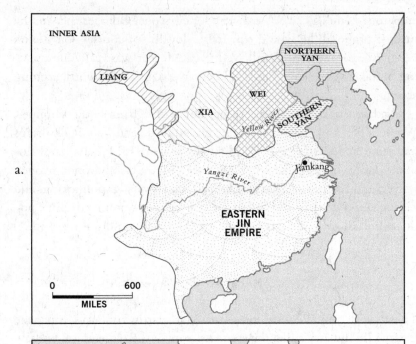

a.

b.

Figure 6.8. The divided East and West: (a) the Eastern Jin and China's major immigrant kingdoms, around 400 CE; (b) Byzantium and Europe's major immigrant kingdoms, around 500 CE

Many of the old, rich aristocratic families of northern China and the western Roman Empire fled to Jiankang or Constantinople with their treasures, but even more stayed amid the ruins of the old empires, perhaps holding their noses like Sidonius, and made what deals they could with their new masters. They swapped their silk robes for woolen pants, their classical poetry for hunting, and assimilated to the new realities.

Some of those realities turned out to be quite good. The superrich aristocrats of former times, with estates scattered over the whole Han or Roman Empire, disappeared, but even with their properties restricted to a single kingdom, some fourth- and fifth-century landowners remained staggeringly wealthy. The old Roman and Chinese elites intermarried with their conquerors, and moved from the crumbling cities to great manors in the countryside.

As the drift toward low-end states accelerated in the fourth century in northern China and the fifth in western Europe, kings allowed their noblemen to seize as rent the surpluses that peasants had formerly handed over to the taxman. If anything, these surpluses might have been growing as population fell and farmers could concentrate their efforts on the best lands. Countryfolk had lost few of the skills they had learned across the centuries and had indeed added new ones. Drainage techniques in the Yangzi Valley and irrigation in the Nile Valley improved after 300; ox-drawn plows multiplied in northern China; and seed drills, moldboard plows, and watermills spread across western Europe.

But despite all the nobles' ostentation and the peasants' ingenuity, the steady thinning of the ranks of bureaucrats, merchants, and managers who had prospered so mightily under the Han and Roman empires meant that the larger economies kept on shrinking at both ends of Eurasia. These characters had often been venal and incompetent, but they really *had* performed a service: by moving goods around they capitalized on different regions' advantages, and without these go-betweens, economies grew more localized and more oriented toward subsistence.

Trade routes contracted and cities shrank. Southern visitors were shocked by the decay of cities in northern China, and in some parts of the old Roman Empire the decline was so sharp that poets wondered whether the great stone ruins decaying all around them could have been built by mortals at all. "Snapped rooftrees, towers tottering, the work of Giants," reads an English verse of around 700 CE. "Rime [mold] scours gatetowers, rime on mortar; shattered are shower shields, roofs ruined. Age underate them."

In the first century CE the emperor Augustus had boasted that he had turned Rome from a city of brick to one of marble, but by the fifth century Europe reverted to a world of wood, with simple shacks thrown up in open spaces between the crumbling shells of old Roman town houses. Nowadays we know quite a lot about these humble homes, but when I started going on digs in England in the 1970s, excavators were still struggling to develop techniques careful enough to recover any traces of them at all.

In this simpler world, coinage, counting, and writing lost their uses. With no one mining copper to supply their mints, the kings of northern China first tried reducing the metal content of their coins (to the point, some claimed, that the coins were so light they could float) and then stopped issuing coins altogether. Account-keeping and census-taking shriveled up and libraries rotted. It was an uneven process, and drawn out across centuries, but in most of northern China and western Europe population fell, thistles and forests reclaimed fields, and life grew shorter and meaner.

PATIENCE AND PUSILLANIMITY

How could this have happened? To most Easterners and Westerners, the answer was obvious: the old ways and old gods had failed.

In China, as soon as the frontiers crumbled, critics had accused the Han of losing the mandate of heaven, millenarian healing cults had convulsed the land, and the most creative minds within the educated elite had begun questioning Confucian certainties. The "Seven Sages of the Bamboo Grove," a group of third-century freethinkers, became icons of a new sensibility, reportedly passing their days in conversation, poetry, music, drinking, and drugs rather than studying the classics and serving the state. According to one story, the sage Ruan Ji, caught in a scandalous breach of etiquette (walking unchaperoned with his sister-in-law), just laughed: "Surely you do not mean to suggest that *li*"—

custom, the foundation of Confucianism—"applies to *me*?" He expanded
on his theme:

> Have you ever seen the lice that inhabit a pair of pants? They jump
> into the depths of the seams, hiding themselves in the cotton wad-
> ding, and believe they have a pleasant place to live. Walking, they do
> not risk going beyond the edge of the seam; moving, they are careful
> not to emerge from the pants leg; and they think they have kept to the
> rules of etiquette. But when the pants are ironed, the flames invade
> the hills . . . then the lice that inhabit the pants cannot escape.
>
> What difference is there between the gentleman who lives within
> a narrow world and the lice that inhabit pants legs?

The moral seriousness of Han court poets now appeared ludicrous;
far better, said the new generation, to withdraw into pastoral, writing
lyrical descriptions of gardens and forests, or even to become a hermit.
Aesthetes who were too busy to retreat to the distant mountains might
just play at being hermits in the gardens of their own villas, or—like
Wang Dao, chief minister at the court in Jiankang around 300—could
hire people to be hermits on their behalf. Painters began celebrating
wild mountains, and in the fourth century the great Gu Kaizhi raised
landscape to the status of a major art form. The Seven Sages and other
theorists elevated form over content, studying the techniques of painting and writing rather than their moral message.

This third-century revolt against tradition was largely negative,
mocking and rejecting convention without offering positive alternatives, but toward the century's end that changed. Eight hundred years
earlier, while Confucianism and Daoism were just getting started in
China, Buddhism had also been spreading across South Asia. The Old
World Exchange brought Buddhism to Chinese attention, probably
when Eastern and South Asian traders mingled in central Asia's oases,
and it is first mentioned in a Chinese text in 65 CE. A few cosmopolitan
intellectuals took it up, but it long remained just one among many exotic philosophies washing in from the steppes.

That changed in the late third century, thanks largely to the central Asian monk-translator Dharmaraksa. Traveling regularly between
Chang'an and the great oasis of Dunhuang, he attracted Chinese intel-

lectuals with new translations of Buddhist texts, putting Indian concepts into language that made sense in China. Like most Axial sages, the Buddha had written nothing down, which left endless scope for debate over what his message was. The earliest forms of Buddhism had emphasized disciplined meditation and self-awareness, but the interpretation that Dharmaraksa promoted, known as Mahayana Buddhism, made salvation less onerous. Dharmaraksa presented the Buddha not as a spiritual seeker but as the incarnation of an eternal principle of enlightenment. The original Buddha, Dharmaraksa insisted, was just the first in a series of Buddhas on this and other worlds. These Buddhas were surrounded by a host of other heavenly figures, particularly Bodhisattvas, mortals who were well on the way to enlightenment but had postponed nirvana to help lesser mortals perfect themselves and escape the cycle of rebirth and suffering.

Mahayana Buddhism could get extreme. Most Buddhist sects believed that a Maitreya ("Future") Buddha would one day lead the masses to liberation, but starting in 401 a stream of wilder-eyed Chinese devotees identified themselves as Buddhas and, teaming up with bandits, rebellious peasants, and/or disaffected officials, went on rampages intended to bring salvation to everyone right now. All ended bloodily.

Mahayana Buddhism's most important contribution, though, was to simplify traditional Buddhism's burdensome demands and open salvation to all. By the sixth century all that the popular "Heaven-Man Teaching" required was for devotees to walk laps around statues of the Buddhas and Bodhisattvas, worship relics (especially the many teeth, bones, and begging bowls said to have belonged to the Buddha), chant, act compassionately, be self-sacrificing, and follow the Five Precepts (thou shalt not kill, steal, commit adultery, drink, or lie). Its teachers conceded that this would not actually lead to nirvana, but it would deliver health, prosperity, and upwardly mobile rebirth. The "Pure Land School" went further, claiming that when believers died, the Bodhisattva of Compassion, working with the Amitabha Buddha, would interrupt the cycle of rebirth and guide them to a Western Paradise where they could pursue nirvana away from the cares of this world.

Indian seekers after nirvana regularly took to the road, begging as they went. Holy wanderers (as opposed to well-heeled hermit-poets) were alien to Chinese traditions, and did not catch on, but a second

Indian path toward enlightenment—monasticism—did. Around 365, Dao'an—a native Chinese Buddhist trained as a Confucian, rather than a central Asian immigrant—drew up a monastic code to fit Chinese society. Monks would wear the tonsure and both monks and nuns took vows of chastity and obedience, earning their keep through labor while pursuing salvation through prayer, meditation, and scholarship. Monasticism could get as extreme as millenarian Buddhism: many monks and nuns injured themselves, imitating—in a small way—the Bodhisattvas' self-sacrifice, and a few even burned themselves alive, sometimes before audiences of thousands, to redeem others' sins. Dao'an's great contribution, though, was to shape monasticism into a religious institution that could partly fill the organizational void created in China by the breakdown of state institutions in the fourth century. Monasteries and convents built watermills, raised money, and even organized defense. As well as being centers of devotion they became oases of stability and even islands of wealth as rich co-religionists gave them land and tenants and dispossessed peasants fled to their protection. Thousands of monasteries popped up in the fifth century; "Today," an official wrote in 509, "there is no place without a monastery."

Buddhism's conquest of China was remarkable. There could have been only a few hundred Buddhists in 65 CE; by the sixth century most Chinese—perhaps 30 million people—were believers. Yet astonishing as this is, at the other end of Eurasia another new religion, Christianity, was growing even faster.

Classical traditions did not crumble as early in the West as in the East, perhaps because Rome's frontiers held longer, and although Western healing cults did arise after the great epidemics of the 160s, they did not favor the kinds of violent revolution popular among Chinese versions. Yet the chaos of the third century did unsettle old ways in the West. Statues carved all over the empire bear silent witness to a new mood, abandoning the stately principles of classical art in favor of strangely proportioned forms with huge, upward-staring eyes, seemingly gazing on another, better place. New religions from the empire's eastern margins—Isis from Egypt, the Undefeated Sun from Syria, Mithras (whose followers wallowed in bulls' blood in underground chambers) perhaps ultimately from Iran, Christianity from Palestine—offered eternal life. People were asking for salvation from this troubled world, not rational explanation of it.

Some philosophers responded to the crisis of values by trying to show that the scholarship of past centuries was still relevant. In their day, scholars such as Porphyry and Plotinus (the latter perhaps the greatest Western thinker since Aristotle) who reinterpreted the Platonic tradition to fit modern times were among the biggest names in the West, but increasingly thinkers were looking for entirely new answers.

Christianity offered something for everyone in this troubled age. Like Mahayana Buddhism, it was a new twist on an old Axial Age idea, offering a version of Axial thought more in tune with the needs of the day. Christianity took over Judaism's sacred books, announcing that its founder, Jesus, was the Messiah predicted there. We might call both Mahayana Buddhism and Christianity "second-wave" Axial religions, offering new kinds of salvation to more people than their first-wave predecessors and making the path toward salvation easier. Equally important, both new religions were ecumenical. Neither Jesus nor the Buddha belonged to a chosen people; they had come to save everyone.

Jesus, like the Buddha, wrote no sacred texts, and as early as the 50s CE the apostle Paul (who never met Jesus) was struggling to get Christians to agree on a few core points about what Christianity actually was. Most followers accepted that they should be baptized, pray to God, renounce other gods, eat together on Sundays, and perform good works, but beyond these basic premises, almost anything was possible. Some held that the God of the Hebrew Bible was merely the last (and lowest) in a series of prior gods. Others thought the world was evil and so God the Creator must be wicked too. Or maybe there were two gods, a malevolent Jewish one and Jesus' wholly good (but unknowable) father. Or two Jesuses, a spiritual one who escaped crucifixion and a bodily one who died on the cross. Maybe Jesus was a woman, some suggested, and maybe women were equal to men. Maybe new revelations could overrule the old ones. Maybe Jesus' Second Coming was imminent, in which case no Christian should have sex; maybe its imminence meant Christians should practice free love; or maybe only people who were martyred in horrible ways would go to heaven, in which case sex was irrelevant.

The Buddha was widely believed to have been pragmatic about transcendence, recommending that people use whichever of his ideas helped and ignore the rest. Multiple paths to nirvana were not a problem. For Christians, however, getting into heaven depended on knowing who God and Jesus were and doing what they wanted, and so the chaos of interpretations forced believers into a frenzy of self-definition. In the late second century most came to agree that there should be bishops who would be treated as descendants of the original apostles with the authority to judge what Jesus meant. Preachers with wilder ideas were damned into oblivion, the New Testament crystallized, and the window on revelations closed. No one could tinker with the Good Book and no one could hear from the Holy Spirit unless the bishops said so; and no one had to renounce marital sex or be martyred, unless they wanted to.

Plenty of points of disputation remained, but by 200 Christianity was becoming a disciplined faith with (reasonably) clear rules about salvation. Like Mahayana Buddhism, it was distinctive enough to get attention, offering practical paths to salvation in troubled times, yet familiar enough to be comprehensible. Learned Greeks even suggested that second-wave Axial Christianity was not so different from first-wave Axial philosophy after all: Plato (the Athenian Moses, some called him) had reasoned his way to the truth and Christians had had truth revealed to them, but it was all the same truth.

When high-end state institutions started breaking down, bishops were well placed to step into the gap, mobilizing their followers to rebuild town walls, fix roads, and negotiate with Germanic raiders. In the countryside conspicuously holy men, renouncing the world as vigorously as any Buddhist, became local leaders. One ascetic achieved empire-wide fame by living in a tomb in the Egyptian desert, fasting, and battling Satan, all the while wearing a hair shirt. His greatest promoter insisted, "He neither bathed his body with water to free himself from filth, nor did he ever wash his feet." Another holy man sat on a fifty-foot column in Syria for forty years, while other renouncers wore animal skins and ate only grass, living (briefly, presumably) as "fools for Christ."

All this struck fastidious Roman gentlemen as bizarre, and even Christians worried about wild men who inspired fanatical followings and answered to no one but God. In 320 an Egyptian holy man named Pachomius found a solution, herding local hermits into the first Christian monastery, where they pursued salvation through labor and prayer under his rigid discipline. Pachomius and the Chinese Dao'an surely knew nothing of each other, but their monasteries were strikingly alike and had similar social consequences. In the fifth century Christian monasteries and convents often moored local economies when larger structures broke down, became centers of learning as classical scholarship waned, and provided monkish militias to keep the peace.

Christianity spread even faster than Buddhism. When Jesus died, around 32 CE, he had a few hundred followers; by 391, when Emperor Theodosius declared Christianity the only legal religion, more than 30 million Romans had converted, although "conversion" is necessarily a loose word. While some highly educated men and women were going through torments of doubt, working through the doctrinal implications with great logic and rigor before accepting the new faith, all around them crowds thousands strong could be won over by Christian or Buddhist wonder-workers in a single afternoon. Consequently, all statistics remain crude; we are doing chainsaw art again. We simply do not know, and probably never will, exactly when and where the pace of conversion accelerated and when and where it slackened, but since we know that both Christianity and Buddhism started with a few hundred followers and eventually had 30-million-plus, Figure 6.9 shows what the *average* growth rates for each religion must have been across these centuries, smoothed out over the whole of China and the Roman Empire. On average, Chinese Buddhism was growing by 2.3 percent each year, meaning that it doubled its following every thirty years, but Christianity grew by 3.4 percent, doubling every twenty years.

The lines in Figure 6.9 march up, while those for social development in Figure 6.1 fall steadily down. The obvious question—is there a connection?—already recommended itself to Edward Gibbon back in 1781. "We may hear without surprise or scandal," he observed, "that the introduction . . . of Christianity, had some influence on the decline and fall of the Roman empire"—but the influence, Gibbon held, was not of the kind that Christians themselves liked to believe. Rather, he suggested, Christianity sapped the empire's vigor:

> The clergy successfully preached the doctrines of patience and pusil-lanimity; the active virtues of society were discouraged; and the last remains of military spirit were buried in the cloister: a large portion of public and private wealth was consecrated to the specious demands of charity and devotion; and the soldiers' pay was lavished on the use-less multitude of both sexes, who could only plead the merits of absti-nence and chastity.

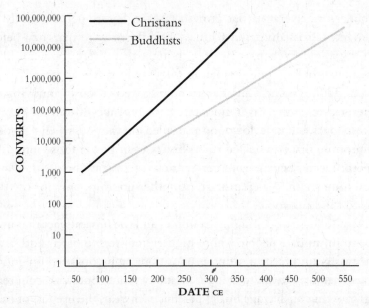

Figure 6.9. Counting souls: the growth of Christianity and Chinese Buddhism, assuming constant rates of change. The vertical scale is logarithmic, as in Figures 3.6 and 3.7, so the constant average rates of growth (3.4 percent per annum for Christianity, 2.3 percent for Buddhism) produce straight lines.

Patience and pusillanimity were as much Buddhist virtues as Christian; so might we extend Gibbon's argument and conclude that ideas—the triumph of priestcraft over politics, revelation over reason—ended the classical world, driving down social development century after century and also narrowing the gap between East and West?

The question cannot be shrugged off lightly, but I think the answer is no. Like first-wave Axial thought, the second-wave Axial religions were more the consequence than the cause of changes in social development. Judaism, Greek philosophy, Confucianism, Daoism, Buddhism, and Jainism all emerged between 600 and 300 BCE, when social development pushed past the level (roughly twenty-four points) at which the Western core had collapsed around 1200 BCE. They were responses to high-end states' reorganization and disenchantment of the world. Second-wave Axial religion was a mirror image of this: as the Old World Exchange destabilized high-end states, people found first-wave thought wanting and salvation religions filled the gap.

Unless the averaged-out growth rates in Figure 6.9 are wildly off the mark, Christianity and Chinese Buddhism were marginal before the Old World Exchange. By 250, though, there were about a million Christians (roughly one Roman in forty), which was apparently some kind of tipping point. Christianity now started seriously annoying the emperors; not only was it competing for revenues in one of Rome's darkest hours, but its jealous God also ruled out the god-when-I'm-dead compromise that had helped rulers justify their power for so long. The emperor Decius began major persecutions in 250, just before the Goths killed him. In 257 Valerian started another pogrom, only for the Persians to kill him, too.

Despite these discouraging examples and the obvious fact that using force to intimidate people whose highest goal was to die as horribly as Jesus was bound to be a losing proposition, emperors tried on and off for another fifty years to wipe Christianity out. But with congregations growing on average by 3.4 percent each year, the miracle of compound interest took church membership to around 10 million members, a quarter of the empire's population, in the 310s. That was apparently a second tipping point: in 312, in the middle of a civil war, the emperor Constantine found God. Instead of trying to squelch Christianity, Constantine worked out a new compromise, just as his predecessors half a millennium earlier had worked out compromises with the equally subversive first-wave Axial thought. Constantine transferred massive wealth to the church; made it tax-exempt, and recognized its hierarchy. In return the church recognized Constantine.

Over the next eighty years the rest of the population turned Christian, aristocrats colonized the church's leadership, and the church and state between them plundered the empire's pagan temples—perhaps the biggest redistribution of wealth the world had yet seen. Christianity was an idea whose time had come. The king of Armenia turned Christian in the 310s, as did Ethiopia's ruler in the 340s. Persia's kings did not, but that was probably because Iranian Zoroastrianism was evolving along similar lines to Christianity anyway.

Chinese Buddhism seems to have passed through rather similar tipping points. In Figure 6.9 it hits the million-member mark around 400, but because conditions were so very different in northern and southern China, the growth of the faith had different consequences in each region. In the unsettled north, Buddhists tended to cluster for safety in the capital cities, which made them very vulnerable to royal pressure. By 400 Northern Wei, the strongest of the kingdoms, had set up a government department to supervise Buddhists, and in 446 it started persecuting them. In southern China, by contrast, instead of concentrating in the capital at Jiankang, Buddhist monks scattered down the Yangzi Valley, where they could get powerful aristocrats to protect them against the court and could force emperors to make concessions. In 402 an emperor even accepted that monks should not have to bow in his presence.

Figure 6.9 suggests that there may have been 10 million Buddhists in China by 500, and when the new faith reached this second tipping point, rulers (in northern China as well as southern) made the same decision as Constantine and lavished wealth, tax exemptions, and honors on the flock's leaders. In the south the genuinely pious emperor Wudi supported vast Buddhist festivals, banned animal sacrifice (people had to consume pastry imitations instead), and sent envoys to India to gather sacred texts. In return, the Buddhist hierarchy recognized Wudi as a Bodhisattva, the redeemer and savior of his people. The kings of Northern Wei got an even better deal, asserting the right to pick their own chief monks and then having the monks pronounce that the kings were reincarnations of the Buddha. Constantine would have been jealous.

Patience and pusillanimity did not cause the decline and fall of East or West. The paradox of social development did that. To some extent the declines and falls followed the script written in the West around 1200 BCE, when the expanding core set off chains of events that no one could control, but to some extent the sheer scale of social development by 160 CE rewrote the script, transforming geography by linking East and West together across central Asia and creating an Old World Exchange of microbes and migrants.

By 160 CE the empires of the classical world were much bigger and stronger than the kingdoms of the Western core had been in 1200 BCE, but so, too, were the disruptions that their primitive version of globalization set off. The classical empires could not cope with the forces they unleashed. Century after century, social development slid. Writing, cities, taxes, and bureaucrats lost their value, and as the old certainties stopped making sense, a hundred million people sought salvation from a world gone wrong by giving new twists to ancient wisdom. Like first-wave Axial thought, second-wave ideas were dangerous, challenging the authority of husbands over wives, rich over poor, and kings over subjects, but once again the mighty made their peace with the subversive, redistributing power and wealth in the process. By 500 CE states were weaker and churches stronger, but life went on.

If I had been writing this book around the year 500 CE I might well have been a long-term lock-in theorist. Every millennium or so, I would have observed, social development undermined itself, and for every two or three steps forward there would be one step back. Disruptions were getting bigger, now affecting the East as well as the West, but the pattern was clear. During steps forward, the West pulled away from the East; during steps back, the gap narrowed; and on it would go, in a series of waves, each cresting higher than the last one, with the West's lead varying but locked in.

But if I had been writing a century later, things would have looked entirely different.

7

∘ ∘ ∘

THE EASTERN AGE

THE EAST TAKES THE LEAD

According to Figure 7.1, 541 ought to be one of the most famous dates in history. In that year (or somewhere around the middle of the sixth century, anyway, allowing for a certain margin of error in the index) the East's social development score overtook the West's, ending a fourteen-thousand-year-old pattern and disproving at a stroke any simple long-term lock-in theory of why the West rules. By 700 the East's score was one-third higher than the West's, and by 1100 the gap—nearly 40 percent—was bigger than it had been for two and a half thousand years (when the advantage had lain with the West).

Why did the East pull ahead in the sixth century? And why did its social development score rise so high over the next half-millennium while the West's steadily fell behind? These questions are crucial to explaining why the West now rules, and as we attempt to answer them in this chapter we will encounter quite a cast of heroes and villains, geniuses and bunglers. Behind all the drama, though, we will find the same simple fact that has driven East-West differences throughout the story: geography.

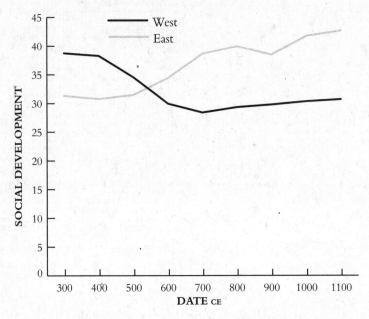

Figure 7.1. The great reversal: the East turns its decline around and for the first time in history pulls ahead of the West

WAR AND RICE

Eastern social development began falling before 100 CE and continued until 400, and by the time it bottomed out it stood lower than it had been for five centuries. States had failed, cities had burned, and migrations—from Inner Asia to northern China, and from northern China to southern—had convulsed the whole core. It was out of these migrations, though, that the Eastern revival began.

In Chapters 4–6 we saw how rising social development transformed geography, uncovering advantages in backwardness and opening highways across the oceans and steppes. Since the third century, though, it had been shown that the relationship also worked in reverse: *falling* social development transformed geography too. As Roman and Chinese cities shrank, literacy declined, armies weakened, and living standards fell, the cores also contracted geographically, and the differences between these contractions largely explain why Eastern social development recovered so quickly while Western development kept falling into the eighth century.

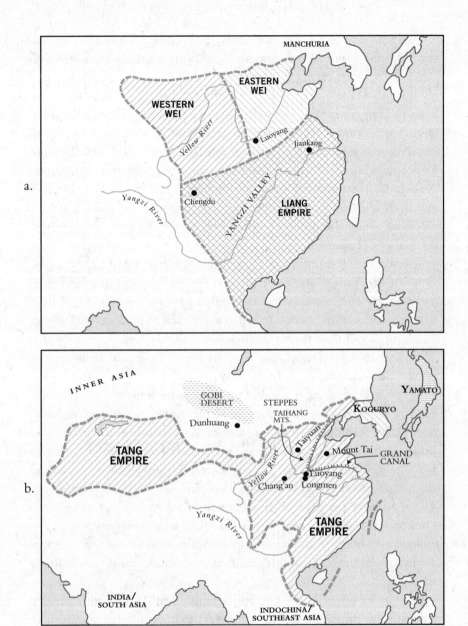

Figure 7.2. The East bounces back, 400–700. Figure 7.2a shows the states
of Western Wei, Eastern Wei, and southern China's Liang dynasty in 541.
The Sui dynasty united all three in 589. Figure 7.2b shows the greatest
extent of the Tang Empire, around 700.

We also saw in Chapter 6 that the Eastern core's old heartland in the Yellow River valley fragmented into warring states after 300 and millions of northerners fled southward. The exodus converted the lands south of the Yangzi from the underdeveloped periphery they had been in Han times into a new frontier. The refugees entered an alien landscape, humid and hot, where their staples of wheat and millet grew poorly but rice flourished. Much of this land was lightly settled, often by people whose customs and languages were very different from those brought by the north Chinese immigrants. Amid the sort of violence and harsh dealing that characterizes most colonial landgrabs, the immigrants' weight of numbers and tighter organization steadily pushed the earlier occupants back.

Between 280 and 464 the number of people listed as taxpayers south of the Yangzi quintupled, but the migration did not just bring more people to the south. It also brought new techniques. According to an agricultural handbook called *The Essential Methods of the Common People*, no fewer than thirty-seven varieties of rice were known by the 530s, and transplantation (growing seedlings in special beds for six weeks, then moving them to flooded paddies) had become the norm. This was backbreaking work, but guaranteed high yields. *The Essential Methods* explains how fertilizers let farmers work fields continuously rather than leaving them fallow, and how watermills—particularly at Buddhist monasteries, which were often built by fast-flowing mountain streams and often had the capital for big investments—made it cheaper to grind grains into flour, mill rice, and press oil from seeds. The result was the gradual development of a new frontier of agricultural opportunities, rather like the one the Romans created when they conquered western Europe in the first century BCE. Gradually, over the course of centuries, the south's rural backwardness was turned into an advantage.

Cheap transport began to complement cheap food. China's rivers were still no substitute for the waterways that the Mediterranean had provided Rome, but little by little human ingenuity made up for this. Underwater archaeologists have not yet provided statistics like those for Roman shipwrecks, but written records suggest that vessels were getting bigger and faster. Paddleboats appeared on the Yangzi in the 490s, and from Chengdu to Jiankang rice fed growing cities, where urban markets encouraged cash crops such as tea (first mentioned in surviving records around 270 and becoming a widespread luxury by 500). Grandees, merchants, and monasteries all got rich on rents, shipping, and milling in the Yangzi Valley.

The ruling court in Jiankang, however, did not get rich. In this regard its situation was less like the Roman Empire's than like eighth-century-BCE Assyria's, where governors and landowners, not the state, captured the fruits of growing population and trade—until, of course, Tiglath-Pileser turned things around. Southern China, however, never got a Tiglath-Pileser. Once in a while an emperor managed to rein in the aristocracy and even tried to reconquer the north, but these efforts always collapsed in civil war. Between 317 and 589 five successive dynasties ruled (after a fashion) from Jiankang.

The Essential Methods suggests that sophisticated agriculture survived in the north into the 530s, but well before then long-distance trade and even coinage had faded away as mounted robbers plundered widely. At first this breakdown produced even more political chaos than in the south, but gradually new rulers began imposing order on the north. Chief among them were the Xianbei, who came from the fringes of the steppes in Manchuria. Like the Parthians who had overrun Iran six centuries earlier, the Xianbei combined nomad and agrarian traditions, and had for generations fought as an equestrian elite while extracting protection money from peasants.

In the ruins of northern China in the 380s the Xianbei set up their own state, called Northern Wei.* Instead of just robbing the Chinese gentry, they worked out deals with them, preserving at least some of the salaried bureaucrats and taxes of the old high-end states. This gave Northern Wei an edge over the disorderly, brawling mobs that ran north China's other states; enough of an edge, in fact, for Northern Wei to unite the whole region in 439.

That said, the deals Northern Wei cut with the surviving remnants of the old Chinese aristocracy remained rather ramshackle. Most Xianbei warriors preferred herding flocks to hobnobbing with literati, and

---

*Once again, the terminology is confusing. The Xianbei borrowed their name from the ancient kingdom of Wei (445–225 BCE) mentioned in Chapter 5. To distinguish the Xianbei state from the earlier kingdom, some historians call it Tuoba Wei (named after the Xianbei clan that ran the state); others prefer Northern Wei, the usage I follow here.

even when the riders did settle down they generally built their own castles to avoid having to rub shoulders with Chinese farmers. Their state remained determinedly low-end. So long as they were just fighting other northern robber states that was fine, but when Xianbei horsemen approached the suburbs of Jiankang in 450 they discovered that although they could win battles and steal everything not nailed down, they could not threaten real cities. Only a proper high-end state with ships, siege engines, and supply trains could do that.

Unable to plunder southern China because they lacked a high-end army, and running out of opportunities to plunder northern China because they already ruled it, the kings of Northern Wei were getting seriously short of resources to buy their supporters' loyalty—a potentially fatal weakness in a low-end state. In the 480s Emperor Xiaowen realized that only one solution remained: to move toward the high end. This he did with a vengeance. He nationalized all land, redistributed it to everyone who would register for taxes and state service, and—to make the Xianbei start thinking and acting like subjects of a high-end state—launched a frontal assault on tradition. Xiaowen banned Xianbei costume, replaced Xianbei with Chinese family names, required all courtiers under thirty to speak Chinese, and moved hundreds of thousands of people to a new city at the hallowed site of Luoyang.

Some Xianbei gave up their ancestral ways and settled into ruling like regular Chinese aristocrats, but others refused. Culture wars escalated into civil wars, and in 534 Northern Wei split into Eastern (modernizing) and Western (traditionalist) states. The traditionalists, clinging to nomadic lifestyles, were able to keep attracting horsemen from the steppes, and soon it looked like their military muscle would overwhelm the revolution Xiaowen had begun. Desperation, however, served as the mother of invention. Where Xiaowen had tried to turn Xianbei warriors into Chinese gentlemen, his successors now did the opposite, giving Chinese soldiers tax breaks, appointing Chinese gentry as generals, and allowing Chinese warriors to take Xianbei names. The peasants and literati learned to fight, and in 577 rolled over the opposition. It had been a long, messy process, but a version of Xiaowen's vision finally triumphed.

The result was a sharply polarized China. In the north a high-end state (renamed the Sui dynasty after a military coup in 581) with a powerful army sat atop a fragmented, run-down economy; in the south, a fragmented state with weak institutions tried, but largely failed, to tap the wealth of a booming economy.

This sounds utterly dysfunctional, but it was in fact perfect for jump-starting social development. In 589 Wendi, the first Sui emperor, built a fleet, took over the Yangzi Valley, and flung a vast army (perhaps half a million men) at Jiankang. Thanks to the extreme military imbalance between north and south, the city fell within weeks. When they realized that Wendi actually intended to tax them, southern China's nobles rose up en masse, reportedly disemboweling—even eating—their Sui governors, but they were defeated within the year. Wendi had conquered southern China without grueling wars that devastated its economy, and an eastern revival took off.

WU'S WORLD

By re-creating a single huge empire, the Sui dynasty did two things at once. First, it allowed the strong state based in northern China to tap the south's new economic frontier; and second, it allowed the south's economic boom to spread all across China.

This was not always deliberate. When the Sui emperors built the greatest monument of the age, the 1,500-mile-long, 130-foot-wide Grand Canal that linked the Yangzi with northern China, they wanted a superhighway for moving armies around. Within a generation, though, it had become China's economic artery, carrying rice from the south to feed northern cities. "By cutting through the Taihang Mountains," seventh-century scholars liked to complain, "Sui inflicted intolerable sufferings on the people"; yet, the scholars conceded, the canal "provided endless benefits to the people . . . The benefits they provide are enormous indeed!"

The Grand Canal functioned like a man-made Mediterranean Sea, changing Eastern geography by finally giving China the kind of waterway ancient Rome had enjoyed. Cheap southern rice fed a northern urban explosion. "Hundreds of houses, thousands of houses—like a great chessboard," the poet Bai Juyi wrote of Chang'an, which once more became China's capital. It sprawled across thirty square miles, "like a huge field planted with rows of cabbages." A million residents thronged tree-lined boulevards up to five times as wide as New York's Fifth Avenue. Nor was Chang'an unique; Luoyang was probably half its size, and a dozen other cities had populations of a hundred thousand.

China's recovery was something of a double-edged sword, though, because the fusion of northern state power and the southern rice frontier cut two ways. On the one hand, a burgeoning bureaucracy organized and policed the urban markets that enriched farmers and merchants, pushing social development upward; on the other, excessive administration put a brake on development by shackling farmers and merchants, regulating every detail of commerce. Officials fixed prices, told people when to buy and sell, and even ruled on how merchants could live (they could not, for instance, ride horses; that was too dignified for mere hucksters).

Civil servants regularly put politics ahead of economics. Instead of allowing people to buy and sell real estate, they preserved Xiaowen's system, claiming all land for the state and merely loaning it to farmers. This forced peasants to register for taxes and kept powerful landlords in check, but tangled everything in red tape. For many years historians suspected that these land laws told us more about ideology than reality; surely, scholars reasoned, no premodern state could handle so much paperwork.* Yet documents preserved by arid conditions at Dunhuang on the edge of the Gobi Desert show that eighth-century managers really did follow these rules.

Farmers, landlords, and speculators of course found ways to evade the regulations, but the civil service steadily swelled to fill out mountains of documentation and went through a revolution of its own. In theory, entrance examinations had made administration the preserve of China's best and brightest since Han times, but in practice aristocratic families always managed to turn high office into a perk of birth. In the seventh century, however, exam scores really did become the only criterion for success. So long as we assume (as most people did) that composing poetry and quoting classical literature are the best guides to administrative talent, China can fairly be said to have de-

---

*"Paperwork" is the right word. Genuine paper, invented in Han China, became widespread in the seventh century.

veloped the most rational selection processes for state service known to history.*

As the old aristocracy's grip on high office slowly loosened, administrative appointments became the surest path to wealth and influence for the gentry, and competition to get into the civil service stiffened. In some years fewer than one candidate in a hundred passed the exams, and stories both sad and comical abound of men retaking the tests for decades. Ambitious families hired tutors, much as they do nowadays to get their teenagers through the exams that winnow out applicants to the most-sought-after universities, and the newly invented printing presses churned out thousands of books of practice questions. Some candidates wore "cheat shirts" with model essays written in the lining. Because grades depended so heavily on literary composition, every young man in a hurry became a poet; and with so many fine minds versifying, this became the golden age of Chinese literature.

The exams created unprecedented social mobility within the educated elite, and some historians even speak of the rise of a kind of "protofeminism" as the new openness expanded to gender relations. We should not exaggerate this trend; the advice to women in *The Family Instructions of the Grandfather*, one of the commonest surviving eighth-century books, would have shocked no one a thousand years earlier—

> *A bride serves her husband*
> *Just as she served her father.*
> *Her voice should not be heard*
> *Nor her body or shadow seen.*
> *With her husband's father and elder brothers*
> *She has no conversation.*

On the other hand, new dowry patterns and liberal (compared to Confucian ideas, anyway) Buddhist attitudes toward female abilities

---

*When Britain reorganized its civil service in the 1880s it introduced self-consciously similar examinations, testing bright young men on their knowledge of Greek and Latin classics before sending them off to govern India, and even now British civil servants are still known as mandarins. Nineteenth-century conservatives saw exams as part of a sinister plot to "Chinesify" Britain.

gave the wealthiest women scope to ignore grandfather's instructions. Take Wu Zetian, who, after one kind of service as a Buddhist nun, took up another (aged thirteen) as a concubine in the emperor's harem, before marrying his son as a junior wife. Wu ran rings around her dizzy, easygoing husband, ruling from behind the bamboo curtain, as the saying went. And when her husband conveniently died in 683, Wu allegedly poisoned the obvious heir, then deposed two of her own sons (one after six weeks, the other after six years). In 690 she pulled back the bamboo curtain to become the only woman who ever sat on China's throne in her own right.

In some ways Wu was the ultimate protofeminist. She founded a research institute to write a *Collection of Biographies of Famous Women* and scandalized conservatives by leading a female procession to Mount Tai for China's most sacred ritual, the Sacrifice to Heaven. Sisterhood had its limits, though—when her husband's senior wife and favorite concubine became a threat while Wu was maneuvering her way to the top, she (again, allegedly) suffocated her own baby, framed her rivals, then punished them by chopping off their arms and legs and drowning them in a vat of wine.

Wu's Buddhism was as contradictory as her protofeminism. She was certainly devout, at one point outlawing butchers' shops and at another personally going beyond Chang'an's city limits to meet a monk returning from collecting sacred texts in India, yet she flagrantly exploited religion for political ends. In 685 her lover—another monk— "found" a text called the Great Cloud Sutra, predicting the rise of a woman of such merit that she would become the universal ruler. Wu took the title Maitreya (Future Buddha) the Peerless, and legend holds that the face of the beautiful Maitreya Buddha statue at Longmen reflects Wu's (Figure 7.3).

Wu had an equally complicated relationship with the civil service. She promoted entrance examinations over family connections, yet the Confucian gentleman scholars whose dominance this guaranteed hated their female ruler with a passion, and she returned the sentiment. Wu purged the scholars, who retaliated by writing official histories making her the archetype of what went wrong when women were on top.

But not even they could conceal the splendor of her reign. She commanded a million-strong army and the resources to send it deep

Figure 7.3. The face of Wu Zetian? Legend has it that this monumental statue of the Future Buddha, carved at Longmen around 700, was modeled on the only woman to rule China in her own name.

into the steppes. More like the Roman army than the Han, it recruited largely within the empire and drew officers from the gentry. It could intimidate internal rivals but elaborate precautions kept its commanders loyal. Any officer who moved even ten men without permission faced a year in prison; any who moved a regiment risked strangulation.

The army took Chinese rule farther into northeast, Southeast, and central Asia than ever before, even intervening in northern India in 648, and China's "soft" power reached further still. In the second through fifth centuries, India had eclipsed China as a cultural center of gravity, its missionaries and traders spreading Buddhism far and wide, and the elites of newly forming Southeast Asian states adopted Indian dress and scripts as well as religion. By the seventh century, though, China's influence was also being felt. A distinctive Indochinese civilization developed in Southeast Asia, Chinese schools of Buddhism shaped thought back in India, and the ruling classes in Korea's and Japan's emerging states learned their Buddhism entirely from China. They aped Chinese dress, town planning, law codes, and writing, and buttressed their power by claiming both approval and descent from China's rulers.

Part of Chinese culture's appeal was its own openness to foreign ideas and ability to blend them into something new. Many of the most powerful people in Wu's world could trace their ancestry back to steppe nomads who had migrated into China, and they maintained their ties to the steppe highway linking East and West. Inner Asian dancers and lutes were all the rage in Chang'an, where fashionistas wore Persian dresses with tight-laced bodices, pleated skirts, and yards of veils. True trendsetters would use only East African "devil slaves" as doormen; "If they do not die," one owner coldly observed, "one can keep them, and after being kept a long time they begin to understand the language of human beings, though they themselves cannot speak it."

The scions of China's great houses broke their bones playing polo, the nomads' game of choice; everyone learned to sit, central-Asian style, on chairs rather than mats; and stylish ladies dallied at the shrines of exotic religions such as Zoroastrianism and Christianity, carried east by the central Asian, Iranian, Indian, and Arab merchants who flocked to Chinese cities. In 2007 a DNA study suggested that one Yu Hong, buried at Taiyuan in northern China in 592, was actually European (though whether he himself migrated all the way from the western to the eastern end of the steppes or whether his ancestors had made the move more slowly remains unclear).

Wu's world was the product of China's unification in 589, which imposed a powerful state on the south and opened a vast realm to southern economic development. That explains why Eastern social development rose so rapidly; but it is only half the explanation for why the Eastern and Western scores crossed around 541. For a full answer we also need to know why Western social development kept falling.

THE LAST OF THEIR BREEDS

On the face of it, Western recovery seemed at least as likely as Eastern in the sixth century. In each core a huge ancient empire had broken down, leaving a smaller empire that claimed legitimate rule over the whole region and a cluster of "barbarian" kingdoms that ignored such claims (Figure 7.4). After the calamities of the fifth century, Byzantium had shored up its frontiers and enjoyed relative calm, and by 527, when a new emperor named Justinian ascended the throne, all signs were positive.

Historians often call Justinian the last of the Romans. He governed with furious energy, overhauling administration, strengthening taxes, and rebuilding Constantinople (the magnificent church Hagia Sophia is part of his legacy). He worked like a demon. Some critics insisted

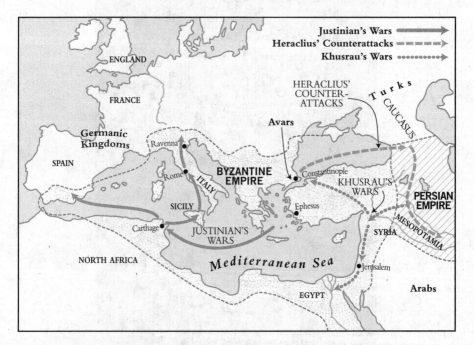

Figure 7.4. The last of their breeds? First Justinian of Byzantium (533–565) and then Khusrau of Persia (603–627) attempt to reunite the Western core; Heraclius of Byzantium strikes back against Khusrau (624–628).

that he really *was* a demon—like some Hollywood vampire, they claimed, he never ate, drank, or slept, although he did have voracious sexual appetites. Some even said they had seen his head separate from his body and fly around on its own as he prowled the corridors at night.

What chiefly drove Justinian, according to gossip, was his wife, Theodora (Figure 7.5), who got even worse press than Wu Zetian. Theodora had been an actress (in antiquity, often a euphemism for prostitute) before marrying Justinian. Rumor had it that her sex drive outdid even his; that she once slept with all the guests at a dinner party and then, when they were exhausted, worked through their thirty servants; and that she used to complain because God had given her only three orifices. Be that as it may, she was very much an empress. When aristocrats opposing Justinian's taxes tried to use rioting sports fans to overthrow him in 532, for instance, it was Theodora who stopped him

Figure 7.5. Worse (or better, depending on your perspective) than Wu? Empress Theodora, as represented on a mosaic at Ravenna in Italy, completed in 547

from fleeing. "Everyone born must die," she pointed out, "but I would not live to see the day when men do not call me 'Your Majesty.' If you seek safety, husband, that is easy . . . but I prefer the old saying—purple [the color of kings] makes the best shroud." Justinian pulled himself together, sent in the army, and never looked back.

The very next year Justinian dispatched his general Belisarius to wrest North Africa from the Vandals. Sixty-five years earlier fireships had sent Byzantium's hopes of retaking Carthage up in smoke, but now it was the Vandals' turn to collapse. Belisarius swept through North Africa, then crossed to Sicily. There the Goths fell apart too, and Justinian's general celebrated Christmas 536 in Rome. All was going perfectly. Yet by the time Justinian died in 565 the reconquest had stalled, the empire was bankrupt, and Western social development had fallen below the East's. What went wrong?

According to Belisarius' secretary Procopius, who left an account called *The Secret History*, it was all the fault of women. Procopius provided a convoluted conspiracy theory worthy of Empress Wu's Confucian civil servants. Belisarius' wife, Antonina, Procopius said, was Empress Theodora's best friend and partner in sexual high jinks. To distract Justinian from the all-too-true gossip about Antonina (and herself), Theodora undermined Belisarius in Justinian's eyes. Convinced that Belisarius was plotting against him, Justinian recalled him—only for the Byzantine army, lost without its general, to be defeated. Justinian sent Belisarius back to save the day; then, paranoid once more, reran the whole foolish cycle (several times).

How much truth Procopius' story holds is anyone's guess, but the real explanation for the reconquest's failure seems to be that despite the similarities between the Eastern and Western cores in the sixth century, the differences mattered more. Strategically, Justinian's position was almost the opposite of Wendi's when he united China. In China, all the northern "barbarian" kingdoms formed a single unit by 577, which Wendi used to overcome the rich but weak south. Justinian, by contrast, was trying to conquer a multitude of mostly poor but strong "barbarian" kingdoms from the rich Byzantine Empire. Reuniting the core in a single campaign, like Wendi's in 589, was impossible.

Justinian also had to deal with Persia. For a century a string of wars with the Huns, conflicts over taxes, and religious upheavals had kept Persia militarily quiet, but the prospect of the Roman Empire rising from the ashes demanded action. In 540 a Persian army broke through Byzantium's weakened defenses and plundered Syria, forcing Justinian to fight on two fronts (which probably had more to do with Belisarius' recall from Italy than any of Antonina's intrigues).

As if this were not enough, an unpleasant new sickness was reported in Egypt in 541. People felt feverish and their groins and armpits swelled. Within a day or so the swellings blackened and sufferers fell into comas and delirium. After another day or two most victims died, raving with pain.

It was the bubonic plague. The sickness reached Constantinople a year later, probably killing a hundred thousand people. The risk of death was so high, Bishop John of Ephesus claimed, that "nobody would go out of doors without a tag bearing his name hung round his neck."

Constantinopolitans said the plague came from Ethiopia, and most historians agree. The bacillus had probably evolved long before 541 around Africa's Great Lakes and become endemic among fleas on black rats in Ethiopia's highlands. Red Sea traders must have carried plenty of Ethiopian rats to Egypt over the years, but because the plague-bearing fleas are only really active when temperatures are between 59 and 68°F, Egypt's heat created an epidemiological barrier—until, apparently, the late 530s.

What happened then is disputed. Tree rings indicate several years of uncommon cold, and Byzantine and Anglo-Saxon watchers of the skies recorded a great comet. Some historians think its tail created a dust veil, lowering temperatures and letting the plague out of its box. Others think volcanic ash was responsible for lowering temperatures. Others still think dust veils and volcanoes have nothing to do with anything.

Yet when all is said and done, neither comets, nor strategy, nor even loose morals by themselves drove Western social development down in the sixth century. The fundamental contrast between East and West, which determined how the shocks of war and disease affected development, was one of maps, not chaps. Justinian's economy was ticking along nicely—Egyptian and Syrian farmers were more productive than ever, and merchants still carried grain and olive oil to Constantinople—but the West had nothing like the East's booming new frontier of rice paddies. When Wendi conquered south China he deployed at least 200,000 troops; at the height of his Italian war, in 551, Justinian could find just 20,000. Wendi's victories captured south China's great wealth, but Justinian's merely won poorer and often war-ravaged lands. Given several generations, a reunited Roman Empire might conceivably have turned the Mediterranean back into a trade superhighway, opened a new economic frontier, and turned social development around; but Justinian did not have that luxury.

Geography doomed Justinian's heroic, vainglorious reconquest before it even began, and his efforts probably only made that doom worse. His troops turned Italy into a wasteland and the traders who fed them carried rats, fleas, and death around the Mediterranean.* The plague slackened after 546, but the bacillus had taken root, and until about 750 no year passed without an outbreak somewhere. Population fell, perhaps by one-third. As had happened when the Old World Exchange unleashed epidemics four hundred years earlier, mass mortality initially rebounded to some people's benefit; with fewer workers around, wages rose for those who survived. But that, of course, only made times harder for the rich (in a remarkably unchristian aside, Bishop John of Ephesus complained in 544 that all these deaths had made the cost of laundry services outrageous), and Justinian responded by pegging wages at preplague levels. This apparently accomplished nothing. Land was abandoned, cities shrank, taxes dwindled, and institutions broke down. Soon everyone was worse off.

Over the next two generations Byzantium imploded. Britain and much of Gaul had dropped out of the Western core in the fifth century; war-torn Italy and parts of Spain followed in the sixth; and then the tidal wave of collapse, rolling slowly from northwest to southeast, engulfed the Byzantine heartland, too. Constantinople's population fell by three quarters, its agriculture, trade, and revenues broke down, and the end looked nigh. By 600 only one man still dreamed of remaking the Western core: King Khusrau II of Persia.

Rome, after all, was not the only Western empire that could be re-created. Back around 500 BCE, when Rome was still a backwater, Persia had united most of the Western core. Now, with Byzantium on its knees, Persia's time seemed to have come again. In 609 Khusrau broke through the decaying frontier fortresses and the Byzantine army

---

*Humans, not rats, spread the plague. Moving on foot, the average rat relocates barely a quarter of a mile during its two-year lifespan; left to rats, the plague would have advanced merely twelve miles per century.

melted away. He took Jerusalem in 614, and with it Christianity's holiest relics: fragments of the True Cross on which Jesus had been cruci-
fied, the Holy Lance that had pierced his side, and the Sacred Sponge
that had refreshed him. Another five years brought Khusrau Egypt,
and in 626, ninety-nine years after Justinian had come to power, Khusrau's armies gazed across the Bosporus at Constantinople itself. The
Avars, nomadic allies he had recruited from the western steppes, swept
through the Balkans and were poised to attack from the other shore.

But Khusrau's dreams collapsed even faster than Justinian's. By 628
he was dead and his empire shattered. Ignoring the armies outside
Constantinople's walls, the Byzantine emperor Heraclius had "borrowed" gold and silver from the church and sailed off to the Caucasus,
where he used the loot to hire his own nomadic cavalry from the Turkic* tribes on the steppes. Horsemen, he reasoned, were what mattered; and since Byzantium no longer had many, he would rent some.
His hired Turks beat off the Persians sent to stop them and devastated
Mesopotamia.

This was all it took to send the tidal wave of collapses rolling over
Persia, too. The ruling class fell apart. Khusrau's own son locked him
up and starved him, then surrendered the lands Khusrau had conquered, sent back the relics he had captured, and even accepted Christianity. Persia dissolved into civil war, going through eight kings in
five years, while Heraclius was hailed as the greatest of all great men.
"Immense joy and indescribable happiness seized the entire universe,"
gushed one contemporary. "Let us all with united voice sing the angelic praises," wrote another: "Glory in the highest to God, and peace
on earth, goodwill to mankind."

The wild swings of fortune in the century after 533 were the death
throes of the ancient Western empires. Absent a new economic frontier
like China's, Khusrau could no more turn around Western social development than had Justinian, and the harder each man tried, the worse
he made things. The last of the Romans and the last of the Persians
hollowed out the Western core with a century of violence, plague, and
economic decline. Just a decade after Heraclius rode into Jerusalem in

---

*Historians use "Turkic" to describe steppe nomads ancestral to the modern Turks,
who migrated to what we now call Turkey only in the eleventh century.

630 to restore the True Cross to its rightful place, all their triumphs and tragedies had ceased to matter.

THE WORD OF THE PROPHET

Without knowing it, Justinian and Khusrau had been following very ancient pattern books. Their struggles to control the core destabilized it and once again drew in people from the margins. Khusrau brought Avars to Constantinople, Heraclius led Turks into Mesopotamia, and both empires hired Arab tribes to guard their desert frontiers, since that was cheaper than paying their own garrisons. The same thinking that had Germanized Rome's borderlands and Xiongnuized China's now Arabized Byzantium's and Persia's mutual boundary, and across the sixth century both empires became more and more involved with Arabia. Each built up Arab client kingdoms, Persia absorbed southern Arabia into its empire, and Byzantium's Ethiopian allies invaded Yemen to balance this. Arabia was being drawn into the core, and Arabs were creating their own kingdoms in the desert, building oasis towns along trade routes, and converting to Christianity.

The great Persian-Byzantine wars convulsed this Arab periphery, and when the empires fell apart, Arab strongmen battled over the ruins. In western Arabia, Mecca and Medina (Figure 7.6) fought through the 620s over trade routes, their war bands fanning out across the desert to find allies and ambush each other's caravans. Old imperial frontiers meant little in this game, and by the time Medina's leader took over Mecca in 630, his raiders were already fighting in Palestine. There Arabs loyal to Medina clashed with Arabs loyal to Mecca while other Arabs, paid by Constantinople, fought both groups.

Most of this would have seemed familiar to, say, an Aramaean tribesman operating in these same desert margins back when the Egyptian and Babylonian empires had collapsed after 1200 BCE: it was simply what happened on the frontiers when states broke down. But one thing would not have seemed familiar to the Aramaean. That was Medina's leader, one Muhammad ibn Abdullah.

Around 610, as Persia was beginning its cataclysmic war on Byzantium, this Muhammad had had a vision. The Archangel Gabriel had

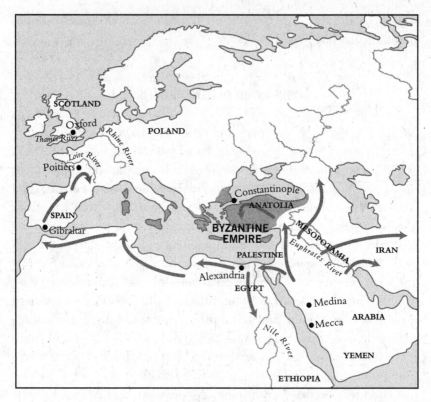

Figure 7.6. Jihad: the Arabs almost reunite the Western core, 632–732.
The arrows show the major Arab invasion routes.

appeared and commanded: "Recite!" Muhammad, understandably
flustered, had insisted he was no reciter, but twice more Gabriel had
commanded him. Then words, unbidden, had come to Muhammad:

> Recite! In the name of your Lord who created—created man from clots
>   of blood.
> Recite! Your Lord is the Most Bountiful One, who by the pen taught
>   man what he did not know.

Muhammad thought madness or demons must have possessed him, but
his wife convinced him otherwise. Across the next twenty-two years
Gabriel returned again and again, sending Muhammad into shivering,
sweating fits and comas and setting God's words free from the prophet's reluctant lips. And what words they were: their beauty, tradition

says, converted people the instant they heard them. "My heart was softened and I wept," said 'Umar, one of the most important converts. "Islam entered into me."

Islam—submission to God's will—was in many ways a classic second-wave Axial religion. Its founder came from the margins of the elite (he was a minor figure in a nouveau riche trading clan) and the margins of empire; he wrote nothing down (the Koran, or "Recitations," was assembled only after his death); he believed that God was unknowable; and he built on earlier Axial thought. He preached justice, equality before God, and compassion toward the weak. All this he shared with earlier Axial thinkers. But in another way, he was a whole new creature: an Axial warrior.

Unlike Buddhism, Confucianism, or Christianity, Islam was born on the edge of collapsing empires and came of age amid constant warfare. Islam was not a religion of violence (the Koran is a good deal less bloody than the Hebrew Bible), but Muslims could not stand aloof from fighting. "Fight for the sake of God those that fight against you," Muhammad had said, "but do not attack them first. God does not love the aggressors"—or, as the American Muslim Malcolm X put it in the twentieth century, "Be peaceful, be courteous, obey the law, respect everyone; but if someone puts his hand on you, send him to the cemetery." Compulsion had no place in spreading religion, but Muslims ("surrenderers" to God) were obliged to defend their faith whenever it was threatened—which, since they were pushing and plundering their way into collapsing empires at the same time as spreading the word, was likely to be quite often.

Thus did Arab migrants find their own advantages of backwardness: the combination of salvation and militarism gave them organization and purpose in a world where both were scarce.

Like many another peripheral people seeking a place in a core, Arabs claimed to have been born to it, as descendants of Abraham's son Ishmael. With their own hands, Muslims claimed, Abraham and Ishmael had built the Ka'ba, Mecca's holiest shrine; Islam was in fact Abraham's original religion, from which Judaism had diverged. The Koran presented Judaism as simply the cousin of Islam; "Who," it asked, "but a foolish man would renounce the faith of Abraham?" All the prophets, from Abraham to Jesus, were valid (although Jesus was no Messiah), and Muhammad was simply the final prophet, putting the seal on the Lord's message and fulfilling the promise of Judaism and Christianity. "Our God and your God is one," Muhammad insisted. There was no necessary conflict between the religions of the book: in fact, the West needed Islam.

Muhammad sent letters to Khusrau and Heraclius explaining all this, but never heard back. No matter; Arabs kept moving into Palestine and Mesopotamia anyway. They came in war bands rather than armies, rarely more than five thousand and probably never more than fifteen thousand strong, hitting and running more than fighting pitched battles; but the few forces that resisted them were rarely much bigger. The empires of the 630s were bankrupt, divided, and incapable of meeting this confusing new threat.

In fact, most people in southwest Asia do not seem to have cared much whether Arab chiefs replaced Byzantine and Persian officials or not. For centuries both empires had persecuted many of their Christian subjects over doctrinal fine print. In the Byzantine Empire, for instance, since 451 the official position had been that Jesus had had two natures, one human and one divine, fused in a single body. Some Egyptian theorists retorted that Jesus had really had just one (purely divine) nature, and by the 630s so many people had died over this question that plenty of One-Nature* Christians in Syria and Egypt positively welcomed the Muslims. Better to have infidel masters to whom the question was meaningless than co-religionists who would unleash holy terror over it.

Just four thousand Muslims invaded Egypt in 639, but Alexandria surrendered without a fight. The mighty Persian Empire, still reeling from a decade of civil wars, collapsed like a house of cards, and the Byzantines retreated into Anatolia, surrendering three-quarters of their empire's tax base. Across the next fifty years Byzantium's high-end institutions evaporated. The empire survived only by quickly finding low-end solutions, relying on local notables to raise armies and on soldiers to grow their own food instead of receiving salaries. By 700 barely fifty thousand people lived at Constantinople, plowing up suburbs to grow crops, going without imports, and bartering instead of using coins.

---

*The technical term is Monophysite, from the Greek for "one nature."

In the space of a century the Arabs swallowed up the wealthiest parts of the Western core. In 674 their armies camped under Constantinople's walls. Forty years later they stood on the banks of the Indus in Pakistan and crossed into Spain, and in 732 a war band reached Poitiers in central France. The migrations from the deserts into the heartland of empires then slowed. A millennium later Gibbon mused:

> A victorious line of march had been prolonged above a thousand miles from the rock of Gibraltar to the banks of the Loire; the repetition of an equal distance would have carried the Saracens [Muslims from North Africa] to the confines of Poland and the Highlands of Scotland: the Rhine is not more impassable than the Nile or Euphrates, and the Arabian fleet might have sailed without a combat into the mouth of the Thames. Perhaps the interpretation of the Koran would now be taught in the schools of Oxford, and her pulpits might demonstrate to a circumcised people the sanctity and truth of the revelation of Mahomet.

"From such calamities Christendom was delivered," Gibbon added, with no little sarcasm. Conventional wisdom in eighteenth-century Britain, like that in seventh-century Constantinople, saw Christianity as the West's defining value and Islam as its antithesis. The rulers of cores probably always picture those who move in from the fringes as barbarians, but Gibbon understood full well that the Arabs were actually part of the larger second-wave Axial transformation of the Western core that had begun with the triumph of Christianity. We can, in fact, out-Gibbon Gibbon, putting the Arabs into a still-longer tradition going all the way back to the Amorites in Mesopotamia in 2200 BCE, and seeing them as they saw themselves: as people who had already been drawn into the core by its conflicts, and who were now claiming their rightful place at its head. They came not to bury the West but to perfect it; not to thwart Justinian's and Khusrau's ambitions, but to fulfill them.

Plenty of political pundits in our own century find it convenient, like Gibbon's eighteenth-century critics, to imagine Islamic civilization as being outside of and opposed to "Western" civilization (by which they generally mean northwest Europe and its overseas colonies). But that ignores the historical realities. By 700 the Islamic world more or less *was* the Western core, and Christendom was merely a periphery along its northern edge. The Arabs had brought into one state roughly as much of the Western core as Rome had done.

The Arab conquests took longer than Wendi's in the East, but because Arab armies were so small and popular resistance generally so limited, they rarely devastated the lands they conquered, and in the eighth century the West's social development finally stopped falling. Now, perhaps, the largely reunited Western core could bounce back like the Eastern core had done in the sixth century, and the East-West gap would narrow again.

THE CENTERS DO NOT HOLD

But that did not happen, as Figure 7.1 shows very clearly. Although both cores were largely reunited by 700 and enjoyed or suffered rather similar political fortunes between the eighth century and the tenth, Eastern social development continued to rise faster than Western.

Both the reunited cores proved politically rickety. Their rulers had to relearn a lesson well known to the Han and Romans, that empires are governed through fudging and compromise, but neither China's Sui dynasty nor the Arabs were very good at this. Like the Han dynasty, the Sui had to worry about nomads (now Turks* rather than Xiongnu), but thanks to the growth of the Eastern core they also had to worry about threats from newly formed states. When Koguryo in what is now Korea opened secret negotiations with the Turks to cooperate in raiding China, the Sui emperor decided he had to act. In 612 he sent a vast army against Koguryo, but bad weather, worse logistics, and atrocious leadership brought about its destruction. In 613 he sent another and in 614 a third. And as he was raising a fourth, rebellions against his demands tore his empire apart.

For a while the horsemen of the apocalypse seemed to be breaking loose again. Warlords divided China, Turkic chieftains played them against one another and plundered at will, and famine and disease

---

*Distant relatives of the Turks at the other end of the steppe highway whom Heraclius hired to invade Mesopotamia in the 620s.

spread. One epidemic arrived across the steppes and another, sounding nastily like bubonic plague, came by sea. But just as bungling idiocy had been enough to start the crisis, good leadership was enough to end it. One Chinese warlord, the Duke of Tang, talked the major Turkic chieftains into backing him against the other Chinese warlords, and by the time the Turks realized their mistake he had proclaimed himself ruler of a new Tang dynasty. In 630 his son exploited a Turkic civil war to extend Chinese rule farther into the steppes than ever before (Figure 7.2b). State control was restored; population movements, famines, and epidemics died down; and the surge in social development that created Wu's world got under way in earnest.

Even more than in Han times, it took firm hands to hold the center together, but humans being what they are, such hands were not always available. It was in fact that most human of emotions, love, that undid the Tang Empire. According to the great poet Bai Juyi, the emperor Xuanzong—"craving beauty that might shake an empire"—fell madly in love with Yang Guifei,* his son's wife, in 740 and made her his concubine. The story sounds suspiciously like that of the love between King You and the snake woman Bao Si that was supposed to have brought down the Western Zhou dynasty fifteen hundred years earlier, but be that as it may, tradition holds that Xuanzong was ready to do anything to please Yang Guifei. One of his bright ideas was to heap honors on her favorites, including a Turkic general named An Lushan, who was fighting on the Chinese side. Ignoring the usual safeguards around military power, Xuanzong allowed An to accumulate control of enormous armies.

Given the complexities of palace intrigues it was inevitable that An would sooner or later fall from favor; and when that came to pass, in 755, An made the obvious move of turning his enormous armies against Chang'an. Xuanzong and Yang fled but the soldiers escorting them, blaming Yang for the civil war, demanded her death. Xuanzong—sobbing, desperate to keep his love out of the soldiers' hands—had his chief eunuch strangle her. "Flowery hairpins fell to the ground, no one picked them up," wrote Bai Juyi.

---

*Guifei actually means "consort"; Yang's own name was Yuhuan, but the title Guifei has stuck.

The Emperor could not save her, he could only cover his face.
And later when he turned to look, the place of blood and tears
Was hidden by a yellow dust blown by a cold wind.

According to legend, Xuanzong hired a seer who tracked down Yang's spirit on an enchanted island. "'Our souls belong together,'" Bai's poem has her tell the emperor; "'somewhere, sometime, on earth or in heaven, we shall surely meet.'"

In the meantime, however, Xuanzong's son crushed the rebellion, but the way he did it—granting other military governors powers as extensive as An's and inviting in Turks from the steppes—was a recipe for further disasters. The frontiers collapsed, tax revenues shriveled, and for generations the empire stumbled back and forth between restorations of order and new uprisings, invasions, and rebellions. In 907 a warlord finally put the Tang dynasty out of its misery by murdering its teenage emperor, and for the next fifty years one large kingdom dominated northern China while eight to ten smaller ones ruled the south.

Xuanzong had exposed China's fundamental political problem: strong emperors had too much power and could override other institutions. With skillful emperors that was fine, but the random distribution of talent and the range of challenges that arose meant that sooner or later disasters were virtually inevitable.

The Western core in a sense had the opposite problem: leadership was too weak. The huge Arab Empire had no emperor. Muhammad had been a prophet, not a king, and people followed him because they were confident that he knew what God wanted. When he died in 632 there was no obvious reason to follow anyone else, and Muhammad's Arab alliance came close to dissolving. To prevent this, several of his friends sat up all night and chose one of their own number as *khalifa* (usually anglicized as caliph), a handily ambiguous word meaning both "deputy" (of God) and "successor" (to Muhammad). The caliph's only claim to lead, though, came from his closeness to the late prophet.

Considering the fractiousness of the Arab chiefs (some of whom wanted to plunder the Persian and Byzantine empires, others to parcel the empires out and settle as landowners, and others still to anoint new prophets), the first few caliphs did remarkably well. They persuaded most Arabs to disturb as little as possible in the Byzantine and Persian empires, keeping conquered peasants in their fields, landlords on their estates, and bureaucrats in their counting houses. The main change they made was to divert the empires' taxes into their own hands, effectively paying Arabs to be professional warriors of God, living in Arab-only garrison cities at strategic points in the conquered lands.

The caliphs could not, though, settle the ambiguity over what a caliph actually was. Were they kings, centralizing revenues and issuing orders, or religious leaders, merely advising independent sheikhs in newly conquered provinces? Should they represent the pre-Islamic tribal elites? Or stand for a Muslim elect of Muhammad's first followers? Or head an egalitarian community of believers? No caliph could please all Muslims all the time, and in 656, when the third caliph was murdered, the difficulties reached crisis proportions. Few of Muhammad's original friends were still alive, and the election devolved on 'Ali, Muhammad's much younger cousin (and son-in-law).

'Ali wanted to restore what he saw as the original spirit of Islam, but his strategy of championing the poor, leaving tax revenues in the soldiers' hands, and sharing plunder more equally infuriated previously privileged groups. Civil war smoldered, but Muslims (at this stage) remained very unwilling to kill one another. In 661 they stepped back from the brink: instead of plunging the whole Arab world into war, 'Ali's disillusioned supporters murdered him. The caliphate now passed to the head of the largest contingent of Arab warriors, who built a capital at Damascus and struggled none-too-successfully to create a conventional empire with centralized taxes and bureaucrats.

In China, Xuanzong's love had triggered political catastrophe; in the West it was brotherly love—or rather, lack of it—that spelled disaster. A new dynasty of caliphs moved the capital to Baghdad in 750 and pursued centralization more effectively, but in 809 a succession dispute between brothers left Caliph al-Ma'mun weak even by Arab standards. He boldly decided to go to the core of the problem: God. Unlike Christians or Buddhists, Muslims had no institutionalized church hierarchy, and while the caliphs had considerable secular power, they had no claim to know more about what God wanted than anyone else. Al-Ma'mun decided to change this by reopening an old wound in Islam.

Back in 680, fewer than twenty years after Muhammad's cousin/son-in-law 'Ali had got himself murdered, 'Ali's own son Husayn had raised the flag of revolt against the caliphs. Few Muslims lifted a finger when Husayn was defeated and killed, but across the next hundred years a faction (*shi'a*) convinced itself that because the current caliphs owed their positions to 'Ali's murder, they were illegitimate. This faction—the Shiites—argued that the blood of Husayn, 'Ali, and Muhammad really did provide privileged knowledge of God, and so only imams, descendants of this line, could lead Islam. Most Muslims (called Sunni because they followed custom, *sunna*) found this story ridiculous, but the Shiites continued elaborating their theology. By the ninth century some Shiites believed that the line of imams was leading to a mahdi, a messiah who would establish God's kingdom on earth.

Al-Ma'mun's bright idea was to adopt the current imam (Husayn's great-great-great-grandson) as his heir, thereby making the Shiites his personal faction. It was a clever, if manipulative, ploy, but it fell through when the imam died within the year and his son proved uninterested in al-Ma'mun's maneuvers. Undaunted, al-Ma'mun unveiled Plan B. Some of the religious theorists he employed in Baghdad, influenced by Greek philosophy, were willing to say that the Koran was a book created by a man, rather than (as most Muslims thought) being part of God's essence. As such, the Koran—and all the clerics who interpreted it—came under the authority of God's earthly deputy, the caliph. Al-Ma'mun set up an Iraqi Inquisition* to bully other scholars into agreeing, but a few hard-core clerics ignored his threats and insisted that the Koran, God's own words, trumped everything—including al-Ma'mun. The struggle dragged on until 848, when the caliphs finally admitted defeat.

The cynicism of al-Ma'mun's Plans A and B weakened the caliphate's authority, but his Plan C shattered it. With religious authority still eluding him, al-Ma'mun decided to be less subtle and simply buy military force—literally, by purchasing Turkic horsemen as a slave army. Like other rulers before him, however, al-Ma'mun and his heirs learned that nomads are basically uncontrollable. By 860 the caliphs were virtually hostages of their own slave army. Without military power or religious support they could no longer generate taxes, and ended up

---

*As was mentioned earlier, historians generally switch from the Greek name Mesopotamia to the Arabic name Iraq for the lands between the Tigris and Euphrates rivers with the seventh-century Muslim conquest.

selling off provinces to emirs: military governors who paid a lump sum, then kept whatever taxes they could extract. In 945 an emir seized Baghdad for himself and the caliphate decomposed into a dozen independent emirates.*

By then the Eastern and Western cores had each fragmented into ten-plus states, yet despite the similarities between the breakdowns in the two cores, Eastern social development continued to rise faster than Western. The explanation once again seems to be that it was not emperors and intellectuals who made history but millions of lazy, greedy, and frightened people looking for easier, more profitable, and safer ways to do things. Regardless of the mayhem that rulers inflicted on them, ordinary people muddled along, making the best of things; and because the geographical realities within which Easterners and Westerners were muddling differed strongly, the political crises in each core ended up having very different consequences.

In the East, the internal migration that had created a new frontier beyond the Yangzi since the fifth century was the real motor behind social development. The restoration of a unified empire in the sixth century had accelerated development's increase, and by the eighth century the upward trend was so robust that it survived the fallout from Xuanzong's love life. Political chaos certainly had negative consequences; a sharp dip in the Eastern score in 900 (Figure 7.1), for instance, was largely the result of rival armies wiping out the million-strong city of Chang'an. But most fighting remained far from the vital rice paddies, canals, and cities, and may actually have accelerated development by sweeping away the government micromanagers who had previously hobbled commerce. Unable to supervise state-owned lands in such troubled times, civil servants started raising money from monopolies and taxes on trade and stopped telling merchants how to do business. There was a transfer of power from the political centers of northern China to the merchants of the south, and merchants, left to their own devices, figured out still more ways to speed up commerce.

---

*Caliphs continued in Baghdad until 1258 (and "shadow caliphs" carried on even later in Cairo), but like the kings of Zhou China after 771 BCE, they were mere figureheads. Emirs would normally mention the caliph in their Friday prayers but otherwise ignore him.

Much of northern China's overseas trade had been state-directed, between the imperial court and the rulers of Japan and Korea, and the collapse of Tang dynasty political power after 755 dissolved these links. Some results were positive; cut off from Chinese models, Japanese elite culture moved in remarkable and original directions, with a whole string of women writing literary masterpieces such as *The Tale of Genji* and *The Pillow Book*. Most results, though, were negative. In northern China, Korea, and Japan economic slowdown and state breakdown went together in the ninth century.

In southern China, by contrast, independent merchants exploited their new freedom from state power. Tenth-century shipwrecks found in the Java Sea since the 1990s contain not only Chinese luxuries but also pottery and glass from South Asia and the Muslim world, hinting at the expansion of markets in this region; and as local elites taxed the flourishing traders, the first strong Southeast Asian states emerged in what is now Sumatra and among the Khmers in Cambodia.

The very different geography of western Eurasia, with no equivalent to the East's rice frontier, meant that its political breakdown also had different consequences. In the seventh century the Arab conquests swept away the old boundary that had separated the Roman world from the Persian (Figure 7.7), setting off something of a boom in the Muslim core. Caliphs expanded irrigation in Iraq and Egypt, and travelers carried crops and techniques from the Indus to the Atlantic. Rice, sugar, and cotton spread across the Muslim Mediterranean, and by alternating crops farmers got two or three harvests from their fields. The Muslims who colonized Sicily even invented classic Western foods such as pasta and ice cream.

However, the gains from overcoming the old barrier between Rome and Persia were increasingly offset by the losses caused by a new barrier across the Mediterranean, separating Islam from Christendom. As the southern and eastern Mediterranean grew more solidly Muslim (as late as 750, barely one person in ten under Arab rule was Muslim; by 950, it was more like nine in ten) and Arabic became its lingua franca, contact with Christendom declined; and then, as the caliphate fragmented after 800, emirs raised barriers within Islam, too. Some of the regions within the Muslim core, such as Spain, Egypt, and Iran, were big enough to get by on internal demand alone, but others declined.

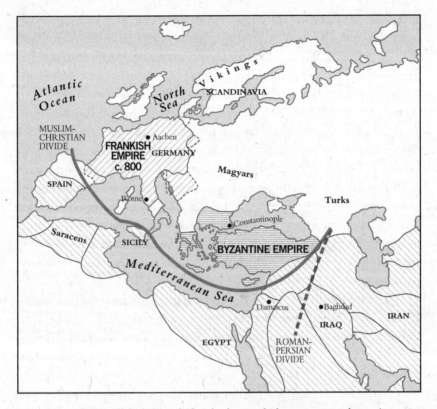

Figure 7.7. The fault line shifts: the heavy dashes represent the major
economic-political-cultural fault line between 100 BCE and 600 CE,
separating Rome from Persia; the solid line shows the major line after
650 CE, separating Islam from Christendom. At the top left is the
Frankish Empire at its peak, around 800; at the bottom the Muslim
world, showing the political divisions around 945.

And while China's ninth-century wars had mostly avoided the economic heartlands, Iraq's fragile irrigation network was devastated by
competing Turkic slave armies and a fourteen-year uprising of African
plantation slaves under a leader who at various times claimed to be a
poet, a prophet, and a descendant of 'Ali.

In the East, Korea and Japan drifted toward political breakdown
when the northern Chinese core went into crisis; similarly, in the West
the Christian periphery fragmented still further as the Muslim core
came apart. Byzantines slaughtered one another by the thousands and

split from the Roman Church over new doctrinal questions (especially whether God approved of images of Jesus, Mary, and the saints), and the Germanic kingdoms, largely cut off from the Mediterranean, began creating their own world.

Some on this far western fringe expected it to become a core in its own right. Since the sixth century the Frankish people had become a regional power, and small trading towns now popped up around the North Sea to satisfy the Frankish aristocracy's insatiable demand for luxuries. Theirs remained a low-end state, with little taxation or administration. Kings who were good at mobilizing their quarrelsome lords could quickly put together large but loose realms embracing much of western Europe, but under weak kings these equally quickly broke down. Kings with too many sons usually ended up dividing their lands among them—which often simply led to wars to reunite the patrimony.

The later eighth century was a particularly good time for the Franks. In the 750s the pope in Rome sought their protection against local bullies, and on Christmas morning, 800, the Frankish king Charlemagne* was even able to get Pope Leo III to kneel before him in St. Peter's and crown him Roman emperor.

Charlemagne vigorously tried to build a kingdom worthy of the title he claimed. His armies carried fire, the sword, and Christianity into eastern Europe and pushed the Muslims back into Spain, while his literate bureaucracy gathered some taxes, assembled scholars at Aachen ("a Rome yet to be," one of his court poets called it), created a stable coinage, and oversaw a trade revival. It is tempting to compare Charlemagne to Xiaowen, who, three centuries before, had moved the Northern Wei kingdom on China's rough frontier toward the high end, jump-starting the process that led to the reunification of the Eastern core. Charlemagne's coronation in Rome certainly speaks of ambitions like Xiaowen's, as do the embassies he sent to seek Baghdad's friendship. So impressed was the caliph, Frankish chronicles say, that he sent Charlemagne an elephant.

Arab sources, however, mention neither Franks nor elephants. Charlemagne was no Xiaowen, and apparently counted for little in the

---

*Charlemagne's actual name was Carolus; Charlemagne is a Gallicized version of Carolus Magnus, "Charles the Great."

caliph's councils. Nor did Charlemagne's claim to be Roman emperor move the Byzantine empress Irene* to abdicate in his favor. The reality was that the Frankish kingdom never moved very far toward the high end. For all Charlemagne's pretensions, he had no chance of reuniting the core or even turning the Christian fringe into a single state.

One of the things Charlemagne did achieve, unfortunately, was to raise social development enough to lure raiders into his empire from the even wilder lands beyond the Christian periphery. By the time he died in 814, Viking longboats from Scandinavia were nosing up rivers into the empire's heart, Magyars on tough little steppe ponies were plundering Germany, and Saracen pirates from North Africa were about to sack Rome itself. Aachen was ill equipped to respond; when Vikings beached their ships and burned villages, royal armies came late or not at all. Increasingly, countryfolk turned to local big men to defend them, and townspeople turned to their bishops and mayors. By the time Charlemagne's three grandsons divided the empire among themselves in 843, kings had ceased to mean much to most of their subjects.

UNDER PRESSURE

As if these strains were not enough, after 900 Eurasia came under a new kind of pressure—literally; as Earth's orbit kept shifting, atmospheric pressure increased over the landmass, weakening the westerlies blowing off the Atlantic into Europe and the monsoons blowing off the Indian Ocean into southern Asia. Averaged across Eurasia, temperatures probably rose 1–2°F between 900 and 1300 and rainfall declined by perhaps 10 percent.

As always, climate change forced people to adapt, but left it up to them to decide just how to do that. In cold, wet northern Europe this so-called Medieval Warm Period was often welcome, and population probably doubled between 1000 and 1300. In the hotter, drier Islamic core, however, it could be less welcome. Overall population in the Muslim world probably fell by 10 percent, but some areas, particularly

*Irene was a worthy rival to Theodora and Wu; she seized the throne in 797 after having her own son's eyes gouged out to disqualify him from ruling.

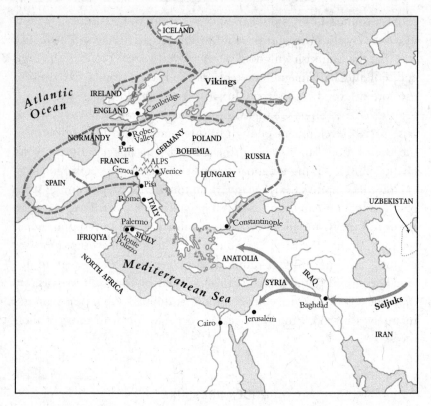

Figure 7.8. Coming in from the cold: the migrations of the Seljuk
Turks (solid arrows) and Vikings/Normans (broken arrows) into
the Western core in the eleventh century

in North Africa, flourished. In 908 Ifriqiya,* roughly modern Tunisia
(Figure 7.8), broke away from the caliphs in Baghdad. Radical Shiites[†]
set up a line of officially infallible caliph-imams, known as Fatimids because they claimed descent (and imamhood) from Muhammad's daughter Fatima. In 969 these Fatimids conquered Egypt, where they built a
great new city at Cairo and invested in irrigation. By 1000 Egypt had
the highest social development in the West, and Egyptian traders were
fanning out across the Mediterranean.

*Ifriqiya is an Arabized version of Africa, the Roman name for Tunisia.

[†]Radical in the sense that they belonged to the Isma'ili Shiite sect, which often used
violence to oppose what it saw as illegitimate Sunni regimes, rather than the "Twelver"
Shiites, who awaited more peacefully the return of the hidden twelfth imam.

We would know precious little about these traders had the Jewish community in Cairo not decided in 1890 to remodel its nine-hundred-year-old synagogue. Like many synagogues, this had a storeroom where worshippers could deposit unwanted documents to avoid risking blasphemy by destroying papers that might have God's name written on them. Normally storerooms were cleared out periodically, but this one had been allowed to fill up with centuries' worth of wastepaper. As the remodeling began, old documents started showing up in Cairo's antiquities markets, and in spring 1896 two English sisters carried a bundle back to Cambridge. There they showed two texts to Solomon Schechter, the University Reader in Talmudics. Initially skeptical, Schechter then had an "Oh my God" moment: one was a Hebrew fragment of the biblical book of Ecclesiasticus, previously known only from Greek translations. The learned doctor descended on Cairo that December and carried off 140,000 documents.

Among them were hundreds of letters to Cairo trading houses, mailed between 1025 and about 1250 from as far afield as Spain and India. The ideological divisions that had formed in the wake of the Arab conquests were crumbling as population growth expanded markets and profits, and clearly meant little to these correspondents, who worried more about the weather, their families, and getting rich than about religion and politics. In this they may have been typical of Mediterranean merchants; though less well documented, commerce was apparently just as international and profitable in Ifriqiya and Sicily, where Muslim Palermo became a boomtown trading with Christian northern Italy.

Even Monte Polizzo, the backcountry Sicilian village where I have been excavating for the last few years, got into the act. As I mentioned in Chapter 5, I went there to study the effects of Phoenician and Greek colonization in the seventh and sixth centuries BCE, but when we started digging in 2000 we found a second village above the ancient houses. This second village had been established around 1000 CE, probably by Muslim immigrants from Ifriqiya, and burned down around 1125. When our botanist sifted through the carbonized seeds excavated in its ruins, he discovered—to everyone's surprise—that one building had been a storeroom full of carefully threshed wheat, with scarcely a weed in it.* This formed a sharp contrast with the seeds we

*I would like to thank Dr. Hans-Peter Stika for his analysis of these finds.

found in the sixth-century-BCE contexts, which were always mixed with plenty of weeds and chaff. That would have made for rather coarse bread, which is what we might expect in a simple farming village where people grew crops for their own tables and did not worry about the occasional unpleasant mouthful. The compulsive winnowing that rid the twelfth-century-CE wheat of all impurities, though, is exactly what we might expect from commercial farmers producing for picky city folk.

The Mediterranean economy was booming indeed if little Monte Polizzo was tied into international networks. But the oldest part of the Muslim core, in southwest Asia, was not doing so well. It was bad enough that since the 860s the Turkic slaves whom Iraqi caliphs had bought for their armies had been launching coups and making themselves sultans, but worse was to come. Since the seventh century Muslim merchants and missionaries had been preaching Muhammad's good news to the Turkic tribes in the steppes, and in 960 the Karluk clan in what is now Uzbekistan—reputedly some 200,000 families—converted to Islam en masse. It was a triumph for the faith but rapidly turned into a nightmare for the politicians. The Karluks founded their own Karakhanid Empire and another Turkic tribe, the Seljuks, followed their conversion with migration, plundering their way across Iran and taking Baghdad in 1055.* By 1079 they had driven the Byzantines out of most of Anatolia and the Fatimids out of Syria.

Muslim southwest Asia diverged rapidly from the flourishing Islamic Mediterranean. The Seljuk Turks assembled a large empire, but it was even more dysfunctional than the caliphate had been. When its fierce first ruler died in 1092 his sons followed steppe traditions by splitting the empire into nine parts and fighting one another. The decisive arm in their wars was cavalry, so the Seljuk kings gave great estates to warlords who could provide mounted followers. These nomad chiefs, predictably, let administration and trade decay and even stopped minting coins. Cities shrank, irrigation canals silted up, and marginal villages were abandoned. In the hot, dry weather of the Medieval Warm Period farmers had to struggle constantly just to keep their precious fields from reverting to steppe and desert, but Seljuk policies made

---

*There are several ways to transliterate Turkic names; some historians prefer Qarluq to Karluk, Qarakhanid to Karakhanid, and Saljuq to Seljuk.

their job harder still. Many of the conquerors, preferring nomadic to urban lifestyles, welcomed the decline of agriculture, and as the twelfth century wore on, more and more Arabs left their fields and joined the Turks in herding flocks.

Alarmed at the spread of radical Shiite theories in these troubled years, scholars in eastern Iran set up schools to develop and teach a coherent Sunni response, which Seljuk lords promoted vigorously in the twelfth century. Its monuments of scholarship—such as al-Ghazali's *Revivification of the Sciences of Religion*, which drew on Greek logic to reconcile Islamic jurisprudence, Sufi mysticism, and Muhammad's revelation—remain foundations of Sunni thought to this day. So successful was the Sunni Revival, in fact, that some Shiites decided that murdering Sunni leaders was the only practical response. Retreating to the mountains of Iran, they formed a secret society known to its enemies as the Assassins (according to legend, so called because its agents smoked hashish to put them in the right frame of mind for murder).

Assassination could not roll back the Sunni Revival, but neither could an intellectual movement—despite its success—hold together a Seljuk state, and without the kind of political organization that the Fatimid kingdoms provided in North Africa, the Seljuk lands buckled under the pressures of the Medieval Warm Period. The timing was unfortunate, because the same weather that posed such challenges in southwest Asia created opportunities for the unruly raiders, traders, and invaders on the Muslim core's European fringe. Equally important, warmer weather brought northern Europe longer growing seasons and higher yields, making previously marginal lands potentially profitable. By the time the Medieval Warm Period wound down, farmers had plowed up vast tracts of what had once been forest, felling perhaps half the trees in western Europe.

Like all episodes of expansion since the spread of farming from the Hilly Flanks, two processes combined to bring advanced agricultural techniques from western into eastern Europe. The first was colonization, often led by the church, normally the only well-organized institution on the frontier. "Give these monks a naked moor or a wild wood," Gerald of Wales wrote, "then let a few years pass and you will find not only beautiful churches, but dwellings of men built around them." Expansion was the Lord's work: according to a recruiting drive in 1108, "pagans are the worst of men but their land is the best, with

368 WHY THE WEST RULES—FOR NOW

meat, honey, and flour . . . here you will be able both to save your souls [by forcing heathens to convert] and, if you will, to acquire very good land to settle."

Sometimes the pagans fled; sometimes they submitted, oftentimes ending up little better than slaves. But like hunter-gatherers confronting farmers or Sicilians confronting Greek colonists thousands of years earlier, sometimes they organized and stood their ground. As Frankish and Germanic farmers moved east, cutting down trees and plowing up pastures, some villagers in Bohemia, Poland, Hungary, and even distant Russia copied their techniques, exploiting the better weather to farm their own lands more intensively. Their chiefs, turning Christian, persuaded or forced them to become tax-paying subjects and fight the colonists (and one another).

The spread of states, churches, and intensive farming across Europe had much in common with the agricultural frontier that had developed south of the Yangzi since the fifth century, but differed in one crucial respect: it did not create major trade flows between the new rural frontier and an older urban core. In the absence of a central European equivalent of China's Grand Canal there was simply no cheap way to get Polish grain to great cities such as Palermo and Cairo. Western Europe's towns were closer to the frontiers and were growing, but remained too few and too small to provide adequate markets. Rather than importing food from eastern Europe, these western European towns generally grew by intensifying local production and exploiting new energy sources.

Watermills, already common in the Muslim core, now spread across the Christian fringe. The number of mills in France's Robec Valley, for instance, quintupled between the tenth century and the thirteenth, and the *Domesday Book*, a census compiled in 1086, says that England had a remarkable 5,624 mills. Farmers also learned the virtues of horses, which eat more than oxen but can pull plows faster and work longer. The balance slowly tipped in horses' favor after 1000, when—for reasons I will return to in Chapter 8—Europeans adopted from Muslims metal horseshoes, which reduced friction, and replaced their clumsy, choking, throat-and-girth harnesses with collar harnesses that quadrupled horses' pulling power. In 1086 just one draft animal in twenty on English barons' lands was a horse; by 1300 one in five was. With this extra horsepower (not to mention extra manure) farmers could reduce the land they left fallow each year, squeezing more from their properties.

Europe's farms remained less productive than Egypt's or China's but they increasingly had surpluses to sell to towns, and the growing towns took on new roles. Many northwest Europeans were serfs, legally bound to work the land of lords who protected them from raiders (and from other lords). In theory, at least, the lords held their own positions as vassals of kings, repaying the kings by fighting as armored cavalry, and kings owed their positions to the church, which dispensed God's approval. But lords, kings, and the church all wanted access to the wealth now accumulating in towns, and townsfolk could often negotiate freedom from feudal obligations in return for surrendering a cut of it.

Like low-end rulers going all the way back to Assyria and the Zhou, European kings were effectively running a protection racket, but their version was even messier than those of most of their predecessors. Towns, nobles, monarchs, and churchmen constantly interfered in one another's affairs, and in the absence of real central authorities, conflict was virtually guaranteed. In 1075, for instance, Pope Gregory VII claimed the right to appoint all bishops in Germany. His goal was to reform the morality of church leaders, but since bishoprics controlled vast slices of Germany's land, the move also had the pleasing side effect of giving Gregory control over much of Germany's resource base. The German emperor Henry IV was horrified, and responded by claiming that as defender of the faith he had the right to depose Gregory—"now not pope," Henry insisted, "but false monk . . . I, Henry, by the grace of God, together with all our bishops, say to you: Descend! Descend!"

Instead of descending, Gregory excommunicated Henry, casting the German emperor outside the Christian faith. In practical terms, that meant Germany's feudal lords could legally ignore their ruler. Now unable to get anything done in his own land, within a year Henry was reduced to kneeling barefoot in the snow for three days outside an Alpine monastery, begging the pope's forgiveness. This he got, then went to war with the pope anyway. No one won. Pope Gregory lost everyone's support after his own mercenaries sacked Rome because he had not paid them; the emperor ended his life on the run from his own son; and the theological dispute was never really resolved.

Eleventh-century Europe was full of such tangled struggles, but little by little, their resolutions gradually made institutions stronger and their spheres of responsibility clearer. Kings increasingly managed to organize, mobilize, and tax people in their territories. One historian has called this process "the formation of a persecuting society": royal officials persuaded people to see themselves as part of a nation (the English, the French, and so on) defined against what they were not—pariahs such as Jews, homosexuals, lepers, and heretics, who, for the first time, were systematically stripped of protection and terrorized. Increasingly effective states emerged from this unpleasant process.

Other historians speak more happily of an "age of cathedrals," as awe-inspiring monuments sprouted all over Europe. In France alone, eighty cathedrals, five hundred abbeys, and tens of thousands of parish churches were built between 1180 and 1270. Over 40 million cubic feet of stone were quarried, more than for Egypt's Great Pyramid.

Scholarship had declined in western Europe along with the Roman Empire and only partially recovered in Charlemagne's France, but after 1000, teachers began clustering around the new cathedrals, setting up schools rather like those of the independent muftis in the Islamic world. Christians who went to study in Muslim Spain brought home with them translations of Aristotle's treatises on logic, preserved for centuries by Arab court scholars. All this strengthened Christian intellectual life, helping theologians think about God in the same sophisticated ways as al-Ma'mun's theorists in ninth-century Baghdad, but it also created new conflicts within the educated elite.

No one illustrates these better than Peter Abelard. A bright young man steeped in the new learning, Abelard showed up in Paris around 1100. Wandering from school to school, he publicly humiliated his pedantic teachers by tripping them up with his Aristotelian logic. Honest but plodding professors saw their careers collapse when twenty-somethings like Abelard used their razor-sharp debating skills to throw convention (and potentially the fates of everyone's souls) into confusion. Inordinately pleased with himself, Abelard set up his own school and promptly seduced and impregnated one of his pupils, the teenage Héloïse. Her family, dishonored, struck back: "One night when I was sound asleep," Abelard coyly put it, "they cut off the organs by which I had committed the deed which they abhorred."

Héloïse and Abelard each withdrew in shame to houses of God, and for twenty years kept up a correspondence, self-justifying on his part, searingly personal on hers. In this enforced retirement Abelard wrote the *Sic et Non*, "Thus and Not-Thus," a kind of handbook for applying logic to Christianity's contradictions; and if Abelard's name became a byword for the dangers of the new learning, he nonetheless forced Christian theorists to reconcile the authority of scripture with Aristotelian rationalism. By 1270, when Thomas Aquinas perfected this in his *On Christian Theology*, Christian learning was quite as sophisticated as that of the Sunni Revival.

Other Europeans did the opposite of Abelard: instead of bringing ideas and institutions from the Muslim core to the Christian fringe, they moved themselves into the Muslim core. Merchants of Venice, Genoa, and Pisa competed with those of Cairo and Palermo for the lucrative Mediterranean trade, buying and selling or stealing and fighting. In Spain, migrants from increasingly crowded northwest Europe helped local Christians push the Muslims back, and all around the Mediterranean Normans (or Norsemen) unleashed a storm of pillage and conquest.

The Normans were descendants of Scandinavia's pagan Vikings, who had flourished as raiders on Europe's far northwest fringe in the ninth century but in the tenth progressed to grander forms of theft. As the Medieval Warm Period opened up the waters of the North Atlantic they took their longboats to Iceland, Greenland, and even Vinland in North America. They settled heavily in Ireland and Britain, and in northern France their chief, Rollo, turned himself into a proper king (of what is now Normandy) by adopting Christianity in 912.

The Normans remained vague on the faith's details, sacrificing a hundred captives at Rollo's funeral in 931, but their violence made them desirable as mercenaries as far away as Constantinople. Hired in 1016 to fight on both sides in the endless wars over southern Italy, Norman bands proceeded to carve out their own state, and pressing on to Sicily in 1061, they pursued an almost genocidal war against its Muslim occupants. If you visit Sicily today you will be hard-pressed to find a single monument from the two centuries of Islamic rule, during which the island was the wonder of the Mediterranean.

The Normans had no particular animus against Islam; they treated fellow Christians just as badly. One Italian writer called them "a savage, barbarous and horrible race of inhuman disposition," and Anna Comnena, a Byzantine princess, was even more appalled. "Whenever battle and war occur," she wrote, "there is a baying in [the Normans'] hearts and they cannot be held back. Not only the soldiers but also their leaders fling themselves irresistibly into the enemy ranks."

Byzantium learned about Normans the hard way. In the ninth and tenth centuries Byzantine strength had revived somewhat as Muslims turned to fighting one another, and in 975 a Byzantine army even came within sight of Jerusalem (it failed to take the holy city but did liberate Jesus' sandals and John the Baptist's hair). But within a century the Byzantines became dangerously dependent on Norman mercenaries, whose unreliability (for all their ferocity, they regularly ran away) contributed to a catastrophic defeat at Turkish hands in 1071. Twenty years later, with Constantinople under Turkish siege, the Byzantine emperor wrote to the pope in Rome, apparently hoping for help in hiring more mercenaries. The pope, though, had other ideas. Seeking to strengthen his own position in his struggles with Europe's kings, he called a summit in 1095 and pitched the idea of an expedition—a crusade—to throw the Turks out of Jerusalem.

There was wild enthusiasm; rather more, in fact, than either the pope or the Byzantines wanted. Tens of thousands of villagers started walking east, plundering central Europe and massacring Jews as they went. Only a few reached Anatolia, where the Turks slaughtered them. None made it to the Holy Land, except as slaves.

Of more practical use were the three armies of French and Norman knights, backed by Genoese merchants, which converged on Jerusalem in 1099. Their timing was impeccable: the Seljuks were too busy fighting one another to offer much resistance, and after heart-stopping feats of bravado the crusaders breached the holy city's walls. For twelve hours they plundered and killed on a scale that shocked even the Normans among them, burning Jews alive and chopping Muslims into pieces (though at least, a Jewish woman observed, the Christians did not follow the Turkish practice of raping their victims first). Finally, at dusk, the conquerors splashed through ankle-deep gore to thank God at the Church of the Holy Sepulcher.

Yet spectacular though it was, this direct assault on the core never seriously threatened Islam. The Christian Kingdom of Jerusalem was steadily rolled back until in 1187 the Muslims recaptured the city. More crusades followed, most failing dismally; in 1204 the fourth, unable to afford ships, ended up renting itself out as muscle to Venetian financiers and sacking not Jerusalem but Constantinople. Neither the crusading movement nor the Byzantine Empire recovered from this disgrace.

The West was changing shape under the pressures of the Medieval Warm Period. The Muslim lands remained the core, but as social development stagnated in southwest Asia, Islam's center of gravity shifted toward the Mediterranean, and even within the Mediterranean there were winners and losers. Egypt became the jewel in the Muslim crown; Byzantium, Rome's last relic, went into terminal decline; and the rude, backward northwest fringe expanded fastest of all.

DARK SATANIC MILLS

Matters could scarcely have been more different in the Eastern core. The Tang Empire had dissolved in 907, but already by 960 China had been reunited. Taizu, the first emperor of the new Song dynasty, was a tough soldier, but saw that the growth of economic and cultural ties between China's regions across the last few centuries had made much of the elite feel that China *should* be one empire. Given the right terms, he reckoned, they would join him rather than fight him. When force was required he readily used it, but unlike earlier efforts to unite either core, most states submitted peacefully and most accepted Song rule.

Taizu also understood that army commanders had brought down most previous dynasties, so he simply got rid of them. Inviting the generals who had put him on the throne to a feast, he "dissolved the militarists' power with a cup of wine," as the official history put it. Publicly toasting the generals for having reached retirement (which was news to the generals), he dismissed them. Rather surprisingly, Taizu got away with this bloodless coup, and from then on when he mobilized the army he usually led it himself.

Shifting from military to civilian government was a brilliant way to tap into the broad desire for peace and unity. Its one drawback was that China did still have enemies, particularly two seminomadic groups, the Khitans and Tanguts, which had built up empires beyond China's northern frontier (Figure 7.9). These could not be dissolved with wine, and after losing an army and almost having an emperor captured, the Song fell back on the old policy of buying peace with gifts.

Up to a point, this worked, and neither the Khitans nor the Tanguts overran the Eastern core like the Seljuks did in the West. Its downside was that the Song, like earlier dynasties, were soon bankrupting themselves paying for gifts and garrisons that did not really keep the peace. By the 1040s they were supporting a million-man army and buying thousands of suits of armor and millions of arrowheads each month—not at all what Taizu had intended.

Some generals hoped that wonder weapons could save China from sliding back into the old standoff with the steppes. Daoist alchemists

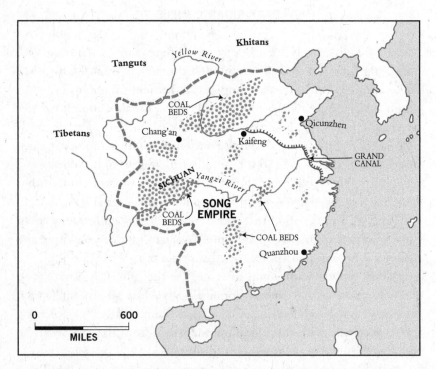

Figure 7.9. The antimilitarist empire: the division of China around 1000 among the Song, Khitan, and Tangut states. China's main coalfields are marked with dots.

had discovered a crude kind of gunpowder around 850 (ironically while looking for elixirs of eternal life); by 950, paintings show people squirting burning powder on one another from bamboo tubes; and in 1044 a military handbook described a "fire drug," packed in paper or bamboo and thrown by catapult. Gunpowder's bark, however, was still worse than its bite, and while it frightened horses it rarely hurt anyone—yet.

In the absence of technological breakthroughs, the Song military simply needed more money. Help came from unlikely directions. One was China's intellectuals. After An Lushan's revolt tipped the country into chaos in 755, many scholars had questioned the enthusiasm for all things foreign, which, as they saw it, had given China nothing but Turkic generals and disorder. The whole five-century period since the fall of the Han started to strike many disillusioned gentry as a barbarous interlude that had corrupted Chinese traditions. Chief among the corrosive alien imports, they argued, was Buddhism.

In 819 the learned gentleman Han Yu sent a "Memorial on the Bone of the Buddha" to the emperor to express his horror at the mass hysteria that broke out when a monastery relocated one of the (many) bones said to be the Buddha's. "Buddhism," Han insisted, "is no more than a cult of barbarian peoples." Back in the days when Buddhism had seduced China, he argued, "officials, being of small worth and knowledge, were unable fully to comprehend the ways of the ancient kings and the exigencies of past and present, and so could not implement the wisdom of the emperor and rescue the age from corruption." Now, however, scholarship was superior. Intellectuals were learning to think, paint, and above all write like the ancients, thereby recapturing antique virtue and saving the nation. "Prose writing must serve as the vehicle for the Way," urged Han, who designed a new writing style to reproduce the crispness and high moral tone of antiquity.

The backlash against Buddhism was controversial but convenient. Buddhist monasteries had accumulated enormous wealth, and when Emperor Wuzong cracked down on Buddhism in the 840s—defrocking monks, closing monasteries, plundering treasures—fiscal pressures may have moved him more than scholarly fulminations. The official persecution made opinions such as Han's respectable. Millions of Buddhists remained, but millions more Chinese, filled with doubts about this imported religion, were energized by the possibility that answers to the

Buddha's great questions—What is the real me? How do I fit into the universe?—lay hidden in plain sight in their own Confucian classics.

A "Neo-Confucian" movement swept through the gentry, and in China's hour of need, with the Khitans and Tanguts pressing in, the empire's finest minds emulated Confucius by stepping forward to advise the ruler. Forget about rebirth and immortality, they insisted; the here-and-now is everything, and fulfillment comes from action in the world. "The true scholar," one concluded, "should be the first to worry about the world's troubles and the last to enjoy its pleasures."

The Neo-Confucians turned classical studies into a program for perfecting society. Men who had the philological and artistic skills to understand ancient culture properly, they claimed, could use antiquity's virtue to save the modern world. Ouyang Xiu, for instance, who had stumbled across Han Yu's writings as a boy, invented his own "ancient prose" style, made a name as a poet, historian, and collector of two-thousand-year-old bronzes, then rose high in the imperial service, championing fiscal and military reforms.

Dozens of equally talented men offered their help to the state, but the most remarkable was Wang Anshi, a leading antiquarian, great prose stylist, and prime minister. Wang's many enemies (who included Ouyang) called him abrasive and repulsively dirty, and in the end drove him into exile and disgrace, but his radical New Policies—an eleventh-century version of the New Deal and Reaganomics rolled into one—brought some real relief. Wang slashed taxes but raised revenues by making collection fairer. He funded massive public works and stimulated growth with "green shoots loans," lending capital to farmers and small merchants. He balanced the budget by shifting from expensive professional soldiers toward cheaper militias. When conservative administrators objected, he found new administrators. He put economics, geography, and law on the civil service exams, established new schools to teach them, and raised salaries for those who made it through.

Extraordinary as the Neo-Confucians' achievements were, though, they paled into insignificance compared with a second development going on at the same time, an economic explosion to rival ancient Rome's. The Medieval Warm Period was a boon almost everywhere in China: lake sediments, the chemistry of stalagmites, and textual records all suggest that the semiarid north got more rain, just what its farmers wanted, while the wet south got less, which suited that region's farmers too. China's population grew to perhaps 100 million by 1100.

By 1100 all thirty-seven of the types of rice mentioned in the sixth-century *Essential Methods of the Common People* had been replaced by even higher-yielding varieties, and farmers regularly squeezed three crops out of their irrigated and manured fields each year by alternating rice with wheat. An expanding network of roads—often finished in stone within cities and sometimes in brick even in the countryside—made it easier to get crops to harbors, and water transport was improving even more dramatically. Chinese shipwrights copied the best features of Persian, Arab, and Southeast Asian vessels, building large oceangoing junks with watertight compartments, four or even six masts, and crews up to a thousand strong. Shipping costs tumbled and merchants organized for large-scale trade. According to a twelfth-century writer,

> The rivers and lakes are linked together so that by means of them one can go everywhere. When a boat leaves its home port, there are no obstacles to its planning a journey of ten thousand *li* [roughly three thousand miles]. Every year the common people use for trading all the grain that is surplus to their requirements for seed and food. Large merchants gather what the lesser households have. Little boats become the dependents of the greater vessels and engage in joint operations, going back and forth selling grain to clear a solid profit.

Almost as important as the actual boats were shipping brokers, middlemen who bought and warehoused cargoes, made loans, and turned ships around quickly. All this, though, took cash, and as the economy grew the government struggled to mint enough bronze coins. Heroic efforts to find new copper sources (and less-heroic ones to debase coins with lead) pushed output up from 300 million coins in 983 to 1.83 billion in 1007, but demand still outran supply.

Greed and laziness saved the day. In the ninth century, when the tea trade started booming and state supervision of commerce declined, dealers from Sichuan began setting up offices in Chang'an where they could exchange the coins they received for their tea for "flying money," paper bills of credit. When they returned to Sichuan the dealers could convert these bills back into cash at the company's head office. Given that a pocketful of flying money was worth forty pocketfuls of bronze coins, the advantages were obvious, and soon merchants were using the bills as cash in their own right. They had invented fiduciary money, tokens whose value depended on trust rather than their metal content. In 1024 the state took the logical next step, printing paper banknotes, and was soon issuing more money in notes than in coin.*

As paper money and credit penetrated the countryside, making buying and selling easier, more peasants grew whatever did best on their land, sold it for cash, then bought whatever they could not produce so easily. A Buddhist monk described stumbling across one of their little markets in a remote village:

> The morning sun not yet risen from the lake,
> Bramble thickets seem for a moment like gates of pine.
> Aged trees steep the precipitous cliffs in gloom;
> The apes' desolate calls float down.
>
> The path turns, and a valley opens
> With a village in the distance barely visible.
> Along the track, shouting and laughing,
> Come farmhands overtaking and overtaken in turn
> Off to match wits a few hours at the market.
>
> The lodges and stores are countless as the clouds.
> They bring linen fabrics and paper-mulberry paper,
> Or drive pullets and sucking-pigs ahead of them.
> Brushes and dustpans are piled this way and that—
> Too many domestic trifles to list them all.
> An elderly man controls the busy trafficking,
> And everyone respects his slightest indications.
> Meticulously careful, he compares

---

*In most years the Song issued about a billion bronze coins plus notes valued at 1.25 billion coins. The notes were fully convertible back to bronze, guaranteed by a reserve of 360 million coins.

The yardsticks one by one,
And turns them over slowly in his hands.

Urban markets were of course far grander and could draw on half a continent of suppliers. Southeast Asian traders linked the port of Quanzhou to the Indonesian Spice Islands and the riches of the Indian Ocean, and imports made their way from there to every town in the empire. To pay for them, family workshops turned out silks, porcelain, lacquer, and paper, and the most successful blossomed into factories. Even villagers could buy what had formerly been luxuries, such as books. By the 1040s, millions of relatively cheap books were rolling off wooden printing presses and making their way into even quite modest buyers' hands. Literacy rates probably rivaled those of Roman Italy a thousand years earlier.

The most momentous changes of all, though, were in textiles and coal, exactly the spheres of activity that would drive the British industrial revolution in the eighteenth century. Eleventh-century textile workers invented a pedal-powered silk-reeling machine, and in 1313 the scholar Wang Zhen's *Treatise on Agriculture* described a large hemp-spinning version, adapted to use either animal or waterpower. It was, Wang noted, "several times cheaper than the women it replaces," and was "used in all parts of north China which manufacture hemp." So moved was Wang by this wizardry that he interrupted his technical account with bursts of poetry:

It takes a spinner many days to spin a hundred catties,
But with waterpower it may be done with supernatural speed! . . .
There is one driving belt for wheels both great and small;
When one wheel turns, the others all turn with it!
The rovings are transmitted evenly from the bobbin rollers,
*The threads wind by themselves onto the reeling frame!**

Comparing eighteenth-century plans for a French flax-spinning machine with Wang's fourteenth-century design, the economic historian Mark Elvin felt compelled to conclude that "the resemblance to Wang [Z]hen's machine is so striking that suspicions of an ultimate

---

*A hundred catties are roughly 130 pounds; rovings are twisted fibers.

Chinese origin for it . . . are almost irresistible." Wang's machine was less efficient than the French one, "but," Elvin concludes, "if the line of advance which it represented had been followed a little further then medieval China would have had a true industrial revolution in the production of textiles over four hundred years before the West."

No statistics survive for Song-era textile production and prices, so we cannot easily test this theory, but we do have information on other industries. Tax returns suggest that iron output increased sixfold between 800 and 1078, to about 125,000 tons—almost as much as the whole of Europe would produce in 1700.[*]

Ironworks clustered around their main market, the million-strong city of Kaifeng, where (among other uses) iron was cast into the countless weapons the army required. Chosen as a capital because it lay conveniently near the Grand Canal, Kaifeng was the city that worked. It lacked the history, tree-lined boulevards, and gracious palaces of earlier capitals and it inspired no great poetry, but in the eleventh century it grew into a crowded, chaotic, and vibrant metropolis. Its raucous bars served wine until dawn,[†] fifty theaters each drew audiences of thousands, and shops even encroached on the city's one great processional avenue. And beyond the walls, foundries burned day and night, dark satanic mills belching fire and smoke, sucking in tens of thousands of trees to smelt ores into iron—so many trees, in fact, that ironmasters bought up and clear-cut entire mountains, driving the price of charcoal beyond the reach of ordinary homeowners. Hundreds of freezing Kaifengers were trampled in fuel riots in 1013.

Kaifeng was apparently entering an ecological bottleneck. There was simply not enough wood in northern China to feed and warm its million bodies and to keep foundries turning out thousands of tons of iron. That left just two options: the people and/or industries could drift away, or someone could innovate and find a new fuel source.

Homo sapiens had always lived by exploiting plants and animals for food, clothes, fuel, and shelter. Over the ages humans had become much more efficient parasites; subjects of the Han and Roman empires

---

[*]Eleventh-century tax registers are extraordinarily difficult to interpret, and some historians think the increase was smaller. None, however, denies that it rose significantly or disputes its consequences for energy use.

[†]After a curfew was lifted in 1063.

in the first centuries CE, for instance, consumed seven or eight times as much energy per person as their Ice Age ancestors had grubbed up fourteen thousand years earlier.* The Han and Romans had also learned to tap winds and waves to move boats, going beyond what plants and animals could do for them, and to apply waterpower to mills. Yet the cold Kaifengers who rioted in 1013 were still basically feeding off other organisms, standing little higher in the Great Chain of Energy than Stone Age hunter-gatherers.

Within a few decades that had begun to change, turning Kaifeng's ironmasters into unwitting revolutionaries. A thousand years earlier, in the days of the Han dynasty, some Chinese had tinkered with coal and gas, but these energy sources had had few obvious applications. Only now, with the voracious forges competing with hearths and homes for fuel, did industrialists push hard at the door between the ancient organic economy and a new world of fossil fuels. Kaifeng was near two of China's biggest coal deposits (Figure 7.9), with easy access via the Yellow River, so it did not take genius—just greed, desperation, and trial and error—to work out how to use coal instead of charcoal to smelt iron ore. It also took capital and labor to locate, dig up, and move the coal, which probably explains why businessmen (who had resources) rather than householders (who did not) led the way.

A poem written around 1080 gives a sense of the transformation. The first verse describes a woman so desperate for fuel that she sells her body for firewood; the second, a coal mine coming to the rescue; the third, a great blast furnace; and the fourth, relief that people can now have their cake and eat it: great iron swords can be cast but the forests will survive.

> *Didn't you see her,*
> *Last winter, when travelers were stopped by the rain and snow,*
> *And city-dwellers' bones were torn by the wind?*

---

*Per capita energy capture rose in the East from an average of roughly 4,000 kilocalories per person per day (for all purposes) around 14,000 BCE (4.29 points on the index of social development) to 27,000 kilocalories in 1 BCE/CE (29.35 points). In the West it rose from roughly the same level around 14,000 BCE to around 31,000 kilocalories (33.70 points) in 1 BCE/CE.

With a half-bundle of damp firewood, "bearing her bedding at
  dawn."*
At twilight she knocked on the gate, but no one wanted her trade.

Who would have thought that in those mountains lay a hidden
  treasure,
In heaps, like black jewels, ten thousand cartloads of coal.
Flowing grace and favor, unknown to all.

The stinking blast—zhenzhen†—disperses;
Once a beginning is made, [production] is vast without limit.
Ten thousand men exert themselves, a thousand supervise.
Pitching ore into the roiling liquid makes it even brighter,
Flowing molten jade and gold, its vigorous potency.

In the Southern Mountains, chestnut forests now breathe easy;
In the Northern Mountains, no need to hammer the hard ore.
They will cast you a sword of a hundred refinings,
To chop a great whale of a bandit to mincemeat.

Coal and iron took off together. One well-documented foundry, at Qicunzhen, employed three thousand workers to shovel 35,000 tons of ore and 42,000 tons of coal into furnaces each year, harvesting 14,000 tons of pig iron at the other end. By 1050 so much coal was being mined that householders were using it too, and when the government overhauled poor relief in 1098 coal was the only fuel its officials bothered to mention. Twenty new coal markets opened in Kaifeng between 1102 and 1106.

By then Eastern social development had risen as high as the peak reached in ancient Rome a millennium earlier. The West, split between a Muslim core and a Christian periphery, now lagged far behind, and would not match this level of social development until the eighteenth century, on the eve of Britain's industrial revolution. Every indication

---

*A euphemism for prostitution.

†The poet's idea of the sound of a bellows.

was, in fact, that a Chinese industrial revolution was brewing within Kaifeng's soot-blackened walls and would turn the huge Eastern lead in social development into Eastern rule. History seemed to be moving down the path that would take Albert to Beijing rather than Looty to Balmoral.

8

⊙ ⊙ ⊙

GOING GLOBAL

THREE BIG THINGS

Everything about China amazed Marco Polo. Its palaces were the best in the world and its rulers the richest. Its rivers supported more ships than all the waters of Christendom combined, carrying more food into its cities than a European could imagine anyone eating. And what food it was, so subtle that Europeans could scarcely believe it. Chinese maidens excelled in modesty and decorum; Chinese wives were angelic; and foreigners who enjoyed the hospitality of the courtesans of Hangzhou never forgot them. Most amazing of all, though, was China's commerce. "I can tell you in all truthfulness," said Marco, "that the business . . . is on such a stupendous scale that no one who hears tell of it without seeing it for himself can possibly credit it."

That, it turned out, was the problem. When Marco returned to Venice in 1295 many of those who thronged to hear his stories did not, in fact, credit them.* But despite its occasional oddities, such as pears that weighed ten pounds, Marco's account is quite consistent with what we see in Figure 8.1. When he went to China its social development was far ahead of the West's.

---

*Even today, a few historians still wonder whether Marco actually went to China.

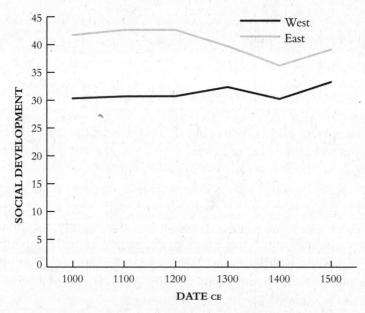

Figure 8.1. A shrinking gap in a shrinking world: trade, travel, and turbulent times bring East and West together again

There were three big things, though, that Marco did not know when he marveled at the East. First, its lead was shrinking, from almost twelve points on the index of social development in 1100 to less than six in 1500. Second, the scenario foreseen at the end of Chapter 7—that Eastern ironmasters and mill owners would begin an industrial revolution, unleashing the power of fossil fuels—had not come to pass. Marco admired the "black stone" that burned in Chinese hearths, but he admired China's fat fish and translucent porcelain just as much. The land he described, for all its marvels, remained a traditional economy. And third, the fact that Marco was there at all was a sign of things to come. Europeans were on the move. In 1492 another Italian, Christopher Columbus, would land in the Americas, even if he remained convinced until his dying day that he had reached China, and in 1513 Columbus's cousin Rafael Perestrello would correct the family's confusion by becoming the first European who actually did sail to China.

Another three centuries would pass between Columbus's landfall and the West regaining the lead in social development from the East. The long period covered by this chapter was not the end of the Eastern age. It was not even the beginning of the end. But it was, without doubt, the end of the beginning.

THE RACE OF SATAN

Kaifeng, January 9, 1127. The city walls shook under the crunch of battering rams and the blast of bombs. No one could really see what was going on in the driving snow but still the Chinese defenders on the ramparts fired great iron bolts from their giant crossbows and sprayed burning gunpowder into the dark, hoping to hit the creaking siege towers coming toward them. Three thousand men from the Jurchen Empire, the latest threat to China's northern borders, had fallen in the first assault on the walls—some burned up, others smashed by stones, more pierced with arrows—but still the attackers gathered up their dead and regrouped. They were used to worse.

Inside the walls, though, where barely a hundred men had fallen, even this scattering of bodies unnerved the defenders. Officers melted away and rumors spread, and all too soon, muffled by the snow, came the rumble of returning siege towers and the deadly hiss of more arrows. We do not know exactly how the panic begin, but suddenly tens of thousands of men were streaming from the battlements, desperate to get away. The enemy was inside, looting, burning, raping, and killing. Many of the palace women drowned themselves rather than endure what lay ahead, but the emperor just waited to be led into captivity.

The fall of Kaifeng was a self-inflicted wound. Despite the eleventh-century economic boom, the Song dynasty's endless war against the Khitans on the northern frontier was a constant financial drain and the emperors kept looking for new ways to pay their bills. Consequently, when in 1115 the "Wild Jurchens" of Manchuria offered to help fight the Khitans, Emperor Huizong eagerly accepted (Figure 8.2). It should have worried him that these Jurchens had gone from being backwoods farmers to fearsome cavalrymen in just twenty years, but it did not. Huizong was a connoisseur of music, a noted painter, and a calligrapher of genius, but no statesman, and his advisers mostly preferred office politics to facing hard facts. By backing the Jurchens, Huizong created a monster that devoured first the Khitans and then Huizong himself. It would have swallowed the desperate remnants of the Song

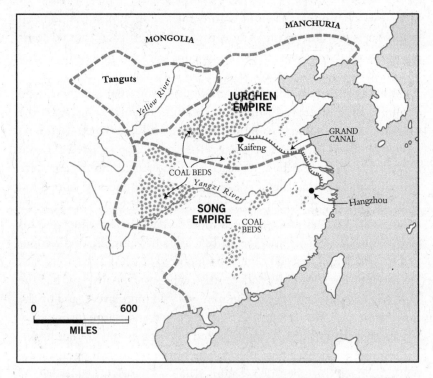

Figure 8.2. Creating monsters: the Jurchen and Song empires in 1141.
Dotted areas show China's main coalfields.

court, too, had they not fled on boats. Only in 1141 did a frontier settle down between the Jurchens, now ruling northern China, and a much-reduced Song state based at Hangzhou.*

The fall of Kaifeng and the disruption of north-south trade that followed meant that social development barely grew at all in the twelfth century. Yet while it stagnated, development did not actually collapse; Kaifeng quickly recovered from the sack, even becoming the Jurchen capital at one point, and Hangzhou grew into the metropolis that so impressed Marco Polo. The coalfields of southern China were not as rich as those of the north, but they were abundant all the same, and twelfth-century industrialists learned how to use cheaper, dirtier coal

*Historians normally divide the Song period into the Northern Song phase (960–1127), when the dynasty ruled most of China from Kaifeng, and a Southern Song phase (1127–1279), when it ruled only southern China from Hangzhou.

in iron production and even how to extract copper from the polluted by-products of ironworking. Trade, paper money, fossil fuels, and commodity production kept growing, and in 1200 a Chinese industrial takeoff still looked as possible as it had a century earlier.

What changed all that was a ferocious young steppelander named Temujin. Born in frozen Mongolia in 1162, Temujin came from the ultimate broken home. His father, Yesugei, had kidnapped Temujin's mother, Hoelun, from her original bridegroom, impregnated her, and named the resulting baby after a man he had killed. So distant were Temujin's parents that they once forgot him when moving camps and waited a year before coming back to look. After they married Temujin off at eight, Yesugei was murdered (not, perhaps, before time) and his fellow tribesmen then cast Hoelun out, stole her animals, and left her to starve. Temujin rushed home and supported Hoelun by hunting rats. He also murdered his older half-brother, who, under tribal law, had the right to marry Hoelun. Next Temujin was sold into slavery, and by the time he escaped, his fiancée had been abducted and was perhaps carrying another man's child. Temujin killed her captors and got her back.

Temujin was a hard man, but had he not been, the Mongols would not have given him the title Genghis Khan*—"Fearless Leader"—and he would not have become history's greatest conqueror. It does not take a therapist to suspect that his path to power (via hunting down and killing his blood brother Jamuka,† transforming Mongol warfare by ignoring the claims of kinship, and siding against his squabbling, alcoholic sons in every dispute) owed something to his early family experiences.

In some ways not much had changed on the steppes in two thousand years. Like so many chiefs before him, Genghis Khan was driven partly by fear (of China) and partly by greed (for its wealth). These motives pushed him into raiding the Jurchen kingdom in northern China and using the loot to bribe other Mongol chiefs to follow him. In other ways, though, a great deal had changed, and not even the khan stood

---

*Historians sometimes call him Chinggis Khan. That is closer to the Mongol pronunciation than Genghis, the name Persian writers used, but Genghis is now conventional.

†According to legend, though, this was only after Jamuka had betrayed him and, on being caught, had asked Temujin to execute him.

above the historical law that you can't step into the same river twice. For half a millennium Chinese, Muslim, and Christian settlers had been pushing towns, irrigation, and the plow into the steppes. Farmers took land from the nomads, but what the nomads took from the farmers was knowledge of their weapons and ways.

The nomads, it transpired, got the better of the deal. Once again the advantages of backwardness came into play, and Genghis Khan— the most brilliant of all nomad chiefs—learned to integrate city-dwelling engineers into his cavalry armies so well that he could storm any fortification as easily as he could defeat any army. He plundered his way from the Pacific to the Volga before his death in 1227 (Figure 8.3), sweeping away obstacles "as lines of writing are effaced from paper," according to a Persian eyewitness. After the Mongols passed though, "those abodes became a dwelling for the owl and the raven; in those places the screech-owls answer each other's cries, and in those halls the winds moan."

Genghis Khan needed no index of social development to tell him that China was the mother lode of plunder. So far as we can tell, he intended to steal everything, drive the peasants off the land, and convert the whole of northern China into winter pastures for his tough steppeland ponies. In 1215 he destroyed more than ninety cities, leaving Beijing burning for a month. After his death in 1227, though, wiser (Chinese) counsels prevailed, insisting that leaving peasants in place and taxing them would pay better.

An opportunity to try the new policy came quickly. Undeterred by the fact that Huizong's alliance with the Jurchens against the Khitans had ended with the Jurchens sacking Kaifeng and kidnapping the emperor, in 1234 a new Song ruler proposed a similar alliance with the Mongols against the Jurchens. The outcome was even worse: the Mongols swallowed the Jurchen Empire and brought China's armies to the brink of collapse.

Only the peculiarities of Mongol politics prevented the Song Empire from falling in the 1230s. When Genghis Khan died in 1227 his son Ögödei had replaced him as Great Khan, but Genghis's grandsons had immediately started maneuvering to see who would succeed Ögödei. Some of them, worried that letting Ögödei conquer China would put too much power in his hands and would favor his son in the succession struggle, pressured the minor Mongol chiefs to back a gigantic

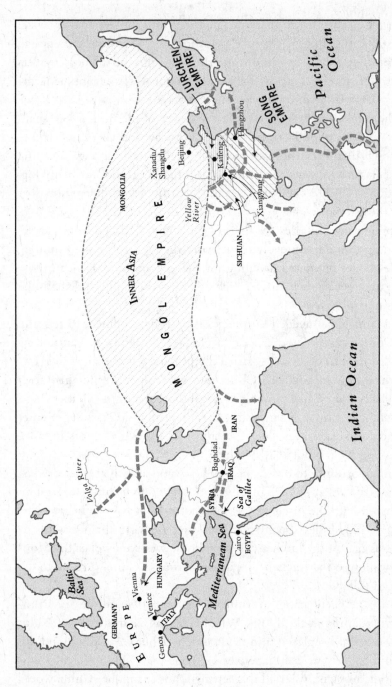

Figure 8.3. **Where the nomads roam**: the boundaries of the Mongol Empire when Genghis Khan died in 1227 and (heavy broken lines) the wars his sons and grandsons waged between then and 1294

raid in the far west instead. In 1237 they got their way, and the main Mongol hordes abruptly wheeled westward.

Europeans literally did not know what hit them. To Matthew Paris, an English chronicler, the invaders were an utter mystery. "Never," he said, "has there been any mode of access to them, nor have they themselves come forth, so as to allow any knowledge of their customs or persons to be gained through common intercourse with other men." Incorrectly interpreting the name Tatars (one of the terms used for the Mongols) as a reference to Tartarus, the ancient Greek name for Hell, Matthew wondered whether they were "an immense horde of that detestable race of Satan." Or maybe, he speculated, they were the Lost Tribes of Israel, finally going home. Despite recognizing that the Mongols did not speak Hebrew and seemed unaware of Mosaic Law, Matthew decided this must be right: having gone astray before Moses received the Ten Commandments, these were Jews who

> followed after strange gods and unknown customs, so now in a more wonderful manner, owing to the vengeance of God, they were unknown to every other nation, and their heart and language was confused, and their life changed to that of the cruel and irrational beast.

Some Christians concluded that the logical defense against the Lost Tribes of Israel was to massacre local Jews, but that produced predictably few results. The Mongols overwhelmed the massed knights of Germany and Hungary and probed as far as Vienna. But then—just as suddenly as they had abandoned China—they departed, turning their ponies around and herding their prisoners off into Inner Asia. The whole point of the European raid had been to influence succession to the khanate, and so when Ögödei died on December 11, 1241, Europe abruptly lost all importance.

When the Mongols did look west again, they sensibly chose a richer target, the Muslim core. It took them just two weeks to breach Baghdad's walls in 1258. They left the last of the caliphs without food or water for three days, then threw him into a pile of gold and told him to eat it. When he did not, he and his heirs were rolled in rugs and trampled to death.*

---

*The Mongols considered this an honorable form of death because it shed no blood.

An Egyptian army finally stopped the Mongols on the shores of the Sea of Galilee in 1260, but by then their rampage had put the seal on two centuries of economic decline in the old Muslim heartlands of Iran, Iraq, and Syria. The Mongols' greatest impact on the West, though, was what they did *not* do. Because they did not sack Cairo it remained the West's biggest and richest city, and because they did not invade western Europe, Venice and Genoa remained the West's greatest commercial centers. Development tumbled in the old Muslim core but continued to rise in Egypt and Italy, and by the 1270s, when Marco Polo set off for China, the Western core had shifted decisively into the Mediterranean lands that the Mongols had spared.

The Mongols definitively abandoned their Western wars when one more khan died and his successor, Khubilai, immortalized by the English poet Coleridge's drug-crazed vision of his palace at Xanadu* ("That sunny dome! Those caves of ice!"), finally determined to finish off China. This was the hardest war the Mongols ever fought, and the most destructive. It took a five-year siege of the great fortress Xiangyang to break Chinese resistance, and by the time Khubilai chased the last Song child-emperor into the sea in 1279, the complex infrastructure that had brought China to the verge of an industrial revolution was breaking down. Eastern social development went into free fall.

Natural disasters certainly contributed to this. After recovering from the Jurchen sack, Kaifeng's real decline began when the Yellow River burst its dykes in 1194, destroying the canals that fed the city, brought in its coal, and carried away its products. But the Yellow River had flooded plenty of times before; the big difference now was that Mongol destruction magnified nature's cruelties. In the 1230s famine and epidemic followed the Mongol armies, carrying off a million people around Kaifeng and perhaps even more in Sichuan, and in the 1270s the death toll was even worse. Overall, the four horsemen of the apocalypse that stalked China in the thirteenth century—migration, state collapse, famine, and disease—reduced the population by perhaps a quarter. Despite Marco Polo's amazement, China was no longer on track toward an industrial takeoff by 1290. In fact, the gap between East and West was closing.

---

*This famous name is actually a misunderstanding of the city's Chinese name, normally transliterated as Shangdu. The site of Khubilai's palace is currently under excavation.

GUNS, GERMS, AND CAST IRON

When Eastern social development had fallen before, from the first un-til the fourth century CE, it had been part of a Eurasia-wide paradox. The sharp rise in social development in the first millennium BCE had effectively shrunk the distance between the cores, and a handful of travelers, traders, and raiders had created overlapping zones of contact across the steppes and Indian Ocean. This Old World Exchange was a consequence of rising development but also generated the forces that would undermine development, and when the Western core failed to break through the hard ceiling around forty-three points, the horsemen of the apocalypse dragged down both cores.

By the ninth century Eastern development had recovered enough to set off a Second Old World Exchange. Merchants, missionaries, and migrants crossed the steppes and Indian Ocean, again building over-lapping zones of contact (Figure 8.4). By Genghis Khan's boyhood years, traders were already carrying not just luxuries such as spices and silk but also bulk foods across the Indian Ocean in quantities even Romans would have envied, and from Hormuz in the Persian Gulf to Majapahit in Java, cosmopolitan merchant cities were flourishing.

The Mongol conquest of the steppes brought stability to a second East-West artery, and Khan Ögödei, eager to turn the new capital he built at Karakorum into a worthy imperial metropolis, reportedly lured merchants there by paying 10 percent over whatever price they asked for their goods. He "would sit," the Persian scholar Rashid al-Din wrote, "every day, after he finished his meal, on a chair outside his court, where every kind of merchandise that was to be found in the world was heaped up in piles."

Along with merchants came clerics, drawn by the Mongols' relaxed attitudes about religion. "Just as God gave different fingers to the hand," Ögödei's successor told a Christian, "so He has given different ways to men." Curious about these ways, in 1254 the khan decided to stage a public debate among Buddhists, Muslims, and Christians. Only in Karakorum could this have happened.

A great crowd gathered to watch the learned doctors, but the ex-periment was not a success. Following Mongol traditions, the contes-tants were served fermented mares' milk between rounds of debate,

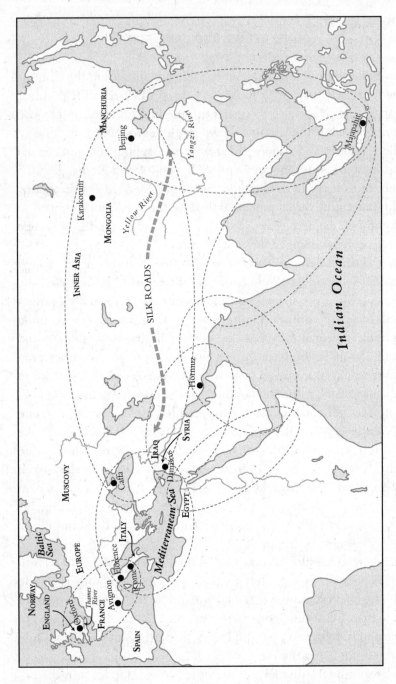

Figure 8.4. The Second Old World Exchange: eight overlapping zones of trade and travel that carried progress and disaster from one end of Eurasia to the other

and as the day wore on, their arguments lost focus. Their dialectical skills blunted by alcohol, the Christians lapsed into singing hymns. The Muslims responded by chanting Koranic verses, and the Buddhists withdrew into silent contemplation. Eventually, too drunk to go on, the Christians and Muslims followed their example.

Despite the failure of interfaith dialogue, Westerners kept coming. Muslim traders carried Eastern goods to Caffa in Crimea, selling them there to Italians, who not only sold them on to north Europeans (Chinese silk first showed up in French markets in 1257) but also followed the goods back to their source. Marco Polo's uncles left Caffa in 1260 and kept moving until they reached Beijing, then made a second trip, with young Marco in tow, in 1274. Missionaries followed, and in 1305 a Christian friar who had just arrived in Beijing could boast that the steppe route was faster and safer than the sea route.

The First Old World Exchange had strung a few gossamer-thin threads end-to-end across Eurasia, but the Second spun a real web, with enough people moving across it to make the centuries after 1100 the first true age of technological transfer. This worked almost entirely to the advantage of the backward West. Something so seemingly obvious as the wheelbarrow, invented in China around the first century CE, made it to Europe only around 1250, and horse collars, used in China since the fifth century CE, arrived there about the same time.

By far the most important technological transfer, though, was cheap cast-iron tools. These appeared in China in the sixth century BCE and were common by the first. Arabs knew about cast iron by the eleventh century CE, but Europeans not until 1380. If you have ever tried moving earth without iron picks and shovels you will know what a difference this made. Once when I was a graduate student on an excavation in Greece the key to our storeroom went missing and we had to start digging without our collection of iron tools. Soil seems remarkably hard and heavy when you approach it like a pre-1380 European. I can vouch that the Second Old World Exchange revolutionized Western energy capture.

So, too, its information technology. Chinese artisans first made paper from mulberry bark in 105 CE, and wood-pulp paper was common by 700. Arabs learned of paper around 750 (reputedly by capturing Chinese papermakers in central Asia) but Italians only started buying it from them after 1150 and making their own in 1276. By then

Chinese publishers had been using engraved woodblocks to print paper books for five centuries and using movable type for two centuries; Europeans only borrowed or reinvented woodblocks around 1375 and movable type around 1430. Chinese and Indian innovations in rigging and steering also moved west, passing through Arab hands into the Mediterranean in the late twelfth century.

Along with ancient technologies such as the wheelbarrow, Westerners also picked up the newest advances. The magnetic compass, first mentioned in a Chinese text in 1119, had reached Arabs and Europeans by 1180, and guns moved even faster. During the thirteenth-century Mongol invasion of China, Eastern craftsmen learned how to make gunpowder oxidize quickly enough that it would explode, not just burn, and started using this nasty new trick to propel arrows from bamboo tubes. The oldest known true gun—a foot-long bronze tube found in Manchuria that could fire lead bullets—probably dates to 1288. In 1326, barely a generation later, a manuscript from Florence described a brass gun, and illustrations painted in a manuscript from Oxford the next year show two crude but unmistakable cannons. The first known Arabic use of guns came soon after, in a war in Spain in 1331. Most likely western Europeans learned about guns directly from Mongols on the steppes and then taught Spanish Muslims. It took another generation, until 1360, for these loud new weapons to work their way back to Egypt.

Over the next few centuries guns would change much in the West, but even so, the most important commodities being moved around in the Second Old World Exchange, as in the First, were germs. "Civilization both in the East and the West was visited by a destructive plague that devastated nations and caused populations to vanish," wrote the Arab historian Ibn Khaldun. "It swallowed up many of the good things of civilization and wiped them out." The Black Death* had arrived.

The plague probably evolved in Inner Asia and spread along the Silk Roads. One Arabic scholar (who himself died of it) said it began on the steppes around 1331, and in that same year an epidemic raged along the middle Yangzi Valley, reportedly killing nine people out of ten.

---

*This name was invented only in 1832; fourteenth-century Europeans spoke of "the great mortality," while Chinese and Arabic sources each used half a dozen names.

We cannot know if this was the same bacillus that devastated Eurasia over the next two decades, but a plague mentioned on Mongolian tombstones in 1338 and 1339 almost certainly was. In 1340 we lose sight of it for a few years; then—abruptly—it was everywhere at once. Sickness gripped China's east coast in 1345, and the next year a Mongol army brought the plague to Caffa in Crimea,* the very city from which Marco Polo's uncles had departed for Beijing nearly a century before. The Second Old World Exchange had come full circle.

In 1347 merchants carried the pestilence to every harbor in the Mediterranean. From England to Iraq the classic symptoms of bubonic plague showed up—"Swellings appeared suddenly in the armpit or the groin, in many cases both," a French chronicler recorded in 1348, "and were infallible signs of death." A pneumonic mutation, spread by coughing, was even deadlier. "People spat bits of blood, and one was covered with blotches and died," a poet in Damascus bluntly commented. He died of plague in 1363.

Author after author describes graveyards too full to accommodate more corpses, priests dropping dead while reading the last rites, and entire villages emptied. "The souls of men have become very cheap," another Damascus poet observed. "Each soul is worth but a kernel"—a gruesome pun on the word "habbah," meaning both "kernel of grain" and "pustule," the bubonic plague's first symptom.

By 1351 the disease had killed a third or even half of all westerners, working its way from the Mediterranean to the fringes of Muscovy, whence it raced back to China. That year the "green-eyed Christian[s]" whom the emperor recruited from Inner Asia to fight rebels brought the plague with them. It killed half the army and then ravaged China every year until 1360. We cannot calculate the death toll, but it was clearly horrendous.

There is no good time for something like the Black Death to visit humanity, but it is hard to think of a worse time than the 1340s. The balmy Medieval Warm Period had drawn to a close, ushering in what

---

*The chronicler Gabriele de' Mussi (who was in Italy at the time) insisted that the Mongols used catapults to hurl plague-ridden corpses into Caffa. Most historians suspect—more prosaically—that rats carried plague-bearing fleas from the besiegers' camp into the city.

climatologists often call the Little Ice Age. From Norway to China, glaciers grew. The Denmark Strait, separating Greenland and Iceland, regularly froze after 1350. Norsemen abandoned their settlements on Greenland and polar bears wandered across the ice bridge to Iceland, which was now cold enough for them. The Baltic Sea froze in 1303 and again in 1306–1307; in 1309–1310 the river Thames in temperate England iced over too. Between 1315 and 1317 it rained so much in northwest Europe that crops rotted in the ground and—a truly astonishing detail—it got too muddy for knights to fight.

With harvests failing and loved ones dying, it was hard not to conclude that God was sending a message. In China endemic banditry turned into religious revolt, directed mainly against the Mongol occupiers. As the alien emperor amused himself with pleasure boats and orgies, messianic cult leaders announced that the Buddha was returning to right the world's wrongs and usher everyone into Paradise. By 1350 the empire was disintegrating.

We know rather little about events in the old Western core in Iraq, whose Mongol rulers were every bit as incompetent as those in China, but in Egypt and Syria the plague may have strengthened Islam. Clearly not everyone bought the official line that the plague was meant to punish only infidels (for believers, death from it was a mercy and a martyrdom)—the chronicler al-Wardi, for instance, wrote, "We ask God's forgiveness for our souls' bad inclination; the plague is surely part of His punishment," and vendors of magical defenses had a field day—but the most popular responses by far were mass prayer sessions, processions to the tombs of holy men, and tougher laws against alcohol and moral laxity.

Things looked much grimmer to many Christians. Not only did God seem to be punishing them—"My mind reels as I prepare to write of the sentence that divine justice, in its infinite mercy, meted out to men," one Italian lamented—but the church itself also seemed to be coming apart. In 1303 a French king had had the pope himself beaten up and thrown in prison, and soon thereafter the papal court relocated to Avignon in France, where it became a byword for corruption and decadence. One pope even made it illegal to say that Jesus had been poor. Eventually some cardinals decamped back to Rome and elected a counterpope, who squabbled with the Avignon pope over every conceivable issue; and for a few debilitating years after 1409 there were actually three rival popes, all claiming to be God's vicar on earth.

Since the church had failed them, people took matters into their own hands. The most creative were the Flagellants:

> Stripped to the waist, they gathered in large groups and bands and marched in procession through the crossroads and squares of cities and good towns. There they formed circles and beat upon their backs with whips, rejoicing as they did so in loud voices and singing hymns . . . Many honorable women and devout matrons, it must be added, had done this penance with whips, marching and singing through towns and churches like the men.

Others favored more traditional remedies such as massacring Jews, even though (as one of the popes pointed out in 1348) Jews were dying as fast as Christians. But nothing worked, and social development in the Western core around the Mediterranean fell as fast in the great plague delivered by the Second Old World Exchange as it had done during the plagues delivered by the First. No wonder the end seemed nigh.

DIFFERENT RIVERS

History looked to be repeating itself. In the first century CE Western social development had risen to a hard ceiling around forty-three points, strained against it, and set off a centuries-long, Old World–wide collapse. Eleven hundred years later, Eastern social development rose to the same level and set off similar disasters. Had von Däniken's aliens from outer space been orbiting Earth again in 1350 they might well have concluded that human history was locked in a series of boom-and-bust cycles, bouncing against an unbreakable hard ceiling.

But like all the spacemen I have imagined so far, they would have been mistaken, because another historical law was also operating. I commented earlier that not even Genghis Khan could step into the same river twice; and neither could the horsemen of the apocalypse. The cores across which the horsemen rode during the Second Old World Exchange were very different from those they had devastated during the First Old World Exchange, which meant that the Second Exchange had very different consequences from the First.

Most obviously, both cores were geographically bigger when the Second Exchange intensified around 1200 than they had been during the First (Figure 8.5), and size mattered. On the one hand, larger cores generated larger disruptions: it is hard to quantify calamity, but the plagues, famines, and migrations that began in the thirteenth century do seem to have been even worse than those that began in the second century. On the other hand, though, larger cores also meant greater depth to absorb shocks and larger reserves to hasten recovery. Japan, Southeast Asia, the Mediterranean Basin, and most of Europe escaped Mongol devastation in the thirteenth century; Japan and Southeast Asia avoided the Black Death in the fourteenth too; and in the very heart of China the Yangzi Delta region seems to have come through the disasters remarkably well.

Economic geography had also changed. Around 100 CE the Western core was richer and more developed than the Eastern, but by 1200 the reverse was true. It was the Eastern core, not the Western, that was now straining against the hard ceiling, and Eastern commercial networks (especially those linking southern China, Southeast Asia, and the Indian Ocean) dwarfed anything in the West.

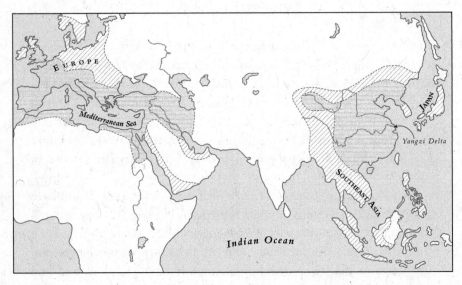

Figure 8.5. Size matters: horizontal lines mark areas in the Eastern and Western cores ruled by states around 100 CE, on the eve of the first Old World crisis, and diagonal lines show where states had spread by 1200, just before the second crisis

Changes in political geography reinforced economics. Back in 100 CE most trade in each core had gone on within the boundaries of a single great empire; by 1200 that was no longer true. Both cores were politically messier than they had been in antiquity, and even when great empires once again consolidated the old heartlands after the Black Death, the political relationships were very different. Any great empire now had to deal with a surrounding ring of smaller states. In the East the relationships were mainly commercial and diplomatic; in the West they were mainly violent.

Put together, these changes meant that the cores not only recovered faster from the Second Old World Exchange than from the First but also recovered in different ways.

In the West the Ottoman Turks quickly rebuilt an empire in the old heartland in the fourteenth century. The Ottomans were just one of dozens of Turkic clans that settled in Anatolia around 1300 after the Mongols had shattered the older Muslim kingdoms (Figure 8.6), but within a few years of the Black Death they had already got the better of their rivals and established a European bridgehead. By the 1380s they were bullying the pitiful remnants of the Byzantine Empire, and by 1396 they scared Christendom so badly that the squabbling popes of Rome and Avignon briefly agreed to join forces in sending a crusade against them.

It was a disaster, but Christian hopes briefly revived when Tamerlane, a Mongol chieftain who made Genghis Khan look well adjusted, led new steppe incursions into the Muslim world. In 1400 the Mongols annihilated Damascus and in 1401 sacked Baghdad, reportedly using the skulls of ninety thousand of its residents as bricks for a series of towers they built around the ruins. In 1402 Tamerlane defeated the Ottomans and threw the sultan into a cage, where he expired of shame and exposure. But then Christian hopes failed. Instead of staying to devastate the remaining Muslim lands, Tamerlane decided that the emperor of distant China had insulted him and swung his horsemen around. He died in 1405 while riding east to avenge the slight.

Saved by the bell, the Ottomans bounced back into business within twenty years, but as they advanced through the Balkans they had to learn some tough lessons. When the Mongols defeated them in 1402 both armies had fought as steppe warriors had done for two thousand years, with clouds of mounted archers enveloping and shooting down

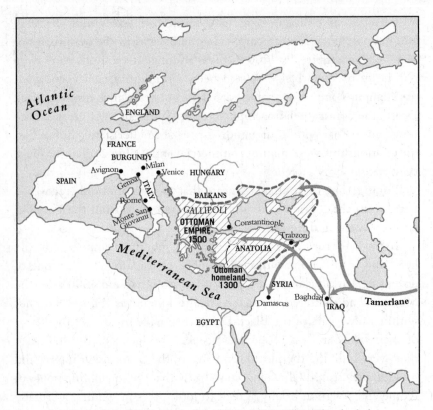

Figure 8.6. The revival of the West, 1350–1500. The shaded
area shows the extent of the Ottoman Turkish empire in 1500—by
which time the Western core was moving decisively
northward and westward.

slower-moving foes. European armies could not compete head-to-head
with these swarms of light horsemen, but they had improved their
newfangled guns to the point that in 1444 a Hungarian army gave the
Ottomans a nasty shock. With small cannons mounted on wagons that
were roped together as mobile forts, Hungarian firepower stopped the
Turkish cavalry in its tracks. Had the Hungarian king not galloped out
ahead of his men and got himself killed he probably would have won
the day.

The Turks, quick learners, figured out the best response: buy European firepower. This new technology was expensive, but even Europe's richest states, such as Venice and Genoa, were paupers next to
the sultans. Hiring Italians as admirals and siege engineers, training

enslaved Christian boys as an elite infantry corps, and recruiting European gunners, the Ottomans were soon on the move again. When they began their 1453 assault on Constantinople, still the greatest fortress on earth and the main barrier to Turkish power, the Turks hired away the Byzantines' top gunner, a Hungarian. This gunner made the Ottomans an iron cannon big enough to throw a thousand-pound stone ball, with a roar loud enough (chroniclers said) to make pregnant women miscarry. The gun in fact cracked on the second day and was useless by the fourth or fifth, but the Hungarian also cast smaller, more practical cannon that succeeded where the giant failed.

For the first and only time in its history, Constantinople's walls failed. Thousands of panic-stricken Byzantines crowded into the church of Hagia Sophia—"the earthly heaven, the second firmament, the vehicle of the cherubim, the throne of the glory of God," Gibbon called it—trusting in a prophecy that when infidels attacked the church an angel would descend, sword in hand, to restore the Roman Empire. But no angel came; Constantinople fell; and with it, Gibbon concluded, the Roman Empire finally expired.*

As the Turks advanced, European kings fought more fiercely against one another as well as against the infidel, and a genuine arms race took off. France and Burgundy led the way in the 1470s, their gunners casting cannons with thicker barrels, forming gunpowder into corns that ignited faster, and using iron rather than stone cannonballs. The result was smaller, stronger, and more portable guns that rendered older weapons obsolete. The new guns were light enough to be loaded onto expensive new warships, driven by sails, not oars, with gun ports cut so low in the hull that iron cannonballs could hole enemy ships right at the waterline.

It was hard for anyone but a king to afford this kind of technology, and slowly but surely western European monarchs bought enough of the new weapons to intimidate the lords, independent cities, and bishops whose messy, overlapping jurisdictions had made earlier European

---

*Hairsplitters might argue that this was not really the end of the Roman Empire: the last Byzantine outpost, at Trabzon, hung on until 1461, and the Holy Roman Empire founded by Charlemagne lingered on, in theory at least, until Napoleon disbanded it in 1806. But most historians follow Gibbon in drawing a line under the Roman Empire in 1453.

states so weak. Along the Atlantic littoral, kings created bigger, stronger states—France, Spain, and England—within which the royal writ ran everywhere and the nation, not far-flung aristocratic clans or popes in Rome, had first claim on people's loyalties. And once they had muscled their lords aside, kings could build up bureaucracies, tax the people directly, and buy more guns—which of course forced neighboring kings to buy more guns too, and pushed everyone to raise still more money.

Once again there were advantages to backwardness, and the struggle steadily pulled the West's center of gravity toward the Atlantic. The cities of northern Italy had long been the most developed part of Europe, but now discovered a disadvantage of forwardness: glorious city-states such as Milan and Venice were too rich and powerful to be bullied into any Italian national state, but not rich or powerful enough to stand alone against genuine national states such as France and Spain. Writers such as Machiavelli rejoiced in this liberty, but its price became crystal clear when a French army invaded Italy in 1494. Italian war-making had declined, as Machiavelli himself conceded, "into such a state of decay that wars were commenced without fear, continued without danger, and concluded without loss." A few dozen up-to-date French cannons now blew away everything in their path. It took them just eight hours to smash the great stone castle of Monte San Giovanni, killing seven hundred Italians for the loss of ten Frenchmen. Italian cities could not begin to compete with the tax revenues of big states such as France. By 1500 the Western core was being reordered from its Atlantic fringe, and war was leading the way.

The Eastern core, by contrast, was reordered from its ancient center in China, and commerce and diplomacy ultimately led the way, even though the rise of new empires began in bloodshed as grim as anything in the West. Zhu Yuanzhang, the founder of the Ming dynasty that reunited China, had been born into poverty in 1328 as Mongol power was falling apart. His parents—migrant laborers on the run from tax collectors—sold four of his brothers and sisters because they could not feed them, and abandoned Yuanzhang, their youngest, with a Buddhist grandfather. The old man filled the boy's head with the messianic visions of the Red Turbans, one of many resistance movements fighting Mongol rule. The end was nigh, the old man insisted, and the Buddha would soon return from Paradise to smite the wicked. Instead, in the locust- and drought-ravaged summer of 1344, disease—quite likely the Black Death—carried off Yuanzhang's whole family.

The teenager attached himself to a Buddhist monastery as a servant, but the monks could barely feed themselves and sent him out to beg or steal for his keep. After wandering southern China's back roads for three or four years he returned to the monastery just in time to see it burned to the ground in the vast, roiling civil wars that accompanied the collapse of Mongol rule. With nowhere else to go, he joined the other monks in hanging around the smoking ruins, starving.

Yuanzhang was an alarming-looking youth, tall, ugly, lantern-jawed, and pockmarked. But he was also smart, tough, and (thanks to the monks) literate; the kind of man, in short, that any bandit would want in his gang. Recruited by a band of Red Turbans as they passed through the neighborhood, he impressed the other thugs and visionaries, married the chief's daughter, and eventually took over the gang.

In a dozen years of grinding warfare Yuanzhang turned his cut-throat crew into a disciplined army and drove the other rebels from the Yangzi Valley. Just as important, he distanced himself from the Red Turbans' wilder prophecies and organized a bureaucracy that could run an empire. In January 1368, just shy of his fortieth birthday, he renamed himself Hongwu ("Vast Military Power") and proclaimed the creation of a Ming ("Brilliant") dynasty.

Hongwu's official pronouncements make it sound as if his whole adult life was a reaction against his terrible, rootless, violent youth. He promoted an image of China as a bucolic paradise of stable, peaceful villages, where virtuous elders supervised self-sufficient farmers, traders dealt only in goods that could not be made locally, and—unlike Hongwu's own family—no one moved around. Hongwu claimed that few people needed to travel more than eight miles from home, and that covering more than thirty-five miles without permission should earn a whipping. Fearing that commerce and coinage would corrode stable relationships, three times he passed laws restricting trade with foreigners to government-approved dealers and even prohibited foreign perfumes lest they seduce the Chinese into illicit exchanges. By 1452 his successors had renewed his laws three more times and had four times banned silver coins out of fear they would make unnecessary commerce too easy.

"For thirty-one years I labored to discharge Heaven's mandate," Hongwu claimed in his will, "tormented by worries and fears, without relaxing for a day." We have to wonder, though, how much of Hongwu's struggle was just in his mind. Hongwu was eager to appear—in contrast to his Mongol predecessors—as an ideal Confucian ruler, but never actually banned foreign trade. His son Yongle even expanded it, assiduously importing Korean virgins for sex (because, he claimed, they were good for his health). But Ming monarchs did insist on keeping trade in official hands. This, they repeatedly announced, protected the (theoretically) stable social order and allowed foreigners to show due deference. "I do not care for foreign things," one ruler explained. "I accept them because they come from far away and show the sincerity of distant peoples." The fact that "tribute" (as the court called trade beyond the borders) was filling the imperial coffers was not worth mentioning.

Despite all the talk, trade flourished. In 1488 a shipwrecked Korean observed that "foreign ships stand as thick as the teeth of a comb" in Hangzhou harbor. Underwater archaeologists have found that merchant ships were getting bigger, and the fact that the emperors felt compelled to renew their laws about illicit trade quite as often as they did strongly suggests that people were ignoring them.

The effects of the commercial boom were far-reaching. Peasant incomes rose once more, families grew, and farmers streamed from their villages to open new lands or work in cities. Local worthies repaired roads, bridges, and canals after the violence of the preceding centuries, merchants carried food along them, and people everywhere rushed to market, selling what they could produce cheaply and buying everything else. By 1487 an official simply took it for granted that people "convert grain into cash, then convert cash into clothing, food, and daily necessities . . . there aren't any people throughout the realm of whom this is not true."

Commerce was interlinking the enlarged Eastern core just as much as war interlinked the states of the West. Population, agriculture, and finance all expanded rapidly in fourteenth-century Japan, and despite the Ming restrictions, trade with China steadily grew. Dealings with Southeast Asia were even more important: revenues from trade funded the rise of states such as Majapahit on Java, which dominated the spice business. Many local rulers came to depend on Chinese support for their thrones.

None of this required the kind of relentless violence that cursed the West, and other than a disastrous attempt to prop up a friendly regime in Vietnam, early Ming monarchs limited their fighting to the steppe frontier. The Mongols remained the only real threat to the dynasty. Had Tamerlane not died in 1405 he might well have overthrown the Ming, and in 1449 other Mongol clans actually captured an emperor. To pursue their steppe wars, though, the Ming felt that they needed not advanced guns but conventional armies with vast supply trains. When Yongle invaded the steppes in 1422, for instance, he took 340,000 donkeys, 117,000 carts, and 235,000 cart pullers to drag the twenty thousand tons of grain his army would eat.

Yongle walked softly but carried a big stick. In 1405 he announced that he was sending ambassadors "to the various foreign countries in the Western [Indian] Ocean to read out the imperial commands and to bestow rewards," enmeshing commerce in a web of diplomacy, but along with them he also sent the biggest fleet the world had ever seen. To build it he summoned 25,000 craftsmen to add vast new dockyards to his capital at Nanjing. Lumberjacks in Sichuan picked out the best fir trees for masts, elm and cedar for hulls, and oak for tillers, then clear-cut entire forests and floated them down the Yangzi to the shipwrights. Laborers built giant dry docks, hundreds of feet long, to work on the great vessels. No detail was overlooked; even the iron nails got a special waterproof coat.

This was no war fleet, but it was designed for shock and awe. At its heart were the biggest wooden ships of all time, perhaps 250 feet long and displacing two thousand tons of ocean; and at its head was history's biggest admiral, the Muslim eunuch Zheng He, said to have been seven feet tall and sixty inches around the belly (in some accounts, nine feet tall and ninety inches in girth).*

More than three hundred vessels set sail, carrying 27,870 men. The plan was to descend on the wealthy cities around the Indian Ocean, whose princes, waking up to find the seas outside their palace windows filled with Chinese sails, would hand over huge "tribute" payments,

---

*Zheng was from the far southwest of China, where Arab merchants had converted many people to Islam. Captured as a boy in 1381 during the Ming dynasty's wars to pacify the region, he was enlisted in the emperor's service and castrated. He seems to have taken all this in his enormous stride.

channeling trade through official channels. But it was also a grand adventure: the sailors seem to have felt they were plunging into a twilight zone, where anything was possible. In Sri Lanka (Figure 8.7) local Muslims showed them the biblical Adam's footprints, while in Vietnam sailors thought they had to dodge the "corpse-head barbarian," a kind of banshee that was

> really a woman belonging to a human family, her only peculiarity being that her eyes have no pupils; at night, when she is sleeping, her head flies away and eats the tapering feces of human infants; the infant, affected by the evil influence which invades its abdomen, inevitably dies; and the flying head returns and unites with its body, just as it was before. If people know of this and wait until the moment the head flies away, and then remove the body to another place, the returning head cannot unite with the body, and then the woman dies.

Other than the threats in their own imaginations, though, the sailors encountered few dangers. The seven Treasure Fleets dispatched between 1405 and 1433 were the grandest projections of state power the world had seen. They did have to fight three times to secure the Straits of Malacca, then as now the world's busiest waterway and then as now infested by pirates, but otherwise used force only when tricked into taking sides in a Sri Lankan civil war. Chinese sailors walked the streets of Mogadishu, which did not impress them ("If one's eyes wander one meets only sighs and sulky glances," one of Zheng's officers wrote; "Desolation, the entire country nothing but hills!"), and Mecca, which did (even if another officer inexplicably thought Islam's holiest shrine looked like a pagoda).

The Treasure Fleets had sailed south and west a good nine thousand miles, but some researchers think this was just the beginning. With their compasses and charts, tankers full of drinking water, and huge stores of food, Zheng's ships could have gone anywhere they wanted; and that, the former submarine captain Gavin Menzies claims in his bestselling book *1421: The Year China Discovered America*, is exactly what they did. Plunging into the uncharted Pacific Ocean, Menzies says, Zheng's lieutenant Zhou Man made landfall in Oregon in summer 1423, then sailed down America's west coast. Menzies suggests that despite losing a ship in San Francisco Bay, Zhou persevered, putting in on

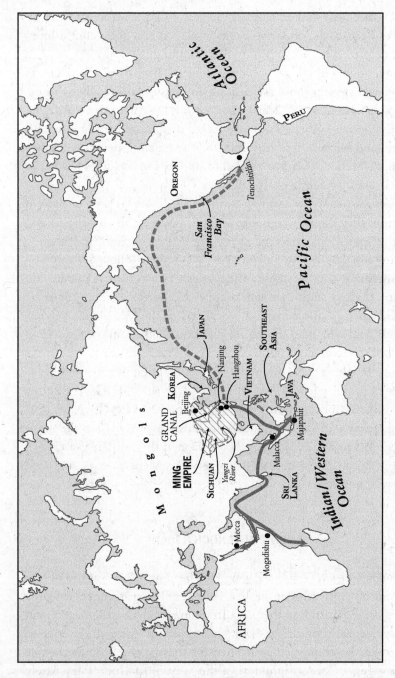

Figure 8.7. The fifteenth-century world as seen from China, showing the Ming diplomatic offensive in the Indian Ocean (solid line) and the route Chinese ships could have taken to reach the New World (broken line)

the Mexican coast and getting all the way to Peru before picking up winds to head back across the Pacific. In October 1423, after a four-month detour, Zhou was safely back in Nanjing.

Conventional historians, Menzies suggests, have overlooked Zhou's feats (as well as even more astonishing voyages that took Zheng's subordinates to the Atlantic Ocean, the North Pole, Antarctica, Australia, and Italy) because Zheng's official records disappeared in the fifteenth century; and because few historians have Menzies's practical knowledge of navigation, they have failed to understand the clues hidden in fifteenth- and sixteenth-century maps.

Historians, however, remain unmoved. Menzies, they concede, is quite right that Zheng's logbooks are lost; but why, the historians ask, does the enormous mass of surviving Ming dynasty literature—including not one but two eyewitness accounts of Zheng's voyages—*never* mention any of these discoveries? How, they wonder, did fifteenth-century ships maintain the speeds Menzies's theory requires? How did Zheng's sailors map the world's coasts the way Menzies claims they did? And why does the actual evidence Menzies musters for Chinese globe-trotting hold up so poorly to scholarly scrutiny?

I have to admit that I am on the side of skeptics; to my mind Menzies's *1421* is on a par with von Däniken's *Chariots of the Gods?* But like von Däniken's speculations—or, for that matter, like the Albert-in-Beijing scenario in the introduction to this book—*1421* has the merit of forcing us to ask *why* things didn't happen this way. It is a critical question, because if they had happened like Menzies says, the West might well not now rule.

ZHENG IN TENOCHTITLÁN

Tenochtitlán, August 13, 1431. Zheng He's head hurt. He was too old for this. And too big. All day he had been sending messengers into the burning city, demanding that his allies stop massacring the Aztecs, but as the sun set through the smoke he had given up. After all, he tried to tell himself, he could not be blamed for the slaughter. These people were savages, indecent, ignorant of the Way or of God. They barely even knew what bronze was. All they seemed to care about was hacking their enemies' chests open with glassy black stones and tearing out their still-beating hearts.

Zheng and his men of course knew the stories of China's ancient Shang dynasty, whose unrighteous rulers so many thousands of years ago had sacrificed humans, and speculation was rife that here beyond the Eastern Ocean was a parallel world—stranger even than the land of corpse-head barbarians—where time had stood still and the Shang still ruled. Heaven, Zheng's men speculated, must have assigned their expedition the role once played by the virtuous Zhou dynasty of antiquity; Zheng was a new King Wu, come to wrest heaven's mandate from the wicked kings of this land and usher in a golden age.

Zheng had not anticipated any of this when the emperor had ordered him into the Eastern Ocean. *Sail beyond the Eastern Ocean to the Isles of Penglai,* the Son of Heaven had said. *Since the Qin First Emperor, men have sought these Isles, where immortals live in palaces of silver and gold, the birds and beasts are pure white, and magic herbs grow. Ten years ago Our admiral Zhou Man set foot in this magical place, and now We command you to bring Us the herbs of immortality.*

Zheng had seen more of the world than anyone who had ever lived. Nothing surprised him anymore, and if he had run into dragons and giant sharks, like the old stories said he would, he would simply have dealt with them. But what he most expected was exactly what he did find at first—nothing. After sailing up the coast of Japan, bestowing titles on its unruly warlords and receiving their tribute, his fleet had run with the wind for two months, chasing an endlessly receding blue horizon where sea and sky merged. And when his nearly mutinous men finally sighted land it was all trees, rain, and mountains, in its way worse even than Africa.

It took more long weeks of drifting down the coast before they found natives who did not run away—natives who in fact sailed out to meet them, bringing marvelous foods they had never tasted before. These hospitable, half-naked barbarians had no herbs of immortality, although they did have pleasantly intoxicating herbs to smoke. Nor did they have palaces of silver and gold, though they seemed to be saying that these things lay inland. And so with just a few hundred men, a few dozen cavalry, and a smattering of native words, Zheng set off to find the immortals.

Sometimes he had to fight, but firebombs had a salutary effect and the savages rarely stood their ground. Even after his powder ran low, horses and steel swords were almost as effective. His best weapons, though, were the natives themselves. They treated his men like gods, carrying their supplies and flocking to fight for them. Zheng could follow the wise tradition of using barbarians to fight barbarians, simply helping "his" barbarians, who called themselves the Purépecha, feed some ancient grudge they bore the neighboring barbarians, the Aztecs. Zheng could not work out what the grudge was, but no matter; step by step, the barbarians' civil war brought him closer to the immortals.

Only when Zheng joined his allies outside the Aztec capital of Tenochtitlán did he finally admit that there were no immortals. Tenochtitlán was grand enough in its own way, with broad, straight streets and stepped pyramids, but there were no pure white animals, no silver-and-gold palaces, and certainly no herbs of eternal life. In fact, death was everywhere. Hideous boils and pustules had started carrying the barbarians off by their thousands, their bodies stinking even before they died. Zheng had seen plagues aplenty, but none like this. Barely one in a hundred of his own men caught it, surely a sign of God's pleasure in Zheng's task.

Right up to the last moment it was touch-and-go what the pestilence would do first—leave Zheng's barbarians too weak to storm Tenochtitlán or the enemy barbarians too weak to defend it. But once again Heaven decided in Zheng's favor, and under cover of the last bombs and crossbow bolts his horsemen had led the charge across the causeways into Tenochtitlán. After a vicious but one-sided struggle in the streets—Aztec stone blades and cotton padding against Chinese steel swords and chain mail—resistance collapsed and the Purépecha set about torturing, raping, and stealing. Itzcoatl, the last Aztec king, they pierced with many darts as he fought at the gate of his palace, then threw him into a fire, carved out his heart before he died, and—horror of horrors—sliced off and ate chunks of his flesh.

Zheng's questions had been answered. These people were not immortals. Nor was he King Wu, initiating a new age of virtue. The only question remaining, in fact, was how he would get all his plunder back to Nanjing.

GREAT MEN AND BUNGLING IDIOTS

In reality, of course, things didn't happen this way, any more than things in 1848 happened the way I described in the introduction. Tenochtitlán did get sacked, its Mesoamerican neighbors did do most of the fighting, and imported diseases did kill most people in the New World. But the sack came in 1521, not 1431; the man who led it was Hernán Cortés, not Zheng He; and the killer germs came from Europe, not Asia. If Zhou Man really had discovered the Americas, as Menzies insists, and if the story really had unfolded the way I just told it, with Mexico becoming part of the Ming Empire, not the Spanish, the modern world might look very different. The Americas might have been tied into a Pacific, not an Atlantic economy; their resources might have fueled an Eastern, not a Western industrial revolution; Albert might have ended up in Beijing rather than Looty in Balmoral; and the West might not rule.

So why did things happen the way they did?

Ming dynasty ships certainly could have sailed to America if their skippers had wanted to. A replica of a Zheng-era junk in fact managed the China–California trip in 1955 (though it could not get back again) and another, the *Princess Taiping*, got within twenty miles of completing a Taiwan–San Francisco round trip in 2009 before a freighter sliced it in two.* If they could do it, why didn't Zheng?

The most popular answer is that things happened the way they did because in the fifteenth century Chinese emperors lost interest in sending ships overseas, while European kings (some, anyway) became very interested in it. And up to a point, that is clearly correct. When Yongle died in 1424 his successor's first act was to ban long-distance voyages. Predictably, the princes of the Indian Ocean stopped sending tribute, so the next emperor sent Zheng back to the Persian Gulf in 1431, only for his successor, Zhengtong, to reverse policy again. In 1436 the court refused repeated requests from the shipyards at Nanjing for more craftsmen, and over the next decade or two the great fleet rotted. By

---

*The crew survived, though they had to be hospitalized for hypothermia after spending hours in the water.

1500 no emperor could have repeated Yongle's voyages even if he had wanted to.

At the other end of Eurasia, royalty was behaving in exactly the opposite way. Portugal's Prince Henry "the Navigator" poured resources into exploration. Some of his motives were calculating (such as lust for African gold) and some otherworldly (such as the belief that somewhere in Africa there was an immortal Christian king named Prester John, who guarded the Gates of Paradise and would save Europe from Islam). All the same, Henry funded expeditions, hired mapmakers, and helped design new ships that were perfect for exploring the west coast of Africa. .

Portuguese exploration was certainly not all smooth sailing. Upon discovering the uninhabited Madeira Islands (Figure 8.8) in 1420, the captain in charge (Christopher Columbus's future father-in-law) released a mother rabbit and her young on Porto Santo, the most promising piece of real estate. Breeding like they do, the bunnies ate everything, forcing the humans to relocate to the densely forested main island of Madeira ("wood" in Portuguese). This island the colonists set alight, compelling them, a chronicler tells us, "with all the men, women, and children, to flee [the fire's] fury and to take refuge in the sea, where they remained up to their necks in the water, and without food or drink for two days and two nights."

But having destroyed the native ecosystem, the Europeans discovered that sugarcane thrived in this charred new world, and Prince Henry put up the money for them to build a mill. Within a generation they were importing African slaves to labor in their plantations, and by the fifteenth century's end the settlers were exporting more than six hundred tons of sugar every year.

Plunging farther into the Atlantic, Portuguese sailors found the Azores, and nudging down the African coast, they reached the Senegal River in 1444. In 1473 their first ship crossed the equator, and in 1482 they reached the Congo River. Here, for a while, headwinds made sailing farther south impossible, but in 1487 Bartolomeu Dias hit on the idea of *volta do mar*, "returning by sea." Swinging far out into the Atlantic, he picked up winds that carried him to what he named the Cape of Storms (known today, more optimistically, as the Cape of Good Hope) at Africa's southern tip, where his terrified sailors mutinied and

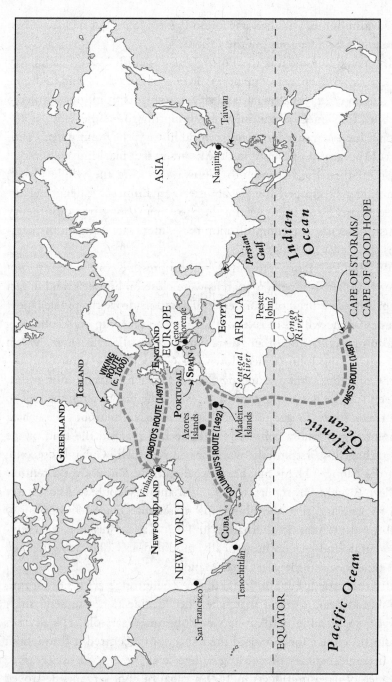

Figure 8.8. The world as seen from Europe, and the paths taken by fifteenth-century European explorers

forced him home. Dias had not found Prester John, but he had shown there could be a sea route to the Orient.

By Yongle's standards the Portuguese expeditions were laughably small (involving dozens of men, not dozens of thousands) and undignified (involving rabbits, sugar, and slaves, not gifts from great princes), but with the benefit of hindsight it is tempting to see the 1430s as a—perhaps the—decisive moment in world history, the point when Western rule became possible. At just the moment that maritime technology began to turn the oceans into highways linking the whole planet, Prince Henry grasped the possibilities and Emperor Zhengtong rejected them. Here, if anywhere, the great man/bungling idiot theory of history seems to accomplish a lot: the planet's fate hung on the decisions these two men made.

Or did it? Henry's foresight was impressive, but certainly not unique. Other European monarchs were close on his heels, and in fact the private enterprise of countless Italian sailors drove the process quite as much as the whims of rulers. If Henry had taken up coin collecting instead of navigating, other rulers would have filled his shoes. When Portugal's king John turned down the Genoese adventurer Christopher Columbus's crazy-sounding scheme to reach India by sailing west, Queen Isabella of Castile stepped in (even if he had to pitch the idea to her three times to get to yes). Within a year Columbus was back, announcing—doubly confused—that he had reached the land of the great khan (his first mistake was that it was actually Cuba; his second, that the Mongol khans had been expelled from China over a century earlier). Panicked by reports of the Castilians' new route to Asia, Henry VII of England sent the Florentine merchant Giovanni Caboto[*] to find a North Atlantic alternative in 1497. Caboto reached icy Newfoundland, and—as enthusiastically muddled as Columbus—insisted that this, too, was the great khan's land.

By the same token, breathtaking as Zhengtong's error now seems, we should bear in mind that when he "decided" not to send shipwrights to Nanjing in 1436 he was only nine years old. His advisers made this choice for him, and their successors repeated it throughout the fifteenth century. According to one story, when courtiers revived the idea of Treasure Fleets in 1477 a cabal of civil servants destroyed

---

[*]Known in Britain as John Cabot.

the records of Zheng's voyages. The ringleader, Liu Daxia, we are told, explained to the minister of war,

> The voyages of [Zheng] to the Western Ocean wasted millions in money and grain, and moreover the people who met their deaths may be counted in the tens of thousands . . . This was merely an action of bad government of which ministers should severely disapprove. Even if the old archives were still preserved they should be destroyed.

Grasping the point—that Liu had deliberately "lost" the documents— the minister rose from his chair. "Your hidden virtue, sir," he exclaimed, "is not small. Surely this seat will soon be yours!"

If Henry and Zhengtong had been different people, making different decisions, history would still have turned out much the same. Maybe instead of asking why particular princes and emperors made one choice rather than another, we should ask why western Europeans embraced risk-taking just as an inward-turned conservatism descended on China. Maybe it was culture, not great men or bungling idiots, that sent Cortés rather than Zheng to Tenochtitlán.

BORN AGAIN

"At the present moment I could almost wish to be young again," the Dutch scholar Erasmus wrote to a friend in 1517,* "for no other reason but this—that I anticipate the near approach of a golden age." Today we know this "golden age" by the name Frenchmen gave it, *la renaissance*, "the rebirth": and as some people see it, this rebirth was precisely the cultural force that suddenly, irreversibly, set Europeans apart from the rest of the world, making men like Columbus and Caboto do what they did. The creative genius of a largely Italian cultural elite— "first-born among the sons of modern Europe," a nineteenth-century historian famously called them—set Cortés on the path to Tenochtitlán.

Historians normally trace the roots of the rebirth back to the twelfth century, when northern Italy's cities shook off German and papal domination and emerged as economic powerhouses. Rejecting their recent

---

*Erasmus was then fifty-one, a ripe old age in the sixteenth century.

history of subjection to foreign rulers, their leaders began wondering how to govern themselves as independent republics, and increasingly concluded that they could find answers in classical Roman literature. By the fourteenth century, when climate change, famine, and disease undermined so many old certainties, some intellectuals expanded their interpretation of the ancient classics into a general vision of social rebirth.

Antiquity, these scholars started claiming, was a foreign country. Ancient Rome had been a land of extraordinary wisdom and virtue, but barbarous "Middle Ages" had intervened between then and modern times, corrupting everything. The only way forward for Italy's newly freed city-states, intellectuals suggested, was by looking backward: they must build a bridge to the past so that the wisdom of the ancients could be born again and humanity perfected.

Scholarship and art would be the bridge. By scouring monasteries for lost manuscripts and learning Latin as thoroughly as the Romans themselves, scholars could think as the Romans had thought and speak as they had spoken; whereupon true humanists (as the born-again called themselves) would recapture the wisdom of the ancients. Similarly, by poking around Roman ruins, architects could learn to re-create the physical world of antiquity, building churches and palaces that would shape lives of the highest virtue. Painters and musicians, who had no Roman relics to study, made their best guesses about ancient models, and rulers, eager to be seen to be perfecting the world, hired humanists as advisers, commissioned artists to immortalize them, and collected Roman antiquities.

The odd thing about the Renaissance was that this apparently reactionary struggle to re-create antiquity in fact produced a wildly untraditional culture of invention and open-ended inquiry. There certainly were conservative voices, banishing some of the more radical thinkers (such as Machiavelli) to drain the bitter cup of exile and intimidating others (such as Galileo) into silence, but they barely blunted the thrust of new ideas.

The payoff was phenomenal. By linking every branch of scholarship, art, and crafts to every other and evaluating them all in the light of antiquity, "Renaissance men"* such as Michelangelo revolutionized

*There were also a few, but only a very few, Renaissance women.

them all at once. Some of these amazing characters, such as Leon Battista Alberti, theorized as brilliantly as they created, and the greatest, such as Leonardo da Vinci, excelled at everything from portraiture to mathematics. Their creative minds moved effortlessly between studios and the corridors of power, taking time off from theorizing to lead armies, hold office, and advise rulers. (In addition to writing *The Prince*, Machiavelli also penned the finest comedies of his age.) Visitors and emigrants spread the new ideas from the Renaissance's epicenter at Florence as far as Portugal, Poland, and England, where distinct local renaissances blossomed.

This was, without a doubt, one of the most astonishing episodes in history. Renaissance Italians did not re-create Rome—even in 1500, Western social development was still a full ten points lower than the Roman peak a millennium and a half earlier. More Italians could now read than in the heyday of the Roman Empire, but Europe's biggest city was just one-tenth the size of ancient Rome; Europe's soldiers, despite being armed with guns, would have struggled to better Caesar's legions; and Europe's richest countries remained less productive than Rome's richest provinces. But none of these quantitative differences necessarily matters if Renaissance Italians really did revolutionize Western culture so thoroughly that they set Europe apart from the rest of the world, inspiring Western adventurers to conquer the Americas while conservative Easterners stayed home.

Chinese intellectuals, I suspect, would have been astonished to hear of this idea. Laying down their inkstones and brushes, I can imagine them patiently explaining to the nineteenth-century European historians who dreamed up this theory that twelfth-century Italians were not the first people to feel disappointed with their recent history and to look to antiquity for ways to perfect modernity. Chinese thinkers—as we saw in Chapter 7—did something very similar four hundred years earlier, looking back past Buddhism to find superior wisdom in Han dynasty literature and painting. Italians turned antiquity into a program for social rebirth in the fifteenth century, but the Chinese had already done so in the eleventh century. Florence in 1500 was crowded with geniuses, moving comfortably between art, literature, and politics, but so was Kaifeng in 1100. Was Leonardo's breadth really more astonishing than that of Shen Kuo, who wrote on agriculture, archaeology, cartography, climate change, the classics, ethnography, geology, mathematics, medicine, metallurgy, meteorology, music, painting, and zoology? As comfortable with the mechanical arts as any Florentine inventor, Shen explained the workings of canal locks and printers' movable type, designed a new kind of water clock, and built pumps that drained a hundred thousand acres of swampland. As versatile as Machiavelli, he served the state as director of the Bureau of Astronomy and negotiated treaties with nomads. Leonardo would surely have been impressed.

The nineteenth-century theory that the Renaissance sent Europe down a unique path seems less compelling if China had had a strikingly similar renaissance of its own four centuries earlier. It perhaps makes more sense to conclude that China and Europe both had Renaissances for the same reason that both had first and second waves of Axial thought: because each age gets the thought it needs. Smart, educated people reflect on the problems facing them, and if they face similar issues they will come up with similar ranges of responses, regardless of where and when they live.*

Eleventh-century Chinese and fifteenth-century Europeans did face rather similar issues. Both groups lived in times of rising social development. Both had a sense that the second wave of Axial thought had ended badly (the collapse of the Tang dynasty and rejection of Buddhism in the East; climate change, the Black Death, and the crisis of the church in the West). Both looked back beyond their "barbarous" recent pasts to glorious antiquities of first-wave Axial thought (Confucius and the Han Empire in the East; Cicero and the Roman Empire in the West). And both groups responded similarly, applying the most

---

*Not everyone agrees. In his most recent book, *1434: The Year a Magnificent Chinese Fleet Sailed to Italy and Ignited the Renaissance*, Gavin Menzies claims that part of Zheng He's fleet visited Venice in 1434, setting off the Italian Renaissance by teaching Alberti and others the secrets of the earlier Chinese Renaissance. The reason Leonardo's inventiveness seems so like Shen Kuo's, Menzies argues, is that Italians were working from Chinese prototypes, particularly Wang Zhen's *Treatise on Agriculture*, mentioned in Chapter 7—which would also explain why eighteenth-century European spinning machines looked so much like earlier Chinese ones! Menzies's *1434* calls for even more suspension of disbelief than his *1421* (most obviously, we have to wonder why the abundant sources from fifteenth-century Italy never mention the magnificent Chinese fleet), and once again I must confess that this is more suspension than I can muster.

advanced scholarship to ancient literature and art and using the results to interpret the world in new ways.

Asking why Europe's Renaissance culture propelled daredevils to Tenochtitlán while China's conservatives stayed home seems to miss the point just as badly as asking why Western rulers were great men while Easterners were bungling idiots. We clearly need to reformulate the question again. If Europe's fifteenth-century Renaissance really did inspire bold exploration, why, we should ask, did China's eleventh-century Renaissance not do the same? Why did Chinese explorers not discover the Americas in the days of the Song dynasty, even earlier than Menzies imagines them going there?

The quick answer is that no amount of Renaissance spirit would have delivered Song adventurers to the Americas unless their ships could make the journey, and eleventh-century Chinese ships probably could not. Some historians disagree; the Vikings, they point out, made it to America around 1000 in longboats that were much simpler than Chinese junks. But a quick glance at a globe (or Figure 8.10) reveals a big difference. Sailing via the Faeroes, Iceland, and Greenland, the Vikings never had to cross more than five hundred miles of open sea to reach America. Terrifying as that must have been, it was nothing compared to the five thousand miles Chinese explorers would have had to cross by sailing with the Kuro Siwo Drift from Japan, past the Aleutian Islands, to make land in northern California (following the Equatorial Counter Current from the Philippines to Nicaragua would mean crossing twice as much open sea).

Physical geography—and, as we will see later in this chapter, other kinds of geography too—just made it easier for western Europeans to cross the Atlantic than for Easterners to cross the Pacific. And while storms might well have blown the occasional Chinese ship as far as America*—and the North Equatorial Current could, conceivably, have

---

*Some historians believe that Xu Fu, the emissary sent by the Qin First Emperor to find the herbs of immortality, reached America's west coast in the 210s BCE. There is, however, no actual evidence, and Tim Severin's bold attempt to repeat Xu's voyage in 1993 was not encouraging—despite having many modern advantages, he had to abandon ship a good thousand miles shy of America. Nor does Thor Heyerdahl's famous balsa raft *Kon-Tiki* inspire confidence. Heyerdahl crossed only half the Pacific, from Peru to Polynesia, and in only one direction, carried by the Equatorial Current. The voyage from Asia to Peru is much longer and tougher.

brought them back again—it was never likely that eleventh-century explorers, however motivated by Renaissance spirit, would find the Americas and return to tell the story.

Only in the twelfth century did shipbuilding and navigation improve to the point that Chinese ships could have reliably made the twelve-thousand-mile round-trip from Nanjing to California; but that, of course, was still nearly four hundred years before Columbus and Cortés. So why were there no twelfth-century Chinese conquistadors?

It may have been because China's Renaissance spirit, whatever exactly we mean by such a term, was in retreat by the twelfth century. Social development stagnated and then tumbled in the thirteenth and fourteenth centuries, and as the preconditions for Renaissance culture disappeared, elite thought did indeed turn increasingly conservative. Some historians think the failure of Wang Anshi's New Policies in the 1070s turned Neo-Confucian intellectuals against engagement with the wider world; some point to the fall of Kaifeng in 1127; others see the causes in entirely different places. But nearly all agree that while intellectuals continued thinking globally, they began acting very locally indeed. Instead of risking their lives in political infighting at the capital, most stayed home. Some organized local academies, arranging lectures and reading groups but declining to train scholars for the state examinations. Others drew up rules for well-ordered villages and family rituals; others still focused on themselves, building perfection one life at a time through "quiet sitting" and contemplation. According to the twelfth-century theorist Zhu Xi,

> If we try to establish our minds in a state free of doubt, then our progress will be facilitated as by the breaking forth of a great river . . . So let us now set our minds on honoring our virtuous natures and pursuing our studies. Let us every day seek to find in ourselves whether we have been remiss about anything in our studies and whether or not we have been lax about anything in our virtuous natures . . . If we urge ourselves on in this way for a year, how can we not develop?

Zhu was a man of his times. He turned down imperial offices and lived modestly, establishing his reputation from the ground up by teaching at a local academy, writing books, and mailing letters explaining his ideas. His one venture into national politics ended in banishment and condemnation of his life's work as "spurious learning." But as external threats mounted in the thirteenth century and Song civil servants cast around for ways to bind the gentry to their cause, Zhu's philosophically impeccable but politically unthreatening elaboration of Confucius started to seem rather useful. His theories were first rehabilitated, then included in state examinations, and finally made the exclusive basis for administrative advancement. Zhu Xi thought became orthodoxy. "Since the time of Zhu Xi the Way has been clearly known," one scholar happily announced around 1400. "There is no more need for writing; what is left is to practice."

Zhu is often called the second-most-influential thinker in Chinese history (after Confucius but ahead of Mao), responsible, depending on the judge's perspective, either for perfecting the classics or for condemning China to stagnation, complacency, and oppression. But this praises or blames Zhu too much. Like all the best theorists, he simply gave the age the ideas it needed, and people used them as they saw fit.

This is clearest in Zhu's thinking on family values. By the twelfth century Buddhism, protofeminism, and economic growth had transformed older gender roles. Wealthy families now often educated their daughters and gave them bigger dowries when they married, which translated into more clout for wives; and as women's financial standing improved, they established the principle that daughters should inherit property like sons. Even among poorer families, commercial textile production was giving women more earning power, which again translated into stronger property rights.

A male backlash began among the rich in the twelfth century, while Zhu was still young. It promoted feminine chastity, wifely dependence, and the need for women to stay in the house's inner quarters (or, if they really had to go out, to be veiled or carried in a curtained chair). Critics particularly attacked widows who remarried, taking their property into other families. By the time Zhu Xi thought was rehabilitated in the thirteenth century, his pious ideal of re-creating perfect Confucian families had come to seem like a useful vehicle to give philosophical shape to these ideas, and when bureaucrats began rolling back property laws that favored women in the fourteenth century they happily announced that it was all in the name of Zhu Xi thought.

Zhu's writings did not cause these changes in women's lives. They were merely one strand of a broader reactionary mood that swept up not just learned civil servants but also people who were most unlikely to have been reading Zhu. For instance, artisans' representations of feminine beauty changed dramatically in these years. Back in the eighth century, in the heyday of Buddhism and protofeminism, one of the most popular styles of ceramic figurines was what art historians rather ungallantly call "fat ladies." Reportedly inspired by Yang Guifei, the courtesan whose charms ignited An Lushan's revolt in 755, they show women solid enough for Rubens doing everything from dancing to playing polo. When twelfth-century artists portrayed women, by contrast, they were generally pale, wan things, serving men or languidly sitting around, waiting for men to come home.

The slender beauties may have been sitting down because their feet hurt. The notorious practice of footbinding—deforming little girls' feet by wrapping them tightly in gauze, twisting and breaking their toes in the interest of daintiness—probably began around 1100, thirty years before Zhu was born. A couple of poems seem to refer to it around then, and soon after 1148 a scholar observed that "women's footbinding began in recent times; it was not mentioned in any books from previous eras."

The earliest archaeological evidence for footbinding comes from the tombs of Huang Sheng and Madame Zhou, women who shuffled off this mortal coil in 1243 and 1274, respectively. Each was buried with her feet bound in six-foot-long gauze strips and accompanied by silk shoes and socks with sharply upturned tips (Figure 8.9). Madame Zhou's skeleton was well-enough preserved to show that her deformed feet matched the socks and sandals: her eight little toes had been twisted under her soles and her two big toes were bent upward, producing a slender-enough foot to fit into her narrow, pointed slippers.

Twelfth-century China did not invent female foot modification. Improving on the way women walk seems to be an almost universal obsession (among men, anyway). The torments visited on Huang and Zhou, though, were orders of magnitude greater than those served up in other cultures. Wearing stilettos will give you bunions; binding your feet will put you in a wheelchair. The pain this practice caused—day in, day out, from cradle to grave—is difficult to imagine. In the very year Madame Zhou was buried, a scholar published the first known criticism of footbinding: "Little girls not yet four or five, who

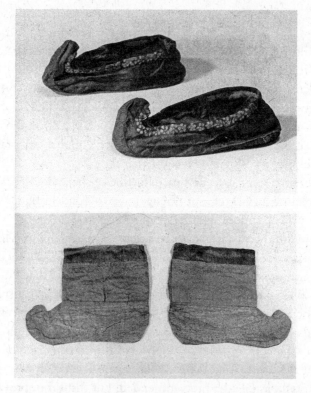

Figure 8.9. Little foot: silk slippers and socks from the tomb of Huang
Sheng, a seventeen-year-old girl buried in 1243, the first
convincingly documented footbinder in history

have done nothing wrong, nevertheless are made to suffer unlimited
pain to bind [their feet] small. I do not know what use this is."

What use indeed? Yet footbinding grew both more common and
more horrific. Thirteenth-century footbinding made feet slimmer;
seventeenth-century footbinding actually made them shorter, collapsing the toes back under the heel into a crippled ball of torn ligaments
and twisted tendons known as a "golden lotus." The photographs of
the mangled feet of the last twentieth-century victims are hard to
look at.*

---

*Whatever his faults, Mao Zedong banned footbinding immediately on assuming
power in 1949.

Blaming all this on Zhu Xi would be excessive. His philosophy did not cause Chinese elite culture to turn increasingly conservative; rather, cultural conservatism caused his ideas to succeed. Zhu Xi thought was just the most visible element of a broader response to military defeat, retrenchment, and falling social development. As the world turned sour in the twelfth century, antiquity became less a source of renewal than a source of refuge, and by the time Madame Zhou died in 1274 the sort of Renaissance spirit that might drive global exploration was sorely lacking.

So does the stagnation and then decline of social development after 1100 explain why Cortés, not Zheng, went to Tenochtitlán? Well, partially. It probably does explain why there were no great voyages of exploration in the twelfth and thirteenth centuries. But by 1405, when Zheng's first Treasure Fleet sailed from Nanjing, Eastern social development was once again rising quickly. The very fact that Yongle kept sending Zheng across the Indian Ocean indicates an expansive mindset. As social development surged upward again, fifteenth-century intellectuals started looking for alternatives to Zhu Xi thought.

The extraordinary Wang Yangming, for instance, tried hard to follow Zhu's rules. In the 1490s Wang spent a week contemplating a bamboo stalk, as Zhu had recommended, but instead of providing insight it made him ill. Wang then had just the kind of epiphany appropriate for a successful, expanding society: he realized that everyone intuitively knows the truth without years of quiet sitting and studying commentaries on Confucius. We can all attain wisdom if we just get out and do something. Wang, as good as his word, became a new Renaissance man, ranking among the period's top generals, administrators, editors of ancient texts, and poets. His followers, rebelling still more against Zhu Xi thought, proclaimed that the streets were full of sages, that everyone could judge right and wrong for themselves, and that getting rich was good. They even advocated women's equality.

The decision to end Zheng's voyages was in fact made not against a background of conservative retrenchment but against one of expansion, innovation, and challenges faced and overcome. There is little to suggest that a rigid, inward-turned mind-set cut off Chinese exploration in the fifteenth century while a dynamic Renaissance culture pushed Europeans across the seas. So what did?

THE ADVANTAGES OF ISOLATION

We have already seen the answer: once again it was maps, not chaps, that took East and West down different paths. Geography just made it easier for Westerners to wash up in the Americas than for Easterners (Figure 8.10).

Europeans' most obvious geographical advantage was physical: the prevailing winds, the placing of islands, and the sheer size of the Atlantic and Pacific oceans made things easier for them. Given time, East Asian explorers would surely have crossed the Pacific eventually, but other things being equal, it was always going to be easier for Viking or Portuguese sailors to reach the New World than for Chinese or Japanese.

In reality, of course, other things are rarely equal, and in the fifteenth century economic and political geography conspired to multiply the advantages that physical geography gave western Europe. Eastern social development was much higher than Western, and thanks to men like Marco Polo, Westerners knew it. This gave Westerners economic incentives to get to the East and tap into the richest markets on earth. Easterners, by contrast, had few incentives to go west. They could rely on everyone else to come to them.

The Arabs were conveniently placed to dominate the western stretches of the Silk Road and Indian Ocean trade routes, and for many centuries Europeans, at the farthest end of both East-West arteries, mostly stayed home and made do with the crumbs that Venetians collected from Arab tables. The Crusades and Mongol conquests began changing the political map, though, easing European access to the East. Greed began trumping sloth and fear, pulling traders (particularly Venetians) down the Red Sea into the Indian Ocean or, like the Polos, across the steppes.

When western European states began moving toward the high end and intensifying their wars after the Black Death, political geography added a push to the economic pull. Rulers along the Atlantic fringe were desperate to buy more cannons and were exhausting the usual ways to get rich (ramping up the bureaucracy to tax their subjects, robbing Jews, plundering neighbors, and so on). They were ready to talk to anyone who could offer them new revenue sources, even the shady, greedy characters who hung around harbors.

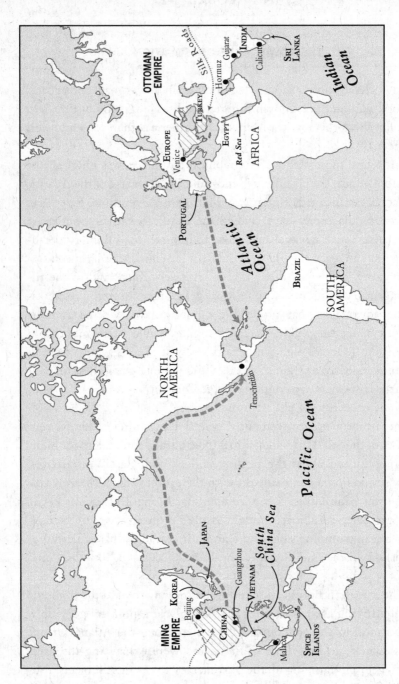

Figure 8.10. A third way of seeing the world: how physical geography stacked the odds in favor of western Europe by putting it just three thousand miles from America, while China had the misfortune to lie twice as far from the New World

The Atlantic kingdoms lay as far as it was possible to get from the Red Sea and Silk Road routes, but captains of all kinds, confident in their marvelous new ships, offered—in return for gifts, loans, and trade monopolies—to turn what had previously been geographical isolation into an advantage. They would find an Atlantic route to the Orient. Some promised to sail around the southern tip of Africa into the Indian Ocean, avoiding the awkward business of dealing with Venetians and Muslims. Others insisted they would simply sail west till they came around the globe and showed up in the East.* (A third approach, sailing over the North Pole, was for obvious reasons less attractive.)

. Most Europeans favored heading south over heading west because they calculated—rightly—that they would have to sail a very long way west to get to the East. If there is any place for bungling idiots in this story, it surely belongs to Columbus, who opened the road to Tenochtitlán by massively underestimating the distance around the globe and refusing to believe that he had the numbers wrong. Conversely, if there is a place for great men, it must go to the Ming emperors' tough-minded advisers who, after calculating the costs and benefits, shut down Zheng's quixotic tours in the 1430s and "lost" their paperwork in the 1470s.

Sometimes a little bungling is a good thing, but in reality neither bungling nor good sense made much difference, because maps left little scope for chaps to do anything except what they did do. When Yongle came to China's throne in 1403 he needed to repair his nation's standing in South Asia. Sending Zheng's Treasure Fleets to Calicut and Hormuz was an expensive way to do this, but it did work; but sending Zheng east into an empty ocean was simply out of the question, no matter how many herbs of immortality might lie there. It was always likely that fifteenth-century China's administrators would eventually shut down the costly voyages into the Indian Ocean, and it was never likely that they would send fleets into the Pacific. Economic geography made exploration irrational.

It is also hard to see how European sailors could not have run into the Americas quite quickly once they struck out across the Atlantic in

*Even in backward Europe, informed opinion had recognized since the twelfth century that the world was round. (The classical Greeks had already known this.)

search of a route to the riches of the East. Columbus and his men needed hearts of oak and intestines of iron to plunge into the unknown, the wind at their backs, with no guarantee of finding another wind to bring them home, but if they had balked, there were brave men aplenty in Europe's ports to try again. And if Queen Isabella had rejected Columbus's third proposal in 1492, Europeans would not have stopped sailing west. Either Columbus would have found another backer or we would simply remember a different mariner—Caboto, perhaps, or the Portuguese Pedro Alvares Cabral, who found Brazil blocking his way to India in 1500—as the great discoverer.

Maps made it as inevitable as things get—as inevitable, say, as when farmers replaced hunter-gatherers or states replaced villages—that the daredevil sailors of the Atlantic fringe would find the Americas sooner rather than later, and certainly sooner than the equally daredevil sailors of the South China Sea.

And once that happened, the consequences were largely predetermined too. European germs, weapons, and institutions were so much more powerful than Native American ones that indigenous populations and states simply collapsed. Had Montezuma or Cortés made other choices, the first conquistadors might well have died on the blood-soaked altars of Tenochtitlán, their hearts hacked from their screaming bodies and offered to the gods, but there would have been more conquistadors right behind them, bringing more smallpox, cannons, and plantations. Native Americans could no more resist European imperialists than native European hunter-gatherers could resist farmers seven or eight millennia earlier.

Geography mattered just as much when Europeans rounded South Africa and sailed into the Indian Ocean, but in different ways. Here Europeans entered a world of higher social development, with ancient empires, long-established trading houses, and its own virulent diseases. Distance and cost—physical and economic geography—kept European incursions as tiny as those to the Americas. The first Portuguese mission to sail around Africa and on to India in 1498 involved just four ships. Its commander, Vasco da Gama, was a nobody, chosen in the expectation he would fail.

Da Gama was a great captain, covering six thousand miles of open sea to catch the winds to take him south of Africa, but he was no politician. He did almost everything possible to justify people's lack of faith in him. His habit of kidnapping and flogging local pilots almost led to disaster before he even left Africa, and when his maltreated guides got him to India he offended the Hindu rulers of Calicut by assuming they were Christians. He insulted them further by offering paltry gifts, and when he finally extracted a cargo of spices and gems he ignored all advice and set sail into contrary winds. Almost half his crew died on the Indian Ocean and scurvy crippled the survivors.

But because profit margins on Asian spices exceeded 100 percent, da Gama still made fortunes for himself and his king in spite of all his blunders. Dozens of Portuguese ships followed in da Gama's wake, exploiting the one advantage they did have: firepower. Slipping as the occasion demanded among trading, bullying, and shooting, the Portuguese found that nothing closed a deal quite like a gun. They seized harbors along the Indian coast as trading enclaves (or pirates' lairs, depending who was talking) and shipped pepper back to Portugal.

Their tiny numbers meant that Portuguese ships were more like mosquitoes buzzing around the great kingdoms of the Indian Ocean than like conquistadors, but after nearly a decade of their biting, the sultans and kings of Turkey, Egypt, Gujarat, and Calicut—egged on by Venice—decided enough was enough. Massing more than a hundred vessels in 1509, they trapped eighteen Portuguese warships against the Indian coast and closed to ram and board them. The Portuguese blasted them into splinters.

Like the Ottomans when they advanced into the Balkans a century earlier, rulers all around the Indian Ocean rushed to copy European guns, only to learn that it took more than just cannons to outshoot the Portuguese. They needed to import an entire military system and transform the social order to make room for new kinds of warriors, which proved just as difficult in sixteenth-century South Asia as it had been three thousand years earlier, when the kings of the Western core had struggled to adapt their armies to chariots. Rulers who moved too slowly had to open port after port to the fierce intruders, and in 1510 the Portuguese cowed the sultan of Malacca, who controlled the straits leading to the Spice Islands themselves, into granting them trading rights. When the sultan rediscovered his backbone and threw them out, the Portuguese seized his whole city. "Whoever is lord of Malacca," observed Tomé Pires, its first Portuguese governor, "has his hand on the throat of Venice."

1521

And not just Venice. "China," Pires wrote,

> is an important, good, and very wealthy country, and the Governor of
> Malacca would not need as much force as they say in order to bring it
> under our rule, because the people are very weak and easy to over-
> come. And the principal people who have often been there affirm that
> with ten ships the Governor of India who took Malacca could take the
> whole of China along the seacoast.

In the giddy years after 1500, almost anything seemed possible to
the adventurers who had crossed the Atlantic and rounded Africa. Why
not simply take over the East now they had got there? So in 1517 the
Portuguese king decided to test Pires's theory, sending him to Guangzhou to propose peace and trade with the Celestial Kingdom. Unfortunately, Pires was about as diplomatic as da Gama, and a three-year
face-off developed, with Pires demanding to meet the emperor and
local officials stalling. Pires finally got his way in 1521, the very year
that Cortés entered Tenochtitlán.

Pires's story, though, ended very differently from Cortés's. On
reaching Beijing, Pires had to wait more weeks for an audience, only
for it to go disastrously wrong. While Pires was negotiating, a letter
arrived from the sultan of Malacca denouncing the Portuguese envoy
for stealing his throne. More letters flooded in from officials Pires had
offended in Guangzhou, accusing him of cannibalism and espionage.
Then, at the worst possible moment, the Chinese emperor dropped
dead. In a swirl of accusations and counteraccusations Pires's party was
clapped in irons.

What happened to Pires remains unclear. One letter from a sailor
imprisoned with him says he died in jail, but another account says he
was banished to a village, where, twenty years later, a Portuguese priest
met his daughter. The cleric insisted that the girl proved her identity
by reciting the Lord's Prayer in Portuguese and told him that Pires
had grown old with a wealthy Chinese wife and only recently died.
But all in all, it is most likely that Pires shared the fate of the rest of the
embassy. After being pilloried and publicly mocked, they were exe-

cuted and dismembered. Each man's penis was chopped off and stuffed in his mouth before his body parts were displayed on spikes around Guangzhou.

Whatever his fate, Pires learned the hard way that despite their guns, here at the real center of the world Europeans still counted for little. They had destroyed the Aztecs and shot their way into the markets of the Indian Ocean, but it took more than that to impress the gatekeepers of All Under Heaven. Eastern social development remained far ahead of Western, and despite Europe's Renaissance, sailors, and guns, in 1521 there was still little to suggest that the West would narrow the gap significantly. Three more centuries would pass before it became clear just what a difference it made that Cortés, not Zheng, had burned Tenochtitlán.

9

◎ ◎ ◎

THE WEST CATCHES UP

THE RISING TIDE

"A rising tide lifts all the boats," said President John F. Kennedy. Never was this truer than between 1500 and 1800, when for three centuries Eastern and Western social development both floated upward (Figure 9.1). By 1700 both were pushing the hard ceiling around forty-three points; by 1750 both had passed it.

Kennedy spoke his famous line in Heber Springs, Arkansas, in a speech to celebrate a new dam. The project struck his critics as the worst kind of pork barrel spending: sure, they observed, the proverbial rising tide lifts all the boats, but it lifts some faster than others. That, too, was never truer than between 1500 and 1800. Eastern social development rose by a quarter, but the West's rose twice as fast. In 1773 (or, allowing a reasonable margin of error, somewhere between 1750 and 1800) Western development overtook the East's, ending the twelve-hundred-year Eastern age.

Historians argue passionately over why the global tide rose so much after 1500 and why the Western boat proved particularly buoyant. In this chapter I suggest that the two questions are linked and that once we set them into their proper context, of the long-term saga of social development, the answers are no longer so mysterious.

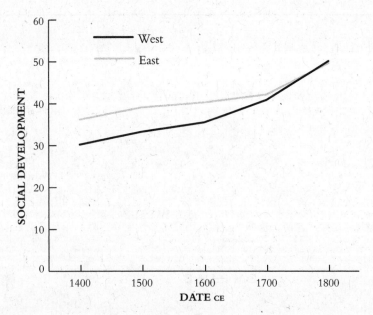

Figure 9.1. Some boats float better than others: in the eighteenth century the rising tide of social development pushed East and West through the ceiling that had always constrained organic economies, but pushed the West harder, further, and faster. In 1773, according to the index, the West regained the lead.

MICE IN A BARN

It took a while to get over Tomé Pires. Not until 1557 did Chinese officials start turning a blind eye to the Portuguese traders who were settling at Macao (Figure 9.2), and although by 1570 other Portuguese traders had set up shop as far around the coasts of Asia as Nagasaki in Japan, their numbers remained pitifully small. To most Westerners, the lands of the Orient remained merely magical names; to most Easterners, Portugal was not even that.

The main impact these European adventurers did have on ordinary Easterners' lives in the sixteenth century was through the extraordinary plants—corn, potatoes, sweet potatoes, peanuts—they brought from the New World. These grew where nothing else would, survived wretched weather, and fattened farmers and their animals wonderfully. Across the sixteenth century millions of acres of them were planted, from Ireland to the Yellow River.

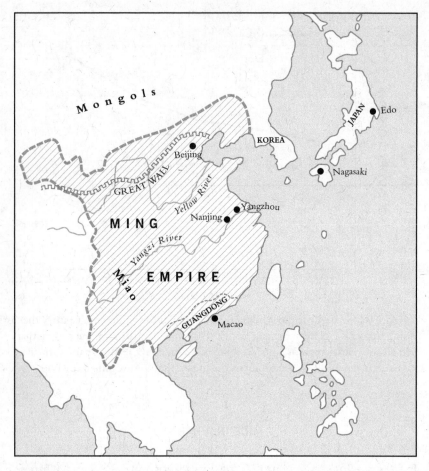

Figure 9.2. A crowded world: the East in an age of rising tides, 1500–1700

They came, perhaps, in the nick of time. The sixteenth century was a golden age for Eastern and Western culture. In the 1590s (admittedly a particularly good decade) Londoners could watch new dramas such as Shakespeare's *Henry V, Julius Caesar,* and *Hamlet* or read inexpensive religious tracts such as John Foxe's gory *Book of Martyrs,* churned out in their thousands by the new printing presses and crammed with woodcuts of true believers at the stake. At the other end of Eurasia, Beijingers could catch Tang Xianzu's twenty-hour-long *Peony Pavilion,* which remains China's most-watched traditional opera, or read *The Journey to the West* (the hundred-chapter tale of Monkey, Pig, and a Shrek-like ogre named Friar Sand, who followed a seventh-century monk to India to find Buddhist sutras, along the way rescuing him from countless cliff-hangers).

But behind the glittering façade all was not well. The Black Death had killed a third or more of the people in the Western and Eastern cores and for about a century after 1350 recurring outbreaks kept population low. Between 1450 and 1600, however, the number of hungry mouths in each region roughly doubled. "Population has grown so much that it is entirely without parallel in history," one Chinese scholar recorded in 1608. In faraway France observers agreed; people were breeding "like mice in a barn," as a proverb put it.

Fear has ever been an engine of social development. More children meant more subdivided fields or more heirs left out in the cold, and always meant more trouble. Farmers weeded and manured more often, dammed streams, and dug wells, or wove and tried to sell more garments. Some settled on marginal land, squeezing a meager living from hillsides, stones, and sand that their parents would never have bothered with. Others abandoned the densely settled cores for wild, underpopulated frontiers. Yet even when they planted the New World wonder crops, there never seemed to be enough to go around.

The fifteenth century, when labor had been scarce and land abundant, increasingly became just a fuzzy memory: happy days, beef and ale, pork and wine. Back then, said the prefect of a county near Nanjing in 1609, everything had been better: "Every family was self-sufficient with a house to live in, land to cultivate, hills from which to cut firewood, gardens in which to grow vegetables." Now, though, "nine out of ten are impoverished . . . Avarice is without limit, flesh injures bone . . . Alas!" A German traveler around 1550 was blunter: "In the past they ate differently at the peasant's house. Then, there was meat and food in profusion." Today, though, "everything is truly changed . . . the food of the most comfortably off peasants is almost worse than that of day laborers and valets in the old days."

In the English fairy tale of Dick Whittington (which, like many such stories, goes back to the sixteenth century), a poor boy and his cat drift from the countryside to London and make good, but in the real world many of the hungry millions that fled to cities merely jumped from the frying pan into the fire. Figure 9.3 shows how urban real wages (that is, consumers' ability to buy basic goods, corrected to account for inflation) changed after 1350. The graph rests on years of

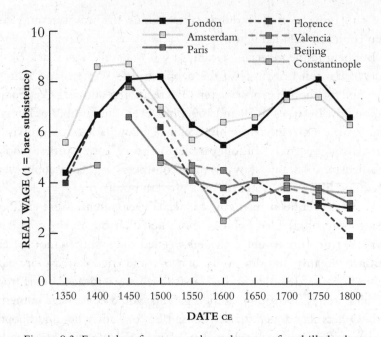

Figure 9.3. For richer, for poorer: the real wages of unskilled urban
workers in six Western cities plus Beijing, 1350–1800. Every city and every
industry had its own story, but almost everywhere we can measure it, after
roughly doubling between 1350 and 1450 workers' purchasing power fell back
to pre-1350 levels by 1550 or 1600. For reasons that will become clear later in
the chapter, after 1600 cities in Europe's northwest increasingly pulled away
from the rest. (Data begin at Paris and Valencia only around 1450 and at
Beijing around 1750, and—not surprisingly—there is a gap in the figures
from Constantinople around 1453, when the Ottomans sacked the city.)
Data from Allen 2006, Figure 2.

painstaking detective work by economic historians, deciphering crumbling records, recorded in a regular Babel of tongues and measured in
an even greater confusion of units. Not until the fourteenth century
do European archives begin providing data good enough to calculate
incomes this precisely, while in China we have to wait until after 1700.
But despite the gaps in the data and the mass of crisscrossing lines,
the Western trend, at least, is clear. Basically, wages roughly doubled
everywhere we have evidence in the century after the Black Death,
then, as population recovered, mostly fell back to pre–Black Death
levels. The Florentines who hauled blocks and raised the soaring dome
of Brunelleschi's cathedral in the 1420s feasted on meat, cheese, and

olives; those who dragged Michelangelo's David into place in 1504 made do with bread. A century later their great-grandchildren were happy to get even that.

By then hunger stalked Eurasia from end to end. A disappointing harvest, an ill-advised decision, or just bad luck could drive poor families to scavenging (in China for chaff and bean pods, tree bark and weeds, in Europe for cabbage stumps, weeds, and grass). A run of disasters could push thousands onto the roads in search of food and the weakest into starvation. It is probably no coincidence that in the original versions of Europe's oldest folktales (like *Dick Whittington*), peasant storytellers dreamed not of golden eggs and magic beanstalks but of actual eggs and beans. All they asked from fairy godmothers was a full stomach.

In both East and West the middling sorts steadily hardened their hearts against tramps and beggars, herding them into poorhouses and prisons, shipping them to frontiers, or selling them into slavery. Callous this certainly was, but those who were slightly better off apparently felt they had troubles enough of their own without worrying about others. As one gentleman observed in the Yangzi Delta in 1545, when times were tough "the stricken [that is, poorest] were excused from paying taxes," but "the prosperous were so pressed that they also became impoverished." Downward social mobility stared the children of once-respectable folk in the face.

The sons of the gentry found new ways to compete for wealth and power in this harder world, horrifying conservatives with their scorn for tradition. "Rare styles of clothing and hats are gradually being worn," a Chinese official noted with alarm; "and there are even those who become merchants!" Worse still, one of his colleagues wrote, even formerly respectable families

are mad for wealth and eminence . . . Taking delight in filing accusations, they use their power to press their cases so hard that you can't distinguish between the crooked and the straight. Favoring lavishness and fine style, they drag their white silk garments as they roam about such that you can't tell who is honored and who base.

In China the civil service became a particular flashpoint. The ranks of the gentry swelled but numbers of administrative positions did not, and as the thorny gates of learning narrowed, the rich found ways to make wealth matter more than scholarship. One county official complained that "poor scholars who hoped to get a place [at the examinations] were dismissed by the officials as though they were famine refugees."

Even for kings, at the very top of the pile, these were tense times. In theory, rising population was good for rulers—more people to tax, more soldiers to enlist—but in practice things were not so simple. Pressed into a corner, hungry peasants might rebel rather than pay taxes, and fractious, feuding nobles often agreed with them. (Failed Chinese civil service candidates developed a particular habit of resurfacing as rebels.)

The problem was as old as kingship itself, and most sixteenth-century kings chose old solutions: centralization and expansion. Japan was perhaps the extreme case. Here political authority had collapsed altogether in the fifteenth century, with villages, Buddhist temples, and even individual city blocks setting up their own governments and hiring toughs to protect them or rob their neighbors.* In the sixteenth century population growth set off ferocious competition for resources, and from lots of little lords there gradually emerged a few big ones. The first Portuguese guns reached Japan in 1543 (a generation ahead of the Portuguese themselves) and by the 1560s Japanese craftsmen were making outstanding muskets of their own, just in time to help already-big lords who could afford to arm their followers get bigger still. In 1582 a single chief, Toyotomi Hideyoshi, made himself shogun over virtually the whole archipelago.

Hideyoshi talked his quarrelsome countrymen into handing over their weapons, promising to melt them down into nails and bolts for the world's biggest statue of the Buddha, twice as tall as the Statue of Liberty. This would "benefit the people not only in this life but in the life hereafter," he explained. (A Christian missionary was unimpressed; Hideyoshi was "crafty and cunning beyond belief," he reported, "depriving the people of their arms under pretext of devotion to Religion.")

*This is the background to Akira Kurosawa's classic film *The Seven Samurai* (1954) and—with a little historical and geographical license—John Sturges's almost-as-classic adaptation *The Magnificent Seven* (1960).

Whatever Hideyoshi's spiritual intent may have been, disarming the people was certainly a huge step toward centralizing the state, greatly easing the task of counting heads, measuring land, and assigning tax and military obligations. By 1587, according to a letter he sent to his wife, Hideyoshi saw expansion as the solution to all his problems and decided to conquer China. Five years later his army—perhaps a quarter-million strong, armed with the latest muskets—landed in Korea and swept all before it.

He faced a Chinese Empire deeply divided over the merits of expansion. Some of the Ming emperors, like Hideyoshi in Japan, pushed to overhaul their empire's rickety finances and expand. They ordered up new censuses, tried to work out who owed taxes on what, and converted complicated labor dues and grain contributions into simple silver payments. Civil servants, however, overwhelmingly shunned all this sound and fury. Centuries of tradition, they pointed out, showed that ideal rulers sat quietly (and inexpensively) at the center, leading by moral example. They did not wage war and certainly did not squeeze money out of the landed gentry, the very families that the bureaucrats themselves came from. Censuses and tax registers, Hideyoshi's pride and joy, could safely be ignored. So what if one prefecture in the Yangzi Valley reported exactly the same number of residents in 1492 as it had done eighty years earlier? The dynasty, scholars insisted, would last ten thousand years whether it counted the people or not.

Activist emperors floundered in a bureaucratic quagmire. Sometimes the results were comical, as when Emperor Zhengde insisted on leading an army against the Mongols in 1517 only for the official in charge of the Great Wall to refuse to open the gates to let him through because emperors belonged in Beijing. Sometimes things were less amusing, as when Zhengde had his senior administrators whipped for stubbornness, killing several in the process.

Few emperors had Zhengde's energy, and rather than take on the bureaucratic and landed interests, most let the tax rolls decay. Short of money, they stopped paying the army (in 1569 the vice-minister for war confessed that he could find only a quarter of the troops on his books). Bribing the Mongols was cheaper than fighting them.

Emperors also stopped paying the navy, even though it was supposed to be suppressing the enormous black market that had sprung up since Hongwu had banned private maritime trade back in the fourteenth century. Chinese, Japanese, and Portuguese smugglers ran lucrative operations up and down the coast, buying the latest muskets, turning piratical, and easily outgunning the underfunded coastguards who intercepted them. Not that the coastguards really tried; kickbacks from smugglers were among their major perks.

China's coast increasingly resembled something out of TV cop shows such as *The Wire*, with dirty money blurring distinctions among violent criminals, local worthies, and shady politicians. One upright but naïve governor learned this the hard way when he actually followed the rules, executing a gang of smugglers even though one of them was a judge's uncle. Strings were pulled. The governor was fired and committed suicide when the emperor issued a warrant for his arrest.

The government effectively lost control of the coast in the 1550s. Smugglers turned into pirate kings, controlling twenty cities and even threatening to loot the royal tombs at Nanjing. In the end it took a whole team of officials, politically savvy as well as incorruptible, to defeat them. With a covert force (known as "Qi's Army" after Qi Jiguang, the most famous of these untouchables) of three thousand musketeers, the reformers fought a shadow war, sometimes with official backing, sometimes not, funded by a prefect of Yangzhou who channeled money to them under the table by squeezing back taxes out of the local elite. Qi's Army showed that when the will was there the empire could still crush challengers, and its success inspired a (brief) era of reform. Transferred to the north, Qi revolutionized the Great Wall's defenses, building stone towers,* filling them with trained musketeers, and mounting cannons on carts like the wagon forts that Hungarians had used against the Ottomans a century before.

In the 1570s Grand Secretary Zhang Zhuzheng, arguably the ablest administrator in Chinese history, updated the tax code, collected arrears, and modernized the army. He promoted bright young men such as Qi and personally oversaw the young emperor Wanli's education. The treasury refilled and the army revived, but when Zhang died in 1582 the bureaucrats struck back. Zhang was posthumously disgraced

---

*If you brave the crowds and peddlers and visit the Great Wall today, the massive stone carapace you will see snaking across the mountains near Beijing is largely the work of Qi and his contemporaries.

and his acolytes fired. The worthy Qi died alone and penniless, abandoned even by his wife.

Emperor Wanli, frustrated at every turn now that his great minister was gone, lost all patience and in 1589 went on strike. Withdrawing into a world of indulgence, he squandered a fortune on clothes and got so fat that he needed help standing up. For twenty-five years he refused to attend imperial audiences, leaving ministers and ambassadors kowtowing to an empty throne. Nothing got done. No officials were hired or promoted. By 1612 half the posts in the empire were vacant and the law courts had backlogs years long.

No wonder Hideyoshi expected an easy victory in 1592. But whether because Hideyoshi made mistakes, because of Korean naval innovations, or because the Chinese army (especially the artillery Qi had established) performed surprisingly well, the Japanese attack bogged down. Some historians think Hideyoshi would still have conquered China had he not died in 1598, but as it was, Hideyoshi's generals immediately rethought expansion. Abandoning Korea, they rushed home to get on with the serious business of fighting one another, and Wanli and his bureaucrats went back to their own serious business of doing not very much at all.

After 1600, the great powers of the Eastern core tacitly agreed that the bureaucrats were right: centralization and expansion were not the answers to their problems. The steppe frontier remained a challenge for China, and European pirates/traders still posed problems in Southeast Asia, but Japan faced so few threats that—alone in the history of the world—it actually stopped using firearms altogether and its skilled gunsmiths went back to making swords (not, alas, plowshares). In the West, however, no one had that luxury.

THE CROWN IMPERIAL

In a way, the Western and Eastern cores looked rather similar in the sixteenth century. In each, a great empire dominated the traditional center (Ming China in the Yellow and Yangzi river valleys in the East, Ottoman Turkey in the eastern Mediterranean in the West) while smaller commercially active states flourished around its edges (in Japan and Southeast Asia in the East, in western Europe in the West). But there the similarities ended. In contrast to the squabbles in Ming China, neither the Ottoman sultans nor their bureaucrats ever doubted that expansion was the answer to their problems. Constantinople had been reduced to fifty thousand people after the Ottoman sack in 1453 but rebounded as it once more became the capital of a great empire. Four hundred thousand urbanites lived there by 1600, and—like Rome so many centuries before—they needed the fruits of the whole Mediterranean to feed themselves. And like ancient Rome's senators, Turkey's sultans resolved that conquest was the best way to guarantee all these dinners.

The sultans carried on a complex dance, keeping one foot in the Western core and one in the steppes. This was the secret of their success. In 1527 Sultan Suleiman reckoned that his army boasted 75,000 cavalry, mostly aristocratic archers of traditional nomad type, and 28,000 Janissaries, Christian slaves trained as musketeers and backed by artillery. To keep the horsemen happy, sultans parceled out conquered lands as fiefs; to keep the Janissaries content—that is, paid in full and on time—they drew up land surveys that would have impressed Hideyoshi, managing cash flows to the last coin.

All this took good management, and a steadily expanding bureaucracy drew in the empire's best and brightest while the sultans adroitly played competing interest groups against one another. In the fifteenth century they often favored the Janissaries, centralizing government and patronizing cosmopolitan culture; in the sixteenth they leaned toward the aristocracy, devolving power and encouraging Islam. Even more important than these nimble accommodations, though, was plunder, which fueled everything. The Ottomans needed war, and usually won.

Their toughest tests came on their eastern front. For years they had confronted a low-grade insurgency in Anatolia (Figure 9.4), where Red-Head* Shiite militants denounced them as corrupt Sunni despots, but this ulcer turned septic when the Persian shah declared himself the descendant of 'Ali in 1501. The Shiite challenge gave focus to the hungry, dispossessed, and downtrodden of the empire, whose violent rage shocked even hard-bitten soldiers: "They destroyed everything—

---

*So called because of their tall red hats with twelve folds, symbolizing the twelve imams whose reigns would culminate in the millennium.

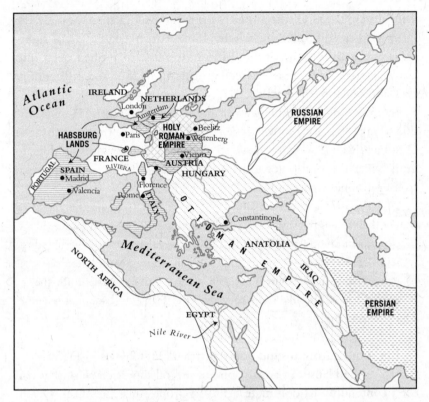

Figure 9.4. The Western empires: the Habsburg, Holy Roman, Ottoman, and Russian empires around 1550

men, women, and children," one sergeant recorded of the rebels. "They even destroyed cats and chickens." The Turkish sultan pressured his religious scholars into declaring the Shiites heretical, and jihads barely let up across the sixteenth century.

Superior firearms gave the Ottomans the edge, and though they never completely defeated Persia they were able to fight it to a standstill and then swing southwest to take the biggest prize of all, Egypt, in 1517. For the first time since the Arab conquests nearly nine centuries earlier, hungry Constantinopolitans now had guaranteed access to the Nile breadbasket.

But like every expansionist power since the Assyrians, the Ottomans found that winning one war just set off another. To reinstate the Egypt-Constantinople grain trade they had to build a fleet to protect their ships, but their victories over the Mediterranean's ferocious pirates

(Muslim as well as Christian) only drew the fleet farther west. By the 1560s Turkey controlled the whole North African coast and was fighting western European navies. Turkish armies also pushed deep into Europe, overwhelming the fierce Hungarians in 1526 and killing their king and much of their aristocracy.

In 1529 Sultan Suleiman was camped outside Vienna. He was unable to take the city, but the siege filled Christians with terror that the Ottomans would soon swallow all Europe. "It makes me shudder to think what the results [of a major war] must be," an ambassador to Constantinople wrote home.

> On their side is the vast wealth of their empire, unimpaired resources, experience and practice in arms, a veteran soldiery, an uninterrupted series of victories . . . On ours are found an empty treasury, luxurious habits, exhausted resources, broken spirits . . . and, worst of all, the enemy are accustomed to victory, we, to defeat. Can we doubt what the result must be?

But some Europeans did doubt, particularly Charles V. He was patriarch of the Habsburg family, one of several superrich clans that had been contending to dominate central Europe since the Black Death. Thanks to astute marriages and the almost preternaturally good timing of their in-laws' deaths, Habsburgs squeezed themselves onto thrones from the Danube to the Atlantic, and in 1516 the whole inheritance—Austria, chunks of Germany and what is now the Czech Republic, southern Italy, Spain, and modern Belgium and Holland—fell into Charles's lap. His many crowns gave him access to Europe's best soldiers, richest cities, and leading financiers, and in 1518 the princes of Germany elected him Holy Roman Emperor too. This particular crown, an odd relic of Europe's messy Middle Ages, was a mixed blessing; as Voltaire famously remarked in the 1750s, the Holy Roman Empire "was neither holy, nor Roman, nor an empire." Herding its squabbling princes normally cost more than the throne was worth, but all the same, whoever sat on the imperial throne was, in principle, Charlemagne's heir—no small matter when rallying Europe against the Turk.

Many observers foresaw only two alternatives for western Europe: conquest by Islam or subjugation by the Habsburgs, the only people strong enough to stop the Turks. Charles's chancellor summed it up in a letter to the emperor in 1519: "God has been very merciful to you. He has raised you above all the kings and princes of Christendom to a power such as no sovereign has enjoyed since your ancestor Charlemagne. He has set you on the way toward a world monarchy, toward the uniting of Christendom under a single shepherd."

Had either the ambassador or the chancellor been right, western Europe would have started looking more like the rest of world's core areas, dominated by a great land empire. But the idea of being shepherded so alarmed Christendom's kings and princes that some launched preemptive wars against Charles to head it off. France even concluded a treaty with the Ottomans against the Habsburgs, and a joint Franco-Turkish fleet bombarded the French Riviera (then under Charles's control) in 1542—all of which, of course, forced Charles to try even harder to shepherd Christendom.

Charles and his son Philip II spent most of their long reigns* fighting other Christians, not Muslims, but rather than turning western Europe into a land empire, their struggle pulled Europe apart, deepening old divisions and creating new ones. When the German monk Martin Luther nailed ninety-five protests about Christian practices to the door of Wittenberg Castle Church on Halloween, 1517, for instance, he was doing nothing extraordinary; this was a traditional way of publicizing theological debates (and compared to many critics of the Church since the Black Death, Luther was positively moderate). But the charged atmosphere turned his religious protest into a political and social earthquake that his contemporaries regularly likened to Turkey's Shiite-Sunni split.

Luther had hoped Charles would support him, but Charles believed that shepherding Christendom required one church, undivided. "A single monk must err if he stands against the opinion of all Christendom," he told Luther. "I am determined to set my kingdoms and dominions, my friends, my body, my blood, my life, my soul upon it." And so he did; but with all Europe up in arms for or against the Habsburgs, denying the differences within Christendom proved disastrous. Sometimes for reasons of principle, sometimes for narrow advantage, and sometimes out of sheer confusion, millions of Christians renounced

*Skipping over various complexities, we can say that they jointly reigned from 1516 through 1598.

the Roman Church. Protestants and Catholics killed one another; Protestants killed other Protestants; and interpretations of protest multiplied. Some Protestants proclaimed the Second Coming, free love, or communism. Many came to bloody, fiery ends. And all, whether their protests were violent or sublime, made the Habsburgs' job harder—and more expensive.

People who believe their enemies to be agents of the Antichrist rarely want to compromise, so small conflicts turned into large ones, large ones refused to end, and costs spiraled upward. In the end, the bottom line for the Habsburgs was the bottom line itself: they simply could not afford to unite western Europe.

Charles, broken by his struggles, retired from his various thrones in 1555–56 and divided them between a cousin, who got Austria and the Holy Roman Empire, and Philip, who got Spain and the other western lands. This was a smart move: by making Habsburg dominion synonymous with Spanish dominion, Philip could streamline administration and focus on the real issue, money.

For forty years Philip labored like Hercules to reform Habsburg finances. He was an odd man, putting in astonishing hours in his custom-built offices outside Madrid but always too busy to find time to actually visit his possessions. But although he counted and taxed his subjects as enthusiastically as Hideyoshi, increased revenues, and soundly defeated France and Turkey, the final victory that would unite western Europe never came any closer. The harder his taxmen squeezed, the more problems mounted. Philip's subjects—breeding like mice in a barn, caught between starvation and the state, and seeing their contributions spent on quarrels in faraway countries with peoples of whom they knew nothing—increasingly fought back.

In the 1560s Philip even managed to push God and Mammon into the same camp. The normally stolid Dutch burghers, persecuted by the Habsburgs for their Protestantism and burdened by heavier taxes, went on an altar-smashing, church-desecrating rampage. Losing the wealthy Netherlands to a nest of Calvinists was unthinkable, so Philip sent in the army, only for the Dutch to raise one of their own. Philip kept winning battles but could not win the war. The Dutch would not consent to pay new taxes to the Habsburgs, but when their faith was at stake they would spend any amount of money and lay down any number of lives to defend it. By the 1580s the war was costing Philip more than the entire empire's income, and unable to afford victory or defeat, he borrowed more heavily from Italian financiers. When he reached the point that he could pay neither his troops nor his creditors, he declared bankruptcy; then did it again, and again. His unpaid armies ran riot, robbing for their keep, and his credit rating collapsed. Spain was not decisively defeated until 1639 (at sea) and 1643 (on land), but when Philip died in 1598 the empire was already ruined, its debt fifteen times its annual revenue.

Two centuries would pass before a western European land empire again looked likely, and by then other western Europeans had set off an industrial revolution that was transforming the world. If the Habsburgs or Turks had united Europe in the sixteenth century, perhaps that industrial revolution would not have happened; perhaps in Charles and Philip, who failed to unite western Europe, or the Ottoman Suleiman, who failed to conquer western Europe, we have finally found the bungling idiots who changed the course of history.

Once again, though, this is too much blame for any one man. The European ambassador who had worried so much about a Turkish takeover had noted that "The only obstacle is Persia, whose position on his rear forces the [Turkish] invader to take precautions"; it was simply beyond the Turks' powers to defeat Persia, the Shiites, *and* the Europeans. Similarly, Charles and Philip failed to become Christendom's shepherds, not because they lost some decisive battle (in fact, they almost always won until the 1580s) or lacked some decisive resource (in fact, they had far more than their fair share of luck, talent, and credit), but because defeating the Turks, schismatic Christians, *and* the other states of western Europe was beyond their organization and wealth. And if the Habsburgs, with all their advantages, could not unite western Europe, then no one could. Western Europe was bound to remain distinct from the band of empires that stretched from Turkey to China.

THE HARD CEILING

Despite the variety of these experiences of empire, social development kept rising in both cores, and in the decades after Hideyoshi and Philip died in 1598 there was every sign that the paradox of development was kicking in again. As so often in the past, the weather contributed to the growing crisis. Cool since 1300, it now turned colder still. Some climatologists blame this on a volcanic eruption in Peru in 1600; others, on weaker sunspot activity. But most agree that the years 1645–1715 were bitterly cold across much of the Old World. From London to Guangdong, diarists and officials complained about snow, ice, and cool summers.

Cold city folk and land-hungry cultivators worked together to make the seventeenth century a disaster for the defenseless, whether that meant forests, wetlands, wildlife, or colonized peoples. Conscience sometimes pricked governments into legislating to defend all these victims, but the colonists pushing the frontiers of the cores outward rarely took much notice. In China so-called shack people invaded mountains and forests, devastating fragile ecologies with sweet potatoes and corn. They drove indigenous groups such as the Miao to the brink of starvation, but when the Miao rebelled, the Chinese state sent in armies to crush them. The Ainu of northern Japan, the Irish in England's oldest colony, and the natives of eastern North America could all tell the same dismal story.

Colonists came because the cores were depleting their own resources. "There will be some trifling income from every foot or inch of earth," one Chinese official insisted, and at both ends of Eurasia governments worked with developers to turn scrub and wetland into pasture and arable land. Another Chinese official laid out the rationale in the 1620s:

> Stop the minor profit of the occupants of reedlands and grasslands! . . . some lazy people, without consideration for the long-term future, go after the minor profits of reeds and reject the great treasure of cultivation of crops. Not only do they not pursue land reclamation themselves, but they also hate others for doing so . . . the marketplaces are more desolate every day, the government revenues fall short of the regular quota. How can we allow this under these circumstances!

Dutch and English entrepreneurs attacked wetlands with equal gusto. Giant state-sponsored drainage programs released vast amounts of fertile soil, but the people who already lived there resisted in court and on the streets. Their (mostly anonymous) protest songs are heart-wrenching:

Behold the great design, which [drainers] do now undermine,
Will make our bodies pine, a prey to crows and vermin;
For they do mean all fens [wetlands] to drain and waters overmaster;
All must be dry and we must die, 'cause Essex calves want pasture.
The feathered fowls have wings to fly to other nations,
But we have no such things to help our transportations;
We must give place (O grievous case!) to horned beasts and cattle
Except that we can all agree to drive them out by battle.

Invasive humans, bringing equally invasive plants and animals, displaced native species or hunted them to extinction, plowing up habitats and clear-cutting forests. One scholar complained in the 1660s that four-fifths of Japan's mountains had been deforested. Only 10 percent of England and Scotland was still wooded around 1550, and by the 1750s more than half those trees were gone too. Ireland, by contrast, was still 12 percent forest in 1600, but colonists eliminated five out of six of those trees by 1700.

Around the big cities the price of wood rose sharply and people turned to alternatives. Near Edo, Japanese salt and sugar makers, potters, and eventually homeowners started burning coal, and those Europeans who could do so substituted peat and coal for charcoal. Just like Kaifengers five hundred years before, Londoners embraced fossil fuels as they were priced out of the market for wood. Most English households outside the capital could still find firewood, but by 1550 the average Londoner was already burning nearly a quarter of a ton of coal each year. By 1610 that had tripled, and by 1650 more than half of Britain's fuel energy came from coal. "London was enveloped in such a cloud of sea-coal," a resident complained in 1659, that "if there be a resemblance of hell on earth, it is in this volcano in a foggy day."

Sadly, he was mistaken, because other Eurasians were making much worse hells for themselves. Climate change was only the first horseman of the apocalypse to break free; the rising pressure on resources also set off state failure as regimes came apart under the stresses. When monarchs cut costs, they alienated their civil servants and soldiers; when they squeezed more out of taxpayers, they alienated their merchants and farmers. Violent protests by the poor had been a fact of life since states were invented, but they now intensified as dispossessed gentry, bankrupt traders, unpaid troops, and failed officials all joined them.

As times got tougher, Western rulers tried to raise the costs of revolt by insisting more firmly that they represented God's will made flesh. Ottoman sultans courted religious scholars more aggressively and western European intellectuals developed theories of "absolutism." Kings' authority, they claimed, came from God's grace alone, and neither parliaments, nor churchmen, nor the will of the people could curtail it. According to the French catchphrase, it was "un roi, une foi, un loi": one king, one faith, one law. Challenging any part of this package deal meant challenging everything good and pure.

But plenty of disgruntled subjects were ready to do just that. In 1622 Osman II, who as Turkey's sultan and caliph was both Muhammad's successor and God's representative on earth, tried to curtail his increasingly expensive Janissaries; they responded by dragging him from his palace, strangling him, and mutilating his divine body. Osman's brother tried to salvage the situation by allying himself with hard-line clerics, even banning coffee and instituting the death penalty for smoking to please them, but in the 1640s the sultans' legitimacy failed completely. In 1648 the Janissaries, now allied with the clerics, executed Sultan Ibrahim the Crazy (perhaps none too soon; he fully deserved his nickname) and fifty years of civil wars began.

The 1640s were a royal nightmare almost everywhere. Anti-absolutist rebellions paralyzed France, and in England Parliament went to war with its pushy king and cut off his head. That let the genie out of the bottle; if a godlike king could be tried and executed, what was not possible? For perhaps the first time since ancient Athens, democratic ideas bubbled up. "The poorest he that is in England hath a life to live as the greatest he," asserted one colonel in the parliamentary army; "every man that is to live under a government ought first by his own consent to put himself under that government."

This was strong stuff for the seventeenth century, but splinter groups of English radicals were even wilder. The Levellers, as one faction called itself, rejected all social distinctions. "None comes into the world with a saddle upon his back," they pointed out, "neither any booted and spurred to ride him." And if hierarchy was unnatural, surely so too was property. Within a year of the king's execution a group calling themselves True Levellers had split off and set up ten communes. Another splinter group, the Ranters, labeled God "that mighty Leveller" and preached permanent revolution—"Overturn, overturn, overturn . . . Have all things in common, or else the plague of God will rot and consume all that you have."

Leveling was an idea whose time had come. Take, for instance, a 1644 report on Levellers who

> sharpened their hoes into swords, and took to themselves the title of "Leveling Kings," declaring that they were leveling the distinction between masters and serfs, titled and mean, rich and poor. The tenants seized hold of their masters' best clothes . . . they would order the masters to kneel and pour the wine for them. They would slap them across the cheeks and say: "We are all of us equally men. What right had you to call us serfs?"

These leveling warlords, however, were not Englishmen; they were in fact rampaging around China's east coast. In East and West alike, the radical challenges to established hierarchy discussed earlier—such as Wang Yangming's to Zhu Xi thought in 1490s China and Martin Luther's to Catholicism in 1510s Europe—combined with state failure to produce new ideas about the equality of man. As we will see, though, these ideas had very different fates in the eighteenth century.

In China, the Ming dynasty was paralyzed by bankruptcy and factionalism, and when famine—a third horseman of the apocalypse—broke loose in 1628, the emperors seemed to have lost the mandate of heaven. Rebels increasingly felt that no act was too extreme. The country dissolved into warlordism in the 1630s; in 1644 Beijing fell. The last Ming emperor hanged himself from a lonely tree behind the palace. "I, feeble and of small virtue, have offended against Heaven," he painted on his robe. "Ashamed to face my ancestors, I die. Removing my imperial cap and with my hair disheveled about my face, I leave to the rebels the dismemberment of my body. Let them not harm my people!"

He was wasting his last words. The warlords no more had the money to pay their swollen armies than did Europe's kings, Turkey's sultans, or the Ming emperor himself, so they turned their men loose to extract payment from civilians. Armies have plundered the innocent since war began, and probably worked out all the possible variations on savagery quite early on, merely repeating them in resounding counter-point through subsequent ages of horror. But all over Eurasia, angry, greedy, and frightened soldiers seem to have plumbed new depths of cruelty in the harsh seventeenth century. Torture, mass executions, and gang rapes fill our sources. When Beijing fell civilians

> were subjected to cruel beatings to extract any silver they might have. Some were tortured with finger or limb presses more than three or four times. And some implicated others, so that thousands of com-moner households were affected . . . people began to lose interest in living.

If anything, the violence unleashed by state failure was even worse in the West. Europe's religious wars reached a terrible climax in Ger-many between 1618 and 1648. From every corner of Christendom came enormous armies; paid irregularly, if at all, they lived off the land, extorting whatever they could. The surviving sources are full of outrages and brutalities. The little town of Beelitz, which had the mis-fortune to be in the path of the Holy Roman Emperor's army in 1637, is as good (or bad) an example as any. A customs officer wrote that after rounding up locals,

> the robbers and murderers took a piece of wood and stuck it down the poor wretches' throats, stirred it and poured in water, adding sand or even human feces, and pitifully tortured the people for money, as transpired with a citizen of Beelitz called David Örtel, who died of it soon after.

Another band of soldiers hung a Beelitzer over a fire and roasted him until he led them to his savings; only for yet another band, hearing that their comrades had scorched money out of him, to carry him back to the fire and hold his face in it "for so long that he died of it and his skin even came off like that of a slaughtered goose."

Historians long assumed that stories like these were religious pro-paganda, too awful to be true, but recent research suggests otherwise. More than 2 million died violently (numbers not matched until the twentieth-century world wars) and maybe ten times as many from the famines and disease—the third and fourth horsemen—that came in the wake of the armies. Both China and central Europe saw population fall by perhaps one-third, like a man-made Black Death.

The plague itself, back in fierce new forms, played its own part. Daniel Defoe's fictionalized *Journal of the Plague Year*, put together fifty years after the facts, vividly described the rumors, panic, and suffering that swept London in 1665, and Chinese doctors' reports are almost as graphic. "Sometimes everyone has swollen neck glands and sometimes everyone's face and head swell up," one recorded in the Yangzi Delta in 1642; or "sometimes everyone suffers from diarrhea and intermittent fever. Or it might be cramps, or pustules, or a rash, or itching scabs, or boils."

Four of the five horsemen of the apocalypse were riding in force, yet as Figure 9.1 shows, there was no seventeenth-century collapse. Social development kept moving up, passing forty-three points, the level where Roman and Song scores had both peaked, in the East in 1710 (give or take twenty-five years, depending on the index's accuracy) and in the West in 1723 (again, thereabouts). By 1800 both East and West were approaching fifty points. Why, we have to ask, did development buck the historical trend?

CLOSING THE STEPPES

Nerchinsk, August 22, 1689. Siberia's short summers can be strangely beautiful. Every year as the ground thaws, dark shoots of grass carpet the gentle hills with green, splashed with red, yellow, and blue wildflowers and butterflies. But this summer was different: along the banks of the Shilka River (Figure 9.5) a tent town sprang up and hundreds of Chinese negotiators, using Christian missionaries to present their terms in Latin, sat down with grizzled Russians to work out a mutual frontier.*

The Russians were far from home. As recently as 1500 Moscow had been just one principality among many in Europe's wild east, struggling to find space between Mongols raiding from the steppes and knights pushing outward from Poland, Germany, and Lithuania. Its thuggish,

---

*They did a good job; the border is still where they set it, on the Amur River. The latest negotiations, in July 2008, moved the line just a mile or two across an island within the river.

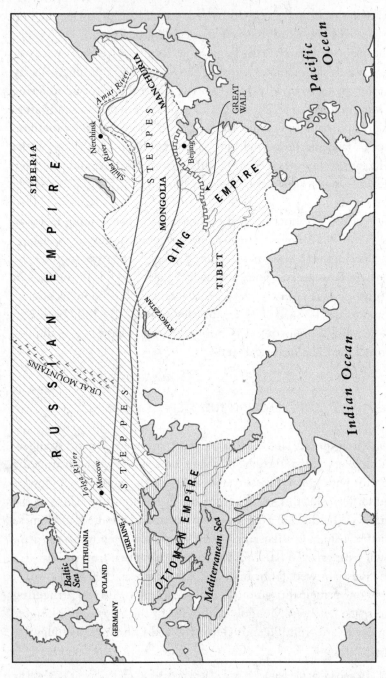

Figure 9.5. The end of the steppes: the empires strike back. By 1750 Russia and China had shut down the steppe highway.

illiterate princes called themselves tsars (that is, caesars), signaling Byzantine and even Roman pretensions, yet they often seemed unsure whether they wanted to be European-style kings or Mongol-style khans. Not until the days of Ivan the Terrible—sadistic even by the disturbing standards of Russian rulers—in the 1550s did Moscow count for much, but Ivan quickly made up for lost time. Musket-toting adventurers crossed the Ural Mountains and in 1598 defeated the local Mongol khan, opening the way to Siberia.

Best known now as the frozen setting of Solzhenitsyn's tales from the gulag, Siberia then struck Russians as a place to get rich. Fur fever gripped them: having long ago hunted their own marten, sable, and ermine into extinction, Europeans would now pay well for their coats. Within forty years Russian fur men, racing across the tundra to feed this lucrative market, stood on the shores of the Pacific. They had strung a thin line of stockades across the edge of Siberia's frozen forests, and from these they ventured out to trap mink or extort skins from the local Stone Age hunters; and though these empty wastes were hardly an empire by the standards of Suleiman or Hideyoshi, taxes on fur saved more than one tsar from disaster.

Russian trappers and Chinese troopers soon clashed along the Amur River, but by the 1680s both sides were ready to talk. Each feared that the other, like so many misguided monarchs before them, would invite in the Mongols as allies and unleash the fifth horseman, steppe migration; and so they came to Nerchinsk.

Their agreement in that Siberian summer formalized one of the great shifts in world history. For two thousand years the steppes had been an East-West highway largely beyond the control of the great agrarian empires. Migrants, microbes, ideas, and inventions had rushed along it, tying together East and West in linked rhythms of development and collapse. Under rare circumstances, and at great cost, conquering kings such as Darius of Persia, the Han emperor Wudi, or the Tang emperor Taizong had imposed their will on the steppes, but these were exceptions. The rule was that agrarian empires paid whatever the nomads asked and hoped for the best.

Guns changed all that. Nomads regularly used firearms (the oldest known gun, from 1288, was found in nomad country in Manchuria*)

*See p. 396 above.

and it was probably Mongols who brought guns from China to the West. But as guns got better (shooting farther and faster) and empires got more organized, generals who could afford to recruit tens of thousands of infantry, arm them with muskets and cannons, and train them to fire volley after volley started defeating nomad cavalry. Around 1500, mounted archers from the steppes still regularly beat infantry from agricultural kingdoms. By 1600, they sometimes did so. But by 1700 it was almost unheard of.

The Russians took the lead. In the 1550s Ivan the Terrible's artillery had swept weak Mongol khanates out of the Volga Basin, and across the next hundred years Russians, Turks, and Poles steadily enclosed the dry Ukrainian steppes with garrisons, ditches, and palisades. Villagers armed with muskets first channeled the nomads' movements and finally cut them off altogether, and at Nerchinsk, Russia and China agreed that no one—not refugees, traders, deserters, and above all not migrating nomads—would move along the steppes without their permission. All would now be subjects of agrarian empires.

The Inner Asians' last hurrah, in 1644, reveals how much had changed. China's Ming dynasty collapsed that year when a warlord took Beijing, and as civil war spiraled out of control, a former Ming general decided that inviting the Manchus—seminomads from Manchuria— to cross the Great Wall and reestablish order would be the lesser of numerous evils. Chinese leaders had a long tradition of bringing Inner Asians into the empire's civil wars, generally with disastrous results. But unlike earlier invaders, the Manchus came not as nomadic cavalry but with an army virtually indistinguishable from China's, based on massed infantry using muskets and cannons copied from the Portuguese.

The Manchus took Beijing unopposed, announced themselves to be a new Qing dynasty, and then spent almost forty years fighting to consolidate their power. These struggles also differed from the aftermaths of earlier steppe invasions. Rather than opening the floodgates for more nomads to come in from the cold, the long struggle just forged a Qing army capable of pushing back into Inner Asia. In 1697 the Qing destroyed a great nomad force deep in Mongolia and in 1720 extended Chinese power for the first time into mountainous Tibet. In the 1750s the Qing imposed a final solution on the nomad problem, dragging their guns, powder, and shot to the borders of modern Kyrgyzstan, where they smashed the last resistance.

In the seventeenth and eighteenth centuries the agrarian empires—above all, Romanov Russia and Qing China—effectively killed one of the horsemen of the apocalypse. Because of this, the pressure of social development against the hard ceiling did not trigger waves of steppe migration the way it had done in the second and twelfth centuries; and because of that, it seems, even the combined weight of state failure, famine, disease, and climate change was not enough to drive the cores into collapse. The steppe highway had been closed, and with it closed an entire chapter of Old World history.

For nomads this was an unmitigated disaster. Those who survived the wars were increasingly hemmed in. Free movement, the foundation of their way of life, came to depend on the whims of distant emperors, and from the eighteenth century onward the once-proud steppe warriors were increasingly reduced to hired hands, thugs such as the Cossacks, deployed to keep unruly peasants in line.

For the empires, though, closing the steppe highway was a triumph. Inner Asia, so long a source of danger, became a new frontier. As nomad raids declined, a million or two Russians and five or ten million Chinese drifted from the crowded cores to new lands along the edges of the steppe frontier. Once there, those tough enough to make it carved up the landscape for farming, mining, and logging, sending raw materials and taxes back to the empires' heartlands. Closing the steppe highway did not just avert collapse; it also began a steppe bonanza, cracking the hard ceiling that had for millennia limited social development to the low forties on the index.

OPENING THE OCEANS

As the Russians and Chinese were closing the old steppe highway, western Europeans were opening a new oceanic highway that would change history even more dramatically.

For a century after western Europeans first crossed the Atlantic and entered the Indian Ocean, their maritime empires did not seem so very unusual. Venetians had been enriching themselves by tapping Indian

Ocean trade since the thirteenth century; by sailing around Africa's southern tip rather than haggling their way across the Turkish Empire, Portuguese sailors simply did the same thing more cheaply and quickly. In the Americas the Spaniards had entered a wholly New World, but what they did there was really quite like what the Russians would later do in Siberia.

Both Spaniards and Russians outsourced everything possible. Ivan the Terrible gave the Stroganov family a monopoly on everything east of the Urals in return for a cut of the takings; Spain's kings gave more or less anyone who asked the right to keep whatever they could find in the Americas so long as the Habsburgs got 20 percent. In both Siberia and America tiny bands of desperadoes fanned out, scattering stockades built at their own expense across mind-boggling expanses of unmapped territory and constantly writing home for more money and more European women.

Where fur fever drove Russians, bullion fever drove Spaniards. Cortés set Spain on this path by sacking Tenochtitlán in 1521, and Francisco Pizarro speeded them further along it. In 1533 he kidnapped the Inca king Atahualpa and as ransom ordered his subjects to stuff a room twenty-two feet long, seventeen feet across, and nine feet high with treasure. Pizarro melted the accumulated artistic triumphs of Andean civilization into ingots—13,420 pounds of gold and 26,000 pounds of silver—and then strangled Atahualpa anyway.

The relatively easy pickings ran out by 1535, but dreams of El Dorado, the Golden King of a realm where treasure lay all around, kept the cutthroats coming. "Every day they did nothing else but think about gold and silver and the riches of the Indies of Peru," one chronicler lamented. "They were like a man in desperation, crazy, mad, out of their minds with greed for gold and silver."

The madness found a new outlet in 1555, when improved techniques for extracting silver suddenly made New World mining highly profitable. Output was prodigious: some fifty thousand tons of American silver reached Europe between 1540 and 1700, two-thirds of it from Potosí, a mountain in what is now Bolivia that turned out to be virtually solid ore. By the 1580s Europe's stock of silver had doubled and the Habsburg take had grown tenfold—even though, as a Spanish visitor to Potosí claimed in 1638, "Every peso coin minted in Potosí has cost the life of ten Indians." In another parallel with Russia, the

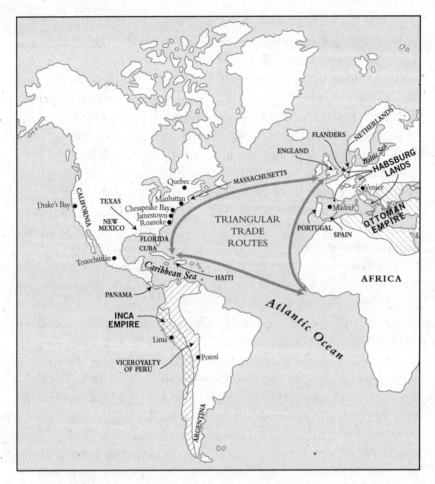

Figure 9.6. The oceanic empires, 1500–1750. The arrows show the major
"triangular trades" of slaves, sugar, rum, food, and manufactured
goods around the Atlantic.

Habsburgs came to look on their conquest of the wild periphery chiefly as a way to finance wars to build a land empire in Europe. "Potosí lives in order to serve the imposing aspirations of Spain," one visitor wrote. "It serves to chastise the Turk, humble the Moor, make Flanders tremble, and terrify England."

The Habsburgs used most of their New World silver to pay their debts to Italian financiers, from whose hands much of the bullion made its way to China, where the booming economy needed all the silver coins it could get. "The king of China could build a palace with the silver bars from Peru which have been carried to his country," one trader thought. Yet although the Habsburg Empire exported silver and the Ming Empire imported it, they otherwise had much in common, worrying more about enlarging their own slice of the economic pie than about enlarging the pie itself. Both empires restricted overseas trade to a chosen few who held easy-to-tax state-backed monopolies.

In theory, Spain allowed just one great galleon full of silver to cross the Atlantic each year, and (again, in theory) regulated trade in other goods just as strictly. In practice, the outcome was like that along China's troubled coasts: those excluded from official sweetheart deals created a huge black market. These "interlopers," like China's smuggling pirates, undersold official dealers by ignoring taxes and shooting anyone who argued.

The French, who bore the brunt of the Habsburgs' European wars in the 1520s–30s, were first into the fray. The earliest recorded pirate attack was in 1536; by the 1550s they were common. "Along the whole coast of [Haiti] there is not a single village that has not been looted by the French," one official complained in 1555. In the 1560s English smugglers also started selling duty-free slaves or landing and robbing mule trains of silver, as opportunities presented themselves. The pickings were good, and within twenty years western Europe's wildest and most desperate men (and a few women) were flocking to join them.

Spain, like China, reacted slowly and halfheartedly. Both empires usually found that ignoring pirates was cheaper than fighting them, and only in the 1560s did Spain, like China, really push back. A decades-long global war on piracy broke out, fought with cutlass and cannon from China to Cuba (and by the Ottomans in the Mediterranean too). In 1575 Spanish and Chinese ships even collaborated against pirates off the Philippines.

By then the Ming and Ottomans had more or less won their pirate wars, but Spain was struggling with the altogether more serious threat of privateering—state-sponsored piracy. Privateers were captains whose rulers gave them licenses and sometimes even ships to plunder the Spaniards, and their nerve knew no limits. In the 1550s the ferocious French privateer Peg-Leg Le Clerc sacked Cuba's main towns and in 1575 England's John Oxenham sailed into the Caribbean, beached his ship near Panama, and dragged two of its cannons across the isthmus. When he reached the Pacific side he cut down trees, built a new ship, took on a crew of runaway slaves, and for a couple of weeks terrorized Peru's defenseless coast.

Oxenham ended up dangling from a rope in Lima, but four years later his old shipmate Francis Drake—equal parts liar, thief, and visionary; in short, the consummate pirate—was back with the even wilder plan of sailing around the bottom of South America and plundering Peru properly. Only one of his six ships made it around Cape Horn, but it was so heavily armed that it instantly established English naval supremacy in the Pacific. Drake proceeded to capture the biggest haul of silver and gold (over twenty-five tons) ever taken from a Spanish vessel, and then, realizing that he could not go back the way he had come, calmly circumnavigated the globe with his loot. Piracy paid: Drake's backers realized a 4,700 percent return on their investment, and using just three-quarters of her share Queen Elizabeth cleared England's entire foreign debt.

Emboldened by success, Spain's rivals sent their own would-be conquistadors to the New World. That went less well. In an extraordinary triumph of hope over experience, France planted a colony at Quebec in 1541 in the expectation of finding gold and spices. Quebec being rather short of both, the colony failed. Nor did the next French effort prosper: copying the Spaniards even more closely, colonists settled almost next door to a Spanish fort in Florida and were promptly massacred.

The first English ventures were equally unrealistic. After terrorizing Peru in 1579 Francis Drake sailed up America's west coast and landed in California (perhaps at the picturesque inlet near San Francisco now known as Drake's Bay). There he informed the locals who met him on the beach that their homeland was now called Nova Albion— New England—and belonged to Queen Elizabeth; whereupon he set off again, never to return.

In 1585 Drake's great rival Walter Raleigh (or Walter Raw Lie, as rivals liked to call him) founded his own colony, Roanoke, in what is now North Carolina. Raleigh was more realistic than Drake and did at least land actual settlers, but his plan to use Roanoke as a pirate lair for raiding Spanish shipping was disastrous. Roanoke was poorly placed, and when Drake sailed past the next year its starving colonists hitched a ride home with him. One of Raleigh's lieutenants dropped a second party at Roanoke (he was supposed to take them to a better site on

Chesapeake Bay, but got lost). No one knows what happened to them; when their governor returned in 1590 he found everyone gone and just a single word—Croatan, their name for Roanoke—carved on a tree.

Life was cheap on this new frontier, and the lives of Native Americans especially so. Spaniards liked to joke that their imperial overlords in Madrid were so inefficient that "if death came from Spain, we would all live forever," but Native Americans probably did not find that very funny. For them death *did* come from Spain. Shielded by the Atlantic and Pacific oceans, they had evolved no defenses against Old World germs, and within a few generations of Columbus's landfall their numbers fell by at least three-quarters. This was the "Columbian Exchange" mentioned in Chapter 6: Europeans got a new continent and Native Americans got smallpox. Although European colonists sometimes visited horrifying cruelty on the people they encountered, death came to natives mostly unseen, as microbes on the breath or in body fluids. It also raced far ahead of the Europeans themselves, transmitted from colonists to natives and then spread inland every time an infected native met one who was still healthy. Consequently, when white men did show their faces, they rarely had much trouble dispossessing the shrunken native populations.

Wherever the land was good, colonists created what the historian and geographer Al Crosby calls "Neo-Europes"—transplanted versions of their homelands, complete with familiar crops, weeds, and animals. And where colonists did not want the land—as in New Mexico, which contained nothing, a Spanish viceroy claimed, but "naked people, false bits of coral, and four pebbles"—their ecological imperialism (another of Crosby's fine phrases) transformed it anyway. From Argentina to Texas, cattle, pigs, and sheep ran off, went wild, bred herds millions strong, and took over the plains.

Better still, colonists created *improved* Europes, where instead of squeezing rent out of surly peasants they could reduce the surviving natives to bondage or—if natives were unavailable—ship in African slaves (the first are attested in 1510; by 1650 they outnumbered Europeans in Spanish America). "Even if you are poor you are better off here than in Spain," one settler wrote home from Mexico, "because here you are always in charge and do not have to work personally, and you are always on horseback."

By building improved Europes the colonists began yet another revolution in the meaning of geography. In the sixteenth century, when
traditional-minded European imperialists had treated the New World
primarily as a source of plunder to finance the struggle for a land empire in Europe, the oceans separating America from the Old World had
been nothing but an annoyance. In the seventeenth century, though,
geographical separation began to seem like a plus. Colonists could exploit the ecological differences between the New World and the Old to
produce commodities that either did not exist in Europe or performed
better in the Americas than at home, then sell them back to European
markets. Instead of being a barrier, the Atlantic was beginning to look
like a highway allowing traders to integrate different worlds.

In 1608 French settlers returned to Quebec, this time as fur traders,
not treasure hunters. They flourished. English settlers at Jamestown
almost starved until they discovered in 1612 that tobacco thrived in
Virginia. The leaf was not as fine as what the Spaniards grew in the
Caribbean, but it was cheap, and soon fortunes were being made. In
1613 Dutch fur traders settled on Manhattan, then bought the whole
island. In the 1620s religious refugees who had fled England for Massachusetts got in on the act too, sending timber for ships' masts back
home. By the 1650s they were sending cattle and dried fish to the Caribbean, where sugar—white gold—was setting off a whole new frenzy.
Settlers and slaves dribbled, then flooded, westward across the Atlantic,
and exotic commodities and taxes washed back eastward.

Up to a point, settlers on new frontiers had always done something
like this. Ancient Greeks sent wheat home from the western Mediterranean; Chinese settlers in the Yangzi Valley shipped rice up the Grand
Canal; and colonists along the edge of the steppe were now dispatching
timber, fur, and minerals to Moscow and Beijing. But the sheer variety
of ecological niches around the Atlantic and the ocean's size—big but
still manageable, given the sophistication of modern shipping—allowed
western Europeans to create something new: an interdependent, inter-
continental economy, linked via overlapping triangular networks of
trade (Figure 9.6).

Rather than just carrying merchandise from A to B, traders could
take western European manufactured goods (textiles, guns, and so on)
to west Africa and exchange them, at a profit, for slaves. Then they

could ship the slaves to the Caribbean and exchange them (again at a profit) for sugar. Finally they could bring the sugar back to Europe, selling it there for more profits, before buying a new consignment of finished goods and setting off to Africa again. Alternatively, Europeans who settled in North America could take rum to Africa and swap it for slaves; then carry the slaves to the Caribbean and exchange them for molasses; then bring the molasses back to North America to make into more rum. Others carried food from North America to the Caribbean (where sugar-producing land was too valuable to waste on growing food for slaves), bought sugar there and carried it to western Europe, finally returning with finished goods for North America.

The advantages of backwardness also contributed. Spain, sixteenth-century Europe's great imperial power, had the most fully developed absolutist monarchy, which generally treated its merchants like cash machines that paid out on demand when threatened and its colonies as sources of plunder. If the Habsburgs had succeeded in forcing their European rivals into a land empire, the Atlantic economy would surely have continued in this vein well into the seventeenth century. Instead, though, merchants from Europe's relatively backward northwestern fringe, where kings were weaker, took matters in a new direction.

Foremost among them were the Dutch. In the fourteenth century the Netherlands had been a waterlogged periphery divided among tiny city-states. In theory the Dutch owed fealty to the Habsburgs, but in practice those busy, distant rulers found that imposing their will on the far northwest was more trouble than it was worth, and left government to the local urban worthies. To survive at all, Dutch cities had to innovate. Lacking wood, they developed peat as an energy source; lacking food, they fished the North Sea and traded their catches for grain around the Baltic Sea; and lacking interfering kings and noblemen, wealthy burghers kept their cities business-friendly. Sound money and sounder policy attracted more money, until by the late sixteenth century the formerly backward Netherlands was Europe's banking hub. Able to borrow at low rates, the Dutch could finance the grinding, endless war of attrition that slowly broke Spanish power.

England moved steadily in the Dutch direction. Before the Black Death, England was already a real kingdom, but its booming wool trade made its merchants more influential than those anywhere outside the Netherlands. Traders took the lead in the seventeenth century in opposing, fighting, and finally beheading their relatively weak ruler, then pushing the government toward building big, state-of-the-art fleets. When a coup d'état/bloodless invasion put a Dutch prince on England's throne in 1688, merchants were among the main beneficiaries.

Spain's grip weakened after 1600 and Dutch and English merchants aggressively pushed into the Atlantic. As Figure 9.3 shows, in 1350 ordinary people's wages had been slightly higher on Europe's Anglo-Dutch northwestern fringe than in the richer but more crowded cities of Italy. After 1600, though, the gap yawned wider and wider. Elsewhere the relentless pressure of hungry mouths drove wages back to pre–Black Death levels, but in the northwest wages came close to returning to where they had been in the golden age of the fifteenth century.

This was not a result of simply extracting wealth from the Americas, as Spain had done, and shipping it to Europe. While experts debate how much of the northwest's new wealth came directly from colonization and trade, even the highest estimates put it below 15 percent (and the lowest at just 5 percent). What was revolutionary about the Atlantic economy was that it changed how people worked.

I have suggested several times in this book that the motors of history are fear, sloth, and greed. Terror tends to trump laziness, and so when population grew after 1450, people leaped into action all over Eurasia out of anxiety about losing status, going hungry, or even starving. But after 1600, greed also began trumping sloth as the Atlantic economy's ecological variety, cheap transport, and open markets brought a world of little luxuries within reach of northwest Europe's everyday folk. By the eighteenth century a man with a little extra cash in his pocket could do more than just buy another loaf of bread; he could get imports such as tea, coffee, tobacco, and sugar, or homemade marvels such as clay pipes, umbrellas, and newspapers. And the same Atlantic economy that generated this bounty also generated people ready to give such a man the cash he needed, because traders would buy every hat, gun, or blanket they could get to ship to Africa or America, and manufacturers would therefore pay people to make them. Some farmers put their families to spinning and weaving; others joined workshops. Some gave up farming altogether; others found that feeding these hungry workers provided steady-enough markets to justify enclosing, draining, and manuring land more intensively and buying more livestock.

The details varied, but northwest Europeans increasingly sold their labor and worked longer hours. And the more they did so, the more sugar, tea, and newspapers they could buy—which meant more slaves dragged across the Atlantic, more acres cleared for plantations, and more factories and shops opened. Sales rose, economies of scale were achieved, and prices fell, opening this world of goods to even more Europeans.

For good or ill, by 1750 the world's first consumer culture had taken shape around the shores of the North Atlantic and was changing millions of lives. Men who would not dare show their faces in a coffee shop unless they sported leather shoes and a pocketwatch—let alone tell their wives that they could not put sugar in the tea when visitors called—were less inclined to take dozens of holy days as holidays or observe the old tradition of "Saint Monday," using that day to sleep off Sunday's hangover. Time was money when there was so much to buy; no more, the novelist Thomas Hardy lamented, did "one-handed clocks sufficiently subdivide the day."

LIKE CLOCKWORK

Two-handed clocks were in fact the least of the demands this new age was making. Westerners wanted to know about seed drills and triangular plows, vacuums and boilers, and clocks that not only had two hands but would keep time even when carried to the far side of the world, allowing sea captains to calculate longitude. For two thousand years—in fact, since the last time Western social development had pressed against the hard ceiling in the low forties on the index—the wise old voices of the ancients had provided guidance for most of life's burning questions. But now it was becoming clear that the classics could not tell people the things they needed to know.

The title of Francis Bacon's 1620 book *Novum Organum* ("New Method") said it all. *Organum* was the label philosophers used for Aristotle's six books on logic; Bacon set out to replace them. "The honour and reverence due to the ancients remains untouched and undiminished," Bacon insisted; his goal, he said, was to "appear merely as a guide to point out the road." Yet once we started down his road, Bacon noted, we would find there was "but one course left . . . to commence a total reconstruction of sciences, arts, and all human knowledge, raised upon the proper foundations."

But what would provide such foundations? Simple, said Bacon (and growing numbers of his peers): observation. Philosophers should get their noses out of books and look instead at the things all around them—stars and insects, cannons and oars, falling apples and wobbling chandeliers. And they should talk to blacksmiths, clockmakers, and mechanics, people who knew how things worked.

When they did so, thought Bacon, Galileo, the French philosopher René Descartes, and legions of lesser-known scholars, they could hardly avoid coming to the same conclusion: that contrary to what most of the ancients said, nature was not a living, breathing organism, with desires and intentions. It was actually mechanical. In fact, it was very like a clock. God was a clockmaker, switching on the interlocking gears that made nature run and then stepping back. And if that was so, then humans should be able to disentangle nature's workings as easily as those of any other mechanism. After all, Descartes mused, "it is not less natural for a clock, made of the requisite number of wheels, to indicate the hours, than for a tree which has sprung from this or that seed, to produce a particular fruit."

This clockwork model of nature—plus some fiendishly clever experimenting and reasoning—had extraordinary payoffs. Secrets hidden since the dawn of time were abruptly, startlingly, revealed. Air, it turned out, was a substance, not an absence; the heart pumped blood around the body, like a water bellows; and, most bewilderingly, Earth was not the center of the universe.

All these discoveries, contradicting the ancients and even scripture, produced firestorms of criticism. Galileo's reward for watching the skies was to be dragged before a papal court in 1633 and browbeaten into retracting what he knew to be true. Yet all that the bullying really accomplished was to accelerate the new thinking's migration from the old Mediterranean core to the northwest, where social development was rising fastest, the shortcomings of ancient thinking seemed clearest, and anxieties about challenging authority were weakest.

Northerners began turning the Renaissance on its head, rejecting antiquity instead of seeking answers in it, and in the 1690s, as social development nudged within a hair's breadth of its peak under the Roman Empire, learned gentlemen in Paris formally debated whether the

Moderns were now surpassing the Ancients. By then the answer was obvious to anyone with eyes to see. Isaac Newton's *Principia Mathematica* had appeared in 1687, using the new tool of calculus that Newton himself developed to express his mechanical model of the heavens mathematically.* It was as incomprehensible (even to educated readers) as Einstein's general theory of relativity would be when he published it in 1905, but all the same, everyone agreed (as they would about relativity) that it marked a new age.

Hyperbole seemed inadequate for such monuments of mind. When called upon to immortalize Newton, England's leading poet, Alexander Pope, exclaimed,

> *Nature, and Nature's laws lay hid in night,*
> *God said* Let Newton be! *And all was* Light.

In reality, the shift from night to day was a little less abrupt. Newton's *Principia* came out just five years after England's last witch-hanging and five years before the Salem witch trials in Massachusetts began. Newton himself, as became clear when thousands of his personal papers were auctioned off in 1936, was as enthusiastic about alchemy as about gravity, remaining convinced to the end that he would turn lead into gold. Nor was he the only seventeenth-century scientist to hold views that today seem distinctly odd. But gradually Westerners were disenchanting the world, dispersing its spirits and devils with mathematics. Numbers became the measure of reality.

According to Galileo,

> Philosophy is written in this grand book, the universe, which stands
> continually open to our gaze . . . It is written in the language of math-
> ematics, and its characters are triangles, circles, and other geometric
> figures without which it is humanly impossible to understand a single
> word of it; without these, one wanders about in a dark labyrinth.

---

*Unless, that is, the German thinker Gottfried Leibniz, who was working on similar mathematical methods in the 1670s, in fact developed calculus first and Newton just stole the credit. Most likely the two thinkers invented calculus independently, but mutual accusations of plagiarism eventually poisoned their relationship.

And what was true of nature, some scientists speculated, might be true of society too. Up to a point, government officials—especially financiers—welcomed this thought. The state, too, could be seen as a machine; statisticians could calculate its revenue flows and ministers could calibrate its intricate gears. But the new ways of thinking were also worrying. Natural science had taken its new turn by exposing ancient authority as arbitrary; would social science do the same to kings and the church?

If scientists were right and observation and logic were really the best tools for understanding God's will, then it stood to reason that they would be the best tools for running governments, too. It was equally reasonable, the English theorist John Locke argued, that in the beginning God had endowed humans with certain natural rights; "Man," he deduced, "hath by nature a power . . . to preserve his property—that is, his life, liberty, and estate—against the injuries and attempts of other men." Therefore, Locke concluded, "The great and chief end . . . of men's uniting into commonwealths, and putting themselves under government, is the preservation of their property." And if that was so, and if man was "by nature all free, equal, and independent, [then] no one can be put out of this estate, and subjected to the political power of another, without his own consent."

These ideas would have been troubling enough if they had been limited to intellectuals arguing in Latin in ivy-clad colleges. But they were not. First in Paris, then more widely, wealthy women sponsored salons where scholars rubbed shoulders with the mighty and new thinking moved back and forth. Amateurs established discussion clubs, inviting lecturers to explain new ideas and demonstrate experiments. Cheaper printing, better distribution, and rising literacy allowed new journals, combining reporting with social criticism and readers' letters, to spread the ferment to tens of thousands of readers. Three centuries before Starbucks, enterprising coffeehouse owners realized that if they provided free newspapers and comfortable chairs, patrons would sit there—reading, arguing, and buying coffee—all day long. Something new was coming into being: public opinion.

Opinion makers liked to say that enlightenment was spreading across Europe, shining illumination into dark recesses obscured by centuries of superstition. But what was enlightenment? The German thinker Immanuel Kant was blunt: "Dare to know! Have the courage to use your own understanding!"

The challenge to established authority was glaring, but rather than fight it, most eighteenth-century monarchs compromised. They insisted that they had been enlightened despots all along, ruling rationally for the common good. "Philosophers should be the teachers of the world and the teachers of princes," the king of Prussia wrote; "they must think logically and we must act logically."

In practice, though, princes often found their subjects' logic annoying. In Britain* kings just had to put up with it, and in Spain they could silence it, but France was sufficiently avant-garde (a French term, after all) to be swarming with enlightened critics yet sufficiently absolutist to imprison them and ban their books from time to time. It was, the historian Thomas Carlyle thought, "a despotism tempered by epigrams"—which made it a perfect garden where enlightenment could blossom.

Of all the books and bons mots that set Paris atwitter in the 1750s, none matched the aggressively enlightened *Encyclopedia or Reasoned Dictionary of the Sciences, the Arts, and the Crafts.* "One must examine and stir up everything, without exception and without caution," wrote one of its editors. "We must trample underfoot all that old foolishness; overturn barriers not put there by reason; restore to the sciences and arts their precious liberty." One bewigged rebel after another insisted that slavery, colonialism, and the legal inferiority of women and Jews were contrary to nature and reason, and from exile in Switzerland in the 1760s the greatest wit of all, Voltaire, challenged even what he labeled "the infamous thing"—the privileges of church and crown.

Voltaire knew exactly where Europeans should be looking for more enlightened models: China. There, he insisted, they would find a truly wise despot, ruling in consultation with a rational civil service, abstaining from pointless wars and religious persecution. They would also find Confucianism, which (unlike Christianity) was a faith of reason, free from superstition and foolish legends.

Voltaire was not entirely wrong, for Chinese intellectuals had already been challenging absolutism for a century before he was born.

---

*In 1707 the Act of Union linked England, Wales, and Scotland into a single kingdom of Great Britain; a separate act added Ireland in 1800.

Printing had created an even broader readership for new ideas than in western Europe, and private scholarly institutes had revived. The most famous of them, the Donglin Academy, confronted the infamous thing even more directly than did Voltaire. In the 1630s its director promoted self-reliance, urging scholars to seek answers through their own judgment, not in older texts,* and one Donglin scholar after another was jailed, tortured, or executed for criticizing the Ming court.

The intellectual critique only intensified when the conquering Qing dynasty took control in 1644. Hundreds of scholars refused to work for the Manchus. One such was Gu Yanwu, a low-level civil servant who never passed the highest examinations. Gu took himself off to the distant frontiers, far from the tyrants' taint. There he turned his back on the metaphysical nitpicking that had dominated intellectual life since the twelfth century and, like Francis Bacon in England, tried instead to understand the world by observing the physical things that real people actually did.

For nearly forty years Gu traveled, filling notebooks with detailed descriptions of farming, mining, and banking. He became famous and others copied him, particularly doctors who had been horrified by their impotence in the face of the epidemics of the 1640s. Collecting case histories of actual sick people, they insisted on testing theories against real results. By the 1690s even the emperor was proclaiming the advantages of "studying the root of a problem, discussing it with ordinary people, and then having it solved."

Eighteenth-century intellectuals called this approach *kaozheng*, "evidential research." It emphasized facts over speculation, bringing methodical, rigorous approaches to fields as diverse as mathematics, astronomy, geography, linguistics, and history, and consistently developing rules for assessing evidence. *Kaozheng* paralleled western Europe's scientific revolution in every way—except one: it did not develop a mechanical model of nature.

Like Westerners, Eastern scholars were often disappointed in the learning they had inherited from the last time social development approached the hard ceiling around forty-three points on the index (in their case under the Song dynasty in the eleventh and twelfth centu-

---

*The director, Chen Zilong, took inspiration from the arguments of Wang Yangming, mentioned on p. 426 above.

ries). But instead of rejecting its basic premise of a universe motivated by spirit (*qi*) and imagining instead one running like a machine, Easterners mostly chose to look back to still more venerable authorities, the texts of the ancient Han dynasty. Even Gu Yanwu was as excited about ancient inscriptions as about mining or agriculture, and many of the doctors gathering case histories rejoiced as much in using them to clarify Han medical texts as in curing people. Instead of turning the Renaissance on its head, Chinese intellectuals chose a Second Renaissance. Many were scholars of brilliance, but because of this choice none became Galileos or Newtons.

This was where Voltaire went wrong. He was holding China up as a model at the very moment it was ceasing to provide one—at exactly the moment, in fact, that some of his rivals in Europe's salons started drawing exactly opposite conclusions about China. Although they had no index to tell them that Western social development had whittled away the East's lead, these men decided that China was not the ideal enlightened empire at all. Rather, it was the antithesis of everything European. Whereas Europeans had learned dynamism, reason, and creativity from ancient Greece and were now surpassing their teacher, China was the land where time stood still.

Thus was the long-term lock-in theory of Western superiority born. The Baron de Montesquieu decided that climate was the ultimate explanation: bracing weather gave Europeans (particularly Frenchmen) "a certain vigor of body and mind, which renders them patient and intrepid, and qualifies them for arduous enterprises," while "the effeminacy of people in hot climates has always rendered them slaves . . . there reigns in Asia a servile spirit, which they have never been able to shake off."

Other Europeans went further. The Chinese were not just servile, they argued: they were a different kind of human. Carolus Linnaeus, the founding father of genetics, claimed to recognize four races of humans—white Europeans, yellow Asians, red Americans, and black Africans; and in the 1770s the philosopher David Hume decided that only the white race was capable of real civilization. Kant even wondered whether yellow people were a proper race at all. Perhaps, he mused, they were merely bastard offspring of interbreeding between Indians and Mongols.

Daring to know, apparently, was for Europeans only.

TRIAL BY TELESCOPE

In 1937 three young scientists-in-training took ship from Nanjing, China's capital, for England. It would have been hard enough under any circumstances to exchange their bustling, chaotic hometown (known as one of the "four furnaces" of China for its steaming humidity) for the hushed cloisters, relentless drizzle, and cutting winds of Cambridge; but the circumstances that summer were particularly tough. The three did not know if they would ever see their families and friends again. A Japanese army was closing in on Nanjing. In December it would butcher thousands of their fellow citizens so brutally that even a Nazi official caught up in the disaster was shocked.

Nor could the three refugees anticipate much of a welcome when they arrived. Nowadays Cambridge's scientific laboratories teem with Chinese students, but in 1937 the legacy of Hume and Kant was still strong. The three caused quite a stir, and Joseph Needham, a rising star at the Biochemistry Institute, was more stirred than anyone. One of the students, Lu Gwei-djen, wrote that "the more he got to know us, the more exactly like himself in scientific grasp and intellectual penetration he found us to be; and this led his inquisitive mind to wonder why therefore had modern science originated only in the western world?"

Needham had no training in languages or history, but he did have one of the sharpest, quirkiest minds in a university famous for both. Lu became his lover and helped him master China's language and past; so desperately did Needham fall in love with Lu's native land, in fact, that in 1942 he forsook the safety of his college for a Foreign Office posting to Chongqing to help China's universities survive the disastrous war with Japan. The BBC wrote to ask him to record his impressions, but Needham did rather more. In the margin of their letter he jotted a query that would change his life: *"Sci. in general in China—why not develop?"*

This question—why, after so many centuries of Chinese scientific preeminence, it was western Europeans who created modern science in the seventeenth century—is now generally known as "the Needham Problem." Needham was still wrestling with it when I got to know him, forty years later (my wife was studying anthropology in the Cambridge college where Lu Gwei-djen—still Needham's lover—held a fellowship, and we rented the upper floor of Dr. Lu's house). He never did solve his problem, but thanks in large part to his decades of work cataloguing Chinese scientific accomplishments we are now vastly better placed to understand what happened than we were in the 1930s.

As we saw in Chapter 7, China had made particularly rapid scientific and technological advances when its social development pressed against the hard ceiling in the eleventh century, but these were derailed when development collapsed. The real question is why, when development again pressed against the hard ceiling in the seventeenth and eighteenth centuries, Chinese intellectuals did not, like Europeans, create mechanical models of nature and unlock its secrets.

The answer, once again, is that intellectuals ask the questions that social development forces onto them: each age gets the thought it needs. Western Europeans, with their new frontier across the oceans, needed precise measurements of standardized space, money, and time, and by the point that two-handed clocks had become the norm Europeans would have to have been positively obtuse not to wonder whether nature itself was a mechanism. Likewise, the West's ruling classes would have needed to be still more obtuse not to see enough advantages in scientific thinking to take a chance on cutting its eccentric, unpredictable thinkers a little slack. Like the first and second waves of Axial thought and the Renaissance, the scientific revolution and Enlightenment were initially consequences, rather than causes, of the West's rising social development.

The East also had its own new frontier on the steppes, of course, but this was a more traditional kind of frontier than the Atlantic, and the need for new thought was correspondingly less pressing. Natural and social philosophers did ask some of the same questions as western Europeans, but the need to recast thought in terms of mechanical models of the universe remained less obvious; and to the Qing rulers, who badly needed to win China's intellectuals over to their new regime, the dangers of indulging radical thought massively outweighed any possible advantages.

The Qing court did everything possible to woo scholars back to state service from their private academies and fact-finding tours of the frontiers. It set up special examinations, paid generously, and flattered mercilessly. The young emperor Kangxi assiduously presented himself as a Confucian, convening a special group of scholars to study the classics with him and in 1670 issuing a "Sacred Edict" demonstrating his seriousness. He funded huge encyclopedias (his *Complete Collection of Illustrations and Writings from the Earliest to Current Times,* published shortly after his death, ran to 800,000 pages),* but instead of stirring up everything, like contemporary French encyclopedias, these books aimed to stir up nothing at all, faithfully preserving ancient texts and providing sinecures for loyalist scholars.

The strategy was a stunning success, and as intellectuals drifted back to state service, they turned *kaozheng* itself into a career path. Candidates for the examinations had to display evidential research, but only scholars with access to good libraries could master it, which effectively blocked everyone outside the narrowest elite from high scores. The lure of profitable niches as state servants was a powerful incentive to conventional thought.

I will postpone until Chapter 10 the most important question— whether, given more time, Chinese intellectuals would have had their own scientific revolution. As things actually turned out, Westerners did not give them time. Jesuit missionaries had been infiltrating China from Macao since the 1570s, and though they came to save souls, not to sell science, they knew that good gifts make for welcome guests. Western clocks were a big hit; so, too, eyeglasses. One of China's greatest poets, whose vision had long been fading, described with joy how

> *Clear glass from across the Western Seas*
> *Is imported through Macao.*
> *Fashioned into lenses big as coins,*
> *They encompass one's vision in a double frame.*
> *I put them on—things suddenly become clear.*
> *I can see the very tips of things!*
> *And read fine print by the dim-lit window*
> *Just like in my youth.*

---

*Its successor, *The Complete Library of the Four Treasuries,* completed in 1782, filled a staggering 36,000 volumes.

The biggest gift the Jesuits brought, though, was astronomy. The missionaries knew that calendars were a weighty matter in China; celebrating the winter solstice on the wrong day could throw the cosmos out of joint just as badly as getting Easter wrong would do in Christendom. So seriously did Chinese officials take this that they would even employ foreigners in the Bureau of Astronomy if the aliens—mostly Arabs and Persians—demonstrably knew more about the stars than did natives.

The Jesuits sensibly saw this as their best route to China's rulers. Jesuit mathematicians had been deeply involved in reforming the Catholic calendar in the 1580s, and although their astronomy was out-of-date by northwest European standards (they resolutely stuck to Earth-centered models of the universe), it was better than anything available in China.

At first all went swimmingly. By 1610 several senior civil servants, impressed by Jesuitical mathematics, secretly converted to Christianity. They openly promoted Western scholarship as superior to Chinese and translated European textbooks. More traditional scholars sometimes took offense at this unpatriotic attitude, though, so in the 1630s the Jesuits' main backer began taking a subtler line. "Melting the material and substance of Western knowledge," he assured his compatriots, "we will cast them into the mold of the [traditional Chinese] Grand Concordance system." Maybe, he even suggested, Western learning was in fact a spin-off from earlier Chinese wisdom.

When the Manchus seized Beijing in 1644 the Jesuits proposed—and won—a public tournament of solar eclipse prediction. Their prestige had never been higher, and for a few heady months in 1656 it even looked as if the emperor might convert to Christianity. Victory seemed at hand, until the teenage monarch grasped that Christians could not keep concubines. He turned Buddhist instead. Traditionalists then struck back, denouncing the Jesuits' leader as a spy.

In 1664 another trial by telescope was ordered, with the Jesuits, the Bureau of Astronomy, and a Muslim astronomer each predicting the time of an upcoming solar eclipse. Two fifteen, said the Bureau; two thirty, said the Muslim; three o'clock, said the Jesuits. Lenses were set up to project the sun's image into a darkened room. Two fifteen came and went with no eclipse. Two thirty: still nothing. But at almost exactly three a shadow began creeping across the fiery disk.

Not good enough, the judges decided, and banned Christianity.

That, it seemed, was that—except for the niggling fact that the Chinese calendar was still wrong. So, as soon as he took the throne in 1668, the emperor Kangxi arranged a rematch. Again the Jesuits won.

Convinced of the Jesuits' superiority, Kangxi threw himself into their teaching, sitting for hours with priests, learning their arithmetic, geometry, and mechanics. He even took up the harpsichord. "I realized that Western mathematics has its uses," the emperor wrote. "On inspection tours later I used these Western methods to show my officials how to make more accurate calculations when planning their river works."

Kangxi recognized that "the 'new methods' of calculating make basic errors impossible" and that "the general principles of Western calendrical science are without error," but still resisted the Jesuits' larger claims for their science and their God. "Even though some of the Western methods are different from our own, and may even be an improvement, there is little about them that is new," Kangxi concluded. "The principles of mathematics all derive from the *Book of Changes*, and the Western methods are Chinese in origin . . . After all," he added, "they know only a fraction of what I know."

In 1704 the pope, worried that the Jesuits were promoting astronomy more vigorously than Christianity, sent an emissary to Beijing to keep a closer eye on them, and Kangxi, worried that this amounted to sedition, sidelined the missionaries. He set up new scientific academies (loosely modeled on the Academy of Sciences in Paris) where Chinese scientists could pursue astronomy and mathematics free from Jesuit influence. The mathematics the Jesuits were teaching, with little algebra and less calculus, was already decades behind northern Europe's, but as soon as Kangxi cut this link with Western science the East-West scholarly gap widened into a chasm.

It is tempting to see Kangxi (Figure 9.7) as the solution to Needham's Problem, the bungling idiot who could have brought Chinese science into the eighteenth century but chose not to. Yet of all the men (and the one woman) who sat on the Celestial Throne, Kangxi is surely among the least-deserving of such a label. Saying that the Jesuits knew only a fraction of what he knew was immodest, but not altogether wrong. Kangxi was a true intellectual, a strong leader, and a man of action (including fathering fifty-six children). He looked at the

Figure 9.7. The great bungler? Kangxi, emperor of China, painted by
the Italian artist Giovanni Gherardi around 1700

Westerners in a larger context. For two thousand years Chinese emperors had recognized that nomad war-making was superior to their
own, and had usually found buying the horsemen off less risky than
fighting them. When that changed, Kangxi was the first to recognize
it, and personally led the campaigns that began closing the steppe highway in the 1690s. With the Westerners, things worked the other way
around. Kangxi had engaged with Westerners since the 1660s, but after 1704 ignoring them started to seem less risky. Some Southeast Asian
rulers had reached the same conclusion in the sixteenth century, and
Japan's shoguns followed suit by 1613. A violent, Christian-tinged uprising in Japan in 1637 only seemed to confirm the wisdom of this
decision to sever links with the West. In this context, Kangxi's decision seemed no bungle.

And in any case, there is another question we must ask. Even if Kangxi had foreseen where Western science would go and had promoted it, could he have kept Eastern social development ahead of Western in the eighteenth century?

The answer is almost certainly no. China did face some of the same problems as northwest Europe, and some of its thinkers did move in similar directions. In the 1750s, for instance, Dai Zhen (like Gu Yanwu, a low-level functionary who never won the highest degree) propounded something like the Western vision of a mechanical nature functioning without intentions or goals and open to empirical analysis. But Dai, an excellent philologist, always grounded his arguments in ancient texts; at the end of the day, preserving the glories of the past seemed more important in China than addressing the kind of questions that global expansion was forcing onto Westerners' attention.

The challenges of the Atlantic frontier produced Westerners who clamored for answers to new kinds of questions. The Newtons and Leibnizes who responded won fame and fortune beyond anything earlier scientists could have imagined, and new kinds of theorists, the likes of Locke and Voltaire, traced out the implications of these advances for the social order. China's new steppe frontier, by contrast, produced much milder challenges. The well-paid scholars in Kangxi's scientific institutes felt no need to invent calculus for themselves or figure out that the earth went around the sun. There seemed to be much more profit in turning mathematics—like medicine—into a branch of classical studies.

East and West each got the thought they needed.

THE IRON LAW

When Kangxi died in 1722, social development was moving higher than ever before. Twice in the past, in the Roman Empire around 100 CE and Song dynasty China a thousand years later, development had reached forty-three points, only to generate disasters that drove it down again. By 1722, though, the steppe highway had been closed. One of the horsemen of the apocalypse was dead and social development did not collapse when it hit the hard ceiling. Instead, the new frontier along the edge of the steppes allowed Eastern development to keep rising, while northwest Europeans, shielded from steppe migrations by the Chinese and Russian empires, opened their own new frontier on the Atlantic. Western development rose even faster than Eastern, passing it in 1773 (or thereabouts). It was a new age at both ends of Eurasia.

Or was it? If someone from Rome or Song China had been transplanted to eighteenth-century London or Beijing he or she would certainly have had many surprises. Such as guns. Or America. Or tobacco, coffee, and chocolate. And as for the fashions—powdered wigs? Manchu pigtails? Corsetry? Bound feet? *O tempora, O mores!* ("Oh the times! Oh, the customs!"), as Cicero liked to say.

Yet more, in fact much more, would have seemed familiar. The modern world's great gunpowder armies were certainly stronger than those of antiquity and far more people could and did read than ever before, but neither East nor West could boast a million-strong city like ancient Rome or medieval Kaifeng.* Most important of all, though, the visitors from the past would have noticed that although social development was moving higher than ever, the *ways* people were pushing it up hardly differed from how Romans and Song Chinese had pushed it up. Farmers were using more manure, digging more ditches, rotating crops, and cutting back on fallow. Craftsmen were burning more wood to cast more metal, and, when wood grew scarce, turning to coal. More and bigger animals were being bred to turn wheels, lift weights, and pull better carts along smoother roads. Wind and water were being harnessed more effectively to crush ores, grind grains, and move boats down straightened rivers and artificial canals. Yet while the Song and Roman visitors would probably have conceded that many things were bigger and better in the eighteenth century than in the eleventh or first, they would not have conceded that things were fundamentally different.

There was the rub. The conquest of the steppes and oceans had not shattered the hard ceiling that the Romans and Song had encountered around forty-three points: they had merely pushed it up a little, and by 1750 there were alarming signs that development was once more

---

*In the East, Beijing had about 650,000 residents in 1722 and Edo (modern Tokyo) probably had slightly more; in the West, London may have had 600,000 people and Istanbul/Constantinople perhaps 700,000.

straining against it. The right-hand side of Figure 9.3, showing real wages, is not a pretty picture. By 1750 living standards were falling everywhere, even in Europe's dynamic northwest. As the Eastern and Western cores strained to push the hard ceiling upward, times were getting harder.

What was to be done? The bureaucrats of Beijing, the salon-goers of Paris, and every self-respecting intellectual in between threw out theories. Some argued that all wealth came from farming, and set about persuading rulers to dole out tax breaks to farmers who drained marshes or terraced hillsides. From Yunnan to Tennessee, shacks and log cabins crept farther into the forests where less-developed communities hunted. Other theorists insisted that all wealth came from trade, so rulers (often the same ones) poured even more resources into beggaring their neighbors by stealing their commerce.

There was immense variation, but on the whole Western rulers (who had been fighting so furiously since the fifteenth century) thought war would solve their problems, while Eastern rulers (who had generally been fighting less furiously) thought it would not. Japan was the extreme case. After pulling out of Korea in 1598 its leaders decided that there were no profits in conquest, and by the 1630s even concluded that overseas trade was merely losing them valuable goods such as silver and copper. Chinese and Dutch (the only Europeans allowed into Japan by 1640) merchants were hemmed into tiny ghettos in Nagasaki, where the only women allowed to join them were Japanese prostitutes. Not surprisingly, foreign trade dwindled.

Protected from aggression by the wide blue sea, Japan flourished until about 1720. Its population doubled and Edo grew into perhaps the world's biggest city. Rice, fish, and soy replaced cheaper foods in most people's diets. And peace reigned: having surrendered their guns to Hideyoshi back in 1587, ordinary Japanese never rearmed. Even the touchy samurai warriors agreed to sort out their quarrels by swordplay alone, which amazed the Westerners who bullied their way into Japan in the 1850s. "These people seemed scarcely to know the use of firearms," one remembered. "It strikes an American, who has from his childhood seen children shoot, that ignorance of arms is an anomaly indicative of primitive innocence and Arcadian simplicity."

After 1720, though, the picture steadily darkened. Japan was full. Without a technological breakthrough there was no way to squeeze more food, fuel, clothing, and housing out of the crowded landscape, and without trade there was no way to bring more in. Japanese farmers displayed astonishing ingenuity, and Japanese officials realized the damage that fuel hunger had done to their forests and actively protected them. Japanese elite culture turned toward an austere, beautiful minimalism that conserved resources. But still food prices rose, famines increased, and hungry mobs protested in the streets. This was no Arcadia.

The only reason Japan could take this extreme path was that China, the one credible threat to its security, moved the same way. China's broad, open frontiers meant that population could continue growing through the eighteenth century, but the Qing, too, increasingly shut out the dangerous world across the waters. In 1760 all foreign trade was restricted to Guangzhou, and when Britain's East India Company sent Lord Macartney to complain about the restrictions in 1793 the emperor Qianlong imperiously replied, "We have never valued ingenious articles, nor do we have the slightest need of your country's manufactures." Further contact, he concluded, "is not in harmony with the regulations of the Celestial Empire [and] . . . is of no advantage to your country."

Few Western rulers shared Qianlong's faith in isolation. The world they lived in was not dominated by a single great empire like Qing China; rather, it was a place of squabbles and constantly shifting balances of power. As most Western rulers saw things, even if the world's wealth was fixed, a nation could always grab a bigger slice of the pie. Every florin, franc, or pound spent on war would pay for itself, and as long as some rulers felt that way, all rulers had to be ready to fight. Western Europe's arms race never stopped.

Europe's merchants of death constantly improved the tools of their trade (better bayonets, prepackaged gunpowder cartridges, faster firing mechanisms), but the real breakthroughs came from organizing violence more scientifically. Discipline—things such as uniforms, agreed-on ranks, and firing squads for officers who just did what they liked (as opposed to ordinary soldiers, who had always been punished brutally)—worked wonders, and adding year-round training created fighting machines that performed complex maneuvers and fired their weapons steadily.

Such orderly dogs of war delivered more kills for the guilder. First the Dutch and then their rivals eliminated the cheap but nasty tradition of outsourcing war to private contractors who hired rabbles of killers, paid them irregularly or never, then turned them loose to extort income from civilians. War remained hell, but acquired at least a few limits.

The same was true at sea, where the curtain came down on the age of the Jolly Roger, walking the plank, and buried treasure. England led the way in a new war on piracy, which, like China's in the sixteenth century, was as much about corruption as about swashbuckling. When the notorious Captain Morgan had ignored an English peace treaty with Spain and sacked Spanish colonies in the Caribbean in 1671, his well-placed backers had helped him to a knighthood and the governorship of Jamaica. By 1701, though, the equally notorious Captain Kidd found himself hauled to London merely for robbing an English ship, and upon arriving learned that his own well-placed backers (including the king) could or would not help him. Spending his last shilling on rum, Captain Kidd was dragged to the gallows, roaring, "I am the innocentest person of all!"—only for the rope to break. Once upon a time that might have saved him, but not now. A second noose did the job. By 1718, when the navy closed in on Blackbeard (Edward Teach), no one even tried to help. Blackbeard took even more killing than Kidd—five musket balls and twenty-five sword strokes—but kill him the sailors did. That year there were fifty pirate raids in the Caribbean; by 1726 there were just six. The age of rampage was over.

All this cost money, and the advances in organization depended on even greater advances in finance. No government could actually afford to feed, pay, and supply soldiers and sailors year-round, but the Dutch again found the solution: credit. It takes money to make money, and because the Netherlands had such steady income from trade and such solid banks to handle its cash, its merchant rulers could borrow bigger sums, faster, at lower interest rates, and pay them back over longer periods than spendthrift rivals.

Once more England followed the Dutch lead. By 1700 both countries had national banks, managing a public debt by selling long-term bonds on a stock exchange, with their governments calming lenders' jitters by committing specific taxes to pay interest on the bonds. The results were spectacular. As Daniel Defoe (the author of *Robinson Crusoe*, that epic of the new oceanic highways) explained,

> Credit makes war, and makes peace; raises armies, fits out navies, fights battles, besieges towns; and, in a word, it is more justly called the sinews of war than the money itself . . . Credit makes the soldier fight without pay, the armies march without provisions . . . and fills the Exchequer and the banks with as many millions as it pleases, upon demand.

Limitless credit meant war without end. Britain had to fight for twenty years to win the biggest slice of the trade pie from the Dutch, but that victory just paved the way for an even greater struggle. France's rulers seemed bent on achieving the kind of land empire that had eluded the Habsburgs, and, British politicians feared, "France will undo us at sea when they have nothing to fear on land." The only answer, Britain's prime minister William Pitt (the Elder) insisted, was to "conquer America through Germany," bankrolling continental coalitions to keep the French tied up in Europe while Britain snapped up its colonies overseas.

Anglo-French wars filled more than half the years between 1689, when France's first attempt to invade England failed, and 1815, when Wellington finally defeated Napoleon at Waterloo. This epic struggle was nothing less than a War of the West, fought for domination of the European core. Great armies volleyed and charged in Germany and dug trenches in Flanders; men-of-war blasted and boarded each other off the stormy French coast and in the sparkling waters of the Mediterranean; and in the forests of Canada and Ohio, the plantations of the Caribbean, and the jungles of west Africa and Bengal, European and (especially) local allies fought dozens of bitter, self-contained little wars that added up to make the War of the West the first worldwide struggle.

There was daring and treachery enough to fill many a book, yet the real story was told in pounds, shillings, and pence. Credit constantly replenished Britain's armies or fleets, but France could not pay its bills. "Our bells are threadbare with ringing of victories," one well-placed Briton bragged in 1759, and in 1763 the exhausted French had no option but to sign away most of their overseas empire (Figure 9.8).

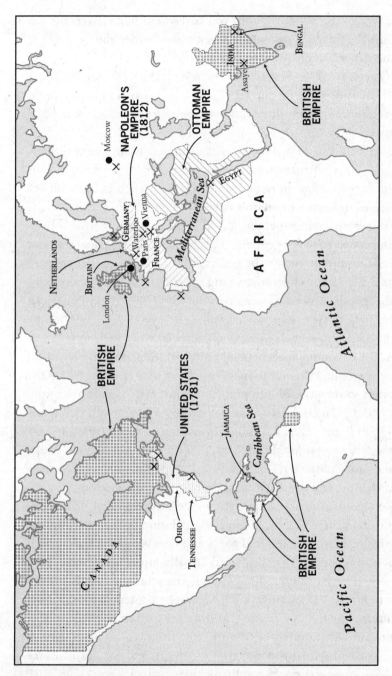

Figure 9.8. All the world's a stage: the global setting of the War of the West, fought by Britain and its allies against France between 1689 and 1815. Crossed swords mark some of the major battles; the British Empire as it was in 1815 is marked by dots.

The War of the West, though, was barely half done. Even Britain was feeling the financial strain, and when a poorly thought-out scheme to get the American colonists to pick up part of the check for the war set off a revolt in 1776, France was there with the cash and ships that made all the difference for the rebels. Not even Britain's credit could master determined rebels three thousand miles from home *and* another great power.

Finance could, though, take away the sting of defeat. In any reasonable world, losing America to revolutionaries who celebrated their pursuit of happiness in language inspired by the French Enlightenment should have bankrupted Britain's Atlantic economy and ushered in a French imperium in Europe. Pitt feared as much, warning that if Britain lost he expected every gentleman in England to sell up and ship out to America, but trade and credit again came to the rescue. Britain paid down its debts, kept its fleets patrolling the sea-lanes, and went on carrying the goods Americans still needed. By 1789 Anglo-American trade was back to prerevolution levels.

For France, however, 1789 was a disaster. To win the American war Louis XVI had run up debts he could not pay, so he now convened his nobles, clergy, and rich commoners to ask for new taxes, only for the commoners to turn the Enlightenment against him, too. Proclaiming the Rights of Man (and, two years later, those of Woman), rich commoners found themselves half stage-managing and half trying to stay out of the way of an unpredictable spiral of revolt and civil war. "Make terror the order of the day!" the radicals shouted, then executed their king, his family, and thousands of their fellow revolutionaries.

Once again reasonable expectations were confounded. Instead of leaving Britain master of the West, the revolution opened the way for new forms of mass warfare, and for a few heady years it looked as if Napoleon, its general of genius, would finally create a European land empire. In 1805 he mustered his Grand Army for the fourth French attempt to invade Britain since 1689; "Let us be masters of the Channel for six hours," he told the troops, "and we are masters of the world!"

Napoleon never got his six hours, and although he made British traders' worst nightmares come true by shutting them out of every harbor in Europe, he could not break their financial power. In 1812 Napoleon controlled a quarter of Europe's population and a French army was in Moscow; two years later he was out of power and a Russian army (on the British payroll) was in Paris; and in 1815 diplomats at the great Congress of Vienna thrashed out terms that would damp down the War of the West for the next ninety-nine years.

Did all these wars in the end make much difference? In a way, yes. In 1683, on the eve of the Anglo-French conflict, Vienna was again under siege by a Turkish army, but by the time the great and the good convened there in 1815 the War of the West had pushed western European firepower, discipline, and finance far ahead of anything else in the world, and Turkish armies came no more. When Napoleon invaded Egypt in 1798 the Ottomans had to rely on Britain to throw him out, and in 1803 fewer than five thousand British troops (half of them recruited locally and trained in European musketry) would scatter ten times their number of South Asians at Assaye. The balance of military power had shifted, spectacularly, toward western Europe.

But in another way, no. Despite all the battles and bombardments, real wages kept falling after 1750. Beginning in the 1770s, a new breed of scholars, calling themselves political economists, brought all the tools of science and enlightenment to bear on the problem. The news they brought back from their researches was not good: there were, they claimed, iron laws governing humanity. First, although empire and conquest might raise productivity and income, people would always convert extra wealth into more babies. The babies' empty bellies would then consume all the extra wealth, and, worse still, when the babies grew up and needed jobs of their own, their competition would drive wages back down to the edge of starvation.

There appeared to be no way out of this cruel cycle. Had the political economists known about the index of social development they would probably have pointed out that although the hard ceiling had been pushed up a little, it remained as hard as ever. They might have been fascinated to learn that the West's score had caught up with the East's in 1773, but would surely have said it did not really matter, because the iron laws forbade either score from rising much further. Political economy had proved scientifically that nothing could ever really change.

But then it did.

10

⊚ ⊛ ⊚

THE WESTERN AGE

WHAT ALL THE WORLD DESIRES

Once in a while a single year seems to shift the ground under our feet. In the West, 1776 was such a moment. In America a tax revolt turned into a revolution; in Glasgow, Adam Smith finished his *Wealth of Nations*, the first and greatest work of political economy; in London, Edward Gibbon's *Decline and Fall of the Roman Empire* hit the bookstores and became an overnight sensation. Great men were doing great things. Yet on March 22 James Boswell—Ninth Laird of Auchinleck, thwarted man of letters, and ambitious hanger-on around the rich and famous— was to be found not in some wit-filled salon but in a coach splashing through the mud toward Soho, an estate outside Birmingham in the English Midlands (Figure 10.1).

From a distance Soho's clock tower, carriageway, and Palladian façade made it look like just the kind of country house Boswell might want to visit for tea and pleasantries, but on closer approach a clattering hubbub of crashing hammers, screeching lathes, and cursing laborers dispelled any such illusions. This was no setting for a Jane Austen novel; it was a factory. And Boswell, despite his privilege and pretensions, wanted to see it, for there was nothing quite like Soho anywhere else in the world.

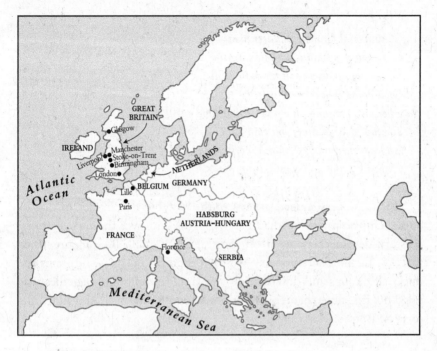

Figure 10.1. Power for sale: the cradle of the nineteenth-century
industrial revolution

Everything at Soho lived up to Boswell's expectations—its hundreds of workmen, "the vastness and the contrivance of some of the machinery," and above all its proprietor, Matthew Boulton ("an *iron chieftain*," Boswell called him). Boswell confided to his journal, "I shall never forget Mr. Bolton's [*sic*] expression to me: 'I sell here, Sir, what all the world desires to have—POWER.'"

It was men like Boulton who gave the lie to political economists' dismal predictions. When Boswell and Boulton met in 1776, Western social development had clawed its way up just forty-five points since Ice Age hunter-gatherers had prowled the tundra in search of a meal; within the next hundred years it soared another *hundred* points. The transformation beggared belief. It turned the world inside out. In 1776 East and West were still neck and neck, barely above the old forty-three-point hard ceiling; a century later, the sale of power had turned the West's lead into Western rule. "'Twas in truth," said the poet Wordsworth in 1805,

. . . an hour
Of universal ferment; mildest men
Were agitated; and commotions, strife
Of passion and opinion fill'd the walls
Of peaceful houses with unquiet sounds.
The soil of common life was at that time
Too hot to tread upon; oft said I then,
And not then only, "what a mockery this
Of history; the past and that to come!"

What mockery indeed, at least of the past; but not, in fact, of that to come. Universal ferment had barely begun, and over the next century Western development went off the scale. Any graph (like Figure 10.2) that can fit the contemporary West's 906 points on its vertical axis reduces all the ups and downs, leads and lags, triumphs and tragedies that filled the first nine chapters of this book to insignificance. And all thanks to what Boulton was selling.

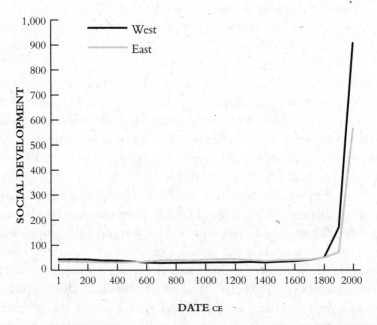

Figure 10.2. Universal ferment: social development across the last two thousand years, showing the Western-led takeoff since 1800 that made mockery of all the drama of the world's earlier history

THE JOY OF STEAM

The world had had power before Boulton, of course. What he was selling was *better* power. For millions of years nearly all the power to move things had come from muscles; and while muscles can be remarkable—they built the pyramids, dug the Grand Canal, and painted the Sistine Chapel—they do have limits. Most obviously, muscles are parts of animals, and animals need food, shelter, and often fuel and clothes. All of these come from plants or other animals, which also require food, shelter, and so on; and everything in this chain ultimately requires land. So as land grew scarce in the eighteenth-century cores, muscles got expensive.

For centuries wind and water power had augmented muscles by pushing boats along and driving millstones. But wind and water have limits too. They are available only in certain places; streams can freeze in winter or run dry in summer; and whenever the air hangs heavy, windmills' sails stop.

What was needed was power that was portable, so people could bring it to their work rather than bringing their work to it; reliable, so it did not depend on the weather; and space-neutral, so it did not consume millions of acres of trees and fields. The ironmasters of eleventh-century Kaifeng had seen that coal offered an answer, but this, too, had a limit. It could release energy only as heat.

The breakthrough—turning heat into motion—came in the eighteenth century and began at the coal mines themselves. Flooding was a constant problem, and while muscles and buckets could drain mineshafts (one ingenious English pit owner yoked five hundred horses to a bucket chain), they were hugely expensive. In hindsight, the solution seems obvious: get the water out with engines that eat coal from the mine rather than animals that eat food. But that was easier said than done.

The Eastern and Western cores both needed coal in the eighteenth century and both faced flooded mineshafts, but it was English engine makers who found the answer. As we saw in Chapter 9, here on northwest Europe's farthest fringe the Atlantic economy had particularly rewarded semiscientific tinkering. This threw up just the kind of men the problem called for, combining business acumen with practical experience of metals and some basic grasp of physics. Such men did exist in China and Japan, but they were rare, and so far as we know none of them even tried to tinker with coal-fired engines.

The first working Western pump, the "Miner's Friend," was patented in England in 1698. It burned coal to boil water and then condensed the steam into a vacuum, whereupon operators opened a valve and the vacuum sucked water up from the mine. Now closing the valve, workers stoked the fires to boil this water, too, into steam; and then repeated the gravity-defying process of boiling and condensing over and over again.

The Miner's Friend was slow, could raise only forty feet of water, and had a distinctly unfriendly tendency to explode, but it was still (usually) cheaper than feeding hundreds of horses. It also inspired more tinkering, but even the improved engines remained horribly wasteful. Because they used the same cylinder to boil water and then cool it to make a vacuum, they had to reheat the cylinder for every stroke of the piston. Even the best engines converted less than 1 percent of the energy in coal into force to pump water.

For decades, this inefficiency restricted steam power to the single job of pumping out coal mines, and even for that, one owner complained, "the vast consumption of fuel of these engines is an immense drawback on the profit of our mines . . . This heavy tax amounts almost to a prohibition." For any business that had to ship coal from mines to factories, steam engines were just too expensive.

Engines were, however, fun for professors. Glasgow University bought a miniature example, but when none of the scholars could get it to work, it made its way in 1765 to the workshop of James Watt, Mathematical Instrument Maker to the University. Watt got it going, but its inefficiency sinned against his craftsman's soul. In between other tasks he obsessed about better ways to evaporate and condense water, until, as he told it,

I had gone to take a walk on a fine Sabbath afternoon . . . when the idea came into my mind, that as steam was an elastic body it would rush into a vacuum, and if a communication was made between the [heated] cylinder and an exhausted vessel, it would rush into it, and might there be condensed without cooling the cylinder . . . I had not

walked further than the Golf-house when the whole thing was arranged in my mind.

It being Sunday, the God-fearing Watt could only sit on his hands, but
on Monday morning he knocked together a new model separating the
condenser from the evaporation cylinder. Instead of alternately heating
and cooling one cylinder, the boiler now stayed hot and the condenser
cold, cutting coal use by nearly four-fifths.

This threw up a host of new problems, but Watt plodded on with
them, year after year. His wife died; his backer went bankrupt; and still
he could not make the engine work reliably. But in 1774, just as Watt
was about to give up tinkering for steadier work, the iron chieftain
Matthew Boulton came to the rescue, buying out Watt's debt-laden
backer and sweeping the engine maker off to Birmingham. Boulton
threw both money and the brilliant metalworker "Iron Mad" Wilkinson at the problem. (Wilkinson believed everything should be made of
iron, including his own coffin.)

Just six months later Watt wrote to his father—in what strikes me
as the second-greatest understatement of all time (I will come to the
greatest later in this chapter)—that his engine was now "rather successful." In a grand public display in March 1776 Watt and Boulton's engine
pumped sixty feet of water from a mineshaft in sixty minutes flat,
burning just a quarter as much coal as older machines.

No wonder Boulton was feeling expansive when Boswell visited
Soho that month. With engines now cost-effective outside the pits
themselves, the sky was the limit. "If we had . . . a hundred small engines . . . and twenty large ones executed, we could readily dispose of
them all," Boulton wrote to Watt. "Let us make hay while the sun
shines."

And so they did, although even they were probably surprised at
some of the customers who came to their door. The first manufacturers
to seize on steam power were makers of cotton cloth. Cotton would
not grow in western Europe, and until the seventeenth century Britons
had normally worn scratchy, sweaty wool year-round, generally dis-
pensing with underwear altogether. Predictably, when traders started
importing light, brightly printed cotton cloth from India, it was a huge
hit. "It crept into our houses, our closets, our bedchambers," Daniel

Defoe recalled in 1708. "Curtains, cushions, chairs, and at last beds themselves were nothing but Callicoes or Indian stuffs."

The importers made fortunes, but money spent on Indian cotton was of course money not spent on British wool. Wool magnates therefore lobbied Parliament to ban cotton cloth, whereupon other Britons imported raw cotton (which was still legal) and wove their own cloth. Unfortunately, they were not as good at this as Indians, and as late as the 1760s the market for British cotton was just one-thirtieth of that for British wool.

Cotton did have one thing going for it, though: the laborious task of spinning its fibers into yarn lent itself to mechanization. For ten thousand years textile production had depended on nimble-fingered women (but only rarely men) to twist wisps of wool or fiber onto spindles. We saw in Chapter 7 that by 1300, Chinese spinners were using water- and animal-powered machines to increase productivity. These machines became more common over the following centuries, steadily pushing up output, but the British move to mechanization abruptly made all the ancient skills redundant. In 1700 a spinster with a pedal-powered wheel needed two hundred hours to produce a pound of yarn;* by 1800, extraordinary devices with even more extraordinary names—Hargreaves's jenny, Arkwright's throstle, Crompton's mule—were doing the same work in three hours (Roberts's self-acting mule, invented in 1824, took just an hour and twenty minutes). The machines' repetitive movements also made them ideal for steam power and for concentration in large factories, and the first spinning mill powered entirely by steam engines (supplied, naturally, by Boulton and Watt) opened in 1785.

Machines made British cotton cheaper, finer, stronger, and more uniform even than Indian, and British exports of finished cloth increased a hundredfold between 1760 and 1815, turning cotton from a minor industry into the source of almost a twelfth of the national income. A hundred thousand men, women, and (especially) children labored twelve or more hours a day, six days a week, in the mills, flooding markets with so much cotton that the price of yarn fell

---

*Spinning wheels reached Europe in the twelfth century; without a wheel, it took a spinster about five hundred hours to spin a pound of yarn.

from thirty-eight shillings per pound in 1786 to under seven shillings in 1807. As prices fell, though, markets expanded. Profits kept booming.

Geography made cotton the perfect industry for Britain. Because its raw materials grew overseas, they did not compete for land at home. Instead Americans, eager for British cash, turned millions of acres into cotton plantations and put hundreds of thousands of slaves to work on them. Production soared from 3,000 bales in 1790 to 178,000 in 1810 and 4.5 million in 1860. British innovations in spinning stimulated American innovations on the plantations, such as Eli Whitney's cotton gin (short for engine), which separated cotton fibers from sticky seeds even more cheaply than slaves' fingers. The American supply of cotton rose to meet British demand, keeping prices low, enriching mill and plantation owners, and creating vast new armies of labor on both sides of the Atlantic.

Back in Britain, technology jumped from industry to industry, stimulating yet more technology. The most important leap was to ironworking, the industry that made the materials that other new industries used. Britain's ironmasters had known how to smelt iron with coke since 1709 (seven centuries behind Chinese metallurgists), but had trouble keeping their furnaces hot enough for coke smelting. After 1776 Boulton and Watt's engines solved the problem by providing steady blasts of air, and within a decade Cort's puddling-and-rolling process (as wonderfully named as anything in cotton spinning) smoothed out the remaining technical difficulties. Following the same path as cotton, ironmakers saw labor costs plummet while employment, productivity, and profits exploded.

Boulton and his competitors had taken the lid off energy capture. Even though their revolution took several decades to unfold (in 1800, British manufacturers still generated three times as much power from waterwheels as from steam engines), it was nonetheless the biggest and fastest transformation in the entire history of the world. In three generations technological change shattered the hard ceiling. By 1870, Britain's steam engines generated 4 million horsepower, equivalent to the work of 40 million men, who—if industry had still depended on muscles—would have eaten more than three times Britain's entire wheat output. Fossil fuel made the impossible possible.

THE GREAT DIVERGENCE

Locals like to call my hometown, Stoke-on-Trent in the English Midlands, the cradle of the industrial revolution. Its great claim to fame comes from being the heart of the Potteries, where Josiah Wedgwood mechanized vase-making in the 1760s. Industrial-scale potting pervaded everything in Stoke. Even my own earliest archaeological experiences as a teenager nearly two centuries later went on in Wedgwood's shadow, working on misfired pots from a vast dump behind the Whieldon factory where Wedgwood had learned his craft.

Stoke was built on coal, iron, and clay, and when I was young most of its workingmen still got up before dawn and headed for the pit, steelworks, or potbank. My grandfather was a steelworker; my father left school for the mines just before his fourteenth birthday. In my own schooldays we were constantly told how the pluck, grit, and ingenuity of our forebears had made Britain great and changed the world. But so far as I remember, no one told us why it was *our* hills and valleys, rather than someone else's in some other place, that had cradled the infant industry.

This question, though, is the front line in arguments over the great divergence between West and East. Was it inevitable that the industrial revolution would happen in Britain (in and around Stoke-on-Trent, in fact) rather than somewhere else in the West? If not, was it inevitable that it would happen in the West rather than somewhere else? Or—for that matter—that it would happen at all?

I grumbled in the introduction to this book that even though these questions are really about whether Western dominance was locked in in the distant past, experts offering answers rarely look back more than four or five hundred years. I hope I have made my point by now that putting the industrial revolution into the long historical perspective sketched in the first nine chapters of this book will provide better answers.

The industrial revolution was unique in how much and how fast it drove up social development, but otherwise it was very like all the upswings in earlier history. Like all those earlier episodes of (relatively) rapidly rising development, it happened in an area that had until recently been rather peripheral to the main story. Since the origins of agriculture, the major cores had expanded through various combinations of colonization and imitation, with populations on the peripheries adopting what worked in the core and sometimes adapting it to very different environments at the margins. Sometimes this process revealed advantages in backwardness, as when fifth-millennium-BCE farmers found that the only way to make a living in Mesopotamia was by irrigation, in the process turning Mesopotamia into a new core; or when cities and states expanded into the Mediterranean Basin in the first millennium BCE, developing new patterns of maritime trade; or when northern Chinese farmers fled southward and turned the area beyond the Yangzi into a new rice frontier after 400 CE.

When the Western core expanded north and west from its Mediterranean heartland in the second millennium CE, western Europeans eventually discovered that new maritime technology could turn their geographical isolation, which had long been a source of backwardness, into an advantage. More by accident than design, western Europeans created new kinds of oceanic empires, and as their novel Atlantic economy drove social development up, it presented entirely new challenges.

There was no guarantee that Europeans would meet these challenges; neither the Romans (in the first century CE) nor the Song Chinese (in the eleventh) had found a way through the hard ceiling. All the signs were that muscles were the ultimate source of power, that no more than 10–15 percent of people would ever be able to read, that cities and armies could never grow beyond about a million members, and that—consequently—social development could never get past the low forties on the index. But in the eighteenth century Westerners brushed these limits aside; by selling power they made mockery of all that had gone before.

Western Europeans succeeded where the Romans and Song failed because three things had changed. First, technology had gone on accumulating. Some skills were lost each time social development collapsed, but most were not, and over the centuries new ones were added. The same-river-twice principle thus kept working: each society that pressed against the hard ceiling between the first century and the eighteenth was different from its predecessors. Each knew and could do more than those that had gone before.

Second, in large part because technology had accumulated, agrarian empires now had effective guns, allowing the Romanovs and Qing to close the steppe highway. Consequently, when social development pressed against the hard ceiling in the seventeenth century, the fifth horseman of the apocalypse—migration—did not ride. It was a struggle, but the cores managed to cope with the other four horsemen and averted collapse. Without this change, the eighteenth century might have been as disastrous as the third and thirteenth.

Third, again largely because technology had accumulated, ships could now sail almost anywhere they wanted, allowing western Europeans to create an Atlantic economy unlike anything seen before. Neither the Romans nor the Song had been in a position to build such a vast engine of commercial growth, so neither had had to confront the kinds of problems that forced themselves on western Europeans' attention in the seventeenth and eighteenth centuries. Newton, Watt, and their colleagues were probably no more brilliant than Cicero, Shen Kuo, and theirs; they just thought about different things.

Eighteenth-century western Europe was better placed than any earlier society to annihilate the hard ceiling; within western Europe, the northwest—with its weaker kings and freer merchants—was better placed than the southwest; and within the northwest, Britain was best placed of all. By 1770 Britain not only had higher wages, more coal, stronger finance, and arguably more open institutions (for middle- and upper-class men, anyway) than anyone else, but—thanks to coming out on top in its wars with the Dutch and French—it also had more colonies, trade, and warships.

It was easier to have an industrial revolution in Britain than anywhere else, but Britain still had no lock-in on industrialization. If—as could easily have happened—it had been French bells, not British, that were worn threadbare by ringing victories in 1759, and if France had stripped Britain of its navy, colonies, and trade rather than Britain stripping France, my elders would not have reared me on stories of how Stoke-on-Trent had midwifed the industrial revolution. The elders in some equally smoke-blackened French city such as Lille might have been spinning that yarn instead. France, after all, had plenty of inventors and entrepreneurs, and even a small shift in national endowments or the decisions of kings and generals might have made a big difference.

Great men, bungling idiots, and dumb luck had a lot to do with why the industrial revolution was British rather than French, but they had much less to do with why the West had an industrial revolution in the first place. To explain that, we have to look at larger forces, because once enough technology had accumulated, once the steppe highway had closed, and once the oceanic highways had opened—by, say, 1650 or 1700—it is hard to imagine what could have stopped an industrial revolution from happening *somewhere* in western Europe. If France or the Low Countries had become the workshop of the world rather than Britain, the industrial revolution might have broken more slowly, perhaps beginning in the 1870s rather than the 1770s. The world we live in today would be different, but western Europe would still have had the original industrial revolution and the West would still rule. I would still be writing this book, but it might be in French rather than English.

Unless, that is, the East had independently industrialized first. Could that have happened if Western industrialization had been slower? Here, of course, I am piling what-ifs on top of what-ifs, but I think the answer is still fairly clear: probably not. Even though Eastern and Western social development scores were neck-and-neck until 1800, there are few signs that the East, if left alone, was moving toward industrialization fast enough to have begun its own takeoff during the nineteenth century.

The East had large markets and intense trade, but these did not work like the West's Atlantic economy, and while ordinary people in the East were not as poor as Adam Smith claimed in his *Wealth of Nations* ("The poverty of the lower ranks of people in China far surpasses that of the most beggarly nations in Europe"), Figure 10.3 shows that they were not rich either. Beijingers* were no worse off than Florentines but much worse off than Londoners. With labor so cheap in China and Japan (and southern Europe), the incentives for the local equivalents of Boulton to invest in machinery were weak. As late as 1880 the up-front costs to open a mine with six hundred Chinese laborers were estimated as $4,272—roughly the price of a single steam pump. Even when they had the option, savvy Chinese investors often preferred cheap muscles to expensive steam.

With so little to gain from tinkering, neither Eastern entrepreneurs nor scholars in the imperial academies showed much interest in boilers

---

*Workers in Tokyo, Suzhou, Shanghai, and Guangzhou all earned slightly less than Beijingers through most of the eighteenth and nineteenth centuries.

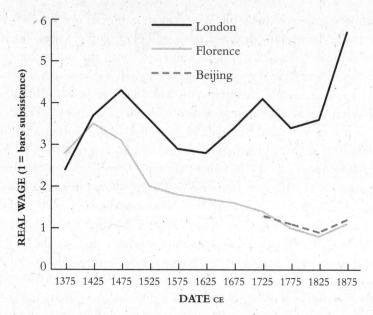

Figure 10.3. Workers of the world, divide: despite their woes, British workers earned much more than non-British between 1780 and 1830 and did better still after 1830. The graph compares the real wages of the unskilled in London, Florence (fairly typical of southern Europe's low wages), and Beijing (exemplifying Chinese and Japanese wages).

and condensers, let alone jennies, throstles, and puddling. To have had its own industrial revolution, the East would have needed to create some equivalent to the Atlantic economy that could generate higher wages and new challenges, stimulating the whole package of scientific thought, mechanical tinkering, and cheap power.

Again, given time, that might have come to pass. Already in the eighteenth century there was a flourishing Chinese diaspora in Southeast Asia; other things being equal, the kind of geographical interdependence that characterized the Atlantic economy might have emerged in the nineteenth century. But other things were not equal. It took Westerners two hundred years to get from Jamestown to James Watt. *If* the East had been left in splendid isolation, *if* it had moved down the same path as the West across the nineteenth and twentieth centuries toward creating a geographically diversified economy, and *if* it had moved at roughly the same pace as the West, a Chinese Watt or Japanese Boulton might at this very moment be unveiling his first steam engine in Shanghai or Tokyo. But none of those ifs eventuated, because once the West's industrial revolution began, it swallowed the world.

THE GRADGRINDS

As late as 1750, the similarities between the Eastern and Western cores were still striking. Both were advanced agrarian economies with complex divisions of labor, extensive trade networks, and growing manufacturing sectors. At both ends of Eurasia rich landowning elites, confident in their order's stability, traditions, and worth, were masters of all they surveyed. Each elite defended its position with elaborate rules of deference and etiquette, and each consumed and produced culture of great subtlety and refinement. Behind all the obvious differences of style and narration, it is hard not to see a certain kinship between sprawling eighteenth-century novels of manners such as Samuel Richardson's *Clarissa* and Cao Xueqin's *Dream of the Red Chamber*.

By 1850 all these similarities were being washed away by one massive difference: the rise in the West of a new, steam-powered class of iron chieftains that, according to its most famous critics, "has pitilessly torn asunder the motley feudal ties that bound man to his 'natural superiors.'" This new class, Marx and Engels went on, "has drowned the most heavenly ecstasies of religious fervor, of chivalrous enthusiasm, of philistine sentimentalism, in the icy water of egotistical calculation."

Opinions differed—violently—over just what this new class was doing, but most agreed that whatever it was, it was changing everything. To some, the millionaires who tapped and sold power were heroes whose "energy and perseverance, guided by sound judgment, [merely] secured their usual reward." Thus Samuel Smiles, author of the Victorian classic *Self-Help*. "In early times," Smiles explained, "the products of skilled industry were for the most part luxuries intended for the few, whereas now"—thanks to the captains of industry—"the most exquisite tools and engines are employed in producing articles of ordinary consumption for the great mass of the community."

To others, though, industrialists were hard-faced, frock-coated brutes, like Dickens's Mr. Gradgrind in *Hard Times*. "Facts alone are wanted in life," Gradgrind insisted. "Plant nothing else, and root out everything else." Dickens had learned about the industrial revolution the hard way, laboring in a boot-black factory while his father languished in debtors' prison, and had strong views on the Gradgrinds. As he saw it, they leached the beauty out of life, herding workers into soul-destroying cities like his imaginary Coketown, "a triumph of fact . . . a town of machinery and tall chimneys, out of which interminable serpents of smoke trailed themselves for ever and ever."

There were certainly real-life Gradgrinds aplenty. The young Friedrich Engels described running into one in 1840s Manchester and lecturing him on the plight of this Coketown's workers. "He listened patiently," said Engels, "and at the corner of the street at which we parted company, he remarked: 'And yet there is a great deal of money made here. Good morning, Sir!'"

The businessman was right: by tapping into the energy trapped in fossil fuels, Boulton and Watt's engines had unleashed a storm of moneymaking. Yet Engels was right too: the workers who made the money saw precious little of it. Between 1780 and 1830 output per laborer grew by more than 25 percent but wages rose barely 5 percent. The rest was skimmed off as profits. Anger mounted in the slums. Workers formed unions and demanded a People's Charter; radicals plotted to blow up the government. Farmworkers, their livelihoods threatened by mechanical threshers, smashed machines and burned hayricks in 1830, signing threatening letters to the gentry under the piratical-sounding name "Captain Swing." Everywhere magistrates and clergymen caught the whiff of Jacobinism, their catchall term for French-style insurrection, and men of property bore down on it with the full weight of the state. Cavalry trampled demonstrators; unionists were jailed; machine breakers were shipped to penal colonies at the farthest fringes of Britain's empire.

To Marx and Engels, the process seemed crystal clear: Western industrialization was driving social development up faster than ever before but was also kicking the paradox of development into warp speed.* By turning men into mere "hands," flesh-and-blood cogs in mills and factories, capitalists were also giving them common cause and making them revolutionaries. "What the bourgeoisie therefore produces, above

---

*Marx and Engels of course used a different terminology, that the shift from a feudal to a capitalist mode of production increased the extraction of surplus labor but heightened the contradictions between base and superstructure.

all," Marx and Engels concluded, "are its own gravediggers . . . Let the ruling classes tremble at a Communist revolution. The proletarians have nothing to lose but their chains. They have a world to win. Workingmen of all countries, unite!"

Marx and Engels believed that capitalists had brought this on themselves by fencing off the countryside and driving the dispossessed into cities to be wage slaves, but they had the facts wrong. Rich landlords did not drive country folk off the land; sex did. The nineteenth century's intensive agriculture actually needed more field hands, not fewer, and the real reason people exchanged farms for cities was reproduction. Life expectancy increased by about three years between 1750 and 1850, and although historians cannot agree why this happened (Fewer outbreaks of plague? More nutritious foods? Better water supplies and sewers? Smarter child-rearing practices? Cotton underwear? Something else completely?), those extra childbearing years meant that unless women married later, had sex in different ways, or aborted/starved their young, they would raise more children. Women did in fact change their behavior, but not enough to cancel out their longer lives, and Britain's population roughly doubled (to about 14 million) between 1780 and 1830. About a million of these extra people stayed on the land, but 6 million sought jobs in towns.

These hard facts of reproduction make the industrial revolution's glass look half-full rather than half-empty: industrialization was traumatic but the alternatives were worse. In the sixteenth century wages had collapsed all over the West when population grew, but British wages actually rose after 1775 and pulled away from everyone else's (Figure 10.3). When Britons did starve en masse, in the horrific 1840s Irish famine, it had more to do with greedy landlords and stupid politicians than with industry (which was strikingly scarce in Ireland).

The irony is that the tide turned in workers' favor in the very years Marx and Engels formulated their doctrines. Since 1780 capitalists had been spending much of their profits on country houses, peerages, and the other trappings of the arriviste, but they had plowed even more back into new machines and mills. By about 1830 these investments were making the mechanically augmented labor of each dirty, malnourished, ill-educated "hand" so profitable that bosses often preferred cutting deals with strikers to firing them and competing with other bosses to find new ones. For the next fifty years wages grew as fast as profits, and in 1848, when Marx and Engels published *The Communist Manifesto*, British workers' pay was finally regaining the heights it had reached after the Black Death.

Like every other age, the 1830s got the thought it needed, and as workers became more valuable the middle classes discovered sympathy—of a kind—for the downtrodden. On the one hand, unemployment came to seem positively wicked, and paupers were herded (for their own good, said the middle classes) into workhouses; on the other, Dickens's picture of these same workhouses made *Oliver Twist* a bestseller and reform became the watchword of the hour. Official commissions decried urban squalor; Parliament banned children under nine from factories and limited under-thirteens to a forty-eight-hour workweek; and the first stumbling steps were taken toward mass education.

These early Victorian reformers can seem hypocritical today, but the very idea of taking practical steps to improve the lives of the poor was revolutionary. The contrast with the Eastern core is particularly strong: in China, where Gradgrinds, Coketowns, and factory hands remained conspicuously rare, learned gentlemen carried on with the centuries-old tradition of sending hand-painted scrolls about utopian reform schemes up to the imperial bureaucrats, who maintained the equally old tradition of ignoring them. Would-be reformists continued to come mostly from the margins of the elite. Hong Liangji (condemned to death for "extreme indecorum" after criticizing government inactivity on social issues) and Gong Zizhen (an eccentric who dressed strangely, used wild calligraphy, and gambled madly), arguably the most constructive social critics, both failed the highest exam multiple times and neither had much impact. Even eminently practical schemes, such as an 1820s program for shipping rice to Beijing by sea to avoid the decay and corruption along the Grand Canal, were allowed to languish.

In the West, but nowhere else, a brave new world of coal and iron was being born, and for the first time in history the possibilities seemed truly limitless. "We consider it a happiness and a privilege to have had our lot cast in the first fifty years of this century," the British journal *The Economist* enthused in 1851; "the period of the last fifty years . . . has witnessed a more rapid and astonishing progress than *all* the centuries which have preceded it. In several vital points the difference between the 18th and the 19th century, is greater than between the first and the 18th, as far as civilised Europe is concerned." Time was speeding up in the West, leaving the rest of the world behind.

ONE WORLD

London, October 2, 1872, 7:45 p.m. It is a famous scene: "Here I am, gentlemen!" announces Phileas Fogg as he strides into his club. Despite being mistaken for a bank robber in Egypt, attacked by Sioux in Nebraska, and drawn into saving a beautiful widow from enforced suicide in India (Figure 10.4), Fogg had done what he said he would do. He had traveled around the world in eighty days, with one second to spare.

It is also a fictional scene, but like all Jules Verne's tales, *Around the World in Eighty Days* was firmly grounded in fact. The aptly named George Train really did travel around the world in eighty days in 1870, and although the fictional Fogg fell back on elephants, sledges, and sailboats when technology let him down,* neither he nor Train could have managed their tours without brand-new triumphs of engineering—the Suez Canal (opened in 1869), the San Francisco–New York railroad (completed the same year), and the Bombay–Calcutta train line† (finished in 1870). The world, as Fogg observed before he set off, was not as big as it used to be.

Rising social development and expanding cores had always gone together as colonists carried new lifestyles outward and people on the peripheries copied, resisted, or ran away from them. The nineteenth century differed only in scale and speed, but these differences changed the course of history. Before the nineteenth century, great empires had dominated this or that part of the world, bending it to their will, but the new technologies stripped away all limits. For the first time, a lead in social development could be turned into global rule.

Converting the energy of fossil fuels into motion annihilated distance. As early as 1804 a British engineer showed that lightweight, high-pressure engines could push carriages along iron rails, and by the

---

*Not, though, on balloons. That detail was added only in 1956, for the wonderful film version starring David Niven.

†Modern Mumbai and Kolkata.

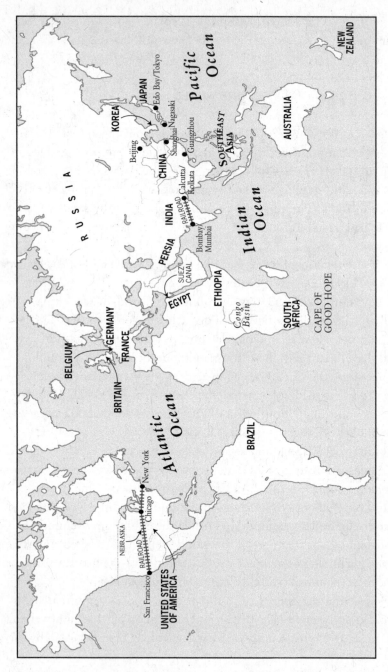

Figure 10.4. Around the world: Western rule shrinks the globe.

1810s similar engines were driving paddleboats. After another generation of inspired fiddling, George Stephenson's famous *Rocket* was puffing along the Liverpool–Manchester railroad at twenty-nine miles per
hour* and boats were paddling across the Atlantic. Social development
transformed geography faster than ever before: freed from wind and
wave, ships could sail not just where they wanted but also when they
wanted, and so long as someone laid the rails, goods could move over
land almost as cheaply as over water.

Technology transformed colonization. More than 5 million Britons
(out of a population of 27 million) emigrated between 1851 and 1880,
mostly to the ultimate new frontier in North America. Between 1850
and 1900 this "white plague," as the historian Niall Ferguson calls it,
felled 168 million acres of American forest, more than ten times Britain's
farmable area. Already in 1799 a traveler had recorded that American
pioneers "have an unconquerable aversion to trees . . . they cut away
all before them without mercy . . . all share the same fate and are involved in the same havoc." A hundred years later their aversion had
only grown, fed by stump-removing machines, flamethrowers, and
dynamite.

An unprecedented agricultural boom fed equally astonishing cities.
In 1800 there were 79,000 New Yorkers; in 1890, 2.5 million. Chicago
meanwhile became the wonder of the world. A prairie town of thirty
thousand in 1850, by 1890 it was the sixth-largest city on earth, more
than a million strong. Chicago made Coketown look genteel. "For
her," one astonished critic wrote,

> all the Central States, all the Great Northwest roared with traffic and
> industry; sawmills screamed; factories, their smoke blackening the
> sky, clashed and flamed; wheels turned, pistons leaped in their cylin-
> ders; cog gripped cog; beltings clasped the drums of mammoth wheels;
> and converters of forges belched into the clouded air their tempest
> breath of molten steel.
>
> It was Empire.

---

*Admittedly this was when empty; with a full thirteen-ton load it managed a statelier
twelve mph.

Emulation did much more than colonization to spread industrial-ization eastward across Europe. In 1860 Britain was still the only thor-oughly industrial economy, producing half the world's iron and textiles, but first in Belgium (which had good coal and iron) and then along an arc from northern France through Germany and Austria, the age of steam and coal took off. By 1910 the former peripheries of Germany and the United States discovered advantages in their backwardness and outstripped their teacher.

Germans, less blessed with coal than Britain, learned to use fuel more efficiently, and lacking workers with that sixth sense—bred by generations of on-the-job training—for just when to close a valve or tighten a bobbin, Germany substituted technical education. Americans, lacking old family firms with accumulated capital, discovered a differ-ent advantage. Selling shares to raise money for huge modern enter-prises effectively separated owners from hired managers, who felt free to experiment with time-and-motion studies, assembly lines, and the new science of management. All this book-learning struck Britons as rather ridiculous, but in new, high-tech industries such as optics and chemistry, knowing a little science and management theory produced better results than going by feel. By 1900 it was Britain, with its faith in improvisation, muddling through, and inspired amateurs, that was starting to look ridiculous.

Germany and the United States led the way in what historians often call the Second Industrial Revolution, applying science to technology more systematically. They quickly made Phileas Fogg's feats seem ar-chaic, turning the twentieth century into an age of oil, automobiles, and aircraft. In 1885 Gottlieb Daimler and Karl Benz figured out how to burn gasoline (hitherto a low-value by-product of the kerosene used in lamps) efficiently in an internal combustion engine, and in the very same year British mechanics perfected the bicycle. Putting light new engines together with robust new chassis yielded cars and planes. In 1896 automobiles were still so slow that hecklers yelled "Get a horse!" at America's first car race, but in 1913 American factories turned out a million vehicles. By then the Wright brothers, two bicycle mechanics from North Carolina, had bolted wings onto a gasoline engine and made it fly.

Oil was transforming geography. "The development of the internal Combustion engine is the greatest the world has ever seen," one British oilman enthused in 1911; "it will supersede steam and that too with almost tragic rapidity." Because oil was lighter than coal, yielded more power, and made things go faster, those who stuck with steam inevitably lost out to those who invested in the new engines. "The first of all necessities," Britain's top naval adviser insisted in 1911, "is SPEED," and bowing to the inevitable, Britain's young first lord of the admiralty—Winston Churchill—switched the Royal Navy from coal to oil. Britain's endless coal reserves were beginning to matter less than access to oil fields in Russia, Persia, Southeast Asia, and above all America.

Communications were changing just as quickly. In 1800 the quickest way to send a message around the world was to put a letter on a boat, but by 1851 Britons and Frenchmen could exchange messages using electrical signals sent down an underwater cable. In 1858 the British queen and American president telegraphed across the Atlantic, and more than once in *Around the World in Eighty Days* everything hinged on a timely telegram. Between 1866 and 1911 the cost of transatlantic telegrams fell by 99.5 percent, but by then such savings were taken for granted. The first telephones started ringing in 1876, just three years after Verne's book came out; in 1895 came wireless telegraphy; in 1906, the radio.

Faster transport and communication drove an explosive growth in markets. Back in the 1770s Adam Smith had realized that wealth depended on the size of markets and the division of labor. If markets are big, everyone can produce what they make cheapest and best, then sell it, using their profits to buy whatever else they need. That, Smith reasoned, would make everyone richer than if they tried to make everything for themselves. The key, Smith argued, was liberalization: economic logic required tearing down the walls that separated people and leaving them to indulge their "propensity to truck, barter, and exchange one thing for another."

But that was easier said than done. Those who produced the cheapest goods in the world, such as British industrialists, were all for free markets, but those who made uncompetitive, overpriced goods—such as British farmers—often thought lobbying Parliament to slap tariffs on more efficient rivals sounded better than switching to new lines of work. It took bloodshed, the fall of a government, and the specter of famine to persuade Britain's rulers to abandon protectionism, but as they did so (and as the average duty on imports fell from over 50 percent around 1825 to under 10 percent fifty years later), global markets took off.

To some, the craze for free markets seemed like madness. British manufacturers were exporting trains, ships, and machines, and British financiers were lending foreigners the money to buy them. Britain was, in effect, building up foreign industries that would challenge its economic dominance. To free traders, however, there was method in the madness. By selling and lending everywhere, even to rivals, Britain created such a big market that it could concentrate on those industrial (and increasingly financial) skills that made the biggest profits. And not just that; British machines helped Americans and Europeans produce the food Britons needed to buy, and the profits foreigners made by selling food to Britain allowed them to buy even more British goods.

The free traders reasoned that everybody—everybody willing to swallow the hard, Gradgrindian logic of liberalization, anyway—would win. Few countries were as enthusiastic as Britain (Germany and the United States in particular shielded their infant industries from British competition), but by the 1870s the Western core was effectively tied into a single financial system. Its various currencies were pegged at fixed rates against gold, making trade more predictable and committing governments to play by the market's rules.

But that was only the beginning. Liberalization would not stop at the borders, sweeping away barriers between nations while leaving the barriers within them intact. Liberalization was a package deal, as Marx and Engels saw most clearly:

> Constant revolutionizing of production, uninterrupted disturbance of all social conditions, everlasting uncertainty and agitation distinguish the bourgeois epoch from all earlier ones. All fixed, fast-frozen relations, with their train of ancient and venerable prejudices and opinions, are swept away, all new-formed ones become antiquated before they can fossilize. All that is solid melts into air, all that is holy is profaned, and man is at last compelled to face with sober senses his real conditions of life and his relations with his kind.

If traditional rules and regulations about how people could dress, whom they should worship, and what jobs they might do interfered with productivity and the growth of the market, those traditions had to go. "The sole end for which mankind are warranted, individually or collectively, in interfering with the liberty of action of any of their number is self-protection," concluded the liberal theorist John Stuart Mill. "Over himself, over his own body and mind, the individual is sovereign." Everything else was up for grabs.

Serfdom, guilds, and other legal restrictions on movement and occupation crumbled. It took a war to end American slavery in 1865, but within a generation the West's other slaveholding states legislated peaceful (and often profitable) ends to that ancient institution. Employers increasingly compromised with workers, and after 1870 most countries legalized trade unions and socialist parties, granted universal male suffrage, and provided free, compulsory primary education. As wages rose, some governments offered saving plans for retirement, public health programs, and unemployment insurance. In return, workers agreed to national service in armies and navies; after all, with so much to protect, who would not be willing to fight?

Liberalization gnawed at even the hoariest prejudices. For nearly two thousand years Christians had persecuted Jews and those who followed Jesus inappropriately, but all of a sudden other people's faiths seemed to be their own business, and certainly no reason to stop them from owning property or voting. In fact, for growing numbers, faith seemed less of an issue altogether, and new creeds such as socialism, evolutionism, and nationalism filled the place religion had so long held. And as if dethroning God were not enough, the solidest prejudice of all, female inferiority, also came under attack. "The principle which regulates the existing social relations between the two sexes—the legal subordination of one sex to the other—is wrong in itself and now one of the chief hindrances to human improvement," wrote Mill. "No slave is a slave to the same lengths, and in so full a sense of the word, as a wife."

Film and fiction often present the Victorian age as a cozy world of candles, roaring hearths, and people who knew their place, but contemporaries experienced it very differently. The nineteenth-century West was "like the sorcerer, who is no longer able to control the powers of the nether world which he has called up by his spells," thought Marx and Engels. Artists and intellectuals reveled in this; conservatives pushed back. Churches took stands (some crude, some clever) against socialism, materialism, and science; landed noblemen defended the privileges of their orders; and anti-Semitism and slavery reared their heads again, sometimes behind new masks. Confrontations could be violent; Marx and Engels in fact only pulled their ideas together in *The Communist Manifesto* in 1848 because revolutions were rocking almost every European capital that year and the hour of apocalypse seemed at hand.

Western society was rapidly shedding the features that as recently as 1750 had made it so like the East. As so often, nothing reveals this as clearly as fiction. You will search early nineteenth-century Chinese literature in vain for the kind of assertive heroines that crowd the pages of European novels. The closest thing to a protest about women's subjugation may be Li Ruzhen's bizarre satire *Flowers in the Mirror*, in which a male merchant is forcibly feminized, even to the point of footbinding. ("His feet lost much of their original shape," Li wrote. "Blood and flesh were squeezed into a pulp . . . little remained of his feet but dry bones and skin, shrunk, indeed, to a dainty size.") Dickens's upwardly mobile heroes are just as hard to find, and Samuel Smiles's self-made men still more so. The mood of Shen Fu's heartrending *Six Records of a Floating Life*—romantic and moving, but crushed by a rigid hierarchy—is much more typical.

The really new thing about the West, though, was that the more it sped itself up and raced down paths utterly unlike those the rest of the world was strolling along, the more it forced the rest of the world to follow its direction and frenetic pace. The market could not sleep; it must expand, integrating ever more activity, or the ravening beast of industry would die. The West's corrosive, liberal acid ate away the barriers within societies and those between them, and no amount of custom, tradition, or imperial edicts could preserve the kind of ancient order that so oppressed Shen Fu. It was one world, ready or not.

NEMESIS

Globalization revealed the secret of the age—that in this new world, to talk of the West merely *leading* the world in social development was to talk nonsense. For millennia the original agricultural cores had expanded largely independently in several parts of the planet, but the upward movement of social development steadily transformed geography, linking the world's cores together.

Already in the sixteenth century new kinds of ships enabled Europeans to overwhelm the Aztecs and Incas, converting the New World's formerly independent cores into a far-flung periphery of a vastly enlarged West. In the eighteenth century Europeans began turning the South Asian core into another such periphery, and in the nineteenth, steamships, railroads, and telegraphs gave the West worldwide reach, transforming geography once again. Britain, the West's great power, could project its will almost anywhere on the planet, and as Westerners extracted more energy from the environment, the proportion of this they turned to war skyrocketed. Western energy capture increased two and a half times between 1800 and 1900, but its military capacity increased tenfold. The industrial revolution turned the West's lead in social development into Western rule.

It was very vexing, therefore, that the East's great powers chose to ignore this, restricting Western traders to tiny enclaves at Guangzhou and Nagasaki. When, as I mentioned in Chapter 9, Britain's Lord Macartney traveled to Beijing in 1793 to demand open markets, Emperor Qianlong firmly rebuffed him—even though, as Macartney acidly observed in his journal, the ordinary Chinese "are all of a trafficking turn, and it seemed at the seaports where we stopped that nothing would be more agreeable to them than to see our ships come often into their harbours."

Matters came to a head in the 1830s. For three centuries Western merchants had been sailing to Guangzhou and swapping silver, the only thing they had that Chinese officials seemed to want, for tea and silk. By the 1780s nearly seven hundred tons of Western silver flowed into Guangzhou each year. Britain's East India Company, however, had discovered that whatever the bureaucrats might say, plenty of Chinese people were also interested in opium, the wonder drug grown in India. Western dealers (particularly the British) pushed the drug hard; by 1832 enough was pouring into Guangzhou—nearly twelve tons—to keep two or three million addicts high year-round (Figure 10.5). Paying for narcotics turned the influx of silver into China into a net outflow of nearly four hundred tons. This was a lot of drugs and a lot of money.

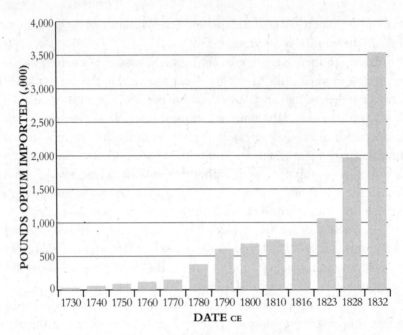

Figure 10.5. Just say yes: the British East India Company's soaring opium sales in Guangzhou, 1730–1832

The dealers insisted that opium "simply did for the upper levels of Chinese society what brandy and champagne did for the same levels in England," but that was not true, and they knew it. Opium left a trail of broken lives as grim as anything in today's inner cities. It also hurt peasants who had never even seen an opium pipe, because the outflow of silver to the drug lords increased the value of the metal, forcing farmers to sell more crops to raise the silver they needed to pay their taxes. By 1832 taxes were effectively twice as high as they had been fifty years before.

Some of Emperor Daoguang's advisers recommended a cynical market solution: legalize opium so that homegrown poppies would undercut British imports, stanching the outflow of silver and increasing tax revenues. But Daoguang was a good Confucian, and instead of caving in to his subjects' baser urges, he wanted to save them from themselves. In 1839 he declared war on drugs.

I said a few words about this first war on drugs in the introduction. At first it went well. Daoguang's drug czar confiscated tons of opium, burned it, and dumped it in the ocean (after writing a suitably classical poem of apology to the sea god for polluting his realm). But then it went less well. The British trade commissioner, recognizing that where the magic of the market would not work that of the gun might do better, dragged his unwilling homeland into a shooting war with China.

What followed was a shocking demonstration of the power of industrial-age warfare. Britain's secret weapon was the *Nemesis*, a brand-new all-iron steamer. Even the Royal Navy had reservations about such a radical weapon; as her captain admitted, just "as the *floating* property of wood, without reference to its shape or fashion, rendered it the most natural material for the construction of ships, so did the *sinking* property of iron make it appear, at first sight, very ill adapted for a similar purpose."

These worries seemed well-founded. The iron hull made the compass malfunction; the *Nemesis* hit a rock even before leaving England; and she almost cracked in two off the Cape of Good Hope. Only by hanging overboard in a howling gale and bolting odd bits of lumber and iron to her sides did her captain keep her afloat. But on reaching Guangzhou all was forgiven. The *Nemesis* lived up to her name, steaming up shallow passages where no wooden ship could go and blasting all opposition to pieces.

In 1842 the British ships closed the Grand Canal, bringing Beijing to the verge of famine. Governor-General Qiying, charged with negotiating peace, assured his emperor that he could still "pass over these small matters and achieve our larger scheme," but in reality he handed the British—then the Americans, then the French, then other Westerners—the access to Chinese ports that they demanded. And when Chinese hostility toward these foreign devils (Figure 10.6) made the concessions less profitable than expected, Westerners pushed for more.

The Westerners also pushed one another, terrified that a commercial rival would gain some concession that would shut their traders out of the new markets. In 1853 their rivalry spilled over into Japan. Commodore Matthew Perry steamed into Edo Bay and demanded the right for American steamships bound for China to refuel there. He brought just four modern ships, but they carried more firepower than all the guns in Japan combined. His ships were "castles that moved freely on the waters," one amazed witness said. "What we'd taken for a conflagration on the sea was really black smoke rising out of [their] smokestacks." Japan granted

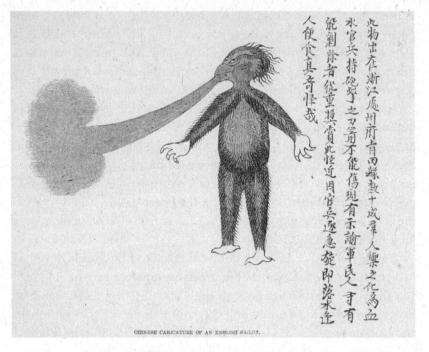

CHINESE CARICATURE OF AN ENGLISH SAILOR.

Figure 10.6. Cultural dissonance: a Chinese sketch of a fire-breathing
British sailor, 1839

Americans the right to trade in two ports; Britain and Russia promptly demanded—and received—the same.

The jockeying for position did not stop there. In an appendix to their 1842 treaty with China, British lawyers had invented a new status, "most favored nation," meaning that anything China gave another Western power, it had to give Britain too. The treaty the United States had signed with China in 1843 included a provision allowing for renegotiation after twelve years, so in 1854 British diplomats claimed the same right. The Qing stalled and Britain went back to war.

Even the British Parliament thought this was a little much. It censured Prime Minister Palmerston; his government fell; but the voters returned him with an increased majority. In 1860 Britain and France occupied Beijing, burned the Summer Palace, and sent Looty back to Balmoral. Not to be outdone in renegotiation, America's consul general bullied Japan into a new treaty by threatening that the alternative was for British ships to open the country to opium.

The West bestrode the world like a colossus in 1860, its reach seemingly unlimited. The ancient Eastern core, which just a century before had boasted the highest social development in the world, was becoming a new periphery to the Western core, just like the former cores in South Asia and the Americas; and North America, now heavily settled by Europeans, was pushing into the core in its own right. Responding to this massive reorganization of geography, Europeans opened still newer frontiers. Their steamships carried the white plague of settlers to South Africa, Australia, and New Zealand, and returned with their holds full of grain and sheep. Africa, still largely a blank space on Western maps as late as 1870, was almost entirely under European rule by 1900.

Looking back on these years in 1919, the economist John Maynard Keynes remembered them as a golden age when

> for . . . the [West's] middle and upper classes, life offered, at a low cost and with the least trouble, conveniences, comforts, and amenities beyond the compass of the richest and most powerful monarchs of other ages. The inhabitant of London could order by telephone, sipping his morning tea in bed, the various products of the whole earth . . . and reasonably expect their early delivery upon his doorstep; he could at the same moment and by the same means adventure his wealth in the natural resources and new enterprises of any quarter of the world; . . . He could secure forthwith, if he wished it, cheap and comfortable means of transit to any country or climate without passport or any other formality . . . and could then proceed abroad to foreign quarters, without knowledge of their religion, language, or customs, bearing coined wealth upon his person, and would consider himself greatly aggrieved and much surprised at the least interference.

But things looked rather different to the novelist Joseph Conrad after he had spent much of 1890 in the Congo Basin. "The conquest of the earth, which mostly means taking it away from those who have a different complexion or slightly flatter noses than ourselves, is not a pretty thing when you look into it too much," he observed in his anticolonialist classic *Heart of Darkness*.

The Congo was certainly the extreme case: King Leopold of Belgium seized it as his personal property and made himself a billionaire by torturing, mutilating, and murdering 5 million or more Congolese to encourage the others to provide him with rubber and ivory. It was hardly unique, though. In North America and Australia white settlers almost exterminated the natives, and some historians blame European imperialism for turning the weak monsoons of 1876–79 and 1896–1902 into catastrophes. Even though crops failed, landlords kept on exporting food to Western markets, and from China to India and Ethiopia to Brazil hunger turned to famine. Dysentery, smallpox, cholera, and the Black Death itself came in its wake, carrying off perhaps 50 million weakened people. Some Westerners raised aid for the starving; some pretended nothing was happening; and some, like *The Economist* magazine, grumbled that famine relief merely taught the hungry that "it is the duty of the Government to keep them alive." Small wonder that the dying whisper of Mr. Kurtz, the evil genius whom Conrad pictured carving out a personal kingdom in the jungle, has come to stand as the epitaph of European imperialism: "The horror! The horror!"*

The East avoided the worst, but still suffered defeat, humiliation, and exploitation at Western hands. China and Japan fell apart as motley crews of patriots, dissidents, and criminals, blaming their governments for everything, took up arms. Religious fanatics and militiamen murdered Westerners who strayed outside their fortified compounds and bureaucrats who appeased these intruders; Western navies bombarded coastal towns in retaliation; rival factions played the Westerners against one another. European weapons flooded Japan, where a British-backed faction overthrew the legitimate government in 1868. In China civil war cost 20 million lives before Western financiers decided that regime change would hurt returns, whereupon an "Ever-Victorious Army" with American and British officers and gunboats helped save the Qing.

Westerners told Eastern governments what to do, seized their assets, and filled their council chambers with advisers. These, not surprisingly, kept down tariffs on Western imports and prices on goods Westerners wanted to buy. Sometimes the process even made Westerners uncomfortable. "I have seen things that made my blood boil in the

---

*Now probably best known from Marlon Brando's delivery in *Apocalypse Now!*, Francis Ford Coppola's re-creation of *Heart of Darkness* in 1960s Vietnam.

way the European powers attempt to degrade the Asiatic nations," Ulysses S. Grant told the Japanese emperor in 1879.

Most Westerners, however, concluded that things were just as they should be, and against this background of Eastern collapse, long-term lock-in theories of Western rule hardened. The East, with its corrupt emperors, groveling Confucians, and billion half-starved coolies, seemed always to have been destined for subjection to the dynamic West. The world appeared to be reaching its final, predestined form.

THE WAR OF THE EAST

The arrogant, self-congratulatory champions of nineteenth-century long-term lock-in theories overlooked one big thing—the logic of their own market-driven imperialism. Just as the market had led British capitalists to build up the industrial infrastructure of their own worst rivals in Germany and the United States, it now rewarded Westerners who poured capital, inventions, and know-how into the East. Westerners stacked the deck in their own favor whenever they could, but capital's relentless quest for new profits also presented opportunities to Easterners who were ready to seize them.

The speed with which Easterners did so was astonishing. In the 1860s Chinese "self-strengthening" and Japanese "civilization and enlightenment" movements set about copying what they saw as the best of the West, translating Western books on science, government, law, and medicine into Chinese and Japanese and sending delegations to the West to look for themselves. Westerners rushed to sell their latest gadgets to Easterners, and Chinese and Japanese Gradgrinds dirtied the countryside with factories.

In a way, this was not so surprising. When Easterners grabbed at the tools that had driven Western social development so high, they were doing just the same thing that Westerners had done six centuries earlier with Eastern tools such as compasses, cast iron, and guns. But in another way, it was very surprising. The Eastern reaction to Western rule differed sharply from the reactions in the former cores in the New World and South Asia, incorporated as Western peripheries across the previous three centuries.

Native Americans never developed indigenous industries and South Asians were much slower to do so than East Asians. Some historians think culture explains this, arguing (more or less explicitly) that while Western culture strongly encourages hard work and rationality, Eastern culture does so only weakly, South Asian culture even less, and other cultures not at all. But this legacy of colonialist mind-sets cannot be right.

When we look at reactions to Western rule within a longer time frame, we in fact see two striking correlations. The first is that those regions that had relatively high social development before Western rule, like the Eastern core, tended to industrialize themselves faster than those that had relatively low development scores; the second, that those regions that avoided direct European colonization tended to industrialize faster than those that did become colonies. Japan had high social development before 1853 and was not colonized; its modernization took off in the 1870s. China had high development and was partly colonized; its modernization took off in the 1950s. India had moderate development and was fully colonized; its modernization did not take off until the 1990s. Sub-Saharan Africa had low development and full colonization, and is only now starting to catch up.

Because the nineteenth-century East was (by preindustrial standards) a world of advanced agriculture, great cities, widespread literacy, and powerful armies, plenty of its residents found ways to adapt Western methods to a new setting. Easterners even adopted Western debates about industrialism. For every Eastern capitalist there was an aging samurai to grumble, "Useless beauty had a place in the old life, but the new asks only for ugly usefulness," and although real wages were creeping up in the cities by 1900, Chinese and Japanese dissenters eagerly formed socialist parties. By 1920 their members included the young Mao Zedong.

Eastern debates over industrialization varied from country to country. Just as happened in the West, there was little or nothing that great men, bungling idiots, culture, or dumb luck could have done to prevent an industrial takeoff once the possibility arose, but—again paralleling the West—these forces had everything to do with deciding which country led the way.

When W. S. Gilbert and Arthur Sullivan presented their comic opera *The Mikado* in London in 1885, they took Japan as the very model of the exotic orient, just the sort of place where little birds died for love and lord high executioners had to cut their own heads off. In reality, though, Japan was already industrializing faster than any previous society in history. Adroitly stage-managing the young new emperor installed in 1868 after the civil war, clever operators in Tokyo managed to keep their country out of wars with Western powers, finance industrialization largely from native capital, and dissuade the angry people from provocative attacks on foreigners. Clumsy operators in Beijing, by contrast, tolerated and even encouraged violence against missionaries, blundered into war with France in 1884 (losing most of their expensive new fleet in an hour), and borrowed—and embezzled—on a ruinous scale.

Japan's elite faced up to the fact that liberalization was a package deal. They put on top hats or crinolines; some discussed adopting the Latin script; others wanted Japan to speak English. They were ready to consider anything that might work. China's Qing rulers, however, were division personified. For forty-six years the dowager empress Cixi ruled from behind the bamboo curtain, opposing any modernization that might endanger the dynasty. Her one flirtation with Western ideas was to divert money intended for rebuilding the fleet into a marble copy of a Mississippi paddleboat for her summer palace (still there and well worth seeing). When her nephew Guangxu tried to rush through a hundred-day reform program in 1898 (streamlining the civil service, updating the examinations, creating modern schools and colleges, coordinating tea and silk production for export, promoting mining and railroads, and Westernizing the army and navy), Cixi announced that Guangxu had asked her to come back as regent, then locked him in the palace and executed his modernizing ministers. Guangxu remained a reformer to his bitter end, poisoned by arsenic as Cixi lay on her own deathbed in 1908.

While China stumbled toward modernity, Japan raced. In 1889 Japan published a constitution giving wealthy men the vote, allowing Western-style political parties, and creating modern government ministries. China approved a constitution only in Cixi's dying days, allowing limited male voting in 1909, but Japan made mass education a priority. By 1890 two-thirds of Japanese boys and one-third of girls received free primary schooling, while China did virtually nothing to educate the masses. Both countries laid their first railroads in 1876, but

Shanghai's governor tore out China's tracks in 1877, fearing that rebels might use them. In 1896 Japan had 2,300 miles of railway; China, just 370. Much the same story could be told about iron, coal, steam, or telegraph lines.

Throughout history, the expansion of cores has often set off ferocious wars on the peripheries to decide which part of the fringe would lead resistance (or assimilation) to the great powers. In the first millennium BCE, for instance, Athens, Sparta, and Macedon warred for a century and a half on the fringes of the Persian Empire; and Chu, Wu, and Yue did the same in southern China as the core in the Yellow River valley grew. In the nineteenth century CE, the process repeated itself when the East became a periphery to the West.

Ever since Japan's abortive effort to conquer China in the 1590s, rulers in the Eastern core had assumed that the costs of interstate war would outweigh the benefits, but the coming of the West turned that assumption on its head. Whichever Eastern nation industrialized, reorganized, and rearmed fastest would be able not just to hold the Western imperialists off but also to hold the rest of the East down.

It was ultimately Japanese industrialization, not British warships, that was China's nemesis. Japan lacked resources; China had plenty. Japan needed markets; China was full of them. Arguments in Tokyo over what should be done were furious and even murderous, but across two generations the country gradually committed to forcing its way into China's materials and markets. By the 1930s Japan's most militant officers had determined to take over the entire Eastern core, turn China and Southeast Asia into colonies, and expel the Western imperialists. A War of the East had begun.

The great difference between this War of the East and the eighteenth-century War of the West, though, was that the War of the East took place in a world where the West already ruled. This complicated everything. Thus in 1895 when Japan swept aside Chinese resistance to its advances in Korea, Germany's Kaiser Wilhelm II reacted by sending his cousin Tsar Nicholas II of Russia a rather awful drawing called "The Yellow Peril" (Figure 10.7), urging him "to cultivate the Asian Continent and to defend Europe from the inroads of the Great Yellow Race." Nicholas responded by confiscating much of the territory Japan had seized from China.

Figure 10.7. "The Yellow Peril," an 1895 drawing based on a sketch by
Kaiser Wilhelm II, aimed, he explained, to encourage Europeans
"to unite in resisting the inroad of Buddhism, heathenism, and
barbarism for the Defense of the Cross."

Other Westerners, though, saw advantages in working with Japan, using its burgeoning power to police the East for them. The first opportunity came in 1900, when a Chinese secret society called the Boxers United in Righteousness rose up against Western imperialism (claiming, among other things, that a hundred days of martial-arts training would make its members bulletproof). It took twenty thousand foreign troops to suppress them; and most of the soldiers—though you would not know it from Western accounts (particularly the 1963 Hollywood blockbuster *55 Days in Peking*)—were Japanese. So pleased was Britain with this outcome that in 1902 it signed a naval alliance recognizing Japan's great-power status in the East. Confident of British neutrality, in 1904 Japan took its revenge on Russia, sinking its Far Eastern fleet and overwhelming its army in the biggest land battle ever fought. When Tsar Nicholas sent his main fleet twenty thousand miles around the Old World to put matters right, Japanese battleships sank it, too.

Fewer than fifty years had passed since Looty relocated to London, but the old Eastern core had responded so dynamically that it could already defeat a Western empire. "What happened . . . in 1904–5," the disgraced Russian commander Aleksei Nikolaevich Kuropatkin concluded, "was nothing more than a skirmish with the advance guard . . . Only with a common recognition that keeping Asia peaceful is a matter of importance to all of Europe . . . can we keep the 'yellow peril' at bay." But Europe ignored his advice.

THE WARS OF THE WORLD

Between 1914 and 1991 the Western core fought the greatest wars in history: the First World War, between 1914 and 1918, to determine whether Germany would create a European land empire; the Second, between 1939 and 1945, over the same question; and the Cold War, between 1947 and 1991, to settle how the United States and Soviet Union would divide the spoils (Figure 10.8). Together these added up to a new War of the West that dwarfed the eighteenth-century version. It subsumed the War of the East, left a hundred million dead, and threatened humanity's very survival. In 1991 the West still ruled, but it seemed to many that Kuropatkin's fears were finally coming true: the East was poised to overtake it.

The story of how the new War of the West began has often been told—how the Ottoman Empire's long decline filled the Balkans with terrorists/freedom fighters; how, through bungling and bad luck, a gang called the Black Hand murdered the heir to Austria's Habsburg throne in June 1914 (the bomb tossed by the would-be assassin bounced off the Austrian archduke's car, only for the chauffeur to take a wrong turn, back up, and stop right in front of a second assassin, who made no mistake); and how the web of treaties designed to keep Europe's peace dragged everyone over the precipice together.

What followed is equally well known—how Europe's modernized states called up their young men in unprecedented numbers, armed them with unprecedented weapons, and bent their vast energies to unprecedented slaughter. Before 1914, some intellectuals had argued that great-power war had become impossible because the world's economies were now so interlinked that the moment war broke out all of

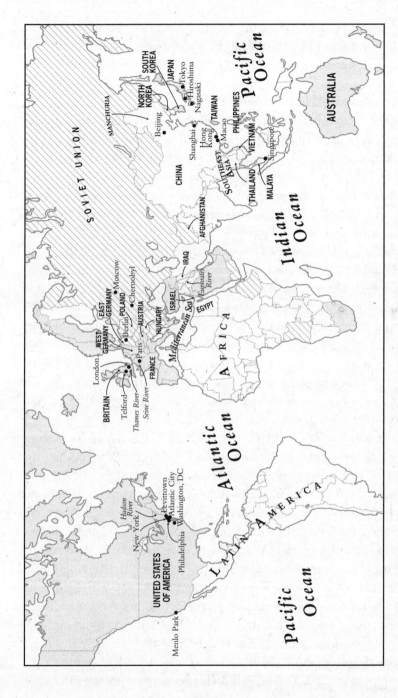

Figure 10.8. The world at war, 1914–1991. Gray shading shows the United States and its major allies around 1980; the Soviet Union and its major allies are indicated by diagonal lines.

them would collapse, ending the conflict. By 1918, though, the lesson seemed to be that only those states that could effectively harness their vast, complex economies could survive the strains of twentieth-century total war.

The war seemed to have shown that the advantage lay with liberal, democratic states, whose citizens were most fully committed to the struggle. Back in the first millennium BCE, Easterners and Westerners had all learned that dynastic empires were the most effective organizations for waging war; now, in the space of a single decade, they learned that these dynastic empires—history's most enduring form of government, with an unbroken heritage from Assyria, Persia, and Qin—were no longer compatible with war.

First to go was China's Qing dynasty. Mired in debt, defeat, and disorder, the boy emperor Puyi's ministers lost control of the army as early as 1911, but when the rebel general Yuan Shikai promoted himself to emperor in 1916—as rebel generals had been doing for two thousand years—he found that he could not hold the country together either. Another military clique restored Puyi in 1917, with no better results. China's imperial history ended a few days later, if not with a whimper then with just a very small bang: a single airplane dropped a bomb on the Forbidden City in Beijing, Puyi was deposed again, and the country descended into anarchy.

Next was Russia's Romanov dynasty. Defeat by Japan had almost toppled Tsar Nicholas in 1905, but the First World War finished the job. In 1917 liberals swept his family from power and in 1918 Bolsheviks shot them. Germany's Hohenzollerns and Austria's Habsburgs quickly followed, escaping the Romanovs' fate only by fleeing their homelands. In Turkey the Ottomans limped on, but only until 1922.

Despite the destruction, World War I strengthened Western rule by sweeping away Europe's archaic dynastic empires and leaving China weaker than ever. The big winners seemed to be France and above all Britain, who not only gobbled up German colonies and pushed their oceanic empires still farther into Africa, the Pacific, and the oil fields of the old Ottoman Empire, but also bullied their Eastern ally Japan into handing over most of the German colonies it had captured. By 1919 more than a third of the world's landmass and almost a third of its population were ruled from either London or Paris.

Yet the great swaths of color that still marked these empires in older atlases when I was a schoolboy were misleading. As well as strengthening Western power, the war redistributed it. Europe had fought beyond its means and the bills overwhelmed even British credit. Inflation hit 22 percent in 1920; the next year unemployment passed 11 percent. Eighty-six million worker-days were lost to strikes. The sun still never set on the British Empire, but it was struggling to stay open for business.

To pay its debts Britain hemorrhaged capital, most of it flowing across the Atlantic. The war had been hell, but the United States had had a hell of a war, emerging as both workshop and banker to the world. Back in the fifteenth century the Western core had shifted from the Mediterranean toward western Europe and in the seventeenth it had shifted again toward the oceanic empires of the northwest. Now, in the twentieth, it moved once more as northwest Europe's bankrupt oceanic empires lost out to a North American empire.

The United States had turned itself into a new kind of organization, one we might call a subcontinental empire. Unlike traditional dynastic empires, it had no ancient aristocracy ruling downtrodden peasants; unlike Europe's oceanic empires, it had no small, liberal, industrialized homeland holding dominion over palm and pine. Rather, after almost exterminating its native population, fighting a brutal civil war, and pushing millions of ex-slaves back into virtual serfdom, Euro-Americans had spread democratic citizenship from sea to shining sea, with prosperous farmers feeding a massive industrial heartland in the northeast and upper Midwest and buying its goods. By 1914 this subcontinental American Empire already rivaled Europe's oceanic empires, and after 1918 its businessmen went global.

The giant sucking sound of European wealth rushing into the United States astonished contemporaries. An American secretary of state observed, "The financial center of the world, which required thousands of years to journey from the banks of the Euphrates to the Thames and the Seine, seems [to be] passing to the Hudson between daybreak and dark." By 1929 Americans held more than $15 billion in foreign investments, almost as much as Britons had owned in 1913, and their global trade was worth almost 50 percent more.

The golden age of global capitalism seemed reborn under American leadership, but there was one crucial difference. Before 1914, thought

Keynes, "the influence of London on credit conditions throughout the world was so predominant that the Bank of England could almost have claimed to be the conductor of the international orchestra," but after 1918 the United States was unwilling to take on the job. Fleeing Europe's contagious rivalries and wars, American politicians left the conductor's podium empty, withdrawing into political isolation worthy of eighteenth-century China or Japan. While times were good the orchestra improvised and muddled through, but when they turned bad its music became cacophony.

In October 1929 a little bungling, a lot of bad luck, and the absence of a conductor turned an American stock market bubble into an international financial disaster. Contagion raced through the capitalist world: banks folded, credit evaporated, and currencies collapsed. Few starved, but by Christmas 1932 one American worker in four was jobless. In Germany it was closer to one in two. Lines of the gray-faced unemployed stretched out, "gazing at their destiny with the same sort of dumb amazement as animals in a trap," the English journalist George Orwell thought. "They simply could not understand what was happening to them."

At least until the mid-1930s everything the liberal democracies did just made things worse. Not only did it seem that the paradox of development had laid the Western core low; it also looked as if the advantages of backwardness were coming into play elsewhere. Russia, for centuries a rather backward periphery, had been reconstituted as the Union of Soviet Socialist Republics. Like the United States, it joined a burgeoning industrial core to a vast agricultural hinterland, but unlike the United States, it promoted state ownership, collective agriculture, and central planning. The Soviet Union mobilized its people more like a modern Western state than like an old dynastic empire, yet its autocrats Lenin and Stalin ruled more like tsars than democratic presidents.

The Soviet Union was a kind of anti-America—a subcontinental empire, but decidedly illiberal. Stalin preached equality but built a centralized economy by forcibly transporting millions of his comrades around his empire and locking another million in gulags. Ideologically suspect ethnic groups and class enemies (often the same thing) were purged. And unlike the failing capitalist economies, the successful Soviet Union did let 10 million of its subjects starve. Yet Stalin was clearly doing something right, for while capitalist industry collapsed between 1928 and 1937, Soviet output quadrupled. "I have seen the future, and it works," the journalist Lincoln Steffens famously told his fellow Americans after visiting the Soviet Union.*

By 1930 it seemed to many that the real lesson of World War I was not that liberal democracy was the shape of the future: it was that the Anglo-Franco-American alliance had won in spite of, not because of, its liberalism. The real answer was subcontinental empire, and the less liberal, the better. Japan, which had profited so much from following liberal models, abandoned them when global markets and its trade-oriented economy went into a tailspin. With unemployment soaring, democracy floundering, and Communist agitation growing, militarists stepped in, baying for an empire Japan could live off. The army—particularly its radical junior officers—went haywire, exploiting the Western democracies' disarray and China's civil wars to annex Manchuria and push toward Beijing. "It is only by bringing about Japanese-Manchurian cooperation and Japanese-Chinese friendship," a lieutenant-colonel explained, "that the Japanese people can become rulers of Asia and be prepared to wage the final and decisive war against the various white races."

Up to a point, militarism paid off. Japan's economy grew by 72 percent in the 1930s; steel output rose eighteenfold. But once again the costs were high. "Cooperation" and "friendship" often meant enslavement and slaughter, and even by the low, dishonest standards of the 1930s, Japanese brutality was shocking. Further, by 1940 it was clear that conquest had not solved Japan's problems, since the war consumed resources even faster than it captured them. Of every five gallons of oil the battleships and bombers burned, four had to be bought from Westerners. The army's plan—keep conquering—brought no relief, and with China becoming a quagmire, an even more alarming naval plan gained traction: to strike into Southeast Asia and liberate its oil and rubber from Western imperialists, even if that meant war with America.

Most alarming of all was the plan coming out of Germany. Defeat, unemployment, and financial collapse scarred the heirs of Goethe and

---

*Steffens visited the Soviet Union in 1919, but apparently composed this endorsement before his trip. Unconcerned by such details, Communists in 1930s Europe and America made it their mantra.

Kant so deeply that they were ready to listen even to a madman blaming the Jews and peddling the panacea of conquest. "The first cause of the stability of our currency is the concentration camp," Adolf Hitler assured his finance minister as he brutalized and banished Germany's Jewish business class and threw trade unionists into jail. Yet there was method in Hitler's madness: deficit spending, state ownership, and rearmament wiped out unemployment and doubled industrial output during the 1930s.

Hitler openly trumpeted his plan to secure Germany's western flank by defeating the oceanic empires and then to replace eastern Europe's Slavs and Jews with sturdy Aryan farmers. His vision of a subcontinental empire centered on Germany went beyond illiberal to downright genocidal; and few Westerners could believe he really meant it. Their self-deception brought on the one thing they most wished to avoid, another all-out war. For a few dark months it looked—for the first time since 1812—like a land empire might unite Europe after all, but in an uncanny echo of Napoleon, Hitler was turned back at the English Channel, in the snows of Moscow, and in the deserts of Egypt. Overreaching, he tried to fold Japan's War of the East into his own War of the West, but instead of knocking Britain out of the war this only brought the United States in. War made bedfellows of the liberal American and illiberal Soviet empires, and despite looting the minerals and labor of Europe and the East, Germany and Japan could not resist these empires' combined money, manpower, and manufactures.

In April 1945 American and Soviet troops joined hands in Germany, embracing, drinking toasts, and dancing together; days later Hitler shot himself and Germany surrendered. In August, as fire rained from the skies and atomic bombs turned Hiroshima and Nagasaki into ash, Japan's god-king broke with all tradition to speak to his people directly. Making what gets my vote as history's greatest understatement, he informed them, "The war situation has developed not necessarily to Japan's advantage." Even then die-hard generals attempted a coup in the hope of fighting on, but on September 2 Japan surrendered too.

Nineteen forty-five simultaneously ended Japan's attempt to win the War of the East and expel the Western imperialists, and Germany's to create a subcontinental empire in Europe, but it also ended the western European oceanic empires. Too drained by total war to resist nationalist revolts any longer, these melted away within a generation. Europe was shattered. Its "economic, social and political collapse," one American officer mused in 1945, seemed "unparalleled in history unless one goes back to the collapse of the Roman Empire."

Western social development did not collapse in 1945, though, because the core was by now so big that not even the greatest war ever fought could wreck all of it. The Soviets had rebuilt their industries beyond Germany's reach, and bombs had barely touched the United States.* By contrast, the devastation visited by Japan on China and by the United States on Japan had gutted the Eastern core, with the consequence that the Second World War—like the First—made Western rule still stronger. There seemed little doubt that Western dominance was here to stay; the question was whether its leadership would be Soviet or American.

These two empires divided the old European core between them, splitting Germany down the middle. American moneymen then hashed out a new international financial system for capitalism and crafted the Marshall Plan, perhaps the most enlightened piece of self-interest on record. If Europeans had money in their pockets, Americans reasoned, they could buy American food, import American machinery to rebuild their own industry, and—most important of all—restrain themselves from voting Communist; so America simply gave them $13.5 billion, one-twentieth of its entire 1948 production.

Western Europeans mostly grabbed America's money, accepted its military leadership, and joined or drifted toward a democratic, pro-trade European union.† (The irony of the United States nudging Europeans toward a pale version of a land empire under West German industrial domination was lost on no one.) Eastern Europeans accepted Soviet

---

*Other than the attack on Pearl Harbor, the only destruction on American soil came from a single Japanese plane (launched from a submarine) that bombed Brookings, Oregon, in 1942.

†This began with the Organization for European Economic Cooperation, founded in 1948, and the 1952 European Coal and Steel Community. These were refounded in 1958 as the European Economic Community and transformed into the European Union by the 1993 Maastricht Treaty.

military leadership and a Communist, inward-turned Council for Mutual Economic Assistance. Instead of pumping resources into eastern Europe and promoting democracy, the Soviets pumped resources out and jailed or shot their opponents, but even so, eastern European output regained prewar levels by 1949. In the American sphere things went better still, and with remarkably few jailings or shootings, output doubled between 1948 and 1964.

The American and Soviet empires were not the first to share the Western core, but atomic weapons made them different from all their predecessors. The Soviets tested a bomb in 1949 and by 1954 both sides had hydrogen bombs a thousand times more violent than the weapon that eviscerated Hiroshima—as far beyond it, Churchill wrote in his diary, as the "atomic bomb itself from the bow and arrow." A Kremlin report concluded that war might "create on the whole globe conditions impossible for life."

Yet the mushroom cloud had a silver lining: "Strange as it may seem," Churchill told the British Parliament, "it is to the universality of potential destruction that I think we may look with hope and even confidence." The doctrine of Mutual Assured Destruction had been born, and although a string of terrifying slip-ups brought the world several times to the brink of Armageddon, in the end the West fought no Third World War.

Instead, it fought a war in the Third World over the ruins of the western European and Japanese empires, waged mostly through proxies (normally rural revolutionaries for the Soviets and thuggish dictators for the Americans). On the face of it, this should have been a walkover for the United States, which bestrode the globe even more colossally than Britain had done a century earlier. In the East in particular, Washington apparently held all the cards. Pumping half a billion dollars into Japan, it created a loyal, prosperous ally, and backed by generous American aid a Nationalist army looked set to defeat Mao Zedong's Communists and finally end China's civil war.

The Nationalists' abrupt collapse in 1949 changed everything, turning the East into the hottest spot of the now-cold War of the West. Stalin encouraged North Korea to invade America's client state South Korea, and when things went badly Mao joined in too. By the time the fighting ground to a halt in 1953, 4 million people had died (including one of Mao's sons) and guerrilla wars were raging in the Philippines, Malaya, and Indochina. American proxies won the first two, as well as a struggle in Indonesia, but by 1968 half a million Americans were on the ground in Vietnam—and losing.

These struggles were simultaneously fronts in the Soviet-American War of the West and wars of national liberation, but were in no sense a renewed War of the East. China and Japan, the East's great powers, saw little to gain from expansion after 1945. China had troubles enough at home, while Japan—in an irony every bit as odd as West Germany's successes in Europe—was busy achieving peacefully many of the goals it had sought violently in 1941. Brilliantly exploiting American support, Japan took advantage of the destruction of its old industries to reorganize, mechanize, and find profitable niches. By 1969 Japan's economy overtook West Germany's, and through the 1970s it steadily gained on the United States.

By then the United States was feeling the strain of the multifront Cold War. Despite dropping more bombs on Vietnam than it had on Germany, America suffered a humiliating defeat, dividing opinion at home and wounding its influence abroad. Soviet proxies started winning wars in Africa, Asia, and Latin America, and even America's successes turned to ashes. Eastern clients that the United States had so assiduously built up were now doing so well that they were invading American markets, while the European allies it defended at such expense now talked of disarmament and going nonaligned. By making Israel a client, Washington drove Arab governments toward the Soviets; and when Israel repulsed Arab invasions in 1973, Arab oil embargoes and price hikes set loose the new monster of stagflation—simultaneous stagnation and inflation.

When I was a teenager in 1970s Britain, my friends and I talked casually of the coming American collapse as we sat around wearing American jeans, watching American films, and playing American guitars. So far as I remember, none of us ever saw a contradiction in this, and I'm pretty certain that it never crossed our minds that far from witnessing the end of the American Empire, we were actually doing our bit to win the War of the West for Washington. The decisive front, it would soon emerge, was not in Vietnam or Angola. It was in the shopping malls.

THE AGE OF EVERYTHING

"Let's be frank about it," Britain's prime minister told voters in 1957. "Most of our people have never had it so good." The British might have lost an empire and failed to find a role, but, like increasing numbers of people around the world, they at least had lots of things. By the 1960s luxuries that had not even existed a century before—radios, televisions, record players, cars, refrigerators, telephones, electric lights (and, what I remember best, the plastic toys)—were everyday items in the Western core (Figure 10.9).

It struck some as an age of vulgarity, a world, one poet put it, where

> . . . *residents from raw estates, brought down*
> *The dead straight miles by stealing flat-faced trolleys,*
> *Push through plate-glass swing doors to their desires—*

Figure 10.9. Never had it so good: the author and his toys, Christmas Day, 1964

*Cheap suits, red kitchen-ware, sharp shoes, iced lollies,**
Electric mixers, toasters, washers, driers—
A cut-price crowd, urban yet simple, dwelling
Where only salesmen and relations come.

Suburbs and satellite cities unfolded around every exit ramp and by-pass, from America's Levittown to Britain's Telford, offending the aesthetes with their boxiness and monotony; but they gave the people what we wanted—a little space, indoor plumbing, and garages for our shiny Fords.

The twentieth century was the age of everything, of material abundance beyond the dreams of avarice. Cheap coal and oil generated electricity for all, turning on engines and lighting up houses at the flick of a switch. More than two thousand years earlier Aristotle had observed that slaves would always be with us, unless people had *automata*—self-moving machines—to do the work for them. Now his fantasy came true, electricity giving even the humblest among us the equivalent of dozens of slaves to fulfill our every demand for entertainment, warmth, and—particularly—food.

This energy revolution turned the sixteenth century's fairy tales of endless feasts into reality. Between 1500 and 1900 wheat yields had roughly doubled in the Western core, thanks to better-organized farming and more draft animals and manure, but by the 1890s farmers were reaching the limits of ingenuity. Adding more animals could drive up productivity only so far, and by 1900 a quarter of North America's farmland was being used to feed horses. Then gasoline came to the rescue. America's first tractor factory opened in 1905, and by 1927 tractors provided as much energy on American farms as horses.

There was no gain without pain. Half of all Americans worked the soil in 1875, but a century later only one in fifty did. Machines ate men, tractoring whole communities off land that could be worked more profitably by a few hired hands and diesel engines. "Snub-nosed monsters," the novelist John Steinbeck called the tractors, "raising dust and sticking their snouts into it, straight down the country, across the country, through fences, through dooryards, in and out of gullies in straight lines."

*Popsicles.

Steinbeck anticipated the wretched of the earth rising in revolution, but when the tidal waves of dispossession that swept surplus Okies westward and black cotton pickers northward receded, most migrants found city jobs that paid better than the rural grind they had fled. The agrobusinessmen who had displaced them now sold them cheap food and invested the profits in chemical fertilizers and herbicides, electric motors to pump water to dry fields, and eventually genetically modified crops that could withstand almost anything. By 2000 each acre of American farmland absorbed eighty times more energy than it had in 1900 and yielded four times as much food.

Where America went today, the world followed tomorrow. A "green revolution" quadrupled global food production between 1950 and 2000. Prices fell steadily, meat replaced grains in diets, and—except when disaster, stupidity, and brutality intervened—starvation was steadily banished.

Like all organisms, humans converted extra energy into offspring, and the world's population almost quadrupled along with the food supply in the twentieth century. But in other ways humans departed from the norm. Instead of turning their entire energy windfall into new bodies, they hoarded some of it in their own bodies. On average, adults were 50 percent bigger by 2000 than they had been in 1900. They grew four inches taller, filled out, and had more energy for work. Growing more robust organs and carrying more fat (in rich countries, too much fat), these bigger humans could resist more disease and trauma. Modern Americans and western Europeans typically live thirty years longer than their great-grandparents and enjoy an extra decade or two before their eyes, ears, and other organs weaken and arthritis freezes their joints. In much of the rest of the world, including China and Japan, life spans have lengthened by closer to forty years. Even in Africa, plagued by AIDS and malaria, average life expectancy was twenty years higher in 2009 than it was around 1900.

The human body has changed more in the last hundred years than in the previous fifty thousand, and—particularly in rich countries—people have learned to intervene to correct the failings that remained. Europeans had been using eyeglasses since 1300, but these now spread all over the globe. Doctors invented new techniques to salvage hearing, keep hearts pumping, reattach limbs, and even intervene in cells.

Public health programs eradicated smallpox and measles as mass killers; garbage collection and clean drinking water did still more.

Figure 10.10, showing what kinds of chronic conditions afflicted veterans from the United States Army, gives a sense of just how much health has improved. Veterans may not be the ideal subset of humanity to study, given the violence of their line of work, but thanks to obsessive military record-keeping they are the best subset we have, and the improvements are stunning.

These veterans were mostly men, but women's lives changed even more. Throughout history, women had been baby-making machines. Because half of their babies died in their first year (most, in fact, in their first week) and only half of those who survived childhood made it to their fortieth birthdays, maintaining a stable population (rearing two offspring to adulthood to replace a mother and her mate) required the average woman to give birth about five times, spending most of her adult life pregnant and/or nursing. But in the twentieth century this high-mortality, low-technology world collapsed.

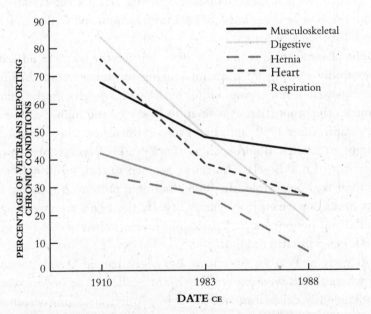

Figure 10.10. Be all that you can be: the health of United States Army veterans, 1910–1988

Even before 1900 bigger, better-fed, stronger women were bearing sturdier babies, feeding them more, and keeping them cleaner. Fewer of their young died, so population grew explosively—until women brought their fertility under control. People had always had ways to avoid conception (legend has it that the eighteenth-century lover Casanova made his own condoms by cutting lemons in half) and birth rates were falling in the richest countries by 1900, but in the twentieth century American technology rose to this challenge too. In 1920 came latex condoms; in 1960 the oral contraceptive; and in rich countries the birth rate dropped below the replacement level of two per couple.

As healthier children and the pill released women from lifetimes of breeding, cheap electrical heating coils for irons and toasters and little motors for washing machines and vacuum cleaners released them from household drudgery too. Pressing a button took care of tasks that previously called for hours of tedious labor. A woman's work was still never done, but by 1960 she could jump in the car (almost every American family had one), drive to the supermarket (where two-thirds of the country's food was sold), store her purchases in the refrigerator (98 percent of houses had them), and put the laundry on before the two or three kids got back from school and settled in front of the TV.

The changes freed women for work outside the home in an economy rapidly shifting from manufacturing toward services, shedding blue-collar labor but crying out for pink-collar workers. In the richest countries the proportion of women in paid jobs and higher education rose steadily after 1960, and, like every era before it, this age got the thought it needed. Books such as *The Feminine Mystique* and *Sexual Politics* urged middle-class American women to seek fulfillment outside their traditional roles. In 1968 a hundred protestors broke up the Miss America pageant in Atlantic City. By the 1990s men were actually sharing housework and parenting (even if their wives and girlfriends generally still did more).

As early as 1951 an American sociologist named David Riesman saw where things were heading. In a story called "The Nylon Wars," simultaneously celebrating and mocking American consumerism, he imagined strategists advising the president that "if allowed to sample the riches of America, the Russian people would not long tolerate masters who gave them tanks and spies instead of vacuum cleaners." The United States drops stockings and cigarettes on the Soviet Union and communism at once collapses.

Reality was almost as strange as fiction. In 1958 the Soviet Union and United States, each confident of overawing the other with its industrial strength, agreed to hold manufacturing expositions in each other's country. To the first, in New York, the Soviets sent tractors, trucks, and mock-ups of rockets to convince the capitalists that resistance was futile. In 1959 the United States struck back brilliantly, dispatching Richard Nixon (then vice president) to Moscow to superintend a fifty-thousand-square-foot exhibit of American home appliances, including an exact copy of a new tract house from Long Island. While puzzled Muscovites looked on, Nixon and Khrushchev squared off across a Westinghouse washing machine.

"Anything that makes women work less is good," Nixon opened, but Khrushchev was ready for him. "You want to keep your women in the kitchen," he countered. "We don't think of women in those terms. We think better of them." Possibly so; more women worked outside the home in the Soviet Union than in the United States. On the other hand, another decade would pass before even half of Soviet households owned a washing machine. After taking the bus back from her factory job, the typical Soviet wife did an additional twenty-eight hours of housework per week. Only one apartment in eight had a vacuum cleaner, though perhaps, good Communists all, the comrades shared them.

Nixon responded with a paean to free enterprise. "We don't have one decision made at the top by one government office," he explained. "We have many different manufacturers and many different kinds of washing machines so that the housewives have a choice . . . Would it not be better to compete in the relative merits of washing machines than in the strength of rockets? . . . We won't thrust it [our lifestyle] upon you," he concluded, "but your grandchildren will see it."

Nixon was right. In 1959 Khrushchev simply denied that American workers lived in such houses, but by the 1980s his grandchildren could see they were being lied to. In a way, the paradox of development was to blame again: most Soviet citizens did now have washing machines and vacuum cleaners, but they also had radios, televisions, and black-market rock music records. They could see for themselves that Americans were pulling even further ahead. A joke started doing the rounds. A train, it said, is carrying former Soviet leaders across the steppes. Suddenly the train stops. Acting true to form, Stalin jumps up and shouts: "Flog the driver!" The driver is flogged but the train does not move. Khrushchev then orders: "Rehabilitate the driver!" This is done, but still nothing happens. Then Brezhnev smiles and suggests: "Let's just pretend the train is moving."

It was bad enough that the subjects of the Soviet Empire could turn on their televisions and see people like me with my guitars and jeans, but what was catastrophic was that they could see that a whole new phase of the industrial revolution was beginning, driven by information technology and generating even greater wealth for those on the right side of the Iron Curtain. The first American computer, the Electronic Numerical Integrator and Calculator (ENIAC), had been unveiled in 1946. It weighed thirty tons and used so much electricity that when it was switched on, lights all over Philadelphia dimmed. Over the next thirty years, International Business Machines (IBM) sold smaller but still monstrous machines to the West's corporations, but the real transformation followed the invention of the microprocessor in 1971.

As so often, the innovators came from the fringes of the elite—in this case, not from ultrarespectable firms such as IBM but, like Steve Wozniak, from garages in places such as suburban Menlo Park in California. Starting with just $91,000 capital and a few geeky friends, Wozniak and his business partner Steve Jobs released their Apple I microcomputer into the world in 1976. By 1982 Apple's sales had reached $583 million and IBM had invented the Personal Computer to compete. By then the Harvard dropouts Bill Gates and Paul Allen had founded Microsoft and relocated to the West Coast. Computing moved into every office and home, getting cheaper and easier every year. It even became fun.

Computers changed how the Western core entertained itself, did business, and waged war. By 1985 there was no walk of Western life computers had not touched—except in the Soviet Empire. Pretending the train was moving was no longer an option.

THE PEOPLE'S PARADISE

Nor was it an option in the East, where America's client states were rapidly pulling away from Communist China. Japan, followed by Taiwan and South Korea, swiftly moved up the economic food chain from the plastic toys I so appreciated in the 1960s to heavy industry and electronics, and as they did so, other Eastern nations (Singapore, Malaysia, Thailand) took their places at the bottom of the ladder. All over the East wages rose. Lives lengthened; babies fattened up; bigger apartments filled with gadgets. There were far fewer televisions in China than in the Soviet Union, but the policy makers in Beijing saw all too clearly the threat posed by outposts of prosperity around their east coast. These "Asian Tigers," as they became known, were an affront. All had more or less one-party rule and all shared China's Confucian and Buddhist background. So if neither authoritarianism nor Eastern cultural traditions prevented meteoric growth, where could the problem lie except with communism itself?

The century of civil war and factional fighting between the 1840s and 1940s had prevented China from following Japan's rapid industrialization, but after his victory in 1949, Mao Zedong quickly adopted Lenin's example and reorganized his realm as a subcontinental empire. Peace brought huge dividends, and just as had happened when the Sui dynasty reunited China in the sixth century, the Song in the tenth, and the Ming in the fourteenth, the economy revived. The Soviet-style Five Year Plan that Mao launched when the Korean War petered out was much less effective than the Asian Tigers' capitalism, but it still more than doubled industrial output and pushed real wages up by a third. Life expectancy at birth soared from thirty-six years in 1950 to fifty-seven in 1957.

There is good reason to think the Chinese economy would have continued growing strongly through the 1960s and '70s if Mao had let it, but, like so many earlier Chinese emperors, Mao mistrusted his bureaucrats. The spurious laws of economics, he insisted, must yield to the truer laws of Marxism, but his planners—with their slide rules and graphs—seemed suspiciously bourgeois. Only when the indomitable will of the masses was unleashed, Mao insisted, would the people's paradise be established.

Mao had come of intellectual age in the 1910s, reading Marx (and Spencer); he was a long-term lock-in theorist, convinced that Eastern inferiority had been set in stone centuries ago. The answer, he decided, was to sweep away the "Four Olds"—old customs, old habits, old culture, and old thinking. Even the family had to go: "The dearest people in the world are our parents," the *China Youth Journal* explained, "yet they cannot be compared with Chairman Mao and the Communist Party . . . which has given us everything." Proclaiming a "Great Leap Forward" in which China would catch up with the West, Mao bundled 99 percent of the population into collective farms with thousands of members. In some places, utopianism ran riot:

> The Party Secretary of Paoma town announced in October 1958 that Socialism would end on November 7th and Communism would begin on November 8th. After the meeting, everyone immediately took to the streets and began grabbing goods out of the shops. When the shelves were bare, they went to other people's homes and took their chickens and vegetables home to eat. People even stopped making a distinction as to which children belonged to whom. Only wives were safe from this sharing because the Party Secretary was unsure about this.

In other places, cynicism prevailed. Some called this the Eat-It-All-Up Period: with every incentive to work and save taken away, many people did neither.

Pressured from higher up to report bigger harvests even though yields were falling, party officials did so and then confiscated ever-larger slices of production to justify their figures. "It is not that there is no food," one commissar insisted. "There is plenty of grain, but 90 percent of the people have ideological problems."

To make matters worse, Mao fell out with Khrushchev. Cut off from Soviet aid, he tried to match Western steel production by pulling 40 million peasants off the land to build backyard foundries, smelting whatever ores they could find locally and even melting their pots and pans to forge homemade steel. Little of what they produced was usable, but no one dared say so.

The countryside became increasingly surreal. "The air," said one reporter, "is filled with the high-pitched melodies of local operas pouring through an amplifier above the site and accompanied by the hum of blowers, the panting of gasoline engines, the honking of heavily laden lorries, and the bellowing of oxen hauling ore and coal."

"Communism is paradise," the peasants were expected to sing; "the People's Communes are the bridge to it." But there was trouble in paradise. When not singing, the people were starving. The following recollection is unusual only in its dispassionate tone:

> No one in our family died. By February 1960, Grandpa's legs were completely swollen. His hair fell out, his body was covered in sores, and he was too weak to open his mouth. A friend came by and drained off some of the sores and this helped. We still had three small goats and an aunt killed two of them secretly to help him. Unfortunately, the cadres discovered this and took the carcasses away.

Even so, Grandpa was lucky. According to another informant,

> The worst thing that happened during the famine was this: parents would decide to allow the old and the young to die first . . . a mother would say to her daughter, "You have to go and see your granny in heaven." They stopped giving the girl-children food. They just gave them water . . . One woman was reported and arrested by the Public Security Bureau. No one in the village criticized her when she returned from a labor camp a few years later.

About 20 million starved between 1958 and 1962. After Mao's death, the Central Committee of the Chinese Communist Party officially concluded that the Great Helmsman had been right 70 percent of the time and wrong 30 percent, but around 1960 the party was much less convinced of this. A technocratic clique sidelined Mao and reintroduced some private property. By 1965 harvests had returned to 1957 levels.

Mao, though, was not beaten. China, like the West, had gone through a postwar baby boom, spawning a huge cohort of impatient teenagers. Affluent youngsters in the liberal Western core exploited their purchasing power to reorient taste around their music, clothes, and sexual mores, but in China Mao reoriented the tastes of angry youngsters around himself. Preaching a permanent "Great Proletarian Cultural Revolution," in 1966 he incited the young to attack everything.

Abandoning schools and colleges, millions of adolescents became rampaging Red Guards, beating and humiliating first their teachers and then anyone else who looked reactionary. While Western youths sang about revolution, Chinese youths lived it. "It was class hatred that made me denounce [my classmate] Li Jianping," one literature student proudly wrote on a poster,

> and that drove the masses to such popular fury. They beat her— a counterrevolutionary element sheltered by the old municipal party committee for so many years—to death with their clubs. It was an immensely satisfying event, to avenge the revolutionary people, to avenge the dead martyrs. Next I am going to settle scores with those bastards who shelter traitors.

Mao tried to direct this rage against his rivals but never really controlled it. With no one safe from denunciation as a counterrevolutionary, people rushed to get their criticisms in first. To many it was just bewildering: one latrine attendant grumbled that he was out of work because too many professors were being forced to clean toilets as re-education. Yet plenty found it exhilarating. Young workers flocked to join the students and factories ground to a halt. Red Guards invited film crews to record them smashing Buddhist statues, Confucian temples, and Han dynasty relics. One gang even occupied the Ministry of Foreign Affairs and appointed its own properly proletarian diplomats.

In 1969, with events apparently lurching toward disaster on the scale of the Great Leap Forward, even Mao lost his nerve. Thousands had died. Millions had had their lives ruined. The Asian Tigers were steadily pulling away from the People's Republic. Relations with the Soviets were so bad that eight hundred Chinese had been killed in border clashes. Mao belatedly distanced himself from the radicals and looked around for a lifeline.

He was thrown one by perhaps the least likely person on earth—the United States' virulently anti-Communist president Richard Nixon. Nixon saw a deal with China as a way to outflank the Soviets in the Cold War, and in 1972, after much back-channel diplomacy, he flew to Beijing and shook Mao's hand. "This was the week that changed the world," Nixon crowed, and in some ways he was right. The prospect of a Washington–Beijing axis terrified Brezhnev so much that within three months of going to China, Nixon was sitting in Moscow making deals.

Mao profited almost as much. By meeting Nixon he signaled support for the pragmatists who hungered after Western technology and opposition to the radicals who had gutted China's educated classes. In one celebrated case, a student won a coveted university place by turning in a blank examination book with a note claiming that revolutionary purity was more valuable than "bookworms who for many years have been taking it easy and have done nothing useful." In a flourish that Soviet jokers might have appreciated, radical bigwigs (allegedly) argued that "a socialist train behind schedule is better than a revisionist train on schedule."

After 1972 the pragmatists pushed back, although it was only after Mao died in 1976 that the tide turned decisively in their favor. Deng Xiaoping, twice purged as a Right Deviationist under Mao and twice rehabilitated, now muscled his rivals aside and showed his true colors. Taking Mao's old mantra "seek truth from facts" as his motto, Deng squarely confronted the most inconvenient truth in China: that the population was growing faster than the economy. To feed all the empty stomachs that came onto the job market each year, China's economy needed to grow by 7 percent every year for at least a generation. The alternative could be famines that would dwarf the Great Leap Forward.

Every experience suggested that given peace and a united government—both largely lacking since the 1840s—China, too, could prosper within the Western-dominated global economy, but Deng went further still, actively pushing China toward integration. To reduce the pressure on resources, he promoted the notorious One Child Policy, which (in theory) required women who had two babies to be sterilized,* and to increase the resources available he embraced the global economy. China joined the World Bank and International Monetary

---

*It is not clear how much impact this actually had. In 1974, the average birth rate had been 4.2 children per woman. By 1980, when the policy got properly established, this had fallen to 2.2. The decline then slowed, taking another fifteen years to fall to 1.0 per woman. China's population will probably peak around 2015.

Fund, opened Special Economic Zones to attract capitalists from Macao, Hong Kong, and Taiwan, and even admitted a Coca-Cola plant to Shanghai.

By 1983 Deng had effectively killed Mao's communes. Peasants were pursuing "sideline" activities for personal gain and businessmen were keeping some of their profits. Farmland still belonged to collectives but families could now lease plots for thirty years and work them privately. Urban property, on longer leases, could even be mortgaged. Output soared, and although liberalization horrified conservatives, there was no going back. "During the 'Cultural Revolution,'" Deng pronounced,

> there was a view that poor communism was preferable to rich capitalism . . . Because I refuted that view, I was brought down . . . [but] the main task of socialism is to develop the productive forces, steadily improve the life of the people, and keep increasing the material wealth of the society . . . To get rich is no sin.

Similar thoughts were also assailing Communists four thousand miles away in Moscow. After the shock of Nixon's trip to China the 1970s had gone rather well for the Soviet Union. When the Arab states drove up the price of oil, the Soviet Union, a massive exporter, benefited too, and with money rolling in, Moscow funded and won a series of proxy wars and overtook America in nuclear arms in 1978. But that was communism's high tide. An intervention to prop up a client regime in Afghanistan turned into a draining war that dragged on through the 1980s. Oil prices fell by two-thirds, and the United States sharply increased military spending, especially on high-tech weapons.

The politburo was already worried that ordinary Russians could see their train was standing still. Its state-run economy could churn out tanks and Kalashnikovs but not computers or cars (another Soviet joke—"How do you double a Lada's* value?" The answer: "Fill up the tank"). Dissent was simmering everywhere. The thought of a new arms race terrified the Soviet Empire's rulers.

---

*A Soviet car.

"We can't go on living like this," Mikhail Gorbachev confessed to his wife, Raisa, as they paced their garden in 1985. Gorbachev would, in a few hours, be named premier of the Soviet Union, yet the garden was the only place he could escape his own snooping spies. Like Deng, Gorbachev knew he had to face reality. The explosion of an antiquated nuclear reactor at Chernobyl in 1986 revealed that the Soviet Union was not just falling behind but actually falling apart, and Gorbachev threw restructuring (*perestroika*) and transparency (*glasnost'*) into high gear—only to rediscover what Marx and Engels had known a century and a half before: liberalization sweeps away *all* fixed, fast-frozen relations, not just those we dislike.

All that was solid melted into air, and Deng and Gorbachev both learned that economic freedoms merely whetted appetites for political ones. Sometimes Deng found the protesters useful allies against hard-line Communists; sometimes he cracked down on them. Gorbachev, though, suspected that trying to use force could cause the whole regime to collapse. When he allowed open elections to the Congress of People's Deputies in spring 1989 and the deputies repaid this by jeering him on live television, he declined to suspend Congress. Instead he flew to Beijing, where protestors against one-party rule cheered him. "In the Soviet Union they have Gorbachev," one student poster read. "In China, we have whom?"

Deng, not amused, declared martial law the day after Gorbachev left. By early June 1989 a million protestors were crammed around Tiananmen Square, some dancing and singing, some dying on hunger strike. Deng branded them the "dregs of society," people determined to "establish a bourgeois republic entirely dependent on the West," and sent in the troops. Pictures flashed around the world of torn bodies, crushed bicycles, and a lone, unknown protestor blocking the path of advancing tanks.

Repression won in China, but even when Hungary and Poland announced multiparty elections, Gorbachev still resisted Deng's lead. Following what one minister called the Sinatra Doctrine, he left the Soviet satellites to do it their way. So astonished was the newly elected Polish prime minister that he fainted during his own inauguration. Testing the limits, Hungarian troops rolled up the barbed wire along their border with Austria. Thousands of East Germans "vacationing" in Hungary abandoned their cars and walked across the border to freedom.

And still Gorbachev did nothing. When he visited Berlin in October, crowds again cheered him and begged him to stay. Over the next few weeks East Germans started dancing on top of the Berlin Wall and chipping at it with hammers and chisels. When no one shot them, thousands crossed into West Berlin. Confused and incompetent, the East German regime disintegrated. Over the next few months Communist dictators all across eastern Europe went the same way and the nations bundled together within the Soviet Union started declaring independence. When even the president of the new Russian Federation announced his intention to quit the union, Gorbachev was left as general secretary of an empire that no longer existed. On Christmas Day, 1991, he bowed to pressure to sign a decree formally dissolving it. The end was almost too perfect: Gorbachev's Soviet pen would not write and he had to borrow one from a CNN cameraman.

The United States had won the War of the West.

EAST WIND, WEST WIND

When dynastic empires proved unable to cope with total war, almost vanishing from the earth between 1917 and 1922, the United States had shown itself a very reluctant leviathan, but when communism proved equally inadequate between 1989 and 1991, Americans were ready to fill the void. Every two years, the Department of Defense reviews its grand strategy in a report called the Defense Planning Guidance. The first draft of the report due in March 1992, just three months after the fall of the Soviet Union, laid out a bold new vision:

> Our first objective is to prevent the reemergence of a new rival, either on the territory of the former Soviet Union or elsewhere, that poses a threat on the order of that posed formerly by the Soviet Union. This . . . requires that we endeavor to prevent any hostile power from dominating a region whose resources would, under consolidated control, be sufficient to generate global power. These regions include

Western Europe, East Asia, the territory of the former Soviet Union, and Southwest Asia.

When "an official who believes this post-cold-war strategy debate should be carried out in the public domain" (as *The New York Times* put it) leaked this draft, the government quickly softened its tone, but something very like the original vision of a world with the United States as its sole superpower came to pass all the same.

The old Soviet Union imploded in a scramble to loot its assets. The breakdown was not as bad as the civil war that had followed the fall of the Romanovs, but Russia, the main successor state, nevertheless saw output fall 40 percent in the 1990s and real wages 45 percent. In 1970 the average Soviet citizen died at sixty-eight, just four years younger than the average western European; by 2000 the average Russian died at sixty-six, twelve years behind residents of the European Union. Russia was still enormous, resource-rich, and the world's biggest nuclear power, and by 2008 the return of strong government and rising energy prices had emboldened it into bullying the former Soviet republics and blackmailing the European Union. But as the Defense Planning Guidance had hoped, Russia posed nothing like the threat of the old Soviet Union.

Nor did the European Union challenge America's dominance of the Western core. To some viewers Europe's lurches toward (then away from) economic and political integration looked like steps toward a mighty subcontinental empire, finally achieving peacefully what the Habsburgs, Bourbons, Napoleon, and Hitler had failed to achieve through violence, but in reality Europe's continuing divisions, slowing economic growth, aging population, and military weakness left it far from superpower status.

Southwest Asia featured in the 1992 planners' minds largely because they feared a hostile state seizing the region's oil fields, as Iraq tried to do in 1990. They ignored the Islamist extremism that had been growing since the 1970s, and (like almost everyone else) were blindsided by the September 11, 2001, attacks on the United States. But it was in the East that the planners' assumptions proved most spectacularly wrong. Within weeks of the Defense Planning Guidance being leaked to the press, America's major Eastern ally, Japan, plunged into recession and its major Eastern rival, China, took off.

A hundred and fifty years had passed since the West began turning the old Eastern core into a periphery, and the lessons were clear to all who had eyes to see. Given peace, responsible government, and willingness to bend to Western power, Easterners could turn the capitalist world economy to their own ends, converting the huge populations and learned elites that had struck nineteenth-century Westerners as evidence of Eastern backwardness into engines of economic growth. Since the 1840s China had had precious little peace, responsibility, or flexibility, but in the 1990s it began to take its rightful place in the global order.

From the unlikely podium of the back of a golf cart in the middle of a theme park, Deng announced that economic reform would no longer "proceed slowly like women with bound feet, but . . . [would] blaze a trail and press forward boldly." The obstacles to red capitalism crumbled. When Mao and Nixon met in the early 1970s the typical American worker was nearly twenty times as productive as the typical undercapitalized Chinese laborer and the United States created 22 percent of the world's goods compared with China's 5 percent. Across the next thirty years American productivity continued to rise, but investment drove China's up three times as fast. By 2000, American workers were less than seven times as productive as Chinese. The United States' share of world production had barely changed, at 21 percent, but China's had nearly tripled, to 14 percent.

China paid a terrible price for this growth. Virtually unregulated factories dumped waste at will, poisoning major rivers. Cancer rates along these waterways were often double the national average. Other rivers, tapped for equally unregulated agriculture, dried up altogether. Logging ran wild and deserts expanded twice as fast as before the 1970s. Protests against government incompetence and endemic corruption became increasingly violent; most years since 2000 the police have recorded around 25,000 "mass incidents" and far more small riots.

In return, though, Deng's program headed off starvation and delivered big income gains. Country folk, who still make up two-thirds of China's population, saw real wages rise about 6 percent per year. The gains, however, were concentrated along the eastern seaboard, and in dirt-poor inland villages the decline of Mao's rudimentary but free education and health care often canceled them out. One result was the biggest migration in history: since the 1990s 150 million people have moved to the cities, creating the equivalent of a new Chicago every year. Relocating to a city typically raised a farmer's income by 50 percent while simultaneously providing manufacturers with labor at a fraction of its cost in rich countries.

Between 1992 and 2007 China's exports increased a dozen-fold and its trade surplus with the United States ballooned from $18 billion to $233 billion. In American discount stores such as Wal-Mart, Chinese-made goods typically filled 90 percent of the shelf space by 2008; rare was the American who did not don at least one piece of made-in-China clothing every morning. *Business Week* magazine observed that "the China price" had become "the three scariest words in U.S. industry." Companies that could not match it went under.

Like nineteenth-century Britain and twentieth-century America, China became the workshop to the world. The financial journalist James Kynge describes overhearing a conversation on a train in Italy between two Chinese businessmen, sounding for all the world like a couple of Gradgrinds wrenched from the pages of Dickens:

> The boss remarked that they had been traveling for an hour and a half and had hardly seen a single factory. "Foreigners like looking at scenery," the young man offered. The boss paused for thought, then asked, "Scenery or production, which is more important?" . . . The boss's curiosity ranged over many subjects . . . Why were foreigners so lazy? What was Europe going to do when it did not have much industry left? Could you really run an economy on services alone? Did European cows really consume two dollars a day in farm subsidies?

Half a century earlier, Mao had claimed, "The direction of the wind in the world has changed . . . At present, it is not the west wind that prevails over the east wind but the east wind that prevails over the west." At the time, he was fooling himself; the 1950s East was very much under the West's wing, divided between Soviet and American spheres. But by 2000 Mao's words were coming true, albeit not in ways he had intended. Western social development was further ahead of Eastern—over three hundred points—than ever before, but whereas

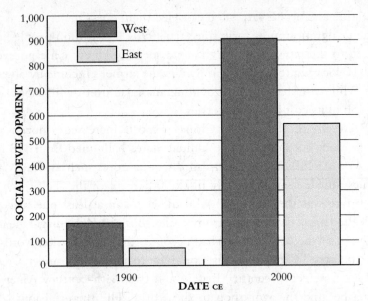

Figure 10.11. Knowing which way the wind blows: Was the twentieth century
both the high point and the end point of Western rule? The West's lead
in social development increased from 101 points in 1900 to 336 in 2000,
but the ratio between the Western and Eastern scores shrank by one-third,
from 2.4:1 in 1900 to 1.6:1 in 2000.

the ratio between the Western and Eastern score had been almost 2.4:1
in 1900, by 2000 it was only a little over 1.6:1. The twentieth century
was both the high point of the Western age and the beginning of
its end.

PART III

◎ ◎ ◎

11

○ ○ ○

WHY THE WEST RULES . . .

WHY THE WEST RULES

The West rules because of geography. Biology tells us why humans push social development upward; sociology tells us how they do this (except when they don't); and geography tells us why the West, rather than some other region, has for the last two hundred years dominated the globe. Biology and sociology provide universal laws, applying to all humans in all times and places; geography explains differences.

Biology tells us that we are animals, and like all living things we exist only because we capture energy from our surroundings. When short of energy, we grow sluggish and die; when filled with it, we multiply and spread out. Like other animals, we are inquisitive but also greedy, lazy, and fearful; we are unlike other animals only in the tools we have for pursuing these moods—the faster brains, more pliable throats, and opposable thumbs that evolution gave us. Using these, we humans have imposed our wills on our environments in ways quite unlike other animals, capturing and organizing ever more energy, spreading villages, cities, states, and empires across the planet.

In the nineteenth and early twentieth centuries plenty of Westerners thought biology was the whole answer to why the West rules. The white European race, they insisted, had evolved further than anyone else. They were mistaken. For one thing, the genetic and skeletal evidence that I discussed in Chapter 1 is unequivocal: there is one kind of human, which evolved gradually in Africa around a hundred thousand years ago and then spread across the globe, making older kinds of humans extinct. The genetic differences between modern humans in different parts of the world are trivial.

For another thing, if Westerners really were genetically superior to everyone else, the graphs of social development that fill Chapters 4–10 would look very different. After taking an early lead, the West would have stayed ahead. But that, of course, is not what happened (Figure 11.1). The West did get a head start at the end of the Ice Age, but its lead grew at some times and shrank at others. Around 550 CE it disappeared altogether, and for the next twelve hundred years the East led the world in social development.

Very few scholars nowadays propagate racist theories that Westerners are genetically superior to everyone else, but anyone who does want

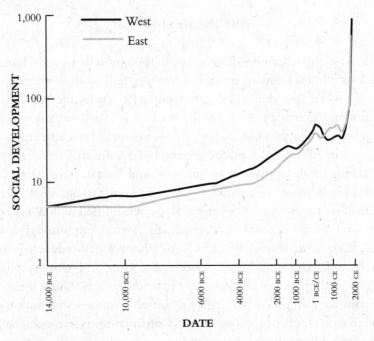

Figure 11.1. The shape of history revisited: Eastern and Western social development and the hard ceiling, 14,000 BCE–2000 CE, shown on a log-linear scale

to take this line will need to show that all the mettle was somehow bred out of Westerners in the sixth century CE, then bred back in in the eighteenth; or that Easterners bred themselves into superiority in the sixth century, then lost it in the eighteenth. That, to put it mildly, is going to be a tough job. Everything suggests that wherever we look, people—in large groups—are all much the same.

We cannot explain why the West rules without starting from biology, since biology explains why social development has kept moving up; but biology alone is not the answer. The next step is to bring in sociology, which tells us *how* social development has increased so much.

As Figure 11.1 shows, this has not been a smooth process. In the introduction, I proposed a "Morris Theorem" (expanding an idea of the great science fiction writer Robert Heinlein) to explain the entire course of history—that change is caused by lazy, greedy, frightened people (who rarely know what they're doing) looking for easier, more profitable, and safer ways to do things. I hope that the evidence presented in Chapters 2–10 has borne this out.

We have seen people constantly tinkering, making their lives easier or richer or struggling to hold on to what they already have as circumstances change, and, in the process, generally nudging social development upward. Yet none of the great transformations in social development—the origins of agriculture, the rise of cities and states, the creation of different kinds of empires, the industrial revolution—was a matter of mere tinkering; each was the result of desperate times calling for desperate measures. At the end of the Ice Age, hunter-gatherers became so successful that they put pressure on the resources that sustained them. Further efforts to find food transformed some of the plants and animals they preyed on into domesticates and transformed some of the foragers into farmers. Some farmers succeeded so well that they put renewed pressure on resources, and to survive—especially when the weather went against them—they transformed their villages into cities and states. Some cities and states succeeded so well that they, too, ran into resource problems and transformed themselves into empires (first land-based, later ruling the steppes and oceans, too). Some of these empires repeated the same cycle, putting pressure on their resources and turning themselves into industrial economies.

History is not just one damn thing after another. In fact, history is the same old same old, a single grand and relentless process of adaptations to the world that always generate new problems that call for further adaptations. Throughout this book I have called this process the paradox of development: rising social development creates the very forces that undermine it.

People confront and solve such paradoxes every day, but once in a while the paradox creates tough ceilings that will yield only to truly transformative change. It is rarely obvious what to do, let alone how to do it, and as a society approaches one of these ceilings a kind of race begins between development and collapse. Societies rarely—perhaps never—simply get stuck at a ceiling and stagnate, their social development unchanging for centuries. Rather, if they do not figure out how to smash the ceiling, their problems spiral out of control. Some or all of what I have called the five horsemen of the apocalypse break loose, and famine, disease, migration, and state collapse—particularly if they coincide with an episode of climate change—will drive development down, sometimes for centuries, even into a dark age.

One of these ceilings comes around twenty-four points on the social development index. This was the level where Western social development stalled and then collapsed after 1200 BCE. The most important ceiling, though, which I have called the hard ceiling, comes around forty-three points. Western development hit this in the first century CE, then collapsed; Eastern development did the same a thousand or so years later. This hard ceiling sets a rigid limit on what agricultural empires can do. The only way to break it is to tap into the stored energy of fossil fuels, as Westerners did after 1750.

Adding sociology to biology explains much of the shape of history, telling us how people have pushed social development upward, why it rises quickly at some times and slowly at others, and why it sometimes falls. Yet even when we put them together, biology and sociology do not tell us why the West rules. To explain that, we need geography.

I have stressed a two-way relationship between geography and social development: the physical environment shapes how social development changes, but changes in social development shape what the physical environment means. Living on top of a coalfield meant very little two thousand years ago, but two hundred years ago it began meaning a lot.

Tapping into coal drove social development up faster than ever before—so fast, in fact, that soon after 1900 new fuels began to displace coal. Everything changes, including the meaning of geography.

So much for my thesis. I want to spend most of this chapter addressing some of the most obvious objections to it, but before turning to that it might be useful to recap the main details of the story that filled Chapters 2–10.

At the end of the Ice Age, around fifteen thousand years ago, global warming marked off a band of Lucky Latitudes (roughly 20–35 degrees north in the Old World and 15 degrees south to 20 degrees north in the New) where an abundance of large, potentially domesticable plants and animals evolved. Within this broad band, one region, the so-called Hilly Flanks of southwest Asia, was luckiest of all. Because it had the densest concentration of potential domesticates it was easier for people who lived there to become farmers than for people anywhere else. So, since people (in large groups) are all much the same, Hilly Flankers were the first to settle in villages and domesticate plants and animals, starting before 9000 BCE. From these first farmers descended the societies of the West. About two thousand years later people in what is now China—where potential domesticates were also plentiful, though not so plentiful as in the Hilly Flanks—moved the same way; from them descend the societies of the East. Over the next few thousand years people independently began domesticating plants and/or animals in half a dozen other parts of the world, each time beginning another regional tradition.

Because Westerners were the first to farm, and because people (in large groups) are all much the same, Westerners were also the first to feel the paradox of development in a serious way and the first to learn what I have called the advantages of backwardness. Rising social development meant bigger populations, more elaborate lifestyles, and greater wealth and military power. Through various combinations of colonization and emulation, societies with relatively high social development expanded at the expense of those with lower development, and farming spread far and wide. To make farming work in new lands such as the sweltering river valleys of Mesopotamia, farmers were forced practically to reinvent it, and in the process of creating irrigation agriculture discovered advantages that made this rather backward frontier even more fruitful than the original agricultural core in the Hilly Flanks. And some time after 4000 BCE, with the biggest farming villages in the crowded Hilly Flanks struggling to manage, it was the Mesopotamians who worked out how to organize themselves into cities and states. About two thousand years later the same process played out in the East too, with the paradox of development exposing somewhat similar advantages of backwardness in the valleys that fed into the Yellow River basin.

The new states had to interact with their neighbors in new ways, which created even more disruptive paradoxes of development along their frontiers. They had to learn to manage these; when they got things wrong—as perhaps happened at Uruk in Mesopotamia around 3100 BCE and Taosi in China around 2300, and definitely happened in the West after 2200 and 1750 BCE—they collapsed in chaos. Each collapse coincided with a period of climate change, which, I suggested, added a fifth horseman of the apocalypse to the four man-made ones.

Rising social development produced worse disruptions and collapses, but it also produced more resilience and greater powers of recovery. After 1550 BCE Western cities and states bounced back from the disasters and expanded around the eastern shores of the Mediterranean Sea. A second great geographical contrast between East and West then came into play; the East had nothing like this extraordinary inland sea, providing cheap and easy transport. But like so much else, the Mediterranean was a paradox, offering both opportunities and challenges. When social development reached about twenty-four points the forces of disruption on this wide-open frontier spun out of control, and around 1200 BCE the horsemen of the apocalypse rode (or, to mix the metaphor, sailed) again. The Western core collapsed even more dramatically than before, ushering in a centuries-long dark age.

Thanks to the paradox of development, the lead in social development that geography had given the West at the end of the Ice Age was long-term but not locked in. Collapses are unpredictable things. Sometimes a few different decisions or a little good luck can postpone, reduce, or even head off disaster; our choices can make a difference. To break through the twenty-four-point ceiling, states had to reorganize themselves and develop a whole new way of thinking about the world, creating what we might call first-wave Axial thought. Because Westerners failed to reorganize and rethink around 1200 BCE, their lead over the East in social development narrowed; and because Westerners and Easterners both succeeded in making the necessary adjustments as development rose in the first millennium BCE, they remained neck and neck for a thousand years.

Westerners and Easterners alike created more centralized states and then full-blown empires, and after 200 BCE reached a scale that began changing the meanings of geography again. In the West the Roman Empire brought the unruly Mediterranean under control and social development spiked up past forty points. By the first century CE it was pressing against the hard ceiling. At the same time, though, the rise of the Roman and Han empires also changed the meaning of the vast spaces that separated East and West. With so much wealth at each end of Eurasia, traders and steppe nomads found new reasons to move around, tentatively linking the cores and beginning the First Old World Exchange. Contacts pushed Eastern and Western development higher still, but they also set off unprecedented disruptions. For the first time, the five horsemen of the apocalypse linked the cores, exchanging microbes as well as goods and ideas. Instead of breaking through the hard ceiling, the Roman and Han empires both came apart after 150 CE.

Both East and West slid into new dark ages in which second-wave Axial thought (Christianity, Islam, and new forms of Buddhism) displaced older first-wave ideas, but in other ways their collapses were quite different. In the West, Germanic invaders broke up the less-developed part of the Roman Empire around the western Mediterranean, and the core retreated into its older and more developed heartland around the eastern Mediterranean. In the East, Inner Asian invaders broke up the older and more developed part of the former Han Empire around the Yellow River, and the core retreated into the less-developed lands beyond the Yangzi River.

This geographical contrast made a world of difference. By 450 CE a new frontier of rice agriculture had begun booming around the Yangzi; by 600 China had been reunited; and over the following century the Grand Canal, linking the Yangzi and Yellow rivers, gave China a system of internal waterways that functioned rather like the Mediterranean had done for ancient Rome. In the West, though, where the Arab invaders were strong enough to break up the old Mediterranean core but not strong enough to remake it, social development kept falling until 700.

Around 541 Eastern development rose above Western (proving beyond all doubt that Western rule was never locked in) and by 1100 was pressing against the hard ceiling. As economic growth outran resources, ironworkers tapped into fossil fuels, inventors created new machines, and Song dynasty intellectuals plunged into a veritable Chinese renaissance. But like Rome a thousand years before, the Song Chinese could not break the hard ceiling.

To some extent, events in the early second millennium BCE paralleled those in the first, but with East and West reversed. Rising development set off a Second Old World Exchange and freed the five horsemen again. Social development fell in both cores, but fell longest and furthest in the East. In the West, the more developed Muslim heartland east of the Mediterranean suffered most, and by 1400 a new core was forming and having its own renaissance in western Europe.

These fragmented, previously peripheral European lands now discovered advantages in their own backwardness. Shipbuilding and gunnery, technologies western Europeans had learned from the East during the Second Old World Exchange, allowed them to turn the Atlantic Ocean into a highway, once again transforming the meanings of geography. Eager to tap into the wealth of the East, Western sailors fanned out and—to their surprise—bumped into the Americas.

Easterners *could* have discovered America in the fifteenth century (some people believe they did) but geography always made it more likely that Westerners would get there first. Easterners had far more to gain by sailing toward the riches of the Indian Ocean than into the empty Pacific and by pushing inland into the steppes, which had been the greatest threat to their security for nearly two thousand years.

In the seventeenth century the expansion of the cores changed the meanings of geography more dramatically than ever before. Centralized empires with muskets and cannons closed the Inner Asian steppe highway that linked East and West, ending nomadic migration and effectively killing one of the horsemen of the apocalypse. On the Atlantic, by contrast, the oceanic highway that western European merchants had opened fueled the rise of new kinds of markets and raised entirely new questions about how the natural world worked. By 1700 social development was again pressing the hard ceiling, but this time, with the full complement of horsemen of the apocalypse unable to ride, disaster was held at bay long enough for western European entrepreneurs to respond to the incentives of the oceanic highway by unleashing the awesome powers of coal and steam.

Given enough time, Easterners would probably have made the same discoveries and had their own industrial revolution, but geography made it much easier for Westerners—which meant that because people (in large groups) are all much the same, Westerners had their industrial revolution first. It was geography that took Looty to Balmoral rather than Albert to Beijing.

NOT WHY THE WEST RULES

But what, you might well ask, about people? The pages of this book have been full of great men (and women), bungling idiots, the beliefs they propounded, and their unremitting conflicts; did none of these in the end matter?

Yes and no. We all have free will, and, as I have repeatedly stressed, our choices do change the world. It is just that most of our choices do not change the world very much. I could, for instance, decide right now to stop writing this book, quit my job, and become a hunter-gatherer. That would certainly make a difference. I would lose my home and, since I know rather little about hunting or gathering, would probably poison myself or starve. A few people around me would be strongly affected, and rather more people would be mildly affected. You, for instance, would have to find something else to read. But otherwise the world would go on. No decision I could conceivably make is going to change whether the West rules.

Of course, if millions of other Americans also decided to walk away from the nine-to-five and take up foraging, my odd individual decision would be transformed from a crazy personal aberration into part of a mass (but still odd) movement that really would make a difference. There are plenty of examples of such mass decisions. At the end of World War II, for instance, half a billion women decided to marry younger than their mothers had done and bear more children. Population soared. Then, thirty years later, a full billion of their own daughters decided to do the opposite, and population growth slowed. Collectively, these choices changed the course of modern history.

They were not, however, just whims. Karl Marx cut to the chase a century and a half ago: "Men [and women] make their own history," he insisted, "but they do not make it just as they please; they do not make it under circumstances chosen by themselves." Twentieth-century women had such good reasons for deciding to have more (and then fewer) babies that they often felt they really had no choice in the matter at all—just as the people who decided to take up farming ten thousand years ago, or to move to cities five thousand years ago, or to get jobs in factories two hundred years ago, must often have felt that there was no real alternative.

There are strong pressures on all of us to make choices that conform to reality. We all know people who ignore these pressures and make eccentric decisions anyway. Often we admire these radicals, rebels, and romantics, but rarely do we follow their lead. Most of us know all too well that predictable conformists tend to fare better (by which I mean win more access to food, shelter, and mates) than Anna Kareninas. Evolution selects for what we call common sense.

That said, eccentric choices clearly can have extraordinary consequences. Take Muhammad, perhaps the extreme case. This rather undistinguished Arab merchant could have chosen to be sensible, blaming his encounter with the Archangel Gabriel around 610 CE on a disorder of the stomach or any of a thousand plausible causes. But instead he chose to listen to his wife, who insisted that the visitation had been real. For years Muhammad looked likely to go the way of most prophets, into ridicule, contempt, and oblivion, but instead he united the Arabs. The caliphs who succeeded him destroyed Persia, shattered Byzantium, and split the West in two.

Everyone agrees that Muhammad was a great man. Few humans have had more impact on history. But even so, the transformation of the Western core in and after the seventh century cannot be ascribed solely to his idiosyncrasy. Arabs had been inventing new versions of monotheism and forming their own states in the desert for some time before Gabriel visited Muhammad. Byzantium and Persia were in desperate trouble well before Muslim war parties started crossing their borders, and the Mediterranean had been coming apart since the third century.

If Muhammad had made different choices, seventh-century Christians might only have had one another to fight, rather than the invading Muslims. Maybe without Muhammad, Western social development would have recovered faster after 750, and maybe it wouldn't, but it would still have taken centuries to catch up with the East. The Western core would have stayed in the eastern Mediterranean whatever Muhammad did; the Turks would still have overrun it in the eleventh century and the Mongols in the thirteenth (and again around 1400); and the core would still have shifted westward toward Italy and then the Atlantic in and after the fifteenth century. If Muhammad had been more normal, the cross, not the crescent, might now inspire the faithful from Morocco to Malaysia—no small thing; but there is no reason to doubt that Europeans would still have conquered the Americas or that the West would now rule.

What is true of Muhammad is probably even truer of the other great men we have met. Assyria's Tiglath-Pileser III and the Qin First Emperor both created terrible, centralized, high-end ancient empires; Europe's Habsburgs and Japan's Hideyoshi both failed to create great land empires in the sixteenth century; England's Glorious Revolution in 1688 and the death of Mao in 1976 both put reformist cliques in power. Yet the most that any of these great men/bungling idiots did was to speed up or slow down processes that were already under way. None really wrestled history down a whole new path. Even Mao, perhaps the most megalomaniac of all, only managed to postpone China's industrial takeoff, giving Deng Xiaoping the opportunity to be remembered as the great man who turned China around. If we could rerun the past like an experiment, leaving everything else the same but substituting bungling idiots for great men (and vice versa), things would have turned out much the same, even if they might have moved at a slightly different pace. Great men (and women) clearly like thinking that by force of will alone they are changing the world, but they are mistaken.

This applies outside politics as well as within. Matthew Boulton and James Watt, for instance, were certainly great men, the latter inventing and the former marketing machines that really did change the world. But they were not *unique* great men, any more than Alexander Graham Bell was unique when he filed a patent for his newly invented telephone on February 14, 1876—the same day that Elisha Gray filed a patent for *his* newly invented telephone. Nor were Boulton and Watt more unique than their acquaintance Joseph Priestley, who discovered oxygen in 1774, a year after a Swedish chemist had also discovered it. Or more unique than the four Europeans who separately discovered sunspots in 1611.

Historians often marvel at the tendency for inventions to come in multiples, the lightbulb going on in several people's brains at almost exactly the same moment. Great ideas often seem to be less the result of brilliance than the logical outcome of having a set of thinkers who share the same questions and methods. So it was with European men of letters in the early seventeenth century; once someone invented the telescope (which nine different men claimed to have done) it would have been remarkable if multiple astronomers had *not* promptly discovered sunspots.

An extraordinary number of modern inventions were made more than once, and the statistician Stephen Stigler even proposed a law that no discovery is ever named after its real discoverer (Stigler's Law, he observed, was actually discovered by the sociologist Robert Merton twenty-five years earlier). Boulton and Watt were ahead of the pack, but there *was* a pack, and if Boulton and Watt had not marketed a relatively fuel-efficient steam engine in the 1770s, one of their many rivals would surely have done so soon after. In fact, the pack might have got in even faster had Watt not finagled an extraordinary patent that excluded all competitors from the field.

Great men/women and bungling idiots are creatures of their times. So should we conclude that some sort of spirit of the age, rather than specific individuals, determined the shape of history by sometimes creating an atmosphere conducive to greatness and other times generating a culture of bungling? Some historians think so, suggesting, for instance, that the real reason the West rules is that Chinese culture turned inward in the fourteenth century, giving up on the world, while European culture turned outward, propelling explorers over the oceans until they washed up in the Americas.

I spent some time on this idea in Chapter 8, suggesting that it just does not make much sense of the facts. Culture is less a voice in our heads telling us what to do than a town hall where we argue about our options. Each age gets the thought it needs, dictated by the kind of problems that geography and social development force on it.

This would explain why the histories of Eastern and Western thought have been broadly similar across the last five thousand years. In both cores the rise of the first states, around 3500 BCE in the West and after 2000 BCE in the East, set off arguments over the nature of and limits on divine kingship. As states in both cores became more bureaucratic, after 750 BCE in the West and 500 BCE in the East, these discussions yielded to first-wave Axial thought, debating the nature of personal transcendence and its relationship to secular authority. By about 200 CE, as the great Han and Roman empires fell apart, these questions in turn gave way to second-wave Axial thought, arguing over how organized churches could save the believer in a chaotic, dangerous world. And when social development revived, by 1000 in China and 1400 in Italy, renaissance questions—how to skip over the disappointing recent past to regain the lost wisdom of the first Axial Age— became more interesting still.

Eastern and Western thought developed so similarly for so long, I suspect, because there was only one path by which social development could keep rising. To break through the twenty-four-point ceiling, Easterners and Westerners both had to centralize their states, which inevitably led intellectuals toward first-wave Axial thought. The decline of these states pushed people toward second-wave Axial thought; their revival led almost inevitably toward renaissances. Each great change pushed people to think the thoughts the age needed.

But what of the great divergence around 1600, when western Europeans moved toward scientific thought while Easterners (plus those Westerners who lived outside the core around the Atlantic's shores) did not? Did this epochal shift in thinking reflect deep cultural differences between Easterners and Westerners rather than simply the age getting the thought it needs?

Some (Western) sociologists think so. When psychologists strap people into functional magnetic resonance imaging machines and ask them to solve problems, these scholars point out, the frontal and parietal areas in Western subjects' brains light up more (indicating that they are working harder to maintain attention) if the question requires placing information within a broad context than if it calls for isolating facts from their background and treating them independently. For Easterners the reverse is true.

What does this difference mean? Isolating facts and treating them independently from their context are hallmarks of modern science (as in the beloved caveat "other things being equal . . ."); perhaps, one theory runs, the contrast in brain function means that Westerners are simply more logical and scientific than Easterners.

But perhaps not. The experiments do not show that Easterners *cannot* separate facts from their background or that Westerners *cannot* put things in perspective; only that each group is less accustomed to thinking that way, and has to work harder to pull it off. Both groups can, and regularly do, perform both kinds of tasks.

In every age and every land we find rationalists and mystics, those who abstract from the details and those who revel in the complexities, and even a few who do all these things at once. What varies is the challenges facing them. When Europeans started creating the Atlantic economy around 1600, they also created new problems for themselves, and mechanical, scientific models of reality turned out to solve these best. Across the next four hundred years these ways of thinking became embedded in Western education, increasingly becoming the default mode of thought. In the East, where the kind of challenges that the Atlantic economy created seemed less pressing until well into the nineteenth century, this process has not yet gone as far.

As recently as the 1960s some Western sociologists argued that Eastern culture—in particular, Confucianism—had prevented those who were steeped in it from developing the entrepreneurial spirit of competition and innovation essential for economic success. In the 1980s, faced with the obvious fact of Japanese economic success, a new generation of sociologists concluded that Confucian values of respect for authority and self-sacrifice for the group did not inhibit capitalism; rather, they actually explained Japan's success. A more sensible conclusion might be that people accommodate their culture to the needs of social development, which, in the late twentieth century, produced Confucian and Communist capitalists as well as liberal ones.

The conclusion that we get the thought we need might also make sense of another odd phenomenon, which psychologists call the Flynn Effect. Since IQ tests began, average scores have steadily moved upward (by about three points per decade). It would be cheering to think that we are all getting smarter, but most likely we are just getting better at thinking in the modern, analytical ways that these tests measure.

Reading books made us more modern than telling stories, and (to the horror of many educators) playing computer games apparently makes us more modern still.

It is certainly true that not all cultures are equally responsive to changing circumstances. The Islamic lands, for instance, have produced notoriously few democracies, Nobel Prize–winning scientists, or diversified modern economies. Some non-Muslims conclude that Islam must be a benighted creed, miring millions in superstition. But if that were true it would be hard to explain why a thousand years ago many of the world's best scientists, philosophers, and engineers were Muslims or why Muslim astronomers outperformed all comers until the sixteenth century.

The real explanation, I suspect, is that since 1700 many Muslims have turned inward in response to military and political defeat, just as many Chinese Confucians did in the thirteenth and fourteenth centuries. Islam remains a broad tent. At one extreme is Turkey, which has modernized so effectively that it is a plausible candidate to join the European Union; at the other we find people such as some of the Taliban, who would kill women for showing their faces in public. Overall, though, as the Muslim world slid from being the core of the West to being an exploited periphery, its social development stagnated in a sense of victimhood. Ending that is modern Islam's great burden; and who knows what advantages the Muslim world might then discover in its backwardness.

Culture and free will are wild cards, complicating the Morris Theorem that change is caused by lazy, greedy, frightened people (who rarely know what they're doing) looking for easier, more profitable, and safer ways to do things. Culture and free will speed up or slow down our reactions to changing circumstances. They deflect and muddy any simple theory. But—as the story that filled Chapters 1–10 shows all too clearly—culture and free will never trump biology, sociology, and geography for long.

BACK TO THE FUTURE

The causes of Western rule are both long-term and short-term, lying in the constantly shifting interplay of geography and social development, but Western rule itself was neither locked-in nor accidental. It would make more sense to call it probable, the most likely result, through most of history, in a game where geography stacked the odds in the West's favor. Western rule, we might say, has often been a good bet.

To explain these rather cryptic comments I want to borrow a method from Robert Zemeckis's 1985 comedy *Back to the Future*. Near the beginning of the movie, a mad professor has combined a giant guitar amplifier, stolen plutonium, and a DeLorean car to create a time machine. When terrorists kill the professor, the teenage Marty McFly (played by Michael J. Fox) gives chase and the time machine/car catapults him back to 1955. There he meets his future parents when they were his age. Disaster strikes—instead of falling in love with his father-to-be, Marty's mother-to-be falls in love with Marty himself. A small dropped stitch in the tapestry of history, we might say, but to Marty it matters very much: unless he can put the past straight before the film ends, he will never be born.

Instead of following the historian's normal method of starting a story at the beginning and telling it until we reach our own times, I think it might be useful to leap McFly-like into the past, and then, just as the movie does, stop to ask what could have happened to prevent the future—let us say the year 2000—from turning out more or less as it did.

I will start two centuries ago, in 1800. Alighting in the age of Jane Austen we will find that it was already overwhelmingly likely that the West would come to rule by 2000. Britain's industrial revolution was under way, science was thriving, and European military power dwarfed everyone else's. Of course, nothing was set in stone; with a bit more luck Napoleon might yet have won his wars or with a bit less luck Britain's rulers might have bungled the challenges of industrialization. Either way, the British takeoff would have been slower, or—as I suggested in Chapter 10—the industrial revolution might have shifted to northern France. There are all kinds of possibilities. It is very hard, though, to see what could plausibly have happened after 1800 to have prevented a Western industrial revolution altogether. And once industrialization got going, it is equally hard to imagine what could have stopped its insatiable markets from going global. "It is . . . in vain," Lord Macartney spluttered when the Chinese government rejected his trade embassy in 1793, "to attempt arresting the progress of human knowledge"—a pompous way to put it, perhaps, but he had a point.

No matter how much we stack the deck against the West, such as by imagining a hundred-year delay in its industrialization and little European imperial expansion until the twentieth century, there is still no obvious reason to think that there would have been an independent Eastern industrial revolution before then. Such an Eastern takeoff would probably have required the rise of a diversified regional economy like the one Westerners had created around the shores of the Atlantic, and that would have taken several centuries to build up. Western rule by 2000 was not locked in in 1800, in the sense of being 100 percent certain, but I suspect it was at least 95 percent probable.

If we leap back another hundred and fifty years from 1800 to 1650, when Newton was still a boy, Western rule by 2000 would look less certain but still likely. Guns were closing the steppes and ships were creating the Atlantic economy. Industrialization remained undreamed-of, but its preconditions were settling into place in western Europe. If the Dutch had won their wars against England in the 1650s, if the Dutch-backed coup in England had fallen through in 1688, or if the French had successfully invaded England in 1689, the particular institutions that wet-nursed Boulton and Watt might never have taken shape; and in that case the industrial revolution might, as I suggested earlier, have taken decades longer or have happened somewhere else in western Europe. But once again it is difficult to see what could plausibly have happened after 1650 to prevent it altogether. Perhaps if Western industrialization had slowed and the Qing rulers had also behaved differently, seventeenth- and eighteenth-century China might have caught up more quickly with European science, but as we saw in Chapter 9, it would have taken more than that for the East to have industrialized first. Western rule by 2000 was less locked in in 1650 than it would be by 1800, but it was still the most plausible outcome—perhaps 80 percent likely?

Another hundred and fifty years earlier, in 1500, the prognosis was murkier still. Western Europeans had ships that could sail to the New World, but their first instinct was simply to plunder it. If the Habsburgs had been even luckier than they actually were (if, perhaps, Luther had never been born, or if Charles V had co-opted him, or if the armada against England had succeeded in 1588 and the Dutch rebellion had then folded), perhaps they really would become the shepherds of Christendom—in which case the Spanish Inquisition might have silenced radical voices such as Newton's and Descartes's, and arbitrary taxation might have destroyed Dutch, English, and French trade the way it destroyed Spanish commerce in historical reality. That is a lot of ifs, though, and for all we know a Habsburg Empire might have had exactly the opposite effect, driving even more Puritans to cross the Atlantic and build cities on hills, kick-starting an Atlantic economy and scientific revolution from the far side.

Alternatively, the Habsburgs could easily have fared worse than they did in reality. If the Ottomans had defeated Shiite Persia more thoroughly, the Turks might have taken Vienna in 1529; minarets and the muezzin might yet have pierced the skies over England and, as Gibbon put it, the interpretation of the Koran might now be taught in the schools of Oxford. A Turkish triumph would perhaps have kept the West's center of gravity in the Mediterranean, leaving the Atlantic economy to wither on the vine—but on the other hand, like the Habsburg victory I imagined a moment ago, it might also have stimulated an even stronger Atlantic world. Another possibility: if the Ottomans and Russians had fought each other more vigorously in the seventeenth century, they might have been too weak to close the Western steppes to nomads. In that case the Qing victories of the seventeenth and eighteenth centuries might have driven the Mongols into Europe, turning the West's seventeenth-century crisis into something as grim as the last days of Rome. With a new dark age in the West, China might, after the passage of enough centuries, have had its own scientific and industrial revolutions as its social development pressed against the hard ceiling. Who knows? One thing is clear, though: in 1500 the odds of Western rule by 2000 were much lower than they would be by 1650, perhaps not much more than fifty-fifty.

Another hundred and fifty years take us back to 1350, in the dark days of the Black Death, and from that vantage point Western rule by 2000 would have looked frankly rather unlikely. The wildest card in the near future was Tamerlane, the Mongol conqueror who burst out of central Asia to devastate India and Persia and then shattered the Ottoman Empire in 1402. At that point Tamerlane decided to turn east to avenge some imagined slight from the Chinese emperor but died before reaching his goal. If instead he had kept riding west after 1402, he might well have devastated Italy, aborting its Renaissance and setting Western development back by centuries. On the other hand, if instead of dying in 1405 on his eastward journey he had hung on a few years longer, he might have repeated Khubilai Khan's brutal conquest of China, holding back Eastern, not Western, development by centuries.

There are plenty of other ways things could have gone. The Ming dynasty founder, Hongwu, could easily have failed to reunite China after its civil wars, leaving a cluster of warring states rather than a great empire in the fifteenth-century Eastern core. Who can say what the consequences would have been? There might have been chaos, but perhaps removing the heavy hand of Ming autocracy would have stimulated even more vigorous maritime trade. I suggested in Chapter 8 that Ming China was never likely to create an Eastern version of the West's later Atlantic economy—geography was too strongly against it—but without the Ming, Eastern colonists and merchants might yet have made a smaller Atlantic-style economy closer to home in Southeast Asia and the Spice Islands. The bottom line, though, is that options were even more open in 1350 than they would be in 1500. Western rule by 2000 was just one of many possibilities, perhaps no more than 25 percent likely.

I could go on; it is fun to play the what-if game. But the point is probably clear. Whether the West would rule by 2000 was a matter of probabilities, not of lock-ins or accidents, and the further back we go, the more wild cards there are. In 1800 it was highly unlikely that different decisions, cultural trends, or accidents would delay Western rule until after 2000; in 1350 that outcome was perfectly plausible. However, it is hard to think of anything happening after 1350 that would have led to the East industrializing before the West or have prevented industrialization altogether.

To find a past that *could* plausibly have led to Eastern rule by 2000 we have to go back a full nine centuries, to 1100. If at that point the Song dynasty emperor Huizong had handled the Jurchen nomads better, saving Kaifeng in 1127, or if the baby Temujin's parents really had forgotten him on the steppes and he had died instead of growing up to be Genghis Khan, who knows what might have happened? Distance and maritime technology probably ruled out a Pacific version of the route to industrialization that Europe followed in the eighteenth century, via an Atlantic economy, but possibly a similar economy could have been created by other means. If China had escaped Jurchen and Mongol devastation, its renaissance culture might have blossomed into a scientific revolution instead of withering into complacency and footbinding. Internal demand from a hundred million Chinese subjects, trade between an agricultural south and an industrial north, and colonization in Southeast Asia might then have been enough to tip the balance. On the other hand, possibly not; until it had the kinds of guns and armies that could close the steppes, China remained open to devastating migrations. It is probably optimistic to think the mandarins could keep so many balls in the air indefinitely. The odds against an Eastern takeoff in the twelfth century were, I suspect, very long.

If we make one last trip in the time machine, plunging back another thousand years before the Song, the great question changes again. Now we have to ask not whether the East might end up ruling by 2000 but whether the Roman Empire might break through the hard ceiling seventeen hundred years before the West actually did so. Frankly, I do not see any way that could have happened. Like the Song, Rome needed not only to find a way through the hard ceiling without the benefits of an Atlantic economy but also to have astonishing luck in evading the five horsemen of the apocalypse. When China's Han Empire fell in the third century, Rome muddled on in a weakened state, only to crack in the fifth century. There were certainly ways Rome might have gotten the better of the Goths and their kindred and carried on with their muddling along, but could the empire then have handled the crisis of the seventh century? And even if some larger Roman Empire had survived, how would that have escaped the long winding down of Western social development? A Roman industrial revolution after 100 looks even less likely than a Song breakthrough after 1100.

What all this adds up to is the conclusion that Western rule by 2000 was neither a long-term lock-in nor a short-term accident. It was more of a long-term probability. It was never very likely, even in 1100, that the East would industrialize first, gain the ability to project its power globally, and turn its lead in social development into rule the way the

West would subsequently do. It was always likely, though, that someone would *eventually* develop guns and empires capable of closing the
steppes, and ships and markets capable of opening the oceans. And
once that happened, it would become increasingly likely that new geographical advantages would lead Westerners into an industrial revolution before Easterners. The only thing that could have prevented it, I
suspect, was a genuine Nightfall moment, the kind of disaster Isaac
Asimov described in the story of that name that I talked about in Chapter 2: a cataclysm that overwhelms all responses, destroying civilization
and hurling humanity back to square one.

NIGHTFALL

But that was never very likely either. The closest the world ever came
to Nightfall before the era of Western rule was around 10,800 BCE,
when a vast icy lake drained into the North Atlantic and lowered its
temperature enough to turn off the Gulf Stream. The twelve-hundred-
year-long mini–ice age that followed, known as the Younger Dryas,
halted social development and snuffed out the first experiments in settled village life and early farming in the Hilly Flanks. The Younger
Dryas makes every episode of global cooling since then seem barely
worth the effort of putting a sweater on.

The consequences of an event on the scale of the Younger Dryas
anytime in the last few thousand years are too horrible to think about
for long. The world's harvests would have failed year after year after
year. Hundreds of millions would have starved. Mass migration would
have emptied much of Europe, North America, and Central Asia. The resulting wars, state failures, and epidemics would have dwarfed anything
known. It would have been as if the five horsemen of the apocalypse had
traded their steeds for tanks. A shrunken, shivering population would
have ended up clustered in villages around the Lucky Latitudes, praying
for rain and scratching a meager living from the dry soil. Thousands of
years of social development would have been wiped off the graph.

Other Nightfall-like paths are imaginable too. Morbidly inclined
astronomers have calculated that if an asteroid a mile or so in diameter
hit the earth, the explosion would be equivalent to 100 billion tons of
TNT going off at once. Opinions differ on just how grim that would

be. It would certainly temporarily fill the upper atmosphere with dust, blocking the sunlight and causing millions to starve. It might release enough nitrogen oxide to degrade the ozone layer and expose the survivors to murderous solar radiation. A two-mile-wide asteroid impact, by contrast, is easier to model. It would be like setting off 2 trillion tons of TNT, which would probably kill everyone.

The good news—obviously—is that no such rocks lay in our path, so there is not much point in depressing ourselves by speculating on just how bad things would have been. Asteroid collisions and ice ages are not like wars or culture: they are (or perhaps we should say until recently were) beyond human control. No bungling idiot, cultural trend, or accident could have conjured up another body of icy water large enough to turn off the Gulf Stream, meaning that a new Younger Dryas was impossible, and even the gloomiest astronomers think we will collide with mile-wide asteroids only once every few hundred thousand years.

There is, in fact, almost nothing that bungling idiots and so on could have done at any point in human history that would have brought on a Nightfall moment. Even the bloodiest wars we have inflicted on ourselves, the twentieth-century Wars of the World, merely confirmed trends that were already under way. In 1900 the United States, a new kind of subcontinental empire with an industrial core, was already challenging western Europe's oceanic empires. The Wars of the World were largely struggles to see who would replace the western Europeans. The United States itself? The Soviet Union, rapidly industrializing by the 1930s? Germany, trying to conquer its own subcontinental empire in the 1940s? In the East, Japan tried to conquer and industrialize a subcontinental empire and expel the West in the 1930s–40s; when that failed, China industrialized the subcontinental empire it already had, disastrously in the 1950s–60s and spectacularly since the 1980s. It is hard to see how Europe's oceanic empires could have survived such competition, particularly when we add the rising tide of nationalism from Africa to Indochina and the steady decline of western Europe's population and industry relative to its challengers'.

If Europe's great powers had not thrown themselves off cliffs in 1914 and 1939 their oceanic empires would surely have lasted longer; if the United States had not fled its global responsibilities in 1919 the oceanic empires may have collapsed even faster. If Hitler had defeated

Churchill and Stalin, things would perhaps have turned out differently; or then again, perhaps they wouldn't. Robert Harris's novel *Fatherland* provides a wonderful illustration. It is a murder mystery set in 1964 Germany, but—as quickly becomes clear—this is a Germany that won the Second World War. Everything seems eerily different. Hitler has killed all of Europe's Jews, not just most of them. His architect Albert Speer has made his master's fantasies material, rebuilding Berlin with an Avenue of Victory twice as long as Paris's Champs Elysées, leading to the biggest building in the world, where the Führer delivers speeches under a dome so high that rain clouds can form inside it. And yet as the story unfolds, the landscape begins to take on an even eerier familiarity. A cold war is under way between the United States and a huge, rickety, totalitarian empire based in eastern Europe. The two empires glower at each other from behind hedges of nuclear missiles, fight proxy wars and manipulate client states in the Third World, and are edging toward détente. In some ways things are not so different from reality after all.

The only way the twentieth-century Wars of the World could plausibly have produced a wildly different outcome was by descending into all-out nuclear war. If Hitler had developed atom bombs he would surely have used them, but since he virtually canceled his nuclear program in 1942, that was never likely. That left the United States free to drop two bombs on Japan with impunity. But once the Soviets tested their first nuclear weapon in 1949, Nightfall became increasingly possible. Even at their peak levels in 1986, all the world's warheads combined only had one-eighth of the destructive power of a two-mile-wide meteor impact, but that was still more than enough to annihilate modern civilization.

It is hard to understand those—like Chairman Mao—who can contemplate nuclear war with anything approaching equanimity. "Let us speculate," he said to the Communist world's leaders in 1957.

> If war broke out, how many people would die? There are 2.7 billion people in the entire world . . . If the worst comes to the worst, perhaps one-half would die. But there would still be one-half left; imperialism would be razed to the ground and the whole world would become socialist. After a number of years, the world's population would once again reach 2.7 billion and certainly become even bigger.

Fortunately for us all, the men who actually made the decisions in the Soviet Union and United States in the 1950s realized that the only way to handle nuclear weapons was through Mutual Assured Destruction, a no-middle-ground doctrine where one false move would mean annihilation all around. The details of how to play this game remained nail-bitingly murky, and there were some close calls, particularly when John F. Kennedy and Nikita Khrushchev tried to work out the rules in the autumn of 1962. Khrushchev, alarmed by American saber rattling, had installed Soviet missiles on Cuba, and Kennedy, worried, had blockaded the island. Soviet warships sailed within a few miles of the American line in the sea; Kennedy sent an aircraft carrier to cut them off. Kennedy suspected at this point that the odds of disaster were reaching one in three or even one in two. And then, around ten in the morning on Wednesday, October 24, they worsened sharply. As Kennedy and his closest advisers sat in strained silence, news came that a Soviet submarine had blocked the American aircraft carrier's path. What could its intention be, if not to attack? Kennedy's "hand went up to his face and covered his mouth," his brother remembered. "He opened and closed his fist. His face seemed drawn, his eyes pained, almost gray." His next move would be to launch four thousand warheads. But the Soviet submarine did not fire. The clock ticked on; and at 10:25 the Soviet ships slowed, then turned back. Night did not fall.

For thirty years brinksmanship and blunders produced an agonizing sequence of glimpses of the outer darkness, but the worst never came to the worst. Since 1986 the number of warheads in the world has fallen by two-thirds, with further big reductions agreed upon in 2010. The thousands of weapons that the Americans and Russians still have could kill everyone on earth with megatons to spare, but Nightfall now seems far less likely than it did during the forty years of Mutual Assured Destruction. Biology, sociology, and geography continue to weave their webs; history goes on.

FOUNDATION

Asimov's story "Nightfall" has not, so far at least, provided a very good model for explaining the onward march of history, but perhaps his *Foundation* novels can do better. Far, far in the future, says Asimov, a young mathematician named Hari Seldon takes a spaceship to Trantor, the mighty capital of a Galactic Empire that has endured for twelve thousand years. There he delivers a scholarly paper at the Decennial Mathematics Convention, explaining the theoretical basis for a new science called psychohistory. In principle, Seldon claims, if we combine regular history, mass psychology, and advanced statistics, we can identify the forces that drive humanity and then project them forward to predict the future.

Promoted from his provincial home planet to a chair at Trantor's greatest university, Seldon works out psychohistory's methods. His major conclusion is that the Galactic Empire is about to fall, leading to a thirty-thousand-year dark age before a Second Empire rises. The emperor promotes Seldon to first minister, from which illustrious position he plans a think tank called the Foundation. While gathering all knowledge into an *Encyclopedia Galactica* its scholars will mastermind a secret plan to restore the empire after just one thousand years.

The *Foundation* novels have delighted science fiction fans for half a century, but Hari Seldon is a standing joke among those professional historians who have heard of him. Only in Asimov's feverish imagination, they maintain, could knowing what has already happened tell you what is going to happen. Many historians deny that there are any big patterns to find in the past, while those who do think there may be such patterns nevertheless tend to feel that detecting them is beyond our powers. Geoffrey Elton, for instance, who held not only the Regius Chair in Modern History at Cambridge University but also famously strong opinions on all matters historical, perhaps spoke for the majority: "Recorded history," he insisted, "amounts to no more than about two hundred generations. Even if there is a larger purpose in history, it must be said that we cannot really expect so far to be able to extract it from the little bit of history we have."

I have tried to show in this book that historians are selling themselves short. We do not have to limit ourselves to the two hundred generations in which people have been writing documents. If we widen our perspective to encompass archaeology, genetics, and linguistics— the kinds of evidence that dominated my first few chapters—we get a whole lot more history. Enough, in fact, to take us back five hundred generations. From such a big chunk of time, I have argued, we really can extract some patterns; and now, like Seldon, I want to suggest that once we do this we really can use the past to foresee the future.

12

◎ ◎ ◎

. . . FOR NOW

IN THE GRAVEYARD OF HISTORY

At the end of Chapter 3 we left Ebenezer Scrooge staring in horror at his own untended tombstone. Clutching the hand of the Ghost of Christmas Yet to Come, he cried out: "Are these the shadows of the things that Will be, or are they shadows of the things that May be, only?"

I suggested that we might well ask the same about Figure 12.1, which shows that if Eastern and Western social development keep on rising at the same speed as in the twentieth century, the East will regain the lead in 2103. But since the pace at which social development has been rising has actually been accelerating since the seventeenth century, Figure 12.1 is really a conservative estimate; the graph might be best interpreted as saying that 2103 is probably the *latest* point at which the Western age will end.

Eastern cities are already as large as Western, and the gap between the total economic output of China and the United States (perhaps the easiest variable to predict) is narrowing rapidly. The strategists on America's National Intelligence Council think China's output will catch up with the United States' in 2036. The bankers at Goldman Sachs think it will happen in 2027; the accountants at Pricewater-houseCoopers, in 2025; and some economists, such as Angus Maddi-

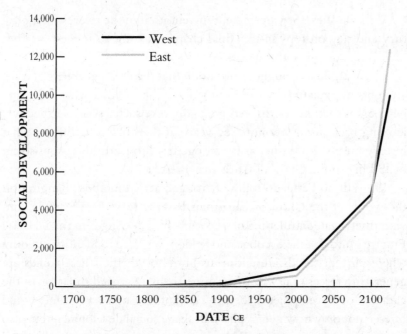

Figure 12.1. Written in stone? If Eastern and Western social development scores carry on rising at the same speed as in the twentieth century, Western rule will end in 2103.

son of the Organization for Economic Cooperation and Development, and the Nobel Prize winner Robert Fogel, opt for even closer dates (2020 and 2016, respectively). It will take longer for the East's war-making capacity, information technology, and per capita energy capture to overtake the West's, but it seems reasonable to suspect that after 2050 Eastern social development will catch up quickly.

Yet nagging doubts do remain. All the expert predictions mentioned above were offered in 2006–2007, on the eve of a financial crisis that these same bankers, accountants, and economists had managed not to foresee; and we should also bear in mind that the whole point of *A Christmas Carol* is that Scrooge's fate is *not* written in stone. "If the courses be departed from," Scrooge assures the Ghost, "the ends will change," and, sure enough, Scrooge pops out of bed on Christmas morning a new man. "He became as good a friend, as good a master, and as good a man," said Dickens, "as the good old City knew, or any other good old city, town, or borough, in the good old world."

Will the West, Scrooge-like, reinvent itself in the twenty-first century and stay on top? In this final chapter, I want to suggest a rather surprising answer to this question.

I have argued throughout this book that the great weakness of most attempts to explain why the West rules and to predict what will happen next is that the soothsayers generally take such a short perspective, looking back just a few hundred years (if that) before telling us what history means. It is rather as if Scrooge tried to learn his lessons solely by talking to the Ghost of Christmas Present.

We will do better to follow Scrooge's actual method, hanging on the words of the Ghost of Christmas Past, or to imitate Hari Seldon, who interrogated millennia of history before peering into the Galactic Empire's future. Like Scrooge and Seldon, we need to identify not only where current trends are taking us but also whether these trends are generating forces that will undermine them. We need to factor in the paradox of development, identify advantages of backwardness, and foresee not only how geography will shape social development but also how social development will change the meanings of geography. And when we do all these things, we will find that the story still has a twist in its tail.

AFTER CHIMERICA

We have been cursed to live in interesting times.

Since about 2000 a very odd relationship has developed between the world's Western core and its Eastern periphery. Back in the 1840s the Western core went global, projecting its power into every nook and cranny in the world and turning what had formerly been an independent Eastern core into a new periphery to the West. The relationship between core and periphery subsequently unfolded along much the same lines as those between cores and peripheries throughout history (albeit on a larger scale), with Easterners exploiting their cheap labor and natural resources to trade with the richer Western core. As often happens on peripheries, some people found advantages in backwardness, and Japan remade itself. In the 1960s several East Asian countries followed it into the American-dominated global market and prospered, and after 1978, when it finally settled into peace, responsibility, and flexibility, so did China. The East's vast, poor populations and indigenous intelligentsias that had struck earlier Western observers as forces of backwardness now began to look like huge advantages. The industrial revolution was finally spreading across the East, and Eastern entrepreneurs were building factories and selling low-cost goods to the West (particularly the United States).

Nothing in this script was particularly new, and for a decade or more all went well (except for Westerners who tried to compete with low-cost East Asian goods). By the 1990s, however, manufacturers in China were discovering—as people on so many peripheries had done before them—that not even the richest core could afford to buy everything that a periphery could potentially export.

What has made the East-West relationship so unusual is the solution to this problem that emerged after 2000. Even though the average American was earning nearly ten times as much as the average Chinese worker, China effectively lent Westerners money to keep buying Eastern goods. It did this by investing some of its huge current-account surplus in dollar-denominated securities such as United States Treasury Bonds. Buying up hundreds of billions of dollars also kept China's currency artificially cheap relative to the United States', making Chinese goods even less expensive for Westerners.

The relationship, economists realized, was rather like a marriage in which one spouse does the saving and investing, the other does the spending, and neither partner can afford a divorce. If China stopped buying dollars, the American currency might collapse and the 800 billion United States dollars that China already held would lose their value. If, on the other hand, Americans stopped buying Chinese goods, their living standards would slide and their easy credit would dry up. An American boycott might throw China into industrial chaos, but China could retaliate by dumping its dollars and ruining the U.S. economy.

The historian Niall Ferguson and the economist Moritz Schularick christened this odd couple "Chimerica," a fusion of China and America that delivered spectacular economic growth but was also a chimera—a dream from which the world eventually had to wake up. Americans could not go on borrowing Chinese money to buy Chinese goods forever. Chimerica's ocean of cheap credit inflated the prices of every kind of asset, from racehorses to real estate, and in 2007 the bubbles started bursting. In 2008 Western economies went into free fall, dragging the rest of the world after them. By 2009, $13 trillion of consumer wealth had evaporated. Chimerica had fallen.

By early 2010, prompt government interventions had headed off a repeat of the 1930s depression, but the consequences of Chimerica's collapse were nonetheless enormous. In the East unemployment spiked, stock markets tumbled, and China's economy expanded barely half as fast in 2009 as it had done in 2007. But that said, China's 7.5 percent growth in 2009 remained well above what economies in the Western core could hope for even in the best years. Beijing had to find $586 billion for a stimulus package, but it at least had the reserves to cover this.

In the West, however, the damage was far worse. The United States piled a $787 billion stimulus on top of its mountain of existing debt and still saw its economy shrink by more than 2 percent in 2009. The International Monetary Fund announced that summer that it expected Chinese economic growth to rebound to 8.5 percent in 2010, while the United States would manage just 0.8 percent. Most alarming of all, the Congressional Budget Office forecast that the United States would not pay off the borrowing for its stimulus package until 2019, by which time the entitlements of its aging population would be dragging its economy down even further.

When the leaders of the world's twenty biggest economies met in April 2009 to craft their response to the crisis, a new wisecrack went around: "After [Tiananmen Square in] 1989 capitalism saved China. After 2009 China saved capitalism." There is much truth to this, but an even better analogy for 2009 might be 1918. That was the year when the sucking sound of power and wealth draining across the Atlantic, from the bankrupt old core in Europe to the thriving new one in the United States, became undeniable. Two thousand and nine may prove to have been the year when the sound of the drain across the Pacific, from bankrupt America to thriving China, became equally audible. Chimerica may have been merely a layover on the road to Eastern rule.

Needless to say, not everyone agrees with this prognosis. Some pundits point out that the United States has made itself over just as thoroughly as Scrooge plenty of times already. All too many critics wrote off the United States in the great depression of the 1930s and the stagflation of the 1970s, only to see it to bounce back to defeat the Nazis in the 1940s and the Soviets in the 1980s. American entrepreneurs and scientists, the optimists insist, will figure something out, and even if the United States does slide into crisis in the 2010s it will get the better of China in the 2020s.

Others stress that China has problems too. Most obviously, as economic success drives up wages, China is losing some of the advantages of its backwardness. In the 1990s low-end manufacturing jobs started migrating from China's coasts to its interior, and are now leaving China altogether for even-lower-wage countries such as Vietnam. Most economists see this as the natural course of China's integration into the global economy, but to a few it is the first sign that China is losing its edge.

Other China bashers see demography as a bigger challenge. Thanks to low birth and immigration rates, the average age is rising faster in China than in America, and by 2040 the entitlements of the elderly may weigh more heavily on China's economy than on that of the United States. China's shortage of natural resources may also slow economic growth, and tensions between the booming cities and languishing countryside may get much worse. If any of these things happen, popular unrest (which is already rising) could get out of control. Ethnic revolts and protests against corruption and environmental catastrophes helped bring down plenty of Chinese dynasties in the past; maybe they will do so again in the near future. And if the Communist party does fall, the country might break apart, just as it did at the end of the Han, Tang, Yuan, and Qing dynasties. The best analogy for China in 2020 might not, after all, be the United States in 1920, soaking up the old core's wealth, but China itself in 1920, sliding into civil war.

Then again, an influential group of Western Panglosses insists, maybe none of these guesses really matters, because all will be for the best regardless. Despite seeing wealth and power drain across the Atlantic in the twentieth century, the typical western European in 2000 is richer than his or her forebear at the height of Europe's imperial grandeur, because the rising capitalist tide has lifted all the boats. In the twenty-first century the drain across the Pacific may lift everyone's boats even higher. Angus Maddison, mentioned above for his calculation that China's gross domestic product will overtake that of the United States in 2020, foresees Chinese incomes tripling (to an average of $18,991 per person) between 2003 and 2030. He expects that American incomes will rise only 50 percent, but because they started from such a high level the typical American in 2030 will earn $58,722, more than three times as much as the typical Chinese. Robert Fogel, who thinks China's economy will outgrow the United States' in 2016, is even more bullish. By 2040, he says, Chinese incomes will reach an astonishing $85,000—but by that time the average American will be making $107,000.*

Most Panglossian of all is what the journalist James Mann calls the "Soothing Scenario," a claim that come what may, prosperity will Westernize the East. Asking whether the West still rules will then be a meaningless question, because the whole world will have become Western. "Trade freely with China," George W. Bush urged in 1999, "and time is on our side."

The only way to flourish in the modern global economy, this argument runs, is to be liberal and democratic—that is, more like the Western core. Japan, Taiwan, South Korea, and Singapore all moved from one-party toward somewhat democratic rule as they grew rich in the late twentieth century, and if the Chinese Communist Party can embrace capitalism, perhaps it can embrace democracy too. Those regions most involved in global trade may already be doing so. In Guangdong and Fujian provinces, for instance, many local officials are nowadays directly elected. National politics certainly remains authoritarian, but the rulers in Beijing have become markedly more responsive to public concerns over natural disasters, public health crises, and corruption.

Many Westerners who have spent time in the East, though, are less impressed with the idea that the East will become culturally Westernized at the very moment that it achieves the power to dominate the globe. Americans, after all, did not start acting more like Europeans after they displaced Europe as the dominant region in the Western core; rather, Europeans began complaining about the Americanization of their own culture.

China's urban elites did find plenty to like in Western culture when they entered the American-dominated global economy in the 1980s.

---

*All figures are in US dollars at 2000 values, adjusted to reflect purchasing power parity.

They dropped the Mao suit, opened English schools, and even (briefly) sipped lattes at a Starbucks in the Forbidden City. The overpriced bars in Beijing's Back Lakes district are as full of hyperactive twenty-somethings checking stock quotes on their cell phones as those in New York or London. The question, though, is whether Westernization will continue if power and wealth carry on draining across the Pacific.

The journalist Martin Jacques suggests not. We are already, he argues, seeing the rise of what he calls "contested modernities" as Easterners and South Asians adapt the industrialism, capitalism, and liberalism invented in the nineteenth-century Western core to their own needs. In the first half of the twenty-first century, Jacques speculates, Western rule will give way to a fragmented global order, with multiple currency zones (dollar-, euro-, and renminbi-denominated) and spheres of economic/military influence (an American sphere in Europe, southwest Asia, and perhaps South Asia, and a Chinese sphere in East Asia and Africa), each dominated by its own cultural traditions (Euro-American, Confucian, and so on). But in the second half of the century, he predicts, numbers will tell; China will rule and the world will be Easternized.

Extrapolating from how China has used its power since the 1990s, Jacques argues that the Sinocentric world of the late twenty-first century will be quite different from the Western world of the nineteenth and twentieth centuries. It will be even more hierarchical, with the old Chinese idea that foreigners should approach the Middle Kingdom as tribute-bearing suppliants replacing Western theories about the nominal equality of states and institutions. It will also be illiberal, dropping the West's rhetoric about universal human values; and statist, brooking no opposition to the powers of political rulers. All over the world, people will forget the glories of the Euro-American past. They will learn Mandarin, not English, celebrate Zheng He, not Columbus, read Confucius instead of Plato, and marvel at Chinese Renaissance men such as Shen Kuo rather than Italians such as Leonardo.

Some strategists think Chinese global rule will follow Confucian traditions of peaceful statecraft and be less militarily aggressive than the West's; others disagree. Chinese history gives no clear guidance. There have certainly been Chinese leaders who opposed war as a policy tool (particularly among the gentry and bureaucracy), but there have been plenty of others who readily used force, including the first few emperors of virtually every dynasty except the Song. Those international-relations theorists who style themselves "realists" generally argue that China's caution since the Korean War owes more to weakness than to Confucius. Beijing's military spending has increased more than 16 percent each year since 2006 and is on target to match America's in the 2020s. Depending on the decisions future leaders make, the East's rise to global rule in the twenty-first century may be even bloodier than the West's in the nineteenth and twentieth.

So there we have it. Maybe great men and women will come to America's aid, preserving Western rule for a few generations more; maybe bungling idiots will interrupt China's rise for a while. Maybe the East will be Westernized, or maybe the West will be Easternized. Maybe we will all come together in a global village, or maybe we will dissolve into a clash of civilizations. Maybe everyone will end up richer, or maybe we will incinerate ourselves in a Third World War.

This mess of contradictory prognoses evokes nothing so much as the story I mentioned in Chapter 4 of the blind men and the elephant, each imagining he was touching something entirely different. The only way to explain why the West rules, I suggested at that point in the book, was by using the index of social development to cast a little light on the scene. I now want to suggest that the same approach can help us see what the elephant will look like a hundred years from now.

2103

So let us look again at Figure 12.1, particularly at the point where the Eastern and Western lines meet in 2103. The vertical axis shows that by then social development will stand at more than five thousand points.

This is an astonishing number. In the fourteen thousand years between the end of the Ice Age and 2000 CE, social development rose nine hundred points. In the next hundred years, says Figure 12.1, it will rise *four thousand points more*. Nine hundred points took us from the cave paintings of Altamira to the atomic age; where will another four thousand take us? That, it seems to me, is the real question. We cannot understand what will come after Chimerica unless we first understand what the world will look like at five thousand points.

In an interview in 2000 the economist Jeremy Rifkin suggested, "Our way of life is likely to be more fundamentally transformed in the next several decades than in the previous thousand years." That sounds extreme, but if Figure 12.1 really does show the shape of the future, Rifkin's projection is in fact a serious understatement. Between 2000 and 2050, according to the graph, social development will rise twice as much as in the previous fifteen thousand years; and by 2103 it will have doubled again. What a mockery, this, of history!

This is where all the prognostications that I discussed in the previous section fall down. All extrapolate from the present into the near future, and all—unsurprisingly—conclude that the future will look much like the present, but with a richer China. If we instead bring the whole weight of history to bear on the question—that is, if we talk to the Ghost of Christmas Past—we are forced to recognize just how unprecedented the coming surge in social development is going to be.

The implications of development scores of five thousand points are staggering. If, for the sake of argument, we assume that the four traits of energy capture, urbanization, information technology, and war-making capacity will each account for roughly the same proportions of the total social development score in 2103 as they did in 2000,[*] then a century from now there will be cities of 140 million people (imagine Tokyo, Mexico City, New York, São Paolo, Mumbai, Delhi, and Shanghai rolled into one) in which the average person consumes 1.3 million kilocalories of energy per day.

A fivefold increase in war-making capacity is even harder to visualize. We already have enough weapons to destroy the world several times over, and rather than simply multiplying nuclear warheads, bombs, and guns, the twenty-first century will probably see technologies that make twentieth-century weapons as obsolete as the machine gun made the musket. Something like "Star Wars," the anti-ballistic-missile shield that American scientists have been working on since the 1980s, will

---

[*] If we assume instead that the balance will shift, positing less dramatic changes in one trait of course just means imagining even more breathtaking transformations in another.

surely become a reality. Robots will do our fighting. Cyberwarfare will become all-important. Nanotechnology will turn everyday materials into impenetrable armor or murderous weapons. And each new form of offense will call forth equally sophisticated defenses.

Most mind-boggling of all, though, are the changes in information technology implied by Figure 12.1. The twentieth century took us from crude radios and telephones to the Internet; it is not so far-fetched to suggest that the twenty-first will give everyone in the developed cores instant access to and total recall of all the information in the world, their brains networked like—or into—a giant computer, with calculating power trillions of times greater than the sum of all brains and machines in our own time.

All these things, of course, sound impossible. Cities of 140 million people surely could not function. There is not enough oil, coal, gas, and uranium in the world to supply billions of people with 1.3 million kilocalories per day. Nano-, cyber-, and robot wars would annihilate us all. And merging our minds with machines—well, we would cease to be human.

And that, I think, is the most important and troubling implication of Figure 12.1.

I have made two general claims in this book. The first was that biology, sociology, and geography jointly explain the history of social development, with biology driving development up, sociology shaping how development rises (or doesn't), and geography deciding where development rises (or falls) fastest; and the second was that while geography determines where social development rises or falls, social development also determines what geography means. I now want to extend these arguments. In the twenty-first century social development promises—or threatens—to rise so high that it will change what biology and sociology mean too. We are approaching the greatest discontinuity in history.

The inventor and futurist Ray Kurzweil calls this the Singularity—"a future period during which the pace of technological change will be so rapid, its impact so deep . . . that technology appears to be expanding at infinite speed." One of the foundations of his argument is Moore's Law, the famous observation made by the engineer (and future chairman of Intel) Gordon Moore in 1965 that with every passing year the miniaturization of computer chips roughly doubled their speed and halved their cost. Forty years ago gigantic mainframes typically performed a few hundred thousand calculations per second and cost several million dollars, but the little thousand-dollar laptop I am now tapping away on can handle a couple of billion per second—a ten-million-fold improvement in price-performance, or a doubling every eighteen months, much as Moore predicted.

If this trend continues, says Kurzweil, by about 2030 computers will be powerful enough to run programs reproducing the 10,000 trillion electrical signals that flash every second among the 22 billion neurons inside a human skull. They will also have the memory to store the 10 trillion recollections that a typical brain houses. By that date scanning technology will be accurate enough to map the human brain neuron by neuron—meaning, say the technology boosters, that we will be able to upload actual human minds onto machines. By about 2045, Kurzweil thinks, computers will be able to host all the minds in the world, effectively merging carbon- and silicon-based intelligence into a single global consciousness. This will be the Singularity. We will transcend biology, evolving into a new, merged being as far ahead of *Homo sapiens* as a contemporary human is of the individual cells that merge to create his/her body.

Kurzweil's enthusiastic vision provokes as much mockery as admiration ("the Rapture for Nerds," some call it), and the odds are that—like all prophets before him—he will be wrong much more often than he is right. But one of the things Kurzweil is surely correct about is that what he calls "criticism from incredulity," simple disbelief that anything so peculiar could happen, is no counterargument. As the Nobel Prize–winning chemist Richard Smalley likes to say, "When a scientist says something is possible, they're probably underestimating how long it will take. But if they say it's impossible, they're probably wrong." Humans are already taking baby steps toward some sort of Singularity, and governments and militaries are taking the prospect of a Singularity seriously enough to start planning for it.

We can, perhaps, already see what some of these baby steps have wrought. I pointed out in Chapter 10 that the industrial revolution set off even bigger changes in what it means to be human than the agricultural revolution had done. Across much of the world, better diets now allow humans to live twice as long as and grow six inches taller than their great-great-grandparents. Few women now spend more than a small part of their lives bearing and rearing babies, and compared with any earlier age, few babies now die in infancy. In the richest countries doctors seem able to perform miracles—they can keep us looking young (in 2008, five million Botox procedures were performed in the United States), control our moods (one in ten Americans has used Prozac), and consolidate everything from cartilage to erections (in 2005 American doctors wrote 17 million prescriptions for Viagra, Cialis, and Levitra). The aging emperors of antiquity, I suspect, would have thought these little purple pills quite as wonderful as anything in Kurzweil's Singularity.

Twenty-first-century genetic research promises to transform humanity even more, correcting copying errors in our cells and growing new organs when the ones we were born with let us down. Some scientists think we are approaching "partial immortalization": like Abraham Lincoln's famous ax (which had its handle replaced three times and its blade twice), each part of us might be renewed while we ourselves carry on indefinitely.

And why stop at just fixing what is broken? You may remember the 1970s television series *The Six Million Dollar Man*, which began with a pilot named Steve Austin (played by Lee Majors) losing an arm, an eye, and both legs in a plane crash. "We can rebuild him—we have the technology," says the voiceover, and Austin quickly reappears as a bionic man who outruns cars, has a Geiger counter in his arm and a zoom lens in his eye, and eventually a bionic girlfriend (Lindsay Wagner) too.

Thirty years on, athletes have already gone bionic. When the golfer Tiger Woods needed eye surgery in 2005, he upgraded himself to better-than-perfect 20/15 vision, and in 2008 the International Association of Athletics Federations even temporarily banned the sprinter Oscar Pistorius from the Olympics because his artificial legs seemed to give him an edge over runners hobbled by having real legs.*

By the 2020s middle-aged folks in the developed cores might see farther, run faster, and look better than they did as youngsters. But they will still not be as eagle-eyed, swift, and beautiful as the next generation. Genetic testing already gives parents opportunities to abort fetuses predisposed to undesirable shortcomings, and as we get better at

*In the end, Pistorius missed qualifying by seven-tenths of a second.

switching specific genes on and off, so-called designer babies engineered for traits that parents like may become an option. Why take
chances on nature's genetic lottery, ask some, if a little tinkering can
give you the baby you want?

Because, answer others, eugenics—whether driven by racist mani-
acs like Hitler or by consumer choice—is immoral. It may also be
dangerous: biologists like to say that "evolution is smarter than you,"
and we may one day pay a price for trying to outwit nature by culling
our herd of traits such as stupidity, ugliness, obesity, and laziness. All
this talk of transcending biology, critics charge, is merely playing at
being God—to which Craig Venter, one of the first scientists to sequence the human genome, reportedly replies: "We're not playing."

Controversy continues, but I suspect that our age, like so many before it, will in the end get the thought it needs. Ten thousand years ago
some people may have worried that domesticated wheat and sheep were
unnatural; two hundred years ago some certainly felt that way about
steam engines. Those who mastered their qualms flourished; those who
did not, did not. Trying to outlaw therapeutic cloning, beauty for all,
and longer life spans does not sound very workable, and banning the
military uses of tinkering with nature sounds even less so.

The United States Defense Advanced Research Projects Agency
(DARPA) is one of the biggest funders of research into modifying humans. It was DARPA that brought us the Internet (then called the
Arpanet) in the 1970s, and its Brain Interface Project is now looking at
molecular-scale computers, built from enzymes and DNA molecules
rather than silicon, that could be implanted in soldiers' heads. The first
molecular computers were unveiled in 2002, and by 2004 better versions were helping to fight cancer. DARPA, however, hopes that more
advanced models will give soldiers some of the advantages of machines
by speeding up their synaptic links, adding memory, and even providing wireless Internet access. In a similar vein, DARPA's Silent Talk
project is working on implants that will decode preverbal electrical
signals within the brain and send them over the Internet so troops can
communicate without radios or e-mail. One National Science Foundation report suggests that such "network-enabled telepathy" will become a reality in the 2020s.

The final component of Kurzweil's Singularity, computers that can
reproduce the workings of biological brains, is moving even faster. In

April 2007 IBM researchers turned a Blue Gene/L supercomputer into a massively parallel cortical simulator that could run a program imitating a mouse's brain functions. The program was only half as complex as a real mouse brain, and ran at only one-tenth of rodent speed, but by November of that year the same lab had already upgraded to mimicking bigger, more complex rat brains.

Half a slowed-down rat is a long way from a whole full-speed human, and the lab team in fact estimated that a human simulation would require a computer four hundred times as powerful, which with 2007 technology would have had unmanageable energy, cooling, and space requirements. Already in 2008, however, the costs were falling sharply, and IBM predicted that the Blue Gene/Q supercomputer, which should be up and running in 2011, would get at least a quarter of the way there. The even more ambitious Project Kittyhawk, linking thousands of Blue Genes, should move closer still in the 2020s.

To insist that this will add up to Kurzweil's Singularity by 2045 would be rash. It might be rasher still, however, to deny that we are approaching a massive discontinuity. Everywhere we look, scientists are assaulting the boundaries of biology. Craig Venter's much-publicized ambition to synthesize life had earned him the nickname "Dr. Frankencell," but in 2010 his team succeeded in manufacturing the genome of a simple bacterium entirely from chemicals and transplanting it into the walls of cells to create JCVI-syn1.0, the earth's first synthetic self-reproducing organism. Genetics even has its own version of Moore's Law, Carlson's Curve:* between 1995 and 2009 the cost of DNA synthesis fell from a dollar per base pair to less than 0.1 cent. By 2020, some geneticists think, building entirely new organisms will be commonplace. Hard as it is to get our minds around the idea, the trends of the last couple of centuries are leading toward a change in what it means to be human, making possible the vast cities, astonishing energy levels, apocalyptic weapons, and science-fiction kinds of information technology implied by social development scores of five thousand points.

This book has been full of upheavals in which social development jumped upward, rendering irrelevant many of the problems that had dominated the lives of earlier generations. The evolution of *Homo sapiens* swept away all previous ape-men; the invention of agriculture made

---

*Named after the geneticist Robert Carlson.

many of the burning issues of hunter-gatherer life unimportant; and the rise of cities and states did the same to the concerns of prehistoric villagers. The closing of the steppe highway and the opening of the oceans ended realities that had constrained Old World development for two thousand years, and the industrial revolution of course made mockery of all that had gone before.

These revolutions have been accelerating, building on one another to drive social development up further and faster each time. If development does leap up by four thousand points in the twenty-first century, as Figure 12.1 predicts, this ongoing revolution will be the biggest and fastest of all. Its core, many futurists agree, lies in linked transformations of genetics, robotics, nanotechnology, and computing, and its consequences will overturn much of what we have known.

But while Figure 12.1 clearly shows the Eastern development score gaining on the West's, you may have noticed that every example I cited in this section—DARPA, IBM, the Six Million Dollar Man—was American. Eastern scientists have made plenty of contributions to the new technologies (robotics, for instance, is as advanced in Japan and South Korea as anywhere), but so far the revolution has been overwhelmingly Western. This might mean that the pundits who point to America's decline and a coming Chinese age will be proved wrong after all: if the United States dominates the new technologies as thoroughly as Britain dominated industrial ones two centuries ago, the genetic/nanotechnology/robotics revolution might shift wealth and power westward even more dramatically than the industrial revolution did.

On the other hand, the underlying shift of wealth from West to East might mean that the current American dominance is just a lag from the twentieth century, and that by the 2020s the big advances will be happening in Eastern labs. China is already using lavish funding to lure its best scientists back from America; perhaps Lenovo, not IBM, will provide the mainframes that host a global consciousness in the 2040s, and Figure 12.1 will be more or less right after all.

Or then again, perhaps the Singularity will render ten-thousand-year-old categories such as "East" and "West" completely irrelevant. Instead of transforming geography, it might abolish it. The merging of mortals and machines will mean new ways of capturing and using energy, new ways of living together, new ways of fighting, and new ways of communicating. It will mean new ways of working, thinking, loving, and laughing; new ways of being born, growing old, and dying. It may even mean the end of all these things and the creation of a world beyond anything our unimproved, merely biological brains can imagine.

Any or all these things may come to pass.

Unless, of course, something prevents them.

THE WORST-CASE SCENARIO

Late in 2006, my wife and I were invited to a conference at Stanford University called "A World at Risk." This star-studded event, featuring some of the world's leading policy makers, took place on a bright winter's day. The sun shone warmly from a clear blue sky as we made our way to the venue. The stock market, house prices, employment, and consumer confidence were at or near all-time highs. It was morning in America.

Over breakfast we heard from former secretaries of state and defense about the nuclear, biological, and terrorist threats facing us. Before lunch we learned about the shocking scale of environmental degradation and the high risk that international security would collapse, and as we ate we were told that global epidemics were virtually inevitable. And then things went downhill. We reeled from session to session in gathering gloom, overwhelmed by expert report after expert report on the rising tide of catastrophe. The conference had been a tour de force, but by the time the after-dinner speaker announced that we were losing the war on terror, the audience could barely even respond.

This day of despair made me think (to put it mildly). In the first century CE and again a thousand years later, social development ran into a hard ceiling and the forces of disruption that development itself had created set off Old World–wide collapses. Are we now discovering a new hard ceiling, somewhere around one thousand points on the index? Are the hoofbeats of the horsemen of the apocalypse overtaking our baby steps toward the Singularity even as you read these words?

The five familiar figures—climate change, famine, state failure, migration, and disease—all seem to be back. The first of these, global warming, is perhaps the ultimate example of the paradox of development, because the same fossil fuels that drove the leap in social development since 1800 have also filled the air with carbon, trapping heat. Our plastic toys and refrigerators have turned the world into a greenhouse. Temperatures have risen 1°F since 1850, with most of the increase coming in the last thirty years; and the mercury in the thermometer just keeps rising.

In the past, higher temperatures often meant better agricultural yields and rising development (as in the Roman and Medieval Warm Periods), but this time may be different. The United Nations Intergovernmental Panel on Climate Change (IPCC) suggested in 2007 that "Altered frequencies and intensities of extreme weather, together with sea level rise, are expected to have mostly adverse effects on natural and human systems . . . warming could lead to some impacts that are abrupt or irreversible." And that may be putting it mildly; the small print in their report is even more alarming.

The air bubbles in the ice caps show that carbon dioxide levels have fluctuated across the last 650,000 years, from just 180 molecules of carbon dioxide per million molecules of air in the ice ages to 290 parts per million (ppm) in warm interglacials. Carbon dioxide never reached 300 ppm—until 1958. By May 2010 it was clocked at 393 ppm, and the IPCC estimates that if present trends continue unchecked, carbon dioxide levels will reach 550 ppm by 2050—higher than they have been for 24 million years—and average temperatures will jump another 5°F. And if energy capture keeps rising as Figure 12.1 implies, the world could get much hotter, much faster.

Even if we stopped pumping out greenhouse gases tomorrow, there is already so much carbon in the air that warming will carry on. We have changed the atmosphere's chemistry. Whatever we do now, the North Pole will melt. Conservative estimates, such as the IPCC's, suggest that the ice will be gone by 2100; the most radical think polar summers will be ice-free by 2013. Most scientists come down around 2040.

As the poles melt, the sea level will rise. The waters are already a good five inches higher than they were in 1900, and the IPCC expects them to rise a further two feet by 2100. The direst predictions for the polar meltdown add another fifty feet to the sea level, drowning millions of square miles of the planet's best farmland and richest cities. The world is shrinking in more ways than we realized.

But despite all the icy meltwater, the seas will keep getting warmer as they absorb heat from the atmosphere, and because the oceans now cool off less in winter than they used to, hurricane and cyclone seasons will get longer and fiercer. Wet places will be wetter, with more violent storms and floods; dry places drier, with more wildfires and dust storms.

Many of us have already had some kind of wake-up call that made global warming personal. Mine came in 2008. Well before California's fire season normally gets going, the air thickened with ash as the forests burned around our house. The sky turned an unearthly orange and the rotors of firefighting helicopters drowned out our voices. We cleared a broad firebreak around our home against future blazes and in the end had only one really close call before the rains came. Or perhaps I should say before the rains *finally* came: the active fire season in the western United States is now seventy-eight days longer than it was in the 1970s. The typical fire burns five times as long as it did thirty years ago. And firefighters predict worse to come.

All this comes under the heading of what the journalist Thomas L. Friedman has called "the really scary stuff we already know." Much worse is what he calls "the even scarier stuff we don't know." The problem, Friedman explains, is that what we face is not global warming but "global weirding." Climate change is nonlinear: everything is connected to everything else, feeding back in ways too bewilderingly complex to model. There will be tipping points when the environment shifts abruptly and irreversibly, but we don't know where they are or what will happen when we reach them.

The scariest of the stuff we don't know is how humans will react. Like all the episodes of climate change in the past, this one will not directly cause collapse. In 2006 the *Stern Review*, a British study, estimated that if we continue business as usual until 2100, climate change will drive global economic output down 20 percent from current levels—a dismal prospect, but not the end of the world as we know it; and even if the direst predictions come true, with temperatures rising 10°F, humanity will muddle through. The real concern is not the weather itself but that long before 2100 people's reactions to climate change will unleash more horsemen of the apocalypse.

The most obvious is famine. The green revolution was perhaps the twentieth century's greatest achievement, increasing food production even faster than population could grow. By 2000 it seemed that if we could just contain the viciousness and stupidity of dictators and war-lords, starvation might yet be banished. But one decade on, that seems less likely. Once again the paradox of development is at work. As wealth rises, farmers feed more and more cheap grain to animals so we can eat expensive meat, or turn more and more acres over to biofuels so we can drive cars without burning oil. The result: the prices of staple foods doubled or tripled between 2006 and 2008 and hungry crowds rioted around Africa and Asia. The combination of the biggest cereal harvest in history (2.3 billion tons) and the financial crisis pushed prices down in 2009, but with the world's population set to reach 9 billion by 2050, the United Nations' Food and Agriculture Organization expects that price volatility and food shortages will only increase.

Geography will continue to be unfair in the twenty-first century. Global warming will raise crop yields in cold, rich countries such as Russia and Canada, but will have the opposite effect in what the U.S. National Intelligence Council calls an "arc of instability" stretching from Africa through Asia (Figure 12.2). Most of the poorest people in the world live in this arc, and declining harvests could potentially un-leash the last three horsemen of the apocalypse.

The National Intelligence Council estimates that between 2008 and 2025 the number of people facing food or water shortages will leap from 600 million to 1.4 billion, most of them in the arc; and not to be outdone in apocalyptic predictions, the *Stern Review* concluded that by 2050 hunger and drought will set 200 million "climate migrants" moving—five times as many as the world's entire refugee population in 2008.

Plenty of people in the Western core already see migration as a threat, even though since the closing of the steppe highway three centuries ago migration has more often been a motor of development than a danger to it.* In 2006 a Gallup poll reported that Americans thought immigration was the country's second-worst problem (after the war in Iraq). To many Americans, the danger of Mexicans smug-gling drugs and taking jobs seems to outweigh all benefits; to many

---

*The obvious example is the United States' rise to power, fueled by moving millions of Europeans and enslaved Africans across the Atlantic and smaller but significant numbers of Chinese and Japanese across the Pacific.

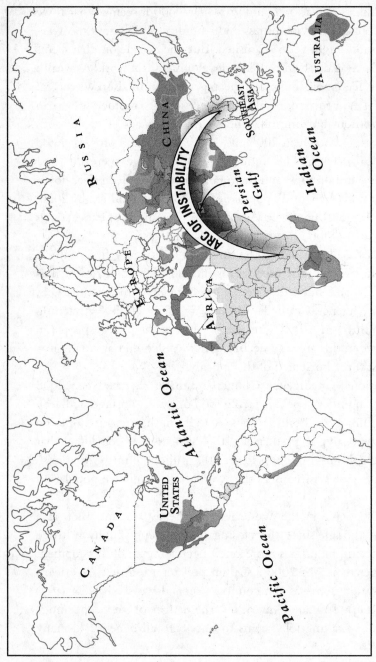

Figure 12.2. The big thirst: the National Intelligence Council's "arc of instability" (stretching from Africa through Asia), plotted against regions likely to face water shortages by 2025. The darkest-shaded areas will face "physical scarcity," defined as having more than 75 percent of their water allocated to agriculture, industry, and/or domestic use. Medium–dark areas will be "approaching physical scarcity," with 60 percent of their water taken up by these purposes, and the lightest areas will face "economic scarcity," with more than 25 percent of their water committed. Rich countries such as the United States, Australia, and China can pipe water from wet areas to dry; poor ones cannot.

Europeans, fears of Islamist terrorism loom just as large. In both regions, nativist lobbies argue that the new settlers are uniquely difficult to assimilate.

Global warming threatens to make even the most lurid fears of anti-immigrant activists come true by the 2020s. Tens of millions of the world's hungriest, angriest, and most desperate people may be fleeing the Muslim world for Europe, and Latin America for the United States. The population movements could dwarf anything in history, reviving the kind of problems that the steppe highway used to present.

Disease, the fourth horseman of the apocalypse, may be one of these problems. Migrations across the steppes spread the plagues of the second and fourteenth centuries, and the greatest pandemic of the twentieth century, the H1N1 influenza of 1918, was spread by a flood of young men under arms between America and Europe. H1N1 killed more people in one year—perhaps 50 million—than the Black Death did in a century, and two or three times as many as AIDS has done in the last thirty years.

Air travel has made disease much harder to contain. After incubating in Africa since at least 1959, AIDS exploded across four continents in the 1980s, and Severe Acute Respiratory Syndrome (SARS) leaped to thirty-seven countries in 2003 within weeks of evolving in southern China. Geneticists sequenced the syndrome's DNA in thirty-one days (as compared to fifteen years for HIV) and aggressive international action nipped it in the bud. By the time epidemiologists identified the so-called swine flu (known as "New H1N1" to distinguish it from the 1918 flu) in 2009, however, it had already spread too widely to be contained.

If swine flu or one of the equally alarming strains of avian flu starts behaving like the H2N2 virus that killed 1–2 million people in 1957, the World Health Organization estimates that it will kill 2–7.4 million people; if it behaves like the 1918 flu, it will kill 200 million. The world is better prepared than it was in 1918, but deaths on even one-tenth of that scale could cause a short-term economic meltdown to make the 2007–2009 financial crisis look trivial. The World Bank guesses that a pandemic would knock 5 percent off global economic output, and some of the "Ten Things You Need to Know About Pandemic Influenza" listed on the World Health Organization's website are even more alarming:

- The world may be on the brink of another pandemic.
- All countries will be affected.
- Medical supplies will be inadequate.
- Large numbers of deaths will occur.
- Economic and social disruption will be great.

As when the horsemen rode in the past, climate change, famine, migration, and disease will probably feed back on one another, unleashing the fifth horseman, state failure. The arc of instability is home to some of the world's most rickety regimes, and as pressure mounts several may collapse as completely as Afghanistan or Somalia, increasing suffering and providing more havens for terrorists. And if instability drags in the cores, whose economies are thoroughly entangled with the arc's resources, we may slide into the mother of all worst-case scenarios.

As early as 1943 an American mission to the Persian Gulf identified the central problem. "The oil in this region," it reported, "is the greatest single prize in all history." Rich nations in the Western core soon reoriented their grand strategies around Gulf oil. When western Europe's power waned in the 1950s, the United States stepped in, covertly or overtly intervening to help friends, harm enemies, and preserve access in the arc. Although less dependent on Gulf oil, the Soviet Union meddled almost as vigorously to deny it to American interests, and when Russia retreated in the 1990s, China's addiction to oil (which accounts for 40 percent of the rise in global demand since 2000) forced it, too, to join the great game.

China's hunger for resources (soybeans, iron, copper, cobalt, timber, and natural gas as well as oil) promises constant clashes with Western interests in the arc of instability in the 2010s. Chinese diplomats stress their country's "peaceful rising" (some tone it down still further to "peaceful development"), but Western anxiety has increased steadily since the 1990s. In 2004, for instance, China's search for iron set off what newspapers quickly dubbed the "great drain robbery," with thieves the world over snatching manhole covers and shipping them to the East to be melted down. Chicago alone lost 150 in one month.

Where would it end? Westerners asked. Today manhole covers, tomorrow the world. According to one poll in 2005, 54 percent of Americans agreed that China's rise was "a threat to world peace"; in a 2007 poll Americans called China the second-greatest threat to global stability, trailing only Iran.

China returns the compliment. When NATO planes bombed China's embassy in Belgrade in 1999, killing three journalists, furious crowds stoned Western embassies in Beijing and firebombed a consulate in Chengdu. "PEOPLE AGONIZED BY CRIMINAL ACT," the *China Daily*'s headline raged. In 2004 the Communist party still insisted on the reality of a "strategic conspiracy of hostile forces to Westernize and cause China to disintegrate."

In 1914, when Europe's great powers faced off over the ruins of the Ottoman Empire in the Balkans, Serbia's Black Hand terrorist gang needed only a pistol to set off World War I. In 2008, a United States commission concluded that "it is more likely than not that a weapon of mass destruction will be used in a terrorist attack somewhere in the world by the end of 2013." With the great powers now facing off over the ruins of Europe's empires in the arc of instability, the havoc al-Qaeda or Hezbollah might wreak with such weapons does not bear thinking about.

The entanglements in the arc are far scarier than those in the Balkans a century ago because they could so easily go nuclear. Israel has built up a large arsenal since about 1970; in 1998 India and Pakistan both tested atomic bombs; and since 2005 the European Union and United States have accused Iran of seeking the same goal. Most observers expect Iran to be nuclear-capable sometime in the 2010s, which may drive up to half a dozen Muslim states* to seek nuclear deterrents. Israel anticipates a nuclear-armed Iran by 2011, but might not wait for matters to reach that point. Israeli warplanes have already destroyed nuclear reactors in Iraq and Syria, and new attacks may follow if Iran's program proceeds.

No American administration could remain neutral in a nuclear confrontation in the arc of instability between its closest friend and bitterest enemy. Nor, perhaps, could Russia or China. Both have opposed Iranian nuclear ambitions but they did let Iran apply to join their

---

*Most likely Egypt, Libya, Saudi Arabia, Syria, Turkey, and the United Arab Emirates.

Shanghai Cooperation Organization,* a loose body working largely to counter American interests in central Asia.

An all-out East-West war would, of course, be catastrophic. For China it would be suicidal: the United States outnumbers it twenty to one in nuclear warheads and perhaps a hundred to one in warheads that can be relied on to reach enemy territory. China tested an antimissile missile in January 2010, but lags far behind American capabilities. The United States has eleven aircraft carrier battle groups to China's zero (although China began building its first carrier in 2009) and an insurmountable lead in military technology. The United States could not, and would not want to, conquer and occupy China, but almost any imaginable war would end with humiliating defeat for China, the fall of the Communist party, and perhaps the country's breakup.

That said, winning a war might be almost as bad for the United States as losing it would be for China. Even a low-intensity conflict would have horrendous costs. If Chimerica splits abruptly and vindictively it will mean financial disaster for both partners. A nuclear exchange would be worse still, turning the west coast of North America and much of China into radioactive ruins, killing hundreds of millions, and throwing the world economy into a tailspin. Worst of all, a Sino-American war could easily drag in Russia, which still has the world's biggest nuclear arsenal.†

Any way we look at it, all-out war is madness. Fortunately, a huge body of expert literature reassures us that in a globalized world such madness is impossible. "No physical force can set at nought the force of credit," says one authority. According to another, the "international movement of capital is the biggest guarantor of world peace." A third adds that fighting "must involve the expenditure of so vast a sum of money and such an interference with trade, that a war would be accompanied or followed by a complete collapse of . . . credit and industry"; it would mean "total exhaustion and impoverishment, industry and trade would be ruined, and the power of capital destroyed."

---

*Formed by China, Kazakhstan, Kyrgyzstan, Russia, Tajikistan, and Uzbekistan in 2001 out of a 1996 "Shanghai Five" that did not include Uzbekistan. Pakistan has also expressed interest in joining.

†Assuming, that is, that Russia's missiles still work. The commander of its strategic nuclear-missile force was sacked in 2009 after a series of missiles failed to take off.

This is comforting—except for the fact that these experts were not talking about the risk of Sino-American conflict in the 2010s. All were writing between 1910 and 1914, insisting the modern world's complicated web of trade and finance ruled out any chance of a great-power war in Europe. We all know how that turned out.

Perhaps the world's statesmen will yank us back from precipice after precipice. Maybe we can avoid a nuclear 1914 for another generation; maybe for fifty years. But is it realistic to think we can keep the bomb out of the hands of terrorists and rogue states forever? Or deter every leader, regardless of national interest, from ever deciding that nuclear war is the best option? Even if we limit proliferation to its current rate, by 2060 there will be close to twenty nuclear powers, several of them in the arc of instability.

Every year we avoid Armageddon the threats from the horsemen of the apocalypse keep building. Pressure on resources will mount, new diseases will evolve, nuclear weapons will proliferate, and—most insidious of all—global weirding will shift the calculus in unpredictable ways. It seems crazily optimistic to think we can juggle all these dangers indefinitely.

We appear to be approaching a new hard ceiling. When the Romans ran up against the original hard ceiling in the first century CE, they faced two possible outcomes: they might find a way through, in which case social development would leap upward, or they might not, in which case the horsemen would drag them down. Their failure began a six-century decline, cutting Western social development more than one-third. In the eleventh century, when Song China reached the same hard ceiling, it, too, failed to break through and Eastern development fell almost one-sixth between 1200 and 1400.

As we press against a new hard ceiling in the twenty-first century, we face the same options but in starker forms. When the Romans and Song failed to find solutions, they had the relative luxury of several centuries of slow decline, but we will not be so lucky. There are many possible paths that our future might follow, but however much they wind around, most seem to lead ultimately to the same place: Nightfall.

What a Singularity will mean for Western rule is open for debate, but what Nightfall will mean seems much clearer. Back in 1949, Einstein told a journalist, "I do not know how the Third World War will

be fought, but I can tell you what they will use in the Fourth—rocks."
After Nightfall, no one will rule.

THE GREAT RACE

Talking to the Ghost of Christmas Past leads to an alarming conclusion: the twenty-first century is going to be a race. In one lane is some
sort of Singularity; in the other, Nightfall. One will win and one will
lose. There will be no silver medal. Either we will soon (perhaps before
2050) begin a transformation even more profound than the industrial
revolution, which may make most of our current problems irrelevant,
or we will stagger into a collapse like no other. It is hard to see how any
intermediate outcome—a compromise, say, in which everyone gets a
bit richer, China gradually overtakes the West, and things otherwise
go on much as before—can work.

This means that the next forty years will be the most important in
history.

What the world needs to do to prevent Nightfall is not really a
mystery. The top priority is to avoid all-out nuclear war, and the way
to do that is for the great powers to reduce their nuclear arsenals. Paradoxically, pursuing total disarmament may be a riskier course, because
nuclear weapons cannot be uninvented. Great powers can always build
new bombs in a hurry, and the really bad guys—terrorists and rulers of
rogue states—will in any case ignore all agreements. Proliferation will
increase the risk that wars will go nuclear across the next thirty to forty
years, but the stablest situation will be one where the great powers have
enough weapons to deter aggression but not enough to kill us all.

The older nuclear powers—the United States, Russia, Britain,
France, China—have been moving in this direction since the 1980s.
During the Cold War the mathematician, pacifist, and meteorologist
(until he abandoned weather research after realizing how much it
helped the air force) Lewis Fry Richardson made a widely cited calculation that there was a 15–20 percent likelihood of a nuclear war before
2000. By 2008, however, the energy scientist Vaclav Smil could offer a
positively sunny estimate that the chance of even a World War II–scale
conflict (killing 50 million people) before 2050 was well under 1 percent, and in January 2010 the *Bulletin of the Atomic Scientists* moved the

minute hand of its celebrated "Doomsday Clock"—indicating how close we stand to Nightfall—back from five minutes to six minutes before midnight.

The second priority is to slow down global weirding. Here things are going less well. In 1997 the world's great and good gathered at Kyoto to work out a solution, and agreed that by 2012 greenhouse gas emissions must be cut to 5.2 percent below their 1990 levels. The proposed cuts, however, fell mostly on rich Western nations, and the United States—the world's biggest polluter in the 1990s—refused to ratify the protocol. To many critics this seemed (as an Indian official put it) like "guys with gross obesity telling guys just emerging from emaciation to go on a major diet," but American policy makers responded that emissions could not be controlled unless India and China (which in 2006 displaced the United States as the world's biggest polluter) made cuts too.

By 2008 the United States and China were both more interested in change, but the political will needed for comprehensive agreements seems to be lacking. The authors of the *Stern Review* estimate that the kind of low-carbon technologies, forest preservation, and energy efficiencies that could avert disaster by holding carbon levels to 450 ppm by 2050 will cost about a trillion dollars. Compared to the price of doing nothing that is trivial, but with their finances in tatters after the 2007–2009 economic crisis, many governments backed away from expensive plans to reduce emissions, and the Copenhagen summit of December 2009 produced no binding agreement.

Despite their obvious differences, nuclear war and global weirding actually both present much the same problem. For five thousand years, states and empires have been the most effective organizations on earth, but as social development has transformed the meaning of geography, these organizations have become less effective. Thomas Friedman has summed it up neatly. "The first era of globalization [roughly 1870–1914] shrank the world from a size 'large' to a size 'medium,'" he observed in 1999, but "this era of globalization [since 1989] is shrinking the world from a size 'medium' to a size 'small.'" Six years later the shrinking had gone so far that Friedman identified a whole new phase, "Globalization 3.0." This, he suggested, "is shrinking the world from a size small to a size tiny and flattening the playing field at the same time."

In this tiny, flattened world, there is no place left to hide. Nuclear weapons and climate change (not to mention terrorism, disease, migration, finance, and food and water supply) are global problems that require global solutions. States and empires, which have sovereignty only within their own frontiers, cannot address them effectively.

Einstein pointed out the obvious solution less than a month after atomic bombs destroyed Hiroshima and Nagasaki in 1945. "The only salvation for civilization and the human race," he told *The New York Times*, "lies in the creation of world government." Publicly mocked as a naïve scientist interfering in matters he did not understand, Einstein put his point more bluntly: "If the idea of world government is not realistic, then there is only one realistic view of our future: wholesale destruction of man by man."

Looking back across the last fifteen thousand years, Einstein does seem to have judged the direction of history correctly. From Stone Age villages through early states such as Uruk and the Shang, early empires such as Assyria and Qin, and oceanic empires such as the British, there has been a clear trend toward bigger and bigger political units. The logical outcome seems to be the rise of an American global empire in the early twenty-first century—or, as the economic balance tilts against the West, a Chinese global empire in the mid or late twenty-first century.

The problem with this logic, though, is that these larger political units have almost always been created through war, precisely the outcome Einstein's world government is supposed to prevent. If the only way to avoid nuclear war is a world government, and if the only way to create a world government is through a Sino-American nuclear war, the outlook is grim.

In fact, though, neither of these propositions is entirely true. Since 1945, nonstate organizations have taken on more and more functions. These organizations range from charities and private multinational corporations that operate beneath the umbrella of states to federations such as the European Union, United Nations, and World Trade Organization that impinge on state sovereignty. States certainly remain the guarantors of security (the United Nations has done little better than the League of Nations at stopping wars) and finance (in 2008–2009 it took government bailouts to save capitalism), and will not fade away anytime soon; but the most effective way to hold back Nightfall for another forty years may be by enmeshing states more deeply with non-state organizations, getting governments to surrender some of their sovereignty in return for solutions that they might be unable to reach independently.

That will be a messy business, and as so often in the past, new challenges will call for new thought. But even if we manage in the next half-century to create institutions that can find global solutions for global problems, this will still only be a necessary rather than a sufficient condition for the Singularity to win the race.

We might compare our situation with what happened in the first, eleventh, and seventeenth centuries, when social development pressed against the hard ceiling at forty-three points on the index. I suggested in Chapter 11 that the only way the Romans or the Song could have broken through in the first and eleventh centuries was by doing what Europe and China did in the seventeenth century: that is, by restructuring geography by closing the steppe highway and creating an oceanic highway. Only then would they have bought themselves security from migrations, raised the kinds of questions that called for a scientific revolution, and begun creating the kinds of incentives that would set off an industrial revolution. Neither the Romans nor the Song, of course, were able to do this, and within a few generations migration, disease, famine, and state failure combined with climate change to set off Eurasia-wide collapses.

When Europeans and Chinese did restructure geography in the seventeenth century, they pushed the hard ceiling upward, though as we saw in Chapter 9 they did not shatter it. By 1750 problems were mounting once again, but by that time British entrepreneurs had used the time that geographical restructuring had bought to begin a revolution in energy capture.

In the twenty-first century we need to follow a similar path. First we must restructure political geography to make room for the kinds of global institutions that might slow down war and global weirding; then we must use the time that buys to carry out a new revolution in energy capture, shattering the fossil-fuel ceiling. Carrying on burning oil and coal like we did in the twentieth century will bring on Nightfall even before the hydrocarbons run out.

Some environmentalists recommend a different approach, urging us to return to simpler lifestyles that reduce energy use enough to halt global weirding, but it is hard to see how this will work. World population will probably grow by another 3 billion before it peaks at 9 billion around 2050, and hundreds of millions of these people are likely to rise out of extreme poverty, using more energy as they do so. David Douglas, the chief sustainability officer at Sun Microsystems, points out that if each of these new people owns just one 60-watt incandescent lightbulb, and if each of them uses it just four hours per day, the world will still need to bring another sixty or so 500-megawatt power plants on line. The International Energy Agency expects world oil demand to rise from 86 million barrels per day in 2007 to 116 million in 2030; and even then, they estimate, 1.4 billion people will still be without electricity.

The double whammy of the world's poor multiplying and getting richer as they do so makes it most unlikely that energy capture will fall over the next fifty years. If we use less energy for fertilizers or for fuel to move food around, hundreds of millions of the poor will starve, which will probably bring on Nightfall faster than anything. But if people do not starve, they will demand more and more energy. In China alone, fourteen thousand new cars hit the roads every day; 400 million people (more than the entire population of the United States) will probably flee low-energy farms for high-energy cities between 2000 and 2030; and the number of travelers vacationing overseas, burning jet fuel and staying in hotels, will probably increase from 34 million in 2006 to 115 million in 2020.

We are not going to reduce energy capture unless catastrophe forces us to—which means that the only way to avoid running out of resources, poisoning the planet, or both, will be by tapping into renewable, clean power.

Atomic energy will probably be a big part of this. Fears about radiation have shackled nuclear programs since the 1970s, but may fall away as the new age gets new thought. Or perhaps solar power will be more important: only one-half of one-billionth of the energy that the sun emits comes to Earth, and roughly one-third of that is reflected back again. Even so, enough solar energy reaches us every hour to power all current human needs for a year—if we could harness it effectively. Alternatively, nanotechnology and genetics may deliver radically new sources of energy. Much of this of course sounds like science fiction, and it will certainly take enormous technological leaps to usher in such an age of abundant clean energy. But if we do not make such leaps—and soon—Nightfall will win the race.

For the Singularity to win, we need to keep the dogs of war on a leash, manage global weirding, and see through a revolution in energy capture. Everything has to go right. For Nightfall to win only one thing needs go wrong. The odds look bad.

THE SHAPE OF THINGS TO COME

Some scientists think they already know who will win the race, because the answer is written in the stars. One day around 1950 (no one remembers exactly when) the physicist Enrico Fermi and three of his colleagues met for lunch at the Los Alamos National Laboratory in New Mexico. After laughing about a *New Yorker* cartoon showing a flying saucer, they moved on to extraterrestrials in general before turning to more conventional scientific topics. Suddenly Fermi burst out: "But where are they?"

It took Fermi's lunch mates a moment or two to realize that he was still worrying about spacemen. Running a few numbers through his head while eating, it had struck him that even if only a vanishingly small proportion of our galaxy's 250 billion stars have habitable planets,[*] outer space should still be teeming with aliens. Earth is relatively young, at less than five billion years, so some of these species should be much older and more advanced than us. Even if their spaceships were as slow as our own, it should have taken them at most 50 million years to explore the whole galaxy. So where were they? Why had they not made contact?

In 1967 the astronomers Iosif Shklovskii and Carl Sagan offered a sobering solution to Fermi's paradox. If just one star in every quarter of a million is orbited by just one habitable planet, they calculated, there would be a million potential alien civilizations in the Milky Way.

---

[*]The International Astronomical Union reported in August 2009 that since the first discovery in 1995 we have now found 360 planets outside our own solar system. None seems likely to support life, but the director of the French Space Agency's planet-hunting program told the Union, "I am really confident that we have an Earth-like planet coming in the next two years."

The fact that we have not heard from any of them,* Shklovskii and Sagan concluded, must mean that advanced civilizations always destroy themselves. The astronomers even suggested that they must invariably do so within a century of inventing nuclear weapons, since otherwise the aliens would have plenty of time to fill the cosmos with signals that we would pick up. All the evidence (or, strictly speaking, the lack of it), then, points to Nightfall by 2045, the centenary of Hiroshima and Nagasaki. (By a slightly unsettling coincidence, 2045 is also the year Kurzweil nominated for the Singularity.)

It is a clever argument, but as always, there is more than one way to do the numbers. A million civilizations rushing into Nightfall is only a guess, and most solutions of the Drake Equation[†] (dreamed up by the astronomer Frank Drake in 1961 as a rough way to calculate the number of civilizations in the galaxy) in fact generate much lower scores. Drake himself calculated that our galaxy has produced just ten advanced civilizations in its entire history, in which case ET could be out there without us knowing.

In the end Fermi's paradox is not very helpful, because the answer to how the great race will turn out lies not in the stars but in our own past. Even if history cannot give us the precise tools of prediction that Asimov imagined in *Foundation*, it does provide some rather solid hints. These, I suspect, are the only real foundation for looking forward.

In the short term, the patterns established in the past suggest that the shift of wealth and power from West to East is inexorable. The transformation of the old Eastern core into a Western periphery in the

---

*Fermi's paradox assumes, of course, that neither von Däniken's spacemen nor the UFO sightings, alien abductions, and so on, that fill certain newspapers are reality-based.

[†]$N = R^* \times f_p \times n_e \times f_l \times f_i \times f_c \times L$, where:

N is the number of civilizations in the galaxy with which communication might be possible,

R^* is the average rate of star formation in the galaxy,

f_p is the fraction of those stars with planets,

n_e is the average number of habitable planets per star that has planets,

f_l is the fraction of those planets where life actually does evolve,

f_i is the fraction of life-forms that evolve intelligence,

f_c is the fraction of those civilizations that develop technologies that produce detectable signs of their existence, and

L is the length of time such civilizations release detectable signals into space.

nineteenth century allowed the East to discover advantages in its back-wardness, and the latest of these—the incorporation of China's vast, poor workforce into the global capitalist economy—is still playing out. Bungling, internal divisions, and external wars may hold China back, as they did so often between the 1840s and 1970s, but sooner or later—probably by 2030, almost certainly by 2040—China's gross domestic product will overtake that of the United States. At some point in the twenty-first century China will use up the advantages of its backward-ness, but when that happens the world's center of economic gravity will probably still remain in the East, expanding to include South and Southeast Asia. The shift in power and wealth from West to East in the twenty-first century is probably as inevitable as the shift from East to West that happened in the nineteenth century.

The West-to-East shift will surely be faster than any in earlier his-tory, but the old Western core currently has a huge lead in per capita energy capture, technology, and military capacity, and will almost cer-tainly maintain its rule in some form through the first half of this cen-tury. So long as the United States is strong enough to act as globocop, major wars should be as rare as they were when Britain was globocop in the nineteenth century. But beginning somewhere between 2025 and 2050, America's lead over the rest of the world will narrow, as Britain's did after about 1870, and the risks of a new world war will increase.

The speed of technological change may well add to the instability by making access to high-tech weapons easier. According to Steven Metz, a professor at the United States Army War College, "We will see if not identical technologies, then parallel technologies being developed [out-side the United States], particularly because of the off-the-shelf nature of it all. We've reached the point where the bad guys don't need to de-velop it; instead they can just buy it." A RAND Corporation report even suggested in 2001 that "the U.S. and its military must include in its planning for possible military conflict the possibility that China may be more advanced technologically and militarily by 2020."

The United States will probably be the first nation to develop a functional antimissile shield, as well as robots and nanoweapons that render human combatants obsolete, cybertechnology that can neutral-ize or seize control of enemy computers and robots, and satellites that militarize space. One risk is that if—as seems probable—the United

States can deploy some or all of these wonder weapons before 2040, its leaders might be tempted to exploit a temporary but enormous technological edge to reverse their long-term strategic decline. Yet I suspect that is unlikely. Even in the feverish atmosphere of the early 1950s the United States resisted the temptation to strike the Soviet Union before it could build up its nuclear arsenal. The real risk is probably that other nations, fearing American military breakthroughs in the next few decades, might prefer striking first to falling even further behind. That kind of thinking played a big part in taking Germany to war in 1914.

It is going to take great statesmanship to preserve the peace in the bewildering twenty-first century. I have argued throughout this book that great men/women and bungling idiots have never played as big a part in shaping history as they have believed they did. Rather than changing the course of history, I suggested, the most that chaps could do was to speed up or slow down the deeper processes driven by maps. Even the most disastrous decisions, such as the wars that Justinian of Byzantium and Khusrau of Persia launched between 530 and 630 CE, just accelerated a collapse that was already under way. Without Justinian's and Khusrau's wars, Western social development might have started recovering sooner, but even with them, development did eventually bounce back.

Since 1945, however, leaders really have had the ability to change history. Khrushchev and Kennedy came close to doing so in 1962. Nuclear weapons leave us no margin of error, no second chance. Mistakes used to cause decline and fall; now they cause Nightfall. For the first time in history, leadership really is decisive. We can only hope that our age, like most before it, gets the thought it needs.

I concluded in Chapter 11 that explanations for why the West rules have to be couched in terms of probabilities, not certainties, and this is even truer of the twenty-first century's great race. Right now the odds are apparently against us, but it does seem to me that if our age is able to get the thought it needs, the odds will steadily shift in the Singularity's favor.

If renewable, clean energy sources replace hydrocarbons across the next fifty years, they should reduce (though certainly not eliminate) the risk of great powers coming to blows over resources or being drawn into feuds in the arc of instability. They should also slow the process of global weirding, reducing the pressures within the arc, and may boost food production even more dramatically than the industrial revolution did. If robotics makes the advances many scientists anticipate, intelligent machines may save wealthy Europe and Japan from demographic disaster, providing cheaply the labor and care that their aging populations need. If nanotechnology similarly lives up to the hype, we might even start cleaning up the air and oceans by the 2040s.

In the end, though, there is only one prediction we can rely on: neither Nightfall nor the Singularity will actually win the great race, because the race will have no finishing line. When we reach 2045 (Kurzweil's estimated time of arrival for the Singularity, and Shklovskii and Sagan's latest date for Nightfall, a century after Hiroshima and Nagasaki) we will not get to declare the end of history and announce a winner. If, as I suspect will happen, we are still holding Nightfall at bay in the mid twenty-first century and social development is soaring past two thousand points, the emerging Singularity will not so much end the race as transform the race—and above all, transform the human race.

Looked at in a really long perspective, the threats that so scare us today seem to have a lot in common with the kinds of forces that have repeatedly pushed evolution into high gear in the past. Time after time, relatively sudden changes in the environment have created conditions in which mutations flourish, transforming the gene pool. About 1.8 million years ago the drying-out of East Africa's forests apparently allowed freaks with big brains to fare better than *Homo habilis*. A brutal phase in the Ice Age about a hundred thousand years ago may have given *Homo sapiens* an equivalent opportunity to shine. And now, in the twenty-first century, something similar is perhaps happening again.

Mass extinctions are already under way, with one species of plant or land animal disappearing every twenty minutes or so. A 2004 study estimated that the cheeriest possible outcome is that 9 percent of the world's 10 million species of plants and land animals will face extinction by 2050, and plenty of biologists expect biodiversity to shrink by as much as one-third or one-half. Some even speak of a sixth mass extinction,* with two-thirds of Earth's species dying out by 2100.

---

*Following the "Big Five" events—the end-Ordovician (about 440 million years ago), Late Devonian (365 million years ago), end-Permian (225 million years ago), end-Triassic (210 million years ago), and end-Cretaceous (65 million years ago) extinctions. Each of these wiped out at least 65 percent of the species on earth.

Humans may be among them; but rather than simply wiping *Homo* off the planet, the harsh conditions of the twenty-first century might act like those 1.8 million or a hundred thousand years ago, creating an opportunity for organisms with new kinds of brains—in this case, brains that merge man and machine—to replace older beings. Far from trampling us, the hoofbeats of the horsemen of the apocalypse might serve to turn our baby steps toward a Singularity into a new great leap.

The Singularity, however, might be every bit as scary as Nightfall. In Kurzweil's vision, the Singularity culminates with the merging of human and machine intelligence in the 2040s, and those of us who live long enough for this might in effect live forever; but some of the humans who have the most experience with this—technologists in the United States Army—doubt that things will stop at that point. The former colonel Thomas Adams, for instance, suspects that war is already moving beyond "human space" as weapons become "too fast, too small, too numerous, and . . . create an environment too complex for humans to direct." Technology, he suggests, is "rapidly taking us to a place where we may not want to go, but probably are unable to avoid." The merging of humans and computers may be just a brief phase before what we condescendingly call "artificial" intelligence replaces *Homo sapiens* as thoroughly as *Homo sapiens* replaced all earlier ape-men.

If this is where a Singularity takes us in the later twenty-first century, it will mean the end of biology as we have known it, and with it the end of sloth, fear, and greed as the motors of history. In that case my Morris Theorem—that change is caused by lazy, greedy, frightened people (who rarely know what they're doing) looking for easier, more profitable, and safer ways to do things—will finally reach its limits.

Sociology as we know it will go the same way, though what kinds of rules will govern a robotic society is anyone's guess; and the Singularity will surely obliterate the old geography. The ancient distinctions between East and West will be irrelevant to robots.

When historians (if such things still exist) look back from 2103 on the shift from carbon- to silicon-based intelligence, it may strike them as inevitable—as inevitable, in fact, as I have claimed that the earlier shifts from foraging to farming, villages to cities, and agriculture to industry were. It may seem just as obvious that the regional traditions that had grown from the original agricultural cores since the end of the Ice Age were bound to merge into a single posthuman world civilization. The early twenty-first century's anxiety over why the West ruled and whether it would keep on doing so might look a little ridiculous.

THE TWAIN MEET

There is a certain irony in all this. I began this book with a what-if story about the Chinese Empire taking Prince Albert to Beijing as a hostage in 1848, and then spent eleven chapters explaining why that didn't happen. The answer to the book's main question, I concluded, is geography; maps, not chaps, sent the little dog Looty to Balmoral rather than Albert to Beijing.

In this chapter I took the argument further, suggesting that explaining why the West rules also largely answers the question of what will happen next. As surely as geography dictated that the West would rule, it also dictates that the East will catch up, exploiting the advantages of its backwardness until its social development overtakes the West's. But here we encounter another irony. Rising social development has always changed the meaning of geography, and in the twenty-first century, development will rise so high that geography will cease to mean anything at all. The only thing that will count is the race between a Singularity and Nightfall. To keep Nightfall at bay we will have to globalize more and more of our concerns, and arguments about which part of the world has the highest social development will matter less and less.

Hence the deepest irony: answering the book's first question (why the West rules) to a great extent also answers the second (what will happen next), but answering the second robs the first of much of its significance. Seeing what is coming next reveals what should, perhaps, have been obvious all along—that the history that really matters is not about the East, the West, or any other subsection of humanity. The important history is global and evolutionary, telling the story of how we got from single-celled organisms to the Singularity.

I have argued throughout the book that neither long-term lock-in nor short-term accident theories explain history very well, but now, once again, I want to go further. In the *really* long run, on the time scale of evolutionary history, neither long-term lock-in nor short-term accident theories actually matter very much. Fifteen thousand years ago, before the Ice Age ended, East and West meant little. A century from now they will once again mean little. Their importance in the intervening era was just a side effect of geography between the age when the first farmers pushed social development past about six points and that when the first machine-enhanced, postbiological creatures push social development past five thousand points. By the time that happens—somewhere, I suspect, between 2045 and 2103—geography will no longer mean very much at all. East and West will be revealed as merely a phase we went through.

Even if everything in this phase had gone as differently as could be imagined—if, say, Zheng He had really gone to Tenochtitlán, if there had been a new kind of Pacific rather than a new kind of Atlantic economy, if there had been a Chinese rather than a British industrial revolution, and if Albert had gone to Beijing rather than Looty to Balmoral—the deep forces of biology, sociology, and geography would still have pushed history in much the same direction. America (or Zhengland, as we might now call it) would have become part of the Eastern rather than the Western core and the West would now be catching up with the East rather than the other way around, but the world would still have shrunk from size large to size small and would still now be shrinking to size tiny. The early twenty-first century would still have been dominated by Chimerica, and whether it fell or not, the race between Nightfall and the Singularity would still be going on. And East and West would still be losing their significance.

This should not be a shocking conclusion. As long ago as 1889, while the world was still shrinking from size large to size medium, a young poet named Rudyard Kipling could already see part of the same truth. Freshly back in London from the far-flung battle line, Kipling got his big break with a ripping yarn of imperial derring-do called "The Ballad of East and West."* It tells the story of Kamal, a border raider who steals an English colonel's mare. The colonel's son leaps

---

*The "East" in Kipling's poem was actually India; he drew no fine distinctions between South Asia and East Asia. They were all east of England.

onto his own horse and pursues Kamal through the desert in a chase of epic proportions ("They have ridden the low moon out of the sky, their hoofs drum up the dawn, / The dun he went like a wounded bull, but the mare like a new-roused fawn"). Finally, though, the Englishman is thrown. Kamal charges back at him, rifle raised. But all ends well: the two men "looked each other between the eyes, and there they found no fault, / They have taken the Oath of the Brother-in-Blood on leavened bread and salt."

Stirring stuff, but it is the poem's opening line—"Oh, East is East, and West is West, and never the twain shall meet"—that gets all the attention, mostly from people quoting it as an example of the nineteenth-century West's insufferable self-satisfaction. Yet that was surely not the effect Kipling was hoping for. What he actually wrote was:

Oh, East is East, and West is West, and never the twain shall meet,
Till Earth and Sky stand presently at God's great Judgment Seat;
But there is neither East nor West, Border, nor Breed, nor Birth,
When two strong men stand face to face,
tho' they come from the ends of the earth!

As Kipling saw it, people (real men, anyway) are all much the same; it is just geography that obscures the truth, requiring us to take a trip to the ends of the earth to figure things out. But in the twenty-first century, soaring social development and a shrinking world are making such trips unnecessary. There will be neither East nor West, border, nor breed, nor birth when we transcend biology. The twain shall finally meet if we can just put off Nightfall long enough.

Can we do that? I think the answer is yes. The great difference between the challenges we face today and those that defeated Song China when it pressed against the hard ceiling a thousand years ago and the Roman Empire another thousand before that is that we now know so much more about the issues involved. Unlike the Romans and the Song, our age may yet get the thought it needs.

On the last page of his book *Collapse*, the biologist and geographer Jared Diamond suggested that there are two forces that might save the world from disaster: archaeologists (who uncover the details of earlier societies' mistakes) and television (which broadcasts their findings). As an archaeologist who watches a lot of television, I certainly agree, but I also want to add a third savior, history. Only historians can draw together the grand narrative of social development; only historians can explain the differences that divide humanity and how we can prevent them from destroying us.

This book, I hope, might help a little in the process.

Appendix: On Social Development

The index of social development is the backbone of this book, holding together the body of facts that archaeologists and historians have accumulated. The index does not itself explain why the West rules, but it does show us the shape of the history that has to be explained. I provide a full account of the index, for those interested in the methods and detailed evidence behind the calculations, at the website www.ianmorris.org; this appendix is intended only as a quick summary of the main technical challenges and the basic results.

FOUR OBJECTIONS

I see four obvious objections to the social development index:

1. Quantifying and comparing social development in different times and places dehumanizes people and we should therefore not do it.
2. Quantifying and comparing societies is a reasonable procedure, but social development in the sense I defined it (as societies' abilities to get things done) is the wrong thing to measure.

3. Social development in the sense I defined it is a useful way to compare East and West, but the four traits I used to measure it (energy capture, organization/urbanization, war-making, and information technology) are not the best ones.
4. These four traits are a good way to measure social development but I have made factual errors and got the measurements wrong.

I addressed objection 1 in Chapter 3. There are plenty of historical and anthropological questions for which quantifying and comparing social development is no help at all, but asking why the West rules is by its nature a comparative and quantitative question. If we want to answer it, we must quantify and compare.

I also said a few words in Chapter 3 about objection 2. Perhaps there are other things we could measure and compare that would work better than social development, but I do not know what they are. I leave it to other historians and anthropologists to identify other objects to measure and to show that they yield better results.

Objection 3 can take three forms—that we should add more traits to my four; that we should use different traits; or that we should look at fewer traits. As I wrote this book I did explore several other traits (for example, area of largest political unit, standards of living [measured through adult stature], transportation speeds, or size of largest monuments), but all had severe evidence problems or failed the test of mutual independence. Most traits in any case show high levels of redundancy through most of history, and any plausible combination of traits will tend to produce much the same final result.

There are plenty of small and two large exceptions to the redundancy rule. The first large exception is what we might call the "nomad anomaly"—the fact that steppe societies normally score low on energy capture, organization, and information technology, but high on war-making. This anomaly helps explain why true nomad societies have been so good at defeating empires but so bad at running them,* and it deserves extensive study, but it does not directly affect the comparisons between the settled, agrarian Eastern and Western cores in this book.

---

*Seminomadic conquerors such as the Parthians, Xianbei, Ottoman Turks, and Manchus have flourished as imperial rulers, but full nomads such as the Xiongnu, Huns,

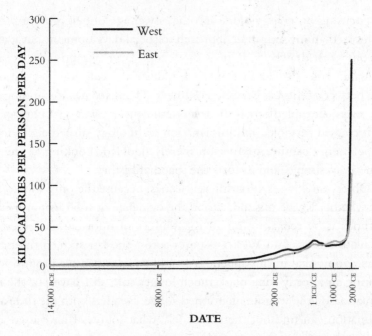

Figure A.1. Energy alone: how East and West compare if we just look
at energy capture per person

Another version of objection 3 would drop organization, war-making, and information technology from the analysis and concentrate only on energy capture, on the grounds that organization, war-making, and information technology are merely ways of *using* energy. Figure A.1 shows what an energy-alone index would look like. It is different from the full index graph in Figure 3.3, but not hugely so. In the energy-alone graph, just like the full social development graph, the West still leads the East for 90 percent of the time, the East still overtakes it between roughly 550 and 1750 CE, there is still a hard ceiling that blocks development around 100 and 1100 CE (at just over 30,000 kilocalories per person per day), postindustrial revolution scores still dwarf those of earlier ages, and in 2000 the West still rules.

---

and Seljuk Turks have not. The closest thing to an exception is the fully nomadic Mongols, but even their record as imperial rulers was decidedly patchy.

Focusing on energy alone has the advantage of being more parsimonious than my four-trait approach to social development, but it also has one great drawback. This is the second large exception to the redundancy rule: the fact that since the industrial revolution the relationship between traits has become nonlinear. Thanks to new technologies, city size quadrupled across the twentieth century, war-making capacity increased fiftyfold, and information technology surged eightyfold, while energy capture per person merely doubled. Looking at energy alone is *too* simple, and distorts the shape of history.

Objection 4 raises very different issues, because the only way to assess whether I have misunderstood the evidence or used inappropriate methods is by reexamining all the sources of information I used to calculate Eastern and Western scores across the last sixteen thousand years. Doing that in this appendix would be an expensive proposition, making an already-long book much longer still, so I have put the information on the website mentioned above. Readers with the time and inclination can find out there precisely what sources I have used and my views on the ambiguities in the evidence.

In what remains of this appendix I will summarize the data, outline quickly how I calculated the scores, and say a few words about margins of error.

ENERGY CAPTURE

I discuss energy capture first and at greatest length because it is quantitatively the most important of the four traits. If we go back far enough in time, the urbanization, war-making, or information-technology scores all fall to zero because human activities were on such a tiny scale that they generate values below 0.01 point on the index. The energy-capture scores by contrast never fall to zero, because humans who capture zero energy die. Keeping body and soul together requires roughly 2,000 kilocalories per capita per day, and since modern Western energy capture is about 228,000 kcal/cap/day (= 250 points), the lowest score possible in theory would be 2.19; and in reality, energy capture has always scored above 4 points since the end of the Ice Age, because much of the energy humans use is in nonfood forms (clothes, shelter, artifacts, fuel, and so on). Until the industrial revolution, the energy capture score typically accounts for 75–90 percent of the total social development scores. In 2000 it still accounted for 28 percent of the Western and 20 percent of the Eastern scores.

The evidence for energy capture ranges from modern statistical digests to literary accounts of farming, industry, and lifestyles, to archaeological evidence for diet, crafts, and quality of life. Combining such varied materials is a challenge, but here, as elsewhere, I have built on the contributions of earlier researchers. As I explained in Chapter 3, Earl Cook's 1971 study of energy flows provides a convenient starting point that can be constantly checked against other estimates. These all converge on contemporary levels in the Western core of around 230,000 kcal/cap/day, which Cook divides into rough categories of feed/food (for domesticated animals as well as humans), home/commerce, industry/agriculture, and transport.

Vaclav Smil (1991, 1994) usefully breaks nonfood consumption down into biomass and fossil fuels, and graphs their development in the Western core over time. Several steps are needed to turn his data into energy-capture scores for the West, but the results come out around 93,000 kcal/cap/day in 1900 and 38,000 in 1800, neatly bracketing Cook's estimate of 77,000 for industrialized Europe in 1860.

The further we move back before 1800 the fewer government-generated statistics are available, but the more that economies relied on biomass fuels, the more we can substitute comparative information gathered by economic historians and anthropologists for official documents. In 1700 the average person in the Western core must have consumed somewhere between 30,000 and 35,000 kcal/day. Our evidence for what Western societies did shows clearly that the further we go back into the previous thousand years the lower that number falls,* though the comparative evidence also makes it clear that Western energy consumption could never have fallen too far below 30,000 kcal/cap/day. There is room for debate, but I doubt that medieval Western

---

*Medievalists may be surprised to see the Western score in Table A.1 stay at 26,000 kcal/cap/day between 1000 and 1400, when (as is well known) western European society was expanding vigorously; but the Western scores in this period actually represent the core in the Muslim eastern Mediterranean, which went through a period of stagnation (described in Chapter 7). Western European energy capture remained below 25,000 kcal/cap/day throughout these centuries, catching up with the Mediterranean world only in the fifteenth century.

Table A.1. Energy capture, kilocalories/person/day
(selected dates)

DATE	WEST	EAST
2000 CE	230	104
1900	92	49
1800	38	36
1700	32	33
1600	29	31
1500	27	30
1400	26	29
1200	26	30.5
1000	26	29.5
800	25	28
600	26	27
400	28	26
200 CE	30	26
1 BCE/CE	31	27
200 BCE	27	24
400	24	22
600	22	20
800	21	18
1000	20	17
1200	21	17
1500	20.5	15
2000	17	11
2500	14	9.5
3000	12	8
3500	11	7.5
4000	10	7
5000	8	6.5
6000	7	6
8000	6	5
10,000	5.5	4
12,000	4.5	4
14,000 BCE	4	4

energy capture ever fell below 25,000 kcal/cap/day, even in the eighth century CE. For reasons I return to below, I do not see how these guesstimates can be more than 5–10 percent wide of the mark.

The impressive ruins of Roman-era houses and monuments, the numbers of shipwrecks, the volume of manufactured goods, the level of industrial pollution in ice cores, and the staggering numbers of animal bones from settlements make it clear that Western energy capture was higher in the first century CE than in the eighth or even the thirteenth, but how much higher? Ingenious calculations by economic historians point toward an answer. Robert Allen (2007a) has shown that in 300 CE real wages (which, for most of the poor in premodern times, closely mirrored energy consumption) in the Western core were comparable to those of southern Europe in the eighteenth century CE, and Walter Scheidel (2008) has suggested that Roman-era wages were comfortably higher than those in much of medieval Europe. Data gathered by Geof Kron (2005) and Nikola Koepke and Joerg Baten (2005, 2008) indicate that stature changed little between the first and eighteenth centuries, and Kron (forthcoming) suggests that ancient housing was typically better than that in the richest parts of eighteenth-century Europe. I have estimated energy capture at around 31,000 kcal/person/day in the years 1 BCE/CE, declining slowly until 500 CE and then faster until 700.

Energy capture must have been lower in the Western core around 1000 BCE not only than in Roman times, but also than in the eighth century CE. The sharpest period of increase came after 300 BCE, as the Mediterranean was integrated into larger political and economic units and the Roman Warm Period raised output, but the mass of archaeological data also shows an earlier period of acceleration after 600 BCE. I have tentatively suggested that in 1000 BCE energy capture may have been as low as 20,000 kcal/cap/day, a slight decline on the levels of the late second millennium BCE, but still above those of the third millennium.

Earlier in prehistory scores were lower still. At the end of the Younger Dryas foragers were probably getting by on about 5,000 kcal/cap/day, but this would have risen sharply (relative to what had gone before) as the climate warmed, plants and animals were domesticated for food, and animals were harnessed for draft power. By 3000 BCE people in established villages in the Hilly Flanks must have been consuming 12,000 kcal/cap/day for their clothes, fuel, farm animals, houses and household goods, and monuments, even if their diets were no better than they had been four millennia earlier.

Calculating Eastern scores is more difficult still, partly because scholars such as Cook and Smil were concerned only with the region of the world that had the highest energy capture, not with regional comparisons. We can begin, though, from the United Nations (2006) estimate that in 2000 CE the average Japanese person consumed 104,000 kilocalories per day (less than half the Western level). In 1900 the Eastern core was still largely agrarian, with Japanese oil use and even coal-powered industry in its infancy. Japanese energy capture may have been around 49,000 kcal/cap/day (again less than half of Western consumption). Across the previous five centuries coal use and agricultural output had risen steadily. In 1600 productivity was higher in the Yangzi Delta than anywhere in the West, but by 1750 Dutch and English agriculture had caught up and Eastern real wages were comparable to those in southern Europe rather than wealthy northern Europe. I have estimated energy capture in the Eastern core around 29,000 kcal/cap/day in 1400 and 36,000 in 1800, with the bulk of the increase coming in the eighteenth century.

There is also debate over how badly the crisis after 1200 impacted Chinese energy use, but there was probably at least a slight dip from the Song-era peak, when consumption probably surpassed 30,000 kcal/cap/day.

As in the West, the archaeological evidence makes it clear that energy capture went through a trough in the mid first millennium CE, but again it is difficult to say just how steep the decline was. The evidence I reviewed in Chapter 5 suggests that Han dynasty energy consumption was higher than anything previously seen in the East but lower than contemporary Roman or later Song levels; I have estimated 27,000 kcal/cap/day in 1 BCE/CE, returning to the same level by 700 CE after a slight fall.

Again paralleling the West, Eastern energy capture in the first millennium BCE saw steady increases, accelerating after about 500 BCE and still more after 300 BCE with the spread of canal networks, trade, and metal tools. Back in 1000 BCE the average energy capture may have been around 17,000 kcal/cap/day; by the time of the Qin First Emperor it was probably more like 26,000.

In prehistoric times Eastern energy capture seems to have passed through much the same thresholds as Western, but began moving upward later and generally ran one to two millennia behind.

ORGANIZATION

Throughout preindustrial history organization was always the second-largest component in social development scores. I used this trait as my main example in Chapter 3, explaining why I use largest city size as a proxy for social organization. There is enough ambiguity in the data and flexibility in definitions that experts disagree over city sizes in every period, and I explain my decisions on the website. In Table A.2 I just summarize some of my main calculations.

WAR-MAKING

Since writing began, people have recorded their wars, and since early prehistory have often buried their dead with weapons. As a result we know a surprising amount even about premodern warfare. The major challenge in scoring war-making capacity is not empirical but conceptual—how we compare radically different fighting systems that are often intended to be incomparable with earlier systems. Most famously, when Britain launched HMS *Dreadnought* in 1906, the whole idea was that its supersized guns and heavy armor meant that no number of 1890-era ships would add up to one post-1906 ship.

The reality, though, is that things never work out so simply. Improvised explosive devices can, under the right circumstances, give even the highest-tech army a run for its money. In principle we can assign scores on a single index to wildly different military systems, even if experts might argue over what those scores should be.

In 2000 CE, the West's unprecedented military power earns 250 points, and is clearly much greater than the East's. Some Eastern armies are large, but weapons systems matter far more than sheer numbers. The United States outspends China 10:1, and outnumbers it 11:0 in carrier groups and 26:1 in nuclear warheads. The qualitative differ-

Table A.2. Population of the largest settlement in each core, thousands (selected dates)

DATE	WEST	EAST
2000 CE	16,700 (New York)	26,700 (Tokyo)
1900	6,600 (London)	1,750 (Tokyo)
1800	900 (London)	1,100 (Beijing)
1700	600 (London, Constantinople)	650 (Beijing)
1600	400 (Constantinople)	700 (Beijing)
1500	100 (Constantinople)	600 (Beijing)
1400	125 (Cairo)	500 (Nanjing)
1200	250 (Baghdad, Cairo, Constantinople)	800 (Hangzhou)
1000	200 (Cordoba)	1,000 (Kaifeng)
800	175 (Damascus)	1,000 (Chang'an)
600	125 (Constantinople)	250 (Daxingcheng)[a]
400	500 (Rome)	150 (Luoyang)
200 CE	800 (Rome)	120 (Luoyang)
1 BCE/CE	1,000 (Rome)	500 (Chang'an)
200 BCE	300 (Alexandria)	125 (Linzi)
500	150 (Babylon)	80 (Luoyang, Linzi)
1000	25 (Susa)	35 (Qi)
1200	80 (Babylon, Thebes)	50 (Anyang)
1500	75 (Uruk, Thebes)	35 (Zhengzhou, Yanshi)
2000	60 (Memphis)	15 (Erlitou)
3000	45+ (Uruk)	2 (Dadiwan)
4000	5 (Uruk, Tell Brak)	<1 (Xipo? Dadiwan?)
6500	3 (Çatalhöyük)	
7500 BCE	1 (Beidha, Basta, Çatalhöyük)	

[a]Renamed Chang'an in the seventh century.

ences between America's M1 battle tanks and precision weapons and China's outdated systems are still greater. Setting the West:East points ratio as low as 10:1 or as high as 50:1 both seem extreme, and I have guessed at 20:1, meaning that the East scores 12.5 points in 2000 as against the West's 250.

Comparing scores in 2000 with those in earlier periods is even more difficult, but by looking at the changes in the size of forces, the speed of their movement, their logistical capacities, the range and destructiveness of their striking power, and the armor and fortifications at their disposal, we can make rough estimates. According to one calculation, the effectiveness of artillery fire increased twentyfold between 1900 and 2000 and that of antitank fire sixtyfold; factoring in all the other changes across the twentieth century, I set the ratio between Western war-making capacity in 2000 and 1900 at 50:1, meaning that the West scores 5 points in 1900 compared with its 250 points in 2000.

Western military power in 1900 was much greater than Eastern, though the gap was certainly not as large as it was by 2000. The British navy had nearly six times the tonnage of the Japanese in 1902, and any one of Europe's great powers had more men under arms than Japan; I set the West:East ratio in 1900 at 5:1, meaning that the East scores just 1 point in 1900 (as compared with the West's 5 points in 1900 and the East's 12.5 points in 2000).

Not everyone will be comfortable with the level of subjectivity in calculations such as these, but the important point is that the West's military capacity in 2000 was so enormous that all other scores—including the West's in 1900 or even the East's in 2000—are necessarily tiny; and, as a result of this, the errors involved in estimation are insignificant. We could double, or cut in half, any or all of the war-making scores for all periods up to 1900 without having a noticeable impact on the total development scores.

The contrast between Western war-making in 1800 and that in 1900 was less than the contrast between 1900 and 2000, but it was still enormous, taking us from the age of sail, cavalry charges, and smooth-bore muzzle-loaded muskets to that of explosive shells, armored oil-powered ships, and machine guns, with tanks and aircraft just around the corner. The nineteenth century probably raised Western war-making capacity by an order of magnitude, and I set the West's war-making capacity at just 0.5 point in 1800. Western warfare at that point was vastly more effective than Eastern, which should perhaps earn just 0.1 point in 1800.

Between 1500 and 1800 Europe went through what historians commonly call a "military revolution," perhaps quadrupling the effectiveness of its war-making. Eastern war-making, by contrast, actually went backward between 1700 (when Kangxi began conquering the steppes) and 1800. In the absence of existential threats, Chinese rulers regularly sought peace dividends by reducing their armed forces and ignoring expensive technological advances. Eastern war-making was not noticeably more effective in 1800 than it had been in 1500, and was much *less* effective than it had been in 1700—which has a lot to do with why Britain's forces swept China's aside so easily in the 1840s.

The advent of gunpowder weapons in the fourteenth century increased war-making capacity in both East and West, though much less dramatically than the inventions of the nineteenth and twentieth centuries would do. In Europe the best armies around 1500 (particularly the Ottomans) were probably twice as effective as those of five centuries earlier, though that had as much to do with size and logistics as with firepower.

The relationship between Western war-making around 1500 and the large, highly organized, but pre-gunpowder forces of the Roman Empire is harder to calculate. One study has estimated that a single jet bomber around 2000 CE had half a million times the killing capacity of a Roman legionary, which we might take as implying that the Western score in 1 BCE/CE would be 0.0005 point; but of course Rome had far more legionaries than the United States has jet bombers, and I estimate the ratio between modern Western and Roman war-making at more like 2,000:1, putting the Western score in 1 BCE/CE at 0.12 point. That makes the Roman war machine at its height a serious rival for fifteenth-century European armies and navies, despite their guns and cannons, but not for the forces of the "military revolution" era. It also means that Roman war-making at its zenith might have competed with that of the Mongols and was superior to that of Tang dynasty China.

In the East, where bronze weapons were still the norm as late as 200 BCE, Han dynasty (200 BCE–200 CE) forces seem to have been less effective than Roman, although Chinese military power declined much less than Western after the Old World Exchange. The armies and navies that the Sui used to reunite China in the sixth century were much stronger than anything in the West, and by the time of Empress Wu around 700 the gap was enormous.

The militaries of the centuries BCE were much weaker than those of the Roman and Han empires. In the East I assume that no force before the time of Erlitou around 1900 BCE was effective enough to score 0.01 point; in the West, Egyptian and Mesopotamian armies probably scored 0.01 point by about 3000 BCE.

Table A.3. War-making capacity, expressed in points on the social development index (selected dates)

DATE	WEST	EAST
2000 CE	250.0	12.5
1900	5.0	1.0
1800	0.50	0.10
1700	0.35	0.15
1600	0.18	0.12
1500	0.13	0.10
1400	0.11	0.11
1200	0.08	0.09
1000	0.06	0.08
800	0.04	0.07
600	0.04	0.09
400	0.09	0.07
200 CE	0.11	0.07
1 BCE/CE	0.12	0.08
200 BCE	0.10	0.07
400	0.09	0.05
600	0.07	0.03
800	0.05	0.02
1000	0.03	0.03
1200	0.04	0.02
1500	0.02	0.01
2000	0.01	0
2500	0.01	0
3000 BCE	0.01	0

INFORMATION TECHNOLOGY

Archaeological and written sources show us what kinds of information technology existed at various periods and it is not too difficult to estimate how much information these media could communicate, at what speeds, and over what distances. The real problem lies in estimating the extent of use of different technologies, which through most of history means how many people could read and write and at what levels of competence.

Moore's Law—that the cost-effectiveness of information technology has doubled every eighteen months or so since about 1950—seems to imply that the score in 2000 should be about a billion times higher than that of 1900, giving us a Western score in 1900 of 0.00000025 point. But that, of course, would overlook both the flexibility of old-fashioned forms of information storage such as printed books (which digital media are only now beginning to challenge) and changes over time in access to the most advanced techniques.

The correct ratio between modern and earlier information technology is much less than a billion to one, though it is clearly enormous, with the consequence that pre-1900 scores (and even more so, pre-1900 margins of error) are even tinier than in the case of war-making. On the other hand, the evidence for just how many people could read, write, and count at various levels of skill is much vaguer than the evidence for war, and my guesstimates are even more impressionistic.

In table A.4 I take a multistep approach to quantifying information technology. First, following common practice among historians, I divide skills into full, medium, and basic. The bars for each category are set low—in terms of literacy, basic means being able to read and write a name; medium, being able to read or write a simple sentence; and full, being able to read and write more connected prose. The Chinese Communist Party's definitions in its 1950 literacy drive (full literacy, being able to recognize 1,000 characters; semiliteracy, recognizing 500–1,000; basic, 300–500) were rather similar.

Second, drawing on the available scholarship, I divide the adult male population at different periods across these three categories. For each 1 percent of men that falls into the full-literacy category I assign 0.5 point; for each percent in the medium category, 0.25 point; and for each percent in the basic category, 0.15 point. I then assign the same scores to women. The evidence for female literacy is poorer than for male, though it is clear that until the twentieth century fewer (usually far fewer) women than men could read and write. Although I am basically guessing before recent times, I hazard estimates of female use of information technology as a percentage of male use. I then assign points to each period based on the amount and level of information technology use.

In 2000, 100 percent of men and women are in the full category in both the Western and Eastern cores,* scoring 100 information technology points for both regions. In 1900, nearly all men in the Western core had at least some literacy (50 percent full, 40 percent medium, and 7 percent basic) and women were almost as well educated, generating a Western score of 63.8 IT points. In the East literacy was also widespread among men, though not at such high levels (I estimate 15 percent full, 60 percent medium, and 10 percent basic), though literate women may have been only a quarter as common. The result is an Eastern score of 30 IT points. As I repeat these calculations further back in history, the possible margin of error around my guesses steadily increases, although the tiny numbers of literate people make the impact of these errors correspondingly small.

The third step is to apply a multiplier for the changing speed and reach of communication technologies. I divide the most advanced tools for handling information into three broad categories: electronic (in use in both East and West by 2000), electrical (in use in the West by 1900), and preelectrical (in use in the West for perhaps eleven thousand years and in the East for perhaps nine thousand years).

Unlike most historians I do not make a strong distinction between print and preprint eras; the main contribution of printing was to produce more and cheaper materials rather than to transform communication the way that the telegraph or Internet would do, and these quantitative changes have already been factored in. For electronic technologies, I use a multiplier of 2.5 for the West and 1.89 for the East, reflecting the relative availability of computers and broadband

---

*I should stress again that my basic, medium, and full literacy categories set the bar much lower than twenty-first-century literacy providers would do. Anyone able to fill out a modern job application or a tax return would rank well up in the full category.

Table A.4. Information technology scores

WESTERN CORE

Dates	MALE CATEGORIES (PERCENTAGES)			Male points	Female (%M)	Literacy points	Multiplier	Total points
	Full (@0.5 pts)	Medium (@0.25 pts)	Basic (@0.15 pts)					
2000 CE	100 (50)	0	0	50	100% = 50	100.0	x 2.5	250.0
1900	40 (20)	50 (12.5)	7 (1.05)	33.6	90% = 30.2	63.8	x 0.05	3.19
1800	20 (10)	25 (6.25)	20 (3)	19.3	50% = 9.65	28.95	x 0.01	0.29
1700	10 (5)	15 (3.75)	25 (3.75)	12.5	10% = 1.25	13.75	x 0.01	0.14
1600	5 (2.5)	10 (2.5)	10 (1.5)	6.5	2% = 0.13	6.63	x 0.01	0.07
1500	4 (2)	8 (2)	6 (0.9)	4.9	2% = 0.10	5.0	x 0.01	0.05
1400	3 (1.5)	6 (1.5)	4 (0.6)	3.6	1% = 0.04	3.64	x 0.01	0.04
1300	3 (1.5)	6 (1.5)	4 (0.6)	3.6	1% = 0.04	3.64	x 0.01	0.04
1200	3 (1.5)	6 (1.5)	4 (0.6)	3.6	1% = 0.04	3.64	x 0.01	0.04
1100	2 (1)	4 (1)	2 (0.3)	2.3	1% = 0.02	2.32	x 0.01	0.02
1000	2 (1)	4 (1)	2 (0.3)	2.3	1% = 0.02	2.32	x 0.01	0.02
600–900	2 (1)	2 (0.5)	1 (0.15)	1.65	1% = 0.02	1.67	x 0.01	0.02
300–500 CE	3 (1.5)	4 (1)	3 (0.45)	2.95	1% = 0.03	2.98	x 0.01	0.03
100 BCE–200 CE	4 (2)	6 (1.5)	5 (0.75)	4.25	1% = 0.04	4.29	x 0.01	0.04
500–200 BCE	2 (1)	3 (0.75)	2 (0.3)	2.05	1% = 0.02	2.07	x 0.01	0.02
900–600 BCE	1 (1)	2 (0.5)	1 (0.15)	1.65	1% = 0.02	1.67	x 0.01	0.02
1100–1000 BCE	1 (1)	1 (0.25)	1 (0.15)	1.4	1% = 0.01	1.41	x 0.01	0.01
2200–1200 BCE	1 (1)	2 (0.5)	1 (0.15)	1.65	1% = 0.02	1.67	x 0.01	0.02

Dates	Full (@0.5 pts)	Medium (@0.25 pts)	Basic (@0.15 pts)	Male points	Female (%M)	Literacy points	Multiplier	Total points
2700–2300 BCE	1 (1)	1 (0.25)	1 (0.15)	1.4	1% = 0.01	1.41	x 0.01	0.01
3300–2800 BCE	0 (1)	1 (0.25)	2 (0.3)	0.55	1% = 0.01	0.56	x 0.01	0.01
6000–3400 BCE	0	0	1 (0.15)	0.15	1% = 0	0.15	x 0.01	0
9000–6100 BCE	0	0	0	0	0	0	x 0.01	0
9300–9000 BCE	0	0	1 (0.15)	0.15	1% = 0	0.15	x 0.01	0

EASTERN CORE

Dates	MALE CATEGORIES (PERCENTAGES)			Male points	Female (%M)	Literacy points	Multiplier	Total points
	Full (@0.5 pts)	Medium (@0.25 pts)	Basic (@0.15 pts)					
2000	100 (50)	0	0	50.0	100% = 50	100.0	x 1.89	189.0
1900	15 (7.5)	60 (15)	10 (1.5)	24.0	25% = 6	30.0	x 0.01	0.3
1800	5 (2.5)	35 (8.75)	10 (1.5)	12.75	5% = 0.64	13.39	x 0.01	0.13
1700	5 (2.5)	20 (5)	10 (1.5)	9	2% = 0.18	9.18	x 0.01	0.09
1600	4 (2)	15 (3.75)	10 (1.5)	7.25	2% = 0.15	7.4	x 0.01	0.07
1500	3 (1.5)	10 (2.5)	10 (1.5)	5.5	2% = 0.11	5.61	x 0.01	0.06
1400	3 (1.5)	10 (2.5)	10 (1.5)	5.5	2% = 0.11	5.61	x 0.01	0.06
1300	3 (1.5)	5 (1.25)	5 (0.75)	3.5	1% = 0.04	3.54	x 0.01	0.04
1200	3 (1.5)	5 (1.25)	5 (0.75)	3.5	1% = 0.04	3.54	x 0.01	0.04
1100	2 (1)	2 (0.5)	3 (0.45)	1.95	1% = 0.02	1.97	x 0.01	0.02
600 BCE–1000 CE	2 (1)	2 (0.5)	2 (0.3)	1.8	1% = 0.02	1.82	x 0.01	0.02
1000–700 BCE	2 (1)	1 (0.25)	1 (0.15)	1.4	1% = 0.01	1.41	x 0.01	0.01
1300–1100 BCE	1 (0.5)	1 (0.25)	1 (0.15)	0.9	1% = 0.01	0.91	x 0.01	0.01
7000–1400 BCE	0	0	1 (0.15)	0.15	1% = 0	0.15	x 0.01	0

communication in West and East in the year 2000. For electrical technologies, having some impact in the West by 1900, I use a multiplier of 0.05; and for preelectrical technologies, in use in all other periods, I use a multiplier of 0.01 in both East and West. Consequently, in 2000 the West scores the maximum possible 250 social development points (100 IT points × 2.5) and the East gets 189 (100 IT points × 1.89); in 1900, the West scores 3.19 points (63.8 × 0.05) and the East 0.3 (30 × 0.01). The Western score reaches the minimum level necessary to register on the index of social development (that is, 0.01 point) only around 3300 BCE; the Eastern, around 1300 BCE.

MARGINS OF ERROR

I spoke repeatedly of estimates and guesses in the previous section, because there is no way to build a social development index without them. One consequence of that is that no index will ever be "right," whether we take that word in the strong sense of meaning that every single detail is completely accurate or in the weaker sense of meaning that all experts will make the same estimates. As a result, there is no point in asking whether the social development scores I have calculated are wrong. Of course they are. The real question is: *How* wrong are they? Are they so wrong that the basic shape of the history of social development as represented in the graphs in Chapters 4–10 is misleading, meaning that this whole book is fatally flawed? Or are the errors in fact relatively trivial?

These questions can in principle be answered easily enough; we simply need to ask (1) just how much we would need to change the scores to make the past look so different that the arguments advanced in this book would cease to hold good and (2) whether such changes are plausible.

Ultimately the only way to do this is by examining the evidence listed on the website (www.ianmorris.org) for each individual calculation I have made, but here I want to address briefly the possibility that systematic errors undermine my claims about the overall shape of history. According to my index (shown on a log-linear scale in Figure 3.7), the West took a lead after 14,000 BCE. The East slowly caught up, and through most of the first millennium BCE the West's lead was narrow. Around 100 BCE the West increased its lead, but in 541 CE the East pulled ahead. It stayed there until 1773. The West then regained the lead, and, if twentieth-century trends continue, will hold it until 2103. Western development has been higher than Eastern for 92.5 percent of the time since the end of the Ice Age.

I suggested in Chapter 3 that overall my scores could err by as much as 10 percent without significantly altering this pattern. Figure A.2a shows how the trends would look if I have consistently underestimated Western development scores by 10 percent and overestimated Eastern scores by the same amount; Figure A.2b shows the outcome if I have underestimated Eastern development scores by 10 percent and overestimated Western scores by the same amount.

The first point to note is that these scores severely strain credibility. Figure A.2a, raising Western and lowering Eastern scores by 10 percent, requires us to accept that the West was more developed than the East in 1400 CE, right before Zheng He sailed on the Indian Ocean; it also means that when Hannibal led his elephants to attack Rome in 218 BCE Western development was already higher than the East's would be in Zheng's time. As if that were not peculiar enough, the graph additionally tells us that the West was more developed when Julius Caesar was murdered in 44 BCE than the East was when China's emperor Qianlong rejected Lord Macartney's trade embassy in 1793.

Figure A.2b is perhaps even more peculiar. The development score it gives to the West in 700 CE, for instance, when the Arabs ruled a vast caliphate from Damascus, is lower than that for the East in the age of Confucius, which cannot be right; and it would make the Western score in 1800, when the industrial revolution was already under way, lower than the Eastern scores under the Song dynasty in 1000–1200, which seems even less likely.

Yet even if historians could swallow such odd conclusions, the shapes of history as represented in Figure A.2 are still not different enough from that in Figure 3.7 to change the basic pattern that needs explaining. Short-term accident theories remain inadequate because even in Figure A.2b the West's score is still higher most of the time (although "most" now means 56 percent rather than 92.5); so, too, long-term lock-in theories, because even in Figure A.2a the East does take the lead for seven centuries. Biology and sociology remain the most plausible explanations for the upward but interrupted movement

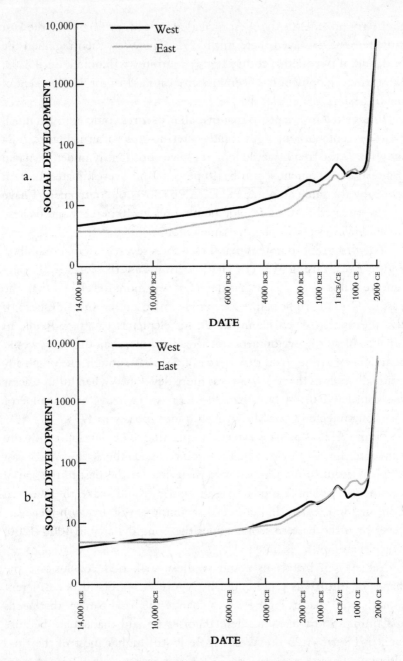

Figure A.2. Error revealed: the implications of systematic errors in social development scores. (a) raises all Western scores by 10 percent and reduces all Eastern scores by the same amount; (b) raises all Eastern scores by 10 percent and reduces all Western scores by the same amount.

of development, while geography remains the most plausible explanation for why the West rules.

To change the fundamental patterns my estimates would need to be 20 percent wide of the mark. Figure A.3a shows how history would look if I have consistently underestimated Western development scores by 20 percent and overestimated Eastern scores by the same amount; Figure A.3b, the outcome if I have underestimated Eastern development scores by 20 percent and overestimated Western scores by the same amount.

This time the patterns are very different. In Figure A.3a the Western score is always higher than the Eastern, making long-term lock-in theories seem very plausible and also invalidating my claim that social development changes the meaning of geography. Figure A.3b, by contrast, effectively reverses the conclusions of my actual index, having the East lead 90 percent of the time since the Ice Age.

If either Figure A.3a or A.3b is correct, everything you have just read in this book is wrong. We can be confident, though, that they are not correct. Figure A.3a, raising Western scores and reducing Eastern scores by 20 percent, tells us that imperial Rome's development in 1 BCE/CE was only five points behind industrial Japan's in 1900, which cannot be true; while Figure A.3b, raising Eastern scores and reducing Western scores by 20 percent, means that Eastern development was higher in pre-Shang times than Western would be under the Persian Empire; that the West caught up with the East only in 1828, on the eve of the Opium War; and that Western rule has already ended (in 2003). None of this seems credible.

Hence my suggestions in Chapter 3 that (a) the margin of error in my estimates is probably less than 10 percent and definitely less than 20 percent, and (b), even if the margin of error does rise to 10 percent, the basic historical patterns I am trying to explain still hold good.

CONCLUSION

I observed several times in Chapter 3 that making a social development index is chainsaw art. The best an index can do is to give us a rough, good-enough approximation that makes the index designer's assumptions explicit. I have argued that the main reason we have for so long

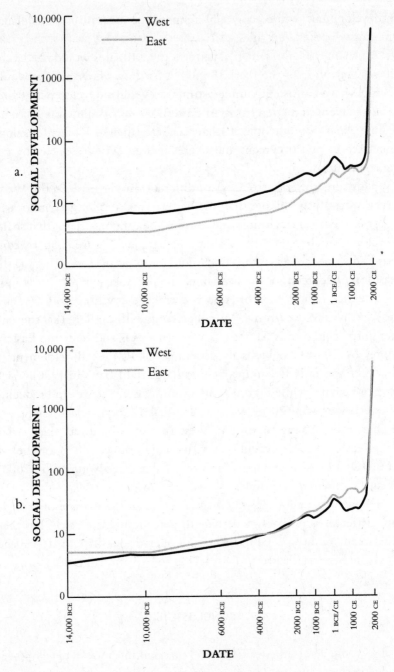

Figure A.3. Even greater error: (a) raises all Western scores and reduces
all Eastern scores by 20 percent, and (b) raises all Eastern scores and reduces
all Western scores by 20 percent

failed to explain why the West rules is that protagonists have defined their terms in different ways and focused on different parts of the problem. The simple act of setting up an index should therefore move the debate forward. Critics of this book who raise the first of the objections I listed at the start of this appendix—that quantitative comparisons are unacceptable because they dehumanize us—will be forced either to find another way to explain why the West rules or to show why we should not be asking that question at all, while critics who raise objections 2 through 4—that I have defined social development badly, used the wrong traits, or misunderstood the evidence—will be forced to come up with better indices of their own. And then, perhaps, we will see some real progress.

Notes

This section provides references for quotations and works mentioned by name in the main text. I refer to sources by the authors' or editors' last names and the date of publication; the full details can be found in the bibliography that follows. For works of the last hundred years or so I provide a precise page number; for older works that have been reprinted in multiple versions with varying page numbers, I give the source's full title and refer to the chapter or other subdivision from which I have taken the quotation. Translations are my own unless indicated otherwise.

The "Further Reading" section suggests books and articles that I have found particularly helpful in writing this book.

INTRODUCTION

11 "I am wearing": Shad Kafuri (August 1994), cited in Jacques 2009, p. 113.
12 "Whatever happens": Hilaire Belloc, *The Modern Traveler* (1898), part 6.
13 "The farther backward": Winston Churchill, cited from http://quotationsbook .com/quote/40770/.
19 "distant marginal peninsula," "Sinocentric world order," and "a third-class seat": Frank 1998, pp. 2, 116, 37.
20 "It's well": William III of England (1690), cited from Goldstone 2006, p. 171.
22 "between that era": Crosby 2004, p. 42; italics in original.
26 "History, *n.*": Bierce 1911, p. 51.
27 "Progress is made": Heinlein 1973, p. 53.
29 "The Art of Biography": Bentley 1905, p. 1.
30 "Soft countries": Herodotus, *History* 9.122.
30 "too uniformly stimulating" and "The people": E. Huntington 1915, p. 134.

32 "None ever wished": Samuel Johnson, *Lives of the Most Eminent English Poets* (1780), section on Milton.

34 "advantages of backwardness": Gerschrenkon 1962.

1. BEFORE EAST AND WEST

39 "When a man": Samuel Johnson, in James Boswell, *Life of Johnson* (1791), vol. 3, entry for September 20, 1777.

39 "necessary": Arthur Young (1761), quoted in Briggs 1994, p. 196.

40 "long one of" etc.: Adam Smith, *Wealth of Nations* (1776), book I, chapter 8.

41 "elastic geography" etc.: Davies 1994, p. 25.

45 "punctuated equilibrium": Gould 2007. The expression goes back to an essay Gould published with Niles Eldredge in 1972.

59 "Are you going": Richard Klein, quoted in "Scientists in Germany Draft Neanderthal Genome," *New York Times*, February 12, 2009, http://www.nytimes.com/2009/02/13/science/13neanderthal.html?_r=1&partner=rss&emc=rss.

62 "What a piece": William Shakespeare, *Hamlet*, Act 2, scene 2.

63 "inquisitive tendrils" and "The very atoms": A. C. Clarke 1968, pp. 16, 17.

71 "one lucky mother": Cann et al. 1987.

72 "modern Chinese man": "Stirring Find in Xuchang," *China Daily*, January 28, 2008, http://www.chinadaily.com/cn/opinion/2008-01/28/content_6424452.htm.

72 "the data": Ke et al. 2001, p. 1151.

73 "Suddenly . . . I made out": Herbert Kühn's 1923 interview with Maria Sanz de Sautuola, in Kühn 1955, pp. 45–46.

74 "so enthusiastic": ibid., p. 46.

2. THE WEST TAKES THE LEAD

85 "cognitive arms race": Pinker 1997, p. 193 (Pinker himself does not subscribe to this theory).

91 "cultivated": Fuller 2007.

93 "You can't step": None of the original works of Heraclitus (flourished c. 500 BCE) survive; Plato quoted this passage in *Cratylus* 402A in the early fourth century BCE.

106 "a small university city": Sahlins 2005, p. 209.

106 "Open the gates," "Thanks to teachers," and "Be a realist": quoted in Quattrocchi and Nairn 1968, pp. 17, 30.

106 "erected a shrine" and "The world's most primitive": Marshall Sahlins, "The Original Affluent Society," first published in French in 1968. The quotations come from an English version published in Sahlins 1972, pp. 39 and 37 and reprinted in Sahlins 2005, pp. 134 and 133.

107 "in different ways": Barker 2006, p. 414.

113 "Free will is for history": Leo Tolstoy, *War and Peace* (1869), Epilogue, part II, chapter 11. Translation modified slightly from http://www.gutenberg.org.

3. TAKING THE MEASURE OF THE PAST

135 "From the remotest past": Spencer 1857, p. 465.

137 "the vanity": Max Weber, cited in Gerth and Mills 1946, p. 66, note.

139 "exist[ing] in a": Charles Darwin, *The Voyage of the Beagle* (1882), chapter 10.

139 agreement among indices: Carneiro 2003, pp. 167–68.

140 "sympathy and even admiration": Sahlins 2005, pp. 22–23.

141 "Evolutionary theories": Shanks and Tilley 1987, p. 164.

141 "We no longer": Ortner 1984, p. 126.

143 "The ships": Lord Robert Jocelyn, cited from Waley 1958, p. 109.

143 "as if the subjects": Armine Mountain, cited from Fay 1997, p. 222.

145 "in science": people regularly attribute these or similar words to Einstein, but no one has been able to trace them back to a source. The strongest claim I have seen is on the One Degree website (http://www.onedegree.ca/2005/04/08/making -einstein-simple), suggesting that the phrase actually comes from a *Reader's Digest* summary of the general theory of relativity. Perhaps it was the most important thing Einstein never said (but should have).

145 "I'm just wondering": Arthur Eddington, quoted in Isaacson 2007, p. 262.

146 Norway and Sierra Leone scores: United Nations Development Programme 2009, Table H, pp. 171, 174 (available at http://hdr.undp.org/en/).

148 $E \times T \rightarrow C$: L. White 1949, p. 368.

149 "Every Communist": taken from Mao Zedong's essay "On Protracted War," written in May 1937, quoted in Short 1999, p. 368.

151 "because no": Naroll 1956, p. 691.

157 "conjectures and refutations": Popper 1963, p. 43.

157 "There could be": Albert Einstein, quoted in ibid., p. 42.

163 "There are three": attributed to Benjamin Disraeli by Mark Twain (Twain 1924, p. 246).

170 "Are these" etc.: Charles Dickens, *A Christmas Carol in Prose* (1843), stave 4.

4. THE EAST CATCHES UP

186 "How can a man": Plutarch, *Life of Alexander* 64.

191 "And they gained": Genesis 47.27, as translated in *The New Oxford Annotated Bible* (1994), p. 63 OT.

193 "Who then": *Sumerian King List*, translated in Kramer 1963, p. 330.

194 "Hunger filled": *The Lamentation over Ur*, lines 390–94, translated in Michalowski 1989.

197 "the kings who": treaty between the Hittites and Amurru, late thirteenth century BCE, translated in Beckman 1999, p. 107.

199 "His Majesty [Ramses] slew": Ramses II's victory inscription, translated in Lichtheim 1973–80, vol. II, p. 62.

204 "The Way": Lü Buwei, *Springs and Autumns of Mr. Lü* 3.5, translated in de Bary and Bloom 1999, p. 239.

205 "But for Yu": *Zuozhuan Commentary*, Duke Zhao Year 1, translated in Legge 1872, p. 578.

205 "the Age of Jade": Chang 1989, p. 42.

206 "During the reign": Lü Buwei, *Springs and Autumns of Mr. Lü*, p. 239.

210 "They tilted": *Classic of Odes*, translated in Waley 1937, no. 240.

213 "Crackmaking": *Jiaguwen heji* 6,664 front, translated in de Bary and Bloom 1999, p. 12.

216 "the watchers": Pylos tablet An 657, translated in Chadwick 1987, pp. 40–42.

216 "it is a matter" and "the enemy's ships": Ugarit tablets RS 20.212 and 18.147, translated in Astour 1965, p. 255.

216 "The foreign countries" etc.: Ramses III, Medinet Habu inscription, translated in Pritchard 1969, pp. 262–63.

217 "The Land": Mursili II, Prayer to the Sun Goddess (*CTH* 376), translated in Pritchard 1969, p. 396.

218 "wasted, bare": Merneptah, Poetical Stela, translated in Lichtheim 1973–80, vol. II, p. 77.

219 "In those days": Judges 21.25, translated in *New Oxford Annotated Bible*, p. 331 OT.

222 "The war chariots": "Great brightness," *Classic of Odes*, translated in Waley 1937, no. 246.

222 "Children of the Sun": G. E. Smith 1915.

5. NECK AND NECK

231 "I come": *Mencius* 7B/4, translated in Lau 2003, p. 158.

232 "In the evening": *Mai zun* inscription, translated in Shaughnessy 1991, p. 207.

232 "The heavens": *Bamboo Annals* 4.4.5, translated in Legge 1865, Prolegomena p. 149.

233 "Cheap iron": Childe 1942, p. 183.

235 "I brought back": Ashur-dan II, translated in Grayson 1991, pp. 134–35.

237 "I built a tower": Ashurnasirpal II, translated in Luckenbill 1926, paragraphs 433, 445, 455, 472.

238 "If such a disruption": Bradley 1999, p. 15.

239 "Phoenician men": Homer, *Odyssey* 15.415–16.

243 "King You": Sima Qian, *Basic Annals* 4.148, from the translation in Nienhauser 1994, p. 74.

246 like a wolf: paraphrased from Lord Byron, "The Destruction of Sennacherib" (1815), stanza 1.

249 "my shepherd": Isaiah 44.28–45.1, translated in *New Oxford Annotated Bible*, p. 927 OT.

250 "the Persians": Herodotus 3.89.

252 "Duke Ling": *Zuozhuan*, Duke Xuan 2nd year, translated in Watson 1989, p. 76.

254 "Would that I": Hesiod, *Works and Days*, lines 174–76, 197–201.

255 "Man, as we": Jaspers 1953, p. 1.

255 "The more . . . in speaking": Confucius, *Analects* 9.11 and 12.3, translated in R. Dawson 1993, pp. 32, 44.

255 "it's beyond me": Plato, *Republic* 506e.

255 "The Way": Laozi, *Daodejing* 1, translated in de Bary and Bloom 1999, pp. 79–80.

257 "I transmit" and "To subdue oneself": Confucius, *Analects* 7.1, 12.1, 7.30, translated in R. Dawson 1993, pp. 24, 44, 26.

257 "act like beggars" and "Regard another's state": *Mozi* 39.2 and 15.11–15, translated in Bloodworth and Bloodworth 2004, p. 31.

258 "For three years," "You can't bear," and "one of the good" etc.: *Zhuangzi* 7, 26, 33, translated in Palmer et al. 2006, pp. 63–64, 239, 299–300.

259 "the enrichment," "If in enterprises," and "A state": *Book of Lord Shang* 8.8 and 20, translated in Duyvendak 1928.

263 "Qin has the same" and "It has the heart": *Stratagems of the Warring States (Zhanguo ce)* chapter 24, p. 869, translated in M. Lewis 2007, p. 40.

263 "Who can be": Polybius 1.1.

265 "[Lord Shang] commanded": Sima Qian, *Shi ji* 68, p. 2230, translated in M. Lewis 2007, p. 30.

266 "To jaw-jaw": Winston Churchill, speech at the White House, June 26, 1954, published in *New York Times*, June 27, 1954, p. 1.

266 "Qin is the": *Stratagems of the Warring States (Zhanguo ce)*, chapter 24, p. 869, translated in M. Lewis 2007, p. 40.

267 "We are the": cited from Paludan 1998, p. 17.

269 "Remember, you are a mortal": Tertullian, *Apology* 33; Jerome, *Letters* 39.2.8 (with discussion in Beard 2007, pp. 85–92).

270 "The Roman custom": Polybius 10.15.

273 "dispatched his adjutant": Fan Ye, *History of the Later Han*, cited from Leslie and Gardiner 1996, p. 43.

274 "In a workshop," "An inner room," and "I casually produced": Wheeler 1955, pp. 170–73.

276 "They have squat bodies": Ammianus Marcellinus, *Histories* 31.2.

277 "violence and neglect": Herodotus 1.106.

278 "Glutton as you are": Herodotus 1.212.

6. DECLINE AND FALL

280 "All is for": Voltaire, *Candide* (1759), chapter 1 and passim.

280 "When the emperor": Han dynasty poet, cited from Lovell 2006, p. 83.

280 "For the eternal": Aelius Aristides, *To Rome* 29, 109.

282 "As things stand": Sima Qian, *Shi ji* 48, translated in Watson 1993, pp. 2–3.

284 "All happy families": Leo Tolstoy, *Anna Karenina* (1875), part I, chapter 1, translation from http://www.gutenberg.org.

286 "I think": Suetonius, *Life of Vespasian* 23.

286 "All right then": *Monty Python's Life of Brian* (1979).

293 stone chambers, etc.: Chuci, cited from Paludan 1998, p. 49.

295 "Columbian Exchange": Crosby 1972.

295 "It appears": cited in Crosby 2004, p. 215.

297 "Recently there have been": He Gong, cited from McNeill 1976, p. 118.

300 "If you lose": Wang Fu, *Discourses of a Hidden Man*, p. 258, translated in M. Lewis 2007, p. 259.

302 "When a new": Fan Ye, *History of the Later Han* 71, p. 2299, cited from Twitchett and Loewe 1986, p. 338.

302 "The Han": Fan Ye, *History of the Later Han* 72, p. 2322, cited from M. Lewis 2007, p. 262.

303 "My armor": Cao Cao, cited from M. Lewis 2007, p. 28.

306 "The dead": *History of the Jin Dynasty*, chapter 107, pp. 2791–92, translated in Graff 2002, p. 63.

307 "awful revolution": Gibbon, *History of the Decline and Fall of the Roman Empire*, vol. 3 (1781), subchapter "General Observations on the Fall of the Roman Empire in the West."

307 "which will ever be": Gibbon, *Decline and Fall*, vol. 1 (1776), chapter 1.

307 "Now was revealed": Tacitus, *Histories* 1.4.

314 "Why ask for a song": Sidonius Apollinaris, *Poems* 12.

314 "All Gaul": Orientus, *Commonitorium* 2.184.

320 "Snapped rooftrees": *The Ruin* (anon.), cited from Dixon 1992, p. 146.

320 coins that float: cited from Dien 2007, p. 217.

320 "Surely you do not" and "Have you ever": Ruan Ji, "Biography of Mr. Great-man," translated in Balazs 1964, p. 238.

323 "Today there is no": *History of Wei* 114.3,045, translated in Gernet 1995, p. 7.

325 "He neither bathed": Athanasius, *Life of Saint Antony* 27.

326 "We may hear" and "The clergy": Gibbon, *Decline and Fall of the Roman Empire*, vol. 3 (1781), subchapter "General Observations on the Fall of the Roman Empire in the West."

7. THE EASTERN AGE

337 "By cutting through": Pi Rixiu, *Quan Tang wen* 797.8363b, translated in Xiong 2006, p. 93.

337 "Hundreds of houses": Bai Juyi, translated in Waley 1961, p. 161. The poem dates to 827.

339 "A bride serves": *Family Instructions of the Grandfather*, translated in Ebrey 1996, p. 127.

342 "If they do not die": Zhu Yu, *Conversations in Pingzhou* 1,119, translated in Duyvendak 1949, p. 24.

345 "Everyone born": Procopius, *History of the Wars* 1.24. The gossip about Justinian's demons and Theodora's orifices comes from the same author's *Secret History* 12.20 and 9.18.

346 "nobody would go": John of Ephesus, quoted in *Pseudo-Dionysus, Chronicle of Zuqnin* 5, translated in Witakowski 1996, p. 93.

348 "Immense joy": Anonymous treatise, "Return of the Relics of the Holy Martyr Anastasius the Persian from Persia to His Monastery" 1.99, translated in Kaegi 2003, p. 206.

348 "Let us all": Sebeos of Armenia, *History* 36, translated in Thomson 1999, p. 73.

350 "Recite!": Koran 96.1–5. A minority of scholars believes that the first recitation was actually verse 74.

351 "My heart": 'Umar, cited in Ibn Ishaq, *Sira* 228, translated in Guillaume 1971, p. 158.

351 "Fight for the sake": Koran 2.190.

351 "Be peaceful": Malcolm X, "Message to the Grassroots," November 1963, cited from DeGroot 2008, p. 117.

351, 352 "Who but" and "Our God": Koran 2.130 and 29.46.

353 "A victorious line": Gibbon, *Decline and Fall of the Roman Empire*, vol. 5 (1788), chapter 52.

355 "craving beauty," "Flowery hairpins," and "Our souls": Bai Juyi, *Everlasting Wrong*, translated by Witter Bynner in Birch 1965, pp. 266, 269.

362 "a Rome": Anon., *Karolus Magnus et Leo Papa*, line 97, translated in Godman 1985, p. 202.

367 "Give these monks": Gerald of Wales, cited from Fagan 2008, p. 36.

367 "pagans are the worst": Anonymous document, cited in Bartlett 1993, pp. 136–37.

369 "now not pope": Henry IV, letter to Gregory VII, January 24, 1076. Translated in Mommsen and Morrison 1962, pp. 151–52.

370 "the formation": R. Moore 1987.

370 "age of cathedrals": Duby 1981.

370 "One night": Peter Abelard, *Story of My Misfortunes*, translated in Muckle 1964, p. 38.

372 "a savage": William of Apulia, *La geste de Robert Guiscard* II.427–28, translated in Bartlett 1993, p. 86.

372 "Whenever battle": Anna Comnena, *Alexiad* 11.6.3, translated in Bartlett 1993, p. 86.

373 "dissolved the militarists' power": Bi Yuan, *Continuation of the Comprehensive Mirror for Aid in Government* (1797), year 2, translated in Mote 1999, p. 103.

375 "Buddhism is no more": Han Yu, "Memorial on the Bone of the Buddha" (819), translated in de Bary and Bloom 1999, pp. 583–84.

376 "The true scholar": Fan Zhongyan, *On Yueyang Tower*, translated in Hucker 1975, p. 364.

377 "The rivers and lakes": Ye Shi, translated in Shiba and Elvin 1970, p. 76.

378 "The morning sun": Daoqian, "On the Way to Guizong Monastery," translated in Shiba and Elvin 1970, p. 357.

379 "several times cheaper": Wang Zhen, *Treatise on Agriculture* 19.13a, 22.4a, translated in Elvin 1973, pp. 195, 198.

379, 380 "the resemblance" and "but if the line": Elvin 1973, p. 198.

381 "Didn't you see her": Su Shi, "Stone Coal" (c. 1080), translated in Wagner 2001b, pp. 51–52. I would like to thank Professor Wagner and Professor Nathan Sivin for discussing this text with me.

8. GOING GLOBAL

384 "I can tell you": Marco Polo, *The Travels*, translated in Latham 1958, p. 223. On palaces, see pp. 125–26; riches, p. 149; the Yangzi, p. 209; bridges, p. 163; food, p. 215; young ladies, p. 196; wives, p. 217; courtesans, p. 216; pears, p. 215; black stone, p. 156; fat fish, p, 215; porcelain, p. 238.

389 "as lines of writing": Yaqut al-Hamawi, translated in Browne 1902, vol. 2, p. 437.

391 "Never has there been" "an immense horde" and "followed after strange gods": Matthew Paris, *English History*, translated in Giles 1852, vol. 1, p. 314.

392 "That sunny dome!": Samuel Taylor Coleridge, *Kubla Khan* (1797), line 47.

393 "would sit": Rashid al-Din, *Assembly of Histories*, translated in Boyle 1971, p. 84.

393 "Just as God": Mongke Khan, audience with William of Rübruck (1254), translated in C. Dawson 1955, p. 195.

396 "Civilization": Ibn Khaldun, *The Muqaddimah*, vol. 1, page 64, cited from Dols 1976, p. 67.

397 "Swellings appeared": Jean de Venette, *Chronicle*, 1348, translated in Kirchner and Morrison 1986, p. 455.

397 "People spat": as-Safadi, cited in Dols 1976, p. 80.

397 "The souls of men": Ibn Nubatah, as quoted by al-Maqrizi, *as-Suluk li-ma'rifat duwal al-muluk*, part II, vol. 3, page 790, cited from Dols 1976, p. 174.

397 "green-eyed Christian[s]": Chuan Heng, *Unofficial History of the Last Yuan Emperor* 23a–b, cited in Dardess 1973, p. 105.

398 "We ask God's forgiveness": Ibn al-Wardi, *Risalat an'naba'*, cited from Dols 1976, p. 114.

398 "My mind reels": Matteo Villani, *Chronicles*, 1348, translated in Kirchner and Morrison 1986, pp. 448–49.

399 "Stripped to the waist": Jean de Venette, *Chronicle*, 1349, translated in Kirchner and Morrison 1986, pp. 457–58.

403 "the earthly heaven": Gibbon, *Decline and Fall of the Roman Empire*, vol. 6 (1788), chapter 68.

404 "into such a state": Niccolò Machiavelli, *Florentine Histories* (1520–25), Book 5, Chapter 1, translation from http://www.gutenberg.org.

406 "For thirty-one years": Hongwu, translated in Carrington-Goodrich 1976, p. 390.

406 "I do not care": Emperor Xuande, *Xuanzong shi lu* (1438) 105, cited in Levathes 1994, p. 173.

406 "foreign ships": Ch'oe Pu, *Diary*, translated in Meskill 1965, p. 135.

406 "convert grain into cash": Qiu Jun, *Supplement to "Expositions on the Great Learning"* (1487) 25.19b, cited from Brook 1998, p. 103.

407 "to the various": Proclamation by Yongle, 1405, quoted by Ma Huan, *Overall Survey of the Ocean's Shores* (1416), Foreword, translated in Mills 1970, p. 69.

408 "corpse-head barbarian": Ma Huan, *Overall Survey*, pp. 5–6, translated in Mills 1970, p. 84. Fei Xin, who accompanied the fleet from 1409 onward, told a similar story (translated in Mills and Ptak 1996, pp. 35–36).

408 "If one's eyes": Fei Xin, *Overall Survey of the Star Raft* (1436), cited from Duyvendak 1949, p. 31. On the Ka'ba, see Mills and Ptak 1996, p. 105.

414 "with all the men": Gomes Eannes de Azurara, *The Chronicle of the Discovery and Conquest of Guinea* II.99, cited from Crosby 2004, p. 76.

417 "The voyages": Gu Qiyuan, *Idle Talk with Guests* (1617), p. 1, cited from Levathes 1994, pp. 179–80.

417 "At the present": Erasmus, Letter 522, translated in Nichols 1904, p. 506.

417 "first-born": Burckhardt 1958 [1860], p. 143.

422 "If we try": Zhu Xi, *Reflections on Things at Hand* (1176), cited from Hucker 1975, p. 371.

423 "Since the time": Xuexuan, translated in Hucker 1975, p. 373.

424 "women's footbinding began": Zhang Bangji, *Mozhuang manlu* 8.5a–b, cited from Ko 2007, p. 111.

424 "Little girls": Che Ruoshui, *Jiaoqi ji* 1.221, cited from Ebrey 1993, p. 40.

431, 432 "Whoever is lord" and "China is an important": Tomé Pires, *Suma Oriental*, translated in Cortesão 1944, pp. lxxvii, 123.

9. THE WEST CATCHES UP

434 "A rising tide": John F. Kennedy, speech at Heber Springs, Arkansas, October 3, 1963 (available at http://www.presidency.ucsb.edu/ws/index.php?pid=9455).

437 "Population has grown": Xie Zhaozhe, *Wuza zu* 4.34a (1608), cited from Ho 1959, p. 262.

437 "like mice": Languedoc expression, cited from Le Roy Ladurie 1972, p. 53.

437 "Every family": Zhang Tao, *Gazetteer of She County* (1609) 6.10b–12a, cited from Brook 1998, pp. 1, 4.

437 "In the past": Heinrich Müller (1560), cited in Braudel 1981–84, vol. 1, pp. 194–95.

439 "the stricken": Wang Wenlu, "Letter to Master Wei of Chengsong" (1545), cited from Brook 1998, p. 106.

439 "Rare styles": *Gazetteer of Shaowu Prefecture* (1543) 2.43b, cited from Brook 1998, p. 144.

439 "are mad for": *Gazetteer of Chongwusuo Citadel* (1542), pp. 39–40, cited from Brook 1998, p. 149.

440 "poor scholars": Zhang Tao, *Gazetteer of She County* (1609) 3.9a, cited from Brook 1998, p. 258.

440 "benefit the people": Toyotomi Hideyoshi, "Sword Collection Edict" (1588) 2, translated in Tsunoda et al. 1964, p. 320.

440 "crafty and cunning": Jesuit Annual Letter (1588), cited from Perrin 1979, p. 27.

444 "They destroyed everything": Sergeant Iskender (1511), cited from Finkel 2005, p. 99.

446 "It makes me shudder": Ogier Ghiselin de Busbecq, Letter 3 (1560), cited from Ross and McLaughlin 1953, p. 255.

446 "was neither holy": Voltaire, *Essay on General History and on the Manners and Spirit of the Nations* (1756), chapter 70.

447 "God has been": Mercurino Gattinara, letter to Charles V, July 12, 1519, cited from Brandi 1939, p. 112.

447 "A single monk": Charles V, Edict of Worms, April 19, 1521, cited from Brandi 1939, p. 132.

449 "The only obstacle": Ogier Ghiselin de Busbecq, Letter 3 (1560), cited from Ross and McLaughlin 1953, p. 255.

450 "There will be": Chang Ying, "Remarks on Real Estate" (published around 1697), cited from John Richards 2003, p. 119.

450 "Stop the minor profit": Official proclamation, seventeenth century, cited from John Richards 2003, p. 120.

451 "Behold the great design": Anonymous song (published 1661), cited from Wiesner-Hanks 2006, p. 409.

451 "London was enveloped": John Evelyn, *A Character of England* (1659), cited from John Richards 2003, p. 235.

452 "The poorest he": Colonel Thomas Rainsborough, spoken at Putney Church, October 29, 1647, cited from Woodhouse 1938 (available at http://oll.liberty fund.org/?option=com_staticxt&staticfile=show.php%3Ftitle=2183).

452 "None comes": Richard Rumbold, spoken at his own execution, London, 1685, cited from Hill 1984, p. 37.

452, 453 "that mighty Leveller" and "Overturn": Abiezer Coppe, *A Fiery Flying Roll* I (1649), pp. 1–5, cited from Hill 1984, p. 43.

453 "sharpened their hoes": cited from Elvin 1973, p. 246.

453 "I, feeble and": Emperor Chongzhen, suicide note (1644), cited from Paludan 1998, p. 187.

454 "were subjected": Liu Shangyou, *A Short Record to Settle My Thoughts* (1644 or 1645), translated in Struve 1993, p. 15.

454 "the robbers and murderers" and "for so long": Peter Thiele, *Account of the Town of Beelitz in the Thirty Years' War*, cited from C. Clark 2006, pp. 32–34.

455 "Sometimes everyone": cited from Spence 1990, pp. 23–24.

460 "Every day": Felipe Guaman Poma, *New Chronicle and Good Government* (1614), cited from Kamen 2003, p. 117.

460 "Every peso": Antonio de la Calancha (1638), cited from Hemming 2004, p. 356.

461 "Potosí lives": cited from Kamen 2003, p. 286.

461 "The king of China": ibid., p. 292.

462 "Along the whole coast": cited from Lane 1998, p. 18.

464 "If death came": The saying has been attributed to several sources, but Cardinal Antoine Perrenot de Granvelle said something very similar in a letter dated May 11, 1573, cited in Kamen 1999, p. 252.

464 "naked people": letter to Juan de Oñate (1605), cited from Kamen 2003, p. 253.

464 "Even if you are poor": settler's letter home to Spain, cited from Kamen 2003, p. 131.

468 "one-handed clocks": Thomas Hardy, *Tess of the D'Urbervilles* (1891), Phase the First, chapter 3.

468 "The honour and reverence" etc.: Francis Bacon, *Novum Organum* (1620), preface.

469 "it is not less natural": René Descartes, *Principles of Philosophy* (1644), chapter 203.

470 "Nature, and Nature's laws": Alexander Pope, "Epitaph: intended for Sir Isaac Newton" (1730). A wit would later add two more lines:

> It did not last; the Devil howling "Ho!
> Let Einstein be!" restored the status quo.
>
> (J. C. Squire, "In Continuation of Pope on Newton" [1926])

470 "Philosophy is written": Galileo Galilei (1605), translated in Drake 1957, pp. 237–38.

471 "Man hath by nature," "The great and chief," and "by nature all": John Locke, *Second Treatise of Civil Government* (1690), chapter 7, section 87; chapter 9, section 124; and chapter 8, section 95.

472 "Dare to know!": Immanuel Kant, "An Answer to the Question: What is Enlightenment?" (1784) (available at http://www.english.upenn.edu/~mgamer/Etexts/kant.html).

472 "Philosophers should be": Frederick II, letter to Christian Wolff (1740), cited from Upton 2001, p. 307.

472 "a despotism": Thomas Carlyle, *History of the French Revolution* (1837), vol. 3, book 7, chapter 7.

472 "One must examine": Denis Diderot, "Encyclopedia [Philosophy]" (1751), translated by Philip Stewart at http://www.hti.umich.edu/d/did.

473 "studying the root": Emperor Kangxi, *Kangxi's Conversations with His Sons* 71b–72 (published 1730), translated in Spence 1974, p. 72.

474 "a certain vigor" etc.: Baron de Montesquieu, *The Spirit of the Laws* (1748), Book 17, translated at http://www.constitution.org/cm/sol11_17.htm#002.

475 "the more he got": Lu Gwei-djen, cited from Winchester 2008, p. 37.

475 *"Sci. in general"*: Joseph Needham (1942), cited from Winchester 2008, p. 57.

475 "the Needham Problem": Boulding 1976, p. 9.

477 "Clear glass": Kong Shangren, *Trying On Glasses* (c. 1690), cited from Strassberg 1997, p. 204.

478 "Melting the material": Xu Guangqi (1631), cited from Elman 2006, p. 30.

479 "I realized" etc.": Emperor Kangxi, various texts, translated in Spence 1974, pp. 72–75.

482 *O tempora, O mores!*: Cicero, *Against Catiline* (63 BCE) 1.1.

483 "These people seemed": Commander John Rodgers, report to the Secretary of the Navy (1865), cited from Perrin 1979, p. 4.

484 "We have never": Emperor Qianlong, letter to George III of Britain (1793), cited from Cranmer-Byng 1963, p. 340.

485 "I am the innocentest": William Kidd (1701), cited from Herman 2004, p. 247.

486 "Credit makes war": Daniel Defoe, *The Complete English Tradesman* (1725), vol. 1, chapter 27.

486 "France will undo us": The Duke of Newcastle (1742), cited from P. Kennedy 1987, p. 98.

486 "conquer America": William Pitt the Elder (1757), cited from Herman 2004, p. 279.

486 "Our bells are threadbare": Horace Walpole, letter to George Montagu, October 21, 1759, cited from W. S. Lewis 1941, pp. 250–51.

488 "Make terror": M. Barère, speech to the National Convention, September 5, 1793, translated in Baker 1987, p. 351.

488 "Let us be masters": Napoleon Bonaparte, speech at Boulogne (1805), cited from J. R. Green 1879, p. 171.

10. THE WESTERN AGE

491 "the vastness," etc.: James Boswell, *Life of Samuel Johnson* (1791), vol. 2. Entry for March 22nd, 1776. Emphasis in original.

491 "'Twas in truth": William Wordsworth, *The Prelude* (1805), Book 9, lines 161–69. Wordsworth was speaking specifically of the French Revolution.

494 "the vast consumption": *Mineralogia Cornubiensis* (1778), cited from Landes 2003, pp. 99–100.

494 "I had gone": James Watt, as told to Robert Hart, 1817 (the walk took place in 1765), cited from Uglow 2002, p. 101.

495 "rather successful": James Watt, letter to James Watt, Sr., December 11, 1774 (James Watt Papers, Birmingham City Archives, 4/60), cited from Uglow 2002, p. 248.

495 "If we had": Matthew Boulton, letter to James Watt, summer 1776, cited from Uglow 2002, p. 256.

495 "It crept into": Daniel Defoe, *Weekly Review*, January 31, 1708, cited from Ferguson 2003, p. 17.

501 "The poverty": Adam Smith, *Wealth of Nations* (1776), book 1, chapter 8.

503 "has pitilessly torn": Karl Marx and Friedrich Engels, *The Communist Manifesto* (1848), chapter 1.

503 "energy and perseverance": Samuel Smiles, *Industrial Biography* (1863), pp. 325, 332.

503 "Facts alone": Charles Dickens, *Hard Times* (1854), chapter 1.

504 "a triumph of fact": ibid., chapter 5.

504 "He listened patiently": Friedrich Engels, *The Condition of the Working Class in England* (1844), chapter 12.

504, 505 "What the bourgeoisie" and "Let the ruling classes": Marx and Engels, *Communist Manifesto*, chapters 1, 4.

506 "We consider it": Anonymous, "The First Half of the Nineteenth Century," *The Economist* 9 (1851), p. 57.

507 "Here I am, gentlemen!": Jules Verne, *Around the World in Eighty Days* (1873), chapter 37.

509 "white plague": Ferguson 2003, p. 59.

509 "have an unconquerable aversion": Isaac Weld, *Travels Through the States of North America and Provinces of Upper and Lower Canada During the Years 1795, 1796, and 1797*, vol. 1 (1799), pp. 232–33, cited from Williams 2003, p. 310.

509 "For her": Frank Norris, *The Pit* (1903), p. 57.

510 "Get a horse!": cited from Yergin 1992, p. 79.

510 "The development": Marcus Samuel, letter to Admiral John Fisher, November 1911, cited from Yergin 1992, pp. 154–55.

511 "The first": Admiral John Fisher, letter to Winston Churchill, 1911, cited from Yergin 1992, p. 155.

511 "propensity to truck": Smith, *Wealth of Nations* (1776), chapter 2.

512 "Constant revolutionizing": Marx and Engels, *Communist Manifesto*, chapter 1.

513 "The sole end" and "Over himself": John Stuart Mill, *On Liberty* (1859), chapter 1.

513 "The principle": John Stuart Mill, *The Subjection of Women* (1869), chapter 1.

513 "like the sorcerer": Marx and Engels, *Communist Manifesto*, chapter 1.

514 "His feet lost": Li Ruzhen, *Flowers in the Mirror* (published 1810s), translated in T. Lin 1965, p. 113.

515 "are all": Lord Macartney (1793), from Cranmer-Byng 1963, p. 153.

516 "simply did": paraphrase of a letter from James Matheson to J. A. Smith (September 24, 1839), cited from Fay 1997, p. 191.

517 "as the *floating* property": Bernard and Hall 1844, p. 6.

517 "pass over these": Governor-General Qiying (1842), cited from Spence 1990, p. 164.

517 "castles that moved": Japanese observers (1853), cited from Feifer 2006, p. 5.

519 "for . . . the [West's] middle": John Maynard Keynes, *The Economic Consequences of the Peace* (1919), chapter 1.

519 "The conquest": Joseph Conrad, *Heart of Darkness* (1902), chapter 1.

520 "it is the duty": *The Economist* 32 (July 1874), p. 802, cited from Davis 2001, p. 37.

520 "The horror! The horror!": Conrad, *Heart of Darkness*, chapter 3.

520 "I have seen things": President Ulysses S. Grant (1879), cited from Feifer 2006, p. 322.

522 "Useless beauty": Sugimoto Etsu Inagaki, recalling a conversation from the 1870s, cited from Feifer 2006, p. 310.

524 "to cultivate": Kaiser Wilhelm II (1895), cited from Ferguson 2007, p. 44.

525 "to unite": Wilhelm II, letter to Tsar Nicholas II (September 26, 1895) (available at http://wwi.lib.byu.edu/index.php/VI_Jagdhaus_Rominten_26/IX/95).

526 "What happened": Commander Aleksei Nikolaevich Kuropatkin (1905), cited from Ferguson 2007, p. 53.

529 "The financial center": Secretary of State John Hay, cited from Frieden 2006, p. 141.

530 "the influence of": Keynes 1930, vol. 2, pp. 306–307.

530 "gazing at their destiny": George Orwell, *The Road to Wigan Pier* (1937), pp. 85–86.

531 "I have seen": Lincoln Steffens (1919), cited from Steffens 1938, p. 463.

531 "It is only": Lieutenant-Colonel Ishiwara Kanji (1932), cited from Totman 2000, p. 424.

532 "The first cause": Adolf Hitler to Hjalmar Schacht (1936), cited from Frieden 2006, p. 204.

532 "The war situation": Emperor Hirohito (August 15, 1954), cited from R. Frank 1999, p. 320.

533 "economic, social and political": John J. McCloy (1945), cited from Judt 2005, p. 39.

534 "atomic bomb itself": Churchill, cited from Reynolds 2000, p. 36.

534 "create on the whole": Internal Kremlin report (1953), cited from Holloway 1994, p. 337.

534 "Strange as it": Churchill, speech to the House of Commons (1955), cited from Gaddis 2005, p. 65.

536 "Let's be frank": Prime Minister Harold Macmillan, speech at Bedford (July 20, 1957), cited from Sandbrook 2005, p. 80.

536 "residents from raw estates": Philip Larkin, "Here" (1964), reprinted in Larkin 2004, p. 79.

537 "Snub-nosed monsters": John Steinbeck, *The Grapes of Wrath* (1939), chapter 5.

540 "if allowed to": Riesman 1964 (first published 1951), p. 64.

541 "Anything that makes" etc.: Richard Nixon and Leonid Brezhnev, the "Kitchen Debate" (Moscow, July 24, 1959), cited from http://teachingamericanhistory .org/library/index.asp?document=176.

542 "Flog the driver!" etc.: joke cited from Reynolds 2000, p. 541n.

544 "The dearest people": *China Youth Journal* (September 27, 1958), cited from Becker 1996, p. 106.

544 "The Party Secretary": Bo Yibo, *Retrospective of Several Big Decisions and Incidents* (1993), cited from Becker 1996, pp. 107–108.

544 "It is not": Lu Xianwen (autumn 1959), cited from Becker 1996, p. 113.

544 "The air is filled": Report from Jiangxi (autumn 1958), cited from Spence 1990, p. 580.

545 "Communism is paradise": Song by Kang Sheng (1958), cited from Becker 1996, p. 104.

545 "No one in our family": Informant, cited from Becker 1996, p. 136.

545 "The worst thing": Informant, cited from Becker 1996, p. 138.

546 "It was class hatred": "Li XX," public poster in Beijing (September 2, 1966), cited from MacFarquhar and Schoenhals 2006, p. 127.

546 "This was the week": President Richard Nixon, toast at a dinner in Shanghai (February 27, 1972), cited from Reynolds 2000, p. 329.

547 "bookworms who": Zhang Tiesheng (1973), cited from Spence 1990, p. 638. In 1976 the "Gang of Four" (an ultraleftist clique including Mao Zedong's widow) was accused of inventing this whole episode.

547 "a socialist train": slogan attributed to the Gang of Four (1976), cited from Spence 1990, p. 651.

548 "During the 'Cultural Revolution'": Deng Xiaoping, speech (September 2, 1986), cited from Gittings 2005, p. 103.

548 "How do you double": cited from "Soviet Cars: Spluttering to a Halt," *The Economist*, July 10, 2008.

549 "We can't go on": Mikhail Gorbachev, private conversation (1985), cited from Gorbachev 1995, p. 165.

549 "In the Soviet Union": Gorbachev 1995, p. 490.

549 "dregs of society": Deng, speech to party leaders and army officers (June 9, 1989), cited from Spence 1990, p. 744.

550 "Our first objective": Zalmay Khalilzad, *Defense Planning Guidance, FY 1994– 1999*, Section IB, cited from http://www/gwu.edu/~nsarchiv/nukevault/ ebb245/index.htm (accessed October 17, 2008).

551 "an official who believes": Patrick Tyler, *New York Times* (March 8, 1992), p. I1, cited from J. Mann 2004, p. 210.

552 "proceed slowly": Deng, speech at Shenzhen Folk Culture Village (1992), cited from Gittings 2005, p. 252.

553 "the China price": *Business Week* (December 6, 2004), p. 104.

553 "The boss remarked": Kynge 2006, pp. 89–90.

553 "The direction of the wind": Mao, speech in Moscow (November 1957), cited from Schram 1969, p. 409.

11. WHY THE WEST RULES . . .

566 "Men make": Marx, *The Eighteenth Brumaire of Louis Napoleon* (1852).

572 "It is . . . in vain": Lord Macartney (1793), from Cranmer-Byng 1963, p. 191.

579 "Let us speculate": Mao, speech in Moscow, November 18, 1957, cited from Short 1999, p. 489.

580 "hand went up": R. F. Kennedy 1969, p. 71.

581 "Recorded history": Elton 1967, p. 62.

12. . . . FOR NOW

582–83 economic output estimates: National Intelligence Council 2008, p. 6; Wilson and Stupnytska 2007; Hawksworth and Cookson 2008; Maddison 2006; Fogel 2007.

583 "If the courses" and "He became": Dickens, *Christmas Carol*, Staves 4 and 5.

585 "Chimerica": Ferguson and Schularick 2007; Ferguson 2009.

586 2010 growth predictions: International Monetary Fund 2009, Table 1.1.

586 Congressional Budget Office: Douglas Elmendorf, cited from "Falls the Shadow: The Deficit and Health Care," *The Economist*, July 25, 2009, p. 25 (available at http://www.economist.com).

586 "After . . . 1989": cited from "May the Good China Preserve Us," *The Economist*, May 23, 2009, p. 47 (available at http://www.economist.com).

587–88 2030 and 2040 incomes calculated from Maddison 2006, Table 5, and Fogel 2007, Tables 1, 2. Maddison expresses GDP in 1990 US$; I have converted these to 2000 US$ using Bureau of Labor Statistics values (http://stats.bls.gov/).

588 "Soothing Scenario": J. Mann 2007, p. 1.
588 "Trade freely": George W. Bush, speech at the Ronald Reagan Library, Simi Valley, California (November 19, 1999), cited in Dietrich 2005, p. 29.
589 "contested modernities": Jacques 2009, p. 100.
591 "Our way of life": Jeremy Rifkin, from an interview conducted in 2000, cited from Singer 2009, p. 105.
592 "a future period": Kurzweil 2005, pp. 5, 24.
593 "the Rapture for Nerds": an expression coined by the science fiction novelist Ken MacLeod in his novel *The Cassini Division* (1998).
593 "criticism from incredulity": Kurzweil 2005, p. 432.
593 "When a scientist": Richard Smalley, cited from Nicholas Thompson, "Down-sizing: Nanotechnology—Why You Should Sweat the Small Stuff," *Washington Monthly*, October 2000 (http://washingtonmonthly.com/features/2000/0010 .thompson.html).
594 "We can rebuild him": *The Six Million Dollar Man*, ABC Television, 1974–78.
595 "We're not playing": Craig Venter, cited from Carr 2008.
595 "network-enabled telepathy": Roco and Bainbridge 2002, p. 19.
599 "Altered frequencies": Intergovernmental Panel on Climate Change 2007, pp. 12–13.
600 "the really scary stuff," "the even scarier stuff," and "global weirding": T. Friedman 2008, pp. 117, 122, 133. Friedman attributes the third expression to Hunter Lovins, cofounder of the Rocky Mountain Institute.
601 "arc of instability": National Intelligence Council 2008, p. 61.
601 "climate migrants": Stern 2006.
601 2006 Gallup poll: "Don't Drink the Water and Don't Breathe the Air," *The Economist*, January 26, 2008, pp. 41–42 (available at http://www.economist.com).
604 "The world may be": World Health Organization, "Ten Things You Need to Know About Pandemic Influenza," http://www.who.int/csr/disease/influenza/ pandemic10things/en/index.html (accessed November 29, 2008).
604 "The oil": *Summary of Report on Near Eastern Oil*, 800.6363/1511–1512 (National Archives, State Department, Washington, DC), February 3, 1943, cited from Yergin 1992, p. 393.
604 "peaceful rising" and "peaceful development": B. Zheng 2005.
604 "great drain robbery": cited from Kynge 2006, p. xiii.
605 "a threat to world peace": Ipsos-Reid poll (April 2005), cited from "Balancing Act: A Survey of China," *The Economist*, Special Report, March 25, 2006, p. 20 (available at http://www.economist.com/specialreports).
605 threat to global stability: Gallup poll (October 2007), cited from "After Bush: A Special Report on America and the World," *The Economist*, March 29, 2008, p. 9 (available at http://www.economist.com/specialreports).
605 "PEOPLE AGONIZED": *China Daily* headline (May 1999), cited from Hessler 2006, p. 20.
605 "strategic conspiracy": Chinese Communist Party resolution (2004), cited from "Balancing Act: A Survey of China," *The Economist*, Special Report, March 25, 2006, p. 15 (available at http://www.economist.com/specialreports).
605 "it is more likely": Graham and Talent 2008, p. xv.
606 "No physical force": Norman Angell, *The Great Illusion* (1910), cited from Ferguson 1998, p. 190.

606 "international movement of capital": Jean Jaurès, cited from Ferguson 1998, p. 190.

606 "must involve the expenditure": Prime Minister Edward Grey in conversation with the Austrian ambassador to Britain, July 1914, cited from Ferguson 1998, p. 191.

606 "total exhaustion": Grey, letter to the German ambassador to Britain, July 24, 1914, cited from Ferguson 1998, p. 191.

607 "I do not know": Albert Einstein, interview with Alfred Werner, *Liberal Judaism* (April–May 1949), cited from Isaacson 2007, p. 494.

608–609 estimates: Richardson 1960; Smil 2008, p. 245, http://www.thebulletin .org/content/doomsday-clock/overview.

609 "guys with gross obesity": Anonymous official in the Indian Foreign Ministry, cited from "Melting Asia," *The Economist*, June 7, 2008, p. 30 (available at http:// www.economist.com).

609 "The first era": T. Friedman 1999, p. xix.

609 "Globalization 3.0": T. Friedman 2005, p. 10.

610 "The only salvation": Albert Einstein, *New York Times*, September 15, 1945, cited from Isaacson 2007, pp. 487–88.

610 "If the idea": Albert Einstein, comment on the film *Where Will You Hide?* (May 1948), Albert Einstein Archives (Hebrew University, Jerusalem) 28-817, cited from Isaacson 2007, p. 494.

612 David Douglas, International Energy Agency: statistics in this and the following paragraph cited from T. Friedman 2008, pp. 31, 73, 59–60.

613 "But where are they?" Enrico Fermi, Los Alamos, circa 1950, cited from Jones 1985, p. 3.

615 "We will see": Steven Metz, interview with Peter Singer, September 19, 2006, cited from Singer 2009, p. 240.

615 "the U.S.": Roger Cliff, *The Military Potential of China's Commercial Technology* (2001), quoted in Singer 2009, p. 246.

618 "human space" etc.: Adams 2001.

621 "They have ridden" etc.: Rudyard Kipling, "The Ballad of East and West," *MacMillan's Magazine*, December 1889.

621 archaeologists and television: Diamond 2005, p. 525.

APPENDIX

634 jet bomber and Roman legionary: Sean Edwards, "Swarming and the Future of Warfare," unpublished PhD dissertation, Pardee Rand Graduate School, 2005, p. 136, cited from Singer 2009, p. 100.

Further Reading

In writing this book I have drawn on the painstaking work of generations of scholars who have assembled, analyzed, and interpreted mountains of data. The scholarly literature on Eastern and Western history is not only virtually endless but also highly argumentative, which means that it is almost impossible to make a statement on any major issue without it being challenged by at least some specialists. Space does not allow for exhaustive bibliographies for all the controversies, even if time allowed me to read them all; but in this section I list the works that have most influenced my thinking.

The works I list combine introductory studies aimed at general readers, more academic overviews, and detailed pieces of research that I found particularly useful. Whenever possible I mention recent works that include detailed bibliographies of their own. The most recent books are available in bookstores and many journal articles are available online, but for the time being most of these studies can be found only in research libraries. I have restricted my references to works in English whenever possible.

With the exception of short articles in newsmagazines, I refer to works by the authors' or editors' last names and the date of publication. Full details are gathered in the bibliography that follows.

Like countless historians before me, I have relied heavily on the Cambridge University Press multivolume histories covering different parts of the world. These are often the best place to find the basic facts, and rather than cite them over and over again, I will simply list the series I have used most heavily:

The Cambridge Ancient History (2nd ed., 14 volumes, 1975–2001)
The Cambridge History of China (10 volumes, 1979–)
The Cambridge History of Egypt (2 volumes, 1980–99)

The Cambridge History of Iran (8 volumes, 1968–91)
The Cambridge History of Islam (2 volumes, 1970)
The Cambridge History of Japan (6 volumes, 1988–99)
The New Cambridge Medieval History (7 volumes, 1995–2006)
The New Cambridge Modern History (12 volumes, 1957–90)
The Cambridge History of Southeast Asia (2 volumes, 1993)

In addition to these series there are also several invaluable single-volume Cambridge histories, which I cite by editors' names and publication dates below.

INTRODUCTION

Our main source for the *Qiying*'s arrival in England is "The Chinese Junk, 'Keying,'" *Illustrated London News* 12, no. 340, April 1, 1848, pp. 220, 222. Anglo-Chinese relations in the 1830s–40s: Fay 1997, Waley 1958. Hong Xiuquan: Spence 1996.

Nature of Western rule: Mandelbaum 2005. Chinese economic takeoff: Jacques 2009.

Chinese-European relations in the sixteenth century: Spence 1983. Eastern theories of Western rule: Fukuzawa 1966 (originally published 1899); Y. Lin 1979.

Westerners have produced hundreds of long-term lock-in theories since the eighteenth century. Diamond 1997, S. Huntington 1996, and Landes 1998 are excellent examples of modern approaches.

Torr 1951 collects Karl Marx's Chinese writings.

On Zheng and Columbus, see Chapter 8. Menzies 2002 presents the case for Zheng's global circumnavigation. Chiasson 2006 claims (even more remarkably) to have found a Chinese colony at Cape Breton, Nova Scotia. For the 1763/1418 map, see http://news.nationalgeographic.com/news/2006/01/0123_060123_chinese_map .html. Fifteenth-century Chinese maps: R. Smith 1996.

Goldstone 2009, Lee and Wang 1999, Pomeranz 2000, and Wong 1997 are the classic Orange County/short-term accident books; Arrighi 2007 explores the implications of their arguments. A. G. Frank 1998 is the most influential of the radical theories; Goody 2004 and Hobson 2004 may be the most extreme. Allen et al. 2005 and Bengtsson et al. 2005 provide quantitative evidence.

Controversies over the California School: the essays collected in *Journal of Asian Studies* 61, 2002, pp. 501–662, and *Canadian Journal of Sociology* 33, 2008, pp. 119–67, provide good examples.

Biology, sociology, and geography: among the studies that have most shaped my thinking are Conway Morris 2003, Coyne 2009, Dawkins 2009, Ehrlich and Ehrlich 2008, and Maynard-Smith and Dawkins 2008 (biology); Boserup 1965, Gerring 2001, North et al. 2009, Smelser and Swedberg 2005, and J. Wood 1998 (social sciences/sociology); Konner 2002, Vermeij 2004, and E. O. Wilson 1975 (interface of biological and social sciences); and Castree et al. 2005, de Blij 2005, Martin 2005, and Matthews and Herbert 2004 (geography). Acemoglu et al. 2002 provide the toughest challenge to geography as an explanation for why the West rules. I would like to thank Jim Robinson for discussing the issues with me.

1. BEFORE EAST AND WEST

Defining the West: Pomeranz 2000, pp. 3–10. History of the universe: Steinhardt and Turok 2007. Humanity's place in it: Christian 2004, Morowitz 2002.

Klein 2009 is the definitive survey of human evolution, covering all the topics in this chapter, and Wrangham 2009, the most readable brief account. Principles of evolution generally: Coyne 2009.

Workings of the brain: Zeman 2008. Reiteration and the FOXP2 gene: P. Lieberman 2007.

Movius Line: Norton and Bae 2008; Petraglia and Shipton 2008. Dmanisi: Lordki-panidze et al. 2007.

Zhoukoudian: Boaz and Ciochon 2004. Flores tools: Brumm et al. 2010. Flores "hobbits": Morwood and van Osterzee 2009, Tocheri 2007, Jungers et al. 2010. Chimpanzee intelligence: Savage-Rumbaugh and Lewin 1994. Central Asian "yeti": Krause et al. 2010.

Neanderthals: Mithen 2005. Distribution: Krause et al. 2007a. Bone breakage and rodeo riders: Berger and Trinkaus 1995. FOXP2 gene: Krause et al. 2007b. *Clan of the Cave Bear*: Auel 1980. Gibraltar: Finlayson et al. 2006. Spiritual life: Renfrew and Morley 2009.

Homo sapiens: Mithen 1996, Fleagle and Gilbert 2008. African Eve: Cann et al. 1987, Ingman et al. 2000. African Adam: P. Underhill et al. 2001.

Body lice: Kittler et al. 2003. A newer DNA study (Kitchen et al. 2010), however, suggests that lice evolved 190,000 years ago, with Neanderthals.

Baby Steps Forward: McBrearty and Brooks 2000, with new evidence in Bouzouggar et al. 2007, Morean et al. 2007, Morgan and Renne 2008, and Vanaeren et al. 2006. Demography and fully modern culture: Powell et al. 2009.

Against *Homo sapiens*/Neanderthal interbreeding: Krings et al. 1997; Caramelli et al. 2003. In favor: Zilhao 2006. Genome evidence: R. Green et al. 2010. Continuing human evolution: Cochran and Harpending 2009, Jakobsson et al. 2008, Voight et al. 2006, E. Wang et al. 2007. Movement out of Africa: Gunz et al. 2009. Dates of migration: Endicott et al. 2009, O'Connell and Allen 2004. First modern humans in China: Shen et al. 2002, 2007, Shang et al. 2007.

Multiregional model: Wolpoff 1996, Wolpoff and Caspari 2002, Cochran and Harpending 2009. New Zhoukoudian finds: Shang et al. 2007. New Xuchang finds:http://www.chinadaily.com/cn/opinion/2008-01/28/content_6424452.htm, with comments http://afp.google.com/article/ALeqM5inq53Ltnn7sNiN7mspQ6t DxCqQOA. Statistical analysis of bones: Manica et al. 2007.

First humans in America: Dillehay et al. 2008, Gilbert et al. 2008, Goebel et al. 2008.

Ancient climate: N. Roberts 1998. Ice core data: EPICA 2004.

Lewis-Williams 2002 provides a lively interpretation of Ice Age cave art and Bahn and Vertut 1997 collect the evidence with fine illustrations. Altamira dates: http://www.timesonline.co.uk/tol/travel/specials/artistic_spain/article 5904206.ece. Hohle Fels figurine: Conrad 2009. Xuchang bird: http://news .xinhuanet.com/english/2009-04/28/content_11274877.htm.

2. THE WEST TAKES THE LEAD

There is a vast literature on the origins of agriculture. The good news is that archaeologists have recently produced several excellent global surveys (especially Mithen 2003, Bellwood 2005, Barker 2006, Fuller 2007, and Cohen et al. 2009), which discuss most of the sites I mention in this chapter. The bad news (in a sense, anyway) is that this field moves so quickly that these works are already out of date. I cite additional works below on details or to update the surveys.

Black Sea flood: Major et al. 2006; Yanko-Hombach et al. 2007.

Energy and history: Smil 1994 remains the classic. Plants and photosynthesis: Morton 2007.

Lost civilizations: Hancock 2003.

Earliest pottery: Boaretto et al. 2009, Kuzmin 2006.

Comets and the Younger Dryas: Kennett et al. 2009.

Nightfall: Asimov 1941.

Hilly Flanks: in addition to the surveys already mentioned, see Cappers and Bottema, eds. 2002; Akkermans and Schwartz 2003; Bar-Yosef 2004.

Domestication of dogs: Savolainen et al. 2002. Garbage and sedentism: Hardy-Smith and Edwards 2004. Eastern sedentism: Liu 2010.

Abu Hureyra: A. Moore et al. 2000; rye and the Younger Dryas, Hillman et al. 2001, Willcox et al. 2008.

Archaeology of religion: Renfrew 1985. Evolutionary psychology of religion: Boyer 1999, Dennett 2007.

Early religious sites in the Hilly Flanks: Baumgarten 2005. Longwangcan: X. Wang 2008.

Fig trees: Kislev et al. 2006. Earliest granaries: Kuijt and Finlayson 2009.

Farming and birth-spacing: Bocquet-Appel and Bar Yosef 2008.

Çatalhöyük: Hodder 2006; http://www.catalhoyuk.com. People domesticating themselves: Hodder 1990.

Marriage, inheritance, and farming: Goody 1976 remains a classic.

Violence in prehistory: LeBlanc and Register 2003, Otterbein 2004. Jericho fortifications: McClellan 2006. Doubts about the original affluent society: D. Kaplan 2000.

Agricultural dispersal across Europe: emphasizing colonization, Renfrew 1987; Cavalli-Sforza et al. 1994; Bellwood 2005. Some essays in Renfrew and Boyle 2000 and Bellwood and Renfrew 2003 move toward consensus.

Inevitability of agriculture: Richerson et al. 2001.

Domestication: Diamond 1997 is the classic account, and Fuller 2007 the most up-to-date. Peru: Dillehay et al. 2007. Oaxaca: Pohl et al. 2007. Indus Valley: Fuller 2006. New Guinea: Denham et al. 2005. Sahara: Marshall and Hildebrand 2002. Bottle gourds: Erickson et al. 2005.

East Asia: in addition to the global surveys, see L. Liu 2004; Chang and Xu 2005, pp. 27–83; Stark 2006, pp. 77–148. Chang's *Archaeology of Ancient China* (1986) has long been the only detailed overview, but Liu and Chen 2010 now supersedes it. Japan: Habu 2004. Korea: Nelson 1993. Barnes 1999 covers China, Korea, and Japan. Bryan Gordon of Carleton College maintains a website on the origins of rice (http://http-server.carleton.ca/~bgordon/Rice/paper_database.htm).

Yangzi Delta sites: Jiang and Liu 2006, Jiang 2008. Pigs: Yuan and Flad 2002, Yuan 2008. Wei valley agricultural tools: Chang and Xu 2005, pp. 60–64. I largely follow Fuller 2007 and Fuller et al. 2007 on Chinese domestication, although G. Lee et al. 2007 and Liu et al. 2007 challenge these arguments (the debate continued in the 2008 online edition of the journal *Antiquity*).

Rice paddies: Zong et al. 2007.

Jiahu: J. Zhang et al. 2004, X. Li et al. 2003. Early Chinese writing: Keightley 2006. 'Ain Ghazal: Schmandt-Besserat 1998. Shamans: Chang 1983. Tarim Basin mummies: Barber 1999. Ancestor worship: Liu 2000.

East Asian agricultural expansion: Bellwood 2005, pp. 128–45; Barker 2006, pp. 199–230; Stark 2006, pp. 77–118; Sanchez-Mazan 2008.

Early farmers' skeletons: C. Larsen 1995, 2006; Armelagos and Harper 2005. Elite cuisines: Goody 1982.

Malinowksi's *A Diary in the Strict Sense of the Term* (1976) describes his time in the Trobriand Islands; Kuper 1983 explains his place in the history of anthropology.

3. TAKING THE MEASURE OF THE PAST

Herbert Spencer: Francis 2007. Trigger 1995 is the best account of the history of archaeology. On archaeology and social evolution more generally: Sanderson 2007, Trigger 1998. Pluciennek 2005 presents the case against evolutionism.

Talcott Parsons's *Societies: Evolutionary and Comparative Perspectives* (1966) is the most important neo-evolutionary study, but archaeologists refer more to Service 1962 and Fried 1967. Social development indices: Naroll 1956 and Carneiro 1962, 1968, and 1970.

Eddington's experiments: Isaacson 2007, pp. 256–62.

Criteria for evaluating traits and indices: Naroll 1956, Gerring 2001.

The UN Human Development Programme's annual reports can be downloaded from http://hdr.undp.org/. Ray 1998, pp. 27–29, neatly summarizes the criticisms.

Contemporary statistics: United Nations Organization 2006, Food and Agriculture Organization 2006, Institute for International Strategic Studies 2009. Earlier energy statistics rely on very scattered data, but Maddison 2003, Allen 2006b, and Allen et al. 2005 and 2007 are valuable. On agriculture, Perkins 1969 and Slicher van Bath 1963 are indispensable. Early industry: Crafts 1985, Mokyr 1999, Morris-Suzuki 1994. Smil 1991 and 1994 are outstanding overviews. Generally, see http://www.ianmorris.org.

Roman pollution: de Callataÿ 2005 summarizes the evidence then available; more recent studies include Boutron et al. 2004, Kylander et al. 2005, and Schettler and Romer 2006, covering the various sources of evidence.

Robert Hartwell's papers from the 1960s remain the standard treatments of Chinese iron and coal, particularly Hartwell 1967. Donald Wagner (2001a, 2001b, 2008) criticizes Hartwell's assumptions and use of evidence but generally accepts his results. I would like to thank Professor Wagner for discussing the issues with me.

Roman consumption: Jongman 2007a.

4. THE EAST CATCHES UP

There are some excellent recent overviews. For Mesopotamia: van de Mieroop 2007, Snell 2007. Egypt: Kemp 2005. Kuhrt 1995 treats both core areas. China: Liu 2004, Chang 1986, and Chang and Xu 2005 are invaluable.

More focused studies:

West—Early Mesopotamia: Postgate 1993. Susa and Eridu: Potts 1999, Pollock 1999. Uruk: Liverani 2006, Rothman 2001. Tell Brak: Ur et al. 2007. Early Egypt: Wilkinson 2003, Wengrow 2006. Pyramids: Lehner 1997. Akkad: Liverani 1993. Syria: Akkermans and Schwartz 2003. Hittites: Bryce 1998, 2002. Aegean: Shelmerdine 2008. Trojan War: Latacz 2004, Strauss 2006. International Age: Liverani 2001. European periphery: Kristiansen and Larsson 2005.

East—Three Dynasties Chronology Project: Y. K. Lee 2002, X. Zhang et al. 2008. Shandong survey: A. Underhill et al. 2002. Chinese music: von Falkenhausen 1993a. Shamanism: Chang 1983, 1989, 1994. Taosi monument: He 2005. Debates over the Xia: von Falkenhausen 1993b, Liu and Xu 2007. Erlitou and early Shang: Liu and Chen 2003. Environmental change: Qiao 2007, A. Rosen 2007. Shang: Thorp 2006. Anyang bronze foundry: Yinxu Team 2008. Oracle bones: Keightley 2000 (with references to that author's many important studies), Flad 2008, A. Smith 2008. Peter Hessler's *Oracle Bones* (2006) is a wonderful personal account of China, weaving historical analysis (particularly of the oracle bones themselves) with pointed reporting. Shang kingship: Puett 2002, Chapter 1, discussing rival theories. On chariots there is great controversy; I generally follow Shaughnessy 1988.

Chariots of the Gods?: von Däniken 1968.

Domestication of the horse: A. Outram et al. 2009.

Disruptions generally: Diamond 2005. McAnany and Yoffee 2010 provide opposed views. G. Schwartz 2006 reviews several of the disruptions of 2200–1200 BCE. Sing 2007 argues that all Western disruptions had ecological causes.

Western disruptions have been studied more than Eastern. Liu 2004, Chapter 2, reviews China's climatic record, and Chapters 6 and 7 look at case studies. For the 2200–2000 BCE Western disruption, see Dalfes et al. 1997. Weiss et al. 1993 discuss Tell Leilan; Cooper 2006 downplays climate change. 1750–1550 BCE: Drews 1988. Hurrians: Wilhelm 1989. Hyksos: Redford 1992. 1200–1000 BCE: Drews 1993 for military factors; Nur and Cline 2000 on earthquakes; Fagan 2004a, Chapter 9, and Sing 2007, pp. 84–89, for references to the numerous discussions of climate.

5. NECK AND NECK

There is a huge literature on early states. I draw particularly on North 1981; Tilly 1992; Turchin 2009; Scheidel, forthcoming.

Overviews of the East: M. Lewis 2007; F. Li 2006, 2009; Nylan and Loewe 2010; von Falkenhausen 2006; Zhao, forthcoming. Overview of the West: *Cambridge Ancient History*, volumes III–IX, provide enormous detail, with volume 2 of Kuhrt 1995 on western Asia.

The following more focused studies are also valuable:

East—Hsu and Linduff 1988, X. Li 1985, and Z. Wang 1982 are thorough but dated; X. Yang 2004 is a partial update. Zhou bronzes: Rawson 1990, J. So 1995. Zhou social organization: F. Li 2003; Chu, Cook and Major 1999. *Zuozhuan*: Pines

2002. Iron: Wagner 1993, 2001c, 2008. Warfare: Kiser and Cai 2003, 2004; M. Lewis 1990; Yates et al. 2009; Zhao 2004. Writing: M. Lewis 1999. Qin law: Hulsewé 1985. Monuments: Wu 1995. Qin and Han: M. Lewis 2007, Loewe 2006, Portal 2007. Hui 2005 is a fascinating comparison of Qin and early modern European state formation.

West—on iron: Wertime and Muhly 1980 has not yet been superseded. Huge controversy surrounds anything to do with early Israel; Provan et al. 2003 generally support the biblical account, while Finkelstein and Silberman 2001, 2006, and Liverani 2005 are more critical. Assyria is not well served by general studies, but see Yamada 2000 on the ninth century, Mattila 2000 on the aristocracy; Oded 1979 on deportations; and Bedford 2009, M. Larsen 1979, Liverani 1995, and Parpola 1997 on the empire. Urartu: Zimansky 1985. Phoenicians: Aubet 2001. Greece: Morris and Powell 2009. Mediterranean colonization: Hodos 2006, Dietler 2010. Monte Polizzo: Morris and Tusa 2004, Mühlenbock 2008. Persia: Bedford 2007, Briant 2002. Alexander: Bosworth 1988. Rome: Eich and Eich 2005, Eckstein 2007. Literacy: W. Harris 1989. Early writing generally: B. Powell 2009. Western empires compared: Morris and Scheidel 2009.

Legitimacy as the difference between mafias and states: Gambetta 1994.

Climate change: Bao et al. 2004, Garcia et al. 2007, Issar 2003, Issar and Zahor 2005, Kvavadze and Connor 2005, P. Zheng et al. 2008. Seasonal mortality: Shaw 1996, Scheidel 2001.

Rise and Fall of the Great Powers: P. Kennedy 1987.

Axial Age: Jaspers 1949 is the foundational study. B. Schwartz 1975 is the clearest introduction and Armstrong 2006 the most readable survey, but Bellah 2005 is the most perceptive comparative study. Some scholars, such as Hall and Ames (1995a, 1995b), emphasize long-term differences between Chinese and Western thought over similarities; others, such as B. Schwartz 1985 and Roetz 1993, see more unity. I find the second approach (particularly as developed by Puett 2002) much more convincing. Background to Confucius: Shaughnessy 1997, von Falkenhausen 2006. Legalists: Fu 1996. Connections between Chinese schools of thought: K. Holloway 2009. Early Greek philosophy: Graham 2006. Greek democracy and its critics: Ober 1998. There are several excellent comparisons of Greek and Chinese thought (for example, Lloyd 2002, Lloyd and Sivin 2002, T. Martin 2009, Shankman and Durant 2000, and Sim 2007). Akhenaten and Moses: Freud 1955, Assmann 2008.

Rome-China contacts: Leslie and Gardiner 1996, Mair 2006. Vagnari DNA: http://www.independent.co.uk/news/science/archaeology/news/ambassador-or-slave-east-asian-skeleton-discovered-in-vagnari-roman-cemetery-1879551.html, *The Independent*, January 26, 2010. Finds in Egypt: Cappers 1999. Finds at Arikamedu: Begley 1996. *Voyage on the Red Sea*: Casson 1989. Silk Roads: F. Wood 2002. Bactria: Holt 1999. Steppe highway: Beckwith 2009, Christian 1998, Kohl 2007, Koryakova and Epimakhov 2007. Parthia: Curtis and Stewart 2007. Nomads and China: Barfield 1989; Di Cosmo 2002; Lovell 2006, pp. 66–116.

6. DECLINE AND FALL

Overviews of the East: M. Lewis 2007, 2009a. West: Garnsey and Saller 1987 remains the best survey of the earlier Roman Empire, and Cameron 1993a, 1993b of the later empire. Since the 1960s many Roman historians have rejected "decline-and-fall" theories of late Roman history (see particularly Brown 1971, 1978), but more recently historians and archaeologists (for example, Goldsworthy 2009, Heather 2005, Jongman 2007b, McCormick 2001, Ward-Perkins 2005) have insisted—as I do here—on the fall in social development after 200 CE.

Han and Roman divine kingship: Puett 2002 and Price 1984. Roman triumphs: Beard 2007. Confucian moral cultivation: Ivanhoe 2000.

Adshead 2000, pp. 4–21, makes interesting comparisons between the Han and Roman empires. Mutschler and Mittag 2009 and Scheidel 2009a are the first systematic English-language studies.

Eastern economic growth: Bray 1984, Hsu 1980, Peng 1999, Wagner 2001c. Western growth: Bowman and Wilson 2009, de Callataÿ 2005, Manning and Morris 2005, Scheidel et al. 2007, Scheidel 2009, A. Wilson 2009, and the ongoing work of the Oxford Roman Economy Project (http://oxrep.classics.ox.ac.uk/index.php). Roman and Han economic growth compared: Scheidel 2009b. Greek and Roman standards of living: Morris 2004, Saller 2002. Han houses: Guo 2010. Comparison of Roman and Han housing: Razeto 2008.

Sources for Figures 6.2 and 6.6: A. Parker 1992, Kylander et al. 2005.

Monte Testaccio: http://ceipac.gh.ub.es/MOSTRA/u_expo.htm (consulted December 4, 2007). Western golden age: Scheidel 2007, Jongman 2007a.

Columbian Exchange: Crosby 1972. The best book on the history of disease remains McNeill 1976. Roman epidemics: Scheidel 2002, Sallares 2007. Athenian plague of 430 BCE: Papagrigorakis et al. 2006.

Climate change: see the works cited in Chapter 5, plus Bao et al. 2004, Garcia et al. 2007, Ge et al. 2003, and B. Yang et al. 2002.

Qiang: M. Wang 1999. Chinese frontiers: Lattimore 1940 remains a classic. Roman frontiers: Whittaker 1994.

China after the Han: De Crespigny 1984; A. Dien 1990, 2007; Eberhard 1965; M. Lewis 2009a; S. Pearce et al. 2001; L. Yang 1961. Stirrups: A. Dien 1986.

Roman animal bones: Jongman 2007b, Ikeguchi 2007. General Western economic decline: McCormick 2001, pp. 25–119; MacMullen 1988, pp. 1–57.

Sassanid Persia: Daryaee 2009. Rome and Persia: Dignas and Winter 2007. Rome's Gothic Wars: Kulikowski 2006. Fifth-century Gaul: Drinkwater and Elton 1992. Fall of the western Roman Empire: Goldsworthy 2009, Heather 2005, Kelly 2009, Ward-Perkins 2005. Post-Roman western Europe: Cameron 1993b, McCormick 2001, McKitterick 2001, Wickham 2005.

Third-century Chinese culture: Balazs 1964, pp. 173–254; Holcombe 1994. Chinese Buddhism: Gernet 1995, X. Liu 1988, Zürcher 2007. Coming of Christianity: Brown 1971, 1978, Lane Fox 1986. Johnson and Johnson 2007 treat Buddhism and Christianity (plus Islam) comparatively. Late Roman art: Elsner 1999, Trimble 2009. Monasticism: Bechert and Gombrich 1984, Dunn 2000. Conversion: MacMullen 1984, Morrison 1992. Figure 6.9 builds on the approach in Hopkins 1998. Imperial adaptations to Christianity: Brown 1992, Fowden 1993.

7. THE EASTERN AGE

Overviews of the East before the Sui dynasty: A. Dien, 1990, 2007; Eisenberg 2008; Gernet 1995; Graff 2002; M. Lewis 2009a; Pearce et al; 2001. Sui dynasty: Wright

1978, Xiong 2006. Tang dynasty: Adshead 2004, M. Lewis 2009b, Perry and Smith 1976, Rozman 1973, Wright and Twitchett 1973, Xiong 2000. "Five Dynasties" period: G. Wang 2007. Northern Song dynasty: Haeger 1975, Hymes and Schirokauer 1993, D. Kuhn 2009. On the whole period 900–1100: Mote 1999.

Essential methods: Bray 2001. Rice in Eastern history generally: Bray 1984, 1986.

Wu Zetian: Guisso 1978, D. Dien 2003, Barrett 2008.

DNA study of Yu Hong: Xie et al. 2007.

Chinese ships: Needham 1971; McGrail 2001, pp. 346–93.

Exams and civil service: Chaffee 1985, Kracke 1968, McMullen 1988.

Eastern expansion: Abramson 2007, Holcombe 2001, Piggott 1997, von Glahn 1987, von Verschuer 2006.

Epidemics in seventh-century China: Twitchett 1979.

Java Sea shipwrecks: Flecker 2002, V. Lieberman 2003.

Elvin 1973, Hartwell 1967 and 1982, and Shiba and Elvin 1970 make the case for rapid economic growth in eleventh-century China. Golas 1988, P. Smith 1994, and Smith and von Glahn 2003 question some parts of this position. Finances: von Glahn 1996, 2004. Coal and iron: Golas 1999; Wagner 2001a, 2008. Trade: P. Smith 1991; Textiles: Bray 1997; Chao 1977; Mokyr 1990, pp. 209–38. Eleventh-century Neo-Confucianism: Bol 1992, 2009; X. Ji 2005; D. Kuhn 2009; T. Lee 2004.

Western social and economic trends to 900: McCormick 2001; Wickham 2005, 2009.

Justinian: Maas 2005, O'Donnell 2008. Byzantine economy (particularly Egypt): Banaji 2001, Hickey 2007, Laiou and Morrison 2007, Sarris 2006. Robert Graves's 1938 novel *Count Belisarius* is still well worth reading. Plague: Keys 2000, Little 2007, S. Rosen 2007, Sarris 2002, Stathakopoulos 2004. Khusrau and Heraclius: Dignas and Winter 2007, Haldon 1997, Kaegi 2003, Whittow 1996.

General accounts of Arabic history: Hourani 2003, Lapidus 2002. Pre-Islamic Arabia: Hoyland 2001. Muhammad: M. Cook 1983, Mattson 2007, Peters 1994. Muslim conquests: Donner 1981, Kaegi 1992, Pourshariati 2008. The caliphate: Crone and Hinds 1986; H. Kennedy 2004a, 2004b, 2007; Madelung 1997; Walmsley 2007. Al-Ma'mun: Cooperson 2005.

Egypt: Walker 2002. Cairo trade documents: Goitein 1967–88. Ghosh 1992 gives a delightful personal account.

Ninth-century Turkish slave armies: M. Gordon 2001. Seljuks: D. Morgan 1988.

Islamic economies: A. Watson 1982.

Charlemagne: Barbero 2004, Hodges and Whitehouse 1983, Verhulst 2002. Sypeck 2006 is an entertaining comparative account. The eighth-century West generally: Hansen and Wickham 2000.

Expansion of Europe: Bartlett 1993, Jordan 2001, McKitterick 2001, R. Moore 2000. Henry IV and Gregory VII: Blumenthal 1988. Persecuting society: R. Moore 1987. Age of cathedrals: Duby 1981. Christian scholarship: Colish 1997. Vikings: Christiansen 2006. Normans in Italy: Matthew 1992, Loud 2000, and the vivid account in Norwich 1992. Italian city-states: D. Waley 1988. Crusades: Maalouf 1984, Tyerman 2006. Old World migrations generally: A. Lewis 1988.

Medieval Warm Period: Fagan 2008 is a readable account; Kerr et al. 2005 treat the causes. Temperatures: Oppo et al. 2009. China: Chu et al. 2002, J. Ji et al. 2005, Qian and Zhu 2002, D. Zhang 1994, P. Zheng et al. 2008.

8. GOING GLOBAL

Marco Polo: Haw 2006, Jackson 1998. Fall of Kaifeng: Lorge 2005, pp. 51–54. Jurchens: Tillman and West 1995. Huizong: Ebrey and Bickford 2006.

Mongols: Allsen 2004, Amitai-Rice and Morgan 2001, di Cosmo et al. 2009, Rossabi 1988. China under the Mongols: Langlois 1981, Smith and von Glahn 2003, and Brook 2010. Recent accounts of the Mongols tend to emphasize the positive results of their opening East-West communications over the negative results of their devastating large parts of Asia.

Movement across the Silk Roads and Indian Ocean: Abu-Lughod 1989; Chaudhuri 1985, 1990; Wood 2002. S. Gordon 2006 describes some individual travelers.

Joseph Needham et al.'s *Science and Civilisation in China*, which began appearing in 1954 and is still ongoing, is a massive (in fact, overwhelming) compendium of Chinese science and technology with explicit discussions of borrowing between West and East. Hobson 2004 describes the major transfers more briefly and perhaps overstates the Western debt to the East. Islamic technology: Hassan and Hill 1986. Guns and ships: Lorge 2005, McNeill 1982, Needham et al. 1986.

There is a massive bibliography on the Black Death in Europe. Benedictow 2004 discusses death rates, Herlihy 1997 considers consequences, and Ziegler 1969 and Hatcher 2008 provide readable narratives. Much less is available on the Muslim world (Dols 1976 is the classic account) or the East. McNeill 1976 remains the best comparative discussion.

Start of the Little Ice Age: Bond et al. 2001; X. Liu et al. 2007; Mangini et al. 2005, 2007; Qian and Zhu 2002; E. Zhang et al. 2004; P. Zheng et al. 2008. Fagan 2004b gives a general account; Jordan 1996 focuses on western Europe.

Crisis of the Christian church: Oakley 1979. Tuchmann 1978 vividly describes fourteenth-century Europe.

Tamerlane: Manz 1989.

Early Ottoman Empire: Barkey 1997, Finkel 2005, Imber 2004, Inalcik and Quataert 1994. Fall of Constantinople: Nicolle et al. 2007, Runciman 1990.

Growth of Southeast Asia: Christie 1998, V. Lieberman 2003.

Rise of the Ming: Dreyer 1982. Zheng He: Levathes 1994, Dreyer 2006. On ships, McGrail 2002, pp. 380–81, 390–92.

Fifteenth-century Mexico: Pollard 1993, M. Smith 2003.

Multiple renaissances: Goody 2010.

Gavin Menzies's arguments: Menzies 2002, 2008, and www.1421.tv and www.gavinmenzies.net. Historians' response: Finlay 2004. A lot of discussion can be found online (for example, http://en.wikipedia.org/wiki/1421_hypothesis and http://www.dightonrock.com/commentsandrebuttalsconcering142.htm).

Princess Taiping: http://www.chinesevoyage.com. On the shipwreck: http://www.chinapost.com.tw/taiwan/national/national-news/2009/04/27/205767/Princess-Taiping.htm.

Henry the Navigator: Russell 2000.

Hongwu: Farmer 1995. Yongle: Tsai 2001.

Neo-Confucian culture: Bol 1992, Hymes and Schirokauer 1993, Ivanhoe 2009, Mote 1999, T. Lee 2004.

Chinese gender relations and footbinding: Birge 2002, Ebrey 1993, Ko 2007. Photographs of bound feet: al-Akl 1932.

Portuguese voyages: Fernandez-Armesto 2006. There is much controversy over how much impact Portugal had on the Indian Ocean in the early sixteenth century; compare the accounts in Bethencourt and Curto 2007 and Subrahmanyam 2007.

9. THE WEST CATCHES UP

General background: Brook 1998 and 2010, Mote 1999, Rowe 2009, the early chapters of Spence 1990, and Struve 2004 for China; V. Lieberman 2003 for Southeast Asia; Cullen 2003 and Totman 1993 for Japan. Braudel 1972 and 1981–84 and Wiesner-Hanks 2006 give readable accounts of Europe. Barkey 2008 and Finkel 2006 review the Ottoman Empire. Historians of this period have produced some fine East-West comparative studies (for example, Brook 2008, Darwin 2008, A. G. Frank 1998, Goldstone 2009, V. Lieberman 1999, Maddison 2005, Pomeranz 2000, Robinson 2010, Wong 1997). Wills 2002 provides a delightful tour of the world in the year 1688.

Real wages: Allen 2001, 2003a; Angeles 2008; Broadberry and Gupta 2006; Pamuk 2007.

Population growth: Ho 1959, Le Roy Ladurie 1972.

European folktales: Darnton 1984, pp. 9–72.

Hideyoshi: Berry 1989; Swope 2005, 2009.

Wanli and Zhang Zhuzheng: R. Huang 1981.

Global war on piracy: Earle 2003, Lane 1998, K. So 1975.

Habsburgs: Ingrau 2000, Kamen 1999, Kann 1980, G. Parker 2001.

Protestant Reformation: Fasolt 2008, MacCullagh 2003. Elton 1963 remains the most readable short account.

Dutch Republic: Israel 1995, Tracy 2008, van Bavel and van Zanden 2004, van Zanden 2002.

Ecology: Allen 2003b, Marks 1998, John Richards 2003.

Seventeenth-century crisis: G. Parker 2009. Levellers: Hill 1984, Mendle 2001. Thirty Years' War: G. Parker 1997, P. Wilson 2009.

Ming/Qing transition: Struve 1993.

Closing the steppes: Perdue 2005, Stevens 1995. Ivan the Terrible: de Madriaga 2008.

Spanish America: Elliott 2006, Kamen 2003. Silver: D. Flynn 1996, Flynn et al. 2003, von Glahn 1996. Columbian Exchange: Crosby 1972. Ecological imperialism: Crosby 2004. Jamestown and early slavery: E. Morgan 1975 is outstanding. Atlantic slavery generally: Blackburn 1997; Inikori 2002, 2007; Mintz 1985.

Industrious revolution: de Vries 2008, Mazumdar 1998, Voth 2001. Consumption: Brewer and Porter 1993, Clunas 1991.

Clocks: Landes 1983.

Scientific revolution: Dear 2001 and Shapin 1994 and 1996 are excellent surveys. Kuhn 1962 remains a classic. Saliba 2007 argues for influences from Muslim science on Europe; Crosby 1997 and Huff 2003 emphasize European developments since the twelfth century. Coffee houses and science: Stewart 1992.

Enlightenment: D. Outram 2005 and Youlton 1992 are reliable, clear introductions; Gay 1966–69 is a classic.

Donglin Academy: Dardess 2002. Qing scholarship and science: Elman 2001, 2006, Sivin 1982.

Joseph Needham and Lu Gwei-djen: Winchester 2008.

Jesuits: Brockey 2007.

Kangxi: Spence 1974. Eighteenth-century Chinese society: Naquin and Rawski 1987. Chinese isolation: Johnston 1995. Qianlong: Elliott and Stearns 2009.

European military revolution: Black 2006, P. Kennedy 1987, McNeill 1982, G. Parker 1996, Rogers 1995. Ottoman warfare: Murphey 1999. Chinese warfare: Lorge 2005, Yates et al. 2009. Japan and guns: Perrin 1979.

Financial crises and fiscal revolutions: Bonney 1999, Goldstone 1991.

British and Dutch commerce and institutions: Brenner 2003, H. Cook 2008, de Vries and van der Woude 1997, Jardine 2008, Pincus 2009.

Anglo-French trade and war: Findlay and O'Rourke 2007, Simms 2008. Mercantilism: Tracy 1990, 1991.

Political economy: the classic texts are Adam Smith's *Wealth of Nations* (1776), Thomas Malthus's *Essay on the Principle of Population* (1st ed., 1798), and David Ricardo's *Principles of Political Economy and Taxation* (1817), all republished many times.

10. THE WESTERN AGE

Bayly 2004 and Darwin 2008 and 2009 are outstanding recent surveys on the global scale, but Eric Hobsbawm's four-volume treatment (1964, 1975, 1987, 1994) remains my favorite. Estimates of economic growth: Maddison 1995, 2001. Western military-fiscal trends: P. Kennedy 1987. China generally: Rowe 2009, Spence 1990. Japan: Cullen 2003, Jansen 2000. Southeast Asia: Owen et al. 2005.

Eighteenth-century science and industry: Jacob 1997; Jacob and Stewart 2004; Mokyr 2002, 2010; R. Porter 2003. Technology: Mokyr 1990, Smil 2005, 2006. Uglow 2002 is a highly readable account of Boulton, Watt, and the characters around them.

The Western industrial revolution remains controversial; compare Acemoglu et al. 2005, Landes 2003 [1969], Mokyr 1999, and Allen 2009. Floud and McCloskey 1994 is the best reference work. Gradualist views: Wrigley 2000, Bayly 2004.

Real wages: Allen 2001, 2007b, 2007c, Allen et al. 2007.

Prices of cotton: Harley 1998.

Resistance to industrialization: the classic accounts are Thompson 1963, 1993, and (on Captain Swing) Hobsbawm and Rudé 1969, although they should be read with the more recent works cited above.

Culture and advantages of backwardness: Weber 1905 is the classic theory; Landes 1998 and G. Clark 2007 offer more sophisticated versions. Acemoglu et al. 2002 stress the role of institutions.

On whether the East was close to an independent industrial revolution around 1800, see the very different arguments in Goldstone 2009, Maddison 2005, Pomeranz 2000, Sivin 1982, Tetlock et al. 2006, and Wong 1997. Inevitability of an Eastern catch-up: Sugihara 2003.

Costs of 1880 Chinese mine: Golas 1999, p. 170.

Nineteenth-century American expansion: Howe 2007, R. White 1993. Environmental impact: Williams 2003.

Oil: Yergin 1992. Free trade: Irwin 1996. Modernism and the speeded-up world: Kern 1983, Gay 2008.

Theories of late nineteenth-century imperialism vary wildly. Cain and Hopkins 2000, Darwin 2009, Davis 2001, Ferguson 2003, and A. Porter 2001 give a sense of the range. Hochschild 1998 is a horrifying account of the Congo. Famines of 1876–79 and 1896–1902: Davis 2001, Cane 2010.

Opium War: see the books listed for the introduction.

Opening of Japan: Feifer 2006 is a readable account. Japan's nineteenth-century transformation: Duus 1976, Jansen 2000. Meiji emperor: Keene 2002. Japanese imperialism: Beasley 1987. Sino-Japanese war: Paine 2003. Guangxu's death: http://www.cnn.com/2008/WORLD/asiapcf/11/04/china.emperor/index.html.

Boxer Rebellion: Preston 1999 is a readable account.

Grouping the conflicts of 1914–91 together: Ferguson 2007. Twentieth-century economy generally: Frieden 2006. World War I: Ferguson 1998, Stevenson 2004, Strachan 2005. Postwar settlement: MacMillan 2002. Great Depression: Eichengreen 1992, Shlaes 2007. Soviet response: Conquest 1986, Figes 1996, Fitzpatrick 1999, Applebaum 2003. Japan: Harries and Harries 1991, Iriye 1987. Nazi Germany: R. Evans 2005, Tooze 2006. World War II: Dower 1986, Ferguson 2007, Overy 1995, A. Roberts 2009, Weinberg 2005. Cold War: Behrman 2008, Eichengreen 2007, Gaddis 2005, Judt 2005, Reynolds 2000, Sheehan 2008, Westad 2005. Mutual Assured Destruction: Krepon 2008. Decolonization: Abernethy 2000, Brendon 2008, P. Clarke 2008, Darwin 2009. European Union: Gillingham 1991, 2003. Material abundance: de Grazia 2005, Fogel 2004, Grigg 1992, Sandbrook 2005. Rising life expectancy: Riley 2001. *Feminine Mystique*: Friedan 1963. *Sexual Politics*: Millett 1970. American suburbs: Hayden 2002. 1980s economic revival: Yergin and Stanislaw 2002.

The *Oxford History of the United States* series (D. Kennedy 1999, Patterson 1997, 2005) is a fine survey of twentieth-century American history. America's geographical advantages: Cumings 2009.

Computers and the Western core in the 1970s–80s: Castells 1996–98, Saxenian 1994, and the entertaining account of Wozniak and Smith 2007.

Postwar Japan: Dower 2000, D. Smith 1995. Maoist China: Becker 1996, P. Clark 2008, MacFarquhar and Schoenhals 2006, Short 1999. Post-Mao China: Gittings 1995, Greenhalgh 2008, Y. Huang 2008, Naughton 1995, Walder 2009, L. Zhang 2008. Nixon and China: Nixon 1967, MacMillan 2008.

Fall of the Soviet Union and post-Soviet Russia: Gaidar 2008, Goldman 2008. 1990s Japan: Amyx 2004, Hutchison and Westermann 2006. The 1992 Defense Planning Guidance and subsequent American policy: J. Mann 2004.

Costs of China's economic boom since the 1990s: Chen and Wu 2006, Chen 2009, Economy 2004, Goldman 2005, Shapiro 2001. Of the many books on China's growth into a trading superpower, Kynge 2006 and Fishman 2006 are among the best.

11. WHY THE WEST RULES . . .

Genetic superiority: some economists do indeed suggest that the European industrial revolution was a result of natural selection. Galor and Moav 2002 are most explicit; G. Clark 2007 comes close to suggesting it for England.

Scientific inventions: Merton 1957, Stigler 1980, and Malcolm Gladwell's highly readable "In the Air," *The New Yorker*, May 12, 2008, pp. 50–60 (available at http://www.newyorker.com/archive).

East-West psychological differences: Hedden et al. 2008. Eastern illogicality: compare Nisbett 2003, Ho and Yan 2007, and McGilchrist 2009. Lloyd 2007 is a balanced discussion of cognitive variation. I'd like to thank Professor Nisbett for discussing this issue with me.

Flynn Effect: Neisser 1998, J. Flynn 2007, and Malcolm Gladwell, "None of the Above: What IQ Doesn't Tell You About Race," *The New Yorker*, December 17, 2007 (available at http://www.newyorker.com/archive).

Confucianism and Japan's failings: J. Hall 1966. Confucianism and Japan's successes: Morishima 1982.

What-ifs: Tetlock et al. 2006, especially the chapters by Goldstone, Pestana, Pomeranz, and Mokyr. Principles of counterfactual analysis: Ferguson 1997, Tetlock and Belkin 1996. I explain my own approach more fully in Morris 2005.

Bungling: Tuchmann 1984 is a must-read.

Nightfall: for the Younger Dryas, see Chapter 2. Asteroids: Brown et al. 2002, Toon et al. 1997, Ward and Asphaug 2000. Disasters generally: Smil 2008. Warheads in 1980: Sakharov 1983.

Hitler winning World War II: Rosenfeld 2005. *Fatherland*: R. Harris 1992. Nuclear weapons: Gaddis et al. 1999. Cuba: Fursenko and Naftali 1997.

Foundation: Asimov published eight short stories in *Astounding Magazine* between May 1942 and January 1950, then collected them into three books published between 1951 and 1953. In the 1980s–90s he wrote two sequels and two prequels. His fullest comments on psychohistory are in *Foundation* (1951) and *Prelude to Foundation* (1988).

12. . . . FOR NOW

Chinese power in the twenty-first century: Jacques 2009, Halper 2010.

Chimerica: Ferguson and Schularick 2007, Ferguson 2009; "A Wary Respect: A Special Report on China and America," *The Economist*, October 24, 2009 (available at http://www.economist.com/specialreports).

America remaking itself: Jack Welch, "Who Will Rule the 21st Century?" *Business Week*, July 2, 2007 (http://www.kurzweilai.net/meme/frame.html?main=memelist .html?m=7%23713).

China's problems: Goldman 2005, Shirk 2007.

Rising tide lifting all boats: Fogel 2007; Maddison 2006, 2007.

Soothing Scenario: J. Mann 2007. China and democracy: Y. Zheng 2004, 2010.

Easternization of the West: Kurlantzick 2007.

International relations realists: Johnston 1995.

Energy: Smil 2006.

Singularity: Kurzweil 2005, with http://www.singularity.com, http://www.kurzweil AI.net, and http://www.singularitysummit.com. Criticisms: Lanier 2000, Richards et al. 2002, McKibben 2003. Moore's Law: G. Moore 1965, 1999, 2003. Brain mapping: http://www.loni.ucla/ICBM/ and http://www.brainmapping.org, constantly updated.

Tiger Woods and Oscar Pistorius: http://www.slate.com/id/2116858/; http://www .slate.com/id/2191801/.

Eugenics debates: writings on augmented bodies and brains tend to be either very upbeat (for example, Naam 2005, R. Green 2007) or very worried about the preservation of identity (for example, Fukuyama 2002, S. Rose 2006). Rifkin 1998, though now a little dated, is more balanced.

Brain Interface Project: http://www.wired.com/dangerroom/2009/05/pentagon-preps-soldier-telepathy-push); Singer 2009, pp. 72–74. Molecular computing: Benenson et al. 2004.

IBM Blue Gene computers: http://www.research.ibm.com/journal/rd49-23.html. Mouse and rat simulations: Frye et al. 2007, Ananthanarayanan and Modha 2007; http://p9.hostingprod.com/@modha.org/blog/2007/11/faq_anatomy_of_a _cortical_simu.html. Energy and cooling requirements: *The Economist Technology Quarterly*, December 6, 2008, pp. 6–8 (available at http://www.economist.com/ specialreports). Project Kittyhawk: Appavoo et al. 2008.

Synthetic life: Gibson et al. 2010 (http://www.sciencemag.org/cgi/content/abstract/ science.1190719).

Carlson's Curve: Robert Carlson, "Open Source Biology and its Impact on Industry," *IEEE Spectrum*, May 2001 (available at http://synthesis.cc/Biol_Tech_2050.pdf); Carlson 2010.

Freeman-Spogli Institute's "World at Risk" conference: http://fsi.stanford.edu/ events/2006_fsi_international_conference_a_world_at_risk/.

Worst-case scenarios generally: Diamond 2005, Smil 2008, Sunstein 2007.

Climate change: Intergovernmental Panel on Climate Change 2007, Smil 2008. Estimates of polar melting: http://news.bbc.co.uk/2/hi/science/nature/7139797 .stm. Global weirding: T. Friedman 2008. Abrupt change: Pearce 2008. *Stern Review*: Stern 2006.

Climate and food: Easterling 2007, Battisti and Naylor 2009, Lobell and Burke 2010. Food: http://www.fao.org/worldfoodsituation/en/, http://www.fao.org/docrep/ 011/ai474e/ai474e13.htm, and http://en.wikipedia.org/wiki/Food_crisis. Regional impacts: Bättig et al. 2007. Water: Pearce 2007.

There is a huge literature on migration into the United States and western Europe, much of it highly partisan. Swain 2007, *The Economist*'s survey of migration ("Open Up: A Special Report on Immigration," *The Economist*, January 5, 2008; available at http://www.economist.com/specialreports), Caldwell 2009, and R. Hsu 2010 make efforts to cover all sides of the questions. Post-2008 trends: Papademetriou and Terrazas 2009.

Migration and disease: http://www.cdc.gov/ncidod/dq/. Influenza: Barry 2005, MacKellar 2007, Davis 2006, http://www.flutrackers.com/forum/index.php and http://www.who.int/en/.

Great-power involvement in the arc of instability: G. Friedman 2004, Oren 2007. China and resources: Zweig and Bi 2005. Peaceful rising: B. Zheng 2005. Terrorist risks: Graham and Talent 2008. Israel and Iran: "The Gathering Storm," *The Economist*, January 7, 2010 (available at http://www.economist.com). Conflict in the twenty-first century: G. Friedman 2009, Fukuyama 2008, Khanna 2008, Krepinevich 2009, Zakaria 2008. Chinese and American military strengths: R. Kaplan 2005. Chinese missile test: http://news.xinhuanet.com/english/2010-01/11/content_12792329 .htm. Chinese aircraft carrier: http://www.cbsnews.com/stories/2009/04/22/world/ main4960774.shtml?source=RSSattr=HOME_4960774.

Nuclear arms reduction: George Schultz et al., "A World Free of Nuclear Weapons," *Wall Street Journal*, January 4, 2007, p. A15 (available at http://www.fcnl.org/issues/item.php?item_id=2252&issue_id=54; "Toward a Nuclear-Free World," *Wall Street Journal*, January 15, 2008 (available at http://online.wsj.com/public/article_print/SB120036422673589947.html); Perkovich and Zaum 2008; Sagan and Miller 2009–2010. Decline of arsenals: Norris and Kristensen 2008, 2009a, b, 2010. Doomsday Clock: http://www.thebulletin.org/content/media-center/announcements/2010/01/14/it-6-minutes-to-midnight.

Reducing consumption: McKibben 2010, Wells 2010.

Kyoto Protocol: text at http://unfccc.int/kyoto-protocol/items/2830.php. Data on emissions since 1990: http://unfccc.int/files/inc/graphics/image/gif/total_excluding_2008.gif; http://co2now.org/. Estimate of costs: Juliette Jowit and Patrick Wintour. "Cost of Tackling Global Climate Change Has Doubled, Warns Stern," *The Guardian*, June 26, 2008 (http://www.guardian.co.uk/environment/2008/jun/26/climatechange.scienceofclimatechange). Some economists (for example, Nordhaus 2007) are critical, but an Australian report (Garnaut 2008) has reached similar conclusions to Stern.

Nonstate organizations: T. Friedman 1999, van Creveld 1999.

Energy issues: Smil 2006.

Fermi Paradox: E. Jones 1985, Webb 2002. Search for extraterrestrials: Impey 2007, P. Davies 2010.

Million civilizations: Shklovskii and Sagan 1968, p. 448. Drake's Equation: http://en.wikipedia.org/wiki/Drake_equation.

High-tech weapons: Adams 2008, Singer 2009.

Extinctions: Thomas et al. 2004. Sixth great extinction: Leakey and Lewin 1995.

Bibliography

Abernethy, David. *The Dynamics of Global Dominance: European Overseas Empires, 1415–1980*. New Haven, CT: Yale University Press, 2000.

Abramson, Marc. *Ethnic Identity in Tang China*. Philadelphia: University of Pennsylvania Press, 2007.

Abu-Lughod, Janet. *Before European Hegemony. The World System AD 1250–1350*. New York: Oxford University Press, 1989.

Acemoglu, Daron, Simon Johnson, and James Robinson. "Reversal of Fortune: Geography and Institutions in the Making of the Modern World Income Distribution." *Quarterly Journal of Economics* 118 (2002), pp. 1231–94.

———. "The Rise of Europe: Atlantic Trade, Institutional Change, and Economic Growth." *American Economic Review* 95 (2005), pp. 546–79.

Adams, Thomas. "Future Warfare and the Decline of Human Decisionmaking." *Parameters: Journal of the US Army War College* 31.4 (2001), p. 57 (15).

———. *The Army After Next: The First Postindustrial Army*. Stanford: Stanford University Press, 2008.

Adshead, Samuel. *China in World History*. 3rd ed. London: Longmans, 2000.

———. *Tang China*. London: Longmans, 2004.

Akkermans, Peter, and Glenn Schwartz. *The Archaeology of Syria*. Cambridge, UK: Cambridge University Press, 2003.

al-Akl, F. M. "Bound Feet in China." *American Journal of Surgery* 18 (1932), pp. 545–50.

Allen, Robert. "The Great Divergence in European Wages and Prices from the Middle Ages to the First World War." *Explorations in Economic History* 38 (2001), pp. 411–48.

———. "Poverty and Progress in Early Modern Europe." *Economic History Review* 56 (2003a), pp. 403–43.

————. "Was There a Timber Crisis in Early Modern Europe?" In *Economia e energia secc. xiii–xviii, Serie II–Atti delle "Settimane di Studi" e altri Convegni*, pp. 469–82. Prato: 34 Istituto Internazionale di Storia Economica "F. Datini," 2003b.

————. "The British Industrial Revolution in Global Perspective: How Commerce Created the Industrial Revolution and Modern Economic Growth," 2006a. http://www.nuffield.ox.ac.uk/General/Members/allen.aspx.

————. "Agricultural Productivity and Rural Incomes in England and the Yangtze Delta, c. 1620–c. 1820," 2006b. http://www.nuffield.ox.ac.uk/General/Members/allen.aspx.

————. "How Prosperous Were the Romans? The Evidence of Diocletian's Price Edict (301 AD)." Oxford University Department of Economics Working Papers 363, 2007a. http://www.nuffield.ox.ac.uk/General/Members/allen.aspx.

————. "Pessimism Preserved: Real Wages in the British Industrial Revolution." Oxford University Department of Economics Working Papers 314, 2007b. http://www.nuffield.ox.ac.uk/General/Members/allen.aspx.

————. "Engels' Pause: A Pessimist's Guide to the British Industrial Revolution." Oxford University Department of Economics Working Papers 315, 2007c. http://www.nuffield.ox.ac.uk/General/Members/allen.aspx.

————. *The British Industrial Revolution in Global Perspective*. Cambridge, UK: Cambridge University Press, 2009.

Allen, Robert, et al. "Wages, Prices, and Living Standards in China, Japan, and Europe, 1738–1925," 2007. http://www.nuffield.ox.ac.uk/General/Members/allen.aspx.

Allen, Robert, Tommy Bengtsson, and Martin Dribe, eds. *Living Standards in the Past: New Perspectives on Well-Being in Asia and Europe*. Oxford: Oxford University Press, 2005.

Allsen, Thomas. *Culture and Conquest in Mongol Eurasia*. Cambridge, UK: Cambridge University Press, 2004.

Amitai-Rice, Reuven, and David Morgan. *The Mongol Empire and its Legacy*. Leiden: E. J. Brill, 2001.

Amyx, Jennifer. *Japan's Financial Crisis*. Princeton: Princeton University Press, 2004.

Ananthanarayanan, Rajagopal, and Dharmendra Modha. "Anatomy of a Cortical Simulator." Paper given at the International Conference for High Performance Computing, Networking, Storage, and Analysis, Reno, NV (November 11, 2007). Available at http://sc07.supercomp.org/schedule/event_detail.php?evid=11063.

Angeles, Luis. "GDP Per Capita or Real Wages? Making Sense of Conflicting Views on Pre-Industrial Europe." *Explorations in Economic History* 45 (2008), pp. 147–63.

Appavoo, Jonathan, Volkmar Uhlig, and Amos Waterland. "Project Kittyhawk: Building a Global-Scale Computer. Blue Gene/P as a Generic Computing Platform." *ACM Sigops Operating System Review*, January 2008. Available at http://domino.research.ibm.com/comm/research_projects.nsf/pages/kittyhawk.index.html.

Applebaum, Anne. *Gulag: A History of the Soviet Camps*. New York: Penguin, 2003.

Armelagos, George, and Kristin Harper. "Genomics at the Origins of Agriculture." *Evolutionary Anthropology* 14 (2005), pp. 68–77, 109–21.

Armstrong, Karen. *The Great Transformation: The Beginning of Our Religious Traditions*. New York: Knopf, 2006.

Arrighi, Giovanni. *Adam Smith in Beijing: Lineages of the Twenty-First Century*. London: Verso, 2007.

Asimov, Isaac. "Nightfall." *Astounding Science Fiction*, September 1941 issue. Cited from Isaac Asimov, *The Complete Short Stories* I, New York: Bantam, 1990, pp. 330–62.

———. *Foundation*. New York: Bantam, 1951.

———. *Prelude to Foundation*. New York: Bantam, 1988.

Assmann, Jan. *Of God and Gods: Egypt, Israel, and the Rise of Monotheism*. Madison: University of Wisconsin Press, 2008.

Astour, Michael. "New Evidence on the Last Days of Ugarit." *American Journal of Archaeology* 69 (1965), pp. 253–58.

Aubet, Maria Eugenia. *The Phoenicians in the West*. 2nd ed. Cambridge, UK: Cambridge University Press, 2001.

Auel, Jean. *The Clan of the Cave Bear*. New York: Crown, 1980.

Bagnall, Roger. *Egypt in Late Antiquity*. Berkeley: University of California Press, 1993.

Bahn, Paul, and Jean Vertut. *Journey Through the Ice Age*. Berkeley: University of California Press, 1997.

Baker, Keith, ed. *The Old Regime and the French Revolution*. Chicago: University of Chicago Press, 1987.

Balazs, Etienne. *Chinese Civilization and Bureaucracy*. New Haven, CT: Yale University Press, 1964.

Banaji, Jairus. *Agrarian Change in Late Antiquity: Gold, Labour, and Aristocratic Dominance*. Oxford: Oxford University Press, 2001.

Bao, Yang, et al. "Evidence for a Late Holocene Warm and Humid Climate Period and Environmental Characteristics in the Arid Zones of Northwest China During 2.2 ~ 1.8 kyr BP." *Journal of Geophysical Research* 109 (2004), 10.1029/2003JD003787.

Barber, Elizabeth. *The Mummies of Ürümchi*. New York: Norton, 1999.

Barbero, Alessandro. *Charlemagne: Father of a Continent*. Berkeley: University of California Press, 2004.

Barfield, Thomas. *The Perilous Frontier: Nomadic Empires and China, 221 BC–AD 1757*. Oxford: Blackwell, 1989.

Barker, Graeme. *The Agricultural Revolution in Prehistory: Why Did Foragers Become Farmers?* Oxford: Oxford University Press, 2006.

Barkey, Karen. *Bandits and Bureaucrats: The Ottoman Route to State Centralization*. Ithaca, NY: Cornell University Press, 1997.

———. *Empire of Difference: The Ottomans in Comparative Perspective*. Cambridge, UK: Cambridge University Press, 2008.

Barnes, Gina. *The Rise of Civilization in East Asia*. London: Thames and Hudson, 1999.

Barrett, T. H. *The Woman Who Discovered Printing*. New Haven, CT: Yale University Press, 2008.

Barry, John. *The Great Influenza*. New York, Penguin, 2005.

Bartlett, Robert. *The Making of Europe: Conquest, Colonization and Cultural Change 950–1350*. Princeton: Princeton University Press, 1993.

Bar-Yosef, Ofer, ed. *East to West—Agricultural Origins and Dispersal into Europe*. Special section of *Current Anthropology* volume 45, 2004.

Bättig, Michèle, et al. "A Climate Change Index: Where Climate Change May Be Most Prominent in the 21st Century." *Geophysical Research Letters* 34 (2007), 201705.

Battisti, David, and Rosamund Naylor. "Historical Warnings of Future Food Insecurity with Unprecedented Seasonal Heat." *Science* 32 (2009), pp. 240–44.

Baumgarten, Jürgen, ed. *The Early Neolithic Origin of Ritual Centers*. Special issue of *Neo-Lithics* 2/05, 2005.

Bayly, Christopher. *The Birth of the Modern World 1780–1914*. Oxford: Blackwell, 2004.

Beard, Mary. *The Roman Triumph*. Cambridge, MA: Harvard University Press, 2007.

Beasley, William. *Japanese Imperialism, 1894–1945*. Oxford: Oxford University Press, 1987.

Bechert, Heinz, and Richard Gombrich, eds. *The World of Buddhism: Buddhist Monks and Nuns in Society and Culture*. New York: Facts on File, 1984.

Becker, Jasper. *Hungry Ghosts: Mao's Secret Famine*. New York: Owl Books, 1996.

Beckman, Gary. *Hittite Diplomatic Texts*. 2nd ed. Atlanta: Scholars Press, 1999.

Beckwith, Christopher. *Empires of the Silk Road: A History of Central Eurasia from the Bronze Age to the Present*. Princeton: Princeton University Press, 2009.

Bedford, Peter. "The Persian Near East." In Walter Scheidel et al., eds., *The Cambridge Economic History of the Greco-Roman World*, pp. 302–29. Cambridge, UK: Cambridge University Press, 2007.

———. "The Neo-Assyrian Empire." In Ian Morris and Walter Scheidel, eds., *The Dynamics of Ancient Empires*, pp. 30–65. New York: Oxford University Press, 2009.

Begley, Vimala. *The Ancient Ports of Arikamedu*. Pondicherry/Arikamedu: École française de l'extrême orient, 1996.

Behrman, Greg. *The Most Noble Adventure: The Marshall Plan and How America Helped Rebuild Europe*. New York: Free Press, 2008.

Bellah, Robert. "What Is Axial About the Axial Age?" *Archives européenes de sociologie* 46 (2005), pp. 69–87.

Bellwood, Peter. *First Farmers: The Origins of Agricultural Societies*. Oxford: Blackwell, 2005.

Bellwood, Peter, and Colin Renfrew, eds. *Examining the Farming/Language Dispersal Hypothesis*. Cambridge, UK: Cambridge University Press, 2003.

Benedictow, Ole. *The Black Death 1346–1353: The Complete History*. Rochester, NY: Boydell Press, 2004.

Benenson, Yaakov, et al. "An Autonomous Molecular Computer for Logical Control of Gene Expression." *Nature* 429 (2004), pp. 423–29.

Bengtsson, Tommy, C. Campbell, and James Lee, eds. *Life Under Pressure: Mortality and Living Standards in Europe and Asia, 1700–1900*. Cambridge, MA: Harvard University Press, 2005.

Bentley, Edmund. *Biography for Beginners*. London: T. W. Laurie, 1905.

Berger, Thomas, and Erik Trinkaus. "Patterns of Trauma Among the Neandertals." *Journal of Archaeological Science* 22 (1995), pp. 841–52.

Bernard, W. D., and W. H. Hall. *Narrative of the Voyages and Services of the Nemesis, 1840 to 1843*, vol. 1. London: H. Colburn, 1844.

Berry, Mary. *Hideyoshi*. Cambridge, MA: Harvard University Press, 1989.

Bethencourt, Francisco, and Diogo Ramada Curto, eds. *Portuguese Oceanic Expansion, 1400–1800*. Cambridge, UK: Cambridge University Press, 2007.

Bierce, Ambrose. *The Devil's Dictionary*. New York: Neale Publishing, 1911. Reissued by Dover, 1993.

Birch, Cyril, ed. *Anthology of Chinese Literature* I: *From Early Times to the Fourteenth Century*. New York: Columbia University Press, 1965.

Birge, Bettina. *Women, Property, and Confucian Reaction in Sung and Yüan China*. Cambridge, UK: Cambridge University Press, 2002.

Black, Jeremy. *Warfare in the Eighteenth Century*. London: Cassell, 2006.

Blackburn, Robin. *The Making of New World Slavery, from the Baroque to the Modern, 1492–1800*. London: Verso, 1997.

Bloodworth, Dennis, and Ching Ping Bloodworth. *The Chinese Machiavelli: 3000 Years of Chinese Statecraft*. 2nd ed. New Brunswick, NJ: Transaction Books, 2004.

Blumenthal, Uta-Renate. *The Investiture Conflict: Church and Monarchy from the Ninth to the Twelfth Century*. Philadelphia: University of Pennsylvania Press, 1988.

Boaretto, Elisabetta, et al. "Radiocarbon Dating of Charcoal and Bone Collagen Associated with Early Pottery at Yuchanyan Cave, Hunan Province, China." *Proceedings of the National Academy of Sciences* 106 (2009), doi: 10.1073/pnas.0900539106.

Boaz, Noel, and Russell Ciochon. *Dragon Bone Hill: An Ice-Age Saga of* Homo erectus. New York: Oxford University Press, 2004.

Bocquet-Appel, Jean-Pierre, and Ofer Bar-Yosef, eds. *The Neolithic Demographic Transition and its Consequences*. Amsterdam: Springer, 2008.

Bol, Peter. *"This Culture of Ours": Intellectual Transitions in T'ang and Sung China*. Stanford: Stanford University Press, 1992.

———. *Neo-Confucianism in History*. Cambridge, MA: Harvard University Press, 2009.

Bond, Gerard, et al. "Persistent Solar Influence on North Atlantic Climate during the Holocene." *Science* 294 (2001), pp. 2130–36.

Bonney, Richard. *The Rise of the Fiscal State in Europe, c. 1200–1815*. Oxford: Oxford University Press, 1999.

Boserup, Esther. *Conditions of Agricultural Growth*. Chicago: Aldine, 1965.

Bosworth, Alan. *Conquest and Empire: The Reign of Alexander the Great*. Cambridge, UK: Cambridge University Press, 1988.

Boulding, Kenneth. "Great Laws of Change." In Anthony Tang, Fred Westfield, and James Worley, eds., *Evolution, Welfare, and Time in Economics*. Lexington, MA: Lexington Books, 1976.

Boutron, C., et al. "Anthropogenic Lead in Polar Snow and Ice Archives." *Comptes Rendus Geoscience* 336 (2004), pp. 847–67.

Bouzouggar, Abdeljalil, et al. "82,000-Year-Old Shell Beads from North Africa." *Proceedings of the National Academy of Sciences* 104 (2007), pp. 9964–69.

Bowman, Alan, and Andrew Wilson, eds. *Quantifying the Roman Economy: Methods and Problems*. Oxford: Oxford University Press, 2009.

Boyer, Pascal. *Religion Explained*. New York: Basic Books, 1999.

Boyle, John, trans. *The Successors of Genghis Khan*. New York: Columbia University Press, 1971.

Bradley, Raymond. *Paleoclimatology*. New York: Academic Press, 1999.

Brandi, Karl. *The Emperor Charles V*. Trans. C. V. Wedgwood. New York: Knopf, 1939.

Braudel, Fernand. *The Mediterranean and the Mediterranean World in the Age of Philip II*. 2 vols. Trans. Siân Reynolds. London: Fontana, 1972.

———. *Civilization and Capitalism, 15th–18th Century*. 3 vols. Trans. Siân Reynolds. New York: Harper and Row, 1981–84.

Bray, Francesca. *Science and Civilisation in China* VI: *Biology and Biological Technology. Part 2: Agriculture*. Cambridge, UK: Cambridge University Press, 1984.

―――. *The Rice Economies: Technology and Development in Asian Societies*. Oxford: Oxford University Press, 1986.

―――. *Technology and Gender: Fabrics of Power in Late Imperial China*. Berkeley: University of California Press, 1997.

―――. "The *Qimin yaoshu* (Essential Techniques for the Common People)." Unpublished paper, 2001.

Brendon, Piers. *The Decline and Fall of the British Empire*. New York: Vintage, 2008.

Brenner, Robert. *Merchants and Revolution: Commercial Change, Political Conflict, and London's Overseas Traders, 1550–1653*. London: Verso, 2003.

Brewer, John, and Roy Porter, eds. *Consumption and the World of Goods*. London: Routledge, 1993.

Briant, Pierre. *From Cyrus to Alexander: A History of the Persian Empire*. Winona Lake, IN: Eisenbrauns, 2002.

Briggs, Asa. *A Social History of England*. London: Penguin, 1994.

Broadberry, Stephen, and Bishnupriya Gupta. "The Early Modern Great Divergence: Wages, Prices and Development in Europe and Asia, 1500–1800." *Economic History Review* 59 (2006), pp. 2–31.

Brockey, Liam. *Journey to the East: The Jesuit Mission to China, 1579–1724*. Cambridge, MA: Harvard University Press, 2007.

Brook, Timothy. *The Confusions of Pleasure: Commerce and Culture in Ming China*. Berkeley: University of California Press, 1998.

―――. *Vermeer's Hat: The Seventeenth Century and the Dawn of the Global World*. New York: Vintage, 2008.

―――. *The Troubled Empire: China in the Yuan and Ming Dynasties*. Cambridge, MA: Harvard University Press, 2010.

Brown, P., et al. "The Flux of Small Near-Earth Objects Colliding with the Earth." *Nature* 420 (2002), pp. 294–96.

Brown, Peter. *The World of Late Antiquity*. London: Thames and Hudson, 1971.

―――. *The Making of Late Antiquity*. Berkeley: University of California Press, 1978.

―――. *Power and Persuasion in Late Antiquity*. Madison: University of Wisconsin Press, 1992.

Browne, Edward. *The Literary History of Persia*. 2 vols. London: Unwin, 1902.

Brumm, Adam, et al. "Hominins on Flores, Indonesia, by One Million Years Ago." *Nature* 464 (2010), pp. 748–52.

Bryce, Trevor. *The Kingdom of the Hittites*. Oxford: Oxford University Press, 1998.

―――. *Life and Society in the Hittite World*. Oxford: Oxford University Press, 2002.

Burckhardt, Jacob. *The Civilization of the Renaissance in Italy*. New York: 1958. 2 vols. First published in German, 1852.

Cain, P. J., and A. G. Hopkins. *British Imperialism, 1688–2000*. New York: Longmans, 2002.

Caldwell, Christopher. *Reflections on the Revolution in Europe: Immigration, Islam, and the West*. New York: Doubleday, 2009.

Cameron, Averil. *The Later Roman Empire*. London: Routledge, 1993a.

―――. *The Mediterranean World in Late Antiquity, AD 395–600*. London: Routledge, 1993b.

Cane, Mark. 2010. "Climate in the Currents of History." In Robinson, ed., 2010.

Cann, Rebecca, et al. "Mitochondrial DNA and Human Evolution." *Nature* 325 (1987), pp. 31–36.

Cappers, René. "Archaeobotanical Evidence of Roman Trade with India." In Himanshu Prabha Ray, ed., *Archaeology of Seafaring*, pp. 51–69. New Delhi: Pragati Publications, 1999.

Cappers, René, and Sytze Bottema, eds. *The Dawn of Farming in the Near East*. Leiden: Brill, 2002.

Caramelli, D., et al. "Evidence for a Genetic Discontinuity between Neandertals and 24,000-Year-Old Anatomically Modern Humans." *Proceedings of the National Academy of Sciences* 100 (2003), pp. 6593–97.

Carlson, Robert. *Biology Is Technology: The Promise, Peril, and Business of Engineering Life*. Cambridge, MA: Harvard University Press, 2010.

Carneiro, Robert. "Scale Analysis as an Instrument for the Study of Cultural Evolution." *Southwestern Journal of Anthropology* 18 (1962), pp. 149–69.

———. "Ascertaining, Testing, and Interpreting Sequences of Cultural Development." *Southwestern Journal of Anthropology* 24 (1968), pp. 354–74.

———. "Scale Analysis, Evolutionary Sequences, and the Rating of Cultures." In Raoul Naroll et al., eds., *A Handbook of Method in Cultural Anthropology*, pp. 834–71. New York: Natural History Press, 1970.

———. *Evolutionism in Cultural Anthropology*. Boulder, CO: Westview Press, 2003.

Carr, Geoffrey. "Shocking Science." In *The World in 2009*, p. 26. London: *The Economist* special publication, 2008.

Carrington-Goodrich, L., ed. *Dictionary of Ming Biography* I. New York: Columbia University Press, 1976.

Casson, Lionel. *The Periplus Maris Erythraei*. Princeton: Princeton University Press, 1989.

Castells, Manuel. *The Information Age: Economy, Society, and Culture*. 3 vols. Oxford: Blackwell, 1996–98.

Castree, N., A. Rogers, and D. Sherman, eds. *Questioning Geography: Fundamental Debates*. Oxford: Blackwell, 2005.

Cavalli-Sforza, Luigi, Paolo Menozzi, and Alberto Piazza. *History and Geography of Human Genes*. Princeton: Princeton University Press, 1994.

Chadwick, John. *Linear B and Related Scripts*. London: British Museum, 1987.

Chaffee, John. *The Thorny Gates of Learning in Sung China: A Social History of Examinations*. 2nd ed. Albany: State University of New York Press, 1995.

Chang, Kwang-chih. *Art, Myth, and Ritual*. Cambridge, MA: Harvard University Press, 1983.

———. *The Archaeology of Ancient China*. 4th ed. New Haven, CT: Yale University Press, 1986.

———. "An Essay on *Cong*." *Orientations* 20 (1989), pp. 37–43.

———. "Shang Shamans." In Willard Peterson et al., *The Power of Culture*, pp. 10–36. Hong Kong: Chinese University Press, 1994.

Chang, Kwang-chih, and Xu Pingfang, eds. *The Formation of Chinese Civilization*. New Haven, CT: Yale University Press, 2005.

Chao, Kang. 1977. *The Development of Cotton Textile Production in China*. Cambridge, MA: Harvard University Press, 1977.

Chaudhuri, K. N. *Trade and Civilisation in the Indian Ocean*. Cambridge, UK: Cambridge University Press, 1985.

———. *Asia Before Europe*. Cambridge, UK: Cambridge University Press, 1990.

Chen, Gang. *Politics of China's Environmental Protection: Problems and Progress.* Beijing: World Scientific Publishing Company, 2009.

Chen, Guidi, and Wu Chuntao. *Will the Boat Sink the Water? The Life of China's Peasants.* New York: PublicAffairs, 2006.

Chiasson, Paul. *The Island of Seven Cities: Where the Chinese Settled When They Discovered America.* New York: St. Martin's Press, 2006.

Childe, V. Gordon. *What Happened in History.* London: Penguin, 1942.

Christian, David. *A History of Russia, Central Asia, and Mongolia* I: *Inner Eurasia from Prehistory to the Mongol Empire.* Oxford: Blackwell, 1998.

———. *Maps of Time: An Introduction to Big History.* Berkeley: University of California Press, 2004.

Christiansen, Eric. *Norsemen in the Viking Age.* Oxford: Blackwell, 2006.

Christie, Jan. "Javanese Markets and the Asian Sea Trade Boom of the 10th to 13th Centuries AD." *Journal of Economic and Social History of the Orient* 41 (1998), pp. 344–81.

Chu, Guoqing, et al. "The 'Medieval Warm Period' Drought Recorded in Lake Huguagyan, Tropical South China." *The Holocene* 15 (2002), pp. 511–16.

Clark, Christopher. *Iron Kingdom: The Rise and Downfall of Prussia, 1600–1947.* Cambridge, MA: Harvard University Press, 2006.

Clark, Gregory. *A Farewell to Alms: A Brief Economic History of the World.* Princeton: Princeton University Press, 2007.

Clark, Paul. *The Chinese Cultural Revolution.* Cambridge, UK: Cambridge University Press, 2008.

Clarke, Arthur C. *2001: A Space Odyssey.* New York: New American Library, 1968.

Clarke, Peter. *The Last Thousand Days of the British Empire: The Demise of a Superpower, 1944–47.* New York: Allen Lane, 2008.

Clunas, Craig. *Superfluous Things: Material Culture and Social Status in Early Modern China.* Cambridge, UK: Cambridge University Press, 1991.

Cochran, Gregory, and Henry Harpending. *The 10,000 Year Explosion: How Civilization Accelerated Human Evolution.* New York: Basic Books, 2009.

Cohen, Mark Nathan, ed. *Rethinking the Origins of Agriculture.* Special section of *Current Anthropology* volume 50, 2009.

Colish, Marcia. *Medieval Foundations of the Western Intellectual Tradition, 400–1400.* New Haven, CT: Yale University Press, 1997.

Conquest, Robert. *Harvest of Sorrow: Soviet Collectivization and the Terror-Famine.* New York: Oxford University Press, 1986.

Conrad, Nicholas. "A New Figurine from the Basal Aurignacian of Hohle Fels Cave in Southwestern Germany." *Nature* 459 (2009), pp. 248–52 (doi: 10.1038/nature07995).

Conway Morris, Simon. *Life's Solution: Inevitable Humans in a Lonely Universe.* Cambridge, UK: Cambridge University Press, 2003.

Cook, Constance, and John Major, eds. *Defining Chu: Image and Reality in Ancient China.* Honolulu: University of Hawaii Press, 1999.

Cook, Earl. "The Flow of Energy in an Industrial Society." *Scientific American* 225 (1971), pp. 135–44.

Cook, Harold. *Matters of Exchange: Commerce, Medicine, and Science in the Dutch Golden Age.* New Haven, CT: Yale University Press, 2007.

Cook, Michael. *Muhammad.* Oxford: Oxford University Press, 1983.

Cooper, Lisa. *Early Urbanism on the Syrian Euphrates*. London: Routledge, 2006.

Cooperson, Michael. *Al Ma'mun*. Oxford: Oneworld, 2005.

Cortesão, Armando. *The Suma Oriental of Tomé Pires*. 2 vols. London: Hakluyt Society, 1944.

Coyne, Jerry. *Why Evolution Is True*. New York: Viking, 2009.

Crafts, Nicholas. *British Economic Growth During the Industrial Revolution*. London: Clarendon Press, 1985.

Cranmer-Byng, J. L., ed. *An Embassy to China: Lord Macartney's Journal, 1793–1794*. London: Longmans, 1963.

Crone, Patricia, and G. Hinds. *God's Caliph: Religious Authority in the First Centuries of Islam*. Cambridge, UK: Cambridge University Press, 1986.

Crosby, Alfred. *The Columbian Exchange: Biological and Cultural Consequences of 1492*. Westport, CT: Westview Press, 1972.

———. *The Measure of Reality: Quantification and Western Society, 1250–1600*. Cambridge, UK: Cambridge University Press, 1997.

———. *Ecological Imperialism: The Biological Expansion of Europe, 900–1900*. 2nd ed. Cambridge, UK: Cambridge University Press, 2004.

Cullen, L. M. *A History of Japan, 1582–1941. Internal and External Worlds*. Cambridge, UK: Cambridge University Press, 2003.

Cumings, Bruce. *Dominion from Sea to Sea: Pacific Ascendancy and American Power*. New Haven, CT: Yale University Press, 2009.

Curtis, Vesta Sarkhosh, and Sarah Stewart, eds. *The Age of the Parthians*. London: I. B. Tauris, 2007.

Dalfes, Nüzhet, et al., eds. *Third Millennium BC Climate Change and Old World Collapse*. Berlin and New York: Springer, 1997.

Dardess, John. *Conquerors and Confucians: Aspects of Political Change in Late Yüan China*. New York: Columbia University Press, 1973.

———. *Blood and History in China: The Donglin Faction and its Repression, 1620–1627*. Honolulu: University of Hawaii Press, 2002.

Darnton, Robert. *The Great Cat Massacre and Other Essays in Cultural History*. New York: Vintage, 1984.

Darwin, John. *After Tamerlane: The Global History of Empire Since 1405*. New York: Allen Lane, 2008.

———. *The Empire Project: The Rise and Fall of the British World-System, 1830–1970*. Cambridge, UK: Cambridge University Press, 2009.

Daryaee, Touraj. *Sasanian Persia*. London: I. B. Tauris, 2009.

Davies, Norman. *Europe: A History*. Oxford: Oxford University Press, 1994.

Davies, Paul. *The Eerie Silence: Reviewing Our Search for Alien Intelligence*. New York: Houghton Mifflin Harcourt, 2010.

Davis, Mike. *Late Victorian Holocausts: El Niño Famines and the Making of the Third World*. New York: Verso, 2001.

———. *The Monster at Our Door: The Global Threat of Avian Flu*. New York: New Press, 2006.

Dawkins, Richard. *The Greatest Show on Earth: The Evidence for Evolution*. New York: Simon and Schuster, 2009.

Dawson, Christopher. 1955. *The Mongol Mission: Narratives and Letters of the Franciscan Missionaries in Mongolia and China in the Thirteenth and Fourteenth Centuries*. New York: Sheed and Ward, 1955.

Dawson, Raymond. *Confucius: The Analects*. Harmondsworth, UK: Penguin, 1993.

Dear, Peter. *Revolutionizing the Sciences: European Knowledge and Its Ambitions, 1500–1700*. Princeton: Princeton University Press, 2001.

de Bary, Theodore, and Irene Bloom, eds. *Sources of Chinese Tradition* I. 2nd ed. New York: Columbia University Press, 1999.

de Blij, Harm. *Why Geography Matters*. New York: Oxford University Press, 2005.

de Callataÿ, François. "The Graeco-Roman Economy in the Super-Long Run: Lead, Copper, and Shipwrecks." *Journal of Roman Archaeology* 18 (2005), pp. 361–72.

de Crespigny, Rafe. *Northern Frontier: The Policies and Strategy of the Later Han Empire*. Canberra: Australian National University, 1984.

de Grazia, Victoria. *Irresistible Empire: America's Advance through 20th-Century Europe*. Cambridge, MA: Harvard University Press, 2005.

DeGroot, Gerard. *The Sixties Unplugged: A Kaleidoscopic History of a Disorderly Decade*. Cambridge, MA: Harvard University Press, 2008.

de Madriaga, Isabel. *Ivan the Terrible*. New Haven, CT: Yale University Press, 2005.

Denham, Tim, et al. "New Evidence and Revised Interpretations of Early Agriculture in Highland New Guinea." *Antiquity* 79 (2005), pp. 839–57.

Dennett, Daniel. *Breaking the Spell: Religion as a Natural Phenomenon*. New York: Penguin, 2007.

de Vries, Jan. *The Industrious Revolution: Consumer Behavior and the Household Economy, 1650 to the Present*. Cambridge, UK: Cambridge University Press, 2008.

de Vries, Jan, and Ad van der Woude. *The First Modern Economy: Success, Failure, and Perseverance in the Dutch Economy, 1500–1815*. Cambridge, UK: Cambridge University Press, 1997.

Diamond, Jared. *Guns, Germs, and Steel: The Fates of Human Societies*. New York: Norton, 1997.

Di Cosmo, Nicola. *Ancient China and Its Enemies*. Cambridge, UK: Cambridge University Press, 2002.

Di Cosmo, Nicola, Allen Frank, and Peter Golden, eds. *The Cambridge History of Inner Asia: The Chingissid Age*. Cambridge, UK: Cambridge University Press, 2009.

———. *Collapse: How Societies Choose to Fail or Succeed*. New York: Viking, 2005.

Dien, Albert. "The Stirrup and its Effect on Chinese History." *Ars Orientalia* 16 (1986), pp. 33–56.

———, ed. *State and Society in Early Medieval China*. Stanford: Stanford University Press, 1990.

———. *Six Dynasties Civilization*. New Haven, CT: Yale University Press, 2007.

Dien, Dora. *Empress Wu Zetian in Fiction and in History: Female Defiance in Confucian China*. Hauppauge, NY: Nova Science, 2003.

Dietler, Michael. *Archaeologies of Colonialism: Consumption, Entanglement, and Violence in Ancient Mediterranean France*. Berkeley: University of California Press, 2010.

Dietrich, John, ed. *The George W. Bush Foreign Policy Reader*. New York: Michael Sharpe, 2005.

Dignas, Beate, and Engelbert Winter. *Rome and Persia in Late Antiquity*. Cambridge, UK: Cambridge University Press, 2007.

Dillehay, Tom, et al. "Preceramic Adoption of Peanut, Squash, and Cotton in Northern Peru." *Science* 316 (2007), pp. 1890–93.

———. "Monte Verde: Seaweed, Food, Medicine, and the Peopling of North America." *Science* 320 (2008), pp. 784–86.

Dixon, Philip. "'The Cities Are Not Populated as Once They Were,'" in John Rich, ed., *The City in Late Antiquity*, pp. 145–60. London: Routledge, 1992.

Dols, Michael. *The Black Death in the Middle East*. Princeton: Princeton University Press, 1976.

Donner, Fred. *The Early Islamic Conquests*. Princeton: Princeton University Press, 1981.

Dower, John. *War Without Mercy*. New York: Pantheon, 1986.

———. *Embracing Defeat: Japan in the Wake of World War II*. New York: Norton, 2000.

Drake, Stillman. *Discoveries and Opinions of Galileo*. New York: Doubleday, 1957.

Drews, Robert. *The Coming of the Greeks*. Princeton: Princeton University Press, 1988.

———. *The End of the Bronze Age*. Princeton: Princeton University Press, 1992.

Dreyer, Edward. *Early Ming China*. Stanford: Stanford University Press, 1982.

———. *Zheng He: China and the Oceans in the Early Ming Dynasty, 1405–1433*. New York: Pearson Longman, 2006.

Drinkwater, John, and Hugh Elton, eds. *Fifth-Century Gaul: A Crisis of Identity?* Cambridge, UK: Cambridge University Press, 1992.

Duby, Georges. *The Age of Cathedrals: Art and Society, 980–1420*. Chicago: University of Chicago Press, 1981.

Dunn, Marilyn. *Emergence of Monasticism from the Desert Fathers to the Early Middle Ages*. Oxford: Blackwell, 2000.

Duus, Peter. *The Rise of Modern Japan*. Boston: Houghton Mifflin, 1976.

Duyvendak, J. J. L. *The Book of Lord Shang*. London: A. Probsthain, 1928.

———. *China's Discovery of Africa*. London: A. Probsthain, 1949.

Earle, Peter. *The Pirate Wars*. New York: St. Martin's, 2003.

Easterling, William, ed. "Climate Change and Food Security." *Proceedings of the National Academy of Sciences* 104 (2007), pp. 19679–714.

Eberhard, Wolfram. *Conquerors and Rulers: Social Forces in Medieval China*. Leiden: E. J. Brill, 1965.

Ebrey, Patricia. *The Inner Quarters: Marriage and the Lives of Chinese Women in the Sung Period*. Berkeley: University of California Press, 1993.

———. *The Cambridge Illustrated History of China*. Cambridge, UK: Cambridge University Press, 1996.

Ebrey, Patricia, and Maggie Bickford, eds. *Emperor Huizong and Late Northern Song China*. Cambridge, MA: Harvard University Press, 2006.

Eckstein, Arthur. *Mediterranean Anarchy, Interstate War, and the Rise of Rome*. Berkeley: University of California Press, 2007.

Economy, Elizabeth. *The River Runs Black: The Environmental Challenge to China's Future*. Ithaca, NY: Cornell University Press, 2004.

Ehrlich, Paul, and Anne Ehrlich. *The Dominant Animal: Human Evolution and the Environment*. New York: Island Press, 2008.

Eich, Armin, and Peter Eich. "War and State-Building in Roman Republican Times." *Scripta Classica Israelica* 24 (2005), pp. 1–33.

Eichengreen, Barry. *Golden Fetters: The Gold Standard and the Great Depression, 1919–1939*. New York: Oxford University Press, 1992.

———. *The European Economy Since 1945*. Princeton: Princeton University Press, 2007.

Eisenberg, Andrew. *Kingship in Early Medieval China*. Leiden: E. J. Brill, 2008.

Elliott, J. H. *Empires of the Atlantic World: Britain and Spain in America, 1492–1830*. New Haven, CT: Yale University Press, 2006.

Elliott, Mark, and Peter Stearns. *Emperor Qianlong: Son of Heaven, Man of the World.* London: Longman, 2009.

Elman, Benjamin. *From Philosophy to Philology: Intellectual and Social Aspects of Change in Late Imperial China.* 2nd ed. Los Angeles: University of California Asian Pacific Monograph Series, 2001.

———. *A Cultural History of Modern Science in China.* Cambridge, MA: Harvard University Press, 2006.

Elsner, Jas. *Imperial Rome and Christian Triumph: The Art of the Roman Empire* AD *100–450.* Oxford: Oxford University Press, 1999.

Elton, Geoffrey. *Reformation Europe.* London: Fontana, 1963.

———. *The Practice of History.* London: Fontana, 1967.

Elvin, Mark. *The Pattern of the Chinese Past.* Stanford: Stanford University Press, 1973.

Endicott, Phillip, et al. "Evaluating the Mitochondrial Timescale of Human Evolution." *Trends in Ecology and Evolution* 24 (2009), pp. 515–21.

EPICA Community Members. "Eight Glacial Cycles from an Antarctic Ice Core." *Nature* 429 (2004), pp. 623–28.

Erickson, David, et al. "An Asian Origin for a 10,000-Year-Old Domesticated Plant from the Americas." *Proceedings of the National Academy of Sciences* 102 (2005), pp. 18315–20.

Evans, Richard. *The Third Reich in Power.* New York: Penguin, 2005.

Fagan, Brian. *The Long Summer: How Climate Changed Civilization.* New York: Basic Books, 2004a.

———. *The Little Ice Age.* New York: Basic Books, 2004b.

———. *The Great Warming: Climate Change and the Rise and Fall of Civilizations.* New York: Bloomsbury Press, 2008.

Farmer, Edward. *Zhu Yuanzhang and Early Ming Legislation: The Reordering of Chinese Society Following the Eras of Mongol Rule.* Leiden: E. J. Brill, 1995.

Fasolt, Constantin. "Hegel's Ghost: Europe, the Reformation, and the Middle Ages." *Viator* 39 (2008), pp. 345–86.

Fay, Peter Ward. *The Opium War, 1840–1842.* 2nd ed. Chapel Hill: University of North Carolina Press, 1997.

Feifer, George. *Breaking Open Japan: Commodore Perry, Lord Abe, and American Imperialism in 1853.* New York: Smithsonian Books, 2006.

Ferguson, Niall, ed. *Virtual History.* New York: Basic Books, 1997.

———. *The Pity of War: Explaining World War I.* New York: Basic Books, 1998.

———. *Empire.* New York: Basic Books, 2003.

———. *The War of the World: Twentieth-Century Conflict and the Descent of the West.* New York: Penguin, 2007.

———. "What 'Chimerica' Hath Wrought." *The American Interest,* January–February 2009, http://www.the-american-interest.com/article.cfm?piece=533.

Ferguson, Niall, and Moritz Schularick. "'Chimerica' and the Global Asset Market Boom." *International Finance* 10.3 (2007), pp. 215–39.

Fernandez-Armesto, Felipe. *Pathfinders: A Global History of Exploration.* New York: Norton, 2006.

Figes, Orlando. *A People's Tragedy: The Russian Revolution, 1891–1924.* New York: Penguin, 1996.

Findlay, Robert, and Kevin O'Rourke. *Power and Plenty: Trade, War, and the World Economy in the Second Millennium.* Princeton: Princeton University Press, 2007.

Finkel, Caroline. *The History of the Ottoman Empire: Osman's Dream*. New York: Basic Books, 2005.

Finkelstein, Israel, and Neil Silberman. *The Bible Unearthed: Archaeology's New Vision of Ancient Israel and the Origin of Its Sacred Texts*. New York: Free Press, 2001.

———. *David and Solomon*. New York: Free Press, 2006.

Finlay, Robert. "How Not to (Re)Write World History: Gavin Menzies and the Chinese Discovery of America." *Journal of World History* 15 (2004), pp. 299–42.

Finlayson, Clive, et al. "Late Survival of Neanderthals at the Southernmost Extreme of Europe." *Nature* 443 (2006), pp. 850–53.

Fishman, Ted. *China, Inc.* New York: Scribner, 2005.

Fitzpatrick, Sheila. *Everyday Stalinism: Ordinary Life in Extraordinary Times—Soviet Russia in the 1930s*. Oxford: Oxford University Press, 1999.

Flad, Rowan. "Divination and Power: A Multiregional View of the Development of Oracle Bone Divination in Early China." *Current Anthropology* 32 (2008), pp. 403–37.

Fleagle, John, and Christopher Gilbert, eds. "Modern Human Origins in Africa." *Evolutionary Anthropology* 17.1 (2008), pp. 1–80.

Flecker, Michael. *The Archaeological Excavation of the Tenth-Century Intan Shipwreck*. Oxford: British Archaeological Reports, 2002.

Floud, Roderick, and Donald McCloskey, eds. *The Economic History of Britain Since 1700*. 2 vols. 2nd ed. Cambridge, UK: Cambridge University Press, 1994.

Flynn, Dennis. *World Silver and Monetary History in the 16th and 17th Centuries*. Aldershot, UK: Variorum, 1996.

Flynn, Dennis, Arturo Giráldez, and Richard von Glahn, eds. *Global Connections and Monetary History, 1470–1800*. Aldershot, UK: Ashgate, 2003.

Flynn, James. *What Is Intelligence? Beyond the Flynn Effect*. Cambridge, UK: Cambridge University Press, 2007.

Fogel, Robert. *The Escape from Hunger and Premature Death, 1700–2100: Europe, America, and the Third World*. Cambridge, UK: Cambridge University Press, 2004.

———. "Capitalism and Democracy in 2040: Forecasts and Speculations." National Bureau of Economic Research Working Paper 13,184, 2007.

Food and Agriculture Organization. *Statistical Yearbook*, vol. 2, part 1. Rome: Food and Agriculture Organization of the United Nations, 2006.

Fowden, Garth. *Empire to Commonwealth: Consequences of Monotheism in Late Antiquity*. Princeton: Princeton University Press, 1993.

Francis, Mark. *Herbert Spencer and the Invention of Modern Life*. Ithaca, NY: Cornell University Press, 2007.

Frank, Andre Gunder. *ReOrient: Global Economy in the Asian Age*. Berkeley: University of California Press, 1998.

Freud, Sigmund. *Moses and Monotheism*. New York: Vintage, 1955. First published in German, 1939.

Fried, Morton. *The Evolution of Political Society*. New York: Random House, 1967.

Friedan, Betty. *The Feminine Mystique*. New York: Dell, 1963.

Frieden, Jeffrey. *Global Capitalism: Its Fall and Rise*. New York: Norton, 2006.

Friedman, George. *America's Secret War: Inside the Hidden Worldwide Struggle Between America and Its Enemies*. New York: Doubleday, 2004.

———. *The Next Hundred Years: A Forecast for the Twenty-First Century*. New York: Doubleday, 2009.

Friedman, Thomas. *The Lexus and the Olive Tree*. New York: Anchor, 1999.

————. *The World Is Flat: A Brief History of the Twenty-First Century.* New York: Farrar, Straus and Giroux, 2005.

————. *Hot, Flat, and Crowded: Why We Need a Green Revolution.* New York: Farrar, Straus and Giroux, 2008.

Frye, James, Rajagopal Ananthanarayanan, and Dharmendra Modha. "Towards Real-Time, Mouse-Scale Cortical Simulations." IBM Research Report RJ10404 (A0702-001), 2007. Available from http://www.modha.org/papers/rj10404.pdf.

Fu, Zhengyuan. *China's Legalists: The Earliest Totalitarians and Their Art of Ruling.* Armonk, NY: Michael Sharpe, 1996.

Fukuyama, Francis. *Our Posthuman Future.* New York: Picador, 2002.

————, ed. *Blindside: How to Anticipate Forcing Events and Wild Cards in Global Politics.* Washington, DC: Brookings Institution, 2008.

Fukuzawa, Yukichi. *The Autobiography of Yukichi Fukuzawa.* New York: Columbia University Press, 1966. Originally published in Japanese in 1899.

Fuller, Dorian. "Agricultural Origins in South Asia." *Journal of World Prehistory* 20 (2006), pp. 1–86.

————. "Contrasting Patterns in Crop Domestication and Domestication Rates." *Annals of Botany* 2007, pp. 1–22.

Fuller, Dorian, Emma Harvey, and Ling Qin. "Presumed Domestication? Evidence for Wild Rice Cultivation and Domestication in the 5th Millennium BC of the Lower Yangtze Region." *Antiquity* 81 (2007), pp. 316–31.

Fursenko, Aleksandr, and Timothy Naftali. *"One Hell of a Gamble": Khrushchev, Castro, and Kennedy, 1958–1964.* New York: Norton, 1997.

Gaddis, John Lewis. *The Cold War: A New History.* New York: Penguin, 2005.

Gaddis, John Lewis, et al., eds. *Cold War Statesmen Confront the Bomb: Nuclear Diplomacy Since 1945.* New York: Oxford University Press, 1999.

Gaidar, Oleg. *Collapse of an Empire.* Berkeley: University of California Press, 2008.

Galor, Oded, and Omer Moav. "Natural Selection and the Origin of Economic Growth." *Quarterly Journal of Economics* 117 (2002), pp. 1133–91.

Garcia, María José, et al. "Late Holocene Environments in Las Tablas de Daimiel (South Central Iberian Peninsula, Spain)." *Vegetation History and Archaeobotany* 16 (2007), pp. 241–50.

Garnaut, Ross. *Garnaut Climate Change Review: Final Report.* 2008. Available at http://www.garnautreview.org.au.

Garnsey, Peter, and Richard Saller. *The Roman Empire.* London: Duckworth, 1987.

Gay, Peter. *The Enlightenment: An Interpretation.* 2 vols. New York: Knopf, 1966–69.

————. *Modernism: The Lure of Heresy.* New York: Norton, 2008.

Ge, Quansheng, et al. "Winter Half-Year Temperature Reconstruction for the Middle and Lower Reaches of the Yellow River and Yangtze River, China, During the Past 2000 Years." *The Holocene* 13 (2003), pp. 933–40.

Gernet, Jacques. *Buddhism in Chinese Society. An Economic History from the Fifth to the Tenth Centuries.* New York: Columbia University Press, 1995.

Gerring, John. *Social Science Methodology.* Cambridge, UK: Cambridge University Press, 2001.

Gerschrenkon, Alexander. *Economic Backwardness in Historical Perspective.* Cambridge, MA: Harvard University Press, 1962.

Gerth, H. H., and C. Wright Mills, eds. *From Max Weber.* New York: Oxford University Press, 1946.

Ghosh, Amitav. *In an Antique Land: History in the Guise of a Traveler's Tale*. New York: Vintage, 1992.

Gibson, Daniel, et al. "Creation of a Bacterial Cell Controlled by a Chemically Synthesized Genome." *Science* 328 (May 20, 2010), doi: 10.1126/science.1190719.

Giles, J. A., ed. *Matthew Paris's English History from the Year 1235 to 1273*. London: H. G. Bohn, 1852.

Gilbert, M. Thomas, et al. "DNA from Pre-Clovis Human Coprolites in Oregon, North America." *Science* 320 (2008), online edition, 120b.

Gillingham, John. *Coal, Steel, and the Rebirth of Europe, 1945–1955*. Cambridge, UK: Cambridge University Press, 1991.

———. *European Integration, 1950–2003: Superstate or New Market Economy?* Cambridge, UK: Cambridge University Press, 2003.

Gittings, John. *The Changing Face of China: From Mao to Market*. Oxford: Oxford University Press, 2005.

Godman, Peter. *Poetry of the Carolingian Renaissance*. Norman: University of Oklahoma Press, 1985.

Goebel, Ted, et al. "The Late Pleistocene Dispersal of Modern Humans in the Americas." *Science* 319 (2008), pp. 1497–1502.

Goitein, Shlomo. *A Mediterranean Society: The Jewish Communities of the Arab World as Portrayed in the Documents of the Cairo Geniza*. 5 vols. Berkeley: University of California Press, 1967–88.

Golas, Peter. "The Sung Economy: How Big?" *Bulletin of Sung-Yuan Studies* 20 (1988), pp. 90–94.

———. *Science and Civilization in China V: Chemistry and Chemical Technology*. Part 13: *Mining*. Cambridge, UK: Cambridge University Press, 1999.

Goldman, Marshall. *Petrostate: Putin, Power, and the New Russia*. New York: Oxford University Press, 2008.

Goldman, Merle. *From Comrade to Citizen: The Struggle for Political Rights in China*. Cambridge, MA: Harvard University Press, 2005.

Goldstone, Jack. *Revolution and Rebellion in the Early Modern World*. Berkeley: University of California Press, 1991.

———. "Europe's Peculiar Path: Would the World be 'Modern' if William III's Invasion of England in 1688 Had Failed?" In Tetlock et al., eds., 2006, pp. 168–96.

———. *Why Europe? The Rise of the West in World History, 1500–1850*. Boston: McGraw-Hill, 2009.

Goldsworthy, Adrian. *How Rome Fell: Death of a Superpower*. New Haven, CT: Yale University Press, 2009.

Goody, Jack. *Production and Reproduction: A Comparative Study of the Domestic Domain*. Cambridge, UK: Cambridge University Press, 1976.

———. *Cooking, Cuisine, and Class*. Cambridge, UK: Cambridge University Press, 1982.

———. *Capitalism and Modernity: The Great Debate*. Cambridge, UK: Cambridge University Press, 2004.

———. *Renaissances: The One or the Many?* Cambridge, UK: Cambridge University Press, 2010.

Gorbachev, Mikhail. *Memoirs*. New York: Doubleday, 1995.

Gordon, Matthew. *The Breaking of a Thousand Swords: A History of the Turkish Military of Samarra (AH 200–275/815–889 CE)*. Albany: State University of New York Press, 2001.

Gordon, Stuart. *When Asia Was the World.* New York: Da Capo, 2008.

Gould, Stephen Jay. *Punctuated Equilibrium.* Cambridge, MA: Harvard University Press, 2007.

Graff, David. *Medieval Chinese Warfare, 300–900.* London: Routledge, 2002.

Graham, Bob, and Jim Talent. *World at Risk: The Report of the Commission on the Prevention of Weapons of Mass Destruction Proliferation and Terrorism.* New York: Vintage, 2008. Available at http://documents.scribd.com/ocs/2avb51ejt0uadzxm2wpt.pdf.

Graham, Daniel. *Explaining the Cosmos: The Ionian Tradition of Scientific Philosophy.* Princeton: Princeton University Press, 2006.

Graves, Robert. *Count Belisarius.* London: Literary Guild, 1938.

Grayson, Kirk. *Assyrian Rulers of the Early First Millennium BC* I. Toronto: University of Toronto Press, 1991.

Green, John Richard. *A History of the English People,* vol. 8. London: Macmillan, 1879.

Green, Richard, et al. "A Draft Sequence of the Neandertal Genome." *Science* 328 (May 7, 2010), pp. 710–22.

Green, Ronald. *Babies by Design: The Ethics of Genetic Choice.* New Haven, CT: Yale University Press, 2007.

Greenhalgh, Susan. *Just One Child: Science and Policy in Deng's China.* Berkeley: University of California Press, 2008.

Grigg, David. *The Transformation of Agriculture in the West.* Oxford: Blackwell, 1992.

Guillaume, Alfred. *The Life of Muhammad.* Lahore: Oxford University Press, 1969.

Guisso, R. *Wu Tse't'ien and the Politics of Legitimation in T'ang China.* Bellingham: University of Western Washington Press, 1978.

Gunz, Philipp, et al. "Early Modern Human Diversity Suggests Subdivided Population Structure and a Complex Out-of-Africa Scenario." *Proceedings of the National Academy of Sciences* 106 (2009), doi: 10.1073/pnas.0901515106.

Guo, Qinghua. *The* Mingqi *Pottery Buildings of Han Dynasty China, 206 BC–AD 220.* Eastbourne, UK: Sussex Academic Press, 2010.

Habu, Junko. *Ancient Jomon of Japan.* Cambridge, UK: Cambridge University Press, 2004.

Haeger, John, ed. *Crisis and Prosperity in Sung China.* Tucson: University of Arizona Press, 1975.

Haldon, John. *Byzantium in the Seventh Century.* 2nd ed. Cambridge, UK: Cambridge University Press: 1997.

Hall, David, and Roger Ames. *Anticipating China: Thinking Through the Narrative of Chinese and Western Culture.* Albany: State University of New York Press, 1995a.

———. *Thinking from the Han: Self, Truth, and Transcendence in Chinese and Western Culture.* Albany: State University of New York Press, 1995b.

Hall, John. "Changing Conceptions of the Modernization of Japan." In Marius Jansen, ed., *Changing Japanese Attitudes Toward Modernization.* Princeton: Princeton University Press, 1966.

Halper, Stefan. *The Beijing Consensus: How China's Authoritarian Model Will Dominate the Twenty-first Century.* New York: Basic Books, 2010.

Hancock, Graham. *Underworld: The Mysterious Origins of Civilization.* London: Three Rivers Press, 2003.

Hansen, Ilse, and Chris Wickham, eds. *The Long Eighth Century.* Leiden: E. J. Brill, 2000.

Hardy-Smith, Tania, and Phillip Edwards. "The Garbage Crisis in Prehistory." *Journal of Anthropological Archaeology* 23 (2004), pp. 253–89.

Harley, Knick. "Cotton Textile Prices and the Industrial Revolution." *Economic History Review*, New Series 51 (1998), pp. 49–83.

Harries, Meirion, and Susie Harries. *Soldiers of the Sun: The Rise and Fall of the Imperial Japanese Army, 1868–1945*. London: Heinemann, 1991.

Harris, Robert. *Fatherland*. New York: Book Club Associates, 1992.

Harris, William. *Ancient Literacy*. Cambridge, MA: Harvard University Press, 1989.

Hartwell, Robert. "A Cycle of Economic Change in Imperial China: Coal and Iron in Northeast China, 750–1350." *Journal of the Economic and Social History of the Orient* 10 (1967), pp. 102–59.

———. "Demographic, Political, and Social Transformation of China, 750–1550." *Harvard Journal of Asiatic Studies* 42 (1982), pp. 365–442.

Hassan, Ahmad, and Donald Hill. *Islamic Technology*. Cambridge, UK: Cambridge University Press, 1986.

Hatcher, John. *The Black Death: A Personal History*. New York: Doubleday, 2008.

Haw, Stephen. *Marco Polo's China: A Venetian in the Realm of Khubilai Khan*. London: Routledge, 2006.

Hawksworth, John, and Gordon Cookson. *The World in 2050: Beyond the BRICs*. London: PricewaterhouseCoopers, March 2008. Available at www.pwc.co.uk/economics.

Hayden, Dolores. *Building Suburbia: Green Fields and Urban Growth*. New York: Pantheon, 2002.

He, Nu. "Monumental Structure from Ceremonial Precinct at Taosi Walled Town." *Chinese Archaeology* 5 (2005), pp. 51–58.

Headrick, Daniel. *Power over Peoples: Technology, Environments, and Western Imperialism, 1400 to the Present*. Princeton: Princeton University Press, 2010.

Heather, Peter. *The Fall of the Roman Empire*. Oxford: Oxford University Press, 2005.

Hedden, Trey, et al. "Cultural Influences on Neural Substrates of Attentional Control." *Psychological Science* 19 (2008), pp. 12–17.

Heinlein, Robert. *Time Enough for Love*. New York: Ace Books, 1973.

Hemming, John. *The Conquest of the Incas*. New York: Penguin, 1970.

Herlihy, David. *The Black Death and the Transformation of the West*. Cambridge, MA: Harvard University Press, 1997.

Herman, Arthur. *To Rule the Waves: How the British Navy Shaped the Modern World*. New York: Harper, 2004.

Hessler, Peter. *Oracle Bones*. New York: Harper, 2006.

Hickey, Todd. "Aristocratic Landholding and the Economy of Byzantine Egypt." In Roger Bagnall, ed., *Egypt in the Byzantine World*, pp. 288–308. Cambridge, UK: Cambridge University Press, 2007.

Hill, Christopher. *The Experience of Defeat: Milton and Some Contemporaries*. New York: Penguin, 1984.

Hillman, Gordon, et al. "New Evidence of Lateglacial Cereal Cultivation at Abu Hureyra on the Euphrates." *The Holocene* 11 (2001), pp. 383–93.

Ho, Mun Chan, and Hektor Yan. "Is There a Geography of Thought for East-West Differences? Why or Why Not?" *Educational Philosophy and Theory* 39 (2007), pp. 383–403.

Ho, Ping-ti. *Studies on the Population of China, 1368–1953*. Cambridge, MA: Harvard University Press, 1959.

Hobsbawm, Eric. *The Age of Revolution, 1789–1848*. New York: Vintage, 1964.

————. *The Age of Capital, 1848–1875.* New York: Vintage, 1975.

————. *The Age of Empire, 1875–1914.* New York: Vintage, 1987.

————. *The Age of Extremes: A History of the World, 1914–1991.* New York: Vintage, 1994.

Hobsbawm, Eric, and George Rudé. *Captain Swing.* London: Penguin, 1969.

Hobson, John. *The Eastern Origins of Western Civilisation.* Cambridge, UK: Cambridge University Press, 2004.

Hochschild, Adam. *King Leopold's Ghost.* New York: Mariner, 1998.

Hodder, Ian. *The Domestication of Europe.* Oxford: Blackwell, 1990.

————. *The Leopard's Tale: Revealing the Mysteries of Çatalhöyük.* London: Thames and Hudson, 2006.

Hodges, Richard, and David Whitehouse. *Mohammad, Charlemagne, and the Origins of Europe.* London: Routledge, 1983.

Hodos, Tamar. *Local Responses to Colonization in the Iron Age Mediterranean.* London: Routledge, 2006.

Holcombe, Charles. *In the Shadow of the Han: Literati Thought and Society at the Beginning of the Southern Dynasties.* Honolulu: University of Hawaii Press, 1994.

————. *The Genesis of East Asia, 221 BC–AD 907.* Honolulu: University of Hawaii Press, 2001.

Holloway, David. *Stalin and the Bomb: The Soviet Union and Atomic Energy, 1939–1956.* New Haven, CT: Yale University Press, 1994.

Holloway, Kenneth. *Guodian: The Newly Discovered Seeds of Chinese Religious and Political Philosophy.* Oxford: Oxford University Press, 2009.

Holt, Frank. *Thundering Zeus: The Making of Hellenistic Bactria.* Berkeley: University of California Press, 1999.

Hopkins, Keith. "Christian Number and its Implications." *Journal of Early Christian Studies* 6 (1998), pp. 185–226.

Hourani, Albert. *A History of the Arab Peoples.* 2nd ed. New York: Warner, 2003.

Howe, Daniel. *What Hath God Wrought: The Transformation of America, 1815–1848.* New York: Oxford University Press, 2007.

Hoyland, Robert. *Arabia and the Arabs: From the Bronze Age to the Coming of Islam.* London: Routledge, 2001.

Hsu, Cho-yun. *Han Agriculture. The Formation of Early Chinese Agrarian Economy (206 BC–AD 220).* Seattle: University of Washington Press, 1980.

Hsu, Cho-yun, and Kathryn Linduff. *Western Chou Civilization.* New Haven, CT: Yale University Press, 1988.

Hsu, Roland. *Ethnic Europe: Mobility, Identity, and Conflict in a Globalized World.* Stanford: Stanford University Press, 2010.

Huang, Ray. *1587, a Year of No Significance: The Ming Dynasty in Decline.* New Haven, CT: Yale University Press, 1981.

Huang, Yasheng. *Capitalism with Chinese Characteristics: Entrepreneurship and the State.* Cambridge, UK: Cambridge University Press, 2008.

Hucker, Charles. *China's Imperial Past.* Stanford: Stanford University Press, 1975.

Huff, Toby. *The Rise of Early Modern Science: Islam, China, and the West.* 2nd ed. Cambridge, UK: Cambridge University Press, 2003.

Hui, Victoria. *War and State Formation in Ancient China and Early Modern Europe.* Cambridge, UK: Cambridge University Press, 2005.

Hulsewé, A. *Remnants of Ch'in Law.* Leiden: E. J. Brill, 1985.

Huntington, Ellsworth. *Civilization and Climate*. 1st ed. New Haven, CT: Yale University Press, 1915.

Huntington, Samuel. *The Clash of Civilizations and the Remaking of World Order*. New York: Simon and Schuster, 1996.

Hutchison, Michael, and Frank Westermann, eds. *Japan's Great Stagnation*. Cambridge, MA: Harvard University Press, 2006.

Hymes, Robert, and Conrad Schirokauer, eds. *Ordering the World: Approaches to State and Society in Sung Dynasty China*. Berkeley: University of California Press, 1993.

Ikeguchi, Mamoru. "The Dynamics of Agricultural Locations in Italy." Unpublished PhD dissertation, King's College, London, 2007.

Imber, Colin. *The Ottoman Empire, 1300–1650: The Structure of Power*. London: Palgrave, 2002.

Impey, Chris. *The Living Cosmos: Our Search for Life in the Universe*. New York: Random House, 2007.

Inalcik, Halil, and Donald Quataert, eds. *An Economic and Social History of the Ottoman Empire, 1300–1914*. Cambridge, UK: Cambridge University Press, 1994.

Ingman, Max, et al. "Mitochondrial Genome Variation and the Origin of Modern Humans." *Nature* 408 (2000), pp. 708–13.

Ingrau, Charles. *The Habsburg Monarchy, 1618–1815*. 2nd ed. Cambridge, UK: Cambridge University Press, 2000.

Inikori, Joseph. *Africans and the Industrial Revolution in England*. Cambridge, UK: Cambridge University Press, 2002.

———. "Africa and the Globalization Process: Western Africa, 1450–1850." *Journal of Global History* 2 (2007), pp. 63–86.

Institute for International Strategic Studies. *The Military Balance 2009*. London: Institute for International Strategic Studies, 2009.

Intergovernmental Panel on Climate Change. *Fourth Assessment Report*. Cambridge, UK: Cambridge University Press, 2007. http://www/ipcc.ch/.

International Monetary Fund. *World Economic Outlook Update*, July 8, 2009 (http://www.imf.org/external/pubs/ft/weo/2009/update/02).

Iriye, Akira. *The Origins of the Second World War in Asia and the Pacific*. London: Longman, 1987.

Irwin, Douglas. *Against the Tide: An Intellectual History of Free Trade*. Princeton: Princeton University Press, 1996.

Isaacson, Walter. *Einstein: His Life and Universe*. New York: Simon and Schuster, 2007.

Israel, Jonathan. *The Dutch Republic: Its Rise, Greatness, and Fall, 1477–1806*. Oxford: Oxford University Press, 1995.

Issar, Arie. *Climate Changes During the Holocene and their Impact on Hydrological Systems*. Cambridge, UK: Cambridge University Press, 2003.

Issar, Arie, and Mattanyah Zahor. *Climate Change—Environment and Civilization in the Middle East*. New York: Springer, 2005.

Ivanhoe, Philip. *Confucian Moral Cultivation*. 2nd ed. Amsterdam: Hackett, 2000.

———, ed. *Readings from the Lu-Wang School of Neo-Confucianism*. Amsterdam: Hackett, 2009.

Jackson, Peter. "Marco Polo and his 'Travels.'" *Bulletin of the School of Oriental and African Studies* 61 (1998), pp. 82–101.

Jacob, Margaret. *Scientific Culture and the Making of the Industrial West*. New York: Oxford University Press, 1997.

Jacob, Margaret, and Larry Stewart. *Practical Matter: Newton's Science in the Service of Industry and Empire*. Cambridge, MA: Harvard University Press, 2004.

Jacques, Martin. *When China Rules the World: The Rise of the Middle Kingdom and the End of the Western World*. London: Allen Lane, 2009.

Jakobsson, Mattias, et al. "Genotype, Haplotype and Copy-Number Variation in Worldwide Human Populations." *Nature* 451 (2008), pp. 998–1003.

Jansen, Marius. *The Making of Modern Japan*. Cambridge, MA: Harvard University Press, 2000.

Jardine, Lisa. *Going Dutch: How England Plundered Holland's Glory*. New York: Harper, 2008.

Jaspers, Karl. *The Origin and Goal of History*. New Haven, CT: Yale University Press, 1953. First published in German, 1949.

Ji, Junfeng, et al. "Asian Monsoon Oscillations in the Northeastern Qinghai-Tibet Plateau Since the Late Glacial as Interpreted from Visible Reflectance of Qinghai Lake Sediments." *Earth and Planetary Science Letters* 233 (2005), pp. 61–70.

Ji, Xiao-bin. *Politics and Conservatism in Northern Song China: The Career and Thought of Sima Guang (AD 1019–1086)*. Hong Kong: Chinese University Press, 2005.

Jiang, Leping. "The Shangshan Site, Pujiang County, Zhejiang." *Chinese Archaeology* 8 (2008), pp. 37–43.

Jiang, Leping, and Li Liu. "New Evidence for the Origins of Sedentism and Rice Domestication in the Lower Yangzi River, China." *Antiquity* 80 (2006), pp. 355–61.

Johnson, Donald, and Jean Johnson. *Universal Religions in World History: The Spread of Buddhism, Christianity, and Islam to 1500*. New York: McGraw-Hill, 2007.

Johnston, Alastair. *Cultural Realism: Strategic Culture and Grand Strategy in Ming China*. Princeton: Princeton University Press, 1995.

Jones, Eric. 1985. " 'Where is Everybody?' An Account of Fermi's Question." Los Alamos Technical Report LA-10311-MS. Available at http://library.lanl.gov/infores/reports/.

Jongman, Willem. "The Early Roman Empire: Consumption." In Walter Scheidel et al., eds., *The Cambridge Economic History of the Greco-Roman World*, pp. 592–618. Cambridge, UK: Cambridge University Press, 2007a.

———. "Gibbon Was Right: The Decline and Fall of the Roman Economy." In Olivier Hekster, Gerda de Kleijn, and Daniëlle Slootjes, eds., *Crises and the Roman Empire*, pp. 183–99. Leiden: E. J. Brill, 2007b.

Jordan, William Chester. *The Great Famine*. Princeton: Princeton University Press, 1996.

———. *Europe in the High Middle Ages*. London: Penguin, 2001.

Judt, Tony. *Postwar: A History of Europe Since 1945*. New York: Penguin Press, 2005.

Jungers, William, et al. "Long-Bone Geometry and Skeletal Biomechanisms in *Homo floresiensis*." Paper delivered at the 79th Annual Meeting of the American Association of Physical Anthropologists, April 2010, *Abstracts of AAPA Poster and Podium Presentations*, pp. 143-44. http://physanth.org/annual-meeting/2010/79th-annual-meeting-2010/2010%20AAPA%20Abstracts.pdf.

Kaegi, Walter. *Byzantium and the Early Islamic Conquests*. Cambridge, UK: Cambridge University Press, 1992.

———. *Heraclius, Emperor of Byzantium*. Cambridge, UK: Cambridge University Press, 2003.

Kamen, Stanley. *Philip of Spain*. New Haven, CT: Yale University Press, 1999.

————. *Empire: How Spain Became a World Power, 1492–1763*. New York: Harper, 2003.

Kann, Robert. *A History of the Habsburg Empire, 1526–1918*. Berkeley: University of California Press, 1980.

Kaplan, David. "The Darker Side of the 'Original Affluent Society.'" *Journal of Anthropological Research* 56 (2000), pp. 301–24.

Kaplan, Robert. "How We Would Fight China." *The Atlantic* 295.5 (June 2005), pp. 49–64.

Ke, Yuehai, et al. "African Origin of Modern Humans in East Asia: A Tale of 12,000 Y Chromosomes." *Science* 292 (2001), pp. 1151–53.

Keene, Donald. *Emperor of Japan: Meiji and His World, 1852–1912*. New York: Columbia University Press, 2002.

Keightley, David. *The Ancestral Landscape: Time, Space, and Community in Late Shang China (ca. 1200–1045 BC)*. Berkeley: University of California Press, 2000.

————. "Marks and Labels: Early Writing in Neolithic and Shang China." In Stark, ed., 2006, pp. 177–201.

Kelly, Christopher. *The End of Empire: Attila the Hun and the Fall of Rome*. New York: Norton, 2009.

Kennedy, David. *Freedom from Fear: The American People in Depression and War, 1929–1945*. New York: Oxford University Press, 1999.

Kennedy, Hugh. *The Prophet and the Age of the Caliphates*. 2nd ed. London: Longmans, 2004a.

————. *When Baghdad Ruled the Muslim World: The Rise and Fall of Islam's Greatest Dynasty*. New York: Da Capo, 2004b.

————. *The Great Arab Conquests*. London: Da Capo, 2007.

Kennedy, Paul. *The Rise and Fall of British Naval Mastery*. London: Allen Lane, 1976.

————. *The Rise and Fall of the Great Powers*. New York: Vintage, 1987.

Kennedy, Robert F. *Thirteen Days: The Cuban Missile Crisis*. New York: Norton, 1969.

Kennett, Douglas, et al. "Nanodiamonds in the Younger Dryas Boundary Sediment Layer." *Science* 323 (2009), p. 94.

Kerr, Richard, et al. "Atlantic Climate Pacemaker for Millennia Past, Decades Hence?" *Science* 309 (2005), pp. 41–42.

Keynes, John Maynard. *A Treatise on Money*. London: Macmillan, 1930.

Keys, David. *Catastrophe: An Investigation into the Origins of Modern Civilization*. New York: Ballantine, 2000.

Khanna, Parag. *The Second World: Empires and Influence in the New Global Order*. New York: Random House, 2008.

Kirchner, Julius, and Karl Morrison, eds. *Medieval Europe*. Chicago: University of Chicago Press, 1986.

Kiser, Edgar, and Yong Cai. "War and Bureaucratization in Qin China." *American Sociological Review* 68 (2003), pp. 511–39.

————. "Early Chinese Bureaucratization in Comparative Perspective: Reply to Zhao." *American Sociological Review* 69 (2004), pp. 608–12.

Kislev, Mordechai, et al. "Early Domesticated Fig in the Jordan Valley." *Science* 312 (2006), pp. 1372–74.

Kitchen, Andrew. "Genetic Analysis of Human Head and Clothing Lice Indicates an Early Origin of Clothing Use in Archaic Hominins." Paper delivered at the

79th Annual Meeting of the American Association of Physical Anthropologists, April 2010, *Abstracts of AAPA Poster and Podium Presentations*, p. 154. http://physanth.org/annual-meeting/2010/79th-annual-meeting-2010/2010%20AAPA%20Abstracts.pdf.

Kittler, Ralf, et al. "Molecular Evolution of *Pediculus Humanus* and the Origin of Clothing." *Current Biology* 13 (2003), pp. 1414–17.

Klein, Richard. *The Human Career.* 3rd ed. Chicago: University of Chicago Press, 2009.

Ko, Dorothy. *Cinderella's Sisters: A Revisionist History of Footbinding.* Berkeley: University of California Press, 2007.

Koepke, Nikola, and Joerg Baten. "The Biological Standard of Living in Europe During the Last Two Millennia." *European Review of Economic History* 9 (2005), pp. 61–95.

———. "Agricultural Specialization and Height in Ancient and Medieval Europe." *Explorations in Economic History* 45 (2008), pp. 127–46.

Kohl, Philip. *The Making of Bronze Age Eurasia.* Cambridge, UK: Cambridge University Press, 2007.

Konner, Melvin. *The Tangled Wing: Biological Constraints on the Human Spirit.* 2nd ed. New York: Holt, Reinhart, and Winston, 2002.

Koryakova, Ludmila, and Andrej Epimakhov. *The Urals and Western Siberia in the Bronze and Iron Ages.* Cambridge, UK: Cambridge University Press, 2007.

Kracke, Edward. *Civil Service in Sung China: 960–1076.* Cambridge, MA: Harvard University Press, 1968.

Kramer, Samuel Noah. *The Sumerians.* Chicago: University of Chicago Press, 1963.

Krause, Johannes, et al. "Neanderthals in Central Asia and Siberia." *Nature* 449 (2007a), pp. 902–904.

———. "The Derived FOXP2 Variant of Modern Humans Was Shared with Neanderthals." *Current Biology* 17 (2007b), pp. 1908–12.

———. "The Complete Mitochondrial DNA Genome of an Unknown Hominin from Southern Siberia." *Nature* 64 (2010), pp. 894–97.

Krepinevich, Andrew. *7 Deadly Scenarios: A Military Futurist Explores War in the 21st Century.* New York: Bantam, 2009.

Krepon, Michael. *Better Safe Than Sorry: The Ironies of Living with the Bomb.* Stanford: Stanford University Press, 2008.

Krings, Matthias, et al. "Neanderthal DNA Sequences and the Origin of Modern Humans." *Cell* 90 (1997), pp. 19–30.

Kristiansen, Kristian, and Thomas Larsson. *The Rise of Bronze Age Society.* Cambridge, UK: Cambridge University Press, 2005.

Kron, Geof. "Anthropometry, Physical Anthropology, and the Reconstruction of Ancient Health, Nutrition, and Living Standards." *Historia* 54 (2005), pp. 68–83.

———. "The Use of Housing Evidence as a Possible Index of Social Equality and Prosperity in Classical Greece and Early Industrial England." Forthcoming.

Kuhn, Dieter. *The Age of Confucian Rule: The Song Transformation of China.* Cambridge, MA: Harvard University Press, 2009.

Kühn, Herbert. *On the Track of Prehistoric Man.* New York: Random House, 1955.

Kuhn, Thomas. *The Structure of Scientific Revolutions.* Chicago: University of Chicago Press, 1962.

Kuhrt, Amelie. *The Ancient Near East*. 2 vols. London: Routledge, 1995.

Kuijt, Ian, and Bill Finlayson. "Evidence for Food Storage and Predomestication Granaries 11,000 Years Ago in the Jordan Valley." *Proceedings of the National Academy of Sciences* 106 (2009), doi: 10.1073/pnas.0812764106.

Kulikowski, Michael. *Rome's Gothic Wars: From the Third Century to Alaric*. Cambridge, UK: Cambridge University Press, 2006.

Kuper, Adam. *Anthropology and Anthropologists*. 2nd ed. London: Routledge, 1983.

Kurlantzick, Joshua. *Charm Offensive: How China's Soft Power Is Transforming the World*. New Haven, CT: Yale University Press, 2007.

Kurzweil, Ray. *The Singularity Is Near: When Humans Transcend Biology*. New York: Vintage, 2005.

Kuzmin, Yaroslav. "Chronology of the Earliest Pottery in East Asia." *Antiquity* 80 (2006), pp. 362–71.

Kvavadze, Eliso, and Simon Connor. "*Zelkova Carpinifolia* (Pallas) K. Koch in Holocene Sediments of Georgia—an Indicator of Climatic Optima." *Review of Palaeobotany and Palynology* 133 (2005), pp. 69–89.

Kylander, M., et al. "Refining the Pre-Industrial Atmospheric Pb Isotope Evolution Curve in Europe Using an 8000-Year-Old Peat Core from NW Spain." *Earth and Planetary Science Letters* 240 (2005), pp. 467–85.

Kynge, James. *China Shakes the World: A Titan's Rise and Troubled Future*. New York: Houghton Mifflin, 2006.

Laiou, Angeliki, and Cécile Morrisson, eds. *The Byzantine Economy*. Cambridge, UK: Cambridge University Press, 2007.

Landes, David. *Revolution in Time: Clocks and the Making of the Modern World*. Cambridge, MA: Harvard University Press, 1983.

———. *The Wealth and Poverty of Nations: Why Some Are So Rich and Some Are So Poor*. New York: Norton, 1998.

———. *The Unbound Prometheus: Technological Change 1750 to the Present*. Rev. ed. Cambridge, UK: Cambridge University Press, 2003.

Lane, Kris. *Pillaging the Empire: Piracy in the Americas, 1500–1750*. Armonk, NY: M. E. Sharpe, 1998.

Lane Fox, Robin. *Pagans and Christians*. New York: Harper and Row, 1986.

Langlois, John, ed. *China Under Mongol Rule*. Princeton: Princeton University Press, 1981.

Lanier, Jaron. "One Half of a Manifesto." *The Edge*, 2000 (http://www.edge.org/3rd_culture/lanier/lanier_index.html).

Lapidus, Ira. *A History of Islamic Societies*. 2nd ed. Cambridge, UK: Cambridge University Press, 2002.

Larkin, Philip. *Collected Poems*. New York: Farrar, Straus and Giroux, 2004.

Larsen, Clark. "Biological Changes in Human Populations with Agriculture." *Annual Review of Anthropology* 24 (1995), pp. 185–213.

———. "The Agricultural Revolution as Environmental Catastrophe." *Quaternary International* 150 (2006), pp. 12–20.

Larsen, Mogens, ed. *Power and Propaganda: A Symposium on Ancient Empires*. Copenhagen: Akademisk Forlag, 1979.

Latacz, Joachim. *Troy and Homer*. Oxford: Oxford University Press, 2004.

Latham, Ronald, trans. *Marco Polo: The Travels*. Harmondsworth, UK: Penguin, 1955.

Lattimore, Owen. *Inner Asian Frontiers of China.* New York: American Geographical Society, 1940.

Lau, D. C. *Mencius.* 2nd ed. Harmondsworth, UK: Penguin, 2003.

Leakey, Richard, and Roger Lewin. *The Sixth Extinction: Patterns of Life and the Future of Mankind.* New York: Doubleday, 1995.

LeBlanc, Steven, and Katherine Register. *Constant Battles: Why We Fight.* New York: St. Martin's Press, 2003.

Lee, Gyoung-ah, et al. "Plants and People from the Early Neolithic to Shang Periods in North China." *Proceedings of the National Academy of Sciences* 104 (2007), pp. 1087–92.

Lee, James and Wang Feng. *One Quarter of Humanity: Malthusian Mythology and Chinese Realities.* Cambridge, MA: Harvard University Press, 1999.

Lee, Thomas, ed. *The New and the Multiple: Sung Senses of the Past.* Hong Kong: Chinese University Press, 2004.

Lee, Yun Kuan. "Special Section: The Xia-Shang-Zhou Chronology Project." *Journal of East Asian Archaeology* 4 (2002), pp. 321–86.

Legge, James, ed. *The Chinese Classics* III: *The Shoo King.* London: Trübner, 1865. Repr. Hong Kong: Hong Kong University Press, 1960.

———. *The Chinese Classics* V: *The Ch'un Ts'ew and the Tso Chuen.* London: Trübner, 1872. Repr. Hong Kong: Hong Kong University Press, 1960.

Lehner, Mark. *The Complete Pyramids.* London: Thames and Hudson, 1997.

Le Roy Ladurie, Emmanuel. *The Peasants of Languedoc.* Trans. John Day. Urbana: University of Illinois Press, 1972.

Leslie, D. D., and K. J. H. Gardiner. *The Roman Empire in Chinese Sources.* Rome: Bardi, 1996.

Levathes, Louise. *When China Ruled the Seas: The Treasure Fleet of the Dragon Throne, 1405–1433.* New York: Oxford University Press, 1994.

Lewis, Archibald. *Nomads and Crusaders, A.D. 1000–1368.* Bloomington: Indiana University Press, 1988.

Lewis, Mark. *Sanctioned Violence in Early China.* Albany: State University of New York Press, 1990.

———. *Writing and Authority in Early China.* Albany: State University of New York Press, 1999.

———. *The Early Chinese Empires: Qin and Han.* Cambridge, MA: Harvard University Press, 2007.

———. *China Between Empires: The Northern and Southern Dynasties.* Cambridge, MA: Harvard University Press, 2009a.

———. *China's Cosmopolitan Empire: The Tang Dynasty.* Cambridge, MA: Harvard University Press, 2009b.

Lewis, W. S., ed. *Horace Walpole's Correspondence* I. New Haven, CT: Yale University Press, 1941.

Lewis-Williams, David. *The Mind in the Cave.* London: Thames & Hudson, 2002.

Li, Feng. "Feudalism and the Western Zhou." *Harvard Journal of Asiatic Studies* 63 (2003), pp. 115–44.

———. *Landscape and Power in Early China: The Crisis and Fall of the Western Zhou, 1045–771 BC.* Cambridge, UK: Cambridge University Press, 2006.

———. *Bureaucracy and the State in Early China: Governing the Western Zhou.* Cambridge, UK: Cambridge University Press, 2009.

Li, Xueqin. *Eastern Zhou and Qin Civilization*. New Haven, CT: Yale University Press, 1985.

Li, Xueqin, et al. "The Earliest Writing?" *Antiquity* 77 (2003), pp. 31–44.

Lichtheim, Miriam, ed. *Ancient Egyptian Literature*. 3 vols. Berkeley: University of California Press, 1973–80.

Lieberman, Philip. "The Evolution of Human Speech." *Current Anthropology* 48 (2007), pp. 39–66.

Lieberman, Victor. *Beyond Binary Histories: Re-imagining Eurasia to c. 1830*. Ann Arbor: University of Michigan Press, 1999.

———. *Strange Parallels: Southeast Asia in Global Context, c. 800–1830*. Cambridge, UK: Cambridge University Press, 2003.

Lin, Tai-yi, trans. *Li Ju-chen, Flowers in the Mirror*. Berkeley: University of California Press, 1965.

Lin, Yusheng. *The Crisis of Chinese Consciousness: Radical Antitraditionalism in the May Fourth Era*. Madison: University of Wisconsin Press, 1979.

Little, Lester, ed. *Plague and the End of Antiquity: The Pandemic of 541–750*. Cambridge, UK: Cambridge University Press, 2007.

Liu, Li. "Ancestor Worship: An Archaeological Investigation of Ritual Activities in Neolithic North China." *Journal of East Asian Archaeology* 2 (2000), pp. 129–64.

———. *The Chinese Neolithic*. Cambridge, UK: Cambridge University Press, 2004.

———. "The Emergence of Sedentism in China." In Markus Reindel et al., eds., *Sedentism: Worldwide Research Perspectives for the Shift of Human Societies from Mobile to Settled Ways of Life*. Wiesbaden: Harrassowitz, 2010.

Liu, Li, and Xingcan Chen. *State Formation in Early China*. London: Routledge, 2003.

———. *The Archaeology of China*. Cambridge, UK: Cambridge University Press, 2010.

Liu, Li, and Hong Xu. "Rethinking Erlitou: Legend, History, and Chinese Archaeology." *Antiquity* 81 (2007), pp. 886–91.

Liu, Li, et al. "Evidence for the Early Beginning (c. 9000 cal. BP) of Rice Domestication in China." *The Holocene* 17 (2007), pp. 1059–68.

Liu, Xiaohong, et al. "Dendroclimatic Temperature Record Derived from Tree-Ring Width and Stable Carbon Isotope Chronologies in the Middle Qilian Mountains, China." *Arctic, Antarctic, and Alpine Research* 39 (2007), pp. 651–57.

Liu, Xinru. *Ancient India and Ancient China: Trade and Religious Exchanges 100–600*. Oxford: Oxford University Press, 1988.

Liverani, Mario, ed. *Akkad, the First World Empire*. Padua: Sargon, 1993.

———, ed. *Neo-Assyrian Geography*. Rome: Eisenbrauns, 1995.

———. *International Relations in the Ancient Near East, 1600–1100 BC*. New York: Palgrave, 2001.

———. *Israel's History and the History of Israel*. London: Equinox, 2005.

———. *Uruk: The First City*. London: Equinox, 2006.

Lloyd, Geoffrey. *The Ambitions of Curiosity: Understanding the World in Ancient Greece and China*. Cambridge, UK: Cambridge University Press, 2002.

———. *Cognitive Variations: Reflections on the Unity and Diversity of the Human Mind*. New York: Oxford University Press, 2007.

Lloyd, Geoffrey, and Nathan Sivin. *The Way and the Word: Science and Medicine in Early China and Greece*. New Haven, CT: Yale University Press, 2002.

Lobell, David, and Marshall Burke, eds. *Climate Change and Food Security: Adapting Agriculture to a Warmer World*. Amsterdam: Springer, 2010.

Loewe, Michael. *The Government of the Qin and Han Empires, 221 BCE–220 CE.* Indianapolis: Hackett, 2006.

Lordkipanidze, David, et al. "Postcranial Evidence from Early *Homo* from Dmanisi, Georgia." *Nature* 449 (2007), pp. 305–10.

Lorge, Peter. *War, Politics and Society in Early Modern China, 900–1795.* London: Routledge, 2005.

Loud, G. *The Age of Robert Guiscard: Southern Italy and the Norman Conquest.* London: Longman, 2000.

Lovell, Julia. *The Great Wall: China Against the World, 1000 BC–AD 2000.* London: Atlantic Books, 2006.

Luckenbill, D. D. *Ancient Records of Assyria and Babylonia* I. Chicago: University of Chicago Press, 1926.

Maalouf, Amin. *The Crusades Through Arab Eyes.* New York: Shocken, 1984.

Maas, Michael, ed. *The Cambridge Companion to the Age of Justinian.* Cambridge, UK: Cambridge University Press, 2005.

MacCullagh, Diarmaid. *The Reformation: A History.* New York: Penguin, 2003.

MacFarquhar, Roderick, and Michael Schoenhals. *Mao's Last Revolution.* Cambridge, MA: Harvard University Press, 2006.

MacKellar, Landis. "Pandemic Influenza: A Review." *Population and Development Review* 33 (2007), pp. 429–51.

MacMillan, Margaret. *Paris 1919: Six Months That Changed the World.* New York: Random House, 2002.

———. *Nixon and Mao: The Week That Changed the World.* New York: Random House, 2008.

MacMullen, Ramsay. *Christianizing the Roman Empire.* New Haven, CT: Yale University Press, 1984.

———. *Corruption and the Decline of Rome.* New Haven, CT: Yale University Press, 1988.

Maddison, Angus. *The World Economy: Historical Statistics.* Paris: Organisation for Economic Co-operation and Development, 2003.

———. *Growth and Interaction in the World Economy: The Roots of Modernity.* Washington, DC: American Enterprise Institute Press, 2005.

———. *Asia in the World Economy 1500–2030.* Canberra: Australian National University Press, 2006.

———. *Chinese Economic Performance in the Long Run: 960–2030.* 2nd ed. Paris: Organisation for Economic Co-operation and Development, 2007.

Madelung, Wilferd. *The Succession to Muhammad: A Study in the Early Caliphate.* Cambridge, UK: Cambridge University Press, 1997.

Mair, Victor, ed. *Contact and Exchange in the Ancient World.* Honolulu: University of Hawaii Press, 2006.

Major, Candace, et al. "The Co-Evolution of Black Sea Level and Composition Through Deglaciation and Its Paleoclimatic Significance." *Quaternary Science Reviews* 25 (2006), pp. 2031–47.

Malinowksi, Bronislaw. *A Diary in the Strict Sense of the Term.* New York: Harcourt, Brace, and World, 1967.

Mandelbaum, Michael. *The Case for Goliath: How America Acts as the World's Government in the 21st Century.* New York: Public Affairs, 2005.

Mangini, A., et al. "Reconstruction of Temperature in the Central Alps During the Past 2000 yr from a δ18O Stalagmite Record." *Earth and Planetary Science Letters* 235 (2005), pp. 741–51.

———. "Persistent Influence of the North Atlantic Hydrography on Central European Winter Temperature During the Last 9000 Years." *Geophysical Research Letters* 34 (2007), pp. 10.1029/2006GL028600.

Manica, Andrea, et al. "The Effect of Ancient Population Bottlenecks on Human Phenotypic Variation." *Nature* 448 (2007), pp. 346–48.

Mann, James. *Rise of the Vulcans: The History of Bush's War Cabinet*. New York: Penguin, 2004.

———. *The China Fantasy*. New York: Penguin, 2008.

Manning, J. G., and Ian Morris, eds. *The Ancient Economy: Evidence and Models*. Stanford: Stanford University Press, 2005.

Manz, Beatrice Forbe. *The Rise and Rule of Tamerlane*. Cambridge, UK: Cambridge University Press, 1989.

Marks, Robert. *Tigers, Rice, Silk, and Silt: Environment and Economy in Late Imperial South China*. Cambridge, UK: Cambridge University Press, 1998.

Marshall, Fiona, and Elisabeth Hildebrand. "Cattle Before Crops." *Journal of World Prehistory* 16 (2002), pp. 99–143.

Martin, Geoffrey. *All Possible Worlds: A History of Geographical Thought*. 4th ed. New York: Oxford University Press, 2005.

Martin, Thomas. *Herodotus and Sima Qian: The First Great Historians of Greece and China*. New York: Bedford/St. Martin's, 2009.

Matthew, Donald. *The Norman Kingdom of Sicily*. Cambridge, UK: Cambridge University Press, 1992.

Matthews, John, and David Herbert, eds. *Unifying Geography*. London: Routledge, 2004.

Mattila, Raiji. *The King's Magnates: A Study of the Highest Officials of the Neo-Assyrian Empire*. Helsinki: Neo-Assyrian Text Corpus Project, 2000.

Mattson, Ingrid. *The Story of the Qur'an*. Oxford: Blackwell, 2007.

Maynard-Smith, John, and Richard Dawkins. *The Theory of Evolution*. 3rd ed. Cambridge, UK: Cambridge University Press, 2008.

Mazumdar, Sucheta. *Sugar and Society in China: Peasants, Technology, and the World Market*. Cambridge, MA: Harvard University Press, 1998.

McAnany, Patricia, and Norman Yoffee, eds. *Questioning Collapse: Human Resilience, Ecological Vulnerability, and the Aftermath of Empire*. Cambridge, UK: Cambridge University Press, 2010.

McBrearty, Sally, and Alison Brooks. "The Revolution That Wasn't: New Interpretation of the Origin of Modern Human Behavior." *Journal of Human Evolution* 39 (2000), pp. 453–563.

McClellan, Thomas. "Early Fortifications: The Missing Walls of Jericho." *Baghdader Mitteilungen* 18 (2006), pp. 593–610.

McCormick, Michael. *Origins of the European Economy: Communications and Commerce, AD 300–900*. Cambridge, UK: Cambridge University Press, 2001.

McGilchrist, Iain. *The Master and His Emissary: The Divided Brain and the Making of the Western World*. New Haven: Yale University Press, 2009.

McGrail, Séan. *Boats of the World from the Stone Age to Medieval Times*. Oxford: Oxford University Press, 2004.

McKibben, Bill. *Enough: Staying Human in an Engineered Age.* New York: Times Books, 2003.

———. *Eaarth: Making Life on a Tough New Planet.* New York: Times Books 2010.

McKitterick, Rosamund. *The Early Middle Ages: Europe, 400–1000.* Oxford: Oxford University Press, 2001.

McMullen, David. *State and Scholars in T'ang China.* Cambridge, UK: Cambridge University Press, 1988.

McNeill, William. *Plagues and Peoples.* New York: Viking, 1976.

———. *The Pursuit of Power.* Chicago: University of Chicago Press, 1982.

Mendle, Michael. *The Putney Debates of 1647: The Army, the Levellers and the English State.* Cambridge, UK: Cambridge University Press, 2001.

Menzies, Gavin. *1421: The Year China Discovered the World.* New York: Bantam, 2002.

———. *1434: The Year a Magnificent Chinese Fleet Sailed to Italy and Ignited the Renaissance.* New York: Bantam, 2008.

Merton, Robert. "Priorities in Scientific Discovery: A Chapter in the Sociology of Science." *American Sociological Review* 22 (1957), pp. 635–59.

Meskill, John, ed. *Ch'oe Pu's Diary: A Record of Drifting Across the Sea.* Tucson: University of Arizona Press, 1965.

Michalowski, Piotr. *The Lamentation Over the Destruction of Sumer and Ur.* Winona Lake, IN: Eisenbrauns, 1989.

Millett, Kate. *Sexual Politics.* New York: Abacus, 1970.

Mills, J. V. G., ed. *Ma Huan, "Overall Survey of the Ocean's Shores" [1433].* Cambridge, UK: Cambridge University Press, 1970.

Mills, J. V. G., and Roderich Ptak, eds. *Hsing-Ch'a Sheng-Lan, The Overall Survey of the Star Raft by Fei Hsin.* Wiesbaden: Harrassowitz Verlag, 1996.

Mintz, Sidney. *Sweetness and Power: The Place of Sugar in Modern History.* New York: Viking, 1985.

Mithen, Steven. *The Prehistory of the Mind: The Cognitive Origins of Art and Science.* London: Thames & Hudson, 1996.

———. *After the Ice: A Global Human History, 20,000–5000 BC.* Cambridge, MA: Harvard University Press, 2003.

———. *The Singing Neanderthals: The Origin of Music, Language, Mind and Body.* London: Weidenfeld and Nicholson, 2005.

Mokyr, Joel. *The Lever of Riches: Technological Creativity and Economic Progress.* New York: Oxford University Press, 1990.

———. "Editor's Introduction: The New Economic History and the Industrial Revolution." In Joel Mokyr, ed., *The British Industrial Revolution: An Economic Perspective,* pp. 1–127. Boulder, CO: Westview Press, 1999.

———. *The Gifts of Athena: Historical Origins of the Knowledge Economy.* Princeton: Princeton University Press, 2002.

———. *The Enlightened Economy: An Economic History of Britain, 1700–1850.* New Haven, CT: Yale University Press, 2010.

Momssen, Theodor, and Karl Morrison. *Imperial Lives and Letters of the Eleventh Century.* New York: Columbia University Press, 1962.

Moore, Andrew, Gordon Hillman, and A. J. Legge. *Village on the Euphrates.* New York: Oxford University Press, 2000.

Moore, Gordon. "Cramming More Components onto Integrated Circuits." *Electronics* 38.8 (April 19, 1965), pp. 114–17. Available at ftp://download.intel.com/research/silicon/moorespaper.pdf.

———. "Our Revolution." 1999. Available at http://www.sia-online.org/downloads/Moore.pdf.

———. "No Exponential Is Forever . . . But We Can Delay 'Forever.'" Paper presented at the International Solid State Circuits Conference, February 10, 2003. Available at ftp://download.intel.com/research/silicon/Gordon_Moore_ISSCC_021003.pdf.

Moore, Robert. *The Formation of a Persecuting Society: Power and Deviance in Western Europe, 950–1250.* Oxford: Blackwell, 1987.

———. *The First European Revolution, c. 970–1215.* Oxford: Blackwell, 2000.

Morean, Curtis, et al. "Early Human Use of Marine Resources and Pigment in South Africa During the Middle Pleistocene." *Nature* 449 (2007), pp. 905–908.

Morgan, David. *Medieval Persia 1040–1797.* London: Longman, 1988.

Morgan, Edmund. *American Slavery, American Freedom.* New York: Norton, 1975.

Morgan, Leah, and Paul Renne. "Diachronous Dawn of Africa's Middle Stone Age: New ^{40}Ar/^{39}Ar Ages from the Ethiopian Rift." *Geology* 36 (2008), pp. 967–70.

Morishima, Michio. *Why Has Japan "Succeeded"?* Cambridge, UK: Cambridge University Press, 1982.

Morowitz, Harold. *The Emergence of Everything: How the World Became Complex.* New York: Oxford University Press, 2004.

Morris, Ian. "Economic Growth in Ancient Greece." *Journal of Institutional and Theoretical Economics* 160 (2004), pp. 709–48.

———. "The Athenian Empire (478–404 BC)." Princeton/Stanford Working Papers in Classics no. 120508, 2005. http://www.princeton.edu/~pswpc/index.html.

Morris, Ian, and Barry Powell. *The Greeks: History, Culture, and Society.* 2nd ed. Upper Saddle River, NJ: Prentice-Hall, 2009.

Morris, Ian, and Walter Scheidel, eds. *The Dynamics of Ancient Empires.* New York: Oxford University Press, 2009.

Morris, Ian, and Sebastiano Tusa. "Scavi sull'acropoli di Monte Polizzo, 2000–2003." *Sicilia Archeologica* 38 (2004), pp. 35–90.

Morrison, Karl. *Understanding Conversion.* Charlottesville: University of Virginia Press, 1992.

Morris-Suzuki, Tessa. *The Technological Transformation of Japan: From the Seventeenth to the Twenty-First Century.* New York: Cambridge University Press, 1994.

Morton, Oliver. *Eating the Sun: How Plants Power the Planet.* New York: Harper, 2007.

Morwood, Mike, and Penny van Oostersee. *A New Human: The Startling Discovery and Strange Story of the "Hobbits" of Flores, Indonesia.* New York: Left Coast, 2007.

Mote, Frederick. *Imperial China, 900–1800.* Berkeley: University of California Press, 1999.

Muckle, Peter, trans. *The Story of Abelard's Adversities.* Toronto: Pontifical Institute of Mediaeval Studies, 1964.

Mühlenbock, Christian. *Fragments from a Mountain Society: Tradition, Innovation, and Interaction at Archaic Monte Polizzo, Sicily.* Gothenburg: University of Gothenburg Press, 2008.

Murphey, Rhoads. *Ottoman Warfare.* London: Routledge, 1999.

Mutschler, Fritz-Heiner, and Achim Mittag, eds. *Conceiving the Empire: China and Rome Compared.* New York: Oxford University Press, 2009.

Naam, Ramez. *More Than Human: Embracing the Promise of Biological Enhancement.* New York: Broadway, 2005.

Naquin, Susan, and Evelyn Rawski. *Chinese Society in the Eighteenth Century.* New Haven, CT: Yale University Press, 1987.

Naroll, Raoul. "A Preliminary Index of Social Development." *American Anthropologist* 58 (1956), pp. 687–715.

National Intelligence Council. *Mapping the Global Future.* Washington, DC: Government Printing Office, 2004. Available at http://www.foia.cia.gov/2020/2020 .pdf.

———. *Global Trends 2025: A Transformed World.* Washington, DC: Government Printing Office, 2008. Available at http://www.dni.gov/nic/NIC_2025_project .html.

Naughton, Barry. *Growing Out of the Plan: Chinese Economic Reform, 1978–1993.* Cambridge, UK: Cambridge University Press, 1995.

Needham, Joseph. *Science and Civilisation in China* IV: *Physics and Physical Technology.* Part 3: *Civil Engineering and Nautics.* Cambridge, UK: Cambridge University Press, 1971.

Needham, Joseph, Ho Ping-yü, Lu Gwei-djen, and Wang Ling. *Science and Civilisation in China* V. *Chemistry and Chemical Technology.* Part 7: *Military Technology; The Gunpowder Epic.* Cambridge, UK: Cambridge University Press, 1986.

Neisser, Ulric, ed. *The Rising Curve: Long-Term Gains in IQ and Related Measures.* New York: American Psychological Association, 1998.

Nelson, Sarah. *The Archaeology of Korea.* Cambridge, UK: Cambridge University Press, 1993.

Nichols, F. M. *The Epistles of Erasmus* II. London: Longmans, Green, 1904.

Nicolle, David, Stephen Turnbull, and John Haldon. *The Fall of Constantinople: The Ottoman Conquest of Byzantium.* London: Osprey, 2007.

Nienhauser, William. *The Grand Scribe's Records* I. Bloomington: Indiana University Press, 1994.

Nisbett, Richard. *The Geography of Thought: How Asians and Westerners Think Differently . . . and Why.* New York: Free Press, 2003.

Nixon, Richard. "Asia After Viet Nam." *Foreign Affairs* 46 (1967), pp. 111–45.

Nordhaus, William. "A Review of the *Stern Review* on the Economics of Climate." *Journal of Economic Literature* 45 (2007), pp. 686–702.

Norris, Robert, and Hans Kristensen. "Chinese Nuclear Forces, 2008." *Bulletin of the Atomic Scientists* 64.2 (2008), pp. 42–45.

———. "Worldwide Deployments of Nuclear Weapons, 2009." *Bulletin of the Atomic Scientists* 65.6 (2009a), pp. 74–81.

———. "US Nuclear Warheads, 1945–2009." *Bulletin of the Atomic Scientists* 65.4 (2009b), pp. 72–81.

———. "Russian Nuclear Forces, 2010." *Bulletin of the Atomic Scientists* 66.1 (2010) pp. 74–81.

North, Douglass. *Structure and Change in Economic History.* New York: Norton, 1981.

North, Douglass, John Wallis, and Barry Weingast. *Violence and Social Orders: A Conceptual Framework for Interpreting Recorded Human History.* Cambridge, UK: Cambridge University Press, 2009.

Norton, Christopher, and Kidong Bae. "The Movius Line Sensu Lato (Norton et al., 2006) Further Assessed and Defined." *Journal of Human Evolution* 55 (2008), pp. 1148–50.

Norwich, John Julius. *The Normans in Sicily*. London: Penguin, 1992.

Nur, Amos, and Eric Cline. "Poseidon's Horses: Plate Tectonics and Earthquake Storms in the Late Bronze Age Aegean and Eastern Mediterranean." *Journal of Archaeological Science* 27 (2000), pp. 43–63.

Nylan, Michael, and Michael Loewe, eds. *China's Early Empires: A Re-Appraisal*. Cambridge, UK: Cambridge University Press, 2010.

Ober, Josiah. *Political Dissent in Democratic Athens*. Princeton: Princeton University Press, 1998.

O'Connell, J., and F. Allen. "Dating the Colonization of Sahul (Pleistocene Australia–New Guinea): A Review of Recent Research." *Journal of Archaeological Science* 31 (2004), pp. 835–53.

Oded, B. *Mass Deportations and Deportees in the Neo-Assyrian Empire*. Wiesbaden: Harrassowitz Verlag, 1979.

O'Donnell, James. *The Ruin of the Roman Empire*. New York: Ecco, 2008.

Oppo, Delia, et al. "2,000-Year-Long Temperature and Hydrology Reconstructions from the Indo-Pacific Warm Pool." *Nature* 460 (2009), pp. 1113–16 (doi: 10.1038/nature08233).

Oren, Michael. *Power, Faith, and Fantasy: America in the Middle East, 1776 to the Present*. New York: Norton, 2007.

Ortner, Sherry. "Theory in Anthropology Since the Sixties." *Comparative Studies in Society and History* 26 (1984), pp. 126–66.

Otterbein, Keith. *How War Began*. College Station: Texas A&M University Press, 2004.

Outram, Alan, et al. "The Earliest Horse Harnessing and Milking." *Science* 323 (2009), pp. 1332–35.

Outram, Dorinda. *The Enlightenment*. 2nd ed. Cambridge, UK: Cambridge University Press, 2005.

Overy, Richard. *Why the Allies Won*. New York: Norton, 1995.

Owen, Norman, et al. *The Emergence of Modern Southeast Asia*. Honolulu: University of Hawaii Press, 2005.

Paine, S. C. M. *The Sino-Japanese War of 1894–1895*. Cambridge, UK: Cambridge University Press, 2003.

Palmer, Martin, Elizabeth Breuilly, Chang Wei Ming, and Jay Ramsay. *The Book of Chuang Tzu*. Harmondsworth, UK: Penguin, 2006.

Paludan, Ann. *Chronicle of the Chinese Emperors*. London: Thames & Hudson, 1998.

Pamuk, Sevket. "The Black Death and the Origins of the 'Great Divergence' Across Europe, 1300–1600." *European Review of Economic History* 11 (2007), pp. 289–317.

Papademetriou, Demetrios, and Aaron Terrazas. *Immigrants and the Current Economic Crisis: Research Evidence, Policy Challenges, and Implications*. Washington, DC: Migration Policy Institute, 2009. Available at www.migrationpolicy.org.

Papagrigorakis, Manolis, et al. "DNA Examination of Ancient Dental Pulp Incriminates Typhoid Fever as a Probable Cause of the Plague of Athens." *International Journal of Infectious Diseases* 10 (2006), pp. 206–14.

Parker, A. J. *Ancient Shipwrecks of the Mediterranean and Roman Provinces*. Oxford: British Archaeological Reports, 1992.

Parker, Geoffrey. *The Military Revolution: Military Innovation and the Rise of the West, 1500–1800.* 2nd ed. Cambridge, UK: Cambridge University Press, 1996.

———. *The Thirty Years' War.* 2nd ed. Cambridge, UK: Cambridge University Press, 1997.

———. *The World Is Not Enough: The Imperial Vision of Philip II of Spain.* Waco, TX: Baylor University Press, 2001.

———. *The World Crisis, 1635–1665.* New York: Basic Books, 2009.

Parpola, Simo, ed. *Assyria 1995: Proceedings of the Tenth Anniversary Symposium of the Neo-Assyrian Text Corpus Project.* Helsinki: Neo-Assyrian Text Corpus Project, 1997.

Parsons, Talcott. *Societies: Evolutionary and Comparative Perspectives.* Englewood Cliffs, NJ: Prentice-Hall, 1966.

Patterson, James. *Grand Expectations: The United States, 1945–1974.* New York: Oxford University Press, 1997.

———. *Restless Giant: The United States from Watergate to Bush vs. Gore.* New York: Oxford University Press, 2005.

Pearce, Fred. *When the Rivers Run Dry. Water—the Defining Crisis of the 21st Century.* Boston: Beacon Press, 2007.

———. *With Speed and Violence: Why Scientists Fear Tipping Points in Climate Change.* Boston: Beacon Press, 2008.

Pearce, Scott, Audrey Spiro, and Patricia Ebrey, eds. *Culture and Power in the Reconstitution of the Chinese Realm, 200–600.* Cambridge, MA: Harvard University Press, 2001.

Peng, Ke. "Coinage and Commercial Development in Classical China, 550–221 BC." Unpublished PhD dissertation, University of Chicago, 1999.

Perdue, Peter. *China Marches West: The Qing Conquest of Central Eurasia.* Cambridge, MA: Harvard University Press, 2005.

Perkins, Dwight. *Agricultural Development in China 1368–1968.* Chicago: Aldine, 1969.

Perkovich, George, and Dominick Zaum. *Abolishing Nuclear Weapons.* London: International Institute for Strategic Studies, Adelphi Paper 396, 2008.

Perrin, Noel. *Giving Up the Gun: Japan's Reversion to the Sword, 1543–1879.* Boston: Godine, 1979.

Perry, John, and Bardwell Smith, eds. *Essays on T'ang Society.* Leiden: E. J. Brill, 1976.

Peters, Francis. *Muhammad and the Origins of Islam.* Albany: State University of New York Press, 1994.

Petraglia, Michael, and Ceri Shipton. "Large Cutting Tool Variation West and East of the Movius Line." *Journal of Human Evolution* 55 (2008), pp. 962–66.

Piggott, Joan. *The Emergence of Japanese Kingship.* Stanford: Stanford University Press, 1997.

Pincus, Steve. *1688: The First Modern Revolution.* New Haven: Yale University Press, 2009.

Pines, Yuri. *Foundations of Confucian Thought: Intellectual Life in the Chunqiu Period, 722–453 BCE.* Honolulu: University of Hawaii Press, 2002.

Pinker, Steven. *How the Mind Works.* New York: Norton, 1997.

Pluciennik, Mark. *Social Evolution.* London: Duckworth, 2005.

Pohl, Mary, et al. "Microfossil Evidence for Pre-Columbian Maize Dispersals in the Neotropics from San Andrés, Tabasco, Mexico." *Proceedings of the National Academy of Sciences* 104 (2007), pp. 6870–75.

Pollard, Helen. *Tariacuri's Legacy: The Prehispanic Tarascan State.* Norman: University of Oklahoma Press, 1993.

Pollock, Susan. *Ancient Mesopotamia.* Cambridge, UK: Cambridge University Press, 1999.

Pomeranz, Kenneth. *The Great Divergence: China, Europe, and the Making of the Modern World Economy.* Princeton: Princeton University Press, 2000.

Popper, Karl. *Conjectures and Refutations.* London: Routledge, 1963.

Portal, Jane, ed. *The First Emperor: China's Terracotta Army.* London: British Museum, 2007.

Porter, Andrew, ed. *The Oxford History of the British Empire* III: *The Nineteenth Century.* Oxford: Oxford University Press, 2001.

Porter, Roy, ed. *The Cambridge History of Science* IV: *The Eighteenth Century.* Cambridge, UK: Cambridge University Press, 2003.

Postgate, Nicholas. *Early Mesopotamia: Society and Economy at the Dawn of History.* Cambridge, UK: Cambridge University Press, 1993.

Potts, Dan. *The Archæology of Elam: Formation and Transformation in an Ancient Iranian State.* Cambridge, UK: Cambridge University Press, 1999.

Pourshariati, Parvaneh. *The Decline and Fall of the Sasanian Empire.* London: I. B. Tauris, 2008.

Powell, Adam, Stephen Shennan, and Mark Thomas. "Late Pleistocene Demography and the Appearance of Modern Human Behavior." *Science* 324 (2009), p. 1298 (doi: 10.1126/science.1170165).

Powell, Barry. *Writing: Theory and History of the Technology of Civilization.* Oxford: Blackwell, 2009.

Preston, Diana. *The Boxer Rebellion.* New York: Berkley Books, 1999.

Price, Simon. *Rituals and Power: The Roman Imperial Cult in Asia Minor.* Cambridge, UK: Cambridge University Press, 1984.

Pritchard, James B., ed. *Ancient Near Eastern Texts Relating to the Old Testament.* 3rd ed. Princeton: Princeton University Press, 1969.

Provan, Iain, V. Philips Long, and Tremper Longman. *A Biblical History of Israel.* Louisville, KY: Westminster John Knox Press, 2003.

Puett, Michael. *To Become a God: Cosmology, Sacrifice, and Self-Divinization in Early China.* Cambridge, MA: Harvard University Press, 2002.

Qian, Weihong, and Zhu, Yafen. "Little Ice Age Climate Near Beijing, China, Inferred from Historical and Stalagmite Records." *Quaternary Research* 57 (2002), pp. 109–19.

Qiao, Yu. "Development of Complex Societies in the Yiluo Region: A GIS-Based Population and Agricultural Area Analysis." *Bulletin of the Indo-Pacific Prehistory Association* 27 (2007), pp. 61–75.

Quattrocchi, Angelo, and Tom Nairn. *The Beginning of the End: France, May 1968.* London: Penguin, 1968.

Rawson, Jessica. *Western Zhou Ritual Bronzes from the Arthur M. Sackler Collections.* 2 vols. Cambridge, MA: Harvard University Press, 1990.

Ray, Debraj. *Development Economics.* Princeton: Princeton University Press, 1998.

Razeto, Anna. 2008. "Life in the Ghetto: Urban Living in Han China and the Roman Mediterranean." Unpublished paper delivered at the conference "State Power and Social Control in Ancient China and Rome," Stanford University, March 19, 2008.

Redford, Donald. *Egypt, Canaan, and Israel in Ancient Times.* Princeton: Princeton University Press, 1992.

Renfrew, Colin. *The Archaeology of Cult*. London: British School at Athens, 1985.
————. *Archaeology and Language*. London: Pelican, 1987.
Renfrew, Colin, and Katie Boyle, eds. *Archaeogenetics*. Cambridge, UK: Cambridge University Press, 2000.
Renfrew, Colin, and Iain Morley, eds. *Becoming Human: Innovation in Prehistoric Material and Spiritual Culture*. Cambridge, UK: Cambridge University Press, 2009.
Reynolds, David. *One World Divisible: A Global History Since 1945*. New York: Norton, 2000.
Richards, Jay, et al. *Are We Spiritual Machines? Ray Kurzweil vs. the Critics of Strong A.I.* Seattle: Discovery Institute, 2002.
Richards, John. *Unending Frontier: An Environmental History of the Early Modern World*. Berkeley: University of California Press, 2003.
Richardson, Lewis Fry. *Statistics of Deadly Quarrels*. Pacific Grove, CA: Boxwood Press, 1960.
Richerson, Peter, Robert Boyd, and Robert Bettinger. "Was Agriculture Impossible During the Pleistocene but Mandatory During the Holocene?" *American Antiquity* 66 (2001), pp. 387–411.
Riesman, David. *Abundance for What?* Garden City, NY: Doubleday, 1964.
Rifkin, Jeremy. 1998. *The Biotech Century: Harnessing the Gene and Remaking the World*. New York: Tarcher, 1998.
Riley, James. *Rising Life Expectancy: A Global History*. Cambridge, UK: Cambridge University Press, 2001.
Roberts, Andrew. *The Storm of War: A New History of the Second World War*. London: Allen Lane, 2009.
Roberts, Neil. *The Holocene*. Oxford: Blackwell, 1998.
Robinson, James, ed. *The Emergence of the Modern World: Comparative History and Science*. New York: Cambridge University Press, 2010.
Roco, Mihail, and William Bainbridge. "Converging Technologies for Improving Human Health: Nanotechnology, Biotechnology, Information Technology, and Cognitive Science." Washington, DC: National Science Foundation, 2002 (http://www.wtec.org/ConvergingTechnologies/1/NBIC_report.pdf).
Roetz, Heiner. *Confucian Ethics of the Axial Age*. Albany: State University of New York Press, 1993.
Rogers, Clifford, ed. *The Military Revolution Debate*. Boulder, CO: Westview Press, 1995.
Rose, Steven. *The Future of the Brain: The Promise and Perils of Tomorrow's Neuroscience*. Oxford: Oxford University Press, 2006.
Rosen, Arlene. "The Role of Environmental Change in the Development of Complex Societies in Early China." *Bulletin of the Indo-Pacific Prehistory Association* 27 (2007), pp. 39–48.
Rosen, Stanley. *Justinian's Flea: Plague, Empire, and the Birth of Europe*. New York: Viking, 2007.
Rosenfeld, Gavriel. *The World Hitler Never Made*. Cambridge, UK: Cambridge University Press, 2005.
Ross, James Bruce and Mary Martin McLaughlin, eds. *The Portable Renaissance Reader*. New York: Penguin, 1953.
Rossabi, Morris. *Khubilai Khan: His Life and Times*. Berkeley: University of California Press, 1988.

Rothman, Mitchell, ed. *Uruk Mesopotamia and Its Neighbors*. Santa Fe, NM: School of American Research, 2001.

Rowe, William. *Saving the World: Chen Hongmou and Elite Consciousness in Eighteenth-Century China*. Stanford: Stanford University Press, 2001.

———. *China's Last Empire: The Great Qing*. Cambridge, MA: Harvard University Press, 2009.

Rozman, Gilbert. *Urban Networks in Ching China and Tokugawa Japan*. Princeton: Princeton University Press, 1973.

Runciman, Steven. *The Fall of Constantinople, 1453*. Cambridge, UK: Cambridge University Press, 1990.

Russell, Peter. *Prince Henry "The Navigator": A Life*. New Haven, CT: Yale University Press, 2000.

Ryan, William, and Walter Pitman. *Noah's Flood*. New York: Simon and Schuster, 1999.

Sagan, Scott, and Steven Miller, eds. *The Global Nuclear Future. Daedalus* 138.4 (2009), pp. 7–171, and 139.1 (2010), pp. 7–140. Cambridge, MA: MIT Press.

Sahlins, Marshall. "La première société d'abondance." *Les temps modernes* 268 (1968), pp. 641–80.

———. *Stone Age Economics*. Chicago: Aldine, 1972.

———. *Culture in Practice*. New York: Zone Books, 2005.

Sakharov, Andrei. "The Danger of Thermonuclear War." *Foreign Affairs* 61 (1983), pp. 1001–1016.

Saliba, George. *Islamic Science and the Making of the European Renaissance*. Cambridge, MA: Harvard University Press, 2007.

Sallares, Robert. 2007. "Ecology." In Walter Scheidel et al., eds., *The Cambridge Economic History of the Greco-Roman World*, pp. 15–37. Cambridge, UK: Cambridge University Press, 2007.

Saller, Richard. "Framing the Debate on the Ancient Economy." In J. G. Manning and Ian Morris, eds., *The Ancient Economy*, pp. 223–38. Stanford: Stanford University Press, 2005.

Sanchez-Mazas, Alicia, ed. *Past Human Migrations in East Asia: Matching Archaeology, Linguistics, and Genetics*. London: Routledge, 2008.

Sandbrook, Dominic. *Never Had It So Good: A History of Britain from Suez to the Beatles*. London: Abacus, 2005.

Sanderson, Stephen. *Evolutionism and Its Critics*. Boulder, CO: Westview Press, 2007.

Sarris, Peter. "The Justinianic Plague: Origins and Effects." *Continuity and Change* 17 (2002), pp. 169–82.

———. *Economy and Society in the Age of Justinian*. Cambridge, UK: Cambridge University Press, 2006.

Savage-Rumbaugh, Sue, and Roger Lewin. *Kanzi: The Ape at the Brink of the Human Mind*. New York: Wiley, 1994.

Savolainen, Peter, et al. "Genetic Evidence for an East Asian Origin of Domestic Dogs." *Science* 298 (2002), pp. 1610–13.

Saxenian, AnnaLee. *Regional Advantage: Culture and Competition in Silicon Valley and Route 128*. Cambridge, MA: Harvard University Press, 1994.

Scheidel, Walter. *Death on the Nile: Disease and the Demography of Roman Egypt*. Leiden: E. J. Brill, 2001.

———. "A Model of Demographic and Economic Change in Roman Egypt After the Antonine Plague." *Journal of Roman Archaeology* 15 (2002), pp. 97–114.

———. "A Model of Real Income Growth in Roman Italy." *Historia* 56 (2007), pp. 322–46.

———. "Real Wages in Ancient and Medieval Economies: Evidence for Living Standards from 2000 BCE to 1300 CE," 2008. http://www.princeton.edu/~pswpc/index.html.

———, ed. *Rome and China: Comparative Perspectives on Ancient World Empires*. New York: Oxford University Press, 2009a.

———. "The Monetary Systems of the Han and Roman Empires." In Walter Scheidel, ed., *Rome and China*, pp. 137–207. New York: Oxford University Press, 2009b.

———. "In Search of Roman Economic Growth." *Journal of Roman Archaeology* 22, 2009c, pp. 46–70.

———. "Studying the State." In Peter Bang and Walter Scheidel, eds., *The Oxford Handbook to the Ancient State*. Oxford: Oxford University Press, forthcoming.

Scheidel, Walter, Ian Morris, and Richard Saller, eds. *The Cambridge Economic History of the Greco-Roman World*. Cambridge, UK: Cambridge University Press, 2007.

Schettler, G., and R. Romer. "Atmospheric Pb-Pollution by Pre-Medieval Mining Detected in the Sediments of the Brackish Karst Lake An Loch Mor, Western Ireland." *Applied Geochemistry* 21 (2006), pp. 58–82.

Schmandt-Besserat, Denise. "'Ain Ghazal 'Monumental' Figures." *Bulletin of the American Schools of Oriental Research* 310 (1998), pp. 1–17.

Scholz, Christopher, et al. "East African Megadroughts Between 135 and 75 Thousand Years Ago and Bearing on Early-Modern Human Origins." *Proceedings of the National Academy of Sciences* 104 (2007), pp. 16416–21.

Schram, Stuart. *The Political Thought of Mao Tse-Tung*. New York: Praeger, 1969.

Schwartz, Benjamin. *The World of Thought in Ancient China*. Cambridge, MA: Harvard University Press, 1985.

Schwartz, Benjamin, ed. *Wisdom, Revelation, and Doubt: Perspectives on the First Millennium BC*. Special edition of *Daedalus*, spring 1975.

Schwartz, Glenn, ed. *After Collapse*. Tucson: University of Arizona Press, 2006.

Service, Elman. *Primitive Social Organization*. 1st ed. New York: Random House, 1962.

Shang, Hong, et al. "An Early Modern Human Tooth from Tianyuan Cave, Zhoukoudian, China." *Proceedings of the National Academy of Sciences* 104 (2007), pp. 6573–78.

Shankman, Steven, and Stephen Durant, eds. *The Siren and the Sage: Knowledge and Wisdom in Ancient Greece and China*. London: Cassell, 2000.

Shanks, Michael, and Christopher Tilley. *Social Theory and Archaeology*. Cambridge: Polity Press, 1987.

Shapin, Steve. 1994. *A Social History of Truth: Credibility and Science in Seventeenth-Century England*. Chicago: University of Chicago Press, 1994.

———. *The Scientific Revolution*. Chicago: University of Chicago Press, 1996.

Shapiro, Judith. *Mao's War Against Nature: Politics and the Environment in Revolutionary China*. Cambridge, UK: Cambridge University Press, 2001.

Shaughnessy, Edward. "Historical Perspectives on the Introduction of the Chariot into China." *Harvard Journal of Asiatic Studies* 48 (1988), pp. 189–237.

———. *Sources of Western Zhou History: Inscribed Bronze Vessels*. Berkeley: University of California Press, 1991.

————. *Before Confucius: Studies in the Creation of the Chinese Classics*. Albany: State University of New York Press, 1997.

Shaw, Brent. "Seasons of Death: Aspects of Mortality in Imperial Rome." *Journal of Roman Studies* 86 (1996), pp. 100–138.

Sheehan, James. *Where Have All the Soldiers Gone?* Boston: Houghton Mifflin, 2008.

Shelmerdine, Cynthia, ed. *The Cambridge Companion to the Aegean Bronze Age*. Cambridge, UK: Cambridge University Press, 2008.

Shen, Guanjen, et al. "U-Series Dating of Liujiang Hominid Site in Guangxi, Southern China." *Journal of Human Evolution* 43 (2002), pp. 817–29.

————. "Mass Spectrometric U-Series Dating of Liabin Hominid Site in Guangxi, Southern China." *Journal of Archaeological Science* 34 (2007), pp. 2109–14.

Shiba, Yoshinobu, and Mark Elvin. *Commerce and Society in Sung China*. Ann Arbor: University of Michigan Press, 1970.

Shklovskii, Iosif, and Carl Sagan. *Intelligent Life in the Universe*. San Francisco: Holden-Day, 1966.

Shlaes, Amity. *The Forgotten Man: A New History of the Great Depression*. New York: HarperCollins, 2007.

Short, Philip. *Mao: A Life*. New York: Owl Books, 1999.

Sim, May. *Remastering Morals with Aristotle and Confucius*. Cambridge, UK: Cambridge University Press, 2007.

Simms, Brendan. *Three Victories and a Defeat: The Rise and Fall of the First British Empire*. New York: Basic Books, 2008.

Sing, Chew. *The Recurring Dark Ages*. Walnut Creek, CA: AltaMira Press, 2007.

Singer, P. W. *Wired for War: The Robotics Revolution and Conflict in the 21st Century*. New York: Penguin, 2009.

Sivin, Nathan. "Why the Scientific Revolution Did Not Take Place in China—Or Didn't It?" *Chinese Science* 5 (1982), pp. 45–66.

Slicher van Bath, B. H. *The Agrarian History of Western Europe, AD 500–1850*. London: Arnold, 1963.

Smelser, Neil, and Richard Swedberg, eds. *The Handbook of Economic Sociology*. 2nd ed. New York: Russell Sage Foundation, 2005.

Smil, Vaclav. *General Energetics: Energy in the Biosphere and Civilization*. New York: Wiley, 1991.

————. *Energy in World History*. Boulder, CO: Westview Press, 1994.

————. *Creating the Twentieth Century: Technical Innovations of 1867–1914 and Their Lasting Impact*. New York: Oxford University Press, 2005.

————. *Transforming the Twentieth Century: Technical Innovations and Their Consequences*. New York: Oxford University Press, 2006.

————. *Global Catastrophes and Trends: The Next Fifty Years*. Cambridge, MA: MIT Press, 2008.

————. *Why America Is Not a New Rome*. Cambridge, MA: MIT Press, 2010.

Smith, Adam. "Writing at Anyang." Unpublished PhD dissertation, University of California–Los Angeles, 2008.

Smith, Dennis. *Japan Since 1945: The Rise of an Economic Superpower*. London: St. Martin's Press, 1995.

Smith, Grafton Elliot. *The Migrations of Early Culture*. Manchester, UK: Manchester University Press, 1915.

Smith, Michael. *The Aztecs*. 2nd ed. Oxford: Blackwell, 2003.

Smith, Paul. *Taxing Heaven's Storehouse: Bureaucratic Entrepreneurship and the Sichuan Tea and Horse Trade, 1074–1224*. Cambridge, MA: Harvard University Press, 1991.

———. "Do We Know as Much as We Need to About the Song Economy? Observations on the Economic Crisis of the Twelfth and Thirteenth Centuries." *Journal of Sung-Yuan Studies* 24 (1994), pp. 327–33.

Smith, Paul, and Richard von Glahn, eds. *The Song-Yuan-Ming Transition in Chinese History*. Cambridge, MA: Harvard University Press, 2003.

Smith, Richard. *Chinese Maps: Images of "All Under Heaven."* New York: Oxford University Press, 1996.

Snell, Daniel, ed. *A Companion to the Ancient Near East*. Oxford: Blackwell, 2007.

So, Jenny. *Eastern Zhou Ritual Bronzes from the Arthur M. Sackler Collections*. Washington, DC: Smithsonian Institution, 1995.

So, Kwan-wai. *Japanese Piracy in Ming China During the 16th Century*. East Lansing: Michigan State University Press, 1975.

Spence, Jonathan. *Emperor of China: Self-Portrait of K'ang-hsi*. New York: Vintage, 1974.

———. *The Memory Palace of Matteo Ricci*. New York: Penguin, 1983.

———. *The Search for Modern China*. New York: Norton, 1990.

———. *God's Chinese Son*. New York: Norton, 1996.

Spencer, Herbert. "Progress: Its Law and Cause." *Westminster Review* 67 (1857), pp. 445–85.

Stark, Miriam, ed. *Archaeology of Asia*. Oxford: Blackwell, 2006.

Stathakopoulos, Dionysios. *Famine and Pestilence in the Late Roman and Early Byzantine Empire*. Burlington, VT: Ashgate, 2004.

Steffens, Lincoln. *The Letters of Lincoln Steffens* I. New York: Harcourt, Brace, & Co., 1938.

Steinhardt, Paul, and Neil Turok. *Endless Universe: Beyond the Big Bang*. New York: Broadway Books, 2007.

Stern, Nicholas. *The Economics of Climate Change: The Stern Review*. Cambridge, UK: Cambridge University Press, 2006. Available at http://www.occ.gov.uk/activities/stern.htm.

Stevens, Carol. *Soldiers on the Steppe: Army Reform and Social Change in Early Modern Russia*. DeKalb: Northern Illinois University Press, 1995.

Stevenson, David. *Cataclysm: The First World War as Political Tragedy*. New York: Basic Books, 2004.

Stewart, Larry. *The Rise of Public Science*. Cambridge, UK: Cambridge University Press, 1992.

Stigler, Stephen. "Stigler's Law of Eponymy." In Thomas Gieryn, ed., *Science and Social Structure*, pp. 147–57. New York: New York Academy of Sciences, 1980.

Strachan, Hew. *The First World War*. New York: Penguin, 2005.

Strassberg, Richard. "Trying On Glasses." In Ronald Pittis and Susan Henders, eds., *Macao: Mysterious Decay and Romance*, pp. 204–205. Hong Kong: Oxford University Press, 1997.

Strauss, Barry. *The Trojan War*. New York: Simon and Schuster, 2006.

Struve, Lynn. *Voices from the Ming-Qing Cataclysm*. New Haven, CT: Yale University Press, 1993.

———, ed. *The Qing Formation in World-Historical Time*. Cambridge, MA: Harvard University Press, 2004.

Subrahmanyam, Sanjay. "The Birth-Pangs of Portuguese Asia: Revisiting the Fateful 'Long Decade,' 1498–1509." *Journal of Global History* 2 (2007), pp. 261–80.

Sugihara, Kaoru. "The East Asian Path of Economic Development: A Long-Term Perspective." In Giovanni Arrighi, Takeshi Hamashita, and Mark Selden, eds., *The Resurgence of East Asia: 500, 150, and 50 Year Perspectives*, pp. 78–123. New York: Routledge, 2003.

Sunstein, Cass. *Worst-Case Scenarios*. Cambridge, MA: Harvard University Press, 2007.

Swain, Carol, ed. *Debating Immigration*. Cambridge, UK: Cambridge University Press, 2007.

Swope, Kenneth. "Crouching Tigers, Secret Weapons: Military Technology Employed During the Sino-Japanese-Korean War, 1592–1598." *Journal of Military History* 69 (2005), pp. 11–42.

———. *A Dragon's Head and a Serpent's Tail: Ming China and the First Great East Asian War, 1592–1598*. Norman: University of Oklahoma Press, 2009.

Sypeck, Jeff. *Becoming Charlemagne: Europe, Baghdad, and the Empires of A.D. 800*. New York: Harper, 2006.

Tetlock, Philip, and Aaron Belkin, eds. *Counterfactual Thought Experiments in World Politics*. Princeton: Princeton University Press, 1996.

Tetlock, Philip, Richard Ned Lebow, and Geoffrey Parker, eds. *Unmaking the West: "What-If" Scenarios That Rewrite World History*. Ann Arbor: University of Michigan Press, 2006.

Thomas, Chris, et al. "Extinction Risk from Climate Change." *Nature* 427 (2004), pp. 145–48.

Thompson, E. P. *The Making of the English Working Class*. London: Penguin, 1963.

———. *Customs in Common: Studies in Traditional Popular Culture*. London: Merlin, 1991.

Thomson, R. W. *The Armenian History Attributed to Sebeos*. Liverpool, UK: Liverpool University Press, 1999.

Thorp, Robert. *China in the Early Bronze Age*. Philadelphia: University of Pennsylvania Press, 2006.

Tillman, Hoyt, and Stephen West, eds. *China Under Jurchen Rule*. Albany: State University of New York Press, 1995.

Tilly, Charles. *Coercion, Capital, and European States, AD 990–1990*. Oxford: Blackwell, 1992.

Tocheri, Matthew, et al. "The Primitive Wrist of *Homo floresiensis* and Its Implications for Hominin Evolution." *Science* 317 (2007), pp. 1743–45.

Toon, O., et al. "Environmental Perturbations Caused by the Impact of Asteroids and Comets." *Review of Geophysics* 35 (1997), pp. 41–78.

Tooze, Adam. *The Wages of Destruction: The Making and Breaking of the Nazi Economy*. New York: Penguin, 2006.

Torr, Dona, ed. *Marx on China, 1855–1860: Articles from the "New York Daily Tribune."* London: Lawrence & Wishart, 1951.

Totman, Conrad. *Early Modern Japan*. Berkeley: University of California Press, 1993.

———. *A History of Japan*. Oxford: Blackwell, 2000.

Tracy, James, ed. *The Rise of Merchant Empires: Long-Distance Trade in the Early Modern World, 1350–1750*. Cambridge, UK: Cambridge University Press, 1990.

———, ed. *The Political Economy of Merchant Empires*. Cambridge, UK: Cambridge University Press, 1991.

———. *The Founding of the Dutch Republic: War, Finance, and Politics in Holland, 1572–1588.* Oxford: Oxford University Press, 2008.

Trigger, Bruce. *A History of Archaeological Thought.* 2nd ed. Cambridge, UK: Cambridge University Press, 1995.

———. *Sociocultural Evolution.* Oxford: Blackwell, 1998.

Trimble, Jennifer. *Replicating Women in the Roman Empire.* Cambridge, UK: Cambridge University Press, 2009.

Tsai, Shih-shan. *Perpetual Happiness: The Ming Emperor Yongle.* Seattle: University of Washington Press, 2001.

Tsunoda, Ryusaku, William de Bary, and Donald Keene, trans. *Sources of Japanese Tradition.* 2 vols. New York: Columbia University Press, 1964.

Tuchmann, Barbara. *The Guns of August.* London: Macmillan, 1962.

———. *A Distant Mirror: The Calamitous Fourteenth Century.* New York: Ballantine, 1978.

———. *The March of Folly: From Troy to Vietnam.* New York: Ballantine, 1984.

Turchin, Peter. "A Theory for Formation of Large Empires." *Journal of Global History* 4 (2009), pp. 191–217.

Twain, Mark. *Autobiography* I. New York: Harper, 1924.

Twitchett, Denis. "Population and Pestilence in T'ang China." In Wolfgang Bauer, ed., *Studia Sino-Mongolica: Festschrift für Herbert Franke*, pp. 35–68. Wiesbaden: Harrassowitz Verlag, 1979.

Twitchett, Denis, and Michael Loewe, eds. *The Cambridge History of China*, vol. 1. Cambridge, UK: Cambridge University Press, 1986.

Tyerman, Christopher. *God's War: A New History of the Crusades.* Cambridge, MA: Harvard University Press, 2006.

Uglow, Jenny. *The Lunar Men.* New York: Farrar, Straus and Giroux, 2002.

Underhill, Anne, et al. "Regional Survey and the Development of Complex Societies in Southeast Shandong, China." *Antiquity* 76 (2002), pp. 745–55.

Underhill, Peter, et al. "The Phylogeography of Y Chromosome Binary Haplotypes and the Origins of Modern Human Populations." *American Journal of Human Genetics* 65 (2001), pp. 43–62.

United Nations Human Development Programme. *Human Development Report 2009. Overcoming Barriers: Human Mobility and Development.* New York: United Nations Development Programme, 2009. http://hdr.undp.org/en/.

United Nations Organization. *2003 Energy Statistics Yearbook.* New York: United Nations Organization, 2006.

Upton, Anthony. *Europe, 1600–1789.* London: Arnold, 2001.

Ur, Jason, et al. "Early Urban Development in the Near East." *Science* 317 (2007), pp. 1188–89.

Vanaeren, Marian, et al. "Middle Paleolithic Shell Beads in Israel and Algeria." *Science* 312 (2006), pp. 1785–88.

van Bavel, Bas, and Jan Luiten van Zanden. "The Jump-Start of the Holland Economy During the Late-Medieval Crisis, c. 1350–c. 1500." *Economic History Review* 57 (2004), pp. 502–32.

van Creveld, Martin. *The Rise and Decline of the State.* Cambridge, UK: Cambridge University Press, 1999.

van de Mieroop, Marc. *A History of the Ancient Near East.* 2nd ed. Oxford: Blackwell, 2007.

van Zanden, Jan Luiten. "The 'Revolt of the Early Modernists' and the 'First Modern Economy': An Assessment." *Economic History Review* 55 (2002), pp. 619–41.

Verhulst, Adriaan. *The Carolingian Economy.* Cambridge, UK: Cambridge University Press, 2002.

Vermeij, Geert. *Nature: An Economic History.* Princeton: Princeton University Press, 2004.

Voight, Benjamin, et al. "A Map of Recent Positive Selection in the Human Genome." *Public Library of Science Biology* 4 (2006), e72.

von Däniken, Erich. *Chariots of the Gods? Was God an Astronaut?* New York: Putnam's, 1968.

von Falkenhausen, Lothar. *Suspended Music: Chime Bells in the Culture of Bronze Age China.* Berkeley: University of California Press, 1993a.

———. "On the Historiographical Orientation of Chinese Archaeology." *Antiquity* 67 (1993b), pp. 839–49.

———. *Chinese Society in the Age of Confucius (1000–250 BC): The Archaeological Evidence.* Los Angeles: Cotsen Institute of Archaeology, 2006.

von Glahn, Richard. *The Country of Streams and Grottoes: Expansion, Settlement, and the Civilizing of the Sichuan Frontier in Song Times.* Cambridge, MA: Harvard University Press, 1987.

———. *Fountain of Fortune: Money and Monetary Policy in China, 1000–1700.* Berkeley: University of California Press, 1996.

———. "Revisiting the Song Monetary Revolution." *International Journal of Asian Studies* 1 (2004), pp. 159–78.

von Verschuer, Charlotte. *Across the Perilous Sea: Japanese Trade with China and Korea from the Seventh to the Sixteenth Centuries.* Ithaca, NY: Cornell University Press, 2006.

Voth, Hans-Joachim. "The Longest Years: New Estimates of Labor Inputs in England, 1760–1830." *Journal of Economic History* 61 (2001), pp. 1065–82.

Wagner, Donald. *Iron and Steel in Ancient China.* Leiden: E. J. Brill, 1993.

———. "The Administration of the Iron Industry in Eleventh-Century China." *Journal of the Economic and Social History of the Orient* 44 (2001a), pp. 175–97.

———. "Blast Furnaces in Song-Yuan China." *East Asian Science, Technology, and Medicine* 18 (2001b), pp. 41–74.

———. *The State and the Iron Industry in Han China.* Copenhagen: Nordic Institute of Asian Studies, 2001c.

———. *Science and Civilisation in China V. Chemistry and Chemical Technology.* Part 11: *Ferrous Metallurgy.* Cambridge, UK: Cambridge University Press, 2008.

Walder, Andrew. *Fractured Rebellion: The Beijing Red Guard Movement.* Cambridge, MA: Harvard University Press, 2009.

Waley, Arthur. *The Book of Songs.* New York: Houghton Mifflin, 1937.

———. "The Fall of Lo-yang." *History Today* 1 (1951), pp. 7–10.

———. *The Opium War Through Chinese Eyes.* London: George Allen & Unwin, 1958.

———. *Chinese Poems.* London: Unwin, 1961.

Waley, Daniel. *The Italian City-Republics.* 3rd ed. London: Weidenfeld and Nicolson, 1988.

Walker, Paul. *Exploring an Islamic Empire: Fatimid History and its Sources.* London: I. B. Tauris, 2002.

Walmsley, Alan. *Early Islamic Syria.* London: Routledge, 2007.

Wang, Eric, et al. "Recent Acceleration of Human Adaptive Evolution." *Proceedings of the National Academy of Sciences* 104 (2007), pp. 20753–58.

Wang, Gungwu. *Divided China: Preparing for Reunification, 883–947.* Singapore: National University of Singapore University, 2007.

Wang, Mingke. "From the Qiang Barbarians to the Qiang Nationality: The Making of a New Chinese Boundary." In Shu-min Huang and Cheng-kuang Hsu, eds., *Imagining China: Regional Division and National Unity*, pp. 43–80. Taipei: Academica Sinica, 1999.

Wang, Xiaoqing. "The Upper Paleolithic Longwangcan Site at Yichuan in Shaanxi." *Chinese Archaeology* 8 (2008), pp. 32–36.

Wang, Zhongshu. *Han Civilization.* New Haven, CT: Yale University Press, 1982.

Ward, Steven, and Erik Asphaug. "Asteroid Impact Tsunami: A Probabilistic Hazard Assessment." *Icarus* 145 (2000), pp. 64–78.

Ward-Perkins, Bryan. *The Fall of Rome and the End of Civilization.* Oxford: Oxford University Press, 2005.

Watson, Andrew. *Agricultural Innovation in the Early Islamic World.* Cambridge, UK: Cambridge University Press, 1982.

Watson, Burton. *The Tso Chuan.* New York: Columbia University Press, 1989.

———. *Records of the Grand Historian: Han Dynasty* I. Rev. ed. New York: Columbia University Press, 1993.

Webb, Stephen. *If the Universe Is Teeming with Aliens . . . Where is Everybody? Fifty Solutions to Fermi's Paradox and the Problem of Extraterrestrial Life.* New York: Springer, 2002.

Weber, Max. *The Protestant Ethic and the Spirit of Capitalism.* New York: Scribner's, 1958. First published in German, 1905.

Weinberg, Gerhard. *A World at Arms: A Global History of World War II.* 2nd ed. Cambridge, UK: Cambridge University Press, 2005.

Weiss, Harvey, et al. "The Genesis and Collapse of North Mesopotamian Civilization." *Science* 261 (1993), pp. 995–1004.

Wells, Spencer. *Pandora's Seed: The Unforeseen Cost of Civilization.* New York: Random House, 2010.

Wengrow, David. *The Archaeology of Early Egypt.* Cambridge, UK: Cambridge University Press, 2006.

Wertime, Theodore, and James Muhly, eds. *The Coming of the Age of Iron.* New Haven, CT: Yale University Press, 1980.

Westad, Odd Arne. *The Global Cold War.* Cambridge, UK: Cambridge University Press, 2005.

Wheeler, Mortimer. *Still Digging: Adventures in Archaeology.* London: Pan, 1955.

White, Leslie. *The Science of Culture.* New York: Farrar, Straus, 1949.

White, Richard. *"It's Your Misfortune and None of My Own": A New History of the American West.* 2nd ed. Norman: University of Oklahoma Press, 1993.

Whittaker, C. R. *Frontiers of the Roman Empire.* Baltimore: Johns Hopkins University Press, 1994.

Whittow, Mark. *The Making of Byzantium, 600–1025.* Berkeley: University of California Press, 1996.

Wickham, Chris. *Framing the Early Middle Ages: Europe and the Mediterranean 400–800.* Oxford: Oxford University Press, 2005.

————. *The Inheritance of Rome: Illuminating the Dark Ages, 400–1000.* New York: Viking, 2009.

Wiesner-Hanks, Merry. *Early Modern Europe 1450–1789.* Cambridge, UK: Cambridge University Press, 2006.

Wilhelm, Gernot. *The Hurrians.* Warminster, UK: Aris and Philips, 1989.

Wilkinson, Toby. *Genesis of the Pharaohs.* London: Routledge, 2003.

Willcox, George, et al. "Early Holocene Cultivation Before Domestication in Northern Syria." *Vegetation History and Archaeobotany* 17 (2008), pp. 313–25.

Williams, Michael. *Deforesting the Earth.* Chicago: University of Chicago Press, 2003.

Wills, John. *1688: A Global History.* New York: Norton, 2002.

Wilson, Andrew. "Indicators for Roman Economic Growth." *Journal of Roman Archaeology* 22, 2009, pp. 46–61.

Wilson, Dominic, and Anna Stupnytska. *The N-11: More Than an Acronym.* Goldman Sachs Global Economics Paper no. 153, March 28, 2007. Available at https://portal.gs.com.

Wilson, Edward O. *Sociobiology: The New Synthesis.* 25th anniversary ed. Cambridge MA: Harvard University Press, 2000.

Wilson, Peter. *The Thirty Years War: Europe's Tragedy.* Cambridge, MA: Harvard University Press, 2009.

Winchester, Simon. *The Man Who Loved China.* New York: Harper, 2008.

Witakowski, Witold. *Pseudo-Dionysius of Tel-Mahre,* Chronicle III. Liverpool: Liverpool University Press, 1996.

Wolpoff, Milford. *Human Evolution.* New York: McGraw-Hill, 1996.

Wolpoff, Milford, and Rachel Caspari. *Race and Human Evolution: A Fatal Attraction.* New York: Simon and Schuster, 2002.

Wong, Bin. *China Transformed: Historical Change and the Limits of European Experience.* Ithaca, NY: Cornell University Press, 1997.

Wood, Frances. *The Silk Road: Two Thousand Years in the Heart of Asia.* Berkeley: University of California Press, 2002.

Wood, James. "A Theory of Preindustrial Population Dynamics." *Current Anthropology* 39 (1998), pp. 99–135.

Woodhouse, A. S. P., ed. *Puritanism and Liberty.* Chicago: University of Chicago Press, 1938.

Wozniak, Steve, and Gina Smith. *iWoz: Computer Geek to Cult Icon.* New York: Norton, 2007.

Wrangham, Richard. *Catching Fire: How Cooking Made Us Human.* New York: Basic Books, 2009.

Wright, Arthur. *The Sui Dynasty: The Unification of China, AD 581–617.* New York: Knopf, 1978.

Wright, Arthur, and Denis Twitchett, eds. *Perspectives on the T'ang.* New Haven, CT: Yale University Press, 1973.

Wrigley, E. A. *Continuity, Chance, and Change: The Character of the Industrial Revolution in England.* Cambridge, UK: Cambridge University Press, 2000.

Wu, Hung. *Monumentality in Early Chinese Art and Architecture.* Stanford: Stanford University Press, 1995.

Xie, C. Z., et al. "Evidence of Ancient DNA Reveals the First European Lineage in Iron Age Central China." *Proceedings of the Royal Society B: Biological Sciences* 274 (2007), pp. 1597–1601.

Xiong, Victor. *Sui-Tang Chang'an: A Study in the Urban History of Medieval China*. Ann Arbor: University of Michigan Press, 2000.

———. *Emperor Yang of the Sui Dynasty*. Albany: State University of New York Press, 2006.

Yamada, Shigeo. *The Construction of the Assyrian Empire*. Leiden: E. J. Brill, 2000.

Yang, B., et al. "General Characteristics of Temperature Variation in China During the Last Two Millennia." *Geophysical Research Letters* 29 (2002), 10.1029/2001GL014485.

Yang, Liensheng. "Notes on the Economic History of the Chin [Jin] Dynasty." In Liensheng Yang, *Studies in Chinese Institutional History*, pp. 119–97. Cambridge, MA: Harvard University Press, 1961.

Yang, Xiaoneng, ed. *New Perspectives on China's Past: Chinese Archaeology in the Twentieth Century*. 2 vols. New Haven, CT: Yale University Press, 2004.

Yanko-Hombach, Virginia, et al., eds. *The Black Sea Flood Question: Changes in Coastline, Climate, and Human Settlement*. Leiden: E. J. Brill, 2007.

Yates, Robin, et al. *Military Culture in Imperial China*. Cambridge, MA: Harvard University Press, 2009.

Yergin, Daniel. *The Prize: The Epic Quest for Oil, Money, and Power*. New York: Free Press, 1992.

Yergin, Daniel, and Joseph Stanislaw. *The Commanding Heights: The Battle for the World Economy*. Rev. ed. New York: Free Press, 2002.

Yinxu Archaeological Team. "The Shang Bronze Foundry-Site at Xiaomintun in Anyang City." *Chinese Archaeology* 8 (2008), pp. 16–21.

Youlton, John, ed. *The Blackwell Companion to the Enlightenment*. Oxford: Blackwell, 1992.

Yuan, Jing. "The Origins and Development of Animal Domestication in China." *Chinese Archaeology* 8 (2008), pp. 1–7.

Yuan, Jing, and Rowan Flad. "Pig Domestication in Ancient China." *Antiquity* 76 (2002), pp. 724–32.

Zakaria, Fareed. *The Post-American World*. New York: Norton, 2008.

Zeman, Adam. *A Portrait of the Brain*. New Haven, CT: Yale University Press, 2008.

Zhang, De'er. "Evidence for the Existence of the Medieval Warm Period in China." *Climatic Change* 26 (1994), pp. 289–97.

Zhang, E., et al. "Quantitative Reconstruction of the Paleosalinity at Qinghai Lake in the Past 900 Years." *Chinese Science Bulletin* 49 (2004), pp. 730–34.

Zhang, Juzhong et al. "The Early Development of Music. Analysis of the Jiahu Bone Flutes." *Antiquity* 78 (2004), pp. 769–78.

Zhang, Lijia. *"Socialism Is Great!" A Worker's Memoir of the New China*. New York: Anchor, 2008.

Zhang, Xuelian, et al. "Establishing and Refining the Archaeological Chronologies of Xinzhai, Erlitou and Erligang Cultures." *Chinese Archaeology* 8 (2008), pp. 197–211.

Zhao, Dingxin. "Spurious Causation in a Historical Process: War and Bureaucratization in Early China." *American Sociological Review* 69 (2004), pp. 603–607.

———. *The Rise of the Qin Empire and Patterns of Chinese History*. Forthcoming.

Zheng, Bijian. "China's 'Peaceful Rise' to Great-Power Status." *Foreign Affairs* 84.5 (2005), pp. 18–24.

Zheng, Pingzhong, et al. "A Test of Climate, Sun, and Culture Relationships from an 1810-Year Chinese Cave Record." *Science* 322 (2008), pp. 940–42.

Zheng, Yongnian. *Will China Become Democratic? Elite, Class and Regime Transition.* Singapore: East Asian Institute, 2004.

———. *The Chinese Communist Party as Organizational Emperor: Culture, Reproduction, and Transformation.* London: Routledge, 2010.

Ziegler, Philip. *The Black Death.* New York: Harper, 1969.

Zilhao, João. "Neandertals and Modern Humans Mixed, and It Matters." *Evolutionary Anthropology* 15 (2006), pp. 183–95.

Zimansky, Paul. *Ecology and Empire: The Structure of the Urartian State.* Chicago: University of Chicago Press, 1985.

Zong, Yeng et al. "Fire and Flood Management of Coastal Swamp Enabled First Rice Paddy Cultivation in Eastern China." *Nature* 449 (2007), pp. 459–63.

Zürcher, Erik. *The Buddhist Conquest of China: The Spread and Adoption of Buddhism in Early Medieval China.* 3rd ed. Leiden: E. J. Brill, 2007.

Zweig, David, and Bi Jianhai. "China's Global Hunt for Energy." *Foreign Affairs* 84.5 (2005), pp. 25–38.

Acknowledgments

Like most books, this one could not have been written without the input of many people besides the author. I probably would never have thought of writing a book like this if I had not spent so long in the open-minded atmosphere of Stanford University's School of Humanities and Sciences, where no one worries too much about traditional academic boundaries. I would like to thank Steve Haber, Ian Hodder, Adrienne Mayor, Josh Ober, Richard Saller, Walter Scheidel, and particularly Kathy St. John for their support, conversation, encouragement, and patience over the years.

Jared Diamond, Constantin Fasolt, Niall Ferguson, Jack Goldstone, John Haldon, Ian Hodder, Agnes Hsu, Mark Lewis, Barnaby Marsh, Neil Roberts, and Richard Saller all read parts of the book while I was writing it, and Eric Chinski, Daniel Crewe, Al Dien, Dora Dien, Martin Lewis, Adrienne Mayor, Josh Ober, Michael Puett, Jim Robinson, Kathy St. John, and Walter Scheidel read the entire manuscript. I am enormously grateful for their comments and advice, and apologetic for the places where I failed to understand it or was too stubborn to take it.

Bob Bellah, Francesca Bray, Mark Elvin, Ian Hodder, Richard Klein, Mark Lewis, Li Liu, Tom McClellan, Douglass North, Walter Scheidel, Nathan Sivin, Adam Smith, Richard Strassberg, Donald Wagner, Barry Weingast, and Zhang Xuelian allowed me to read unpublished or recently published writings, and, in addition to everyone I have already mentioned, conversations with Chip Blacker, David Christian, Paul David, Lance Davis, Paul Ehrlich, Peter Garnsey, David Graff, David Kennedy, Kristian Kristiansen, David Laitin, Geoffrey Lloyd, Steve Mithen, Colin Renfrew, Marshall Sahlins, Jim Sheehan, Steve Shennan, Peter Temin, Lothar von Falkenhausen, Chris Wickham, Bin Wong, Gavin Wright, Victor Xiong, Xiaoneng Yang, Dingxin Zhao, and Yiqun Zhou helped me think through various ideas in the book. Participants in the "Ancient Mediterranean and Chinese Empires" and "First Great Divergence" conferences at Stanford and at talks in Abu Dhabi, Anaheim, Athens (Greece), Austin, Big Sky (Montana), Cambridge (MA and UK), Los Angeles, Medford, Montreal, New Haven, Seattle, Stanford, and Victoria (British Columbia) also listened to parts of the argument and made very helpful suggestions.

Stanford's School of Humanities and Sciences provided financial support that made it possible for me to see the book through. I would like to thank Michele Angel for drawing the final versions of the maps and graphs and Pat Powell for securing permissions to reproduce pictures and texts previously published elsewhere.

Last but certainly not least, the book would never have been written without the encouragement of Sandy Dijkstra and the team at the Sandra Dijkstra Literary Agency; my editors, Eric Chinski at Farrar, Straus and Giroux and Daniel Crewe at Profile Books; and Eugenie Cha at FSG.

Index

IAN MORRIS is the Jean and Rebecca Willard Professor in Classics and History at Stanford University. He has published ten scholarly books and has directed excavations in Greece and Italy. He lives in the Santa Cruz Mountains in California.